PEARSON

ALWAYS LEARNING

Hugh D. Young • Roger A. Freedman

Sears and Zemansky's University Physics
with Modern Physics

Volume 1

with Contributions by A. Lewis Ford
Custom Edition for the University of Victoria

Taken from:
Sears and Zemansky's University Physics with Modern Physics, Thirteenth Edition
by Hugh D. Young and Roger A. Freedman
with Contributions by A. Lewis Ford

Cover Photo: Courtesy of Seamas Culligan.

Taken from:

Sears and Zemansky's University Physics with Modern Physics, Thirteenth Edition
by Hugh D. Young and Roger A. Freedman
with Contributions by A. Lewis Ford

Published by Addison-Wesley
San Francisco, California 94111

This special edition published in cooperation with Pearson Learning Solutions.

Pearson Learning Solutions, 501 Boylston Street, Suite 900, Boston, MA 02116
A Pearson Education Company
www.pearsoned.com

Printed in the United States of America

11 12 13 14 15 V0TX 19 18 17 16 15

000200010271759537

BK

PEARSON

ISBN 10: 1-269-20593-5
ISBN 13: 978-1-269-20593-1

BRIEF CONTENTS

DETAILED CONTENTS

UNITS, PHYSICAL QUANTITIES, AND VECTORS

1

? Being able to predict the path of a thunderstorm is essential for minimizing the damage it does to lives and property. If a thunderstorm is moving at 20 km/h in a direction 53° north of east, how far north does the thunderstorm move in 1 h?

LEARNING GOALS

By studying this chapter, you will learn:

- Three fundamental quantities of physics and the units physicists use to measure them.
- How to keep track of significant figures in your calculations.
- The difference between scalars and vectors, and how to add and subtract vectors graphically.
- What the components of a vector are, and how to use them in calculations.
- What unit vectors are, and how to use them with components to describe vectors.
- Two ways of multiplying vectors.

Physics is one of the most fundamental of the sciences. Scientists of all disciplines use the ideas of physics, including chemists who study the structure of molecules, paleontologists who try to reconstruct how dinosaurs walked, and climatologists who study how human activities affect the atmosphere and oceans. Physics is also the foundation of all engineering and technology. No engineer could design a flat-screen TV, an interplanetary spacecraft, or even a better mousetrap without first understanding the basic laws of physics.

The study of physics is also an adventure. You will find it challenging, sometimes frustrating, occasionally painful, and often richly rewarding. If you've ever wondered why the sky is blue, how radio waves can travel through empty space, or how a satellite stays in orbit, you can find the answers by using fundamental physics. You will come to see physics as a towering achievement of the human intellect in its quest to understand our world and ourselves.

In this opening chapter, we'll go over some important preliminaries that we'll need throughout our study. We'll discuss the nature of physical theory and the use of idealized models to represent physical systems. We'll introduce the systems of units used to describe physical quantities and discuss ways to describe the accuracy of a number. We'll look at examples of problems for which we can't (or don't want to) find a precise answer, but for which rough estimates can be useful and interesting. Finally, we'll study several aspects of vectors and vector algebra. Vectors will be needed throughout our study of physics to describe and analyze physical quantities, such as velocity and force, that have direction as well as magnitude.

1.1 The Nature of Physics

Physics is an *experimental* science. Physicists observe the phenomena of nature and try to find patterns that relate these phenomena. These patterns are called physical theories or, when they are very well established and widely used, physical laws or principles.

CAUTION **The meaning of the word "theory"** Calling an idea a theory does *not* mean that it's just a random thought or an unproven concept. Rather, a theory is an explanation of natural phenomena based on observation and accepted fundamental principles. An example is the well-established theory of biological evolution, which is the result of extensive research and observation by generations of biologists.

To develop a physical theory, a physicist has to learn to ask appropriate questions, design experiments to try to answer the questions, and draw appropriate conclusions from the results.

1.2 Solving Physics Problems

At some point in their studies, almost all physics students find themselves thinking, "I understand the concepts, but I just can't solve the problems." But in physics, truly understanding a concept *means* being able to apply it to a variety of problems. Learning how to solve problems is absolutely essential; you don't *know* physics unless you can *do* physics.

Problem-Solving Strategy 1.1 Solving Physics Problems

IDENTIFY *the relevant concepts:* Use the physical conditions stated in the problem to help you decide which physics concepts are relevant. Identify the **target variables** of the problem—that is, the quantities whose values you're trying to find, such as the speed at which a projectile hits the ground, the intensity of a sound made by a siren, or the size of an image made by a lens. Identify the known quantities, as stated or implied in the problem. This step is essential whether the problem asks for an algebraic expression or a numerical answer.

SET UP *the problem:* Given the concepts you have identified and the known and target quantities, choose the equations that you'll use to solve the problem and decide how you'll use them. Make sure that the variables you have identified correlate exactly with those in the equations. If appropriate, draw a sketch of the situation described in the problem. (Graph paper, ruler, protractor, and compass will help you make clear, useful sketches.) As best you can, estimate what your results will be and, as appropriate, predict what the physical behavior of a system will be. The worked examples in this book include tips on how to make these kinds of estimates and predictions. If this seems challenging, don't worry—you'll get better with practice!

EXECUTE *the solution:* This is where you "do the math." Study the worked examples in the PHYS 110 workbook to see what's involved in this step.

EVALUATE *your answer:* Compare your answer with your estimates, and reconsider things if there's a discrepancy. If your answer includes an algebraic expression, assure yourself that it represents what would happen if the variables in it were taken to extremes. For future reference, make note of any answer that represents a quantity of particular significance. Ask yourself how you might answer a more general or more difficult version of the problem you have just solved.

Idealized Models

In everyday conversation we use the word "model" to mean either a small-scale replica, such as a model railroad, or a person who displays articles of clothing (or the absence thereof). In physics a **model** is a simplified version of a physical system that would be too complicated to analyze in full detail.

For example, suppose we want to analyze the motion of a thrown baseball (Fig. 1.1a). How complicated is this problem? The ball is not a perfect sphere (it has raised seams), and it spins as it moves through the air. Wind and air resistance influence its motion, the ball's weight varies a little as its distance from the center of the earth changes, and so on. If we try to include all these things, the analysis gets hopelessly complicated. Instead, we invent a simplified version of the problem. We neglect the size and shape of the ball by representing it as a point object, or **particle.** We neglect air resistance by making the ball move in a vacuum, and we make the weight constant. Now we have a problem that is simple enough to deal with (Fig. 1.1b).

We have to overlook quite a few minor effects to make an idealized model, but we must be careful not to neglect too much. If we ignore the effects of gravity completely, then our model predicts that when we throw the ball up, it will go in a straight line and disappear into space. A useful model is one that simplifies a problem enough to make it manageable, yet keeps its essential features.

The validity of the predictions we make using a model is limited by the validity of the model. For example, Galileo's prediction about falling bodies (see Section 1.1) corresponds to an idealized model that does not include the effects of air resistance. This model works fairly well for a dropped cannonball, but not so well for a feather.

Idealized models play a crucial role throughout this book. Watch for them in discussions of physical theories and their applications to specific problems.

1.1 To simplify the analysis of (a) a baseball in flight, we use (b) an idealized model.

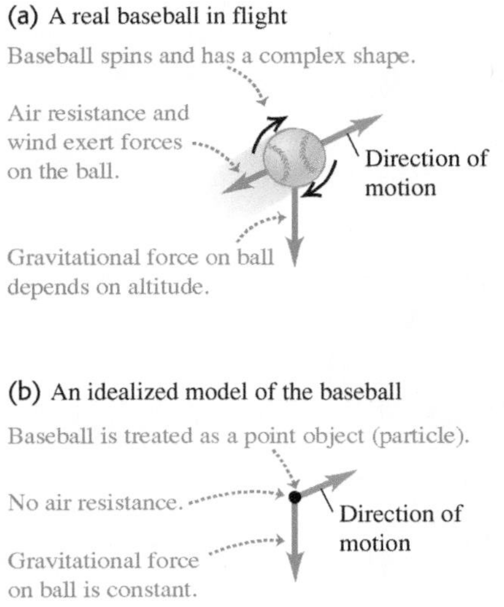
(a) A real baseball in flight
Baseball spins and has a complex shape.
Air resistance and wind exert forces on the ball.
Direction of motion
Gravitational force on ball depends on altitude.
(b) An idealized model of the baseball
Baseball is treated as a point object (particle).
No air resistance.
Direction of motion
Gravitational force on ball is constant.

1.3 Standards and Units

As we learned in Section 1.1, physics is an experimental science. Experiments require measurements, and we generally use numbers to describe the results of measurements. Any number that is used to describe a physical phenomenon quantitatively is called a **physical quantity.** For example, two physical quantities that describe you are your weight and your height. Some physical quantities are so fundamental that we can define them only by describing how to measure them. Such a definition is called an **operational definition.** Two examples are measuring a distance by using a ruler and measuring a time interval by using a stopwatch. In other cases we define a physical quantity by describing how to calculate it from other quantities that we *can* measure. Thus we might define the average speed of a moving object as the distance traveled (measured with a ruler) divided by the time of travel (measured with a stopwatch).

When we measure a quantity, we always compare it with some reference standard. When we say that a Ferrari 458 Italia is 4.53 meters long, we mean that it is 4.53 times as long as a meter stick, which we define to be 1 meter long. Such a standard defines a **unit** of the quantity. The meter is a unit of distance, and the second is a unit of time. When we use a number to describe a physical quantity, we must always specify the unit that we are using; to describe a distance as simply "4.53" wouldn't mean anything.

To make accurate, reliable measurements, we need units of measurement that do not change and that can be duplicated by observers in various locations. The system of units used by scientists and engineers around the world is commonly called "the metric system," but since 1960 it has been known officially as the **International System,** or **SI** (the abbreviation for its French name, *Système International*). Appendix A gives a list of all SI units as well as definitions of the most fundamental units.

Time

From 1889 until 1967, the unit of time was defined as a certain fraction of the mean solar day, the average time between successive arrivals of the sun at its highest point in the sky. The present standard, adopted in 1967, is much more precise. It is based on an atomic clock, which uses the energy difference between the two lowest energy states of the cesium atom. When bombarded by microwaves of precisely the proper frequency, cesium atoms undergo a transition from one of these states to the other. One **second** (abbreviated s) is defined as the time required for 9,192,631,770 cycles of this microwave radiation.

Length

In 1960 an atomic standard for the meter was also established, using the wavelength of the orange-red light emitted by atoms of krypton (^{86}Kr) in a glow discharge tube. Using this length standard, the speed of light in vacuum was measured to be 299,792,458 m/s. In November 1983, the length standard was changed again so that the speed of light in vacuum was *defined* to be precisely 299,792,458 m/s. Hence the new definition of the **meter** (abbreviated m) is the distance that light travels in vacuum in 1/299,792,458 second. This provides a much more precise standard of length than the one based on a wavelength of light.

Mass

The standard of mass, the **kilogram** (abbreviated kg), is defined to be the mass of a particular cylinder of platinum–iridium alloy kept at the International Bureau of Weights and Measures at Sèvres, near Paris. An atomic standard of mass would be more fundamental, but at present we cannot measure masses on an atomic scale with as much accuracy as on a macroscopic scale. The *gram* (which is not a fundamental unit) is 0.001 kilogram.

Unit Prefixes

Once we have defined the fundamental units, it is easy to introduce larger and smaller units for the same physical quantities. In the metric system these other units are related to the fundamental units (or, in the case of mass, to the gram) by multiples of 10 or $\frac{1}{10}$. Thus one kilometer (1 km) is 1000 meters, and one centimeter (1 cm) is $\frac{1}{100}$ meter. We usually express multiples of 10 or $\frac{1}{10}$ in exponential notation: $1000 = 10^3$, $\frac{1}{1000} = 10^{-3}$, and so on. With this notation, $1\text{ km} = 10^3\text{ m}$ and $1\text{ cm} = 10^{-2}\text{ m}$.

The names of the additional units are derived by adding a **prefix** to the name of the fundamental unit. For example, the prefix "kilo-," abbreviated k, always means a unit larger by a factor of 1000; thus

$$\begin{aligned} 1\text{ kilometer} &= 1\text{ km} = 10^3\text{ meters} = 10^3\text{ m} \\ 1\text{ kilogram} &= 1\text{ kg} = 10^3\text{ grams} = 10^3\text{ g} \\ 1\text{ kilowatt} &= 1\text{ kW} = 10^3\text{ watts} = 10^3\text{ W} \end{aligned}$$

A table on the inside back cover of this book lists the standard SI prefixes, with their meanings and abbreviations.

Table 1.1 gives some examples of the use of multiples of 10 and their prefixes with the units of length, mass, and time. Figure 1.2 shows how these prefixes are used to describe both large and small distances.

The British System

Finally, we mention the British system of units. These units are used only in the United States and a few other countries, and in most of these they are being replaced by SI units. British units are now officially defined in terms of SI units, as follows:

Length: 1 inch = 2.54 cm (exactly)

Force: 1 pound = 4.448221615260 newtons (exactly)

Table 1.1 Some Units of Length, Mass, and Time

Length	Mass	Time
1 nanometer = 1 nm = 10^{-9} m (a few times the size of the largest atom)	1 microgram = 1 μg = 10^{-6} g = 10^{-9} kg (mass of a very small dust particle)	1 nanosecond = 1 ns = 10^{-9} s (time for light to travel 0.3 m)
1 micrometer = 1 μm = 10^{-6} m (size of some bacteria and living cells)	1 milligram = 1 mg = 10^{-3} g = 10^{-6} kg (mass of a grain of salt)	1 microsecond = 1 μs = 10^{-6} s (time for space station to move 8 mm)
1 millimeter = 1 mm = 10^{-3} m (diameter of the point of a ballpoint pen)	1 gram = 1 g = 10^{-3} kg (mass of a paper clip)	1 millisecond = 1 ms = 10^{-3} s (time for sound to travel 0.35 m)
1 centimeter = 1 cm = 10^{-2} m (diameter of your little finger)		
1 kilometer = 1 km = 10^{3} m (a 10-minute walk)		

1.2 Some typical lengths in the universe. **(f)** is a scanning tunneling microscope image of atoms on a crystal surface; **(g)** is an artist's impression.

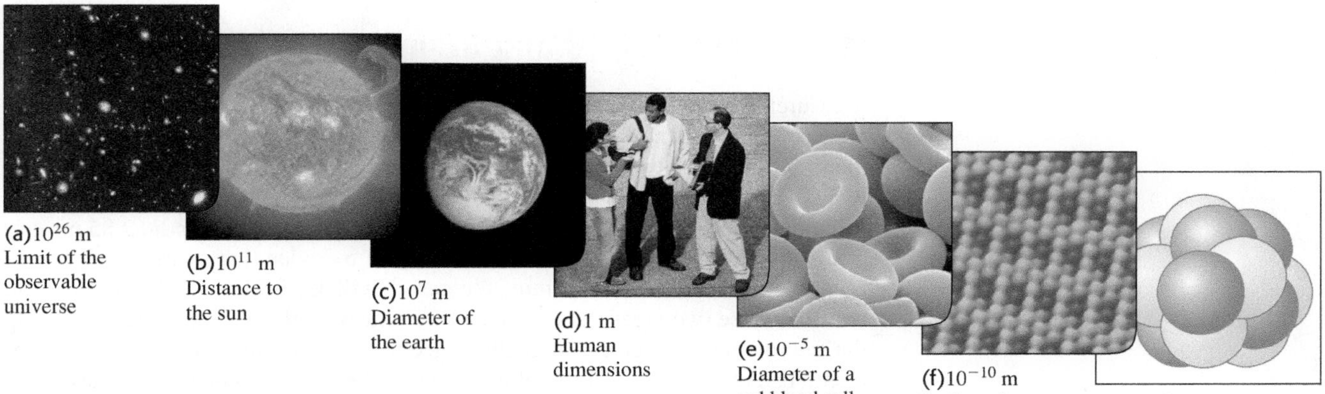

(a) 10^{26} m Limit of the observable universe

(b) 10^{11} m Distance to the sun

(c) 10^{7} m Diameter of the earth

(d) 1 m Human dimensions

(e) 10^{-5} m Diameter of a red blood cell

(f) 10^{-10} m Radius of an atom

(g) 10^{-14} m Radius of an atomic nucleus

The newton, abbreviated N, is the SI unit of force. The British unit of time is the second, defined the same way as in SI. In physics, British units are used only in mechanics and thermodynamics; there is no British system of electrical units.

In this book we use SI units for all examples and problems, but we occasionally give approximate equivalents in British units. As you do problems using SI units, you may also wish to convert to the approximate British equivalents if they are more familiar to you. But you should try to *think* in SI units as much as you can.

1.4 Unit Consistency and Conversions

We use equations to express relationships among physical quantities, represented by algebraic symbols. Each algebraic symbol always denotes both a number and a unit. For example, d might represent a distance of 10 m, t a time of 5 s, and v a speed of 2 m/s.

An equation must always be **dimensionally consistent.** You can't add apples and automobiles; two terms may be added or equated only if they have the same units. For example, if a body moving with constant speed v travels a distance d in a time t, these quantities are related by the equation

$$d = vt$$

If d is measured in meters, then the product vt must also be expressed in meters. Using the above numbers as an example, we may write

$$10\ \text{m} = \left(2\,\frac{\text{m}}{\not{\text{s}}}\right)(5\ \not{\text{s}})$$

Because the unit 1/s on the right side of the equation cancels the unit s, the product has units of meters, as it must. In calculations, units are treated just like algebraic symbols with respect to multiplication and division.

CAUTION **Always use units in calculations** When a problem requires calculations using numbers with units, *always* write the numbers with the correct units and carry the units through the calculation as in the example above. This provides a very useful check. If at some stage in a calculation you find that an equation or an expression has inconsistent units, you know you have made an error somewhere. In this book we will *always* carry units through all calculations, and we strongly urge you to follow this practice when you solve problems.

1.5 Uncertainty and Significant Figures

Measurements always have uncertainties. If you measure the thickness of the cover of a hardbound version of this book using an ordinary ruler, your measurement is reliable only to the nearest millimeter, and your result will be 3 mm. It would be *wrong* to state this result as 3.00 mm; given the limitations of the measuring device, you can't tell whether the actual thickness is 3.00 mm, 2.85 mm, or 3.11 mm. But if you use a micrometer caliper, a device that measures distances reliably to the nearest 0.01 mm, the result will be 2.91 mm. The distinction between these two measurements is in their **uncertainty.** The measurement using the micrometer caliper has a smaller uncertainty; it's a more accurate measurement. The uncertainty is also called the **error** because it indicates the maximum difference there is likely to be between the measured value and the true value. The uncertainty or error of a measured value depends on the measurement technique used.

We often indicate the **accuracy** of a measured value—that is, how close it is likely to be to the true value—by writing the number, the symbol $\pm$, and a second number indicating the uncertainty of the measurement. If the diameter of a steel rod is given as 56.47 ± 0.02 mm, this means that the true value is unlikely to be less than 56.45 mm or greater than 56.49 mm. In a commonly used shorthand notation, the number 1.6454(21) means 1.6454 ± 0.0021. The numbers in parentheses show the uncertainty in the final digits of the main number.

We can also express accuracy in terms of the maximum likely **fractional error** or **percent error** (also called *fractional uncertainty* and *percent uncertainty*). A resistor labeled "47 ohms $\pm$ 10%" probably has a true resistance that differs from 47 ohms by no more than 10% of 47 ohms—that is, by about 5 ohms. The resistance is probably between 42 and 52 ohms. For the diameter of the steel rod given above, the fractional error is (0.02 mm)/(56.47 mm), or about 0.0004; the percent error is (0.0004)(100%), or about 0.04%. Even small percent errors can sometimes be very significant.

In many cases the uncertainty of a number is not stated explicitly. Instead, the uncertainty is indicated by the number of meaningful digits, or **significant figures,** in the measured value. We gave the thickness of the cover of this book as 2.91 mm, which has three significant figures. By this we mean that the first two digits are known to be correct, while the third digit is uncertain. The last digit is in the hundredths place, so the uncertainty is about 0.01 mm. Two values with the *same* number of significant figures may have *different* uncertainties; a distance given as 137 km also has three significant figures, but the uncertainty is about 1 km.

When you use numbers that have uncertainties to compute other numbers, the computed numbers are also uncertain. When numbers are multiplied or divided, the number of significant figures in the result can be no greater than in the factor with the fewest significant figures. For example, $3.1416 \times 2.34 \times 0.58 = 4.3$. When we add and subtract numbers, it's the location of the decimal point that matters, not the number of significant figures. For example, $123.62 + 8.9 = 132.5$. Although 123.62 has an uncertainty of about 0.01, 8.9 has an uncertainty of about 0.1. So their sum has an uncertainty of about 0.1 and should be written as 132.5, not 132.52. Table 1.2 summarizes these rules for significant figures.

As an application of these ideas, suppose you want to verify the value of π, the ratio of the circumference of a circle to its diameter. The true value of this ratio to ten digits is 3.141592654. To test this, you draw a large circle and measure its circumference and diameter to the nearest millimeter, obtaining the values 424 mm and 135 mm (Fig. 1.3). You punch these into your calculator and obtain the quotient $(424\text{ mm})/(135\text{ mm}) = 3.140740741$. This may seem to disagree with the true value of π, but keep in mind that each of your measurements has three significant figures, so your measured value of π can have only three significant figures. It should be stated simply as 3.14. Within the limit of three significant figures, your value does agree with the true value.

In the examples and problems in this book we usually give numerical values with three significant figures, so your answers should usually have no more than three significant figures. (Many numbers in the real world have even less accuracy. An automobile speedometer, for example, usually gives only two significant figures.) Even if you do the arithmetic with a calculator that displays ten digits, it would be wrong to give a ten-digit answer because it misrepresents the accuracy of the results. Always round your final answer to keep only the correct number of significant figures or, in doubtful cases, one more at most. In Example 1.1 it would have been wrong to state the answer as 341.01861 m/s. Note that when you reduce such an answer to the appropriate number of significant figures, you must *round,* not *truncate.* Your calculator will tell you that the ratio of 525 m to 311 m is 1.688102894; to three significant figures, this is 1.69, not 1.68.

When we calculate with very large or very small numbers, we can show significant figures much more easily by using **scientific notation,** sometimes called **powers-of-10 notation.** The distance from the earth to the moon is about 384,000,000 m, but writing the number in this form doesn't indicate the number of significant figures. Instead, we move the decimal point eight places to the left (corresponding to dividing by 10^8) and multiply by 10^8; that is,

$$384{,}000{,}000\text{ m} = 3.84 \times 10^8\text{ m}$$

In this form, it is clear that we have three significant figures. The number 4.00×10^{-7} also has three significant figures, even though two of them are zeros. Note that in scientific notation the usual practice is to express the quantity as a number between 1 and 10 multiplied by the appropriate power of 10.

When an integer or a fraction occurs in a general equation, we treat that number as having no uncertainty at all. For example, in the equation $v_x^2 = v_{0x}^2 + 2a_x(x - x_0)$, the coefficient 2 is *exactly* 2. We can consider this coefficient as having an infinite number of significant figures (2.000000...). The same is true of the exponent 2 in v_x^2 and v_{0x}^2.

Finally, let's note that **precision** is not the same as *accuracy.* A cheap digital watch that gives the time as 10:35:17 A.M. is very *precise* (the time is given to the second), but if the watch runs several minutes slow, then this value isn't very *accurate.* On the other hand, a grandfather clock might be very accurate (that is, display the correct time), but if the clock has no second hand, it isn't very precise. A high-quality measurement is both precise *and* accurate.

Table 1.2 Using Significant Figures

Multiplication or division:
Result may have no more significant figures than the starting number with the fewest significant figures:

$$\frac{0.745 \times 2.2}{3.885} = 0.42$$

$$1.32578 \times 10^7 \times 4.11 \times 10^{-3} = 5.45 \times 10^4$$

Addition or subtraction:
Number of significant figures is determined by the starting number with the largest uncertainty (i.e., fewest digits to the right of the decimal point):

$$27.153 + 138.2 - 11.74 = 153.6$$

1.3 Determining the value of π from the circumference and diameter of a circle.

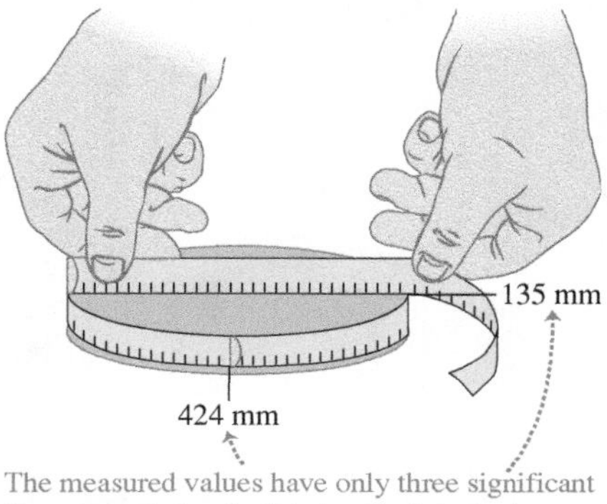

The measured values have only three significant figures, so their calculated ratio (π) also has only three significant figures.

1.6 Vectors and Vector Addition

Some physical quantities, such as time, temperature, mass, and density, can be described completely by a single number with a unit. But many other important quantities in physics have a *direction* associated with them and cannot be described by a single number. A simple example is describing the motion of an airplane: We must say not only how fast the plane is moving but also in what direction. The speed of the airplane combined with its direction of motion together constitute a quantity called *velocity.* Another example is *force,* which in physics means a push or pull exerted on a body. Giving a complete description of a force means describing both how hard the force pushes or pulls on the body and the direction of the push or pull.

When a physical quantity is described by a single number, we call it a **scalar quantity.** In contrast, a **vector quantity** has both a **magnitude** (the "how much" or "how big" part) and a direction in space. Calculations that combine scalar quantities use the operations of ordinary arithmetic. For example, $6\text{ kg} + 3\text{ kg} = 9\text{ kg}$, or $4 \times 2\text{ s} = 8\text{ s}$. However, combining vectors requires a different set of operations.

To understand more about vectors and how they combine, we start with the simplest vector quantity, **displacement.** Displacement is simply a change in the position of an object. Displacement is a vector quantity because we must state not only how far the object moves but also in what direction. Walking 3 km north from your front door doesn't get you to the same place as walking 3 km southeast; these two displacements have the same magnitude but different directions.

We usually represent a vector quantity such as displacement by a single letter, such as $\vec{A}$ in Fig. 1.4a. In this book we always print vector symbols in ***boldface italic type with an arrow above them.*** We do this to remind you that vector quantities have different properties from scalar quantities; the arrow is a reminder that vectors have direction. When you handwrite a symbol for a vector, *always* write it with an arrow on top. If you don't distinguish between scalar and vector quantities in your notation, you probably won't make the distinction in your thinking either, and hopeless confusion will result.

We always *draw* a vector as a line with an arrowhead at its tip. The length of the line shows the vector's magnitude, and the direction of the line shows the vector's direction. Displacement is always a straight-line segment directed from the starting point to the ending point, even though the object's actual path may be curved (Fig. 1.4b). Note that displacement is not related directly to the total *distance* traveled. If the object were to continue on past P_2 and then return to P_1, the displacement for the entire trip would be *zero* (Fig. 1.4c).

1.4 Displacement as a vector quantity. A displacement is always a straight-line segment directed from the starting point to the ending point, even if the path is curved.

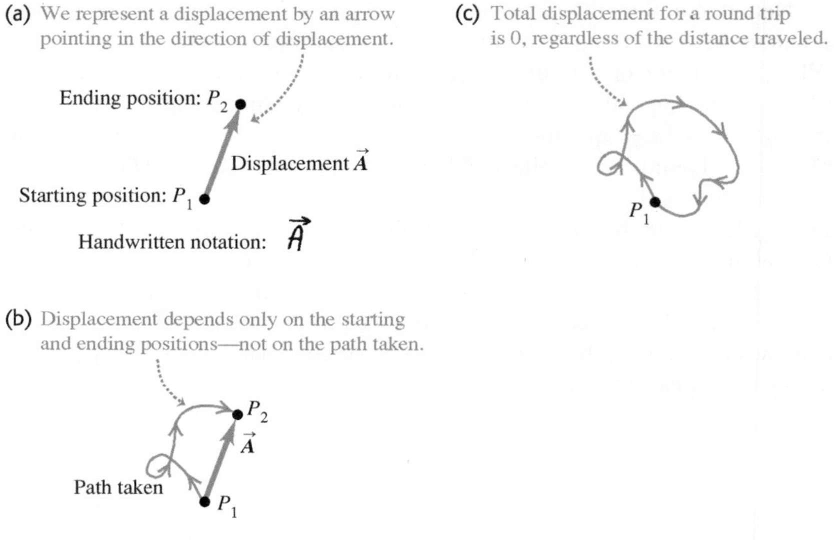
(a) We represent a displacement by an arrow pointing in the direction of displacement.
Ending position: P_2
Displacement $\vec{A}$
Starting position: P_1
Handwritten notation: $\vec{A}$
(c) Total displacement for a round trip is 0, regardless of the distance traveled.
P_1
(b) Displacement depends only on the starting and ending positions—not on the path taken.
P_2
$\vec{A}$
Path taken
P_1

1.5 The meaning of vectors that have the same magnitude and the same or opposite direction.

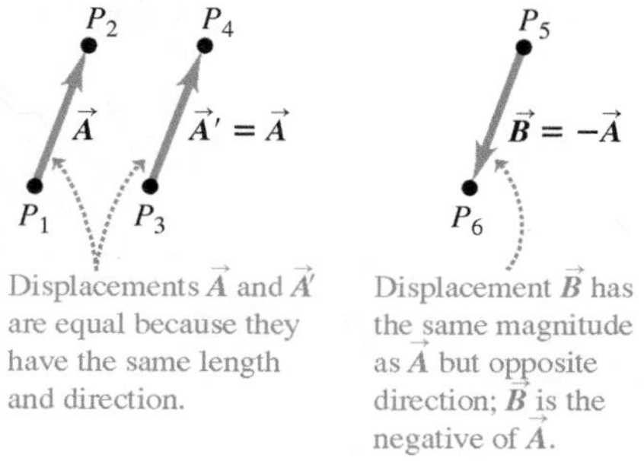

If two vectors have the same direction, they are **parallel.** If they have the same magnitude *and* the same direction, they are *equal,* no matter where they are located in space. The vector $\vec{A}'$ from point P_3 to point P_4 in Fig. 1.5 has the same length and direction as the vector $\vec{A}$ from P_1 to P_2. These two displacements are equal, even though they start at different points. We write this as $\vec{A}' = \vec{A}$ in Fig. 1.5; the boldface equals sign emphasizes that equality of two vector quantities is not the same relationship as equality of two scalar quantities. Two vector quantities are equal only when they have the same magnitude *and* the same direction.

The vector $\vec{B}$ in Fig. 1.5, however, is not equal to $\vec{A}$ because its direction is *opposite* to that of $\vec{A}$. We define the **negative of a vector** as a vector having the same magnitude as the original vector but the *opposite* direction. The negative of vector quantity $\vec{A}$ is denoted as $-\vec{A}$, and we use a boldface minus sign to emphasize the vector nature of the quantities. If $\vec{A}$ is 87 m south, then $-\vec{A}$ is 87 m north. Thus we can write the relationship between $\vec{A}$ and $\vec{B}$ in Fig. 1.5 as $\vec{A} = -\vec{B}$ or $\vec{B} = -\vec{A}$. When two vectors $\vec{A}$ and $\vec{B}$ have opposite directions, whether their magnitudes are the same or not, we say that they are **antiparallel.**

We usually represent the *magnitude* of a vector quantity (in the case of a displacement vector, its length) by the same letter used for the vector, but in *light italic type* with *no* arrow on top. An alternative notation is the vector symbol with vertical bars on both sides:

$$(\text{Magnitude of } \vec{A}) = A = |\vec{A}| \tag{1.1}$$

The magnitude of a vector quantity is a scalar quantity (a number) and is *always positive.* Note that a vector can never be equal to a scalar because they are different kinds of quantities. The expression "$\vec{A} = 6$ m" is just as wrong as "2 oranges = 3 apples"!

When drawing diagrams with vectors, it's best to use a scale similar to those used for maps. For example, a displacement of 5 km might be represented in a diagram by a vector 1 cm long, and a displacement of 10 km by a vector 2 cm long. In a diagram for velocity vectors, a vector that is 1 cm long might represent a velocity of magnitude 5 m/s. A velocity of 20 m/s would then be represented by a vector 4 cm long.

Vector Addition and Subtraction

Suppose a particle undergoes a displacement $\vec{A}$ followed by a second displacement $\vec{B}$. The final result is the same as if the particle had started at the same initial point and undergone a single displacement $\vec{C}$ (Fig. 1.6a). We call displacement $\vec{C}$ the **vector sum,** or **resultant,** of displacements $\vec{A}$ and $\vec{B}$. We express this relationship symbolically as

$$\vec{C} = \vec{A} + \vec{B} \tag{1.2}$$

1.6 Three ways to add two vectors. As shown in (b), the order in vector addition doesn't matter; vector addition is commutative.

(a) We can add two vectors by placing them head to tail.

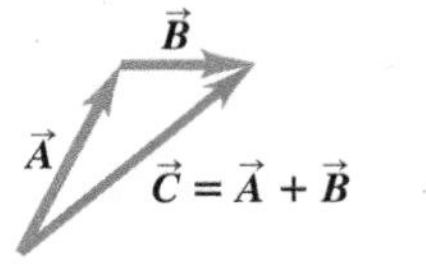

(b) Adding them in reverse order gives the same result.

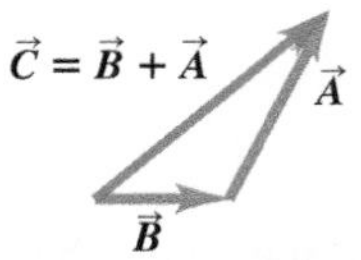

(c) We can also add them by constructing a parallelogram.

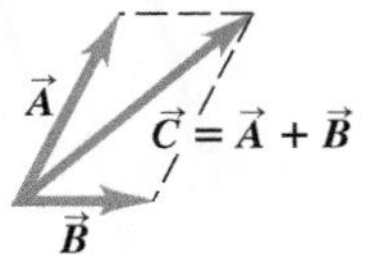

The boldface plus sign emphasizes that adding two vector quantities requires a geometrical process and is not the same operation as adding two scalar quantities such as $2 + 3 = 5$. In vector addition we usually place the *tail* of the *second* vector at the *head,* or tip, of the *first* vector (Fig. 1.6a).

If we make the displacements $\vec{A}$ and $\vec{B}$ in reverse order, with $\vec{B}$ first and $\vec{A}$ second, the result is the same (Fig. 1.6b). Thus

$$\vec{C} = \vec{B} + \vec{A} \quad \text{and} \quad \vec{A} + \vec{B} = \vec{B} + \vec{A} \tag{1.3}$$

This shows that the order of terms in a vector sum doesn't matter. In other words, vector addition obeys the commutative law.

Figure 1.6c shows another way to represent the vector sum: If vectors $\vec{A}$ and $\vec{B}$ are both drawn with their tails at the same point, vector $\vec{C}$ is the diagonal of a parallelogram constructed with $\vec{A}$ and $\vec{B}$ as two adjacent sides.

CAUTION **Magnitudes in vector addition** It's a common error to conclude that if $\vec{C} = \vec{A} + \vec{B}$, then the magnitude C should equal the magnitude A plus the magnitude B. In general, this conclusion is *wrong;* for the vectors shown in Fig. 1.6, you can see that $C < A + B$. The magnitude of $\vec{A} + \vec{B}$ depends on the magnitudes of $\vec{A}$ and $\vec{B}$ *and* on the angle between $\vec{A}$ and $\vec{B}$ (see Problem 1.90). Only in the special case in which $\vec{A}$ and $\vec{B}$ are *parallel* is the magnitude of $\vec{C} = \vec{A} + \vec{B}$ equal to the sum of the magnitudes of $\vec{A}$ and $\vec{B}$ (Fig. 1.7a). When the vectors are *antiparallel* (Fig. 1.7b), the magnitude of $\vec{C}$ equals the *difference* of the magnitudes of $\vec{A}$ and $\vec{B}$. Be careful about distinguishing between scalar and vector quantities, and you'll avoid making errors about the magnitude of a vector sum.

When we need to add more than two vectors, we may first find the vector sum of any two, add this vectorially to the third, and so on. Figure 1.8a shows three vectors $\vec{A}$, $\vec{B}$, and $\vec{C}$. In Fig. 1.8b we first add $\vec{A}$ and $\vec{B}$ to give a vector

1.7 (a) Only when two vectors $\vec{A}$ and $\vec{B}$ are parallel does the magnitude of their sum equal the sum of their magnitudes: $C = A + B$. (b) When $\vec{A}$ and $\vec{B}$ are antiparallel, the magnitude of their sum equals the *difference* of their magnitudes: $C = |A - B|$.

(a) The sum of two parallel vectors

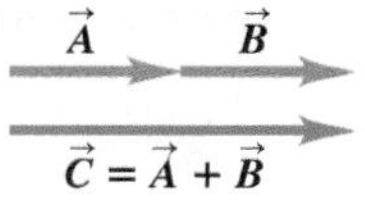

(b) The sum of two antiparallel vectors

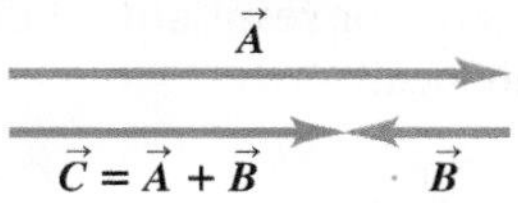

1.8 Several constructions for finding the vector sum $\vec{A} + \vec{B} + \vec{C}$.

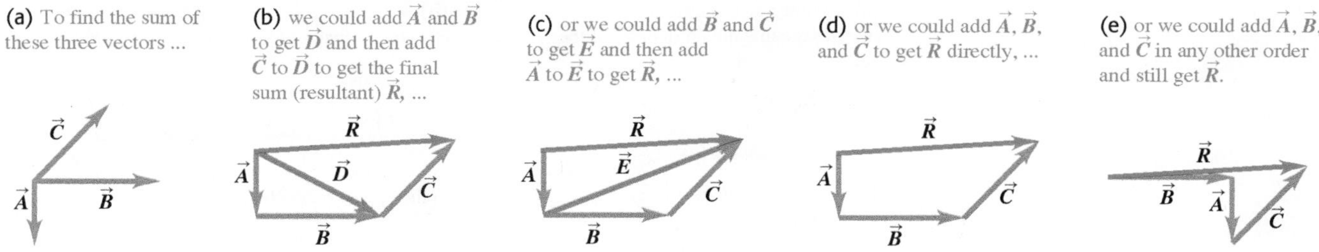
(a) To find the sum of these three vectors ...
(b) we could add $\vec{A}$ and $\vec{B}$ to get $\vec{D}$ and then add $\vec{C}$ to $\vec{D}$ to get the final sum (resultant) $\vec{R}$, ...
(c) or we could add $\vec{B}$ and $\vec{C}$ to get $\vec{E}$ and then add $\vec{A}$ to $\vec{E}$ to get $\vec{R}$, ...
(d) or we could add $\vec{A}$, $\vec{B}$, and $\vec{C}$ to get $\vec{R}$ directly, ...
(e) or we could add $\vec{A}$, $\vec{B}$, and $\vec{C}$ in any other order and still get $\vec{R}$.
$\vec{C}$
$\vec{A}$
$\vec{B}$
$\vec{R}$
$\vec{D}$
$\vec{E}$

sum $\vec{D}$; we then add vectors $\vec{C}$ and $\vec{D}$ by the same process to obtain the vector sum $\vec{R}$:

$$\vec{R} = (\vec{A} + \vec{B}) + \vec{C} = \vec{D} + \vec{C}$$

Alternatively, we can first add $\vec{B}$ and $\vec{C}$ to obtain vector $\vec{E}$ (Fig. 1.8c), and then add $\vec{A}$ and $\vec{E}$ to obtain $\vec{R}$:

$$\vec{R} = \vec{A} + (\vec{B} + \vec{C}\,) = \vec{A} + \vec{E}$$

We don't even need to draw vectors $\vec{D}$ and $\vec{E}$; all we need to do is draw $\vec{A}$, $\vec{B}$, and $\vec{C}$ in succession, with the tail of each at the head of the one preceding it. The sum vector $\vec{R}$ extends from the tail of the first vector to the head of the last vector (Fig. 1.8d). The order makes no difference; Fig. 1.8e shows a different order, and we invite you to try others. We see that vector addition obeys the associative law.

We can *subtract* vectors as well as add them. To see how, recall that vector $-\vec{A}$ has the same magnitude as $\vec{A}$ but the opposite direction. We define the difference $\vec{A} - \vec{B}$ of two vectors $\vec{A}$ and $\vec{B}$ to be the vector sum of $\vec{A}$ and $-\vec{B}$:

$$\vec{A} - \vec{B} = \vec{A} + (-\vec{B}) \tag{1.4}$$

Figure 1.9 shows an example of vector subtraction.

A vector quantity such as a displacement can be multiplied by a scalar quantity (an ordinary number). The displacement $2\vec{A}$ is a displacement (vector quantity) in the same direction as the vector $\vec{A}$ but twice as long; this is the same as adding $\vec{A}$ to itself (Fig. 1.10a). In general, when a vector $\vec{A}$ is multiplied by a scalar c, the result $c\vec{A}$ has magnitude $|c|A$ (the absolute value of c multiplied by the magnitude of the vector $\vec{A}$). If c is positive, $c\vec{A}$ is in the same direction as $\vec{A}$; if c is negative, $c\vec{A}$ is in the direction opposite to $\vec{A}$. Thus $3\vec{A}$ is parallel to $\vec{A}$, while $-3\vec{A}$ is antiparallel to $\vec{A}$ (Fig. 1.10b).

1.9 To construct the vector difference $\vec{A} - \vec{B}$, you can either place the tail of $-\vec{B}$ at the head of $\vec{A}$ or place the two vectors $\vec{A}$ and $\vec{B}$ head to head.

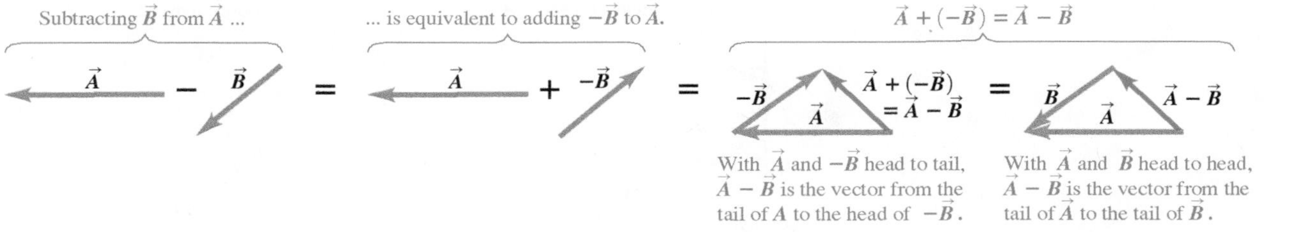
Subtracting $\vec{B}$ from $\vec{A}$ ...
... is equivalent to adding $-\vec{B}$ to $\vec{A}$.
$\vec{A} + (-\vec{B}) = \vec{A} - \vec{B}$
$\vec{A}$
$\vec{B}$
$-\vec{B}$
$\vec{A} + (-\vec{B}) = \vec{A} - \vec{B}$
$\vec{A} - \vec{B}$
With $\vec{A}$ and $-\vec{B}$ head to tail, $\vec{A} - \vec{B}$ is the vector from the tail of $\vec{A}$ to the head of $-\vec{B}$.
With $\vec{A}$ and $\vec{B}$ head to head, $\vec{A} - \vec{B}$ is the vector from the tail of $\vec{A}$ to the tail of $\vec{B}$.

1.10 Multiplying a vector (a) by a positive scalar and (b) by a negative scalar.

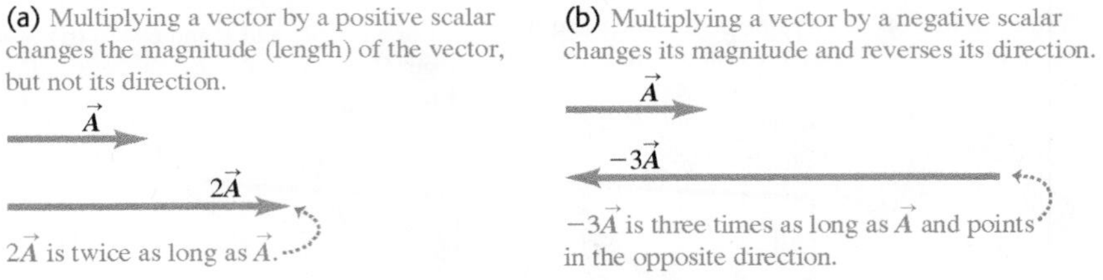

(a) Multiplying a vector by a positive scalar changes the magnitude (length) of the vector, but not its direction.
$\vec{A}$
$2\vec{A}$
$2\vec{A}$ is twice as long as $\vec{A}$.
(b) Multiplying a vector by a negative scalar changes its magnitude and reverses its direction.
$\vec{A}$
$-3\vec{A}$
$-3\vec{A}$ is three times as long as $\vec{A}$ and points in the opposite direction.

A scalar used to multiply a vector may also be a physical quantity. For example, you may be familiar with the relationship $\vec{F} = m\vec{a}$; the net force $\vec{F}$ (a vector quantity) that acts on a body is equal to the product of the body's mass m (a scalar quantity) and its acceleration $\vec{a}$ (a vector quantity). The direction of $\vec{F}$ is the same as that of $\vec{a}$ because m is positive, and the magnitude of $\vec{F}$ is equal to the mass m (which is positive) multiplied by the magnitude of $\vec{a}$. The unit of force is the unit of mass multiplied by the unit of acceleration.

1.7 Components of Vectors

In Section 1.6 we added vectors by using a scale diagram and by using properties of right triangles. Measuring a diagram offers only very limited accuracy, and calculations with right triangles work only when the two vectors are perpendicular. So we need a simple but general method for adding vectors. This is called the method of *components.*

To define what we mean by the components of a vector $\vec{A}$, we begin with a rectangular (Cartesian) coordinate system of axes (Fig. 1.11a). We then draw the vector with its tail at O, the origin of the coordinate system. We can represent any vector lying in the xy-plane as the sum of a vector parallel to the x-axis and a vector parallel to the y-axis. These two vectors are labeled $\vec{A}_x$ and $\vec{A}_y$ in Fig. 1.11a; they are called the **component vectors** of vector $\vec{A}$, and their vector sum is equal to $\vec{A}$. In symbols,

$$\vec{A} = \vec{A}_x + \vec{A}_y \tag{1.5}$$

Since each component vector lies along a coordinate-axis direction, we need only a single number to describe each one. When $\vec{A}_x$ points in the positive x-direction, we define the number A_x to be equal to the magnitude of $\vec{A}_x$. When $\vec{A}_x$ points in the negative x-direction, we define the number A_x to be equal to the negative of that magnitude (the magnitude of a vector quantity is itself never negative). We define the number A_y in the same way. The two numbers A_x and A_y are called the **components** of $\vec{A}$ (Fig. 1.11b).

1.11 Representing a vector $\vec{A}$ in terms of (a) component vectors $\vec{A}_x$ and $\vec{A}_y$ and (b) components A_x and A_y (which in this case are both positive).

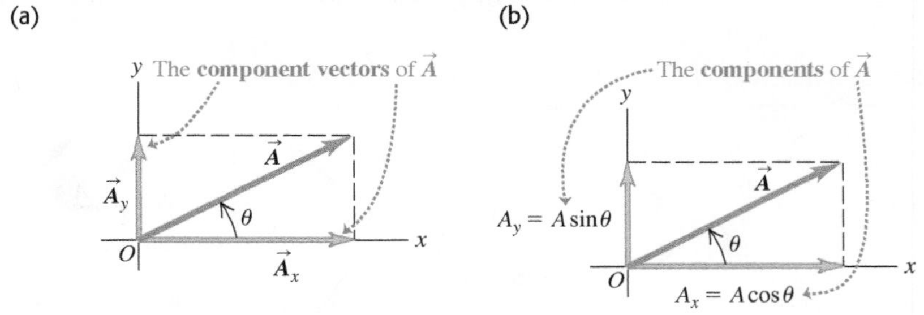

(a)
y The component vectors of $\vec{A}$
$\vec{A}$
$\vec{A}_y$
θ
O
$\vec{A}_x$
x
(b)
The components of $\vec{A}$
y
$\vec{A}$
$A_y = A\sin\theta$
θ
O
$A_x = A\cos\theta$
x

CAUTION **Components are not vectors** The components A_x and A_y of a vector $\vec{A}$ are just numbers; they are *not* vectors themselves. This is why we print the symbols for components in light italic type with *no* arrow on top instead of in boldface italic with an arrow, which is reserved for vectors.

We can calculate the components of the vector $\vec{A}$ if we know its magnitude A and its direction. We'll describe the direction of a vector by its angle relative to some reference direction. In Fig. 1.11b this reference direction is the positive x-axis, and the angle between vector $\vec{A}$ and the positive x-axis is θ (the Greek letter theta). Imagine that the vector $\vec{A}$ originally lies along the $+x$-axis and that you then rotate it to its correct direction, as indicated by the arrow in Fig. 1.11b on the angle θ. If this rotation is from the $+x$-axis toward the $+y$-axis, as shown in Fig. 1.11b, then θ is *positive;* if the rotation is from the $+x$-axis toward the $-y$-axis, θ is *negative.* Thus the *$+y$-axis* is at an angle of 90°, the $-x$-axis at 180°, and the $-y$-axis at 270° (or $-90°$). If θ is measured in this way, then from the definition of the trigonometric functions,

$$\frac{A_x}{A} = \cos\theta \qquad \text{and} \qquad \frac{A_y}{A} = \sin\theta$$

$$A_x = A\cos\theta \qquad \text{and} \qquad A_y = A\sin\theta \tag{1.6}$$

(θ measured from the $+x$-axis, rotating toward the $+y$-axis)

In Fig. 1.11b A_x and A_y are positive. This is consistent with Eqs. (1.6); θ is in the first quadrant (between 0° and 90°), and both the cosine and the sine of an angle in this quadrant are positive. But in Fig. 1.12a the component B_x is negative. Again, this agrees with Eqs. (1.6); the cosine of an angle in the second quadrant is negative. The component B_y is positive ($\sin\theta$ is positive in the second quadrant). In Fig. 1.12b both C_x and C_y are negative (both $\cos\theta$ and $\sin\theta$ are negative in the third quadrant).

CAUTION **Relating a vector's magnitude and direction to its components** Equations (1.6) are correct *only* when the angle θ is measured from the positive x-axis as described above. If the angle of the vector is given from a different reference direction or using a different sense of rotation, the relationships are different. Be careful!

Doing Vector Calculations Using Components

Using components makes it relatively easy to do various calculations involving vectors. Let's look at three important examples.

1. Finding a vector's magnitude and direction from its components. We can describe a vector completely by giving either its magnitude and direction or its x- and y-components. Equations (1.6) show how to find the components if we know the magnitude and direction. We can also reverse the process: We can find

1.12 The components of a vector may be positive or negative numbers.

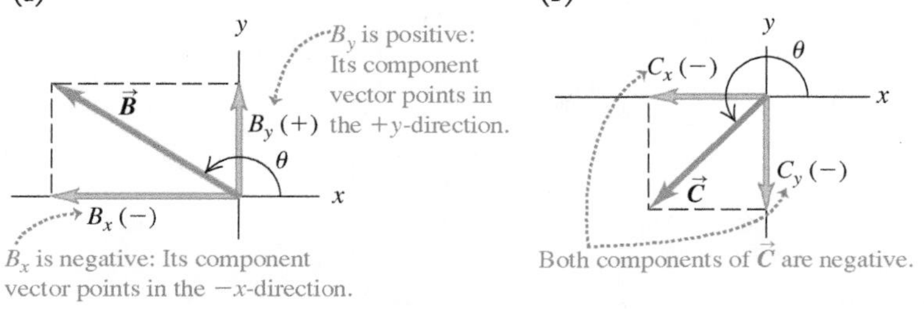
(a)
y
x
$\vec{B}$
B_y (+)
θ
B_x (−)
B_y is positive: Its component vector points in the $+y$-direction.
B_x is negative: Its component vector points in the $-x$-direction.
(b)
y
x
θ
C_x (−)
C_y (−)
$\vec{C}$
Both components of $\vec{C}$ are negative.

the magnitude and direction if we know the components. By applying the Pythagorean theorem to Fig. 1.11b, we find that the magnitude of vector $\vec{A}$ is

$$A = \sqrt{A_x^2 + A_y^2} \tag{1.7}$$

(We always take the positive root.) Equation (1.7) is valid for any choice of x-axis and y-axis, as long as they are mutually perpendicular. The expression for the vector direction comes from the definition of the tangent of an angle. If θ is measured from the positive x-axis, and a positive angle is measured toward the positive y-axis (as in Fig. 1.11b), then

$$\tan\theta = \frac{A_y}{A_x} \quad \text{and} \quad \theta = \arctan\frac{A_y}{A_x} \tag{1.8}$$

We will always use the notation arctan for the inverse tangent function. The notation $\tan^{-1}$ is also commonly used, and your calculator may have an INV or 2ND button to be used with the TAN button.

CAUTION **Finding the direction of a vector from its components** There's one slight complication in using Eqs. (1.8) to find θ: Any two angles that differ by 180° have the same tangent. Suppose $A_x = 2$ m and $A_y = -2$ m as in Fig. 1.13; then $\tan\theta = -1$. But both 135° and 315° (or −45°) have tangents of −1. To decide which is correct, we have to look at the individual components. Because A_x is positive and A_y is negative, the angle must be in the fourth quadrant; thus $\theta = 315°$ (or −45°) is the correct value. Most pocket calculators give $\arctan(-1) = -45°$. In this case that is correct; but if instead we have $A_x = -2$ m and $A_y = 2$ m, then the correct angle is 135°. Similarly, when A_x and A_y are both negative, the tangent is positive, but the angle is in the third quadrant. You should *always* draw a sketch like Fig. 1.13 to check which of the two possibilities is the correct one.

2. Multiplying a vector by a scalar. If we multiply a vector $\vec{A}$ by a scalar c, each component of the product $\vec{D} = c\vec{A}$ is the product of c and the corresponding component of $\vec{A}$:

$$D_x = cA_x \qquad D_y = cA_y \qquad (\text{components of } \vec{D} = c\vec{A}) \tag{1.9}$$

For example, Eq. (1.9) says that each component of the vector $2\vec{A}$ is twice as great as the corresponding component of the vector $\vec{A}$, so $2\vec{A}$ is in the same direction as $\vec{A}$ but has twice the magnitude. Each component of the vector $-3\vec{A}$ is

1.13 Drawing a sketch of a vector reveals the signs of its x- and y-components.

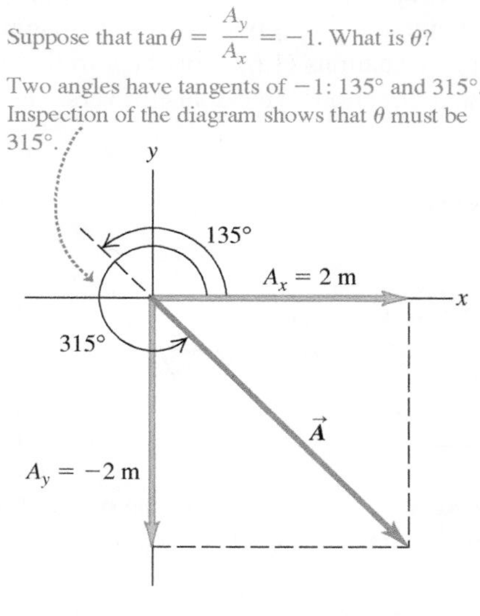
Suppose that $\tan\theta = \frac{A_y}{A_x} = -1$. What is θ?
Two angles have tangents of −1: 135° and 315°. Inspection of the diagram shows that θ must be 315°.
y
x
135°
315°
$A_x = 2$ m
$A_y = -2$ m
$\vec{A}$

1.14 Finding the vector sum (resultant) of $\vec{A}$ and $\vec{B}$ using components.

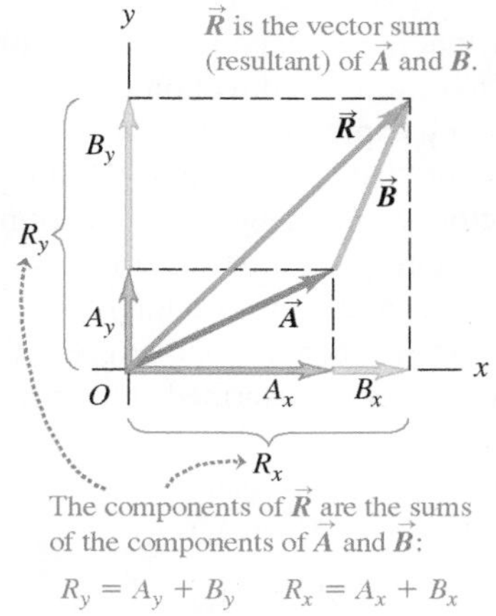

three times as great as the corresponding component of the vector $\vec{A}$ but has the opposite sign, so $-3\vec{A}$ is in the opposite direction from $\vec{A}$ and has three times the magnitude. Hence Eqs. (1.9) are consistent with our discussion in Section 1.6 of multiplying a vector by a scalar (see Fig. 1.8).

3. Using components to calculate the vector sum (resultant) of two or more vectors. Figure 1.14 shows two vectors $\vec{A}$ and $\vec{B}$ and their vector sum $\vec{R}$, along with the x- and y-components of all three vectors. You can see from the diagram that the x-component R_x of the vector sum is simply the sum $(A_x + B_x)$ of the x-components of the vectors being added. The same is true for the y-components. In symbols,

$$R_x = A_x + B_x \qquad R_y = A_y + B_y \qquad (\text{components of } \vec{R} = \vec{A} + \vec{B}) \tag{1.10}$$

Figure 1.14 shows this result for the case in which the components A_x, A_y, B_x, and B_y are all positive. You should draw additional diagrams to verify for yourself that Eqs. (1.10) are valid for *any* signs of the components of $\vec{A}$ and $\vec{B}$.

If we know the components of any two vectors $\vec{A}$ and $\vec{B}$, perhaps by using Eqs. (1.6), we can compute the components of the vector sum $\vec{R}$. Then if we need the magnitude and direction of $\vec{R}$, we can obtain them from Eqs. (1.7) and (1.8) with the A's replaced by R's.

We can extend this procedure to find the sum of any number of vectors. If $\vec{R}$ is the vector sum of $\vec{A}, \vec{B}, \vec{C}, \vec{D}, \vec{E}, \ldots$, the components of $\vec{R}$ are

$$\begin{aligned} R_x &= A_x + B_x + C_x + D_x + E_x + \cdots \\ R_y &= A_y + B_y + C_y + D_y + E_y + \cdots \end{aligned} \tag{1.11}$$

We have talked only about vectors that lie in the xy-plane, but the component method works just as well for vectors having any direction in space. We can introduce a z-axis perpendicular to the xy-plane; then in general a vector $\vec{A}$ has components A_x, A_y, and A_z in the three coordinate directions. Its magnitude A is

$$A = \sqrt{A_x^2 + A_y^2 + A_z^2} \tag{1.12}$$

Again, we always take the positive root. Also, Eqs. (1.11) for the components of the vector sum $\vec{R}$ have an additional member:

$$R_z = A_z + B_z + C_z + D_z + E_z + \cdots$$

We've focused on adding *displacement* vectors, but the method is applicable to all vector quantities. When we study the concept of force, we'll find that forces are vectors that obey the same rules of vector addition that we've used with displacement.

1.8 Unit Vectors

A **unit vector** is a vector that has a magnitude of 1, with no units. Its only purpose is to *point*—that is, to describe a direction in space. Unit vectors provide a convenient notation for many expressions involving components of vectors. We will always include a caret or "hat" (^) in the symbol for a unit vector to distinguish it from ordinary vectors whose magnitude may or may not be equal to 1.

In an *x-y* coordinate system we can define a unit vector $\hat{\imath}$ that points in the direction of the positive *x*-axis and a unit vector $\hat{\jmath}$ that points in the direction of the positive *y*-axis (Fig. 1.15a). Then we can express the relationship between component vectors and components, described at the beginning of Section 1.7, as follows:

$$\begin{aligned}\vec{A}_x &= A_x\hat{\imath}\\ \vec{A}_y &= A_y\hat{\jmath}\end{aligned} \tag{1.13}$$

Similarly, we can write a vector $\vec{A}$ in terms of its components as

$$\vec{A} = A_x\hat{\imath} + A_y\hat{\jmath} \tag{1.14}$$

Equations (1.13) and (1.14) are vector equations; each term, such as $A_x\hat{\imath}$, is a vector quantity (Fig. 1.15b).

Using unit vectors, we can express the vector sum $\vec{R}$ of two vectors $\vec{A}$ and $\vec{B}$ as follows:

$$\begin{aligned}\vec{A} &= A_x\hat{\imath} + A_y\hat{\jmath}\\ \vec{B} &= B_x\hat{\imath} + B_y\hat{\jmath}\\ \vec{R} &= \vec{A} + \vec{B}\\ &= (A_x\hat{\imath} + A_y\hat{\jmath}) + (B_x\hat{\imath} + B_y\hat{\jmath})\\ &= (A_x + B_x)\hat{\imath} + (A_y + B_y)\hat{\jmath}\\ &= R_x\hat{\imath} + R_y\hat{\jmath}\end{aligned} \tag{1.15}$$

Equation (1.15) restates the content of Eqs. (1.10) in the form of a single vector equation rather than two component equations.

If the vectors do not all lie in the *xy*-plane, then we need a third component. We introduce a third unit vector $\hat{k}$ that points in the direction of the positive *z*-axis (Fig. 1.16). Then Eqs. (1.14) and (1.15) become

$$\begin{aligned}\vec{A} &= A_x\hat{\imath} + A_y\hat{\jmath} + A_z\hat{k}\\ \vec{B} &= B_x\hat{\imath} + B_y\hat{\jmath} + B_z\hat{k}\end{aligned} \tag{1.16}$$

1.15 (a) The unit vectors $\hat{\imath}$ and $\hat{\jmath}$. (b) Expressing a vector $\vec{A}$ in terms of its components.

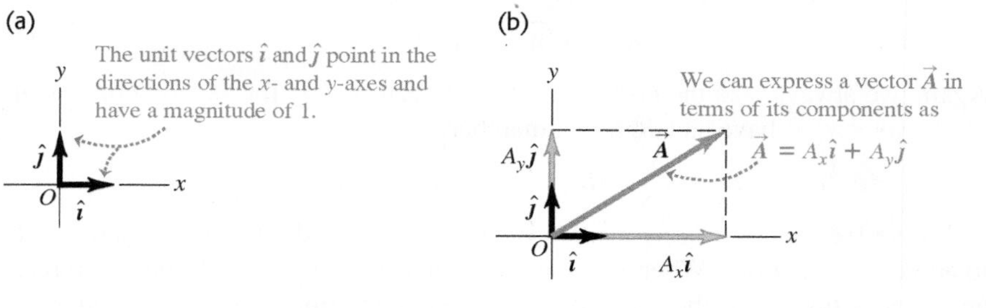

1.16 The unit vectors $\hat{\imath}$, $\hat{\jmath}$, and $\hat{k}$.

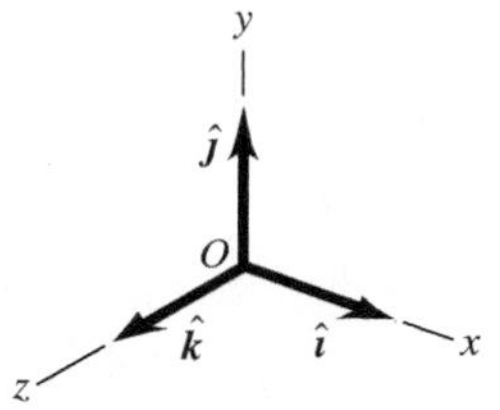

$$\vec{R} = (A_x + B_x)\hat{\imath} + (A_y + B_y)\hat{\jmath} + (A_z + B_z)\hat{k}$$
$$= R_x\hat{\imath} + R_y\hat{\jmath} + R_z\hat{k} \qquad (1.17)$$

1.9 Products of Vectors

Vector addition develops naturally from the problem of combining displacements and will prove useful for calculating many other vector quantities. We can also express many physical relationships by using *products* of vectors. Vectors are not ordinary numbers, so ordinary multiplication is not directly applicable to vectors. We will define two different kinds of products of vectors. The first, called the *scalar product,* yields a result that is a scalar quantity. The second, the *vector product,* yields another vector.

Scalar Product

The **scalar product** of two vectors $\vec{A}$ and $\vec{B}$ is denoted by $\vec{A} \cdot \vec{B}$. Because of this notation, the scalar product is also called the **dot product.** Although $\vec{A}$ and $\vec{B}$ are vectors, the quantity $\vec{A} \cdot \vec{B}$ is a scalar.

To define the scalar product $\vec{A} \cdot \vec{B}$ we draw the two vectors $\vec{A}$ and $\vec{B}$ with their tails at the same point (Fig. 1.17a). The angle ϕ (the Greek letter phi) between their directions ranges from 0° to 180°. Figure 1.17b shows the projection of the vector $\vec{B}$ onto the direction of $\vec{A}$; this projection is the component of $\vec{B}$ in the direction of $\vec{A}$ and is equal to $B\cos\phi$. (We can take components along any direction that's convenient, not just the x- and y-axes.) We define $\vec{A} \cdot \vec{B}$ to be the magnitude of $\vec{A}$ multiplied by the component of $\vec{B}$ in the direction of $\vec{A}$. Expressed as an equation,

$$\vec{A} \cdot \vec{B} = AB\cos\phi = |\vec{A}||\vec{B}|\cos\phi \qquad \text{(definition of the scalar (dot) product)} \qquad (1.18)$$

Alternatively, we can define $\vec{A} \cdot \vec{B}$ to be the magnitude of $\vec{B}$ multiplied by the component of $\vec{A}$ in the direction of $\vec{B}$, as in Fig. 1.17c. Hence $\vec{A} \cdot \vec{B} = B(A\cos\phi) = AB\cos\phi$, which is the same as Eq. (1.18).

The scalar product is a scalar quantity, not a vector, and it may be positive, negative, or zero. When ϕ is between 0° and 90°, $\cos\phi > 0$ and the scalar product is positive (Fig. 1.18a). When ϕ is between 90° and 180° so that $\cos\phi < 0$, the component of $\vec{B}$ in the direction of $\vec{A}$ is negative, and $\vec{A} \cdot \vec{B}$ is negative (Fig. 1.18b). Finally, when $\phi = 90°$, $\vec{A} \cdot \vec{B} = 0$ (Fig. 1.18c). *The scalar product of two perpendicular vectors is always zero.*

For any two vectors $\vec{A}$ and $\vec{B}$, $AB\cos\phi = BA\cos\phi$. This means that $\vec{A} \cdot \vec{B} = \vec{B} \cdot \vec{A}$. The scalar product obeys the commutative law of multiplication; the order of the two vectors does not matter.

1.17 Calculating the scalar product of two vectors, $\vec{A} \cdot \vec{B} = AB\cos\phi$.

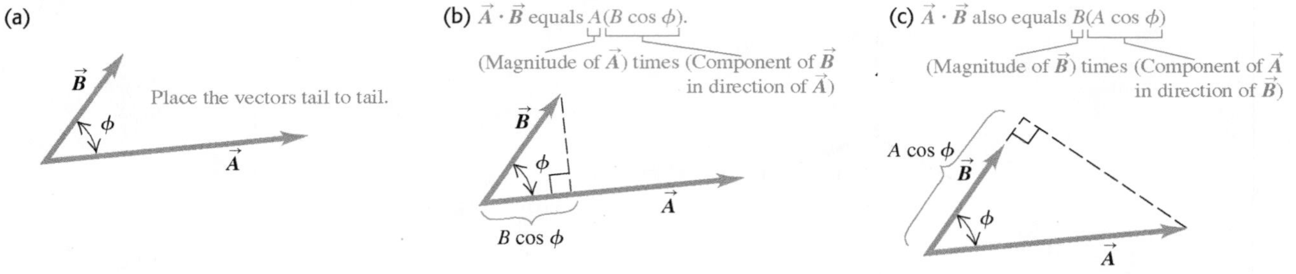
(a)
Place the vectors tail to tail.
$\vec{B}$
ϕ
$\vec{A}$
(b) $\vec{A} \cdot \vec{B}$ equals $A(B\cos\phi)$.
(Magnitude of $\vec{A}$) times (Component of $\vec{B}$ in direction of $\vec{A}$)
$B\cos\phi$
(c) $\vec{A} \cdot \vec{B}$ also equals $B(A\cos\phi)$
(Magnitude of $\vec{B}$) times (Component of $\vec{A}$ in direction of $\vec{B}$)
$A\cos\phi$

1.18 The scalar product $\vec{A} \cdot \vec{B} = AB\cos\phi$ can be positive, negative, or zero, depending on the angle between $\vec{A}$ and $\vec{B}$.

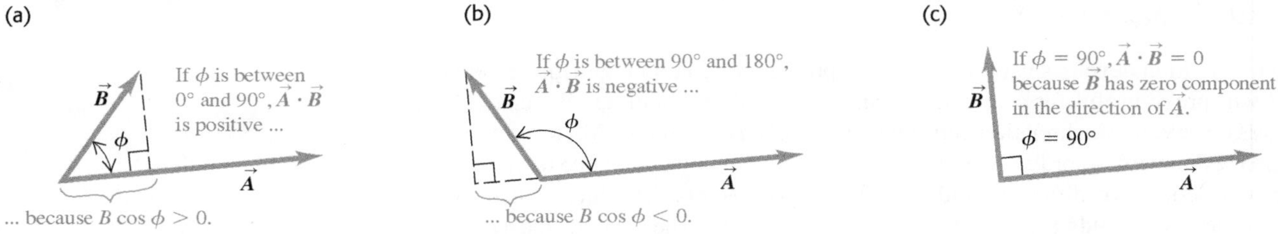
(a)
If ϕ is between 0° and 90°, $\vec{A} \cdot \vec{B}$ is positive ...
... because $B\cos\phi > 0$.
(b)
If ϕ is between 90° and 180°, $\vec{A} \cdot \vec{B}$ is negative ...
... because $B\cos\phi < 0$.
(c)
If $\phi = 90°$, $\vec{A} \cdot \vec{B} = 0$ because $\vec{B}$ has zero component in the direction of $\vec{A}$.
$\phi = 90°$

We will use the scalar product to describe work done by a force. When a constant force $\vec{F}$ is applied to a body that undergoes a displacement $\vec{s}$, the work W (a scalar quantity) done by the force is given by

$$W = \vec{F} \cdot \vec{s}$$

The work done by the force is positive if the angle between $\vec{F}$ and $\vec{s}$ is between 0° and 90°, negative if this angle is between 90° and 180°, and zero if $\vec{F}$ and $\vec{s}$ are perpendicular. (This is another example of a term that has a special meaning in physics; in everyday language, "work" isn't something that can be positive or negative.) In later chapters we'll use the scalar product for a variety of purposes, from calculating electric potential to determining the effects that varying magnetic fields have on electric circuits.

Calculating the Scalar Product Using Components

We can calculate the scalar product $\vec{A} \cdot \vec{B}$ directly if we know the x-, y-, and z-components of $\vec{A}$ and $\vec{B}$. To see how this is done, let's first work out the scalar products of the unit vectors. This is easy, since $\hat{\imath}$, $\hat{\jmath}$, and $\hat{k}$ all have magnitude 1 and are perpendicular to each other. Using Eq. (1.18), we find

$$\begin{aligned} \hat{\imath} \cdot \hat{\imath} &= \hat{\jmath} \cdot \hat{\jmath} = \hat{k} \cdot \hat{k} = (1)(1)\cos 0° = 1 \\ \hat{\imath} \cdot \hat{\jmath} &= \hat{\imath} \cdot \hat{k} = \hat{\jmath} \cdot \hat{k} = (1)(1)\cos 90° = 0 \end{aligned} \qquad (1.19)$$

Now we express $\vec{A}$ and $\vec{B}$ in terms of their components, expand the product, and use these products of unit vectors:

$$\begin{aligned}\vec{A}\cdot\vec{B} &= (A_x\hat{\imath} + A_y\hat{\jmath} + A_z\hat{k})\cdot(B_x\hat{\imath} + B_y\hat{\jmath} + B_z\hat{k})\\ &= A_x\hat{\imath}\cdot B_x\hat{\imath} + A_x\hat{\imath}\cdot B_y\hat{\jmath} + A_x\hat{\imath}\cdot B_z\hat{k}\\ &\quad + A_y\hat{\jmath}\cdot B_x\hat{\imath} + A_y\hat{\jmath}\cdot B_y\hat{\jmath} + A_y\hat{\jmath}\cdot B_z\hat{k}\\ &\quad + A_z\hat{k}\cdot B_x\hat{\imath} + A_z\hat{k}\cdot B_y\hat{\jmath} + A_z\hat{k}\cdot B_z\hat{k}\\ &= A_xB_x\hat{\imath}\cdot\hat{\imath} + A_xB_y\hat{\imath}\cdot\hat{\jmath} + A_xB_z\hat{\imath}\cdot\hat{k}\\ &\quad + A_yB_x\hat{\jmath}\cdot\hat{\imath} + A_yB_y\hat{\jmath}\cdot\hat{\jmath} + A_yB_z\hat{\jmath}\cdot\hat{k}\\ &\quad + A_zB_x\hat{k}\cdot\hat{\imath} + A_zB_y\hat{k}\cdot\hat{\jmath} + A_zB_z\hat{k}\cdot\hat{k}\end{aligned} \qquad (1.20)$$

From Eqs. (1.19) we see that six of these nine terms are zero, and the three that survive give simply

$$\vec{A}\cdot\vec{B} = A_xB_x + A_yB_y + A_zB_z \quad \text{(scalar (dot) product in terms of components)} \qquad (1.21)$$

Thus *the scalar product of two vectors is the sum of the products of their respective components.*

The scalar product gives a straightforward way to find the angle ϕ between any two vectors $\vec{A}$ and $\vec{B}$ whose components are known. In this case we can use Eq. (1.21) to find the scalar product of $\vec{A}$ and $\vec{B}$.

Vector Product

The **vector product** of two vectors $\vec{A}$ and $\vec{B}$, also called the **cross product,** is denoted by $\vec{A}\times\vec{B}$. As the name suggests, the vector product is itself a vector. We'll use this product to describe torque and angular momentums.

To define the vector product $\vec{A}\times\vec{B}$, we again draw the two vectors $\vec{A}$ and $\vec{B}$ with their tails at the same point (Fig. 1.19a). The two vectors then lie in a plane. We define the vector product to be a vector quantity with a direction perpendicular to this plane (that is, perpendicular to both $\vec{A}$ and $\vec{B}$) and a magnitude equal to $AB\sin\phi$. That is, if $\vec{C} = \vec{A}\times\vec{B}$, then

$$C = AB\sin\phi \quad \text{(magnitude of the vector (cross) product of } \vec{A} \text{ and } \vec{B}\text{)} \qquad (1.22)$$

We measure the angle ϕ from $\vec{A}$ toward $\vec{B}$ and take it to be the smaller of the two possible angles, so ϕ ranges from 0° to 180°. Then $\sin\phi \geq 0$ and C in Eq. (1.22) is never negative, as must be the case for a vector magnitude. Note also that when $\vec{A}$ and $\vec{B}$ are parallel or antiparallel, $\phi = 0$ or 180° and $C = 0$. That is, *the vector product of two parallel or antiparallel vectors is always zero.* In particular, *the vector product of any vector with itself is zero.*

CAUTION **Vector product vs. scalar product** Be careful not to confuse the expression $AB\sin\phi$ for the magnitude of the vector product $\vec{A}\times\vec{B}$ with the similar expression $AB\cos\phi$ for the scalar product $\vec{A}\cdot\vec{B}$. To see the difference between these two expressions, imagine that we vary the angle between $\vec{A}$ and $\vec{B}$ while keeping their magnitudes constant. When $\vec{A}$ and $\vec{B}$ are parallel, the magnitude of the vector product will be zero and the scalar product will be maximum. When $\vec{A}$ and $\vec{B}$ are perpendicular, the magnitude of the vector product will be maximum and the scalar product will be zero.

1.19 (a) The vector product $\vec{A} \times \vec{B}$ determined by the right-hand rule. (b) $\vec{B} \times \vec{A} = -\vec{A} \times \vec{B}$; the vector product is anticommutative.

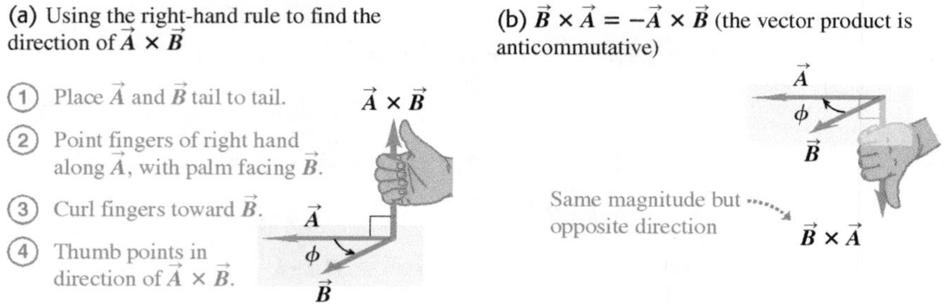
(a) Using the right-hand rule to find the direction of A × B
1 Place A and B tail to tail.
2 Point fingers of right hand along A, with palm facing B.
3 Curl fingers toward B.
4 Thumb points in direction of A × B.
A × B
A
ϕ
B
(b) B × A = −A × B (the vector product is anticommutative)
A
ϕ
B
Same magnitude but opposite direction
B × A

There are always *two* directions perpendicular to a given plane, one on each side of the plane. We choose which of these is the direction of $\vec{A} \times \vec{B}$ as follows. Imagine rotating vector $\vec{A}$ about the perpendicular line until it is aligned with $\vec{B}$, choosing the smaller of the two possible angles between $\vec{A}$ and $\vec{B}$. Curl the fingers of your right hand around the perpendicular line so that the fingertips point in the direction of rotation; your thumb will then point in the direction of $\vec{A} \times \vec{B}$. Figure 1.19a shows this **right-hand rule** and describes a second way to think about this rule.

Similarly, we determine the direction of $\vec{B} \times \vec{A}$ by rotating $\vec{B}$ into $\vec{A}$ as in Fig. 1.19b. The result is a vector that is *opposite* to the vector $\vec{A} \times \vec{B}$. The vector product is *not* commutative! In fact, for any two vectors $\vec{A}$ and $\vec{B}$,

$$\vec{A} \times \vec{B} = -\vec{B} \times \vec{A} \tag{1.23}$$

Just as we did for the scalar product, we can give a geometrical interpretation of the magnitude of the vector product. In Fig. 1.20a, $B \sin\phi$ is the component of vector $\vec{B}$ that is *perpendicular* to the direction of vector $\vec{A}$. From Eq. (1.22) the magnitude of $\vec{A} \times \vec{B}$ equals the magnitude of $\vec{A}$ multiplied by the component of $\vec{B}$ perpendicular to $\vec{A}$. Figure 1.20b shows that the magnitude of $\vec{A} \times \vec{B}$ also equals the magnitude of $\vec{B}$ multiplied by the component of $\vec{A}$ perpendicular to $\vec{B}$. Note that Fig. 1.20 shows the case in which ϕ is between 0° and 90°; you should draw a similar diagram for ϕ between 90° and 180° to show that the same geometrical interpretation of the magnitude of $\vec{A} \times \vec{B}$ still applies.

Calculating the Vector Product Using Components

If we know the components of $\vec{A}$ and $\vec{B}$, we can calculate the components of the vector product using a procedure similar to that for the scalar product. First we work out the multiplication table for the unit vectors $\hat{\imath}$, $\hat{\jmath}$, and $\hat{k}$, all three of which

1.20 Calculating the magnitude $AB \sin\phi$ of the vector product of two vectors, $\vec{A} \times \vec{B}$.

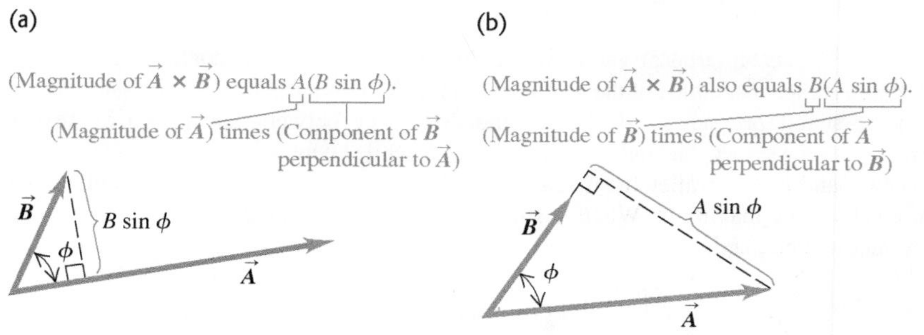
(a)
(Magnitude of A × B) equals A(B sin ϕ).
(Magnitude of A) times (Component of B perpendicular to A)
B
B sin ϕ
ϕ
A
(b)
(Magnitude of A × B) also equals B(A sin ϕ).
(Magnitude of B) times (Component of A perpendicular to B)
A sin ϕ
B
ϕ
A

are perpendicular to each other (Fig. 1.21a). The vector product of any vector with itself is zero, so

$$\hat{\imath} \times \hat{\imath} = \hat{\jmath} \times \hat{\jmath} = \hat{k} \times \hat{k} = \mathbf{0}$$

The boldface zero is a reminder that each product is a zero *vector*—that is, one with all components equal to zero and an undefined direction. Using Eqs. (1.22) and (1.23) and the right-hand rule, we find

$$\begin{aligned} \hat{\imath} \times \hat{\jmath} &= -\hat{\jmath} \times \hat{\imath} = \hat{k} \\ \hat{\jmath} \times \hat{k} &= -\hat{k} \times \hat{\jmath} = \hat{\imath} \\ \hat{k} \times \hat{\imath} &= -\hat{\imath} \times \hat{k} = \hat{\jmath} \end{aligned} \tag{1.24}$$

You can verify these equations by referring to Fig. 1.21a.

Next we express $\vec{A}$ and $\vec{B}$ in terms of their components and the corresponding unit vectors, and we expand the expression for the vector product:

$$\begin{aligned} \vec{A} \times \vec{B} &= (A_x\hat{\imath} + A_y\hat{\jmath} + A_z\hat{k}) \times (B_x\hat{\imath} + B_y\hat{\jmath} + B_z\hat{k}) \\ &= A_x\hat{\imath} \times B_x\hat{\imath} + A_x\hat{\imath} \times B_y\hat{\jmath} + A_x\hat{\imath} \times B_z\hat{k} \\ &\quad + A_y\hat{\jmath} \times B_x\hat{\imath} + A_y\hat{\jmath} \times B_y\hat{\jmath} + A_y\hat{\jmath} \times B_z\hat{k} \\ &\quad + A_z\hat{k} \times B_x\hat{\imath} + A_z\hat{k} \times B_y\hat{\jmath} + A_z\hat{k} \times B_z\hat{k} \end{aligned} \tag{1.25}$$

We can also rewrite the individual terms in Eq. (1.25) as $A_x\hat{\imath} \times B_y\hat{\jmath} = (A_xB_y)\hat{\imath} \times \hat{\jmath}$, and so on. Evaluating these by using the multiplication table for the unit vectors in Eqs. (1.24) and then grouping the terms, we get

$$\vec{A} \times \vec{B} = (A_yB_z - A_zB_y)\hat{\imath} + (A_zB_x - A_xB_z)\hat{\jmath} + (A_xB_y - A_yB_x)\hat{k} \tag{1.26}$$

Thus the components of $\vec{C} = \vec{A} \times \vec{B}$ are given by

$$C_x = A_yB_z - A_zB_y \qquad C_y = A_zB_x - A_xB_z \qquad C_z = A_xB_y - A_yB_x \tag{1.27}$$

(components of $\vec{C} = \vec{A} \times \vec{B}$)

The vector product can also be expressed in determinant form as

$$\vec{A} \times \vec{B} = \begin{vmatrix} \hat{\imath} & \hat{\jmath} & \hat{k} \\ A_x & A_y & A_z \\ B_x & B_y & B_z \end{vmatrix}$$

1.21 (a) We will always use a right-handed coordinate system, like this one. (b) We will never use a left-handed coordinate system (in which $\hat{\imath} \times \hat{\jmath} = -\hat{k}$, and so on).

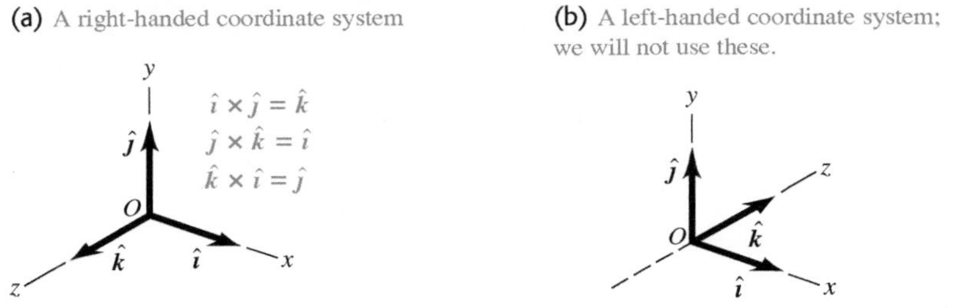

If you aren't familiar with determinants, don't worry about this form.

With the axis system of Fig. 1.21a, if we reverse the direction of the z-axis, we get the system shown in Fig. 1.21b. Then, as you may verify, the definition of the vector product gives $\hat{\boldsymbol{\imath}} \times \hat{\boldsymbol{\jmath}} = -\hat{\boldsymbol{k}}$ instead of $\hat{\boldsymbol{\imath}} \times \hat{\boldsymbol{\jmath}} = \hat{\boldsymbol{k}}$. In fact, all vector products of the unit vectors $\hat{\boldsymbol{\imath}}$, $\hat{\boldsymbol{\jmath}}$, and $\hat{\boldsymbol{k}}$ would have signs opposite to those in Eqs. (1.24). We see that there are two kinds of coordinate systems, differing in the signs of the vector products of unit vectors. An axis system in which $\hat{\boldsymbol{\imath}} \times \hat{\boldsymbol{\jmath}} = \hat{\boldsymbol{k}}$, as in Fig. 1.21a, is called a **right-handed system.** The usual practice is to use *only* right-handed systems, and we will follow that practice throughout this book.

CHAPTER 1 SUMMARY

Physical quantities and units: Three fundamental physical quantities are mass, length, and time. The corresponding basic SI units are the kilogram, the meter, and the second. Derived units for other physical quantities are products or quotients of the basic units. Equations must be dimensionally consistent; two terms can be added only when they have the same units.

Significant figures: The accuracy of a measurement can be indicated by the number of significant figures or by a stated uncertainty. The result of a calculation usually has no more significant figures than the input data. When only crude estimates are available for input data, we can often make useful order-of-magnitude estimates.

Significant figures in magenta

$$\pi = \frac{C}{2r} = \frac{0.424\ \text{m}}{2(0.06750\ \text{m})} = 3.14$$

$$123.62 + 8.9 = 132.5$$

Scalars, vectors, and vector addition: Scalar quantities are numbers and combine with the usual rules of arithmetic. Vector quantities have direction as well as magnitude and combine according to the rules of vector addition. The negative of a vector has the same magnitude but points in the opposite direction.

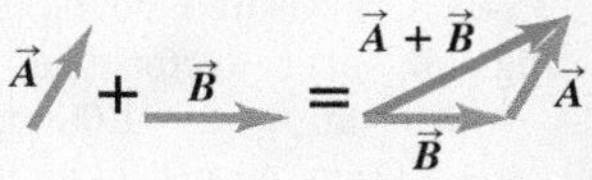

Vector components and vector addition: Vector addition can be carried out using components of vectors. The x-component of $\vec{R} = \vec{A} + \vec{B}$ is the sum of the x-components of $\vec{A}$ and $\vec{B}$, and likewise for the y- and z-components.

$$R_x = A_x + B_x$$
$$R_y = A_y + B_y \qquad (1.10)$$
$$R_z = A_z + B_z$$

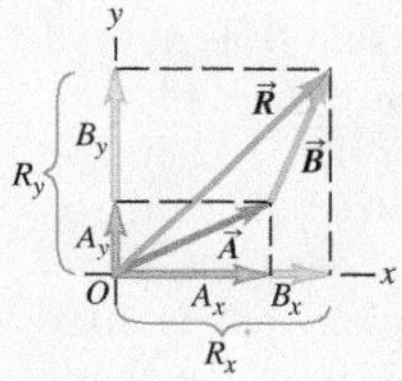

Unit vectors: Unit vectors describe directions in space. A unit vector has a magnitude of 1, with no units. The unit vectors $\hat{\imath}$, $\hat{\jmath}$, and $\hat{k}$, aligned with the x-, y-, and z-axes of a rectangular coordinate system, are especially useful.

$$\vec{A} = A_x\hat{\imath} + A_y\hat{\jmath} + A_z\hat{k} \qquad (1.16)$$

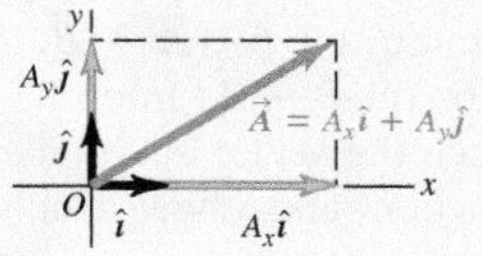

Scalar product: The scalar product $C = \vec{A}\cdot\vec{B}$ of two vectors $\vec{A}$ and $\vec{B}$ is a scalar quantity. It can be expressed in terms of the magnitudes of $\vec{A}$ and $\vec{B}$ and the angle ϕ between the two vectors, or in terms of the components of $\vec{A}$ and $\vec{B}$. The scalar product is commutative; $\vec{A}\cdot\vec{B} = \vec{B}\cdot\vec{A}$. The scalar product of two perpendicular vectors is zero.

$$\vec{A}\cdot\vec{B} = AB\cos\phi = |\vec{A}||\vec{B}|\cos\phi \qquad (1.18)$$
$$\vec{A}\cdot\vec{B} = A_xB_x + A_yB_y + A_zB_z \qquad (1.21)$$

Scalar product $\vec{A}\cdot\vec{B} = AB\cos\phi$

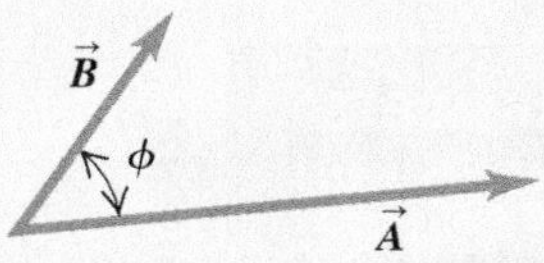

Vector product: The vector product $\vec{C} = \vec{A}\times\vec{B}$ of two vectors $\vec{A}$ and $\vec{B}$ is another vector $\vec{C}$. The magnitude of $\vec{A}\times\vec{B}$ depends on the magnitudes of $\vec{A}$ and $\vec{B}$ and the angle ϕ between the two vectors. The direction of $\vec{A}\times\vec{B}$ is perpendicular to the plane of the two vectors being multiplied, as given by the right-hand rule. The components of $\vec{C} = \vec{A}\times\vec{B}$ can be expressed in terms of the components of $\vec{A}$ and $\vec{B}$. The vector product is not commutative; $\vec{A}\times\vec{B} = -\vec{B}\times\vec{A}$. The vector product of two parallel or antiparallel vectors is zero.

$$C = AB\sin\phi \qquad (1.22)$$
$$C_x = A_yB_z - A_zB_y$$
$$C_y = A_zB_x - A_xB_z \qquad (1.27)$$
$$C_z = A_xB_y - A_yB_x$$

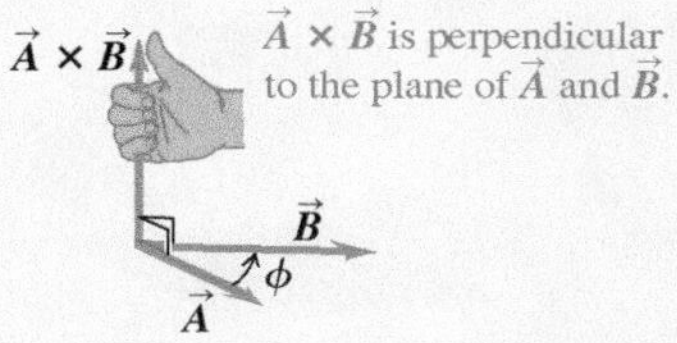

(Magnitude of $\vec{A}\times\vec{B}$) = $AB\sin\phi$

Problems

•, ••, •••: Problems of increasing difficulty. **CP**: Cumulative problems incorporating material from earlier chapters. **CALC**: Problems requiring calculus. **BIO**: Biosciences problems.

1.1 •• How many nanoseconds does it take light to travel 1.00 ft in vacuum? (This result is a useful quantity to remember.)

1.2 •• The density of gold is 19.3 g/cm^3. What is this value in kilograms per cubic meter?

1.3 • How many years older will you be 1.00 gigasecond from now? (Assume a 365-day year.)

1.4 •• A useful and easy-to-remember approximate value for the number of seconds in a year is $\pi \times 10^7$. Determine the percent error in this approximate value. (There are 365.24 days in one year.)

1.5 •• Let the angle θ be the angle that the vector $\vec{A}$ makes with the $+x$-axis, measured counterclockwise from that axis. Find the angle θ for a vector that has the following components: (a) $A_x = 2.00$ m, $A_y = -1.00$ m; (b) $A_x = 2.00$ m, $A_y = 1.00$ m; (c) $A_x = -2.00$ m, $A_y = 1.00$ m; (d) $A_x = -2.00$ m, $A_y = -1.00$ m.

1.6 • For the vectors $\vec{A}$ and $\vec{B}$, use the method of components to find the magnitude and direction of (a) the vector sum $\vec{A} + \vec{B}$; (b) the vector sum $\vec{B} + \vec{A}$; (c) the vector difference $\vec{A} - \vec{B}$; (d) the vector difference $\vec{B} - \vec{A}$.

1.7 •• Vector $\vec{A}$ is 2.80 cm long and is 60.0° above the x-axis in the first quadrant. Vector $\vec{B}$ is 1.90 cm long and is 60.0° below the x-axis in the fourth quadrant (Fig. P1.7). Use components to find the magnitude and direction of (a) $\vec{A} + \vec{B}$; (b) $\vec{A} - \vec{B}$; (c) $\vec{B} - \vec{A}$. In each case, sketch the vector addition or subtraction and show that your numerical answers are in qualitative agreement with your sketch.

Figure P1.7

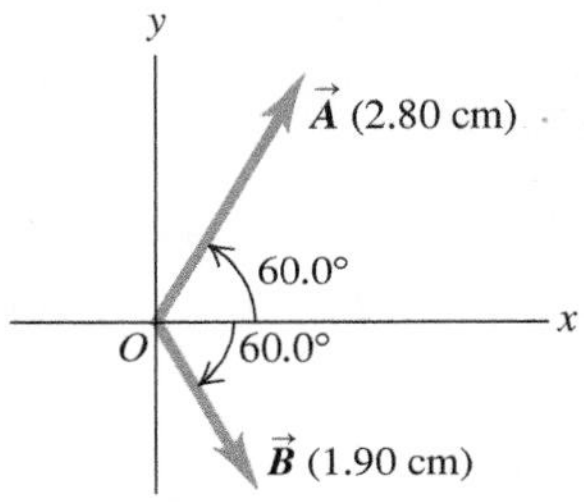

1.8 •• Given two vectors $\vec{A} = 4.00\hat{\imath} + 7.00\hat{\jmath}$ and $\vec{B} = 5.00\hat{\imath} - 2.00\hat{\jmath}$, (a) find the magnitude of each vector; (b) write an expression for the vector difference $\vec{A} - \vec{B}$ using unit vectors; (c) find the magnitude and direction of the vector difference $\vec{A} - \vec{B}$. (d) In a vector diagram show $\vec{A}$, $\vec{B}$, and $\vec{A} - \vec{B}$, and also show that your diagram agrees qualitatively with your answer in part (c).

1.9 •• (a) Write each vector in Fig. P1.9 in terms of the unit vectors $\hat{\imath}$ and $\hat{\jmath}$. (b) Use unit vectors to express the vector $\vec{C}$, where $\vec{C} = 3.00\vec{A} - 4.00\vec{B}$. (c) Find the magnitude and direction of $\vec{C}$.

Figure P1.9

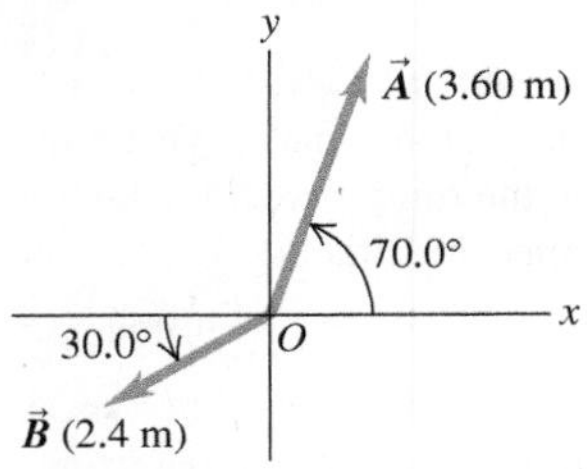

1.10 • For the vectors $\vec{A}$, $\vec{B}$, and $\vec{C}$, find the scalar products (a) $\vec{A} \cdot \vec{B}$; (b) $\vec{B} \cdot \vec{C}$; (c) $\vec{A} \cdot \vec{C}$.

1.11 • For the vectors $\vec{A}$ and $\vec{D}$, (a) find the magnitude and direction of the vector product $\vec{A} \times \vec{D}$; (b) find the magnitude and direction of $\vec{D} \times \vec{A}$.

1.12 • For the two vectors $\vec{A}$ and $\vec{B}$ in Fig. P1.9, (a) find the scalar product $\vec{A} \cdot \vec{B}$; (b) find the magnitude and direction of the vector product $\vec{A} \times \vec{B}$.

Answers

Chapter Opening Question ?

Take the $+x$-axis to point east and the $+y$-axis to point north. Then what we are trying to find is the y-component of the velocity vector measured from the $+x$-axis toward the $+y$-axis. From Eqs. (1.6) we have $v_y = v \sin\theta = (20 \text{ km/h}) \sin 53° = 16$ km/h. So the thunderstorm moves 16 km north in 1 h.

NEWTON'S LAWS OF MOTION—EQUILIBRIUM

2

? This pit crew member is pushing a race car forward. Is the race car pushing back on him? If so, does it push back with the same magnitude of force or a different amount?

LEARNING GOALS

By studying this chapter, you will learn:

- What the concept of force means in physics, and why forces are vectors.
- The significance of the net force on an object, and what happens when the net force is zero.
- How the forces that two bodies exert on each other are related.

We've seen how to use the language and mathematics of *vectors* to describe the location of objects, and more generally to describe quantities where information about direction is important. But why is this so important? Why does it matter which direction an object is being pulled or pushed? Why is it harder to push a chair across the floor if somebody is sitting on it? The answers to these and similar questions will lead us to study about **equilibrium,** the relationship between the various forces applied to objects whose motion does not change.

The rules which explain how objects respond to forces applied to them were clearly stated for the first time by Sir Isaac Newton (1642–1727); today we call them **Newton's laws of motion.** The first law states that when the net force on a body is zero, its motion doesn't change. The second law relates force to acceleration when the net force is *not* zero. The third law is a relationship between the forces that two interacting bodies exert on each other.

Newton did not *derive* the three laws of motion, but rather *deduced* them from a multitude of experiments performed by other scientists, especially Galileo Galilei (who died the same year Newton was born). These laws are truly fundamental, for they cannot be deduced or proved from other principles. Newton's laws are the foundation of **classical mechanics** (also called **Newtonian mechanics**); using them, we can understand most familiar kinds of motion. Newton's laws need modification only for situations involving extremely high speeds (near the speed of light) or very small sizes (such as within the atom).

Newton's laws are very simple to state, yet many students find these laws difficult to grasp and to work with. The reason is that before studying physics, you've spent years walking, throwing balls, pushing boxes, and doing dozens of things that involve motion. Along the way, you've developed a set of "common sense" ideas about motion and its causes. But many of these "common sense" ideas don't stand up to logical analysis. A big part of the job of this chapter—and of the rest of our study of physics—is helping you to recognize how "common sense" ideas can sometimes lead you astray, and how to adjust your understanding of the physical world to make it consistent with what experiments tell us.

2.1 Force and Interactions

2.1 Some properties of forces.

- A force is a push or a pull.
- A force is an interaction between two objects or between an object and its environment.
- A force is a vector quantity, with magnitude and direction.

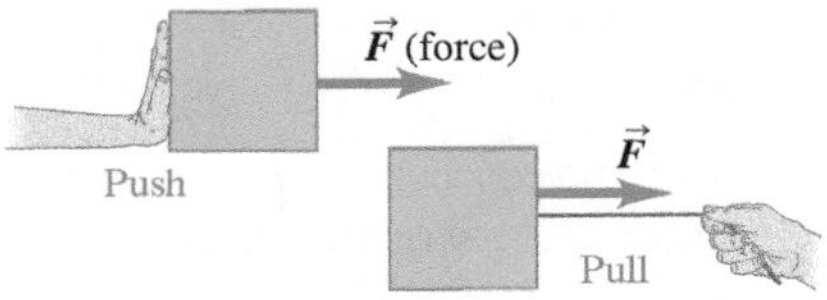

In everyday language, a **force** is a push or a pull. A better definition is that a force is an *interaction* between two bodies or between a body and its environment (Fig. 2.1). That's why we always refer to the force that one body *exerts* on a second body. When you push on a car that is stuck in the snow, you exert a force on the car; a steel cable exerts a force on the beam it is hoisting at a construction site; and so on. As Fig. 2.1 shows, force is a *vector* quantity; you can push or pull a body in different directions.

When a force involves direct contact between two bodies, such as a push or pull that you exert on an object with your hand, we call it a **contact force.** Figures 2.2a, 2.2b, and 2.2c show three common types of contact forces. The **normal force** (Fig. 2.2a) is exerted on an object by any surface with which it is in contact. The adjective *normal* means that the force always acts perpendicular to the surface of contact, no matter what the angle of that surface. By contrast, the **friction force** (Fig. 2.2b) exerted on an object by a surface acts *parallel* to the surface, in the direction that opposes sliding. The pulling force exerted by a stretched rope or cord on an object to which it's attached is called a **tension force** (Fig. 2.2c). When you tug on your dog's leash, the force that pulls on her collar is a tension force.

In addition to contact forces, there are **long-range forces** that act even when the bodies are separated by empty space. The force between two magnets is an example of a long-range force, as is the force of gravity (Fig. 2.2d); the earth pulls a dropped object toward it even though there is no direct contact between the object and the earth. The gravitational force that the earth exerts on your body is called your **weight.**

To describe a force vector $\vec{F}$, we need to describe the *direction* in which it acts as well as its *magnitude,* the quantity that describes "how much" or "how hard" the force pushes or pulls. The SI unit of the magnitude of force is the *newton,* abbreviated N.

2.2 Four common types of forces.

(a) **Normal force $\vec{n}$:** When an object rests or pushes on a surface, the surface exerts a push on it that is directed perpendicular to the surface.

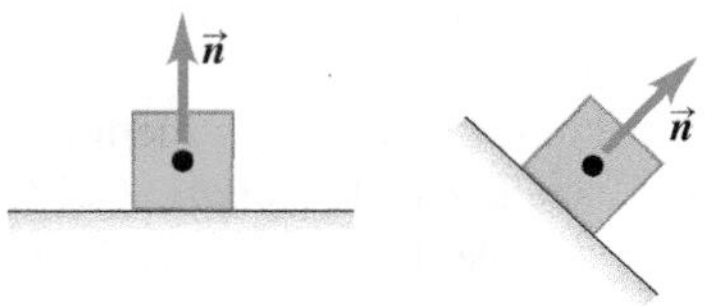

(b) **Friction force $\vec{f}$:** In addition to the normal force, a surface may exert a frictional force on an object, directed parallel to the surface.

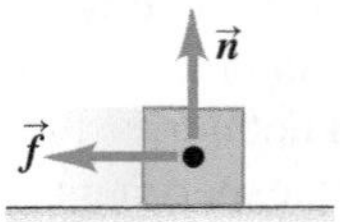

(c) **Tension force $\vec{T}$:** A pulling force exerted on an object by a rope, cord, etc.

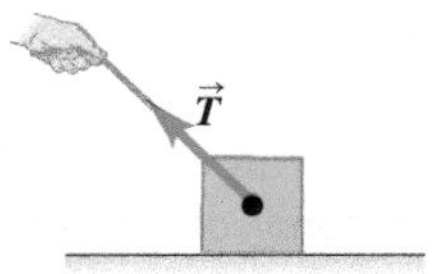

(d) **Weight $\vec{w}$:** The pull of gravity on an object is a long-range force (a force that acts over a distance).

A common instrument for measuring force magnitudes is the *spring balance.* It consists of a coil spring enclosed in a case with a pointer attached to one end. When forces are applied to the ends of the spring, it stretches by an amount that depends on the force. We can make a scale for the pointer by using a number of identical bodies with weights of exactly 1 N each. When one, two, or more of these are suspended simultaneously from the balance, the total force stretching the spring is 1 N, 2 N, and so on, and we can label the corresponding positions of the pointer 1 N, 2 N, and so on. Then we can use this instrument to measure the magnitude of an unknown force. We can also make a similar instrument that measures pushes instead of pulls.

Figure 2.3 shows a spring balance being used to measure a pull or push that we apply to a box. In each case we draw a vector to represent the applied force. The length of the vector shows the magnitude; the longer the vector, the greater the force magnitude.

2.3 Using a vector arrow to denote the force that we exert when (a) pulling a block with a string or (b) pushing a block with a stick.

(a) A 10-N pull directed 30° above the horizontal

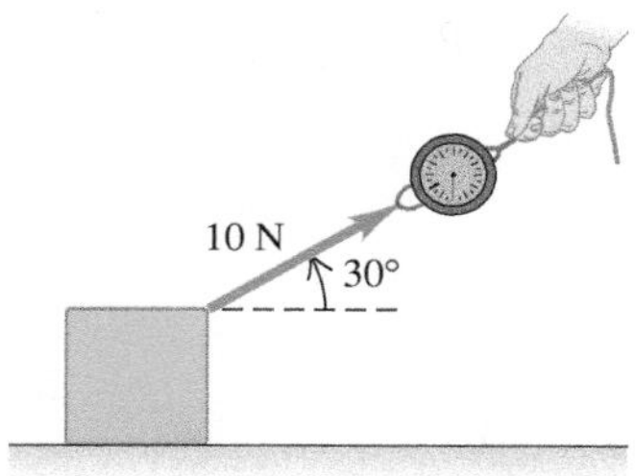
10 N
30°

(b) A 10-N push directed 45° below the horizontal

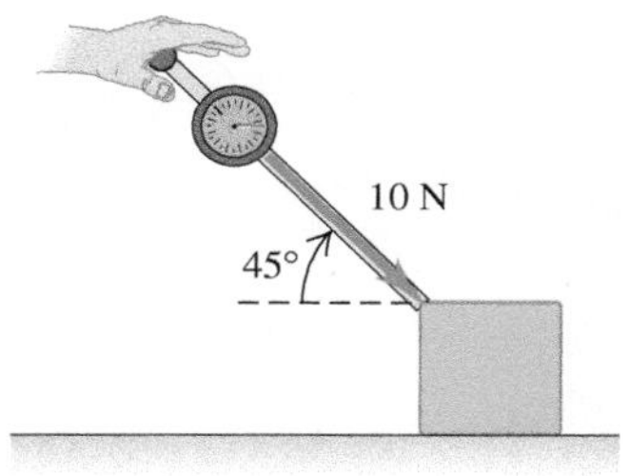
10 N
45°

Superposition of Forces

When you throw a ball, there are at least two forces acting on it: the push of your hand and the downward pull of gravity. Experiment shows that when two forces $\vec{F}_1$ and $\vec{F}_2$ act at the same time at the same point on a body (Fig. 2.4), the effect on the body's motion is the same as if a single force $\vec{R}$ were acting equal to the vector sum of the original forces: $\vec{R} = \vec{F}_1 + \vec{F}_2$. More generally, *any number of forces applied at a point on a body have the same effect as a single force equal to the vector sum of the forces.* This important principle is called **superposition of forces.**

The principle of superposition of forces is of the utmost importance, and we will use it throughout our study of physics. For example, in Fig. 2.5a, force $\vec{F}$ acts on a body at point O. The component vectors of $\vec{F}$ along the x and y axes are $\vec{F}_x$ and $\vec{F}_y$. When $\vec{F}_x$ and $\vec{F}_y$ are applied simultaneously, as in Fig. 2.5b, the effect is exactly the same as the effect of the original force $\vec{F}$. Hence *any force can be replaced by its component vectors, acting at the same point.*

It's frequently more convenient to describe a force $\vec{F}$ in terms of its x- and y-components F_x and F_y rather than by its component vectors (recall that *component vectors* are vectors, but *components* are just numbers). For the case shown in Fig. 2.5, both F_x and F_y are positive; for other orientations of the force $\vec{F}$, either F_x or F_y may be negative or zero.

Our coordinate axes don't have to be vertical and horizontal. Figure 2.6 shows a crate being pulled up a ramp by a force $\vec{F}$, represented by its components F_x and F_y parallel and perpendicular to the sloping surface of the ramp.

2.4 Superposition of forces.

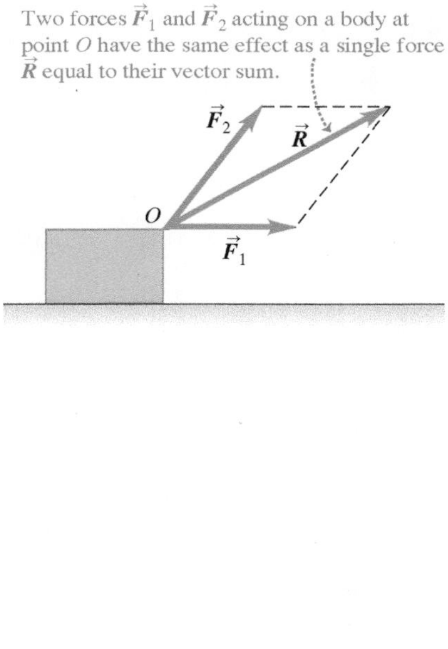
Two forces $\vec{F}_1$ and $\vec{F}_2$ acting on a body at point O have the same effect as a single force $\vec{R}$ equal to their vector sum.
$\vec{F}_2$
$\vec{R}$
O
$\vec{F}_1$

2.5 The force $\vec{F}$, which acts at an angle θ from the x-axis, may be replaced by its rectangular component vectors $\vec{F}_x$ and $\vec{F}_y$.

(a) Component vectors: $\vec{F}_x$ and $\vec{F}_y$
Components: $F_x = F\cos\theta$ and $F_y = F\sin\theta$

(b) Component vectors $\vec{F}_x$ and $\vec{F}_y$ together have the same effect as original force $\vec{F}$.

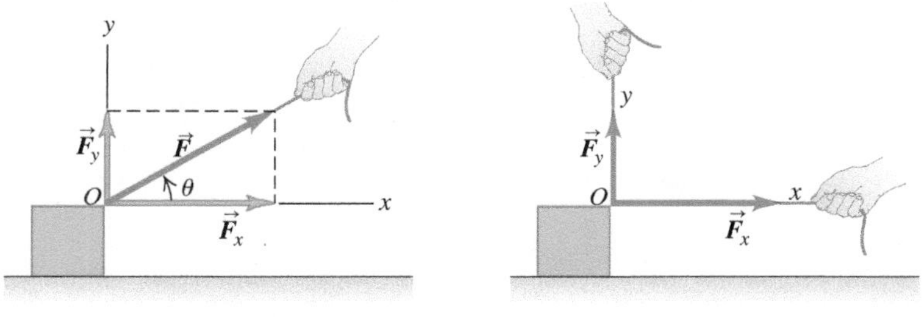
y
$\vec{F}_y$
$\vec{F}$
O
θ
x
$\vec{F}_x$
y
$\vec{F}_y$
O
x
$\vec{F}_x$

CAUTION **Using a wiggly line in force diagrams** In Fig. 2.6 we draw a wiggly line through the force vector $\vec{F}$ to show that we have replaced it by its x- and y-components. Otherwise, the diagram would include the same force twice. We will draw such a wiggly line in any force diagram where a force is replaced by its components.

We will often need to find the vector sum (resultant) of *all* the forces acting on a body. We call this the **net force** acting on the body. We will use the Greek letter Σ (capital sigma, equivalent to the Roman S) as a shorthand notation for a sum. If the forces are labeled $\vec{F}_1$, $\vec{F}_2$, $\vec{F}_3$, and so on, we abbreviate the sum as

$$\vec{R} = \vec{F}_1 + \vec{F}_2 + \vec{F}_3 + \cdots = \sum \vec{F} \qquad (2.1)$$

We read $\sum \vec{F}$ as "the vector sum of the forces" or "the net force." The component version of Eq. (2.1) is the pair of component equations

$$R_x = \sum F_x \qquad R_y = \sum F_y \qquad (2.2)$$

Here $\sum F_x$ is the sum of the x-components and $\sum F_y$ is the sum of the y-components (Fig. 2.7). Each component may be positive or negative, so be careful with signs when you evaluate these sums.

Once we have R_x and R_y we can find the magnitude and direction of the net force $\vec{R} = \sum \vec{F}$ acting on the body. The magnitude is

$$R = \sqrt{R_x^2 + R_y^2}$$

and the angle θ between $\vec{R}$ and the $+x$-axis can be found from the relationship $\tan\theta = R_y/R_x$. The components R_x and R_y may be positive, negative, or zero, and the angle θ may be in any of the four quadrants.

In three-dimensional problems, forces may also have z-components; then we add the equation $R_z = \sum F_z$ to Eq. (2.2). The magnitude of the net force is then

$$R = \sqrt{R_x^2 + R_y^2 + R_z^2}$$

2.6 F_x and F_y are the components of $\vec{F}$ parallel and perpendicular to the sloping surface of the inclined plane.

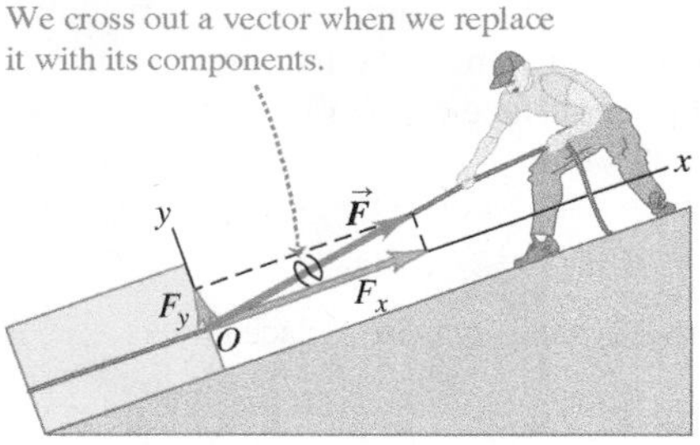
We cross out a vector when we replace it with its components.
y
x
F
Fx
Fy
O

2.7 Finding the components of the vector sum (resultant) $\vec{R}$ of two forces $\vec{F}_1$ and $\vec{F}_2$.

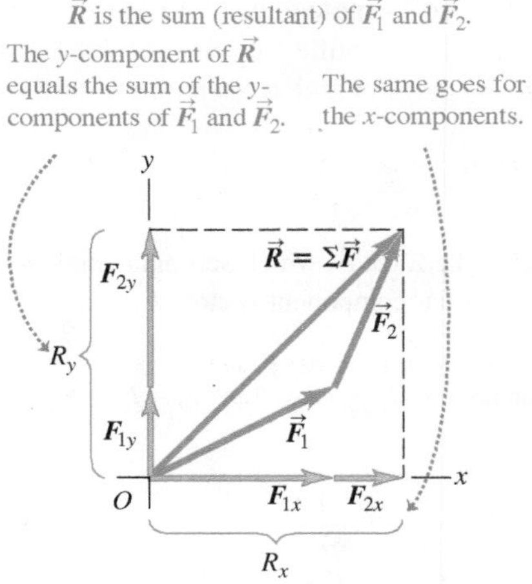
R is the sum (resultant) of F1 and F2.
The y-component of R equals the sum of the y-components of F1 and F2.
The same goes for the x-components.
y
R = ΣF
F2y
F2
Ry
F1y
F1
x
O
F1x
F2x
Rx

2.2 Newton's First Law

How do the forces that act on a body affect its motion? To begin to answer this question, let's first consider what happens when the net force on a body is *zero.* You would almost certainly agree that if a body is at rest, and if no net force acts on it (that is, no net push or pull), that body will remain at rest. But what if there is zero net force acting on a body in *motion*?

To see what happens in this case, suppose you slide a hockey puck along a horizontal tabletop, applying a horizontal force to it with your hand. After you stop pushing, the puck *does not* continue to move indefinitely; it slows down and stops. To keep it moving, you have to keep pushing (that is, applying a force). You might come to the "common sense" conclusion that bodies in motion naturally come to rest and that a force is required to sustain motion.

But now imagine pushing the puck across a smooth surface of ice. After you quit pushing, the puck will slide a lot farther before it stops. Put it on an air-hockey table, where it floats on a thin cushion of air, and it moves still farther. In each case, what slows the puck down is *friction,* an interaction between the lower surface of the puck and the surface on which it slides. Each surface exerts a frictional force on the puck that resists the puck's motion; the difference in the three cases is the magnitude of the frictional force. The ice exerts less friction than the tabletop, so the puck travels farther. The gas molecules of the air-hockey table exert the least friction of all. If we could eliminate friction completely, the puck would never slow down, and we would need no force at all to keep the puck moving once it had been started. Thus the "common sense" idea that a force is required to sustain motion is *incorrect.*

Experiments like the ones we've just described show that when *no* net force acts on a body, the body either remains at rest *or* moves with constant velocity in a straight line. Once a body has been set in motion, no net force is needed to keep it moving. We call this observation *Newton's first law of motion:*

Newton's first law of motion: **A body acted on by no net force moves with constant velocity (which may be zero) and zero acceleration.**

The tendency of a body to keep moving once it is set in motion results from a property called **inertia.** You use inertia when you try to get ketchup out of a bottle by shaking it. First you start the bottle (and the ketchup inside) moving forward; when you jerk the bottle back, the ketchup tends to keep moving forward and, you hope, ends up on your burger. The tendency of a body at rest to remain at rest is also due to inertia. You may have seen a tablecloth yanked out from under the china without breaking anything. The force on the china isn't great enough to make it move appreciably during the short time it takes to pull the tablecloth away.

It's important to note that the *net* force is what matters in Newton's first law. For example, a physics book at rest on a horizontal tabletop has two forces acting on it: an upward supporting force, or normal force, exerted by the tabletop (see Fig. 2.2a) and the downward force of the earth's gravitational attraction (a long-range force that acts even if the tabletop is elevated above the ground; see Fig. 2.2d). The upward push of the surface is just as great as the downward pull of gravity, so the *net* force acting on the book (that is, the vector sum of the two forces) is zero. In agreement with Newton's first law, if the book is at rest on the tabletop, it remains at rest. The same principle applies to a hockey puck sliding on a horizontal, frictionless surface: The vector sum of the upward push of the surface and the downward pull of gravity is zero. Once the puck is in motion, it continues to move with constant velocity because the *net* force acting on it is zero.

Here's another example. Suppose a hockey puck rests on a horizontal surface with negligible friction, such as an air-hockey table or a slab of wet ice. If the puck is initially at rest and a single horizontal force $\vec{F}_1$ acts on it, the puck starts to move. If the puck is in motion to begin with, the force changes its speed, its direction, or both, depending on the direction of the force. In this case the net force is equal to $\vec{F}_1$, which is *not* zero. (There are also two vertical forces: the earth's gravitational attraction and the upward normal force exerted by the surface. But as we mentioned earlier, these two forces cancel.)

Now suppose we apply a second force $\vec{F}_2$, equal in magnitude to $\vec{F}_1$ but opposite in direction. The two forces are negatives of each other, $\vec{F}_2 = -\vec{F}_1$, and their vector sum is zero:

$$\sum \vec{F} = \vec{F}_1 + \vec{F}_2 = \vec{F}_1 + (-\vec{F}_1) = \mathbf{0}$$

Again, we find that if the body is at rest at the start, it remains at rest; if it is initially moving, it continues to move in the same direction with constant speed. These results show that in Newton's first law, *zero net force is equivalent to no force at all.* This is just the principle of superposition of forces that we saw in Section 2.1.

When a body is either at rest or moving with constant velocity (in a straight line with constant speed), we say that the body is in **equilibrium.** For a body to be in equilibrium, it must be acted on by no forces, or by several forces such that their vector sum—that is, the net force—is zero:

$$\sum \vec{F} = \mathbf{0} \qquad \text{(body in equilibrium)} \tag{2.3}$$

For this to be true, each component of the net force must be zero, so

$$\sum F_x = 0 \qquad \sum F_y = 0 \qquad \text{(body in equilibrium)} \tag{2.4}$$

We are assuming that the body can be represented adequately as a point particle. When the body has finite size, we also have to consider *where* on the body the forces are applied. We will discuss this in Chapter 3.

Inertial Frames of Reference

Suppose you are in a bus that is traveling on a straight road and speeding up. If you could stand in the aisle on roller skates, you would start moving *backward* relative to the bus as the bus gains speed. If instead the bus was slowing to a stop, you would start moving forward down the aisle. In either case, it looks as though Newton's first law is not obeyed; there is no net force acting on you, yet your velocity changes. What's wrong?

The point is that the bus is accelerating with respect to the earth and is *not* a suitable frame of reference for Newton's first law. This law is valid in some frames of reference and not valid in others. A frame of reference in which Newton's first law *is* valid is called an **inertial frame of reference.** The earth is at least approximately an inertial frame of reference, but the bus is not. (The earth is not a completely inertial frame, owing to the acceleration associated with its rotation and its motion around the sun. These effects are quite small, however.) Because Newton's first law is used to define what we mean by an inertial frame of reference, it is sometimes called the *law of inertia.*

Figure 2.8 helps us understand what you experience when riding in a vehicle that's accelerating. In Fig. 2.8a, a vehicle is initially at rest and then begins to

2.8 Riding in an accelerating vehicle.

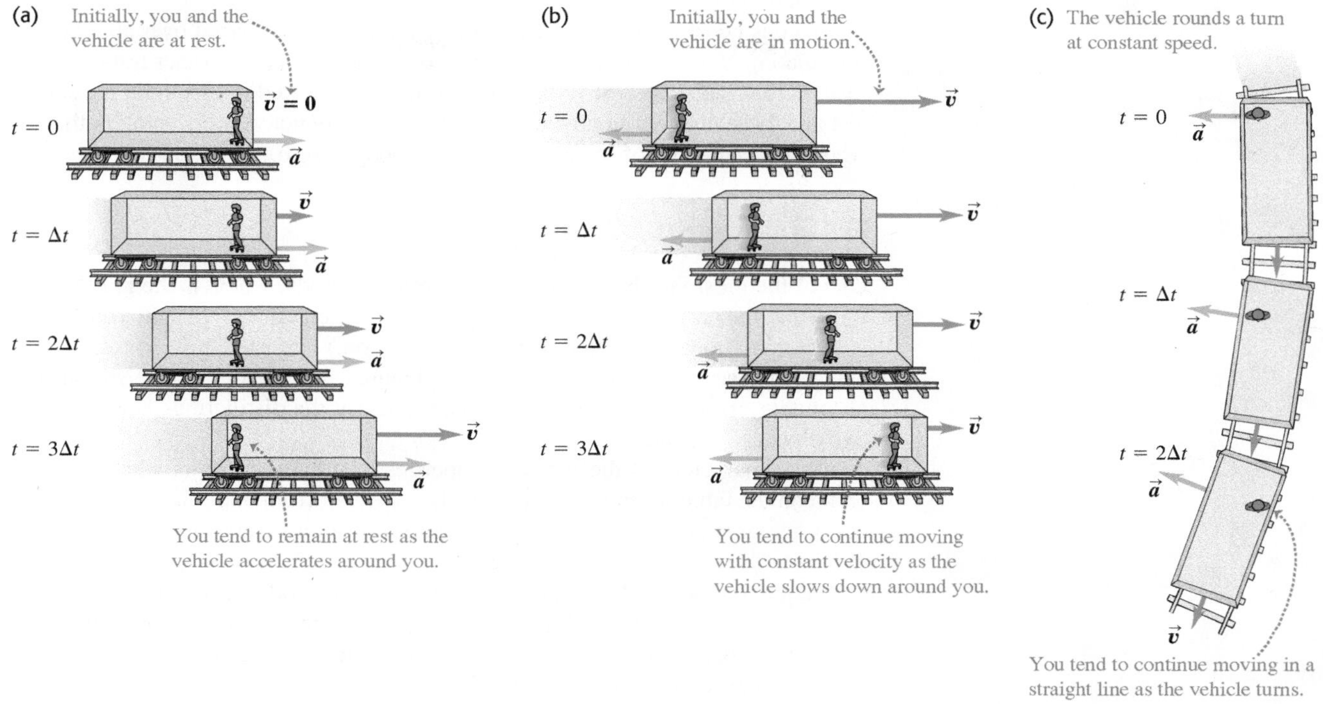
(a) Initially, you and the vehicle are at rest.
$\vec{v} = 0$
$t = 0$
$\vec{a}$
$t = \Delta t$
$\vec{v}$
$\vec{a}$
$t = 2\Delta t$
$\vec{v}$
$\vec{a}$
$t = 3\Delta t$
$\vec{v}$
$\vec{a}$
You tend to remain at rest as the vehicle accelerates around you.
(b) Initially, you and the vehicle are in motion.
$t = 0$
$\vec{v}$
$\vec{a}$
$t = \Delta t$
$\vec{v}$
$\vec{a}$
$t = 2\Delta t$
$\vec{v}$
$\vec{a}$
$t = 3\Delta t$
$\vec{v}$
$\vec{a}$
You tend to continue moving with constant velocity as the vehicle slows down around you.
(c) The vehicle rounds a turn at constant speed.
$t = 0$
$\vec{a}$
$t = \Delta t$
$\vec{a}$
$t = 2\Delta t$
$\vec{a}$
$\vec{v}$
You tend to continue moving in a straight line as the vehicle turns.

accelerate to the right. A passenger on roller skates (which nearly eliminate the effects of friction) has virtually no net force acting on her, so she tends to remain at rest relative to the inertial frame of the earth. As the vehicle accelerates around her, she moves backward relative to the vehicle. In the same way, a passenger in a vehicle that is slowing down tends to continue moving with constant velocity relative to the earth, and so moves forward relative to the vehicle (Fig. 2.8b). A vehicle is also accelerating if it moves at a constant speed but is turning (Fig. 2.8c). In this case a passenger tends to continue moving relative to the earth at constant speed in a straight line; relative to the vehicle, the passenger moves to the side of the vehicle on the outside of the turn.

In each case shown in Fig. 2.8, an observer in the vehicle's frame of reference might be tempted to conclude that there *is* a net force acting on the passenger, since the passenger's velocity *relative to the vehicle* changes in each case. This conclusion is simply wrong; the net force on the passenger is indeed zero. The vehicle observer's mistake is in trying to apply Newton's first law in the vehicle's frame of reference, which is *not* an inertial frame and in which Newton's first law isn't valid. In this book we will use *only* inertial frames of reference.

We've mentioned only one (approximately) inertial frame of reference: the earth's surface. But there are many inertial frames. If we have an inertial frame of reference A, in which Newton's first law is obeyed, then *any* second frame of reference B will also be inertial if it moves relative to A with constant velocity. Observers in frames A and B will disagree about the velocity of P, but they will agree that P has a constant velocity (zero acceleration) and has zero net force acting on it.

There is no single inertial frame of reference that is preferred over all others for formulating Newton's laws. If one frame is inertial, then every other frame moving relative to it with constant velocity is also inertial. Viewed in this light, the state of rest and the state of motion with constant velocity are not very different; both occur when the vector sum of forces acting on the body is zero.

2.3 Mass and Weight

One of the most familiar forces is the *weight* of a body, which is the gravitational force that the earth exerts on the body. (If you are on another planet, your weight is the gravitational force that planet exerts on you.) Unfortunately, the terms *mass* and *weight* are often misused and interchanged in everyday conversation. It is absolutely essential for you to understand clearly the distinctions between these two physical quantities.

Mass characterizes the *inertial* properties of a body. Mass is what keeps the china on the table when you yank the tablecloth out from under it. The greater the mass, the greater the force needed to cause a given acceleration; this is reflected in Newton's second law, $\sum\vec{F} = m\vec{a}$.

Weight, on the other hand, is a *force* exerted on a body by the pull of the earth. Mass and weight are related: Bodies having large mass also have large weight. A large stone is hard to throw because of its large *mass,* and hard to lift off the ground because of its large *weight.*

To understand the relationship between mass and weight, note that a freely falling body has an acceleration of magnitude g. Newton's second law tells us that a force must act to produce this acceleration. If a 1-kg body falls with an acceleration of 9.8 m/s^2 the required force has magnitude

$$F = ma = (1\ \text{kg})(9.8\ \text{m/s}^2) = 9.8\ \text{kg}\cdot\text{m/s}^2 = 9.8\ \text{N}$$

The force that makes the body accelerate downward is its weight. Any body near the surface of the earth that has a mass of 1 kg *must* have a weight of 9.8 N to give it the acceleration we observe when it is in free fall. More generally, a body with mass m must have weight with magnitude w given by

$$w = mg \qquad \text{(magnitude of the weight of a body of mass } m) \tag{2.5}$$

Hence the magnitude w of a body's weight is directly proportional to its mass m. The weight of a body is a force, a vector quantity, and we can write Eq. (2.5) as a vector equation (Fig. 2.9):

2.9 The relationship of mass and weight.

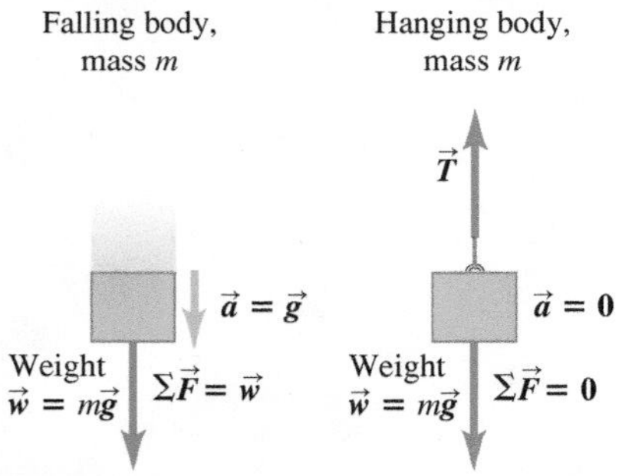
Falling body,
mass m
Hanging body,
mass m
$\vec{T}$
$\vec{a} = \vec{g}$
$\vec{a} = 0$
Weight
$\vec{w} = m\vec{g}$
$\Sigma\vec{F} = \vec{w}$
Weight
$\vec{w} = m\vec{g}$
$\Sigma\vec{F} = 0$

• The relationship of mass to weight: $\vec{w} = m\vec{g}$.
• This relationship is the same whether a body is falling or stationary.

$$\vec{w} = m\vec{g} \tag{2.6}$$

Remember that g is the *magnitude* of $\vec{g}$, the acceleration due to gravity, so g is always a positive number, by definition. Thus w, given by Eq. (2.9), is the *magnitude* of the weight and is also always positive.

CAUTION **A body's weight acts at all times** It is important to understand that the weight of a body acts on the body *all the time,* whether it is in free fall or not. If we suspend an object from a rope, it is in equilibrium, and its acceleration is zero. But its weight, given by Eq. (2.6), is still pulling down on it (Fig. 2.9). In this case the rope pulls up on the object, applying an upward force. The *vector sum* of the forces is zero, but the weight still acts.

Variation of g with Location

We will use $g = 9.80\ \text{m/s}^2$ for problems set on the earth (or, if the other data in the problem are given to only two significant figures, $g = 9.8\ \text{m/s}^2$). In fact, the value of g varies somewhat from point to point on the earth's surface—from about 9.78 to $9.82\ \text{m/s}^2$—because the earth is not perfectly spherical and because of effects due to its rotation and orbital motion. At a point where $g = 9.80\ \text{m/s}^2$, the weight of a standard kilogram is $w = 9.80\ \text{N}$. At a different point, where $g = 9.78\ \text{m/s}^2$, the weight is $w = 9.78\ \text{N}$ but the mass is still 1 kg. The weight of a body varies from one location to another; the mass does not.

If we take a standard kilogram to the surface of the moon, where the acceleration of free fall (equal to the value of g at the moon's surface) is $1.62\ \text{m/s}^2$, its weight is 1.62 N, but its mass is still 1 kg (Fig. 2.10). An 80.0-kg astronaut has a weight on earth of $(80.0\ \text{kg})(9.80\ \text{m/s}^2) = 784\ \text{N}$, but on the moon the astronaut's weight would be only $(80.0\ \text{kg})(1.62\ \text{m/s}^2) = 130\ \text{N}$.

2.10 The weight of a 1-kilogram mass (a) on earth and (b) on the moon.

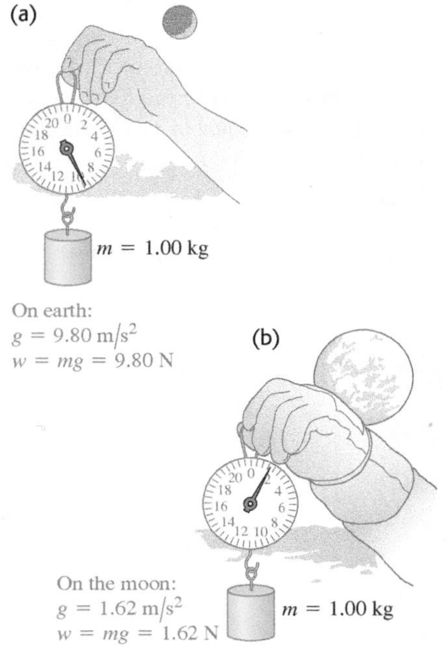

(a)
$m = 1.00$ kg
On earth:
$g = 9.80\ \text{m/s}^2$
$w = mg = 9.80$ N
(b)
On the moon:
$g = 1.62\ \text{m/s}^2$
$w = mg = 1.62$ N
$m = 1.00$ kg

Measuring Mass and Weight

One way to compare masses is by comparing their accelerations when they are subjected to the same net force. Usually, however, the easiest way to measure the mass of a body is to measure its weight, often by comparing with a standard. Equation (2.5) says that two bodies that have the same weight at a particular location also have the same mass. We can compare weights very precisely; the familiar equal-arm balance (Fig. 2.11) can determine with great precision (up to 1 part in 10^6) when the weights of two bodies are equal and hence when their masses are equal.

The concept of mass plays two rather different roles in mechanics. The weight of a body (the gravitational force acting on it) is proportional to its mass; we call the property related to gravitational interactions *gravitational mass.* On the other hand, we call the inertial property that appears in Newton's second law the *inertial mass.* If these two quantities were different, the acceleration due to gravity might well be different for different bodies. However, extraordinarily precise experiments have established that in fact the two *are* the same to a precision of better than one part in 10^{12}.

2.11 An equal-arm balance determines the mass of a body (such as an apple) by comparing its weight to a known weight.

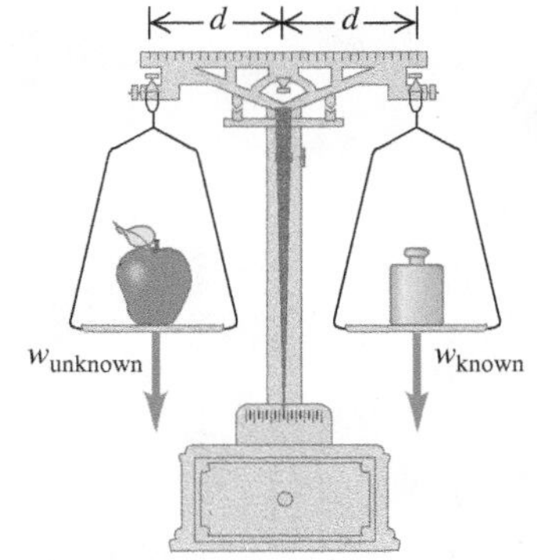

d
d
w_{unknown}
w_{known}

CAUTION **Don't confuse mass and weight** The SI units for mass and weight are often misused in everyday life. Incorrect expressions such as "This box weighs 6 kg" are nearly universal. What is meant is that the *mass* of the box, probably determined indirectly by *weighing,* is 6 kg. Be careful to avoid this sloppy usage in your own work! In SI units, weight (a force) is measured in newtons, while mass is measured in kilograms.

2.4 Newton's Third Law

A force acting on a body is always the result of its interaction with another body, so forces always come in pairs. You can't pull on a doorknob without the doorknob pulling back on you. When you kick a football, the forward force that your foot exerts on the ball launches it into its trajectory, but you also feel the force the ball exerts back on your foot. If you kick a boulder, the pain you feel is due to the force that the boulder exerts on your foot.

In each of these cases, the force that you exert on the other body is in the opposite direction to the force that body exerts on you. Experiments show that whenever two bodies interact, the two forces that they exert on each other are always *equal in magnitude* and *opposite in direction.* This fact is called *Newton's third law of motion:*

Newton's third law of motion: If body A exerts a force on body B (an "action"), then body B exerts a force on body A (a "reaction"). These two forces have the same magnitude but are opposite in direction. These two forces act on *different* bodies.

2.12 If body A exerts a force $\vec{F}_{A \text{ on } B}$ on body B, then body B exerts a force $\vec{F}_{B \text{ on } A}$ on body A that is equal in magnitude and opposite in direction: $\vec{F}_{A \text{ on } B} = -\vec{F}_{B \text{ on } A}$.

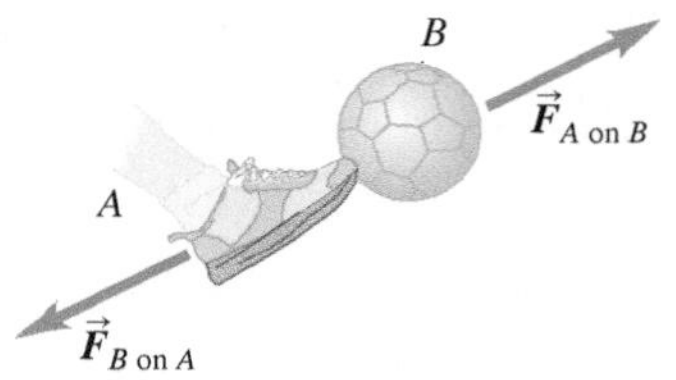

For example, in Fig. 2.12 $\vec{F}_{A \text{ on } B}$ is the force applied *by* body A (first subscript) *on* body B (second subscript), and $\vec{F}_{B \text{ on } A}$ is the force applied *by* body B (first subscript) *on* body A (second subscript). The mathematical statement of Newton's third law is

$$\vec{F}_{A \text{ on } B} = -\vec{F}_{B \text{ on } A} \quad \text{(Newton's third law of motion)} \tag{2.7}$$

It doesn't matter whether one body is inanimate (like the soccer ball in Fig. 2.12) and the other is not (like the kicker): They necessarily exert forces on each other that obey Eq. (2.7).

In the statement of Newton's third law, "action" and "reaction" are the two opposite forces (in Fig. 2.12, $\vec{F}_{A \text{ on } B}$ and $\vec{F}_{B \text{ on } A}$); we sometimes refer to them as an **action–reaction pair.** This is *not* meant to imply any cause-and-effect relationship; we can consider either force as the "action" and the other as the "reaction." We often say simply that the forces are "equal and opposite," meaning that they have equal magnitudes and opposite directions.

CAUTION **The two forces in an action–reaction pair act on different bodies** We stress that the two forces described in Newton's third law act on *different* bodies. This is important in problems involving Newton's first or second law, which involve the forces that act on a single body. For instance, the net force on the soccer ball in Fig. 2.12 is the vector sum of the weight of the ball and the force $\vec{F}_{A \text{ on } B}$ exerted by the kicker. You wouldn't include the force $\vec{F}_{B \text{ on } A}$ because this force acts on the kicker, not on the ball.

In Fig. 2.12 the action and reaction forces are *contact* forces that are present only when the two bodies are touching. But Newton's third law also applies to *long-range* forces that do not require physical contact, such as the force of gravitational attraction. A table-tennis ball exerts an upward gravitational force on the earth that's equal in magnitude to the downward gravitational force the earth exerts on the ball. When you drop the ball, both the ball and the earth accelerate toward each other. The net force on each body has the same magnitude, but the earth's acceleration is microscopically small because its mass is so great. Nevertheless, it does move!

A body that has pulling forces applied at its ends is said to be in *tension*. The **tension** at any point is the magnitude of force acting at that point (see Fig. 2.2c). The tension at the right end of the rope equals the magnitude of $\vec{F}_R$ and the tension at the left end equals the magnitude of $\vec{F}_L$. If the rope is in equilibrium and if no forces act except at its ends, the tension is the *same* at both ends and throughout the rope. Thus, if the magnitudes of $\vec{F}_L$ and $\vec{F}_R$ are 50 N each, the tension in the rope is 50 N (*not* 100 N). The *total* force vector $\vec{F}_L + \vec{F}_R$ acting on the rope in this case is zero!

We emphasize once more a fundamental truth: The two forces in an action–reaction pair *never* act on the same body. Remembering this simple fact can often help you avoid confusion about action–reaction pairs and Newton's third law.

2.5 Free-Body Diagrams

Newton's three laws of motion contain all the basic principles we need to solve a wide variety of problems in mechanics. These laws are very simple in form, but the process of applying them to specific situations can pose real challenges. In this brief section we'll point out three key ideas and techniques to use in any problems involving Newton's laws.

1. *Newton's first (and second) law applies to a specific body.* Whenever you use Newton's first law, $\sum \vec{F} = \mathbf{0}$, for an equilibrium situation (or Newton's second law, $\sum \vec{F} = m\vec{a}$, for a nonequilibrium situation), you must decide at the beginning to which body you are referring. This decision may sound trivial, but it isn't.
2. *Only forces acting on the body matter.* The sum $\sum \vec{F}$ includes all the forces that act *on* the body in question. Hence, once you've chosen the body to analyze, you have to identify all the forces acting on it. Don't get confused between the forces acting on a body and the forces exerted by that body on some other body. For example, to analyze a person walking, you would include in $\sum \vec{F}$ the force that the ground exerts on the person as he walks, but *not* the force that the person exerts on the ground. These forces form an action–reaction pair and are related by Newton's third law, but only the member of the pair that acts on the body you're working with goes into $\sum \vec{F}$.
3. *Free-body diagrams are essential to help identify the relevant forces.* A **free-body diagram** is a diagram showing the chosen body by itself, "free" of its surroundings, with vectors drawn to show the magnitudes and directions of all the forces applied to the body by the various other bodies that interact with it. We have already shown some free-body digrams in Figs. 2.9 . Be careful to include all the forces acting *on* the body, but be equally careful *not* to include any forces that the body exerts on any other body. In particular, the two forces in an action–reaction pair must *never* appear in the same free-body diagram because they never act on the same body. Furthermore, forces that a body exerts on itself are never included, since these can't affect the body's motion.

CAUTION **Forces in free-body diagrams** When you have a complete free-body diagram, you *must* be able to answer this question for each force: What other body is applying this force? If you can't answer that question, you may be dealing with a nonexistent force. Be especially on your guard to avoid nonexistent forces such as "the force of acceleration" or "the $m\vec{a}$ force."

When a problem involves more than one body, you have to take the problem apart and draw a separate free-body diagram for each body.

2.6 Using Newton's First Law: Particles in Equilibrium

We'll begin with equilibrium problems, in which we analyze the forces that act on a body at rest or moving with constant velocity. We learned that a body is in *equilibrium* when it is at rest or moving with constant velocity in an inertial frame of reference. A hanging lamp, a kitchen table, an airplane flying straight and level at a constant speed—all are examples of equilibrium situations. In this section we consider only equilibrium of a body that can be modeled as a particle. The essential physical principle is Newton's first law: When a particle is in equilibrium, the *net* force acting on it—that is, the vector sum of all the forces acting on it—must be zero:

$$\sum \vec{F} = \mathbf{0} \quad \text{(particle in equilibrium, vector form)} \tag{2.8}$$

We most often use this equation in component form:

$$\sum F_x = 0 \qquad \sum F_y = 0 \quad \text{(particle in equilibrium, component form)} \tag{2.9}$$

2.7 Frictional Forces

We've seen several problems where a body rests or slides on a surface that exerts forces on the body. Whenever two bodies interact by direct contact (touching) of their surfaces, we describe the interaction in terms of *contact forces.* The normal force is one example of a contact force; in this section we'll look in detail at another contact force, the force of friction.

Friction is important in many aspects of everyday life. The oil in a car engine minimizes friction between moving parts, but without friction between the tires and the road we couldn't drive or turn the car. Air drag—the frictional force exerted by the air on a body moving through it—decreases automotive fuel economy but makes parachutes work. Without friction, nails would pull out, light bulbs would unscrew effortlessly, and hockey would be hopeless.

Kinetic and Static Friction

When you try to slide a heavy box of books across the floor, the box doesn't move at all unless you push with a certain minimum force. Then the box starts moving, and you can usually keep it moving with less force than you needed to get it started. If you take some of the books out, you need less force than before to get it started or keep it moving. What general statements can we make about this behavior?

First, when a body rests or slides on a surface, we can think of the surface as exerting a single contact force on the body, with force components perpendicular and parallel to the surface (Fig. 2.13). The perpendicular component vector is the normal force, denoted by $\vec{n}$. The component vector parallel to the surface (and perpendicular to $\vec{n}$) is the **friction force,** denoted by $\vec{f}$. If the surface is frictionless, then $\vec{f}$ is zero but there is still a normal force. (Frictionless surfaces are an unattainable idealization, like a massless rope. But we can approximate a surface as frictionless if the effects of friction are negligibly small.) The direction of the friction force is always such as to oppose relative motion of the two surfaces.

2.13 When a block is pushed or pulled over a surface, the surface exerts a contact force on it.

The friction and normal forces are really components of a single contact force.

Contact force
Normal-force component n
Friction-force component f
Push or pull
Weight

The kind of friction that acts when a body slides over a surface is called a **kinetic friction force** $\vec{f}_\text{k}$. The adjective "kinetic" and the subscript "k" remind us that the two surfaces are moving relative to each other. The *magnitude* of the kinetic friction force usually increases when the normal force increases. This is why it takes more force to slide a box across the floor when it's full of books than when it's empty. Automotive brakes use the same principle: The harder the brake pads are squeezed against the rotating brake disks, the greater the braking effect. In many cases the magnitude of the kinetic friction force f_k is found experimentally to be approximately *proportional* to the magnitude n of the normal force. In such cases we represent the relationship by the equation

$$f_k = \mu_k n \quad \text{(magnitude of kinetic friction force)} \tag{2.10}$$

where μ_k (pronounced "mu-sub-k") is a constant called the **coefficient of kinetic friction.** The more slippery the surface, the smaller this coefficient. Because it is a quotient of two force magnitudes, μ_k is a pure number without units.

CAUTION **Friction and normal forces are always perpendicular** Remember that Eq. (2.10) is *not* a vector equation because $\vec{f}_k$ and $\vec{n}$ are always perpendicular. Rather, it is a scalar relationship between the magnitudes of the two forces.

Equation (2.10) is only an approximate representation of a complex phenomenon. On a microscopic level, friction and normal forces result from the intermolecular forces (fundamentally electrical in nature) between two rough surfaces at points where they come into contact (Fig. 2.14). As a box slides over the floor, bonds between the two surfaces form and break, and the total number of such bonds varies; hence the kinetic friction force is not perfectly constant. Smoothing the surfaces can actually increase friction, since more molecules are able to interact and bond; bringing two smooth surfaces of the same metal together can cause a "cold weld." Lubricating oils work because an oil film between two surfaces (such as the pistons and cylinder walls in a car engine) prevents them from coming into actual contact.

2.14 The normal and friction forces arise from interactions between molecules at high points on the surfaces of the block and the floor.

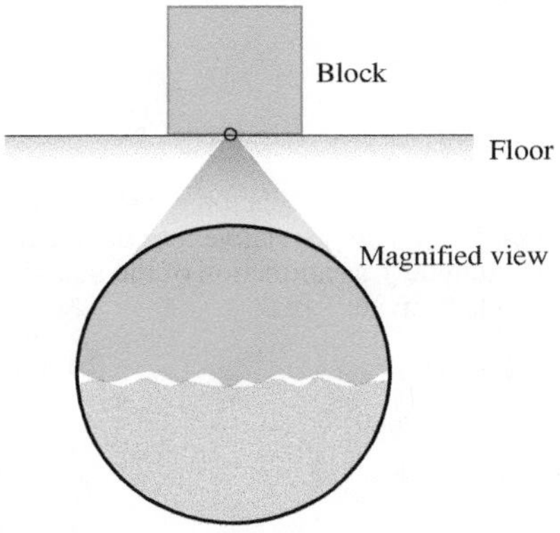
Block
Floor
Magnified view

On a microscopic level, even smooth surfaces are rough; they tend to catch and cling.

Table 2.1 lists some representative values of μ_k. Although these values are given with two significant figures, they are only approximate, since friction forces can also depend on the speed of the body relative to the surface. For now we'll ignore this effect and assume that μ_k and f_k are independent of speed, in order to concentrate on the simplest cases. Table 2.1 also lists coefficients of static friction; we'll define these shortly.

Friction forces may also act when there is *no* relative motion. If you try to slide a box across the floor, the box may not move at all because the floor exerts an equal and opposite friction force on the box. This is called a **static friction force** $\vec{f}_s$. In Fig. 2.15a, the box is at rest, in equilibrium, under the action of its weight $\vec{w}$ and the upward normal force $\vec{n}$. The normal force is equal in magnitude to the weight ($n = w$) and is exerted on the box by the floor. Now we tie a rope to the box (Fig. 2.15b) and gradually increase the tension T in the rope. At first the box remains at rest because the force of static friction f_s also increases and stays equal in magnitude to T.

At some point T becomes greater than the maximum static friction force f_s the surface can exert. Then the box "breaks loose" (the tension T is able to break the bonds between molecules in the surfaces of the box and floor) and starts to slide. Figure 2.15c shows the forces when T is at this critical value. If T exceeds this value, the box is no longer in equilibrium. For a given pair of surfaces the maximum value of f_s depends on the normal force. Experiment shows that in many cases this maximum value, called $(f_s)_{max}$, is approximately *proportional* to n; we call the proportionality factor μ_s the **coefficient of static friction.** Table 2.1 lists

Table 2.1 Approximate Coefficients of Friction

Materials	Coefficient of Static Friction, μ_s	Coefficient of Kinetic Friction, μ_k
Steel on steel	0.74	0.57
Aluminum on steel	0.61	0.47
Copper on steel	0.53	0.36
Brass on steel	0.51	0.44
Zinc on cast iron	0.85	0.21
Copper on cast iron	1.05	0.29
Glass on glass	0.94	0.40
Copper on glass	0.68	0.53
Teflon on Teflon	0.04	0.04
Teflon on steel	0.04	0.04
Rubber on concrete (dry)	1.0	0.8
Rubber on concrete (wet)	0.30	0.25

some representative values of μ_s. In a particular situation, the actual force of static friction can have any magnitude between zero (when there is no other force parallel to the surface) and a maximum value given by $\mu_s n$. In symbols,

$$f_s \le \mu_s n \quad \text{(magnitude of static friction force)} \tag{2.11}$$

Like Eq. (2.10), this is a relationship between magnitudes, *not* a vector relationship. The equality sign holds only when the applied force T has reached the critical value at which motion is about to start (Fig. 2.15c). When T is less than this value (Fig. 2.15b), the inequality sign holds. In that case we have to use the equilibrium conditions ($\Sigma\vec{F} = \mathbf{0}$) to find f_s. If there is no applied force ($T = 0$) as in Fig. 2.16a, then there is no static friction force either ($f_s = 0$).

As soon as the box starts to slide (Fig. 2.15d), the friction force usually *decreases* (Fig. 2.15e); it's easier to keep the box moving than to start it moving. Hence the coefficient of kinetic friction is usually *less* than the coefficient of static friction for any given pair of surfaces, as Table 2.1 shows.

In some situations the surfaces will alternately stick (static friction) and slip (kinetic friction). This is what causes the horrible sound made by chalk held at the wrong angle while writing on the blackboard and the shriek of tires sliding on asphalt pavement. A more positive example is the motion of a violin bow against the string.

When a body slides on a layer of gas, friction can be made very small. In the linear air track used in physics laboratories, the gliders are supported on a layer of air. The frictional force is velocity dependent, but at typical speeds the effective coefficient of friction is of the order of 0.001.

2.15 (a), (b), (c) When there is no relative motion, the magnitude of the static friction force f_s is less than or equal to $\mu_s n$. (d) When there is relative motion, the magnitude of the kinetic friction force f_k equals $\mu_k n$. (e) A graph of the friction force magnitude f as a function of the magnitude T of the applied force. The kinetic friction force varies somewhat as intermolecular bonds form and break.

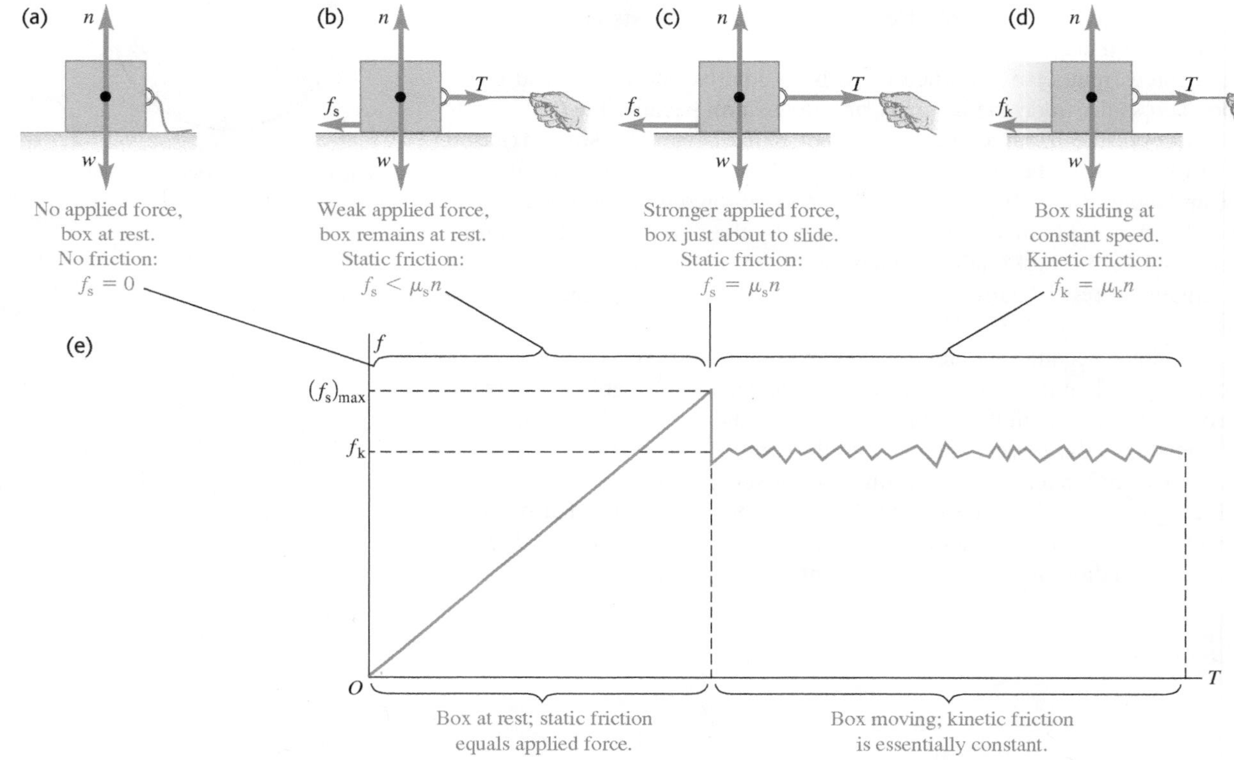

CHAPTER 2 SUMMARY

Force as a vector: Force is a quantitative measure of the interaction between two bodies. It is a vector quantity. When several forces act on a body, the effect on its motion is the same as when a single force, equal to the vector sum (resultant) of the forces, acts on the body.

$$\vec{R} = \vec{F}_1 + \vec{F}_2 + \vec{F}_3 + \cdots = \sum \vec{F} \quad (2.1)$$

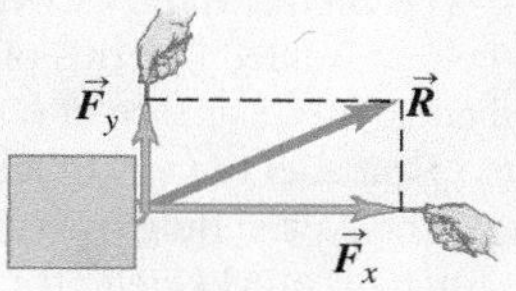

The net force on a body and Newton's first law: Newton's first law states that when the vector sum of all forces acting on a body (the *net force*) is zero, the body is in equilibrium and has zero acceleration. If the body is initially at rest, it remains at rest; if it is initially in motion, it continues to move with constant velocity. This law is valid only in inertial frames of reference.

$$\sum \vec{F} = 0 \quad (2.3)$$

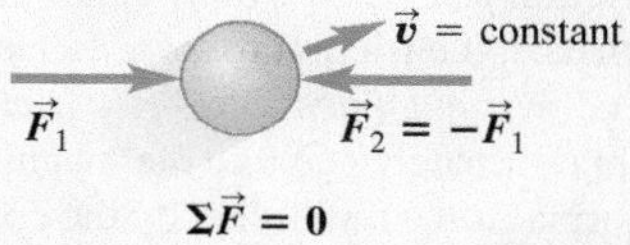

Weight: The weight $\vec{w}$ of a body is the gravitational force exerted on it by the earth. Weight is a vector quantity. The magnitude of the weight of a body at any specific location is equal to the product of its mass m and the magnitude of the acceleration due to gravity g at that location. While the weight of a body depends on its location, the mass is independent of location.

$$w = mg \quad (2.5)$$

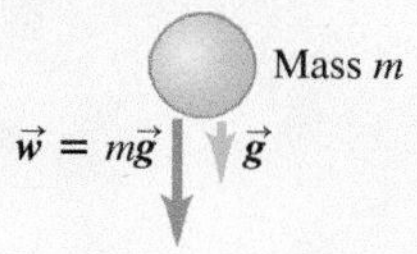

Newton's third law and action–reaction pairs: Newton's third law states that when two bodies interact, they exert forces on each other that at each instant are equal in magnitude and opposite in direction. These forces are called action and reaction forces. Each of these two forces acts on only one of the two bodies; they never act on the same body.

$$\vec{F}_{A \text{ on } B} = -\vec{F}_{B \text{ on } A} \quad (2.7)$$

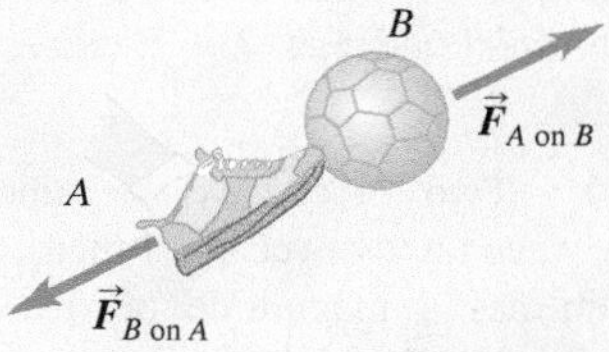

Using Newton's first law: When a body is in equilibrium in an inertial frame of reference—that is, either at rest or moving with constant velocity—the vector sum of forces acting on it must be zero (Newton's first law). Free-body diagrams are essential in identifying the forces that act on the body being considered.

Newton's third law (action and reaction) is also frequently needed in equilibrium problems. The two forces in an action–reaction pair *never* act on the same body.

The normal force exerted on a body by a surface is *not* always equal to the body's weight.

$$\sum \vec{F} = 0 \quad \text{(vector form)} \quad (2.8)$$

$$\sum F_x = 0 \qquad \sum F_y = 0 \quad \text{(component form)} \quad (2.9)$$

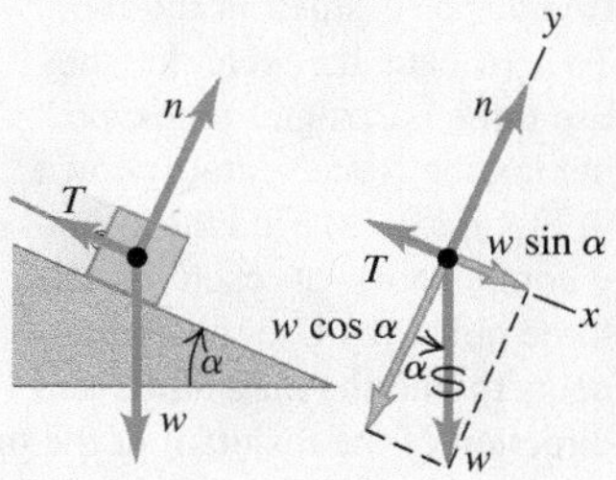

Friction: The contact force between two bodies can always be represented in terms of a normal force $\vec{n}$ perpendicular to the surface of contact and a friction force $\vec{f}$ parallel to the surface.

When a body is sliding over the surface, the friction force is called *kinetic* friction. Its magnitude f_k is approximately equal to the normal force magnitude n multiplied by the coefficient of kinetic friction μ_k. When a body is *not* moving relative to a surface, the friction force is called *static* friction. The *maximum* possible static friction force is approximately equal to the magnitude n of the normal force multiplied by the coefficient of static friction μ_s. The *actual* static friction force may be anything from zero to this maximum value, depending on the situation. Usually μ_s is greater than μ_k for a given pair of surfaces in contact.

Magnitude of kinetic friction force:

$$f_k = \mu_k n \quad (2.10)$$

Magnitude of static friction force:

$$f_s \leq \mu_s n \quad (2.11)$$

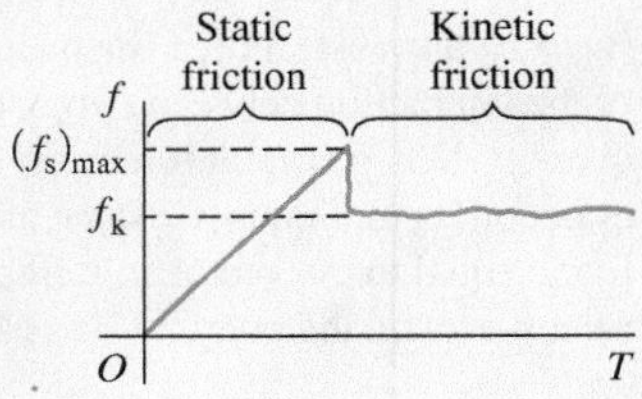

Problems

•, ••, •••: Problems of increasing difficulty. **CP**: Cumulative problems incorporating material from earlier chapters. **CALC**: Problems requiring calculus. **BIO**: Biosciences problems.

2.1 • Two forces have the same magnitude F. What is the angle between the two vectors if their sum has a magnitude of (a) $2F$? (b) $\sqrt{2}F$? (c) zero? Sketch the three vectors in each case.

2.2 • Workmen are trying to free an SUV stuck in the mud. To extricate the vehicle, they use three horizontal ropes, producing the force vectors shown in Fig. P2.2. (a) Find the x- and y-components of each of the three pulls. (b) Use the components to find the magnitude and direction of the resultant of the three pulls.

Figure **P2.2**

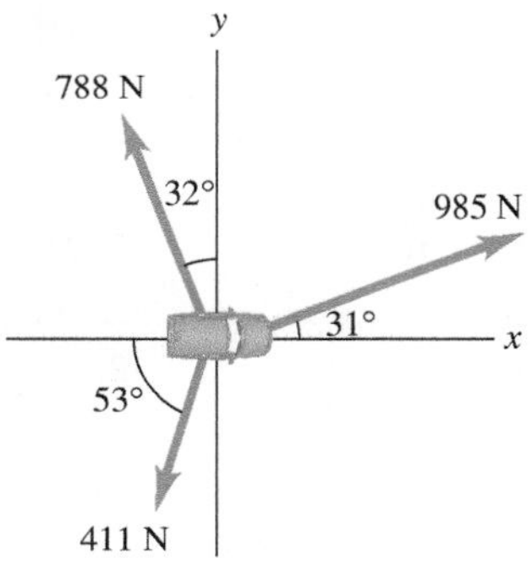

2.3 • **BIO** **Jaw Injury.** Due to a jaw injury, a patient must wear a strap (Fig. P2.3) that produces a net upward force of 5.00 N on his chin. The tension is the same throughout the strap. To what tension must the strap be adjusted to provide the necessary upward force?

Figure **P2.3**

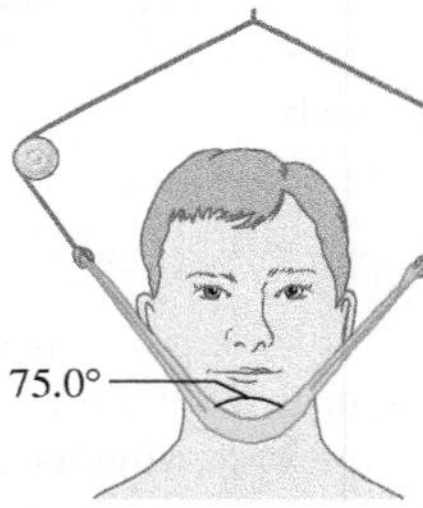

2.4 • At the surface of Jupiter's moon Io, the acceleration due to gravity is $g = 1.81 \text{ m/s}^2$. A watermelon weighs 44.0 N at the surface of the earth. (a) What is the watermelon's mass on the earth's surface? (b) What are its mass and weight on the surface of Io?

2.5 Boxes A and B are in contact on a horizontal, frictionless surface, as shown in Fig. P2.5. Box A has mass 20.0 kg and box B has mass 5.0 kg. A horizontal force of 100 N is exerted on box A. What is the magnitude of the force that box A exerts on box B?

Figure **P2.5**

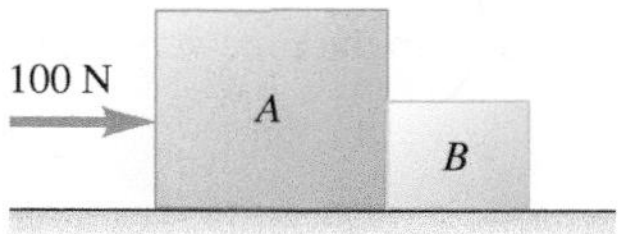
100 N
A
B

2.6 •• Two crates, A and B, sit at rest side by side on a frictionless horizontal surface. The crates have masses m_A and m_B. A horizontal force $\vec{F}$ is applied to crate A and the two crates move off to the right. (a) Draw clearly labeled free-body diagrams for crate A and for crate B. Indicate which pairs of forces, if any, are third-law action–reaction pairs. (b) If the magnitude of force $\vec{F}$ is less than the total weight of the two crates, will it cause the crates to move? Explain.

2.7 •• A person pulls horizontally on block B in Fig. P2.7, causing both blocks to move together as a unit. While this system is moving, make a carefully labeled free-body diagram of block A if (a) the table is frictionless and (b) there is friction between block B and the table and the pull is equal to the friction force on block B due to the table.

Figure **P2.7**

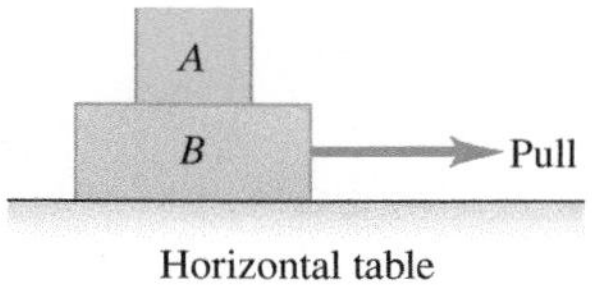
A
B
Pull
Horizontal table

2.8 •• A skier of mass 65.0 kg is pulled up a snow-covered slope at constant speed by a tow rope that is parallel to the ground. The ground slopes upward at a constant angle of 26.0° above the horizontal, and you can ignore friction. (a) Draw a clearly labeled free-body diagram for the skier. (b) Calculate the tension in the tow rope.

2.9 • Two 25.0-N weights are suspended at opposite ends of a rope that passes over a light, frictionless pulley. The pulley is attached to a chain that goes to the ceiling. (a) What is the tension in the rope? (b) What is the tension in the chain?

2.10 •• A picture frame hung against a wall is suspended by two wires attached to its upper corners. If the two wires make the same angle with the vertical, what must this angle be if the tension in each wire is equal to 0.75 of the weight of the frame? (Ignore any friction between the wall and the picture frame.)

2.11 •• A 1130-kg car is held in place by a light cable on a very smooth (frictionless) ramp, as shown in Fig. P2.11. The cable makes an angle of 31.0° above the surface of the ramp, and the ramp itself rises at 25.0° above the horizontal. (a) Draw a free-body diagram for the car. (b) Find the tension in the cable. (c) How hard does the surface of the ramp push on the car?

Figure **P2.11**

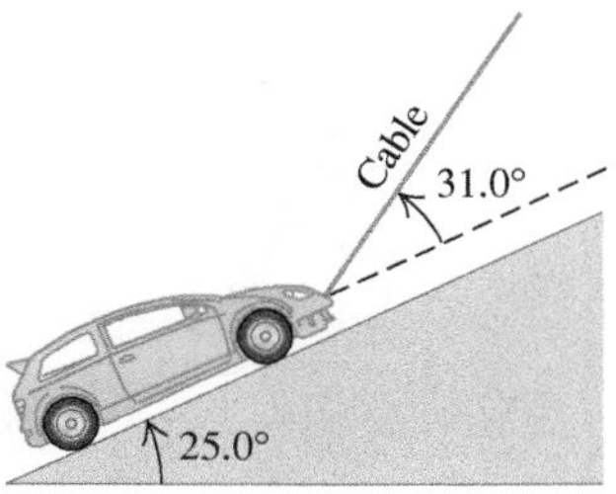
Cable
31.0°
25.0°

2.12 • In a laboratory experiment on friction, a 135-N block resting on a rough horizontal table is pulled by a horizontal wire. The pull gradually increases until the block begins to move and continues to increase thereafter. Figure P2.12 shows a graph of the friction force on this block as a function of the pull. (a) Identify the regions of the graph where static and kinetic friction occur. (b) Find the coefficients of static and kinetic friction between the block and the table. (c) Why does the graph slant upward in the first part but then level out? (d) What would the graph look like if a 135-N brick were placed on the box, and what would the coefficients of friction be in that case?

Figure **P2.12**

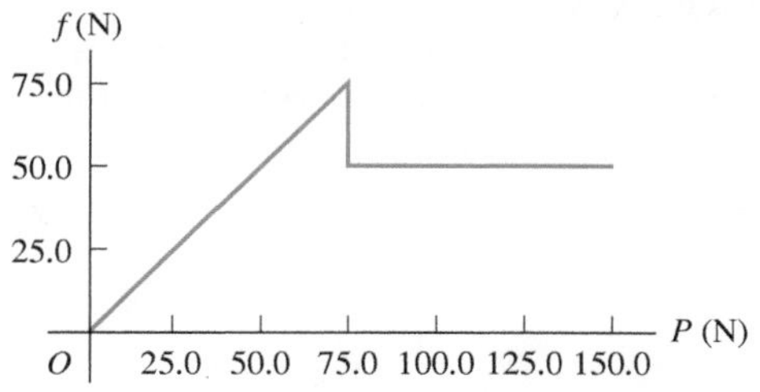
f (N)
75.0
50.0
25.0
O
25.0 50.0 75.0 100.0 125.0 150.0
P (N)

2.13 •• A box of bananas weighing 40.0 N rests on a horizontal surface. The coefficient of static friction between the box and the surface is 0.40, and the coefficient of kinetic friction is 0.20. (a) If no horizontal force is applied to the box and the box is at rest, how large is the friction force exerted on the box? (b) What is the magnitude of the friction force if a monkey applies a horizontal force of 6.0 N to the box and the box is initially at rest? (c) What minimum horizontal force must the monkey apply to start the box in motion? (d) What minimum horizontal force must the monkey apply to keep the box moving at constant velocity once it has been started? (e) If the monkey applies a horizontal force of 18.0 N, what is the magnitude of the friction force and what is the box's acceleration?

2.14 •• You are lowering two boxes, one on top of the other, down the ramp shown in Fig. P2.14 by pulling on a rope parallel to the surface of the ramp. Both boxes move together at a constant speed of 15.0 cm/s. The coefficient of kinetic friction between the ramp and the lower box is 0.444, and the coefficient of static friction between the two boxes is 0.800. (a) What force do you need to exert to accomplish this? (b) What are the magnitude and direction of the friction force on the upper box?

Figure **P2.14**

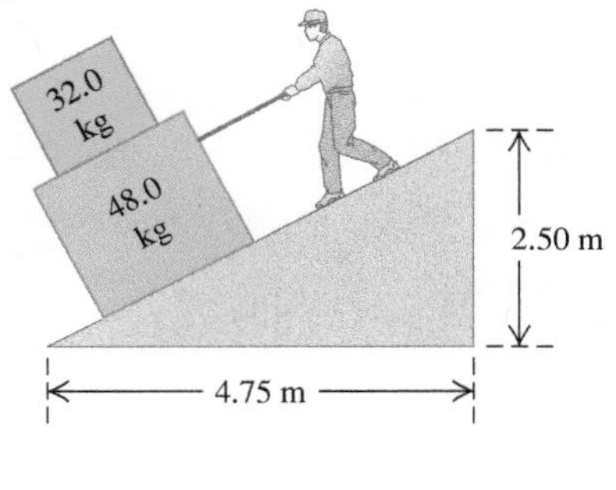
32.0 kg
48.0 kg
2.50 m
4.75 m

2.15 •• A uniform cable of weight w hangs vertically downward, supported by an upward force of magnitude w at its top end. What is the tension in the cable (a) at its top end; (b) at its bottom end; (c) at its middle? Your answer to each part must include a free-body diagram. (*Hint:* For each question choose the body to analyze to be a section of the cable or a point along the cable.) (d) Graph the tension in the rope versus the distance from its top end.

Answers

Chapter Opening Question ?

Newton's third law tells us that the car pushes on the crew member just as hard as the crew member pushes on the car, but in the opposite direction. This is true whether the car's engine is on and the car is moving forward partly under its own power, or the engine is off and being propelled by the crew member's push alone. The force magnitudes are different in the two situations, but in either case the push of the car on the crew member is just as strong as the push of the crew member on the car.

ROTATIONAL EQUILIBRIUM 3

? The cables in many modern suspension bridges are at angles to the bridge deck. How can engineers determine the expected amount of stress on each cable while they are designing the bridge?

LEARNING GOALS

By studying this chapter, you will learn:

- What is meant by the torque produced by a force.
- The conditions that must be satisfied for a body or structure to be in equilibrium.
- What is meant by the center of gravity of a body, and how it relates to the body's stability.
- How to solve problems that involve rigid bodies in equilibrium.

In this chapter we will define a new physical quantity, *torque,* that describes the twisting or turning effort of a force. Any building, from a multistory skyscraper to the humblest shed, must be designed so that it won't topple over. Similar concerns arise with a suspension bridge, a ladder leaning against a wall, or a crane hoisting a bucket full of concrete. We wish to develop a way to analyze the conditions that must be satisfied so that structures like this do not topple.

A body that can be modeled as a *particle* is in equilibrium whenever the vector sum of the forces acting on it is zero. But for the situations we've just described, that condition isn't enough. If forces act at different points on an extended body, an additional requirement must be satisfied to ensure that the body has no tendency to *rotate:* The sum of the *torques* about any point must be zero. This requirement is based on the principles of rotational dynamics. We can compute the torque due to the weight of a body using the concept of center of gravity, which we introduce in this chapter.

Rigid bodies don't bend, stretch, or squash when forces act on them. But the rigid body is an idealization; all real materials are *elastic* and do deform to some extent. Elastic properties of materials are tremendously important. You want the wings of an airplane to be able to bend a little, but you'd rather not have them break off. The steel frame of an earthquake-resistant building has to be able to flex, but not too much. Many of the necessities of everyday life, from rubber bands to suspension bridges, depend on the elastic properties of materials.

3.1 Which of these three equal-magnitude forces is most likely to loosen the tight bolt?

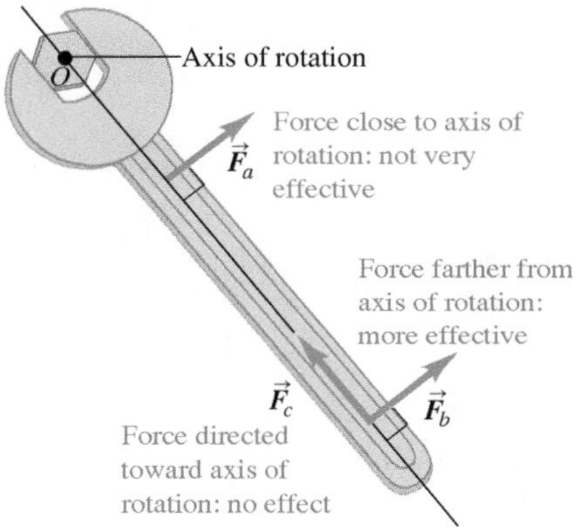

Axis of rotation
O
$\vec{F}_a$
Force close to axis of rotation: not very effective
Force farther from axis of rotation: more effective
$\vec{F}_b$
$\vec{F}_c$
Force directed toward axis of rotation: no effect

3.1 Torque

We know that forces acting on a body can affect its **translational motion**—that is, the motion of the body as a whole through space. Now we want to learn which aspects of a force determine how effective it is in causing or changing *rotational* motion. The magnitude and direction of the force are important, but so is the point on the body where the force is applied. In Fig. 3.1 a wrench is being used to loosen a tight bolt. Force $\vec{F}_b$, applied near the end of the handle, is more effective than an equal force $\vec{F}_a$ applied near the bolt. Force $\vec{F}_c$ doesn't do any good at all; it's applied at the same point and has the same magnitude as $\vec{F}_b$, but it's directed along the length of the handle. The quantitative measure of the tendency of a force to cause or change a body's rotational motion is called *torque;* we say that $\vec{F}_a$ applies a torque about point O to the wrench in Fig. 3.1, $\vec{F}_b$ applies a greater torque about O, and $\vec{F}_c$ applies zero torque about O.

Figure 3.2 shows three examples of how to calculate torque. The body in the figure can rotate about an axis that is perpendicular to the plane of the figure and passes through point O. Three forces, $\vec{F}_1$, $\vec{F}_2$, and $\vec{F}_3$, act on the body in the plane of the figure. The tendency of the first of these forces, $\vec{F}_1$, to cause a rotation about O depends on its magnitude F_1. It also depends on the *perpendicular* distance l_1 between point O and the **line of action** of the force (that is, the line along which the force vector lies). We call the distance l_1 the **lever arm** (or **moment arm**) of force $\vec{F}_1$ about O. The twisting effort is directly proportional to both F_1 and l_1, so in this case we define the **torque** (or *moment*) of the force $\vec{F}_1$ with respect to O as the product $F_1 l_1$. We use the Greek letter τ (tau) for torque. In general, for a force of magnitude F whose line of action is a perpendicular distance l from O, the magnitude of the torque is

$$\tau = Fl \tag{3.1}$$

Physicists usually use the term "torque," while engineers usually use "moment" (unless they are talking about a rotating shaft). Both groups use the term "lever arm" or "moment arm" for the distance l.

The lever arm of $\vec{F}_1$ in Fig. 3.2 is the perpendicular distance l_1, and the lever arm of $\vec{F}_2$ is the perpendicular distance l_2. The line of action of $\vec{F}_3$ passes through point O, so the lever arm for $\vec{F}_3$ is zero and its torque with respect to O is zero. In the same way, force $\vec{F}_c$ in Fig. 10.1 has zero torque with respect to point O; $\vec{F}_b$ has a greater torque than $\vec{F}_a$ because its lever arm is greater.

3.2 The torque of a force about a point is the product of the force magnitude and the lever arm of the force.

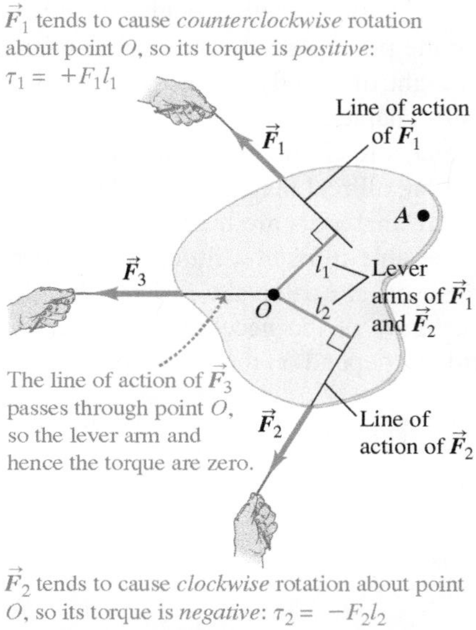
$\vec{F}_1$ tends to cause *counterclockwise* rotation about point O, so its torque is *positive*: $\tau_1 = +F_1 l_1$
Line of action of $\vec{F}_1$
$\vec{F}_1$
A
$\vec{F}_3$
l_1
l_2
O
Lever arms of $\vec{F}_1$ and $\vec{F}_2$
The line of action of $\vec{F}_3$ passes through point O, so the lever arm and hence the torque are zero.
$\vec{F}_2$
Line of action of $\vec{F}_2$
$\vec{F}_2$ tends to cause *clockwise* rotation about point O, so its torque is *negative*: $\tau_2 = -F_2 l_2$

CAUTION **Torque is always measured about a point** Note that torque is *always* defined with reference to a specific point. If we shift the position of this point, the torque of each force may also change. For example, the torque of force $\vec{F}_3$ in Fig. 3.2 is zero with respect to point O, but the torque of $\vec{F}_3$ is *not* zero about point A. It's not enough to refer to "the torque of $\vec{F}$"; you must say "the torque of $\vec{F}$ with respect to point X" or "the torque of $\vec{F}$ about point X."

Force $\vec{F}_1$ in Fig. 3.2 tends to cause *counterclockwise* rotation about O, while $\vec{F}_2$ tends to cause *clockwise* rotation. To distinguish between these two possibilities, we need to choose a positive sense of rotation. The fact that the sign is significant is a clue that torque is a vector quantity. With the choice that *counterclockwise torques are positive and clockwise torques are negative,* the torques of $\vec{F}_1$ and $\vec{F}_2$ about O are

$$\tau_1 = +F_1 l_1 \qquad \tau_2 = -F_2 l_2$$

Figure 3.2 shows this choice for the sign of torque. We will often use the symbol ⊕ to indicate our choice of the positive sense of rotation.

The SI unit of torque is the newton-meter. In our discussion of work and energy we called this combination the joule. But torque is *not* work or energy, and torque should be expressed in newton-meters, *not* joules.

Figure 3.3 shows a force $\vec{F}$ applied at a point P described by a position vector $\vec{r}$ with respect to the chosen point O. There are three ways to calculate the torque of this force:

1. Find the lever arm l and use $\tau = Fl$.
2. Determine the angle ϕ between the vectors $\vec{r}$ and $\vec{F}$; the lever arm is $r\sin\phi$, so $\tau = rF\sin\phi$.
3. Represent $\vec{F}$ in terms of a radial component F_{rad} along the direction of $\vec{r}$ and a tangential component F_{tan} at right angles, perpendicular to $\vec{r}$. (We call this a tangential component because if the body rotates, the point where the force acts moves in a circle, and this component is tangent to that circle.) Then $F_{tan} = F\sin\phi$ and $\tau = r(F\sin\phi) = F_{tan}r$. The component F_{rad} produces *no* torque with respect to O because its lever arm with respect to that point is zero (compare to forces $\vec{F}_c$ in Fig. 3.1 and $\vec{F}_3$ in Fig. 3.2).

Summarizing these three expressions for torque, we have

$$\tau = Fl = rF\sin\phi = F_{tan}r \quad \text{(magnitude of torque)} \tag{3.2}$$

Torque as a Vector

Angular velocity and angular acceleration can be represented as vectors; the same is true for torque. To see how to do this, note that the quantity $rF\sin\phi$ in

3.3 Three ways to calculate the torque of the force $\vec{F}$ about the point O. In this figure, $\vec{r}$ and $\vec{F}$ are in the plane of the page and the torque vector $\vec{\tau}$ points out of the page toward you.

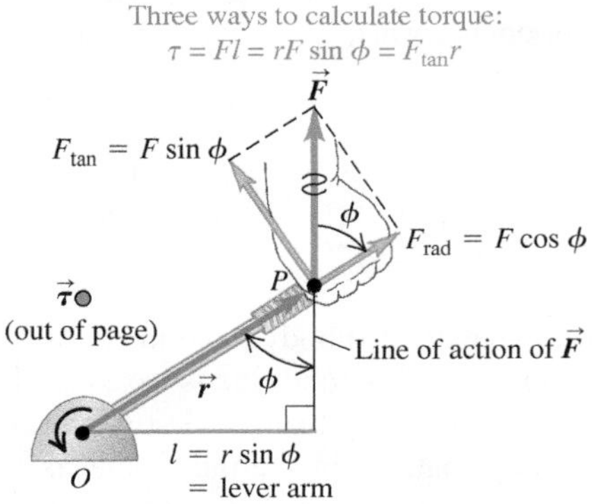

3.4 The torque vector $\vec{\tau} = \vec{r} \times \vec{F}$ is directed along the axis of the bolt, perpendicular to both $\vec{r}$ and $\vec{F}$. The fingers of the right hand curl in the direction of the rotation that the torque tends to cause.

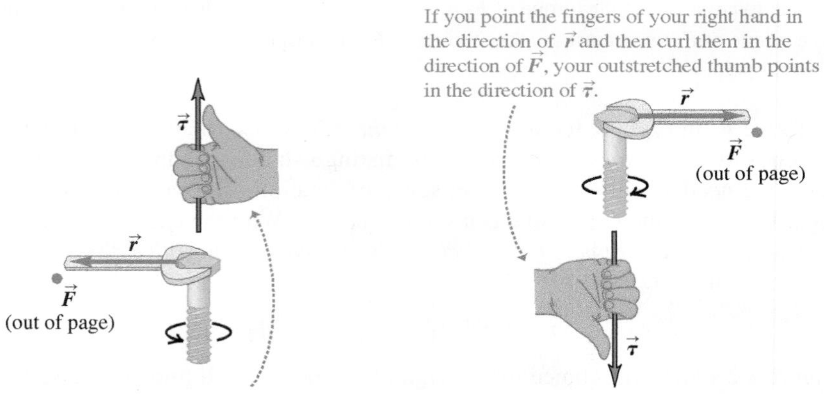
If you point the fingers of your right hand in the direction of $\vec{r}$ and then curl them in the direction of $\vec{F}$, your outstretched thumb points in the direction of $\vec{\tau}$.
$\vec{\tau}$
$\vec{r}$
$\vec{F}$
(out of page)
$\vec{r}$
$\vec{F}$
(out of page)
$\vec{\tau}$

Eq. (3.2) is the magnitude of the *vector product* $\vec{r} \times \vec{F}$. (You should go back and review that definition.) We now generalize the definition of torque as follows: When a force $\vec{F}$ acts at a point having a position vector $\vec{r}$ with respect to an origin O, as in Fig. 3.3, the torque $\vec{\tau}$ of the force with respect to O is the *vector* quantity

$$\vec{\tau} = \vec{r} \times \vec{F} \qquad \text{(definition of torque vector)} \qquad (3.3)$$

The torque as defined in Eq. (3.2) is just the magnitude of the torque vector $\vec{r} \times \vec{F}$. The direction of $\vec{\tau}$ is perpendicular to both $\vec{r}$ and $\vec{F}$. In particular, if both $\vec{r}$ and $\vec{F}$ lie in a plane perpendicular to the axis of rotation, as in Fig. 3.3, then the torque vector $\vec{\tau} = \vec{r} \times \vec{F}$ is directed along the axis of rotation, with a sense given by the right-hand rule. Figure 3.4 shows the direction relationships.

In diagrams that involve $\vec{r}$, $\vec{F}$, and $\vec{\tau}$, it's common to have one of the vectors oriented perpendicular to the page. (Indeed, by the very nature of the cross product, $\vec{\tau} = \vec{r} \times \vec{F}$ *must* be perpendicular to the plane of the vectors $\vec{r}$ and $\vec{F}$.) We use a dot (•) to represent a vector that points out of the page (see Fig. 3.3) and a cross (**×**) to represent a vector that points into the page.

In the following sections we will usually be concerned with rotation of a body about an axis oriented in a specified constant direction. In that case, only the component of torque along that axis is of interest, and we often call that component the torque with respect to the specified *axis*.

3.2 Conditions for Equilibrium

A particle is in *equilibrium*—that is, the particle does not accelerate—in an inertial frame of reference if the vector sum of all the forces acting on the particle is zero, $\sum \vec{F} = \mathbf{0}$. For an *extended* body, the equivalent statement is that the center of mass of the body has zero acceleration if the vector sum of all external forces acting on the body is zero. This is often called the **first condition for equilibrium.** In vector and component forms,

$$\sum \vec{F} = \mathbf{0}$$
$$\sum F_x = 0 \qquad \sum F_y = 0 \qquad \sum F_z = 0 \qquad \text{(first condition for equilibrium)} \qquad (3.4)$$

A second condition for an extended body to be in equilibrium is that the body must have no tendency to *rotate.* This condition is based on the dynamics of rotational motion in exactly the same way that the first condition is based on Newton's first law. A rigid body that, in an inertial frame, is not rotating about a

3.5 To be in static equilibrium, a body at rest must satisfy *both* conditions for equilibrium: It can have no tendency to accelerate as a whole or to start rotating.

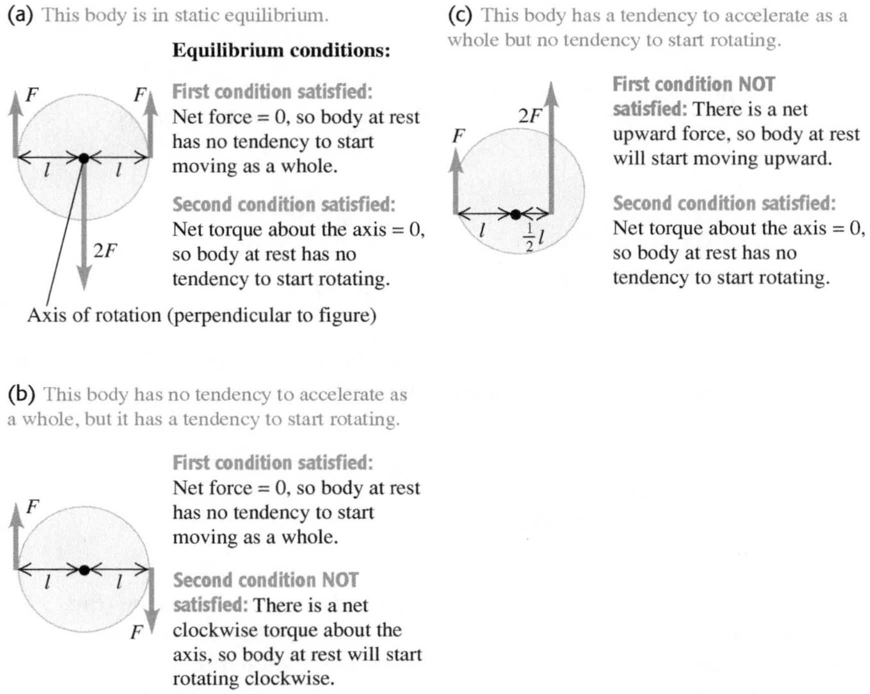
(a) This body is in static equilibrium.
Equilibrium conditions:
F
F
l
l
2F
First condition satisfied: Net force = 0, so body at rest has no tendency to start moving as a whole.
Second condition satisfied: Net torque about the axis = 0, so body at rest has no tendency to start rotating.
Axis of rotation (perpendicular to figure)
(b) This body has no tendency to accelerate as a whole, but it has a tendency to start rotating.
F
l
l
F
First condition satisfied: Net force = 0, so body at rest has no tendency to start moving as a whole.
Second condition NOT satisfied: There is a net clockwise torque about the axis, so body at rest will start rotating clockwise.
(c) This body has a tendency to accelerate as a whole but no tendency to start rotating.
2F
F
l
½l
First condition NOT satisfied: There is a net upward force, so body at rest will start moving upward.
Second condition satisfied: Net torque about the axis = 0, so body at rest has no tendency to start rotating.

certain point has zero angular momentum about that point. If it is not to start rotating about that point, the rate of change of angular momentum must *also* be zero. This means that the sum of torques due to all the external forces acting on the body must be zero. A rigid body in equilibrium can't have any tendency to start rotating about *any* point, so the sum of external torques must be zero about any point. This is the **second condition for equilibrium:**

$$\sum \vec{\tau} = \mathbf{0} \quad \text{about any point} \qquad \text{(second condition for equilibrium)} \qquad (3.5)$$

The sum of the torques due to all external forces acting on the body, with respect to any specified point, must be zero.

In this chapter we will apply the first and second conditions for equilibrium to situations in which a rigid body is at rest (no translation or rotation). Such a body is said to be in **static equilibrium** (Fig. 3.5). But the same conditions apply to a rigid body in uniform *translational* motion (without rotation), such as an airplane in flight with constant speed, direction, and altitude. Such a body is in equilibrium but is not static.

3.3 Center of Gravity

In most equilibrium problems, one of the forces acting on the body is its weight. We need to be able to calculate the *torque* of this force. The weight doesn't act at a single point; it is distributed over the entire body. But we can always calculate the torque due to the body's weight by assuming that the entire force of gravity (weight) is concentrated at a point called the **center of gravity** (abbreviated "cg"). The acceleration due to gravity decreases with altitude; but if we can ignore this variation over the vertical dimension of the body, then the body's center of gravity is identical to its *center of mass* (abbreviated "cm").

First let's review the definition of the center of mass. For a collection of particles with masses $m_1, m_2, \ldots$ and coordinates $(x_1, y_1, z_1), (x_2, y_2, z_2), \ldots$, the coordinates x_{cm}, y_{cm}, and z_{cm} of the center of mass are given by

$$x_{cm} = \frac{m_1x_1 + m_2x_2 + m_3x_3 + \cdots}{m_1 + m_2 + m_3 + \cdots} = \frac{\sum_i m_ix_i}{\sum_i m_i}$$

$$y_{cm} = \frac{m_1y_1 + m_2y_2 + m_3y_3 + \cdots}{m_1 + m_2 + m_3 + \cdots} = \frac{\sum_i m_iy_i}{\sum_i m_i} \quad \text{(center of mass)} \tag{3.6}$$

$$z_{cm} = \frac{m_1z_1 + m_2z_2 + m_3z_3 + \cdots}{m_1 + m_2 + m_3 + \cdots} = \frac{\sum_i m_iz_i}{\sum_i m_i}$$

Also, x_{cm}, y_{cm}, and z_{cm} are the components of the position vector $\vec{r}_{cm}$ of the center of mass, so Eqs. (3.6) are equivalent to the vector equation

$$\vec{r}_{cm} = \frac{m_1\vec{r}_1 + m_2\vec{r}_2 + m_3\vec{r}_3 + \cdots}{m_1 + m_2 + m_3 + \cdots} = \frac{\sum_i m_i\vec{r}_i}{\sum_i m_i} \tag{3.7}$$

3.6 The center of gravity (cg) and center of mass (cm) of an extended body.

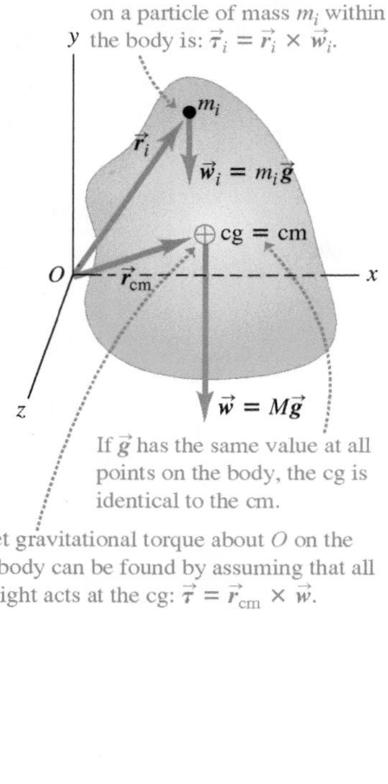
The gravitational torque about O on a particle of mass m_i within the body is: $\vec{\tau}_i = \vec{r}_i \times \vec{w}_i$.
y
m_i
$\vec{r}_i$
$\vec{w}_i = m_i\vec{g}$
cg = cm
O
$\vec{r}_{cm}$
x
z
$\vec{w} = M\vec{g}$
If $\vec{g}$ has the same value at all points on the body, the cg is identical to the cm.
The net gravitational torque about O on the entire body can be found by assuming that all the weight acts at the cg: $\vec{\tau} = \vec{r}_{cm} \times \vec{w}$.

Now consider the gravitational torque on a body of arbitrary shape (Fig. 3.6). We assume that the acceleration due to gravity $\vec{g}$ is the same at every point in the body. Every particle in the body experiences a gravitational force, and the total weight of the body is the vector sum of a large number of parallel forces. A typical particle has mass m_i and weight $\vec{w}_i = m_i\vec{g}$. If $\vec{r}_i$ is the position vector of this particle with respect to an arbitrary origin O, then the torque vector $\vec{\tau}_i$ of the weight $\vec{w}_i$ with respect to O is, from Eq. (3.3),

$$\vec{\tau}_i = \vec{r}_i \times \vec{w}_i = \vec{r}_i \times m_i\vec{g}$$

The *total* torque due to the gravitational forces on all the particles is

$$\begin{aligned}\vec{\tau} &= \sum_i \vec{\tau}_i = \vec{r}_1 \times m_1\vec{g} + \vec{r}_2 \times m_2\vec{g} + \cdots \\ &= (m_1\vec{r}_1 + m_2\vec{r}_2 + \cdots) \times \vec{g} \\ &= \left(\sum_i m_i\vec{r}_i\right) \times \vec{g}\end{aligned}$$

When we multiply and divide this by the total mass of the body,

$$M = m_1 + m_2 + \cdots = \sum_i m_i$$

we get

$$\vec{\tau} = \frac{m_1\vec{r}_1 + m_2\vec{r}_2 + \cdots}{m_1 + m_2 + \cdots} \times M\vec{g} = \frac{\sum_i m_i\vec{r}_i}{\sum_i m_i} \times M\vec{g}$$

The fraction in this equation is just the position vector $\vec{r}_{cm}$ of the center of mass, with components x_{cm}, y_{cm}, and z_{cm}, as given by Eq. (3.7), and $M\vec{g}$ is equal to the total weight $\vec{w}$ of the body. Thus

$$\vec{\tau} = \vec{r}_{cm} \times M\vec{g} = \vec{r}_{cm} \times \vec{w} \tag{3.8}$$

The total gravitational torque, given by Eq. (3.8), is the same as though the total weight $\vec{w}$ were acting on the position $\vec{r}_{cm}$ of the center of mass, which we also call the *center of gravity.* **If $\vec{g}$ has the same value at all points on a body, its center of gravity is identical to its center of mass.** Note, however, that the center of mass is defined independently of any gravitational effect.

3.7 Finding the center of gravity of an irregularly shaped body—in this case, a coffee mug.

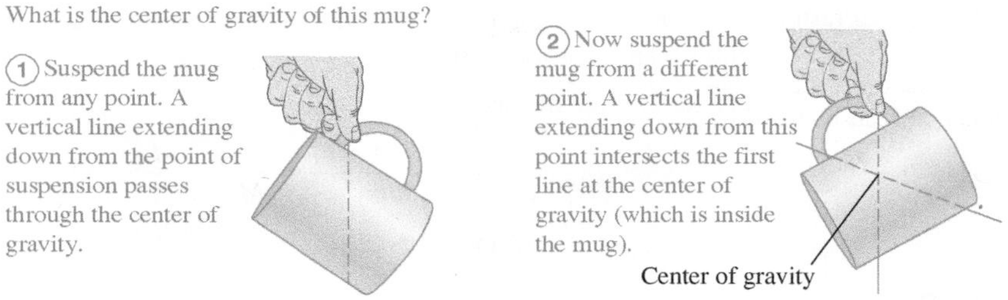
What is the center of gravity of this mug?
1 Suspend the mug from any point. A vertical line extending down from the point of suspension passes through the center of gravity.
2 Now suspend the mug from a different point. A vertical line extending down from this point intersects the first line at the center of gravity (which is inside the mug).
Center of gravity

While the value of $\vec{g}$ does vary somewhat with elevation, the variation is extremely slight. Hence we will assume throughout this chapter that the center of gravity and center of mass are identical unless explicitly stated otherwise.

Finding and Using the Center of Gravity

We can often use symmetry considerations to locate the center of gravity of a body, just as we did for the center of mass. The center of gravity of a homogeneous sphere, cube, circular sheet, or rectangular plate is at its geometric center. The center of gravity of a right circular cylinder or cone is on its axis of symmetry.

For a body with a more complex shape, we can sometimes locate the center of gravity by thinking of the body as being made of symmetrical pieces. For example, we could approximate the human body as a collection of solid cylinders, with a sphere for the head. Then we can locate the center of gravity of the combination with Eqs. (3.6), letting $m_1, m_2, \ldots$ be the masses of the individual pieces and $(x_1, y_1, z_1), (x_2, y_2, z_2), \ldots$ be the coordinates of their centers of gravity.

When a body acted on by gravity is supported or suspended at a single point, the center of gravity is always at or directly above or below the point of suspension. If it were anywhere else, the weight would have a torque with respect to the point of suspension, and the body could not be in rotational equilibrium. Figure 3.7 shows how to use this fact to determine experimentally the location of the center of gravity of an irregular body.

Using the same reasoning, we can see that a body supported at several points must have its center of gravity somewhere within the area bounded by the supports. This explains why a car can drive on a straight but slanted road if the slant angle is relatively small (Fig. 3.8a) but will tip over if the angle is too steep (Fig. 3.8b). The truck in Fig. 3.8c has a higher center of gravity than the car and will tip over on a shallower incline. When a truck overturns on a highway and blocks traffic for hours, it's the high center of gravity that's to blame.

The lower the center of gravity and the larger the area of support, the more difficult it is to overturn a body. Four-legged animals such as deer and horses

3.8 In (a) the center of gravity is within the area bounded by the supports, and the car is in equilibrium. The car in (b) and the truck in (c) will tip over because their centers of gravity lie outside the area of support.

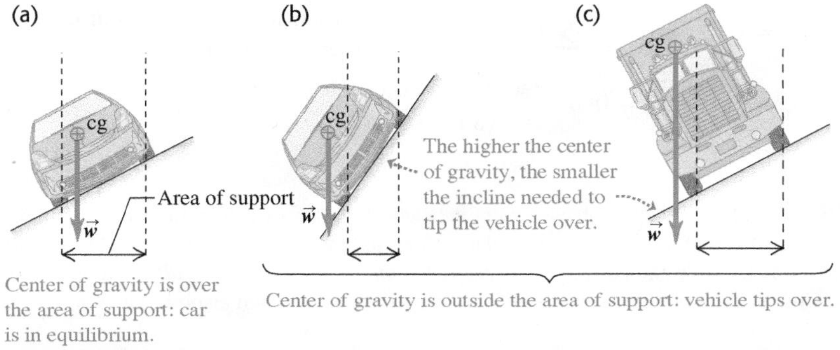
(a)
(b)
(c)
cg
cg
cg
Area of support
$\vec{w}$
$\vec{w}$
$\vec{w}$
The higher the center of gravity, the smaller the incline needed to tip the vehicle over.
Center of gravity is over the area of support: car is in equilibrium.
Center of gravity is outside the area of support: vehicle tips over.

Example 3.1 Walking the plank

A uniform plank of length $L = 6.0$ m and mass $M = 90$ kg rests on sawhorses separated by $D = 1.5$ m and equidistant from the center of the plank. Cousin Throckmorton wants to stand on the right-hand end of the plank. If the plank is to remain at rest, how massive can Throckmorton be?

SOLUTION

IDENTIFY and SET UP: To just balance, Throckmorton's mass m must be such that the center of gravity of the plank–Throcky system is directly over the right-hand sawhorse (Fig. 3.9). We take the origin at C, the geometric center and center of gravity of the plank, and take the positive x-axis horizontally to the right. Then the centers of gravity of the plank and Throcky are at $x_P = 0$ and $x_T = L/2 = 3.0$ m, respectively, and the right-hand sawhorse is at $x_S = D/2$. We'll use Eqs. (3.6) to locate the center of gravity x_{cg} of the plank–Throcky system.

3.9 Our sketch for this problem.

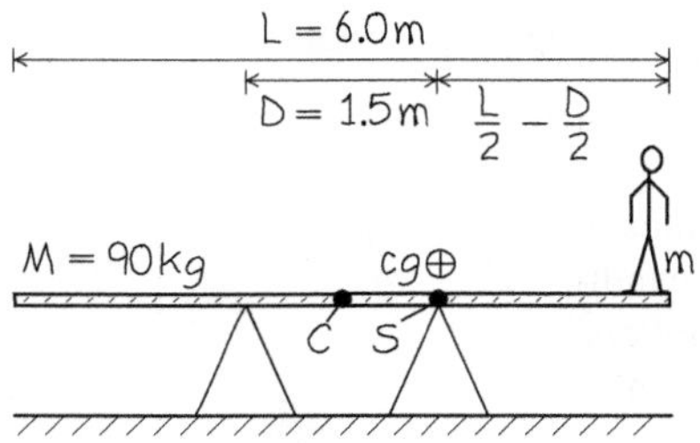

EXECUTE: From the first of Eqs. (3.6),

$$x_{cg} = \frac{M(0) + m(L/2)}{M + m} = \frac{m}{M + m}\frac{L}{2}$$

We set $x_{cg} = x_S$ and solve for m:

$$\frac{m}{M + m}\frac{L}{2} = \frac{D}{2}$$

$$mL = (M + m)D$$

$$m = M\frac{D}{L - D} = (90\text{ kg})\frac{1.5\text{ m}}{6.0\text{ m} - 1.5\text{ m}} = 30\text{ kg}$$

EVALUATE: As a check, let's repeat the calculation with the origin at the right-hand sawhorse. Now $x_S = 0$, $x_P = -D/2$, and $x_T = (L/2) - (D/2)$, and we require $x_{cg} = x_S = 0$:

$$x_{cg} = \frac{M(-D/2) + m[(L/2) - (D/2)]}{M + m} = 0$$

$$m = \frac{MD/2}{(L/2) - (D/2)} = M\frac{D}{L - D} = 30\text{ kg}$$

The result doesn't depend on our choice of origin.

A 60-kg adult could stand only halfway between the right-hand sawhorse and the end of the plank. Can you see why?

have a large area of support bounded by their legs; hence they are naturally stable and need only small feet or hooves. Animals that walk erect on two legs, such as humans and birds, need relatively large feet to give them a reasonable area of support. If a two-legged animal holds its body approximately horizontal, like a chicken or the dinosaur *Tyrannosaurus rex,* it must perform a delicate balancing act as it walks to keep its center of gravity over the foot that is on the ground. A chicken does this by moving its head; *T. rex* probably did it by moving its massive tail.

3.4 Solving Rigid-Body Equilibrium Problems

There are just two key conditions for rigid-body equilibrium: The vector sum of the forces on the body must be zero, and the sum of the torques about any point must be zero. To keep things simple, we'll restrict our attention to situations in which we can treat all forces as acting in a single plane, which we'll call the xy-plane. Then we can ignore the condition $\sum F_z = 0$ in Eqs. (3.4), and in Eq. (3.5) we need consider only the z-components of torque (perpendicular to the plane). The first and second conditions for equilibrium are then

$$\sum F_x = 0 \quad \text{and} \quad \sum F_y = 0 \quad \text{(first condition for equilibrium, forces in } xy\text{-plane)}$$

$$\sum \tau_z = 0 \quad \text{(second condition for equilibrium, forces in } xy\text{-plane)} \qquad (3.9)$$

CAUTION **Choosing the reference point for calculating torques** In equilibrium problems, the choice of reference point for calculating torques in $\sum \tau_z$ is completely arbitrary. But once you make your choice, you must use the *same* point to calculate *all* the torques on a body. Choose the point so as to simplify the calculations as much as possible.

Example 3.2 Will the ladder slip?

Sir Lancelot, who weighs 800 N, is assaulting a castle by climbing a uniform ladder that is 5.0 m long and weighs 180 N (Fig. 3.10a). The bottom of the ladder rests on a ledge and leans across the moat in equilibrium against a frictionless, vertical castle wall. The ladder makes an angle of 53.1° with the horizontal. Lancelot pauses one-third of the way up the ladder. (a) Find the normal and friction forces on the base of the ladder. (b) Find the minimum coefficient of static friction needed to prevent slipping at the base. (c) Find the magnitude and direction of the contact force on the base of the ladder.

SOLUTION

IDENTIFY and SET UP: The ladder–Lancelot system is stationary, so we can use the two conditions for equilibrium to solve part (a). In part (b), we need the relationship among the static friction force, the coefficient of static friction, and the normal force. In part (c), the contact force is the vector sum of the normal and friction forces acting at the base of the ladder, found in part (a). Figure 3.10b shows the free-body diagram, with x- and y-directions as shown and with counterclockwise torques taken to be positive. The ladder's center of gravity is at its geometric center. Lancelot's 800-N weight acts at a point one-third of the way up the ladder.

The wall exerts only a normal force n_1 on the top of the ladder. The forces on the base are an upward normal force n_2 and a static friction force f_s, which must point to the right to prevent slipping. The magnitudes n_2 and f_s are the target variables in part (a). These magnitudes are related by $f_s \le \mu_s n_2$; the coefficient of static friction μ_s is the target variable in part (b).

EXECUTE: (a) From Eqs. (3.9), the first condition for equilibrium gives

$$\sum F_x = f_s + (-n_1) = 0$$
$$\sum F_y = n_2 + (-800\ \text{N}) + (-180\ \text{N}) = 0$$

These are two equations for the three unknowns n_1, n_2, and f_s. The second equation gives $n_2 = 980$ N. To obtain a third equation, we use the second condition for equilibrium. We take torques about point B, about which n_2 and f_s have no torque. The 53.1° angle creates a 3-4-5 right triangle, so from Fig. 3.10b the lever arm for the ladder's weight is 1.5 m, the lever arm for Lancelot's weight is 1.0 m, and the lever arm for n_1 is 4.0 m. The torque equation for point B is then

$$\sum \tau_B = n_1(4.0\ \text{m}) - (180\ \text{N})(1.5\ \text{m}) - (800\ \text{N})(1.0\ \text{m}) + n_2(0) + f_s(0) = 0$$

Solving for n_1, we get $n_1 = 268$ N. We substitute this into the $\sum F_x = 0$ equation and get $f_s = 268$ N.

(b) The static friction force f_s cannot exceed $\mu_s n_2$, so the *minimum* coefficient of static friction to prevent slipping is

$$(\mu_s)_{\min} = \frac{f_s}{n_2} = \frac{268\ \text{N}}{980\ \text{N}} = 0.27$$

(c) The components of the contact force $\vec{F}_B$ at the base are the static friction force f_s and the normal force n_2, so

$$\vec{F}_B = f_s\hat{\imath} + n_2\hat{\jmath} = (268\ \text{N})\hat{\imath} + (980\ \text{N})\hat{\jmath}$$

The magnitude and direction of $\vec{F}_B$ (Fig. 11.9c) are

$$F_B = \sqrt{(268\ \text{N})^2 + (980\ \text{N})^2} = 1020\ \text{N}$$
$$\theta = \arctan\frac{980\ \text{N}}{268\ \text{N}} = 75^\circ$$

EVALUATE: As Fig. 3.10c shows, the contact force $\vec{F}_B$ is *not* directed along the length of the ladder. Can you show that if $\vec{F}_B$ were directed along the ladder, there would be a net counterclockwise torque with respect to the top of the ladder, and equilibrium would be impossible?

As Lancelot climbs higher on the ladder, the lever arm and torque of his weight about B increase. This increases the values of n_1, f_s, and the required friction coefficient $(\mu_s)_{\min}$, so the ladder is more and more likely to slip as he climbs. A simple way to make slipping less likely is to use a larger ladder angle (say, 75° rather than 53.1°). This decreases the lever arms with respect to B of the weights of the ladder and Lancelot and increases the lever arm of n_1, all of which decrease the required friction force.

If we had assumed friction on the wall as well as on the floor, the problem would be impossible to solve by using the equilibrium conditions alone. (Try it!) The difficulty is that it's no longer adequate to treat the body as being perfectly rigid. Another problem of this kind is a four-legged table; there's no way to use the equilibrium conditions alone to find the force on each separate leg.

3.10 (a) Sir Lancelot pauses a third of the way up the ladder, fearing it will slip. (b) Free-body diagram for the system of Sir Lancelot and the ladder. (c) The contact force at B is the superposition of the normal force and the static friction force.

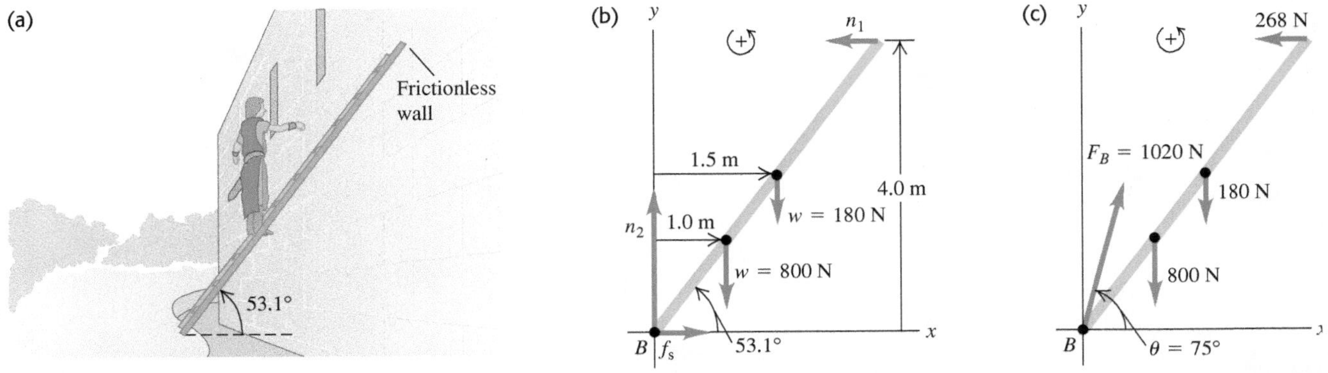

CHAPTER 3 SUMMARY

Torque: When a force $\vec{F}$ acts on a body, the torque of that force with respect to a point O has a magnitude given by the product of the force magnitude F and the lever arm l. More generally, torque is a vector $\vec{\tau}$ equal to the vector product of $\vec{r}$ (the position vector of the point at which the force acts) and $\vec{F}$.

$$\tau = Fl \tag{3.2}$$

$$\vec{\tau} = \vec{r} \times \vec{F} \tag{3.3}$$

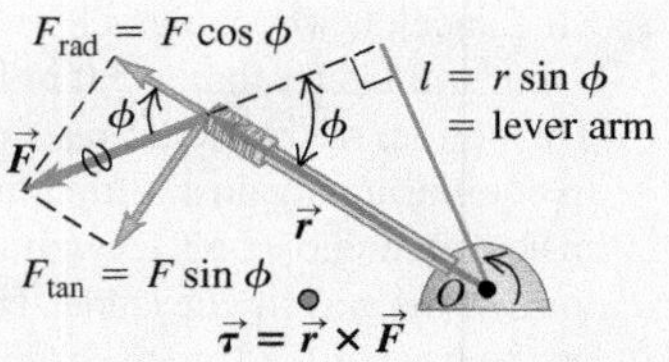

Conditions for equilibrium: For a rigid body to be in equilibrium, two conditions must be satisfied. First, the vector sum of forces must be zero. Second, the sum of torques about any point must be zero. The torque due to the weight of a body can be found by assuming the entire weight is concentrated at the center of gravity, which is at the same point as the center of mass if $\vec{g}$ has the same value at all points. (See Examples 3.1 and 3.2.)

$$\sum F_x = 0 \qquad \sum F_y = 0 \qquad \sum F_z = 0 \tag{3.4}$$

$$\sum \vec{\tau} = \mathbf{0} \quad \text{about } any \text{ point} \tag{3.5}$$

$$\vec{r}_{cm} = \frac{m_1\vec{r}_1 + m_2\vec{r}_2 + m_3\vec{r}_3 + \cdots}{m_1 + m_2 + m_3 + \cdots} \tag{3.7}$$

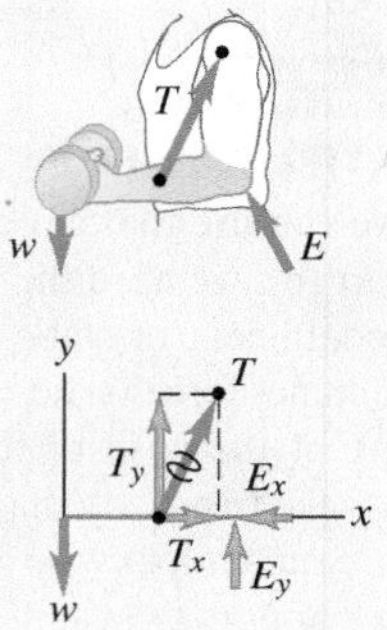

Center of mass: The position vector of the center of mass of a system of particles, $\vec{r}_{cm}$, is a weighted average of the positions $\vec{r}_1, \vec{r}_2, \ldots$ of the individual particles.

$$\vec{r}_{cm} = \frac{m_1\vec{r}_1 + m_2\vec{r}_2 + m_3\vec{r}_3 + \cdots}{m_1 + m_2 + m_3 + \cdots} = \frac{\sum_i m_i \vec{r}_i}{\sum_i m_i} \tag{8.29}$$

Problems

•, ••, •••: Problems of increasing difficulty. **CP**: Cumulative problems incorporating material from earlier chapters. **CALC**: Problems requiring calculus. **BIO**: Biosciences problems.

3.1 • Calculate the net torque about point O for the two forces applied as in Fig. P3.1. The rod and both forces are in the plane of the page.

Figure **P3.1**

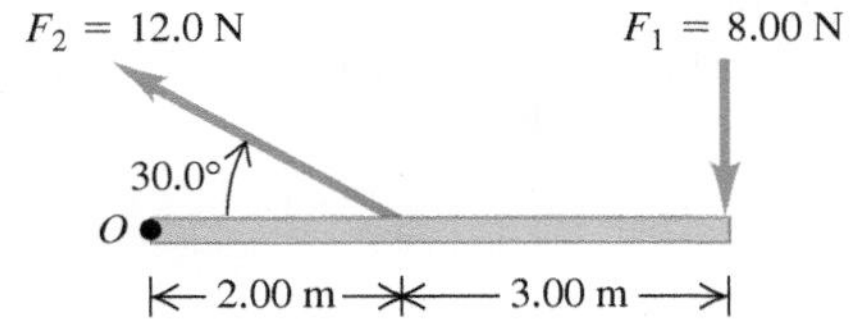

3.2 • In Fig. P3.2, forces $\vec{A}$, $\vec{B}$, $\vec{C}$, and $\vec{D}$ each have magnitude 50 N and act at the same point on the object. (a) What torque (magnitude and direction) does each of these forces exert on the object about point P? (b) What is the total torque about point P?

Figure **P3.2**

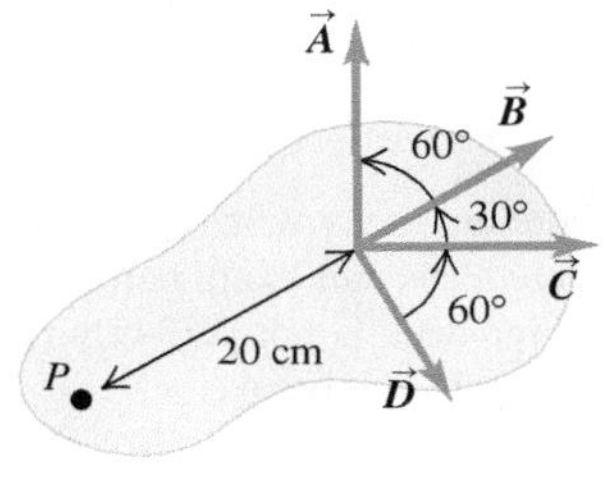

3.3 •• A 0.120-kg, 50.0-cm-long uniform bar has a small 0.055-kg mass glued to its left end and a small 0.110-kg mass glued to the other end. The two small masses can each be treated as point masses. You want to balance this system horizontally on a fulcrum placed just under its center of gravity. How far from the left end should the fulcrum be placed?

3.4 •• **Raising a Ladder.** A ladder carried by a fire truck is 20.0 m long. The ladder weighs 2800 N and its center of gravity is at its center. The ladder is pivoted at one end (A) about a pin (Fig. P3.4); you can ignore the friction torque at the pin. The ladder is raised into position by a force applied by a hydraulic piston at C. Point C is 8.0 m from A, and the force $\vec{F}$ exerted by the piston makes an angle of 40° with the ladder. What magnitude must $\vec{F}$ have to just lift the ladder off the support bracket at B? Start with a free-body diagram of the ladder.

Figure **P3.4**

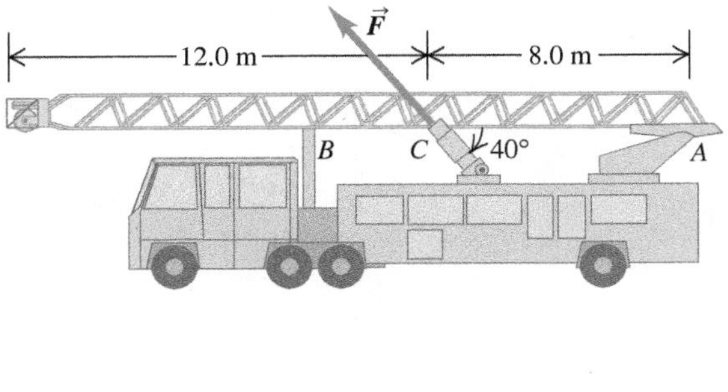

3.5 •• A 60.0-cm, uniform, 50.0-N shelf is supported horizontally by two vertical wires attached to the sloping ceiling (Fig. P3.5). A very small 25.0-N tool is placed on the shelf midway between the points where the wires are attached to it. Find the tension in each wire. Begin by making a free-body diagram of the shelf.

Figure **P3.5**

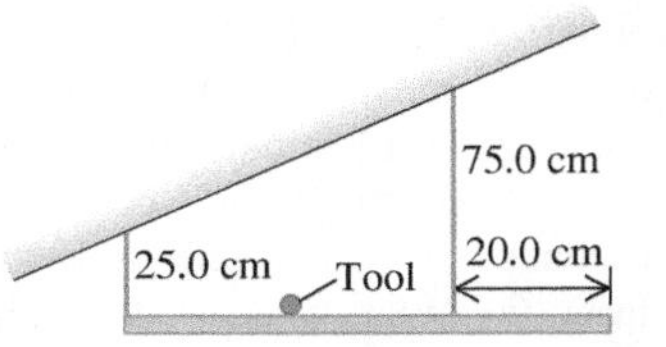

3.6 • A diving board 3.00 m long is supported at a point 1.00 m from the end, and a diver weighing 500 N stands at the free end (Fig. P3.6). The diving board is of uniform cross section and weighs 280 N. Find (a) the force at the support point and (b) the force at the left-hand end.

Figure **P3.6**

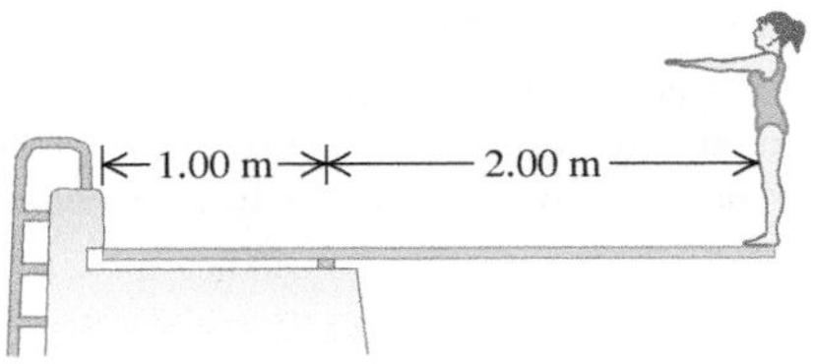

3.7 • Find the tension T in each cable and the magnitude and direction of the force exerted on the strut by the pivot in each of the arrangements in Fig. P3.7. In each case let w be the weight of the suspended crate full of priceless art objects. The strut is uniform and also has weight w. Start each case with a free-body diagram of the strut.

Figure **P3.7**

(a) (b)

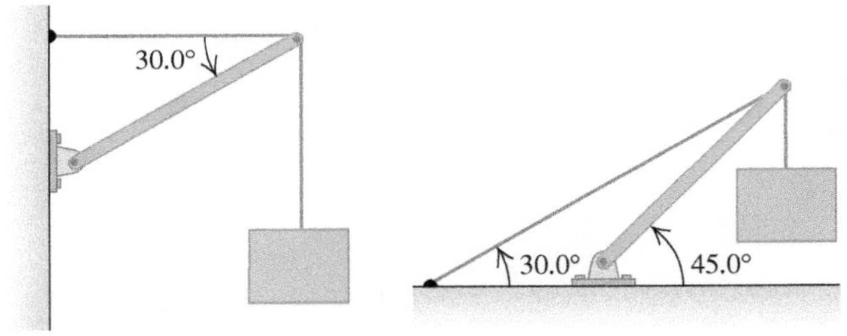

3.8 ••• **Mountain Climbing.** Mountaineers often use a rope to lower themselves down the face of a cliff (this is called *rappelling*). They do this with their body nearly horizontal and their feet pushing against the cliff (Fig. P3.8). Suppose that an 82.0-kg climber, who is 1.90 m tall and has a center of gravity 1.1 m from his feet, rappels down a vertical cliff with his body raised 35.0° above the horizontal. He holds the rope 1.40 m from his feet, and it makes a 25.0° angle with the cliff face. (a) What tension does his rope need to support? (b) Find the horizontal and vertical components of the force that the cliff face exerts on the climber's feet. (c) What minimum coefficient of static friction is needed to prevent the climber's feet from slipping on the cliff face if he has one foot at a time against the cliff?

Figure **P3.8**

3.9 •• A uniform, 8.0-m, 1500-kg beam is hinged to a wall and supported by a thin cable attached 2.0 m from the free end of the beam, (Fig. P3.9). The beam is supported at an angle of 30.0° above the horizontal. (a) Draw a free-body diagram of the beam. (b) Find the tension in the cable. (c) How hard does the beam push inward on the wall?

Figure **P3.9**

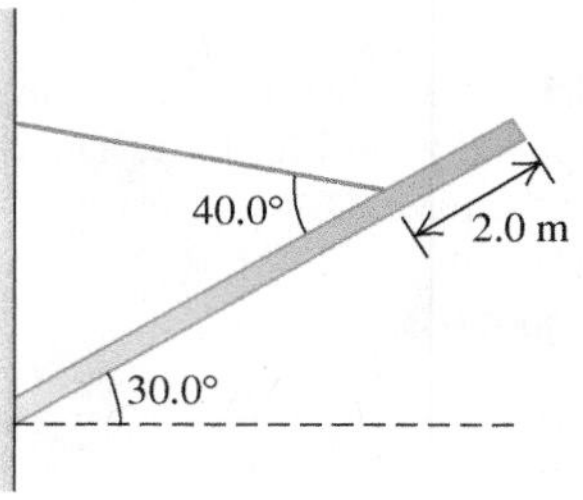

Answers

Chapter Opening Question ?

By applying the conditions for both rotational and translational equilibrium to the array of wires in a suspension bridge it is possible to determine the expected tension in each wire. The reason there are many wires is that the individual wires have a maximum force they can exert before stretching or breaking, and that the bridge deck is not perfectly rigid; if it is held in only one place it will bend and break.

MOTION IN TWO OR THREE DIMENSIONS

4

? If a cyclist is going around a curve at constant speed, is he accelerating? If so, in which direction is he accelerating?

LEARNING GOALS

By studying this chapter, you will learn:

- How to represent the position of a body in two or three dimensions using vectors.
- How to determine the vector velocity of a body from a knowledge of its path.
- How to find the vector acceleration of a body, and why a body can have an acceleration even if its speed is constant.
- How to interpret the components of a body's acceleration parallel to and perpendicular to its path.
- How to describe the curved path followed by a projectile.
- The key ideas behind motion in a circular path, with either constant speed or varying speed.

What determines where a batted baseball lands? How do you describe the motion of a roller coaster car along a curved track or the flight of a circling hawk? Which hits the ground first: a baseball that you simply drop or one that you throw horizontally?

We can't answer these kinds of questions using the techniques of this chapter, in which particles moved only along a straight line. Instead, we need to extend our descriptions of motion to two- and three-dimensional situations. We'll use vectors to describe this motion. In the analysis, we'll use the vector quantities displacement, velocity, and acceleration. It's important to note that these quantities do not have to all be in a straight line. We'll find that several important kinds of motion take place in two dimensions only—that is, in a *plane.* We can describe these motions with two components of position, velocity, and acceleration.

4.1 Position and Velocity Vectors

To describe the *motion* of a particle in space, we must first be able to describe the particle's *position.* Consider a particle that is at a point P at a certain instant. The **position vector** $\vec{r}$ of the particle at this instant is a vector that goes from the origin of the coordinate system to the point P (Fig. 4.1). The Cartesian coordinates x, y, and z of point P are the x-, y-, and z-components of vector $\vec{r}$. Using the unit vectors we introduced in Section 1.8, we can write

$$\vec{r} = x\hat{\imath} + y\hat{\jmath} + z\hat{k} \quad \text{(position vector)} \tag{4.1}$$

During a time interval Δt the particle moves from P_1, where its position vector is $\vec{r}_1$, to P_2, where its position vector is $\vec{r}_2$. The change in position (the displacement) during this interval is $\Delta\vec{r} = \vec{r}_2 - \vec{r}_1 = (x_2 - x_1)\hat{\imath} + (y_2 - y_1)\hat{\jmath} +$

4.1 The position vector $\vec{r}$ from the origin to point P has components x, y, and z. The path that the particle follows through space is in general a curve (Fig. 4.2).

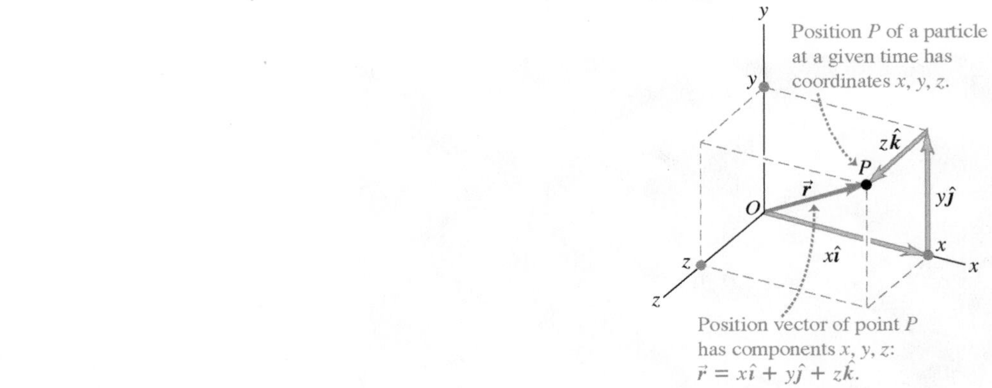
y
Position P of a particle at a given time has coordinates x, y, z.
zk̂
P
r
yĵ
O
x
xî
z
x
z
Position vector of point P has components x, y, z:
r = xî + yĵ + zk̂.

$(z_2 - z_1)\hat{k}$. We define the **average velocity** $\vec{v}_{av}$ during this interval in the same way we did for straight-line motion, as the displacement divided by the time interval:

$$\vec{v}_{av} = \frac{\vec{r}_2 - \vec{r}_1}{t_2 - t_1} = \frac{\Delta\vec{r}}{\Delta t} \quad \text{(average velocity vector)} \qquad (4.2)$$

Dividing a vector by a scalar is really a special case of *multiplying* a vector by a scalar; the average velocity $\vec{v}_{av}$ is equal to the displacement vector $\Delta\vec{r}$ multiplied by $1/\Delta t$, the reciprocal of the time interval. Note that the x-component of Eq. (4.2) is $v_{av\text{-}x} = (x_2 - x_1)/(t_2 - t_1) = \Delta x/\Delta t$. This is the expression for average x-velocity that we found for one-dimensional motion.

We now define **instantaneous velocity**: It is the limit of the average velocity as the time interval approaches zero, and it equals the instantaneous rate of change of position with time. The key difference is that position $\vec{r}$ and instantaneous velocity $\vec{v}$ are now both vectors:

$$\vec{v} = \lim_{\Delta t \to 0} \frac{\Delta\vec{r}}{\Delta t} = \frac{d\vec{r}}{dt} \quad \text{(instantaneous velocity vector)} \qquad (4.3)$$

The *magnitude* of the vector $\vec{v}$ at any instant is the *speed* v of the particle at that instant. The *direction* of $\vec{v}$ at any instant is the same as the direction in which the particle is moving at that instant.

Note that as $\Delta t \to 0$, points P_1 and P_2 in Fig. 4.2 move closer and closer together. In this limit, the vector $\Delta\vec{r}$ becomes tangent to the path. The direction of $\Delta\vec{r}$ in this limit is also the direction of the instantaneous velocity $\vec{v}$. This leads to an important conclusion: *At every point along the path, the instantaneous velocity vector is tangent to the path at that point* (Fig. 4.3).

It's often easiest to calculate the instantaneous velocity vector using components. During any displacement $\Delta\vec{r}$, the changes Δx, Δy, and Δz in the three coordinates of the particle are the *components* of $\Delta\vec{r}$. It follows that the components v_x, v_y, and v_z of the instantaneous velocity $\vec{v}$ are simply the time derivatives of the coordinates x, y, and z. That is,

$$v_x = \frac{dx}{dt} \qquad v_y = \frac{dy}{dt} \qquad v_z = \frac{dz}{dt} \quad \text{(components of instantaneous velocity)} \qquad (4.4)$$

The x-component of $\vec{v}$ is $v_x = dx/dt$, which is the same the expression for instantaneous velocity for straight-line motion.

4.2 The average velocity $\vec{v}_{av}$ between points P_1 and P_2 has the same direction as the displacement $\Delta\vec{r}$.

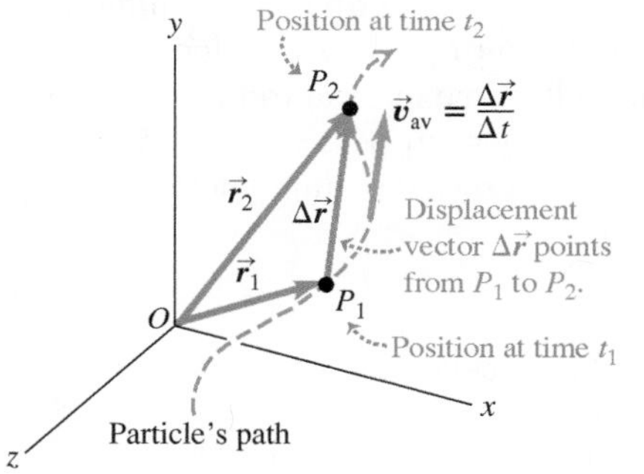

4.3 The vectors $\vec{v}_1$ and $\vec{v}_2$ are the instantaneous velocities at the points P_1 and P_2 shown in Fig. 4.2.

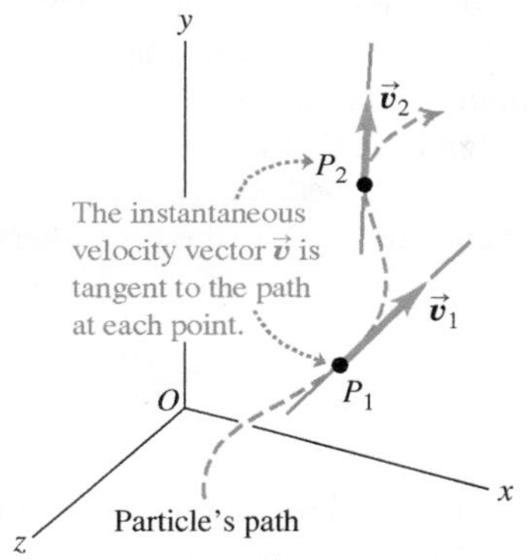

We can also get Eq. (4.4) by taking the derivative of Eq. (4.1). The unit vectors $\hat{\imath}$, $\hat{\jmath}$, and $\hat{k}$ are constant in magnitude and direction, so their derivatives are zero, and we find

$$\vec{v} = \frac{d\vec{r}}{dt} = \frac{dx}{dt}\hat{\imath} + \frac{dy}{dt}\hat{\jmath} + \frac{dz}{dt}\hat{k} \tag{4.5}$$

This shows again that the components of $\vec{v}$ are dx/dt, dy/dt, and dz/dt.

The magnitude of the instantaneous velocity vector $\vec{v}$—that is, the speed—is given in terms of the components v_x, v_y, and v_z by the Pythagorean relation:

$$|\vec{v}| = v = \sqrt{v_x^2 + v_y^2 + v_z^2} \tag{4.6}$$

Figure 4.4 shows the situation when the particle moves in the xy-plane. In this case, z and v_z are zero. Then the speed (the magnitude of $\vec{v}$) is

$$v = \sqrt{v_x^2 + v_y^2}$$

and the direction of the instantaneous velocity $\vec{v}$ is given by the angle α (the Greek letter alpha) in the figure. We see that

$$\tan\alpha = \frac{v_y}{v_x} \tag{4.7}$$

(We always use Greek letters for angles. We use α for the direction of the instantaneous velocity vector to avoid confusion with the direction θ of the *position* vector of the particle.)

4.4 The two velocity components for motion in the xy-plane.

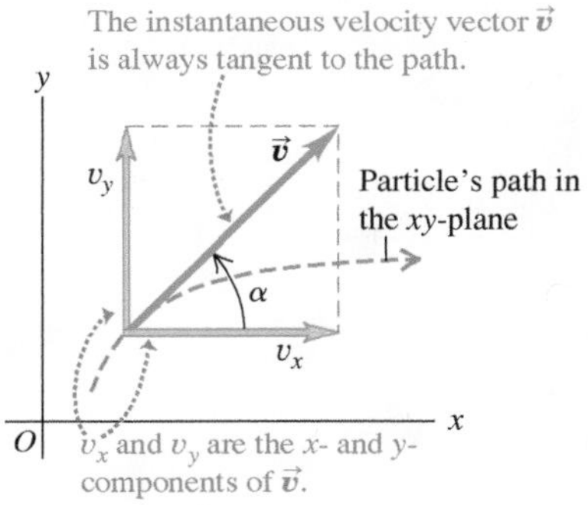

The instantaneous velocity vector is usually more interesting and useful than the average velocity vector. From now on, when we use the word "velocity," we will always mean the instantaneous velocity vector $\vec{v}$ (rather than the average velocity vector). Usually, we won't even bother to call $\vec{v}$ a vector; it's up to you to remember that velocity is a vector quantity with both magnitude and direction.

4.2 The Acceleration Vector

Now let's consider the *acceleration* of a particle moving in space. Since we now treat velocity as a vector, acceleration will describe changes in the velocity magnitude (that is, the speed) *and* changes in the direction of velocity (that is, the direction in which the particle is moving).

In Fig. 4.5a, a car (treated as a particle) is moving along a curved road. The vectors $\vec{v}_1$ and $\vec{v}_2$ represent the car's instantaneous velocities at time t_1, when the car is at point P_1, and at time t_2, when the car is at point P_2. The two velocities may differ in both magnitude and direction. During the time interval from t_1 to t_2, the *vector change in velocity* is $\vec{v}_2 - \vec{v}_1 = \Delta\vec{v}$, so $\vec{v}_2 = \vec{v}_1 + \Delta\vec{v}$ (Fig. 4.5b). We define the **average acceleration** $\vec{a}_{av}$ of the car during this time interval as the velocity change divided by the time interval $t_2 - t_1 = \Delta t$:

$$\vec{a}_{av} = \frac{\vec{v}_2 - \vec{v}_1}{t_2 - t_1} = \frac{\Delta\vec{v}}{\Delta t} \qquad \text{(average acceleration vector)} \qquad (4.8)$$

Average acceleration is a *vector* quantity in the same direction as the vector $\Delta\vec{v}$ (Fig. 4.5c). The x-component of Eq. (4.8) is $a_{av\text{-}x} = (v_{2x} - v_{1x})/(t_2 - t_1) = \Delta v_x/\Delta t$, the average acceleration in straight-line motion.

We define the **instantaneous acceleration** $\vec{a}$ (a *vector* quantity) at point P_1 as the limit of the average acceleration vector when point P_2 approaches point P_1, so $\Delta\vec{v}$ and Δt both approach zero (Fig. 4.6). The instantaneous acceleration is also equal to the instantaneous rate of change of velocity with time:

$$\vec{a} = \lim_{\Delta t \to 0} \frac{\Delta\vec{v}}{\Delta t} = \frac{d\vec{v}}{dt} \qquad \text{(instantaneous acceleration vector)} \qquad (4.9)$$

4.5 (a) A car moving along a curved road from P_1 to P_2. (b) How to obtain the change in velocity $\Delta\vec{v} = \vec{v}_2 - \vec{v}_1$ by vector subtraction. (c) The vector $\vec{a}_{av} = \Delta\vec{v}/\Delta t$ represents the average acceleration between P_1 and P_2.

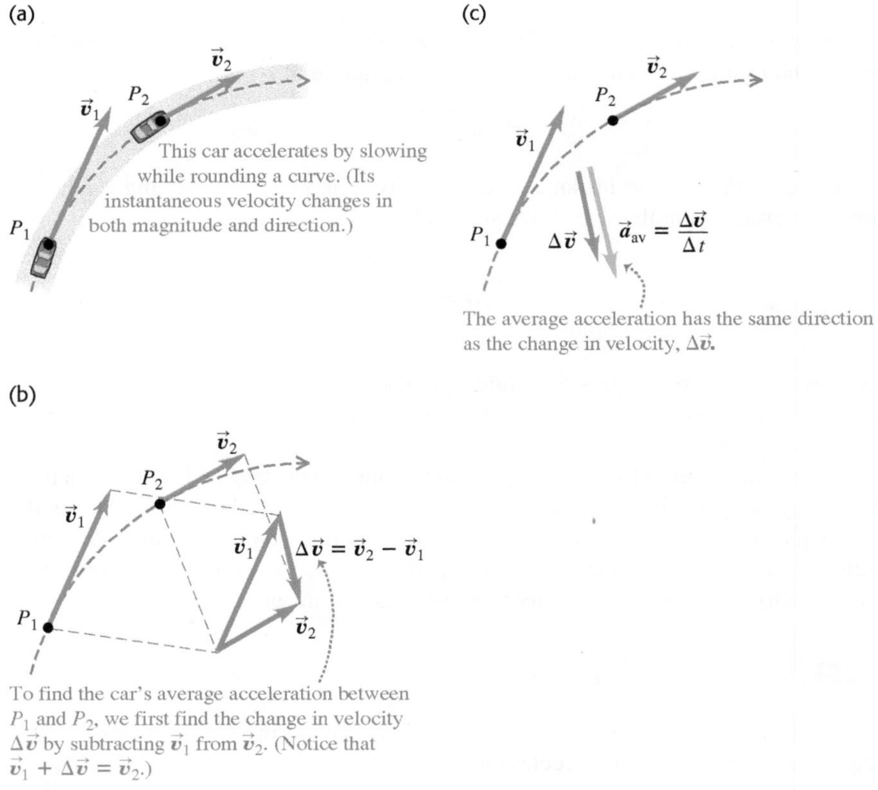
(a)
This car accelerates by slowing while rounding a curve. (Its instantaneous velocity changes in both magnitude and direction.)
(c)
The average acceleration has the same direction as the change in velocity, Δv.
(b)
To find the car's average acceleration between P1 and P2, we first find the change in velocity Δv by subtracting v1 from v2. (Notice that v1 + Δv = v2.)

4.6 (a) Instantaneous acceleration $\vec{a}$ at point P_1 in Fig. 4.6. (b) Instantaneous acceleration for motion along a straight line.

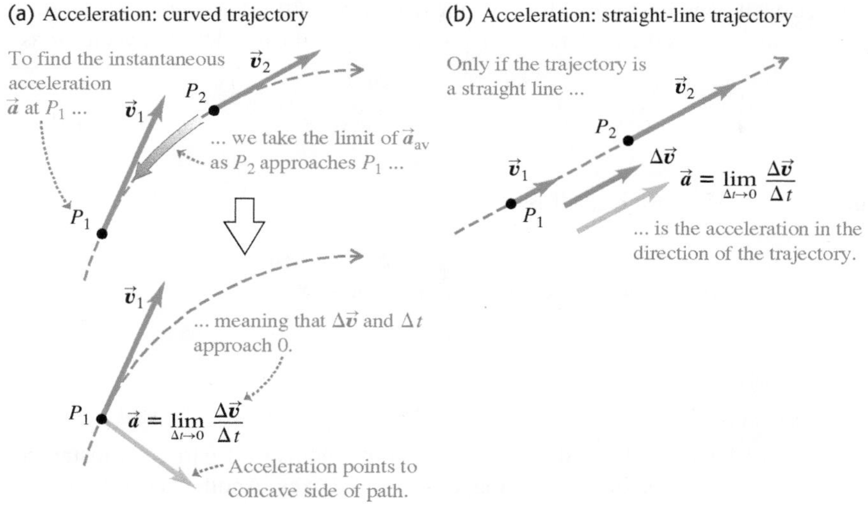
(a) Acceleration: curved trajectory
To find the instantaneous acceleration $\vec{a}$ at P_1 ...
$\vec{v}_2$
P_2
$\vec{v}_1$
... we take the limit of $\vec{a}_{av}$ as P_2 approaches P_1 ...
P_1
$\vec{v}_1$
... meaning that $\Delta\vec{v}$ and Δt approach 0.
P_1
$\vec{a} = \lim_{\Delta t \to 0} \frac{\Delta\vec{v}}{\Delta t}$
Acceleration points to concave side of path.
(b) Acceleration: straight-line trajectory
Only if the trajectory is a straight line ...
$\vec{v}_2$
P_2
$\Delta\vec{v}$
$\vec{v}_1$
$\vec{a} = \lim_{\Delta t \to 0} \frac{\Delta\vec{v}}{\Delta t}$
P_1
... is the acceleration in the direction of the trajectory.

The velocity vector $\vec{v}$, as we have seen, is tangent to the path of the particle. The instantaneous acceleration vector $\vec{a}$, however, does *not* have to be tangent to the path. Figure 4.6a shows that if the path is curved, $\vec{a}$ points toward the concave side of the path—that is, toward the inside of any turn that the particle is making. The acceleration is tangent to the path only if the particle moves in a straight line (Fig. 4.6b).

CAUTION **Any particle following a curved path is accelerating** When a particle is moving in a curved path, it always has nonzero acceleration, even when it moves with constant speed. This conclusion may seem contrary to your intuition, but it's really just contrary to the everyday use of the word "acceleration" to mean that speed is increasing. The more precise definition given in Eq. (4.9) shows that there is a nonzero acceleration whenever the velocity vector changes in any way, whether there is a change of speed, direction, or both. ?

To convince yourself that a particle has a nonzero acceleration when moving on a curved path with constant speed, think of your sensations when you ride in a car. When the car accelerates, you tend to move inside the car in a direction *opposite* to the car's acceleration. Thus you tend to slide toward the back of the car when it accelerates forward (speeds up) and toward the front of the car when it accelerates backward (slows down). If the car makes a turn on a level road, you tend to slide toward the outside of the turn; hence the car has an acceleration toward the inside of the turn.

We will usually be interested in the instantaneous acceleration, not the average acceleration. From now on, we will use the term "acceleration" to mean the instantaneous acceleration vector $\vec{a}$.

Each component of the acceleration vector is the derivative of the corresponding component of velocity:

$$a_x = \frac{dv_x}{dt} \qquad a_y = \frac{dv_y}{dt} \qquad a_z = \frac{dv_z}{dt} \qquad \text{(components of instantaneous acceleration)} \tag{4.10}$$

In terms of unit vectors,

$$\vec{a} = \frac{dv_x}{dt}\hat{\imath} + \frac{dv_y}{dt}\hat{\jmath} + \frac{dv_z}{dt}\hat{k} \tag{4.11}$$

The x-component of Eqs. (4.10) and (4.11), $a_x = dv_x/dt$, is the expression for instantaneous acceleration in one dimension.

Since each component of velocity is the derivative of the corresponding coordinate, we can express the components a_x, a_y, and a_z of the acceleration vector $\vec{a}$ as

$$a_x = \frac{d^2x}{dt^2} \qquad a_y = \frac{d^2y}{dt^2} \qquad a_z = \frac{d^2z}{dt^2} \tag{4.12}$$

The acceleration vector $\vec{a}$ itself is

$$\vec{a} = \frac{d^2x}{dt^2}\hat{\imath} + \frac{d^2y}{dt^2}\hat{\jmath} + \frac{d^2z}{dt^2}\hat{k} = \frac{d^2\vec{r}}{dt^2} \tag{4.13}$$

Parallel and Perpendicular Components of Acceleration

Equations (4.10 and 4.12) tell us about the components of a particle's instantaneous acceleration vector $\vec{a}$ along the x-, y-, and z-axes. Another useful way to think about $\vec{a}$ is in terms of its component *parallel* to the particle's path—that is, parallel to the velocity—and its component *perpendicular* to the path—and hence perpendicular to the velocity (Fig. 4.7). That's because the parallel component $a_\parallel$ tells us about changes in the particle's *speed,* while the perpendicular component $a_\perp$ tells us about changes in the particle's *direction of motion.* To see why the parallel and perpendicular components of $\vec{a}$ have these properties, let's consider two special cases.

In Fig. 4.8a the acceleration vector is in the same direction as the velocity $\vec{v}_1$, so $\vec{a}$ has only a parallel component $a_\parallel$ (that is, $a_\perp = 0$). The velocity change $\Delta\vec{v}$

4.7 The acceleration can be resolved into a component $a_\parallel$ parallel to the path (that is, along the tangent to the path) and a component $a_\perp$ perpendicular to the path (that is, along the normal to the path).

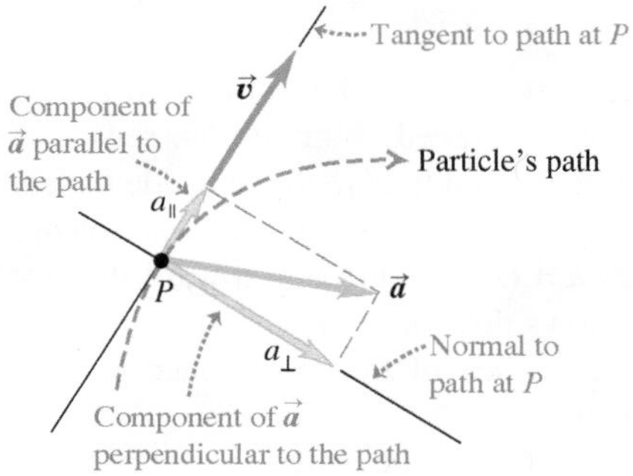

4.8 The effect of acceleration directed **(a)** parallel to and **(b)** perpendicular to a particle's velocity.

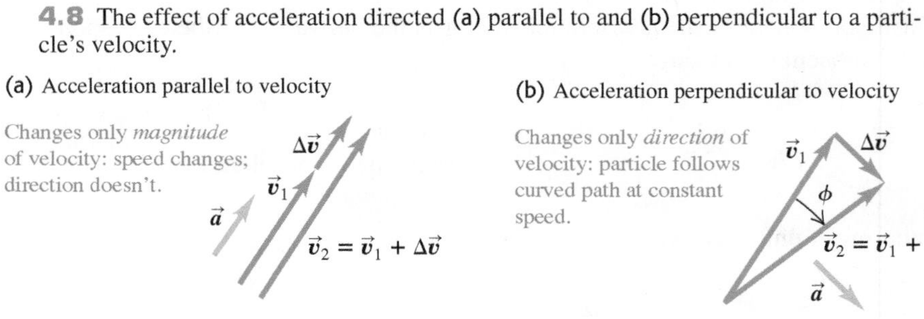

4.9 Velocity and acceleration vectors for a particle moving through a point P on a curved path with (a) constant speed, (b) increasing speed, and (c) decreasing speed.

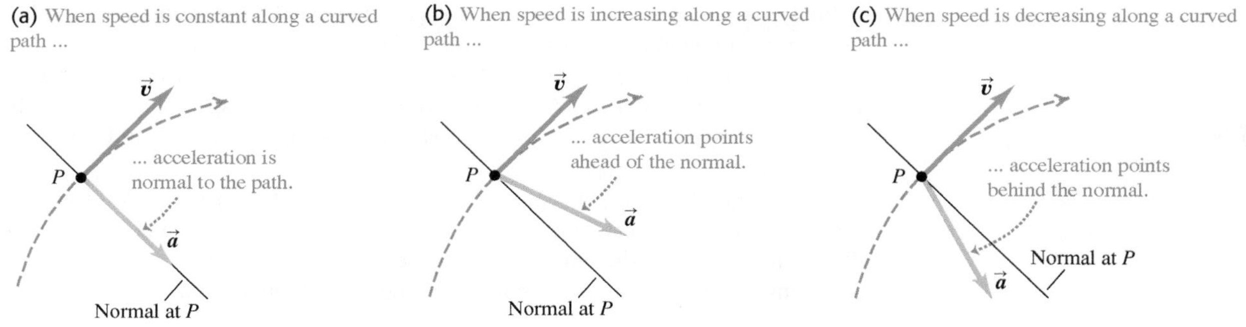

during a small time interval Δt is in the same direction as $\vec{a}$ and hence in the same direction as $\vec{v}_1$. The velocity $\vec{v}_2$ at the end of Δt is in the same direction as $\vec{v}_1$ but has greater magnitude. Hence during the time interval Δt the particle in Fig. 4.8a moved in a straight line with increasing speed (compare Fig. 4.6b).

In Fig. 4.8b the acceleration is *perpendicular* to the velocity, so $\vec{a}$ has only a perpendicular component $a_\perp$ (that is, $a_\parallel = 0$). In a small time interval Δt, the velocity change $\Delta\vec{v}$ is very nearly perpendicular to $\vec{v}_1$, and so $\vec{v}_1$ and $\vec{v}_2$ have different directions. As the time interval Δt approaches zero, the angle ϕ in the figure also approaches zero, $\Delta\vec{v}$ becomes perpendicular to *both* $\vec{v}_1$ and $\vec{v}_2$, and $\vec{v}_1$ and $\vec{v}_2$ have the same magnitude. In other words, the speed of the particle stays the same, but the direction of motion changes and the path of the particle curves.

In the most general case, the acceleration $\vec{a}$ has components *both* parallel and perpendicular to the velocity $\vec{v}$, as in Fig. 4.7. Then the particle's speed will change (described by the parallel component $a_\parallel$) *and* its direction of motion will change (described by the perpendicular component $a_\perp$) so that it follows a curved path.

Figure 4.9 shows a particle moving along a curved path for three different situations: constant speed, increasing speed, and decreasing speed. If the speed is constant, $\vec{a}$ is perpendicular, or *normal,* to the path and to $\vec{v}$ and points toward the concave side of the path (Fig. 4.9a). If the speed is increasing, there is still a perpendicular component of $\vec{a}$, but there is also a parallel component having the same direction as $\vec{v}$ (Fig. 4.9b). Then $\vec{a}$ points ahead of the normal to the path. (This was the case in Example 4.2.) If the speed is decreasing, the parallel component has the direction opposite to $\vec{v}$, and $\vec{a}$ points behind the normal to the path (Fig. 4.9c; compare Fig. 4.6a). We will use these ideas again in Section 4.10 when we study the special case of motion in a circle.

4.3 Displacement, Time, and Average Velocity

Suppose a drag racer drives her AA-fuel dragster along a straight track (Fig. 4.10). To study the dragster's motion, we need a coordinate system. We choose the x-axis to lie along the dragster's straight-line path, with the origin O at the starting line. We also choose a point on the dragster, such as its front end, and represent the entire dragster by that point. Hence we treat the dragster as a **particle.**

A useful way to describe the motion of the particle that represents the dragster is in terms of the change in the particle's coordinate x over a time interval. Suppose that 1.0 s after the start the front of the dragster is at point P_1, 19 m from the origin, and 4.0 s after the start it is at point P_2, 277 m from the origin. The *displacement* of the particle is a vector that points from P_1 to P_2. Figure 4.10 shows that this vector points along the x-axis. The x-component of the displacement is the change in the value of x, $(277 \text{ m} - 19 \text{ m}) = 258 \text{ m}$, that took place during the time interval of $(4.0 \text{ s} - 1.0 \text{ s}) = 3.0 \text{ s}$. We define the dragster's **average velocity** during this time interval as a *vector* quantity whose x-component is the change in x divided by the time interval: $(258 \text{ m})/(3.0 \text{ s}) = 86 \text{ m/s}$.

In general, the average velocity depends on the particular time interval chosen. For a 3.0-s time interval *before* the start of the race, the average velocity would be zero because the dragster would be at rest at the starting line and would have zero displacement.

Let's generalize the concept of average velocity. At time t_1 the dragster is at point P_1, with coordinate x_1, and at time t_2 it is at point P_2, with coordinate x_2. The displacement of the dragster during the time interval from t_1 to t_2 is the vector from P_1 to P_2. The x-component of the displacement, denoted Δx, is the change in the coordinate x:

$$\Delta x = x_2 - x_1 \tag{4.14}$$

The dragster moves along the x-axis only, so the y- and z-components of the displacement are equal to zero.

CAUTION **The meaning of Δx** Note that Δx is *not* the product of Δ and x; it is a single symbol that means "the change in the quantity x." We always use the Greek capital letter Δ (delta) to represent a *change* in a quantity, equal to the *final* value of the quantity minus the *initial* value—never the reverse. Likewise, the time interval from t_1 to t_2 is Δt, the change in the quantity t: $\Delta t = t_2 - t_1$ (final time minus initial time).

The x-component of average velocity, or **average x-velocity,** is the x-component of displacement, Δx, divided by the time interval Δt during which the displacement occurs. We use the symbol $v_{\text{av-}x}$ for average x-velocity (the subscript "av" signifies average value and the subscript x indicates that this is the x-component):

$$v_{\text{av-}x} = \frac{x_2 - x_1}{t_2 - t_1} = \frac{\Delta x}{\Delta t} \quad \text{(average } x\text{-velocity, straight-line motion)} \tag{4.15}$$

As an example, for the dragster $x_1 = 19 \text{ m}$, $x_2 = 277 \text{ m}$, $t_1 = 1.0 \text{ s}$, and $t_2 = 4.0 \text{ s}$, so Eq. (4.15) gives

$$v_{\text{av-}x} = \frac{277 \text{ m} - 19 \text{ m}}{4.0 \text{ s} - 1.0 \text{ s}} = \frac{258 \text{ m}}{3.0 \text{ s}} = 86 \text{ m/s}$$

The average x-velocity of the dragster is positive. This means that during the time interval, the coordinate x increased and the dragster moved in the positive x-direction (in Fig. 4.10).

4.10 Positions of a dragster at two times during its run.

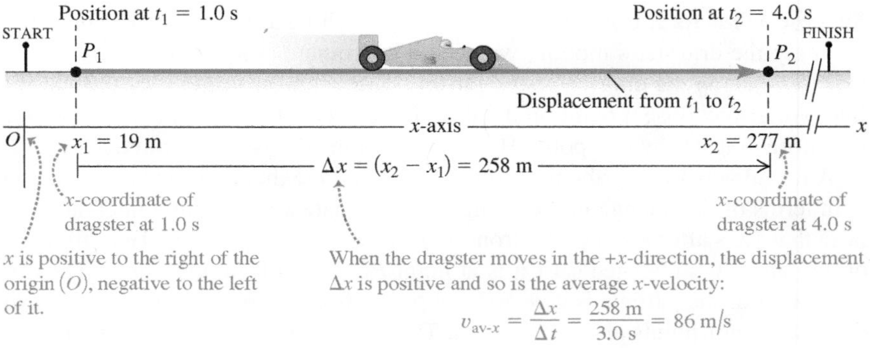

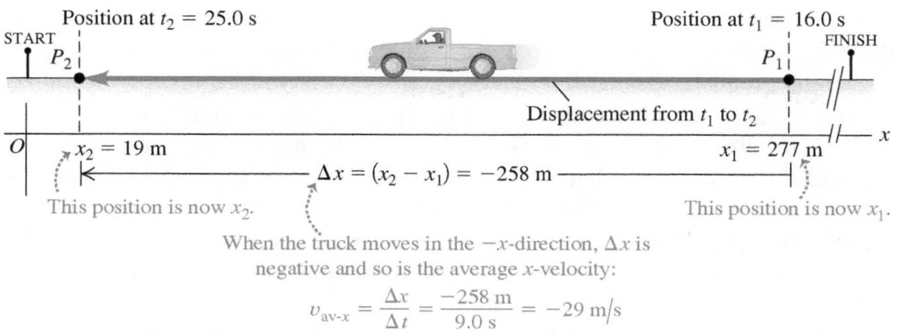

4.11 Positions of an official's truck at two times during its motion. The points P_1 and P_2 now indicate the positions of the truck, and so are the reverse of Fig. 4.10.

If a particle moves in the *negative* x-direction during a time interval, its average velocity for that time interval is negative. For example, suppose an official's truck moves to the left along the track (Fig. 4.11). The truck is at $x_1 = 277$ m at $t_1 = 16.0$ s and is at $x_2 = 19$ m at $t_2 = 25.0$ s. Then $\Delta x = (19\text{ m} - 277\text{ m}) = -258$ m and $\Delta t = (25.0\text{ s} - 16.0\text{ s}) = 9.0$ s. The x-component of average velocity is $v_{av\text{-}x} = \Delta x/\Delta t = (-258\text{ m})/(9.0\text{ s}) = -29$ m/s. Table 4.1 lists some simple rules for deciding whether the x-velocity is positive or negative.

Table 4.1 Rules for the Sign of x-Velocity

If the x-coordinate is:	. . . the x-velocity is:
Positive & increasing (getting more positive)	Positive: Particle is moving in $+x$-direction
Positive & decreasing (getting less positive)	Negative: Particle is moving in $-x$-direction
Negative & increasing (getting less negative)	Positive: Particle is moving in $+x$-direction
Negative & decreasing (getting more negative)	Negative: Particle is moving in $-x$-direction

Note: These rules apply to both the average x-velocity $v_{av\text{-}x}$ and the instantaneous x-velocity v_x.

CAUTION **Choice of the positive x-direction** You might be tempted to conclude that positive average x-velocity must mean motion to the right, as in Fig. 4.10, and that negative average x-velocity must mean motion to the left, as in Fig. 4.11. But that's correct *only* if the positive x-direction is to the right, as we chose it to be in Figs. 4.10 and 4.11. Had we chosen the positive x-direction to be to the left, with the origin at the finish line, the dragster would have negative average x-velocity and the official's truck would have positive average x-velocity. In most problems the direction of the coordinate axis will be yours to choose. Once you've made your choice, you *must* take it into account when interpreting the signs of $v_{av\text{-}x}$ and other quantities that describe motion!

With straight-line motion we sometimes call Δx simply the displacement and $v_{av\text{-}x}$ simply the average velocity. But be sure to remember that these are really the x-components of vector quantities that, in this special case, have *only* x-components.

Figure 4.12 is a graph of the dragster's position as a function of time—that is, an ***x-t* graph.** The curve in the figure *does not* represent the dragster's path in space; as Fig. 4.10 shows, the path is a straight line. Rather, the graph is a pictorial way to represent how the dragster's position changes with time. The points p_1 and p_2 on the graph correspond to the points P_1 and P_2 along the dragster's path. Line p_1p_2 is the hypotenuse of a right triangle with vertical side $\Delta x = x_2 - x_1$

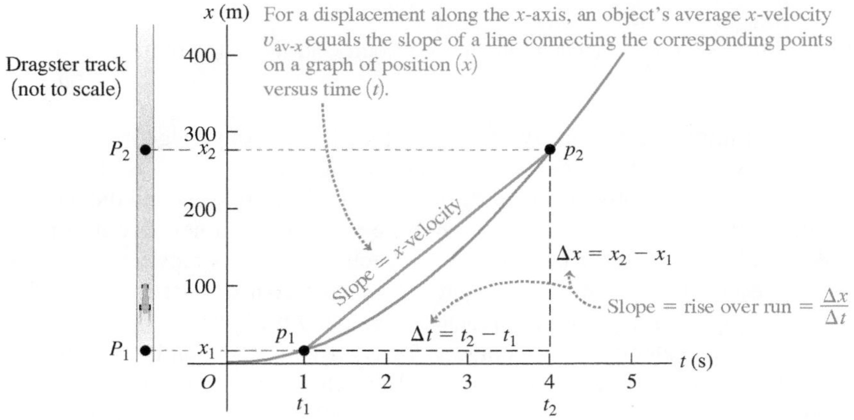

4.12 The position of a dragster as a function of time.

and horizontal side $\Delta t = t_2 - t_1$. The average x-velocity $v_{\text{av-}x} = \Delta x/\Delta t$ of the dragster equals the *slope* of the line p_1p_2—that is, the ratio of the triangle's vertical side Δx to its horizontal side Δt.

The average x-velocity depends only on the total displacement $\Delta x = x_2 - x_1$ that occurs during the time interval $\Delta t = t_2 - t_1$, not on the details of what happens during the time interval. At time t_1 a motorcycle might have raced past the dragster at point P_1 in Fig. 4.10, then blown its engine and slowed down to pass through point P_2 at the same time t_2 as the dragster. Both vehicles have the same displacement during the same time interval and so have the same average x-velocity.

If distance is given in meters and time in seconds, average velocity is measured in meters per second (m/s). Other common units of velocity are kilometers per hour (km/h), feet per second (ft/s), miles per hour (mi/h), and knots (1 knot = 1 nautical mile/h = 6080 ft/h).

4.4 Instantaneous Velocity

Sometimes the average velocity is all you need to know about a particle's motion. For example, a race along a straight line is really a competition to see whose average velocity, $v_{\text{av-}x}$, has the greatest magnitude. The prize goes to the competitor who can travel the displacement Δx from the start to the finish line in the shortest time interval, Δt.

But the average velocity of a particle during a time interval can't tell us how fast, or in what direction, the particle was moving at any given time during the interval. To do this we need to know the **instantaneous velocity,** or the velocity at a specific instant of time or specific point along the path.

CAUTION **How long is an instant?** Note that the word "instant" has a somewhat different definition in physics than in everyday language. You might use the phrase "It lasted just an instant" to refer to something that lasted for a very short time interval. But in physics an instant has no duration at all; it refers to a single value of time.

To find the instantaneous velocity of the dragster in Fig. 4.10 at the point P_1, we move the second point P_2 closer and closer to the first point P_1 and compute the average velocity $v_{\text{av-}x} = \Delta x/\Delta t$ over the ever-shorter displacement and time interval. Both Δx and Δt become very small, but their ratio does not necessarily become small. In the language of calculus, the limit of $\Delta x/\Delta t$ as Δt approaches zero is called the **derivative** of x with respect to t and is written dx/dt. *The instantaneous velocity is the limit of the average velocity as the time interval approaches zero; it equals the instantaneous rate of change of position with time.* We use the symbol v_x, with no "av" subscript, for the instantaneous velocity along the x-axis, or the **instantaneous x-velocity:**

$$v_x = \lim_{\Delta t \to 0} \frac{\Delta x}{\Delta t} = \frac{dx}{dt} \quad \text{(instantaneous } x\text{-velocity, straight-line motion)} \tag{4.16}$$

The time interval Δt is always positive, so v_x has the same algebraic sign as Δx. A positive value of v_x means that x is increasing and the motion is in the positive x-direction; a negative value of v_x means that x is decreasing and the motion is in the negative x-direction. A body can have positive x and negative v_x, or the reverse; x tells us where the body is, while v_x tells us how it's moving. The rules that we presented in Table 4.1 (Section 4.3) for the sign of average x-velocity $v_{\text{av-}x}$ also apply to the sign of instantaneous x-velocity v_x.

Instantaneous velocity, like average velocity, is a vector quantity; Eq. (4.16) defines its x-component. In straight-line motion, all other components of instantaneous velocity are zero. In this case we often call v_x simply the instantaneous velocity. When we use the term "velocity," we will always mean instantaneous rather than average velocity.

The terms "velocity" and "speed" are used interchangeably in everyday language, but they have distinct definitions in physics. We use the term **speed** to denote distance traveled divided by time, on either an average or an instantaneous basis. Instantaneous *speed,* for which we use the symbol v with *no* subscripts, measures how fast a particle is moving; instantaneous *velocity* measures how fast *and* in what direction it's moving. Instantaneous speed is the magnitude of instantaneous velocity and so can never be negative. For example, a particle with instantaneous velocity $v_x = 25\ \text{m/s}$ and a second particle with $v_x = -25\ \text{m/s}$ are moving in opposite directions at the same instantaneous speed 25 m/s.

CAUTION **Average speed and average velocity** Average speed is *not* the magnitude of average velocity. When César Cielo set a world record in 2009 by swimming 100.0 m in 46.91 s, his average speed was $(100.0\ \text{m})/(46.91\ \text{s}) = 2.132\ \text{m/s}$. But because he swam two lengths in a 50-m pool, he started and ended at the same point and so had zero total displacement and zero average *velocity!* Both average speed and instantaneous speed are scalars, not vectors, because these quantities contain no information about direction.

Finding Velocity on an x-t Graph

We can also find the x-velocity of a particle from the graph of its position as a function of time. Suppose we want to find the x-velocity of the dragster in Fig. 4.10 at point P_1. As point P_2 in Fig. 4.10 approaches point P_1, point p_2 in the x-t graphs of Figs. 4.13a and 4.13b approaches point p_1 and the average x-velocity is calculated over shorter time intervals Δt. In the limit that $\Delta t \rightarrow 0$, shown in Fig. 4.13c, the slope of the line p_1p_2 equals the slope of the line tangent to the curve at point p_1. Thus, *on a graph of position as a function of time for straight-line motion, the instantaneous x-velocity at any point is equal to the slope of the tangent to the curve at that point.*

If the tangent to the x-t curve slopes upward to the right, as in Fig. 4.13c, then its slope is positive, the x-velocity is positive, and the motion is in the positive x-direction. If the tangent slopes downward to the right, the slope of the x-t graph and the x-velocity are negative, and the motion is in the negative x-direction. When the tangent is horizontal, the slope and the x-velocity are zero. Figure 4.14 illustrates these three possibilities.

Figure 4.14 actually depicts the motion of a particle in two ways: as (a) an x-t graph and (b) a **motion diagram** that shows the particle's position at various

4.13 Using an x-t graph to go from (a), (b) average x-velocity to (c) instantaneous x-velocity v_x. In (c) we find the slope of the tangent to the x-t curve by dividing any vertical interval (with distance units) along the tangent by the corresponding horizontal interval (with time units).

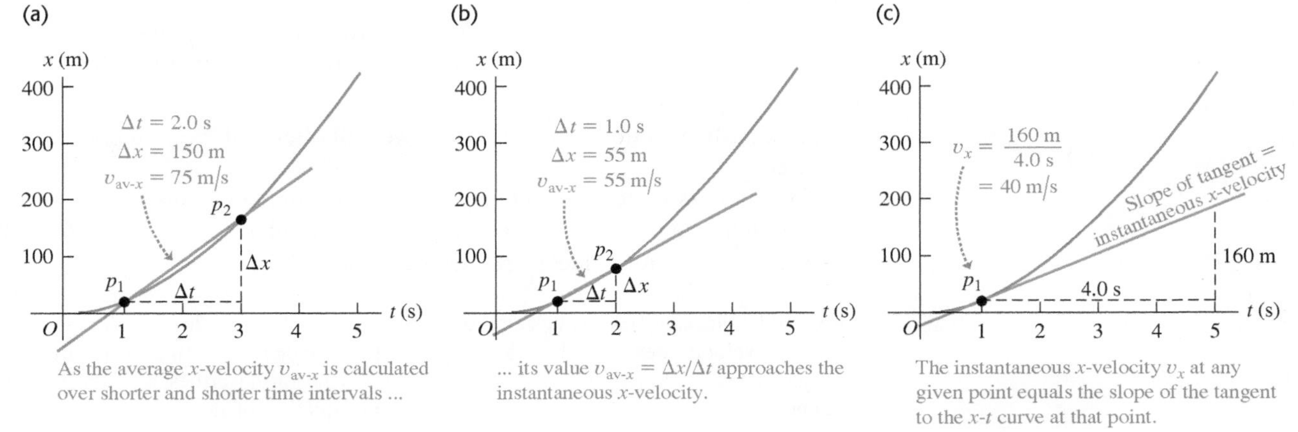

4.14 (a) The x-t graph of the motion of a particular particle. The slope of the tangent at any point equals the velocity at that point. (b) A motion diagram showing the position and velocity of the particle at each of the times labeled on the x-t graph.

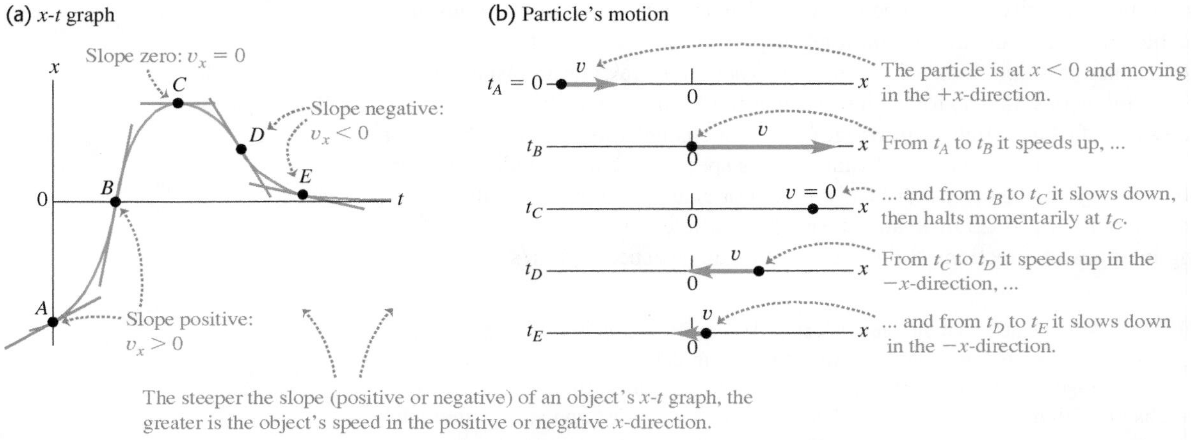

instants (like frames from a video of the particle's motion) as well as arrows to represent the particle's velocity at each instant. We will use both x-t graphs and motion diagrams in this chapter to help you understand motion. You will find it worth your while to draw *both* an x-t graph and a motion diagram as part of solving any problem involving motion.

4.5 Average and Instantaneous Acceleration

Just as velocity describes the rate of change of position with time, *acceleration* describes the rate of change of velocity with time. Like velocity, acceleration is a vector quantity. When the motion is along a straight line, its only nonzero component is along that line. As we'll see, acceleration in straight-line motion can refer to either speeding up or slowing down.

Average Acceleration

Let's consider again a particle moving along the x-axis. Suppose that at time t_1 the particle is at point P_1 and has x-component of (instantaneous) velocity v_{1x}, and at a later time t_2 it is at point P_2 and has x-component of velocity v_{2x}. So the x-component of velocity changes by an amount $\Delta v_x = v_{2x} - v_{1x}$ during the time interval $\Delta t = t_2 - t_1$.

We define the **average acceleration** of the particle as it moves from P_1 to P_2 to be a vector quantity whose x-component $a_{av\text{-}x}$ (called the **average *x*-acceleration**) equals Δv_x, the change in the x-component of velocity, divided by the time interval Δt:

$$a_{av\text{-}x} = \frac{v_{2x} - v_{1x}}{t_2 - t_1} = \frac{\Delta v_x}{\Delta t} \quad \text{(average } x\text{-acceleration, straight-line motion)} \tag{4.17}$$

For straight-line motion along the x-axis we will often call $a_{av\text{-}x}$ simply the average acceleration.

If we express velocity in meters per second and time in seconds, then average acceleration is in meters per second per second, or $(\text{m/s})/\text{s}$. This is usually written as m/s^2 and is read "meters per second squared."

CAUTION **Acceleration vs. velocity** Be very careful not to confuse acceleration with velocity! Velocity describes how a body's position changes with time; it tells us how fast and in what direction the body moves. Acceleration describes how the velocity changes with time; it tells us how the speed and direction of motion are changing. It may help to remember the phrase "acceleration is to velocity as velocity is to position." It can also help to imagine yourself riding along with the moving body. If the body accelerates forward and gains speed, you feel pushed backward in your seat; if it accelerates backward and loses speed, you feel pushed forward. If the velocity is constant and there's no acceleration, you feel neither sensation.

Instantaneous Acceleration

We can now define **instantaneous acceleration** following the same procedure that we used to define instantaneous velocity. As an example, suppose a race car driver is driving along a straightaway as shown in Fig. 4.15. To define the instantaneous acceleration at point P_1, we take the second point P_2 in Fig. 4.15 to be closer and closer to P_1 so that the average acceleration is computed over shorter and shorter time intervals. *The instantaneous acceleration is the limit of the average acceleration as the time interval approaches zero.* In the language of calculus, *instantaneous acceleration equals the derivative of velocity with time.* Thus

$$a_x = \lim_{\Delta t \to 0} \frac{\Delta v_x}{\Delta t} = \frac{dv_x}{dt} \quad \text{(instantaneous } x\text{-acceleration, straight-line motion)} \tag{4.18}$$

Note that a_x in Eq. (4.18) is really the x-component of the acceleration vector, or the **instantaneous *x*-acceleration;** in straight-line motion, all other components of this vector are zero. From now on, when we use the term "acceleration," we will always mean instantaneous acceleration, not average acceleration.

Finding Acceleration on a v_x-t Graph or an x-t Graph

In Section 4.4 we interpreted average and instantaneous x-velocity in terms of the slope of a graph of position versus time. In the same way, we can interpret average and instantaneous x-acceleration by using a graph with instantaneous velocity v_x on the vertical axis and time t on the horizontal axis—that is, a **v_x-t graph** (Fig. 4.16). The points on the graph labeled p_1 and p_2 correspond to points P_1 and

4.15 A Grand Prix car at two points on the straightaway.

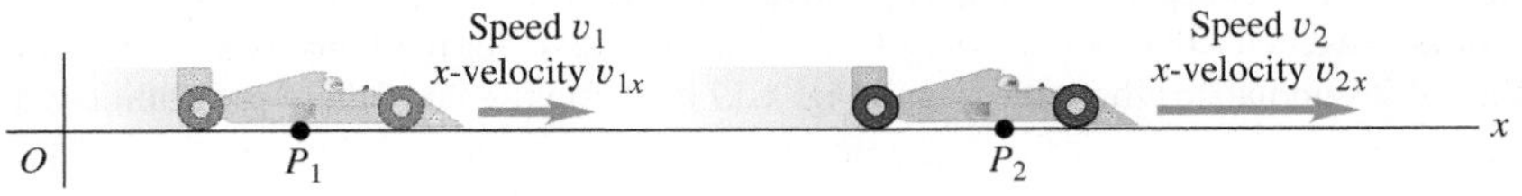

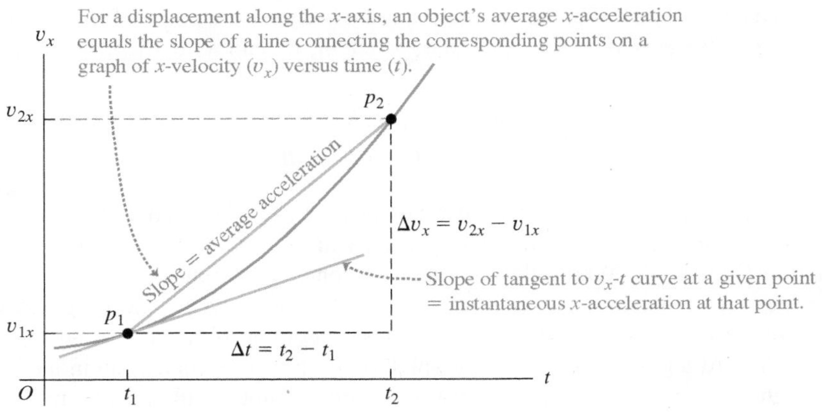

4.16 A v_x-t graph of the motion in Fig. 4.15.

4.17 (a) A v_x-t graph of the motion of a different particle from that shown in Fig. 4.14. The slope of the tangent at any point equals the x-acceleration at that point. (b) A motion diagram showing the position, velocity, and acceleration of the particle at each of the times labeled on the v_x-t graph. The positions are consistent with the v_x-t graph; for instance, from t_A to t_B the velocity is negative, so at t_B the particle is at a more negative value of x than at t_A.

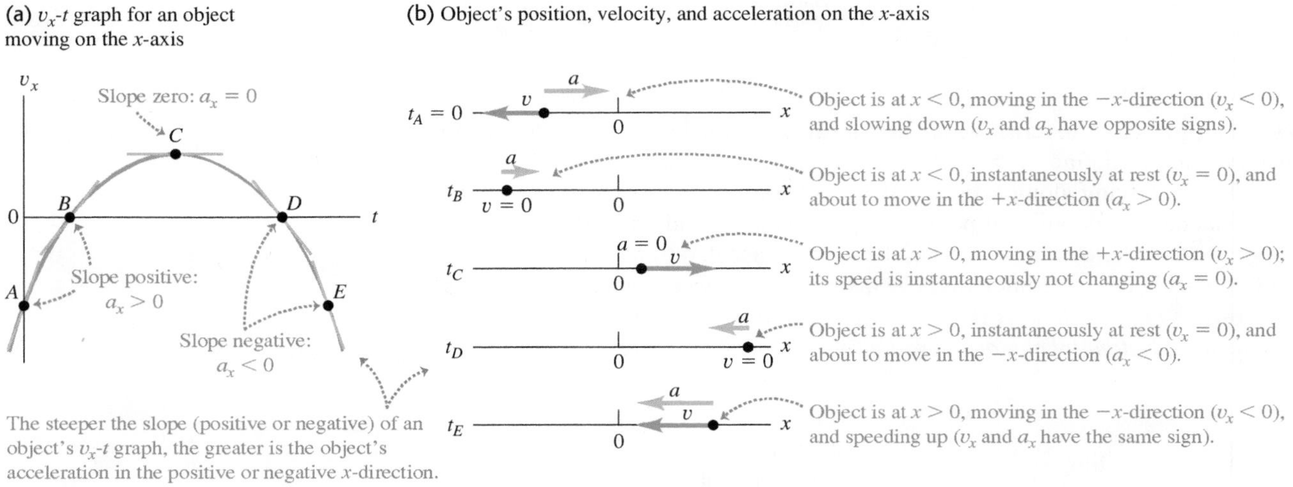
(a) v_x-t graph for an object moving on the x-axis
(b) Object's position, velocity, and acceleration on the x-axis
v_x
Slope zero: $a_x = 0$
C
B
D
0
t
A
E
Slope positive: $a_x > 0$
Slope negative: $a_x < 0$
The steeper the slope (positive or negative) of an object's v_x-t graph, the greater is the object's acceleration in the positive or negative x-direction.
$t_A = 0$
t_B
t_C
t_D
t_E
a
v
$v = 0$
$a = 0$
x
Object is at $x < 0$, moving in the $-x$-direction ($v_x < 0$), and slowing down (v_x and a_x have opposite signs).
Object is at $x < 0$, instantaneously at rest ($v_x = 0$), and about to move in the $+x$-direction ($a_x > 0$).
Object is at $x > 0$, moving in the $+x$-direction ($v_x > 0$); its speed is instantaneously not changing ($a_x = 0$).
Object is at $x > 0$, instantaneously at rest ($v_x = 0$), and about to move in the $-x$-direction ($a_x < 0$).
Object is at $x > 0$, moving in the $-x$-direction ($v_x < 0$), and speeding up (v_x and a_x have the same sign).

P_2 in Fig. 4.15. The average x-acceleration $a_{\text{av-}x} = \Delta v_x/\Delta t$ during this interval is the slope of the line p_1p_2. As point P_2 in Fig. 4.15 approaches point P_1, point p_2 in the v_x-t graph of Fig. 4.16 approaches point p_1, and the slope of the line p_1p_2 approaches the slope of the line tangent to the curve at point p_1. Thus, *on a graph of x-velocity as a function of time, the instantaneous x-acceleration at any point is equal to the slope of the tangent to the curve at that point.* Tangents drawn at different points along the curve in Fig. 4.16 have different slopes, so the instantaneous x-acceleration varies with time.

CAUTION **The signs of x-acceleration and x-velocity** By itself, the algebraic sign of the x-acceleration does *not* tell you whether a body is speeding up or slowing down. You must compare the signs of the x-velocity and the x-acceleration. When v_x and a_x have the *same* sign, the body is speeding up. If both are positive, the body is moving in the positive direction with increasing speed. If both are negative, the body is moving in the negative direction with an x-velocity that is becoming more and more negative, and again the speed is increasing. When v_x and a_x have *opposite* signs, the body is slowing down. If v_x is positive and a_x is negative, the body is moving in the positive direction with decreasing speed; if v_x is negative and a_x is positive, the body is moving in the negative direction with an x-velocity that is becoming less negative, and again the body is slowing down. Table 4.2 summarizes these ideas, and Fig. 4.17 illustrates some of these possibilities.

Table 4.2 Rules for the Sign of x-Acceleration

If x-velocity is:	. . . x-acceleration is:
Positive & increasing (getting more positive)	Positive: Particle is moving in $+x$-direction & speeding up
Positive & decreasing (getting less positive)	Negative: Particle is moving in $+x$-direction & slowing down
Negative & increasing (getting less negative)	Positive: Particle is moving in $-x$-direction & slowing down
Negative & decreasing (getting more negative)	Negative: Particle is moving in $-x$-direction & speeding up

Note: These rules apply to both the average x-acceleration $a_{\text{av-}x}$ and the instantaneous x-acceleration a_x.

The term "deceleration" is sometimes used for a decrease in speed. Because it may mean positive or negative a_x, depending on the sign of v_x, we avoid this term.

We can also learn about the acceleration of a body from a graph of its *position* versus time. Because $a_x = dv_x/dt$ and $v_x = dx/dt$, we can write

$$a_x = \frac{dv_x}{dt} = \frac{d}{dt}\left(\frac{dx}{dt}\right) = \frac{d^2x}{dt^2} \tag{4.19}$$

That is, a_x is the second derivative of x with respect to t. The second derivative of any function is directly related to the *concavity* or *curvature* of the graph of that function (Fig. 4.18). Where the x-t graph is concave up (curved upward), the x-acceleration is positive and v_x is increasing; at a point where the x-t graph is concave down (curved downward), the x-acceleration is negative and v_x is decreasing. At a point where the x-t graph has no curvature, such as an inflection point, the x-acceleration is zero and the velocity is not changing. Figure 4.18 shows all three of these possibilities.

4.18 (a) The same *x-t* graph as shown in Fig. 4.14a. The *x*-velocity is equal to the *slope* of the graph, and the acceleration is given by the *concavity* or *curvature* of the graph. (b) A motion diagram showing the position, velocity, and acceleration of the particle at each of the times labeled on the *x-t* graph.

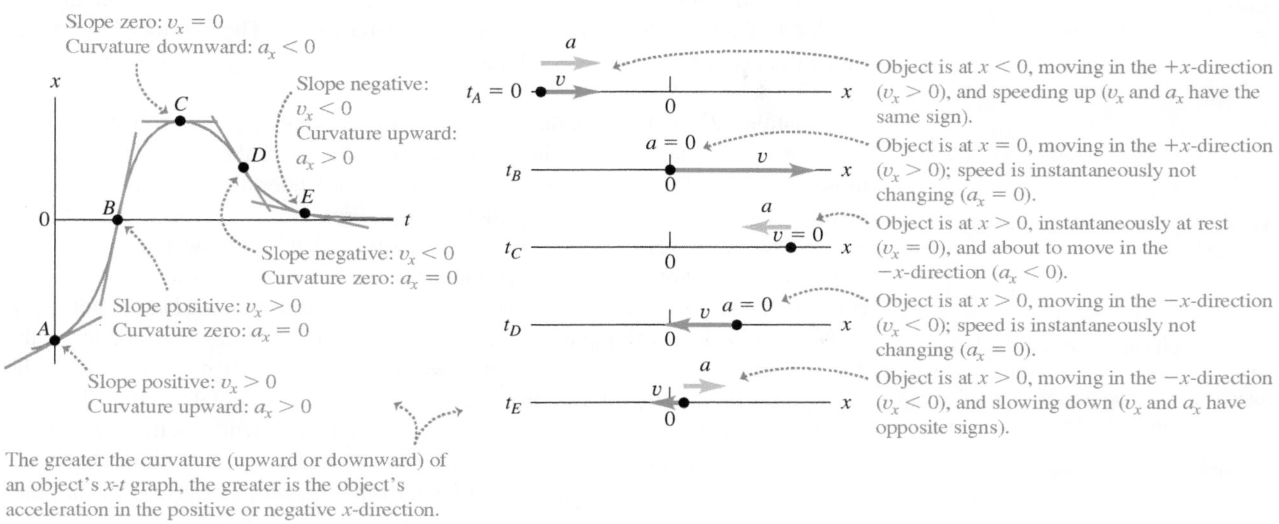

(a) x-t graph
(b) Object's motion
Slope zero: $v_x = 0$
Curvature downward: $a_x < 0$
Slope negative: $v_x < 0$
Curvature upward: $a_x > 0$
Slope negative: $v_x < 0$
Curvature zero: $a_x = 0$
Slope positive: $v_x > 0$
Curvature zero: $a_x = 0$
Slope positive: $v_x > 0$
Curvature upward: $a_x > 0$
The greater the curvature (upward or downward) of an object's x-t graph, the greater is the object's acceleration in the positive or negative x-direction.
Object is at $x < 0$, moving in the $+x$-direction ($v_x > 0$), and speeding up (v_x and a_x have the same sign).
Object is at $x = 0$, moving in the $+x$-direction ($v_x > 0$); speed is instantaneously not changing ($a_x = 0$).
Object is at $x > 0$, instantaneously at rest ($v_x = 0$), and about to move in the $-x$-direction ($a_x < 0$).
Object is at $x > 0$, moving in the $-x$-direction ($v_x < 0$); speed is instantaneously not changing ($a_x = 0$).
Object is at $x > 0$, moving in the $-x$-direction ($v_x < 0$), and slowing down (v_x and a_x have opposite signs).

Examining the curvature of an *x-t* graph is an easy way to decide what the *sign* of acceleration is. This technique is less helpful for determining numerical values of acceleration because the curvature of a graph is hard to measure accurately.

4.6 Motion with Constant Acceleration

The simplest kind of accelerated motion is straight-line motion with *constant* acceleration. In this case the velocity changes at the same rate throughout the motion. As an example, a falling body has a constant acceleration if the effects of the air are not important. The same is true for a body sliding on an incline or along a rough horizontal surface, or for an airplane being catapulted from the deck of an aircraft carrier.

Figure 4.19 is a motion diagram showing the position, velocity, and acceleration for a particle moving with constant acceleration. Figures 4.20 and 4.21 depict this same motion in the form of graphs. Since the *x*-acceleration is constant, the **a_x-*t* graph** (graph of *x*-acceleration versus time) in Fig. 4.20 is a horizontal line. The graph of *x*-velocity versus time, or v_x-*t* graph, has a constant *slope* because the acceleration is constant, so this graph is a straight line (Fig. 4.21).

When the *x*-acceleration a_x is constant, the average *x*-acceleration $a_{\text{av-}x}$ for any time interval is the same as a_x. This makes it easy to derive equations for the position *x* and the *x*-velocity v_x as functions of time. To find an expression for v_x, we first replace $a_{\text{av-}x}$ in Eq. (4.17) by a_x:

$$a_x = \frac{v_{2x} - v_{1x}}{t_2 - t_1} \tag{4.20}$$

Now we let $t_1 = 0$ and let t_2 be any later time t. We use the symbol v_{0x} for the *x*-velocity at the initial time $t = 0$; the *x*-velocity at the later time t is v_x. Then Eq. (4.20) becomes

$$a_x = \frac{v_x - v_{0x}}{t - 0} \quad \text{or}$$

4.19 A motion diagram for a particle moving in a straight line in the positive *x*-direction with constant positive *x*-acceleration a_x. The position, velocity, and acceleration are shown at five equally spaced times.

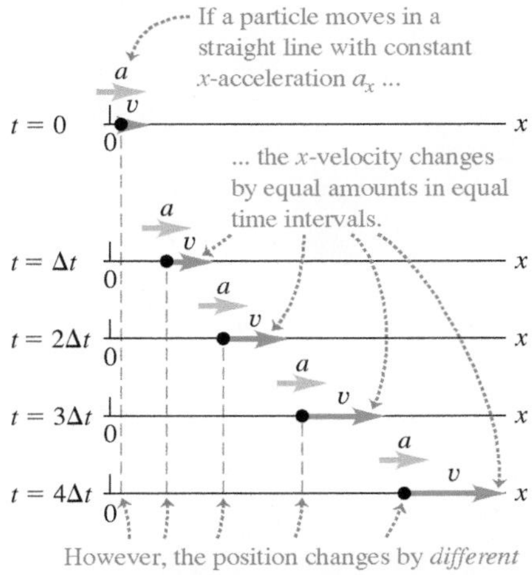

If a particle moves in a straight line with constant x-acceleration a_x ...
... the x-velocity changes by equal amounts in equal time intervals.
$t = 0$
$t = \Delta t$
$t = 2\Delta t$
$t = 3\Delta t$
$t = 4\Delta t$
However, the position changes by *different* amounts in equal time intervals because the velocity is changing.

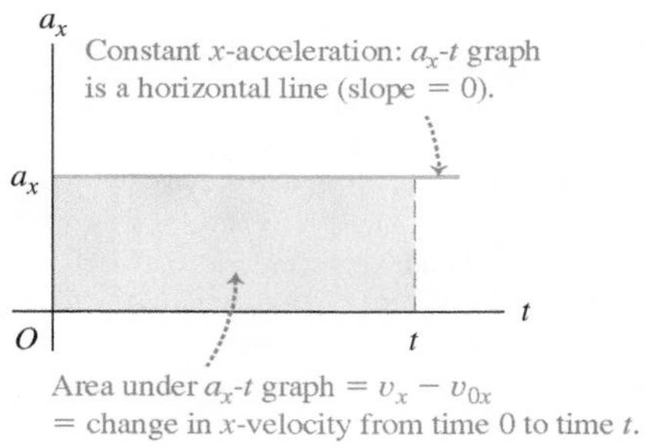
a_x
Constant x-acceleration: a_x-t graph is a horizontal line (slope = 0).
a_x
O
t
t
Area under a_x-t graph = $v_x - v_{0x}$
= change in x-velocity from time 0 to time t.

4.20 An acceleration-time (a_x-t) graph for straight-line motion with constant positive x-acceleration a_x.

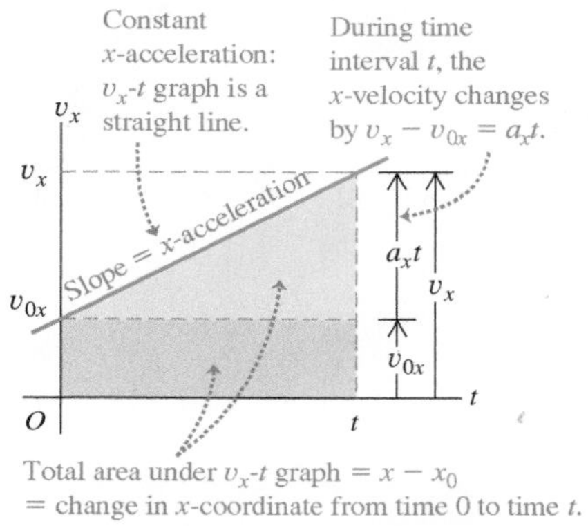
Constant x-acceleration: v_x-t graph is a straight line.
During time interval t, the x-velocity changes by $v_x - v_{0x} = a_x t$.
v_x
v_x
Slope = x-acceleration
$a_x t$
v_x
v_{0x}
v_{0x}
O
t
t
Total area under v_x-t graph = $x - x_0$
= change in x-coordinate from time 0 to time t.

4.21 A velocity-time (v_x-t) graph for straight-line motion with constant positive x-acceleration a_x. The initial x-velocity v_{0x} is also positive in this case.

$$v_x = v_{0x} + a_x t \qquad \text{(constant } x\text{-acceleration only)} \tag{4.21}$$

In Eq. (4.21) the term $a_x t$ is the product of the constant rate of change of x-velocity, a_x, and the time interval t. Therefore it equals the *total* change in x-velocity from the initial time $t = 0$ to the later time t. The x-velocity v_x at any time t then equals the initial x-velocity v_{0x} (at $t = 0$) plus the change in x-velocity $a_x t$ (Fig. 4.21).

Equation (4.21) also says that the change in x-velocity $v_x - v_{0x}$ of the particle between $t = 0$ and any later time t equals the *area* under the a_x-t graph between those two times. You can verify this from Fig. 4.20: Under this graph is a rectangle of vertical side a_x, horizontal side t, and area $a_x t$. From Eq. (4.21) this is indeed equal to the change in velocity $v_x - v_{0x}$. In Section 4.8 we'll show that even if the x-acceleration is not constant, the change in x-velocity during a time interval is still equal to the area under the a_x-t curve, although in that case Eq. (4.21) does not apply.

Next we'll derive an equation for the position x as a function of time when the x-acceleration is constant. To do this, we use two different expressions for the average x-velocity $v_{\text{av-}x}$ during the interval from $t = 0$ to any later time t. The first expression comes from the definition of $v_{\text{av-}x}$, Eq. (4.15), which is true whether or not the acceleration is constant. We call the position at time $t = 0$ the *initial position*, denoted by x_0. The position at the later time t is simply x. Thus for the time interval $\Delta t = t - 0$ the displacement is $\Delta x = x - x_0$, and Eq. (4.15) gives

$$v_{\text{av-}x} = \frac{x - x_0}{t} \tag{4.22}$$

We can also get a second expression for $v_{\text{av-}x}$ that is valid only when the x-acceleration is constant, so that the x-velocity changes at a constant rate. In this case the average x-velocity for the time interval from 0 to t is simply the average of the x-velocities at the beginning and end of the interval:

$$v_{\text{av-}x} = \frac{v_{0x} + v_x}{2} \qquad \text{(constant } x\text{-acceleration only)} \tag{4.23}$$

(This equation is *not* true if the x-acceleration varies during the time interval.) We also know that with constant x-acceleration, the x-velocity v_x at any time t is given by Eq. (4.21). Substituting that expression for v_x into Eq. (4.23), we find

$$v_{\text{av-}x} = \tfrac{1}{2}(v_{0x} + v_{0x} + a_x t)$$

$$= v_{0x} + \tfrac{1}{2}a_x t \qquad \text{(constant } x\text{-acceleration only)} \tag{4.24}$$

Finally, we set Eqs. (4.22) and (4.24) equal to each other and simplify:

$$v_{0x} + \tfrac{1}{2}a_x t = \frac{x - x_0}{t} \qquad \text{or}$$

$$x = x_0 + v_{0x}t + \tfrac{1}{2}a_x t^2 \qquad \text{(constant } x\text{-acceleration only)} \tag{4.25}$$

Here's what Eq. (4.25) tells us: If at time $t = 0$ a particle is at position x_0 and has x-velocity v_{0x}, its new position x at any later time t is the sum of three terms—its initial position x_0, plus the distance $v_{0x}t$ that it would move if its x-velocity were constant, plus an additional distance $\frac{1}{2}a_x t^2$ caused by the change in x-velocity.

A graph of Eq. (4.25)—that is, an x-t graph for motion with constant x-acceleration (Fig. 4.23a)—is always a *parabola*. Figure 4.23b shows such a graph. The curve intercepts the vertical axis (x-axis) at x_0, the position at $t = 0$. The slope of the tangent at $t = 0$ equals v_{0x}, the initial x-velocity, and the slope of the tangent at any time t equals the x-velocity v_x at that time. The slope and x-velocity are continuously increasing, so the x-acceleration a_x is positive; you can also see this because the graph in Fig. 4.23b is concave up (it curves upward). If a_x is negative, the x-t graph is a parabola that is concave down (has a downward curvature).

If there is zero x-acceleration, the x-t graph is a straight line; if there is a constant x-acceleration, the additional $\frac{1}{2}a_xt^2$ term in Eq. (4.25) for x as a function of t curves the graph into a parabola (Fig. 4.23a). We can analyze the v_x-t graph in the same way. If there is zero x-acceleration this graph is a horizontal line (the x-velocity is constant); adding a constant x-acceleration gives a slope to the v_x-t graph (Fig. 4.23b).

Just as the change in x-velocity of the particle equals the area under the a_x-t graph, the displacement—that is, the change in position—equals the area under the v_x-t graph. To be specific, the displacement $x - x_0$ of the particle between $t = 0$ and any later time t equals the area under the v_x-t graph between those two times. In Fig. 4.21 we divide the area under the graph into a dark-colored rectangle (vertical side v_{0x}, horizontal side t, and area $v_{0x}t$) and a light-colored right triangle (vertical side a_xt, horizontal side t, and area $\frac{1}{2}(a_xt)(t) = \frac{1}{2}a_xt^2$). The total area under the v_x-t graph is

$$x - x_0 = v_{0x}t + \frac{1}{2}a_xt^2$$

in agreement with Eq. (4.25).

The displacement during a time interval is always equal to the area under the v_x-t curve. This is true even if the acceleration is *not* constant, although in that case Eq. (4.25) does not apply.

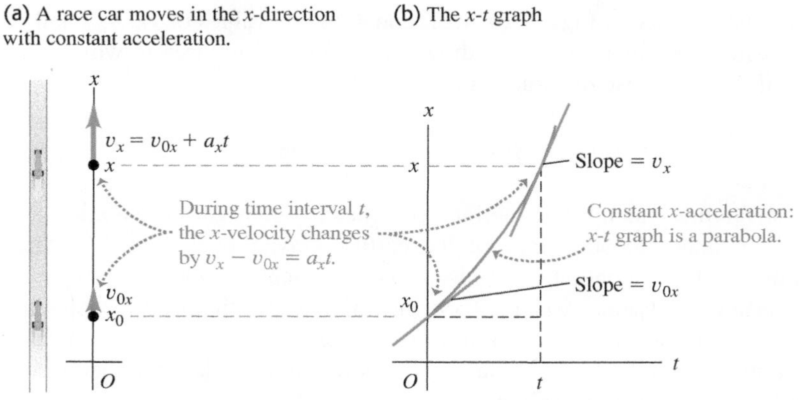

4.22 (a) Straight-line motion with constant acceleration. (b) A position-time (x-t) graph for this motion (the same motion as is shown in Figs. 4.19, 4.20, and 4.21). For this motion the initial position x_0, the initial velocity v_{0x}, and the acceleration a_x are all positive.

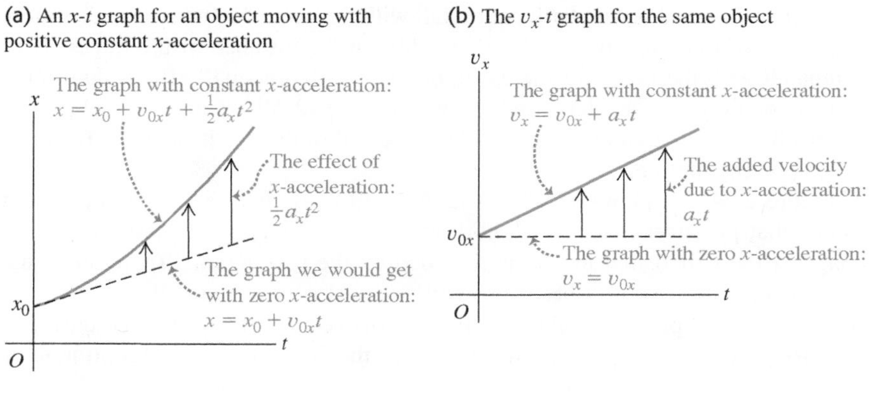

4.23 (a) How a constant x-acceleration affects a body's (a) x-t graph and (b) v_x-t graph.

It's often useful to have a relationship for position, x-velocity, and (constant) x-acceleration that does not involve the time. To obtain this, we first solve Eq. (4.21) for t and then substitute the resulting expression into Eq. (4.25):

$$t = \frac{v_x - v_{0x}}{a_x}$$

$$x = x_0 + v_{0x}\left(\frac{v_x - v_{0x}}{a_x}\right) + \frac{1}{2}a_x\left(\frac{v_x - v_{0x}}{a_x}\right)^2$$

We transfer the term x_0 to the left side and multiply through by $2a_x$:

$$2a_x(x - x_0) = 2v_{0x}v_x - 2v_{0x}^2 + v_x^2 - 2v_{0x}v_x + v_{0x}^2$$

Finally, simplifying gives us

$$v_x^2 = v_{0x}^2 + 2a_x(x - x_0) \quad \text{(constant } x\text{-acceleration only)} \quad (4.26)$$

We can get one more useful relationship by equating the two expressions for $v_{\text{av-}x}$, Eqs. (4.22) and (4.23), and multiplying through by t. Doing this, we obtain

$$x - x_0 = \left(\frac{v_{0x} + v_x}{2}\right)t \quad \text{(constant } x\text{-acceleration only)} \quad (4.27)$$

Table 4.3 Equations of Motion with Constant Acceleration

Equation		Includes Quantities			
$v_x = v_{0x} + a_xt$	(4.21)	t		v_x	a_x
$x = x_0 + v_{0x}t + \frac{1}{2}a_xt^2$	(4.25)	t	x		a_x
$v_x^2 = v_{0x}^2 + 2a_x(x - x_0)$	(4.26)		x	v_x	a_x
$x - x_0 = \left(\frac{v_{0x} + v_x}{2}\right)t$	(4.27)	t	x	v_x	

Note that Eq. (4.27) does not contain the x-acceleration a_x. This equation can be handy when a_x is constant but its value is unknown.

Equations (4.21), (4.25), (4.26), and (4.27) are the *equations of motion with constant acceleration* (Table 4.3). By using these equations, we can solve *any* problem involving straight-line motion of a particle with constant acceleration.

For the particular case of motion with constant x-acceleration depicted in Fig. 4.19 and graphed in Figs. 4.20, 4.21, and 4.22, the values of x_0, v_{0x}, and a_x are all positive. We invite you to redraw these figures for cases in which one, two, or all three of these quantities are negative.

4.7 Freely Falling Bodies

The most familiar example of motion with (nearly) constant acceleration is a body falling under the influence of the earth's gravitational attraction. Such motion has held the attention of philosophers and scientists since ancient times. In the fourth century B.C., Aristotle thought (erroneously) that heavy bodies fall faster than light bodies, in proportion to their weight. Nineteen centuries later, Galileo argued that a body should fall with a downward acceleration that is constant and independent of its weight.

Experiment shows that if the effects of the air can be neglected, Galileo is right; all bodies at a particular location fall with the same downward acceleration, regardless of their size or weight. If in addition the distance of the fall is small compared with the radius of the earth, and if we ignore small effects due to the earth's rotation, the acceleration is constant. The idealized motion that results under all of these assumptions is called **free fall,** although it includes rising as well as falling motion.

Figure 4.24 is a photograph of a falling ball made with a stroboscopic light source that produces a series of short, intense flashes. As each flash occurs, an image of the ball at that instant is recorded on the photograph. There are equal time intervals between flashes, so the average velocity of the ball between successive flashes is proportional to the distance between corresponding images. The increasing distances between images show that the velocity is continuously

4.24 Multiflash photo of a freely falling ball.

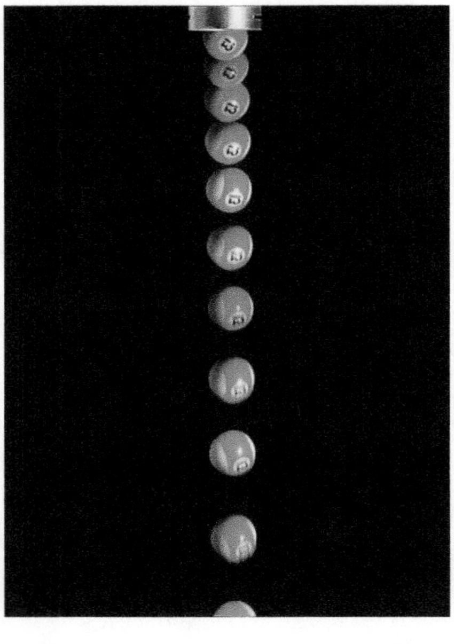

changing; the ball is accelerating downward. Careful measurement shows that the velocity change is the same in each time interval, so the acceleration of the freely falling ball is constant.

The constant acceleration of a freely falling body is called the **acceleration due to gravity,** and we denote its magnitude with the letter g. We will frequently use the approximate value of g at or near the earth's surface:

$$g = 9.8\ \text{m/s}^2 = 980\ \text{cm/s}^2 = 32\ \text{ft/s}^2 \qquad \text{(approximate value near the earth's surface)}$$

The exact value varies with location, so we will often give the value of g at the earth's surface to only two significant figures. On the surface of the moon, the acceleration due to gravity is caused by the attractive force of the moon rather than the earth, and $g = 1.6\ \text{m/s}^2$. Near the surface of the sun, $g = 270\ \text{m/s}^2$.

CAUTION **g is always a positive number** Because g is the *magnitude* of a vector quantity, it is always a *positive* number. If you take the positive direction to be upward and in most situations involving free fall, the acceleration is negative (downward) and equal to $-g$. Be careful with the sign of g, or else you'll have no end of trouble with free-fall problems.

4.8 Velocity and Position by Integration

This section is intended for students who have already learned a little integral calculus. We analyzed the special case of straight-line motion with constant acceleration. When a_x is not constant, as is frequently the case, the equations that we derived in that section are no longer valid. But even when a_x varies with time, we can still use the relationship $v_x = dx/dt$ to find the x-velocity v_x as a function of time if the position x is a known function of time. And we can still use $a_x = dv_x/dt$ to find the x-acceleration a_x as a function of time if the x-velocity v_x is a known function of time.

In many situations, however, position and velocity are not known functions of time, while acceleration is. How can we find the position and velocity in straight-line motion from the acceleration function $a_x(t)$?

We first consider a graphical approach. Figure 4.25 is a graph of x-acceleration versus time for a body whose acceleration is not constant. We can divide the time interval between times t_1 and t_2 into many smaller intervals, calling a typical one Δt. Let the average x-acceleration during Δt be $a_{\text{av-}x}$. From Eq. (4.17) the change in x-velocity Δv_x during Δt is

$$\Delta v_x = a_{\text{av-}x}\,\Delta t$$

Graphically, Δv_x equals the area of the shaded strip with height $a_{\text{av-}x}$ and width Δt—that is, the area under the curve between the left and right sides of Δt. The

4.25 An a_x-t graph for a body whose x-acceleration is not constant.

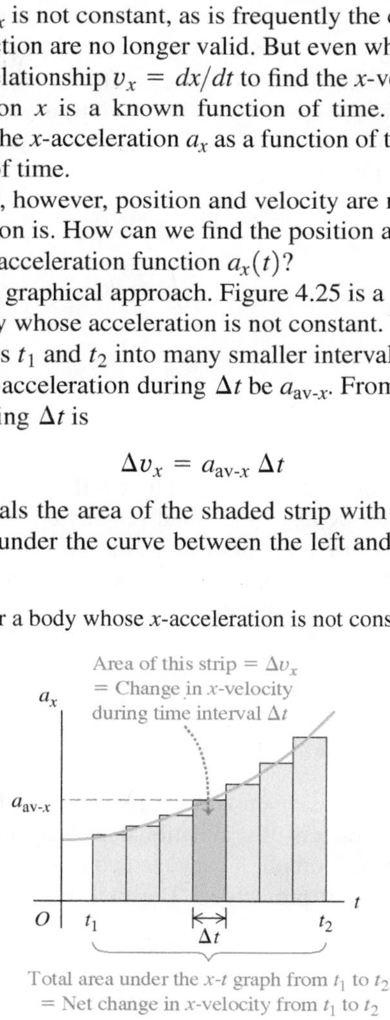

total change in x-velocity during any interval (say, t_1 to t_2) is the sum of the x-velocity changes Δv_x in the small subintervals. So the total x-velocity change is represented graphically by the *total* area under the a_x-t curve between the vertical lines t_1 and t_2. (In Section 4.6 we showed this for the special case in which the acceleration is constant.)

In the limit that all the Δt's become very small and their number very large, the value of $a_{\text{av-}x}$ for the interval from any time t to $t + \Delta t$ approaches the instantaneous x-acceleration a_x at time t. In this limit, the area under the a_x-t curve is the *integral* of a_x (which is in general a function of t) from t_1 to t_2. If v_{1x} is the x-velocity of the body at time t_1 and v_{2x} is the velocity at time t_2, then

$$v_{2x} - v_{1x} = \int_{v_{1x}}^{v_{2x}} dv_x = \int_{t_1}^{t_2} a_x\, dt \tag{4.28}$$

The change in the x-velocity v_x is the time integral of the x-acceleration a_x.

We can carry out exactly the same procedure with the curve of x-velocity versus time. If x_1 is a body's position at time t_1 and x_2 is its position at time t_2, from Eq. (4.15) the displacement Δx during a small time interval Δt is equal to $v_{\text{av-}x}\,\Delta t$, where $v_{\text{av-}x}$ is the average x-velocity during Δt. The total displacement $x_2 - x_1$ during the interval $t_2 - t_1$ is given by

$$x_2 - x_1 = \int_{x_1}^{x_2} dx = \int_{t_1}^{t_2} v_x\, dt \tag{4.29}$$

The change in position x—that is, the displacement—is the time integral of x-velocity v_x. Graphically, the displacement between times t_1 and t_2 is the area under the v_x-t curve between those two times. [This is the same result that we obtained in Section 4.6 for the special case in which v_x is given by Eq. (4.21).]

If $t_1 = 0$ and t_2 is any later time t, and if x_0 and v_{0x} are the position and velocity, respectively, at time $t = 0$, then we can rewrite Eqs. (4.28) and (4.29) as follows:

$$v_x = v_{0x} + \int_0^t a_x\, dt \tag{4.30}$$

$$x = x_0 + \int_0^t v_x\, dt \tag{4.31}$$

Here x and v_x are the position and x-velocity at time t. If we know the x-acceleration a_x as a function of time and we know the initial velocity v_{0x}, we can use Eq. (4.30) to find the x-velocity v_x at any time; in other words, we can find v_x as a function of time. Once we know this function, and given the initial position x_0, we can use Eq. (4.31) to find the position x at any time.

4.9 Projectile Motion

A **projectile** is any body that is given an initial velocity and then follows a path determined entirely by the effects of gravitational acceleration and air resistance. A batted baseball, a thrown football, a package dropped from an airplane, and a bullet shot from a rifle are all projectiles. The path followed by a projectile is called its **trajectory.**

To analyze this common type of motion, we'll start with an idealized model, representing the projectile as a particle with an acceleration (due to gravity) that is constant in both magnitude and direction. We'll neglect the effects of air resistance and the curvature and rotation of the earth. Like all models, this one has limitations. Curvature of the earth has to be considered in the flight of long-range missiles, and air resistance is of crucial importance to a sky diver. Nevertheless, we can learn a lot from analysis of this simple model. For the remainder of this chapter the phrase "projectile motion" will imply that we're ignoring air resistance.

Projectile motion is always confined to a vertical plane determined by the direction of the initial velocity (Fig. 4.26). This is because the acceleration due to gravity is purely vertical; gravity can't accelerate the projectile sideways. Thus projectile motion is *two-dimensional.* We will call the plane of motion the xy-coordinate plane, with the x-axis horizontal and the y-axis vertically upward.

The key to analyzing projectile motion is that we can treat the x- and y-coordinates separately. The x-component of acceleration is zero, and the y-component is constant and equal to $-g$. (By definition, g is always positive; with our choice of coordinate directions, a_y is negative.) So *we can analyze projectile motion as a combination of horizontal motion with constant velocity and vertical motion with constant acceleration.* Figure 4.27 shows two projectiles with different x-motion but identical y-motion; one is dropped from rest and the other is projected horizontally, but both projectiles fall the same distance in the same time.

We can then express all the vector relationships for the projectile's position, velocity, and acceleration by separate equations for the horizontal and vertical components. The components of $\vec{a}$ are

$$a_x = 0 \qquad a_y = -g \qquad \text{(projectile motion, no air resistance)} \tag{4.32}$$

Since the x-acceleration and y-acceleration are both constant, we can use Eqs. (4.21), (4.25), (4.26), and (4.27) directly. For example, suppose that at time $t = 0$ our particle is at the point (x_0, y_0) and that at this time its velocity components have the initial values v_{0x} and v_{0y}. The components of acceleration are $a_x = 0$, $a_y = -g$. Considering the x-motion first, we substitute 0 for a_x in Eqs. (4.21) and (4.25). We find

$$v_x = v_{0x} \tag{4.33}$$

$$x = x_0 + v_{0x}t \tag{4.34}$$

For the y-motion we substitute y for x, v_y for v_x, v_{0y} for v_{0x}, and $a_y = -g$ for a_x:

$$v_y = v_{0y} - gt \tag{4.35}$$

$$y = y_0 + v_{0y}t - \tfrac{1}{2}gt^2 \tag{4.36}$$

It's usually simplest to take the initial position (at $t = 0$) as the origin; then $x_0 = y_0 = 0$. This might be the position of a ball at the instant it leaves the thrower's hand or the position of a bullet at the instant it leaves the gun barrel.

Figure 4.28 shows the trajectory of a projectile that starts at (or passes through) the origin at time $t = 0$, along with its position, velocity, and velocity components at equal time intervals. The x-component of acceleration is zero, so v_x is constant. The y-component of acceleration is constant and not zero, so v_y changes by equal amounts in equal times, just the same as if the projectile were launched vertically with the same initial y-velocity.

We can also represent the initial velocity $\vec{v}_0$ by its magnitude v_0 (the initial speed) and its angle α_0 with the positive x-axis. In terms of these quantities, the components v_{0x} and v_{0y} of the initial velocity are

$$v_{0x} = v_0 \cos\alpha_0 \qquad v_{0y} = v_0 \sin\alpha_0 \tag{4.37}$$

4.26 The trajectory of an idealized projectile.

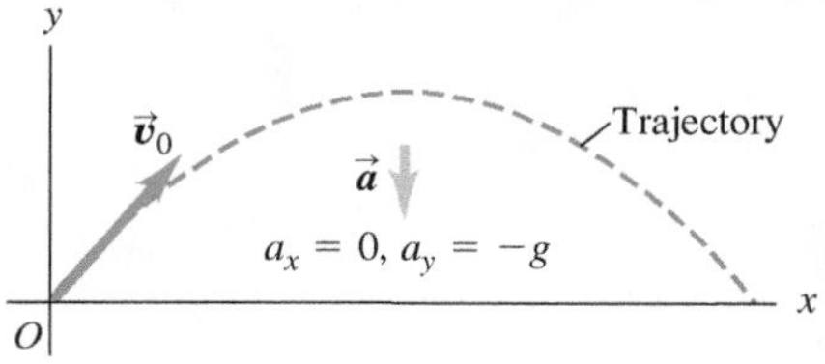
• A projectile moves in a vertical plane that contains the initial velocity vector $\vec{v}_0$.
• Its trajectory depends only on $\vec{v}_0$ and on the downward acceleration due to gravity.
y
$\vec{v}_0$
Trajectory
$\vec{a}$
$a_x = 0,\ a_y = -g$
O
x

4.27 The red ball is dropped from rest, and the yellow ball is simultaneously projected horizontally; successive images in this stroboscopic photograph are separated by equal time intervals. At any given time, both balls have the same y-position, y-velocity, and y-acceleration, despite having different x-positions and x-velocities.

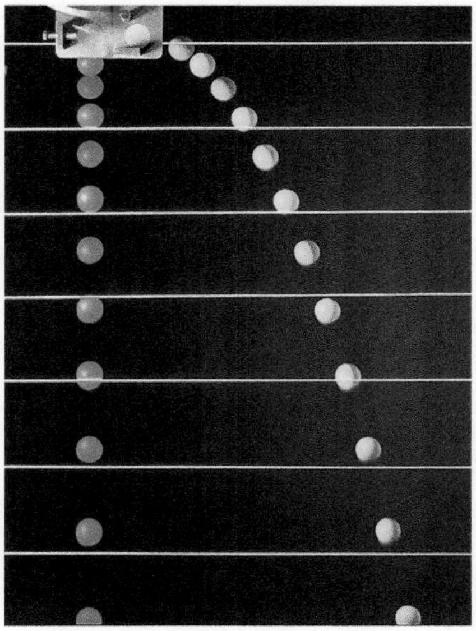

4.28 If air resistance is negligible, the trajectory of a projectile is a combination of horizontal motion with constant velocity and vertical motion with constant acceleration.

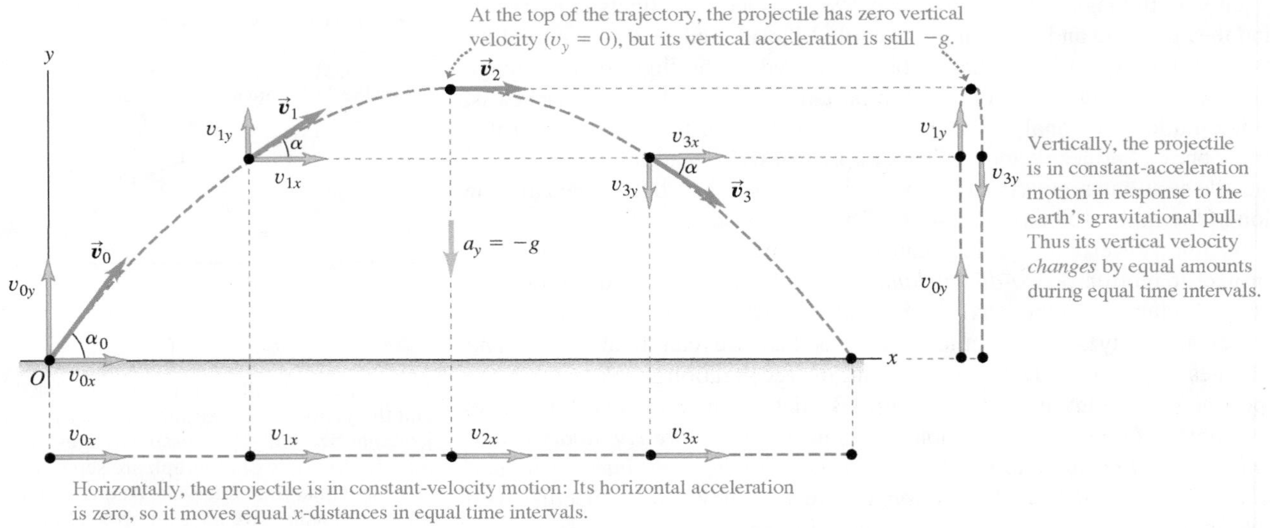
At the top of the trajectory, the projectile has zero vertical velocity ($v_y = 0$), but its vertical acceleration is still $-g$.
$\vec{v}_2$
$\vec{v}_1$
v_{1y}
α
v_{1x}
v_{3x}
α
v_{3y}
$\vec{v}_3$
$a_y = -g$
$\vec{v}_0$
v_{0y}
α_0
O
v_{0x}
x
y
v_{1y}
v_{3y}
v_{0y}
Vertically, the projectile is in constant-acceleration motion in response to the earth's gravitational pull. Thus its vertical velocity *changes* by equal amounts during equal time intervals.
v_{0x}
v_{1x}
v_{2x}
v_{3x}
Horizontally, the projectile is in constant-velocity motion: Its horizontal acceleration is zero, so it moves equal x-distances in equal time intervals.

If we substitute these relationships in Eqs. (4.33) through (4.36) and set $x_0 = y_0 = 0$, we find

$$x = (v_0 \cos\alpha_0)t \qquad \text{(projectile motion)} \tag{4.38}$$

$$y = (v_0 \sin\alpha_0)t - \tfrac{1}{2}gt^2 \qquad \text{(projectile motion)} \tag{4.39}$$

$$v_x = v_0 \cos\alpha_0 \qquad \text{(projectile motion)} \tag{4.40}$$

$$v_y = v_0 \sin\alpha_0 - gt \qquad \text{(projectile motion)} \tag{4.41}$$

These equations describe the position and velocity of the projectile in Fig. 4.28 at any time t.

We can get a lot of information from Eqs. (4.38) through (4.41). For example, at any time the distance r of the projectile from the origin (the magnitude of the position vector $\vec{r}$) is given by

$$r = \sqrt{x^2 + y^2} \tag{4.42}$$

The projectile's speed (the magnitude of its velocity) at any time is

$$v = \sqrt{v_x^2 + v_y^2} \tag{4.43}$$

The *direction* of the velocity, in terms of the angle α it makes with the positive x-direction (see Fig. 4.28), is given by

$$\tan\alpha = \frac{v_y}{v_x} \tag{4.44}$$

The velocity vector $\vec{v}$ is tangent to the trajectory at each point.

We can derive an equation for the trajectory's shape in terms of x and y by eliminating t. From Eqs. (4.38) and (4.39), which assume $x_0 = y_0 = 0$, we find $t = x/(v_0 \cos\alpha_0)$ and

$$y = (\tan\alpha_0)x - \frac{g}{2v_0^2\cos^2\alpha_0}x^2 \tag{4.45}$$

4.29 Air resistance has a large cumulative effect on the motion of a baseball. In this simulation we allow the baseball to fall below the height from which it was thrown (for example, the baseball could have been thrown from a cliff).

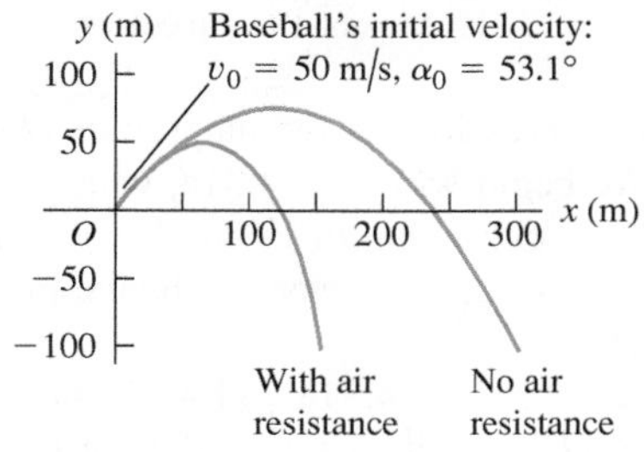
y (m)
Baseball's initial velocity:
$v_0 = 50$ m/s, $\alpha_0 = 53.1°$
100
50
O
−50
−100
100
200
300
x (m)
With air resistance
No air resistance

Don't worry about the details of this equation; the important point is its general form. Since v_0, $\tan \alpha_0$, $\cos \alpha_0$, and g are constants, Eq. (4.45) has the form

$$y = bx - cx^2$$

where b and c are constants. This is the equation of a *parabola.* In our simple model of projectile motion, the trajectory is always a parabola.

When air resistance *isn't* always negligible and has to be included, calculating the trajectory becomes a lot more complicated; the effects of air resistance depend on velocity, so the acceleration is no longer constant. Figure 4.29 shows a computer simulation of the trajectory of a baseball both without air resistance and with air resistance proportional to the square of the baseball's speed. We see that air resistance has a very large effect; the maximum height and range both decrease, and the trajectory is no longer a parabola.

4.10 Motion in a Circle

When a particle moves along a curved path, the direction of its velocity changes. This means that the particle *must* have a component of acceleration perpendicular to the path, even if its speed is constant. In this section we'll calculate the acceleration for the important special case of motion in a circle.

Uniform Circular Motion

When a particle moves in a circle with *constant speed,* the motion is called **uniform circular motion.** A car rounding a curve with constant radius at constant speed, a satellite moving in a circular orbit, and an ice skater skating in a circle with constant speed are all examples of uniform circular motion (Fig. 4.30c;

4.30 A car moving along a circular path. If the car is in uniform circular motion as in (c), the speed is constant and the acceleration is directed toward the center of the circular path (compare Fig. 4.9).

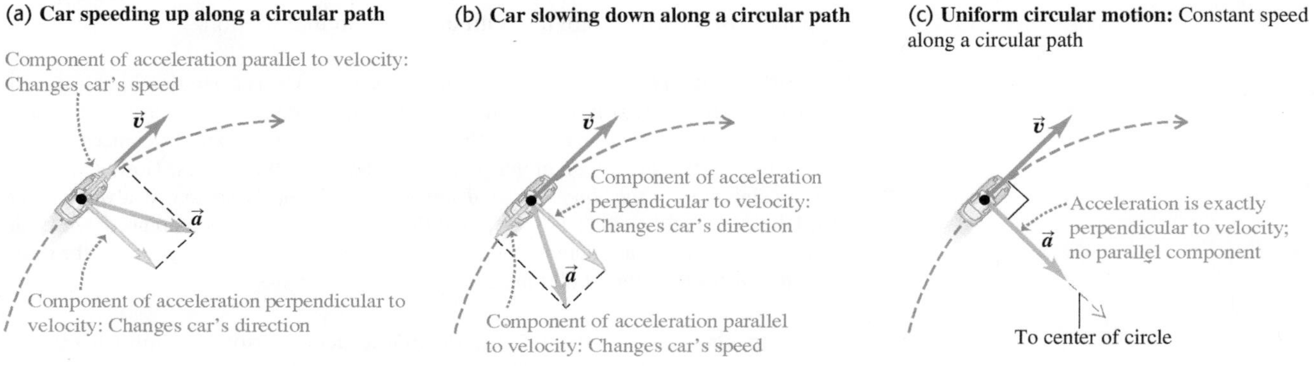
(a) Car speeding up along a circular path
Component of acceleration parallel to velocity: Changes car's speed
$\vec{v}$
$\vec{a}$
Component of acceleration perpendicular to velocity: Changes car's direction
(b) Car slowing down along a circular path
$\vec{v}$
Component of acceleration perpendicular to velocity: Changes car's direction
$\vec{a}$
Component of acceleration parallel to velocity: Changes car's speed
(c) Uniform circular motion: Constant speed along a circular path
$\vec{v}$
Acceleration is exactly perpendicular to velocity; no parallel component
$\vec{a}$
To center of circle

4.31 Finding the velocity change $\Delta\vec{v}$, average acceleration $\vec{a}_{av}$, and instantaneous acceleration $\vec{a}_{rad}$ for a particle moving in a circle with constant speed.

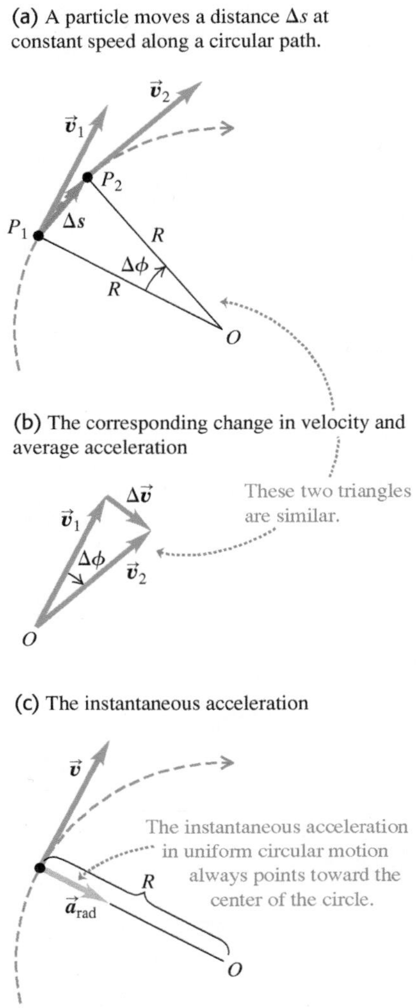

compare Fig. 4.9a). There is no component of acceleration parallel (tangent) to the path; otherwise, the speed would change. The acceleration vector is perpendicular (normal) to the path and hence directed inward (never outward!) toward the center of the circular path. This causes the direction of the velocity to change without changing the speed.

We can find a simple expression for the magnitude of the acceleration in uniform circular motion. We begin with Fig. 4.31a, which shows a particle moving with constant speed in a circular path of radius R with center at O. The particle moves from P_1 to P_2 in a time Δt. The vector change in velocity $\Delta\vec{v}$ during this time is shown in Fig. 4.31b.

The angles labeled $\Delta\phi$ in Figs. 4.31a and 4.31b are the same because $\vec{v}_1$ is perpendicular to the line OP_1 and $\vec{v}_2$ is perpendicular to the line OP_2. Hence the triangles in Figs. 4.31a and 4.31b are *similar.* The ratios of corresponding sides of similar triangles are equal, so

$$\frac{|\Delta\vec{v}|}{v_1} = \frac{\Delta s}{R} \quad \text{or} \quad |\Delta\vec{v}| = \frac{v_1}{R}\Delta s$$

The magnitude a_{av} of the average acceleration during Δt is therefore

$$a_{av} = \frac{|\Delta\vec{v}|}{\Delta t} = \frac{v_1}{R}\frac{\Delta s}{\Delta t}$$

The magnitude a of the *instantaneous* acceleration $\vec{a}$ at point P_1 is the limit of this expression as we take point P_2 closer and closer to point P_1:

$$a = \lim_{\Delta t \to 0} \frac{v_1}{R}\frac{\Delta s}{\Delta t} = \frac{v_1}{R} \lim_{\Delta t \to 0} \frac{\Delta s}{\Delta t}$$

If the time interval Δt is short, Δs is the distance the particle moves along its curved path. So the limit of $\Delta s/\Delta t$ is the speed v_1 at point P_1. Also, P_1 can be any point on the path, so we can drop the subscript and let v represent the speed at any point. Then

$$a_{rad} = \frac{v^2}{R} \quad \text{(uniform circular motion)} \tag{4.46}$$

We have added the subscript "rad" as a reminder that the direction of the instantaneous acceleration at each point is always along a radius of the circle (toward the center of the circle; see Figs. 4.30c and 4.31c). So we have found that *in uniform circular motion, the magnitude a_{rad} of the instantaneous acceleration is equal to the square of the speed v divided by the radius R of the circle. Its direction is perpendicular to $\vec{v}$ and inward along the radius.*

Because the acceleration in uniform circular motion is always directed toward the center of the circle, it is sometimes called **centripetal acceleration.** The word "centripetal" is derived from two Greek words meaning "seeking the center." Figure 4.32a shows the directions of the velocity and acceleration vectors at several points for a particle moving with uniform circular motion.

CAUTION **Uniform circular motion vs. projectile motion** The acceleration in uniform circular motion (Fig. 4.32a) has some similarities to the acceleration in projectile motion without air resistance (Fig. 4.32b), but there are also some important differences. In both kinds of motion the *magnitude* of acceleration is the same at all times. However, in uniform circular motion the *direction* of $\vec{a}$ changes continuously so that it always points toward the center of the circle. (At the top of the circle the acceleration points down; at the bottom of the circle the acceleration points up.) In projectile motion, by contrast, the direction of $\vec{a}$ remains the same at all times.

We can also express the magnitude of the acceleration in uniform circular motion in terms of the **period** T of the motion, the time for one revolution (one

4.32 Acceleration and velocity (a) for a particle in uniform circular motion and (b) for a projectile with no air resistance.

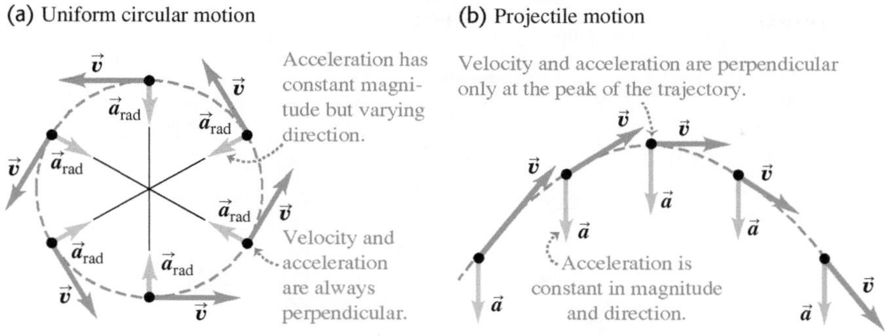
(a) Uniform circular motion
Acceleration has constant magnitude but varying direction.
Velocity and acceleration are always perpendicular.
(b) Projectile motion
Velocity and acceleration are perpendicular only at the peak of the trajectory.
Acceleration is constant in magnitude and direction.

complete trip around the circle). In a time T the particle travels a distance equal to the circumference $2\pi R$ of the circle, so its speed is

$$v = \frac{2\pi R}{T} \tag{4.47}$$

When we substitute this into Eq. (4.46), we obtain the alternative expression

$$a_{\text{rad}} = \frac{4\pi^2 R}{T^2} \quad \text{(uniform circular motion)} \tag{4.48}$$

Nonuniform Circular Motion

We have assumed throughout this section that the particle's speed is constant as it goes around the circle. If the speed varies, we call the motion **nonuniform circular motion.** In nonuniform circular motion, Eq. (4.46) still gives the *radial* component of acceleration $a_{\text{rad}} = v^2/R$, which is always *perpendicular* to the instantaneous velocity and directed toward the center of the circle. But since the speed v has different values at different points in the motion, the value of a_{rad} is not constant. The radial (centripetal) acceleration is greatest at the point in the circle where the speed is greatest.

In nonuniform circular motion there is also a component of acceleration that is *parallel* to the instantaneous velocity (see Figs. 4.30a and 4.30b). This is the component $a_{\parallel}$ that we discussed in Section 4.2; here we call this component a_{tan} to emphasize that it is *tangent* to the circle. The tangential component of acceleration a_{tan} is equal to the rate of change of *speed.* Thus

$$a_{\text{rad}} = \frac{v^2}{R} \quad \text{and} \quad a_{\text{tan}} = \frac{d|\vec{v}|}{dt} \quad \text{(nonuniform circular motion)} \tag{4.49}$$

The tangential component is in the same direction as the velocity if the particle is speeding up, and in the opposite direction if the particle is slowing down (Fig. 4.33). If the particle's speed is constant, $a_{\text{tan}} = 0$.

CAUTION **Uniform vs. nonuniform circular motion** Note that the two quantities

$$\frac{d|\vec{v}|}{dt} \quad \text{and} \quad \left|\frac{d\vec{v}}{dt}\right|$$

are *not* the same. The first, equal to the tangential acceleration, is the rate of change of speed; it is zero whenever a particle moves with constant speed, even when its direction of motion changes (such as in *uniform* circular motion). The second is the magnitude of the vector acceleration; it is zero only when the particle's acceleration *vector* is zero—that is, when the particle moves in a straight line with constant speed. In *uniform* circular motion $|d\vec{v}/dt| = a_{\text{rad}} = v^2/r$; in *nonuniform* circular motion there is also a tangential component of acceleration, so $|d\vec{v}/dt| = \sqrt{a_{\text{rad}}^2 + a_{\text{tan}}^2}$.

4.33 A particle moving in a vertical loop with a varying speed, like a roller coaster car.

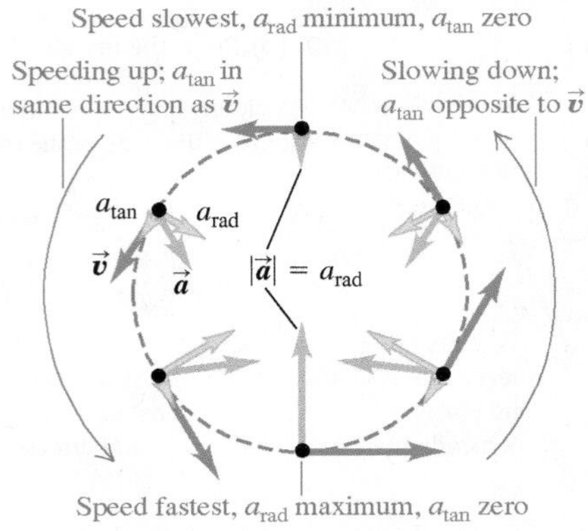

CHAPTER 4 SUMMARY

Position, velocity, and acceleration vectors: The position vector $\vec{r}$ of a point P in space is the vector from the origin to P. Its components are the coordinates x, y, and z.

The average velocity vector $\vec{v}_{av}$ during the time interval Δt is the displacement $\Delta\vec{r}$ (the change in the position vector $\vec{r}$) divided by Δt. The instantaneous velocity vector $\vec{v}$ is the time derivative of $\vec{r}$, and its components are the time derivatives of x, y, and z. The instantaneous speed is the magnitude of $\vec{v}$. The velocity $\vec{v}$ of a particle is always tangent to the particle's path.

The average acceleration vector $\vec{a}_{av}$ during the time interval Δt equals $\Delta\vec{v}$ (the change in the velocity vector $\vec{v}$) divided by Δt. The instantaneous acceleration vector $\vec{a}$ is the time derivative of $\vec{v}$, and its components are the time derivatives of v_x, v_y, and v_z.

The component of acceleration parallel to the direction of the instantaneous velocity affects the speed, while the component of $\vec{a}$ perpendicular to $\vec{v}$ affects the direction of motion.

$$\vec{r} = x\hat{\imath} + y\hat{\jmath} + z\hat{k} \quad (4.1)$$

$$\vec{v}_{av} = \frac{\vec{r}_2 - \vec{r}_1}{t_2 - t_1} = \frac{\Delta\vec{r}}{\Delta t} \quad (4.2)$$

$$\vec{v} = \lim_{\Delta t \to 0} \frac{\Delta\vec{r}}{\Delta t} = \frac{d\vec{r}}{dt} \quad (4.3)$$

$$v_x = \frac{dx}{dt} \quad v_y = \frac{dy}{dt} \quad v_z = \frac{dz}{dt} \quad (4.4)$$

$$\vec{a}_{av} = \frac{\vec{v}_2 - \vec{v}_1}{t_2 - t_1} = \frac{\Delta\vec{v}}{\Delta t} \quad (4.8)$$

$$\vec{a} = \lim_{\Delta t \to 0} \frac{\Delta\vec{v}}{\Delta t} = \frac{d\vec{v}}{dt} \quad (4.9)$$

$$a_x = \frac{dv_x}{dt} \quad a_y = \frac{dv_y}{dt} \quad a_z = \frac{dv_z}{dt} \quad (4.10)$$

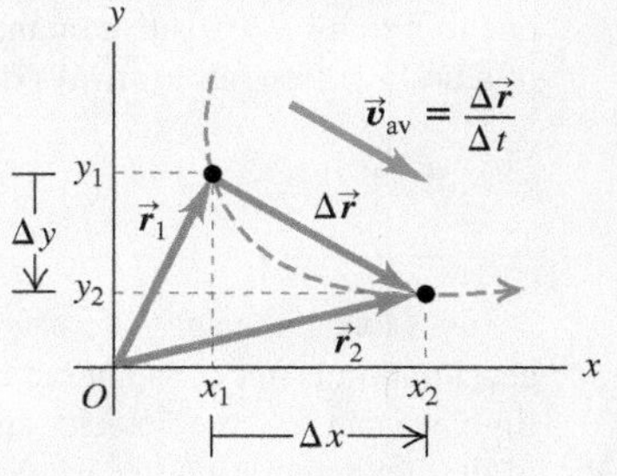

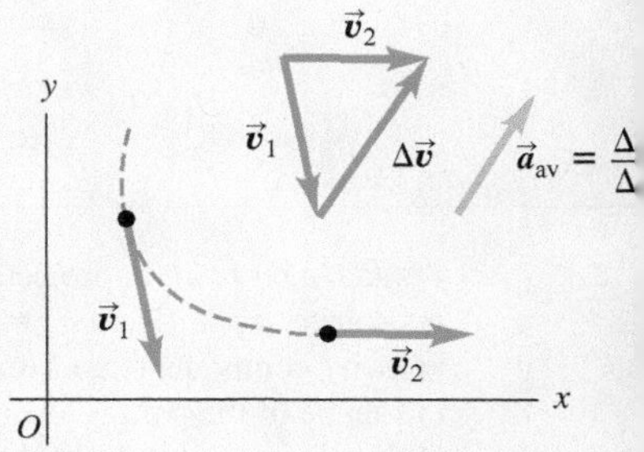

Straight-line motion, average and instantaneous x-velocity: When a particle moves along a straight line, we describe its position with respect to an origin O by means of a coordinate such as x. The particle's average x-velocity $v_{av\text{-}x}$ during a time interval $\Delta t = t_2 - t_1$ is equal to its displacement $\Delta x = x_2 - x_1$ divided by Δt. The instantaneous x-velocity v_x at any time t is equal to the average x-velocity for the time interval from t to $t + \Delta t$ in the limit that Δt goes to zero. Equivalently, v_x is the derivative of the position function with respect to time.

$$v_{av\text{-}x} = \frac{x_2 - x_1}{t_2 - t_1} = \frac{\Delta x}{\Delta t} \quad (4.15)$$

$$v_x = \lim_{\Delta t \to 0} \frac{\Delta x}{\Delta t} = \frac{dx}{dt} \quad (4.16)$$

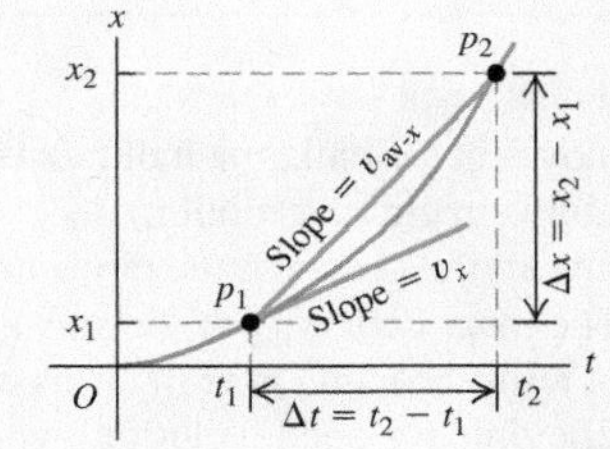

Average and instantaneous x-acceleration: The average x-acceleration $a_{av\text{-}x}$ during a time interval Δt is equal to the change in velocity $\Delta v_x = v_{2x} - v_{1x}$ during that time interval divided by Δt. The instantaneous x-acceleration a_x is the limit of $a_{av\text{-}x}$ as Δt goes to zero, or the derivative of v_x with respect to t.

$$a_{av\text{-}x} = \frac{v_{2x} - v_{1x}}{t_2 - t_1} = \frac{\Delta v_x}{\Delta t} \quad (4.17)$$

$$a_x = \lim_{\Delta t \to 0} \frac{\Delta v_x}{\Delta t} = \frac{dv_x}{dt} \quad (4.18)$$

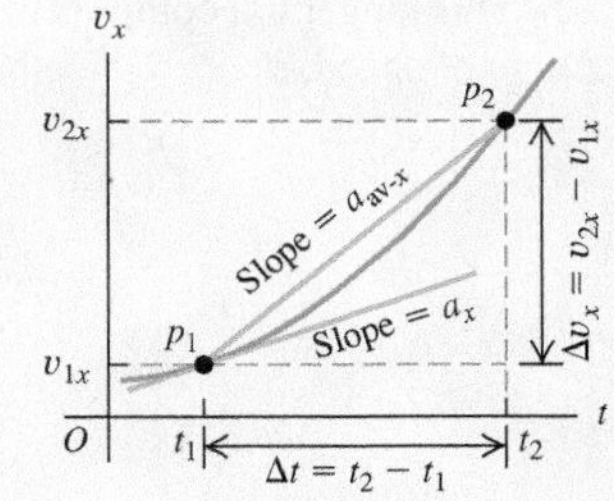

Straight-line motion with constant acceleration: When the x-acceleration is constant, four equations relate the position x and the x-velocity v_x at any time t to the initial position x_0, the initial x-velocity v_{0x} (both measured at time $t = 0$), and the x-acceleration a_x.

Constant x-acceleration only:

$$v_x = v_{0x} + a_x t \quad (4.21)$$

$$x = x_0 + v_{0x}t + \tfrac{1}{2}a_x t^2 \quad (4.25)$$

$$v_x^2 = v_{0x}^2 + 2a_x(x - x_0) \quad (4.26)$$

$$x - x_0 = \left(\frac{v_{0x} + v_x}{2}\right)t \quad (4.27)$$

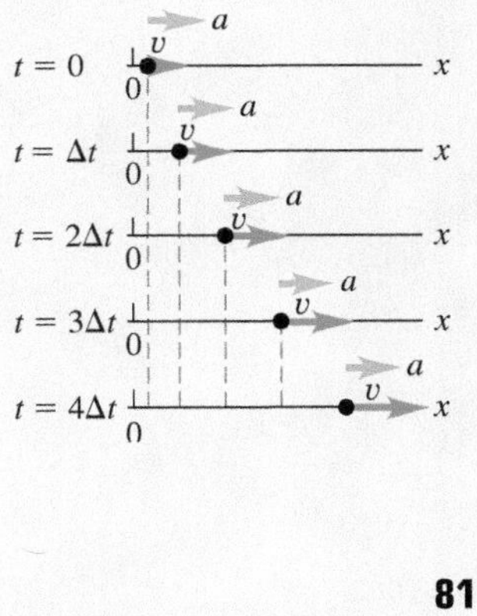

Freely falling bodies: Free fall is a case of motion with constant acceleration. The magnitude of the acceleration due to gravity is a positive quantity, g. The acceleration of a body in free fall is always downward.

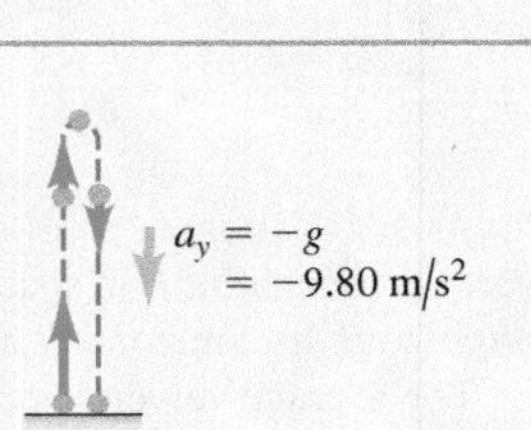

Straight-line motion with varying acceleration: When the acceleration is not constant but is a known function of time, we can find the velocity and position as functions of time by integrating the acceleration function.

$$v_x = v_{0x} + \int_0^t a_x\,dt \tag{4.30}$$

$$x = x_0 + \int_0^t v_x\,dt \tag{4.31}$$

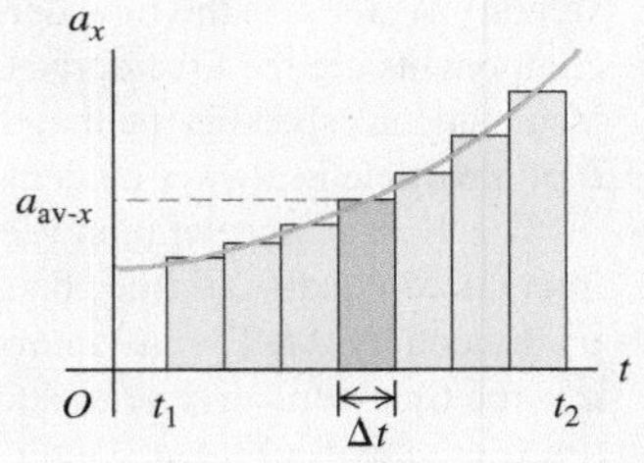

Projectile motion: In projectile motion with no air resistance, $a_x = 0$ and $a_y = -g$. The coordinates and velocity components are simple functions of time, and the shape of the path is always a parabola. We usually choose the origin to be at the initial position of the projectile.

$$x = (v_0 \cos \alpha_0)t \tag{4.38}$$

$$y = (v_0 \sin \alpha_0)t - \tfrac{1}{2}gt^2 \tag{4.39}$$

$$v_x = v_0 \cos \alpha_0 \tag{4.40}$$

$$v_y = v_0 \sin \alpha_0 - gt \tag{4.41}$$

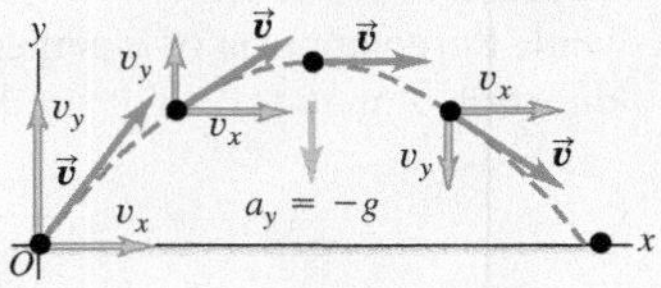

Uniform and nonuniform circular motion: When a particle moves in a circular path of radius R with constant speed v (uniform circular motion), its acceleration $\vec{a}$ is directed toward the center of the circle and perpendicular to $\vec{v}$. The magnitude a_{rad} of the acceleration can be expressed in terms of v and R or in terms of R and the period T (the time for one revolution), where $v = 2\pi R/T$.

If the speed is not constant in circular motion (nonuniform circular motion), there is still a radial component of $\vec{a}$ given by Eq. (4.46) or (4.48), but there is also a component of $\vec{a}$ parallel (tangential) to the path. This tangential component is equal to the rate of change of speed, dv/dt.

$$a_{\text{rad}} = \frac{v^2}{R} \tag{4.46}$$

$$a_{\text{rad}} = \frac{4\pi^2 R}{T^2} \tag{4.48}$$

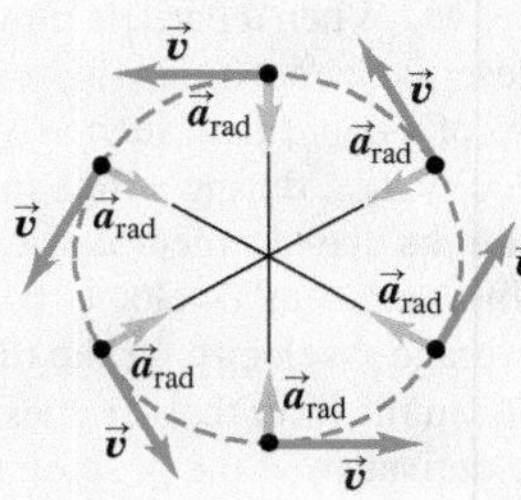

Problems

•, ••, •••: Problems of increasing difficulty. **CP**: Cumulative problems incorporating material from earlier chapters. **CALC**: Problems requiring calculus. **BIO**: Biosciences problems.

4.1 •• **CALC** A web page designer creates an animation in which a dot on a computer screen has a position of $\vec{r} = [4.0\text{ cm} + (2.5\text{ cm/s}^2)t^2]\hat{\imath} + (5.0\text{ cm/s})t\hat{\jmath}$. (a) Find the magnitude and direction of the dot's average velocity between $t = 0$ and $t = 2.0$ s. (b) Find the magnitude and direction of the instantaneous velocity at $t = 0$, $t = 1.0$ s, and $t = 2.0$ s. (c) Sketch the dot's trajectory from $t = 0$ to $t = 2.0$ s, and show the velocities calculated in part (b).

Figure **P4.2**

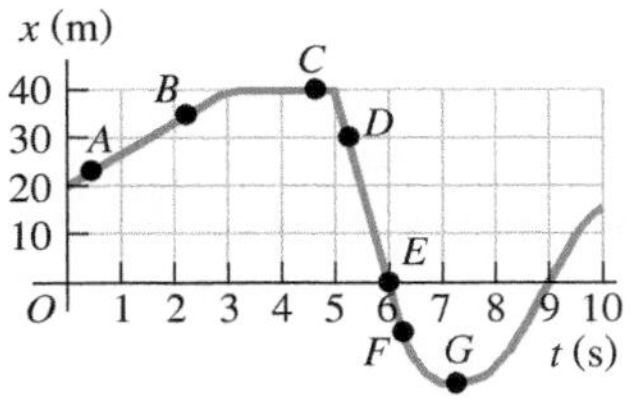

4.2 •• A test car travels in a straight line along the x-axis. The graph in Fig. P4.2 shows the car's position x as a function of time. Find its instantaneous velocity at points A through G.

4.3 •• **Launch of the Space Shuttle.** At launch the space shuttle weighs 4.5 million pounds. When it is launched from rest, it takes 8.00 s to reach 161 km/h, and at the end of the first 1.00 min its speed is 1610 km/h. (a) What is the average acceleration (in m/s^2) of the shuttle (i) during the first 8.00 s, and (ii) between 8.00 s and the end of the first 1.00 min? (b) Assuming the acceleration is constant during each time interval (but not necessarily the same in both intervals), what distance does the shuttle travel (i) during the first 8.00 s, and (ii) during the interval from 8.00 s to 1.00 min?

4.4 •• You throw a glob of putty straight up toward the ceiling, which is 3.60 m above the point where the putty leaves your hand. The initial speed of the putty as it leaves your hand is 9.50 m/s. (a) What is the speed of the putty just before it strikes the ceiling? (b) How much time from when it leaves your hand does it take the putty to reach the ceiling?

4.5 •• **CALC** The position of a particle between $t = 0$ and $t = 2.00$ s is given by $x(t) = (3.00\text{ m/s}^3)t^3 - (10.0\text{ m/s}^2)t^2 + (9.00\text{ m/s})t$. (a) Draw the x-t, v_x-t, and a_x-t graphs of this particle. (b) At what time(s) between $t = 0$ and $t = 2.00$ s is the particle instantaneously at rest? Does your numerical result agree with the v_x-t graph in part (a)? (c) At each time calculated in part (b), is the acceleration of the particle positive or negative? Show that in each case the same answer is deduced from $a_x(t)$ and from the v_x-t graph. (d) At what time(s) between $t = 0$ and $t = 2.00$ s is the velocity of the particle instantaneously not changing? Locate this point on the v_x-t and a_x-t graphs of part (a). (e) What is the particle's greatest distance from the origin ($x = 0$) between $t = 0$ and $t = 2.00$ s? (f) At what time(s) between $t = 0$ and $t = 2.00$ s is the particle *speeding up* at the greatest rate? At what time(s) between $t = 0$ and $t = 2.00$ s is the particle *slowing down* at the greatest rate? Locate these points on the v_x-t and a_x-t graphs of part (a).

4.6 • An automobile and a truck start from rest at the same instant, with the automobile initially at some distance behind the truck. The truck has a constant acceleration of 2.10 m/s^2, and the automobile an acceleration of 3.40 m/s^2. The automobile overtakes the truck after the truck has moved 40.0 m. (a) How much time does it take the automobile to overtake the truck? (b) How far was the automobile behind the truck initially? (c) What is the speed of each when they are abreast? (d) On a single graph, sketch the position of each vehicle as a function of time. Take $x = 0$ at the initial location of the truck.

4.7 • A major leaguer hits a baseball so that it leaves the bat at a speed of 30.0 m/s and at an angle of 36.9° above the horizontal. You can ignore air resistance. (a) At what *two* times is the baseball at a height of 10.0 m above the point at which it left the bat? (b) Calculate the horizontal and vertical components of the baseball's velocity at each of the two times calculated in part (a). (c) What are the magnitude and direction of the baseball's velocity when it returns to the level at which it left the bat?

4.8 • A Ferris wheel with radius 14.0 m is turning about a horizontal axis through its center (Fig. P4.8). The linear speed of a passenger on the rim is constant and equal to 7.00 m/s. What are the magnitude and direction of the passenger's acceleration as she passes through (a) the lowest point in her circular motion? (b) The highest point in her circular motion? (c) How much time does it take the Ferris wheel to make one revolution?

4.9 ••• **BIO** **Spiraling Up.** It is common to see birds of prey rising upward on thermals. The paths they take may be spiral-like. You can model the spiral motion as uniform circular motion combined with a constant upward velocity. Assume a bird completes a circle of radius 6.00 m every 5.00 s and rises vertically at a constant rate of 3.00 m/s. Determine: (a) the speed of the bird relative to the ground; (b) the bird's acceleration (magnitude and direction); and (c) the angle between the bird's velocity vector and the horizontal.

Figure **P4.8**

4.10 ••• **Look Out!** A snowball rolls off a barn roof that slopes downward at an angle of 40° (Fig. P4.10). The edge of the roof is 14.0 m above the ground, and the snowball has a speed of 7.00 m/s as it rolls off the roof. Ignore air resistance. (a) How far from the edge of the barn does the snowball strike the ground if it doesn't strike anything else while falling? (b) Draw x-t, y-t, v_x-t, and v_y-t graphs for the motion in part (a). (c) A man 1.9 m tall is standing 4.0 m from the edge of the barn. Will he be hit by the snowball?

Figure P4.10

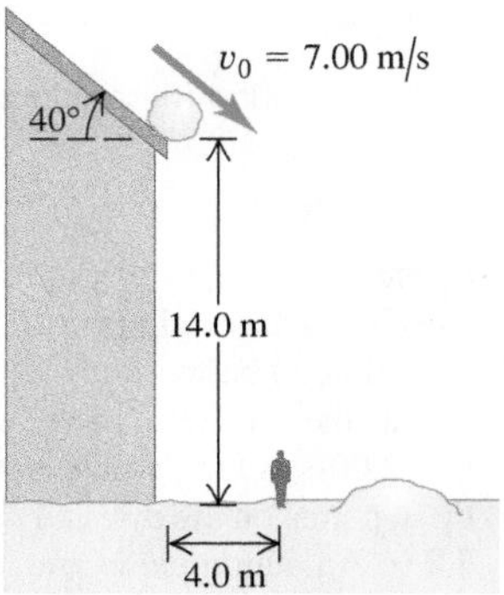
$v_0 = 7.00$ m/s
40°
14.0 m
4.0 m

Answers

Chapter Opening Question ?

A cyclist going around a curve at constant speed has an acceleration directed toward the inside of the curve (see Section 4.2, especially Fig. 4.9a).

NEWTON'S SECOND LAW OF MOTION

5

? This pit crew member is pushing a race car forward. Is the race car pushing back on him? If so, does it push back with the same magnitude of force or a different amount?

LEARNING GOALS

By studying this chapter, you will learn:

- What the concept of force means in physics, and why forces are vectors.
- The significance of the net force on an object, and what happens when the net force is zero.
- The relationship among the net force on an object, the object's mass, and its acceleration.
- How the forces that two bodies exert on each other are related.

In Chapter 1 we discussed how we could use vectors to describe quantities, like positions and forces, where both the direction and magnitude are important. In Chapters 2 and 3 we learned how objects in equilibrium were subject to no net force and no net torque. In chapter 4 we discussed the (vector) concepts of velocity and acceleration. We are now in position to discuss how objects respond to non-zero net forces, and to understand why objects accelerate. We will learn what causes bodies to move the way that they do: for example, why is it harder to control a car on wet ice than on dry concrete?

In this chapter, we will start to study the subject of dynamics: the relationship of motion and the forces that cause it. We will learn to apply Newton's second law, which relates force to acceleration when the net force is non-zero. Using Newton's laws, we can understand and analyze most familiar kinds of motion – Newton's laws need modification only for situations involving extremely high speeds (near the speed of light) or very small sizes (where quantum effects become important).

5.1 Newton's Second Law

Newton's first law tells us that when a body is acted on by zero net force, it moves with constant velocity and zero acceleration. In Fig. 5.1a, a hockey puck is sliding to the right on wet ice. There is negligible friction, so there are no horizontal forces acting on the puck; the downward force of gravity and the upward normal force exerted by the ice surface sum to zero. So the net force

$\sum\vec{F}$ acting on the puck is zero, the puck has zero acceleration, and its velocity is constant.

But what happens when the net force is *not* zero? In Fig. 5.1b we apply a constant horizontal force to a sliding puck in the same direction that the puck is moving. Then $\sum\vec{F}$ is constant and in the same horizontal direction as $\vec{v}$. We find that during the time the force is acting, the velocity of the puck changes at a constant rate; that is, the puck moves with constant acceleration. The speed of the puck increases, so the acceleration $\vec{a}$ is in the same direction as $\vec{v}$ and $\sum\vec{F}$.

In Fig. 5.1c we reverse the direction of the force on the puck so that $\sum\vec{F}$ acts opposite to $\vec{v}$. In this case as well, the puck has an acceleration; the puck moves more and more slowly to the right. The acceleration $\vec{a}$ in this case is to the left, in the same direction as $\sum\vec{F}$. As in the previous case, experiment shows that the acceleration is constant if $\sum\vec{F}$ is constant.

We conclude that *a net force acting on a body causes the body to accelerate in the same direction as the net force.* If the magnitude of the net force is constant, as in Figs. 5.1b and 5.1c, then so is the magnitude of the acceleration.

These conclusions about net force and acceleration also apply to a body moving along a curved path. For example, Fig. 5.2 shows a hockey puck moving in a horizontal circle on an ice surface of negligible friction. A rope is attached to the puck and to a stick in the ice, and this rope exerts an inward tension force of constant magnitude on the puck. The net force and acceleration are both constant in magnitude and directed toward the center of the circle. The speed of the puck is constant, so this is uniform circular motion.

Figure 5.3a shows another experiment to explore the relationship between acceleration and net force. We apply a constant horizontal force to a puck on a

5.1 Exploring the relationship between the acceleration of a body and the net force acting on the body (in this case, a hockey puck on a frictionless surface).

(a) A puck moving with constant velocity (in equilibrium): $\sum\vec{F} = 0$, $\vec{a} = 0$

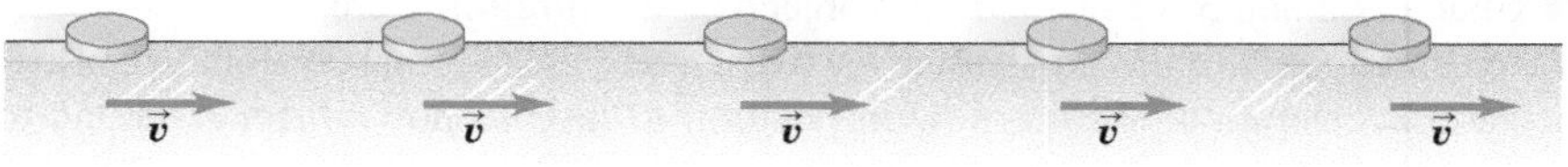

(b) A constant net force in the direction of motion causes a constant acceleration in the same direction as the net force.

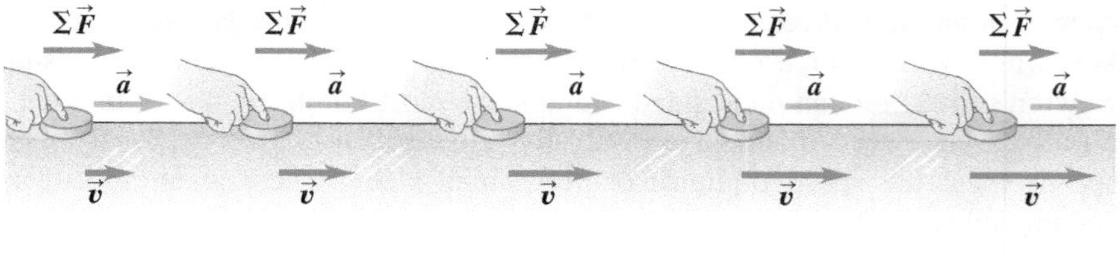

(c) A constant net force opposite the direction of motion causes a constant acceleration in the same direction as the net force.

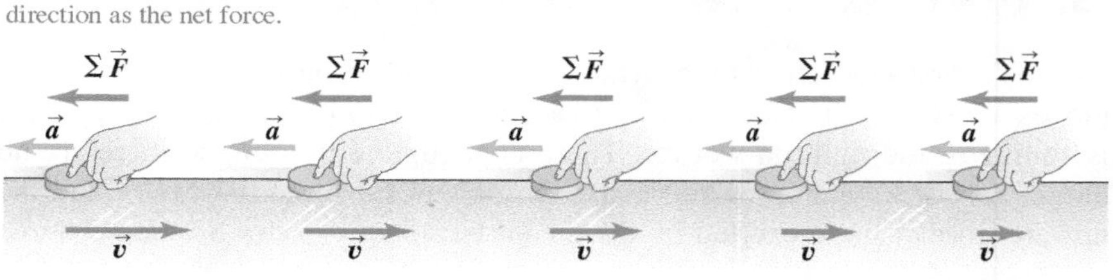

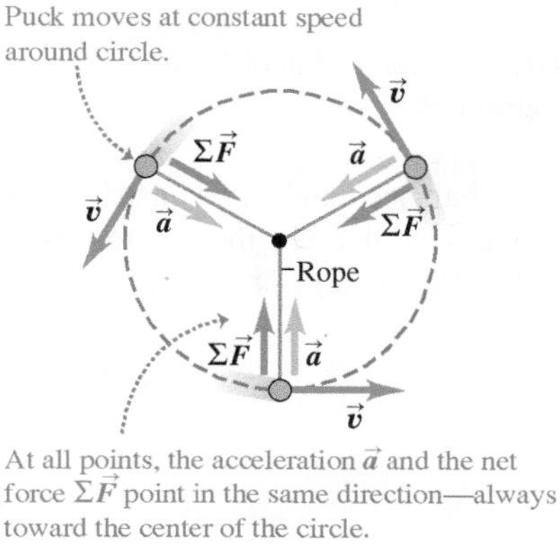

Puck moves at constant speed around circle.
$\vec{v}$
$\Sigma\vec{F}$
$\vec{a}$
Rope
At all points, the acceleration $\vec{a}$ and the net force $\Sigma\vec{F}$ point in the same direction—always toward the center of the circle.

5.2 A top view of a hockey puck in uniform circular motion on a frictionless horizontal surface.

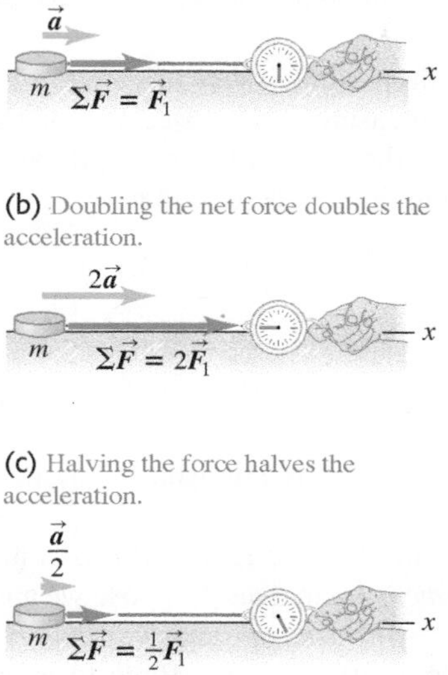

$\vec{a}$
m
$\Sigma\vec{F} = \vec{F}_1$
x
$2\vec{a}$
$\Sigma\vec{F} = 2\vec{F}_1$
$\frac{\vec{a}}{2}$
$\Sigma\vec{F} = \frac{1}{2}\vec{F}_1$

5.3 For a body of a given mass m, the magnitude of the body's acceleration is directly proportional to the magnitude of the net force acting on the body.

(a) A constant net force $\Sigma\vec{F}$ causes a constant acceleration $\vec{a}$.

(b) Doubling the net force doubles the acceleration.

(c) Halving the force halves the acceleration.

frictionless horizontal surface, using the spring balance with the spring stretched a constant amount. As in Figs. 5.1b and 5.1c, this horizontal force equals the net force on the puck. If we change the magnitude of the net force, the acceleration changes in the same proportion. Doubling the net force doubles the acceleration (Fig. 5.3b), halving the net force halves the acceleration (Fig. 5.3c), and so on. Many such experiments show that *for any given body, the magnitude of the acceleration is directly proportional to the magnitude of the net force acting on the body.*

Mass and Force

Our results mean that for a given body, the *ratio* of the magnitude $|\Sigma\vec{F}|$ of the net force to the magnitude $a = |\vec{a}|$ of the acceleration is constant, regardless of the magnitude of the net force. We call this ratio the *inertial mass,* or simply the **mass,** of the body and denote it by m. That is,

$$m = \frac{|\sum\vec{F}|}{a} \quad \text{or} \quad |\sum\vec{F}| = ma \quad \text{or} \quad a = \frac{|\sum\vec{F}|}{m} \qquad (5.1)$$

Mass is a quantitative measure of inertia. The last of the equations in Eqs. (5.1) says that the greater its mass, the more a body "resists" being accelerated. When you hold a piece of fruit in your hand at the supermarket and move it slightly up and down to estimate its heft, you're applying a force and seeing how much the fruit accelerates up and down in response. If a force causes a large acceleration, the fruit has a small mass; if the same force causes only a small acceleration, the fruit has a large mass. In the same way, if you hit a table-tennis ball and then a basketball with the same force, the basketball has much smaller acceleration because it has much greater mass.

The SI unit of mass is the **kilogram.** Tthe kilogram is officially defined to be the mass of a cylinder of platinum–iridium alloy kept in a vault near Paris. We can use this standard kilogram, along with Eqs. (5.1), to define the **newton:**

One newton is the amount of net force that gives an acceleration of 1 meter per second squared to a body with a mass of 1 kilogram.

This definition allows us to calibrate the spring balances and other instruments used to measure forces. Because of the way we have defined the newton, it is related to the units of mass, length, and time. For Eqs. (5.1) to be dimensionally consistent, it must be true that

$$1 \text{ newton} = (1 \text{ kilogram})(1 \text{ meter per second squared})$$

or

$$1 \text{ N} = 1 \text{ kg} \cdot \text{m/s}^2$$

We will use this relationship many times in the next few chapters, so keep it in mind.

We can also use Eqs. (5.1) to compare a mass with the standard mass and thus to *measure* masses. Suppose we apply a constant net force $\sum \vec{F}$ to a body having a known mass m_1 and we find an acceleration of magnitude a_1 (Fig. 5.4a). We then apply the same force to another body having an unknown mass m_2, and we find an acceleration of magnitude a_2 (Fig. 5.4b). Then, according to Eqs. (5.1),

$$m_1 a_1 = m_2 a_2$$

$$\frac{m_2}{m_1} = \frac{a_1}{a_2} \quad \text{(same net force)} \tag{5.2}$$

For the same net force, the ratio of the masses of two bodies is the inverse of the ratio of their accelerations. In principle we could use Eq. (5.2) to measure an unknown mass m_2, but it is usually easier to determine mass indirectly by measuring the body's *weight.*

When two bodies with masses m_1 and m_2 are fastened together, we find that the mass of the composite body is always $m_1 + m_2$ (Fig. 5.4c). This additive property of mass may seem obvious, but it has to be verified experimentally. Ultimately, the mass of a body is related to the number of protons, electrons, and neutrons it contains. This wouldn't be a good way to *define*

5.4 For a given net force $\sum \vec{F}$ acting on a body, the acceleration is inversely proportional to the mass of the body. Masses add like ordinary scalars.

(a) A known force $\sum \vec{F}$ causes an object with mass m_1 to have an acceleration $\vec{a}_1$.

(b) Applying the same force $\sum \vec{F}$ to a second object and noting the acceleration allow us to measure the mass.

(c) When the two objects are fastened together, the same method shows that their composite mass is the sum of their individual masses.

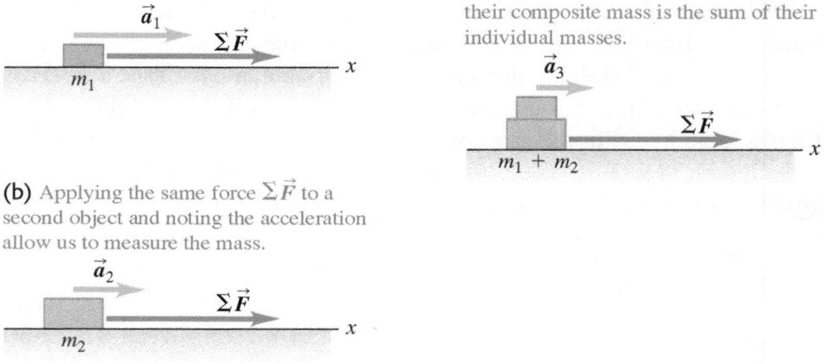

mass because there is no practical way to count these particles. But the concept of mass is the most fundamental way to characterize the quantity of matter in a body.

Stating Newton's Second Law

We've been careful to state that the *net* force on a body is what causes that body to accelerate. Experiment shows that if a combination of forces $\vec{F}_1$, $\vec{F}_2$, $\vec{F}_3$, and so on is applied to a body, the body will have the same acceleration (magnitude and direction) as when only a single force is applied, if that single force is equal to the vector sum $\vec{F}_1 + \vec{F}_2 + \vec{F}_3 + \cdots$. In other words, the principle of superposition of forces also holds true when the net force is not zero and the body is accelerating.

Equations (5.1) relate the magnitude of the net force on a body to the magnitude of the acceleration that it produces. We have also seen that the direction of the net force is the same as the direction of the acceleration, whether the body's path is straight or curved. Newton wrapped up all these relationships and experimental results in a single concise statement that we now call *Newton's second law of motion:*

Newton's second law of motion: If a net external force acts on a body, the body accelerates. The direction of acceleration is the same as the direction of the net force. The mass of the body times the acceleration of the body equals the net force vector.

In symbols,

$$\sum \vec{F} = m\vec{a} \qquad \text{(Newton's second law of motion)} \qquad (5.3)$$

An alternative statement is that the acceleration of a body is in the same direction as the net force acting on the body, and is equal to the net force divided by the body's mass:

$$\vec{a} = \frac{\sum \vec{F}}{m}$$

Newton's second law is a fundamental law of nature, the basic relationship between force and motion.

Equation (5.3) has many practical applications. You've actually been using it all your life to measure your body's acceleration. In your inner ear, microscopic hair cells sense the magnitude and direction of the force that they must exert to cause small membranes to accelerate along with the rest of your body. By Newton's second law, the acceleration of the membranes—and hence that of your body as a whole—is proportional to this force and has the same direction. In this way, you can sense the magnitude and direction of your acceleration even with your eyes closed!

Using Newton's Second Law

There are at least four aspects of Newton's second law that deserve special attention. First, Eq. (5.3) is a *vector* equation. Usually we will use it in component form, with a separate equation for each component of force and the corresponding component of acceleration:

$$\sum F_x = ma_x \qquad \sum F_y = ma_y \qquad \sum F_z = ma_z \qquad \text{(Newton's second law of motion)} \qquad (5.4)$$

This set of component equations is equivalent to the single vector equation (5.3). Each component of the net force equals the mass times the corresponding component of acceleration.

Second, the statement of Newton's second law refers to *external* forces. By this we mean forces exerted on the body by other bodies in its environment. It's impossible for a body to affect its own motion by exerting a force on itself; if it were possible, you could lift yourself to the ceiling by pulling up on your belt! That's why only external forces are included in the sum $\sum\vec{F}$ in Eqs. (5.3) and (5.4).

Third, Eqs. (5.3) and (5.4) are valid only when the mass m is *constant*. It's easy to think of systems whose masses change, such as a leaking tank truck, a rocket ship, or a moving railroad car being loaded with coal. But such systems are better handled by using the concept of momentum.

Finally, Newton's second law is valid only in inertial frames of reference, just like the first law. Thus it is not valid in the reference frame of any of the accelerating vehicles; relative to any of these frames, the passenger accelerates even though the net force on the passenger is zero. We will usually assume that the earth is an adequate approximation to an inertial frame, although because of its rotation and orbital motion it is not precisely inertial.

CAUTION **$m\vec{a}$ is not a force** You must keep in mind that even though the vector $m\vec{a}$ is equal to the vector sum $\sum\vec{F}$ of all the forces acting on the body, the vector $m\vec{a}$ is *not* a force. Acceleration is a *result* of a nonzero net force; it is not a force itself. It's "common sense" to think that there is a "force of acceleration" that pushes you back into your seat when your car accelerates forward from rest. But *there is no such force;* instead, your inertia causes you to tend to stay at rest relative to the earth, and the car accelerates around you. The "common sense" confusion arises from trying to apply Newton's second law where it isn't valid, in the noninertial reference frame of an accelerating car. We will always examine motion relative to *inertial* frames of reference only.

In learning how to use Newton's second law, we will begin in this chapter with examples of straight-line motion. Then we will consider more general cases and develop more detailed problem-solving strategies.

Some Notes on Units

A few words about units are in order. In the cgs metric system (not used in this book), the unit of mass is the gram, equal to 10^{-3} kg, and the unit of distance is the centimeter, equal to 10^{-2} m. The cgs unit of force is called the *dyne:*

$$1\text{ dyne} = 1\text{ g}\cdot\text{cm/s}^2 = 10^{-5}\text{ N}$$

In the British system, the unit of force is the *pound* (or pound-force) and the unit of mass is the *slug*. The unit of acceleration is 1 foot per second squared, so

$$1\text{ pound} = 1\text{ slug}\cdot\text{ft/s}^2$$

The official definition of the pound is

$$1\text{ pound} = 4.448221615260\text{ newtons}$$

It is handy to remember that a pound is about 4.4 N and a newton is about 0.22 pound. Another useful fact: A body with a mass of 1 kg has a weight of about 2.2 lb at the earth's surface.

Table 5.1 lists the units of force, mass, and acceleration in the three systems.

Table 5.1 Units of Force, Mass, and Acceleration

System of Units	Force	Mass	Acceleration
SI	newton (N)	kilogram (kg)	m/s^2
cgs	dyne (dyn)	gram (g)	cm/s^2
British	pound (lb)	slug	ft/s^2

5.2 Using Newton's Second Law: Dynamics of Particles

We are now ready to discuss *dynamics* problems. In these problems, we apply Newton's second law to bodies on which the net force is *not* zero. These bodies are *not* in equilibrium and hence are accelerating. The net force on the body is equal to the mass of the body times its acceleration:

$$\sum \vec{F} = m\vec{a} \qquad \text{(Newton's second law, vector form)} \tag{5.5}$$

We most often use this relationship in component form:

$$\sum F_x = ma_x \qquad \sum F_y = ma_y \qquad \text{(Newton's second law, component form)} \tag{5.6}$$

CAUTION **$m\vec{a}$ doesn't belong in free-body diagrams** Remember that the quantity $m\vec{a}$ is the *result* of forces acting on a body, *not* a force itself; it's not a push or a pull exerted by anything in the body's environment. When you draw the free-body diagram for an accelerating body (like the fruit in Fig. 5.5a), make sure you *never* include the "$m\vec{a}$ force" because *there is no such force* (Fig. 5.5c). You should review Section 5.1 if you're not clear on this point. Sometimes we draw the acceleration vector $\vec{a}$ *alongside* a free-body diagram, as in Fig. 5.5b. But we *never* draw the acceleration vector with its tail touching the body (a position reserved exclusively for the forces that act on the body).

Apparent Weight and Apparent Weightlessness

When a passenger with mass m rides in an elevator with y-acceleration a_y, a scale shows the passenger's apparent weight to be

$$n = m(g + a_y)$$

When the elevator is accelerating upward, a_y is positive and n is greater than the passenger's weight $w = mg$. When the elevator is accelerating downward, a_y is negative and n is less than the weight. If the passenger doesn't know the elevator is accelerating, she may feel as though her weight is changing; indeed, this is just what the scale shows.

5.5 Correct and incorrect free-body diagrams for a falling body.

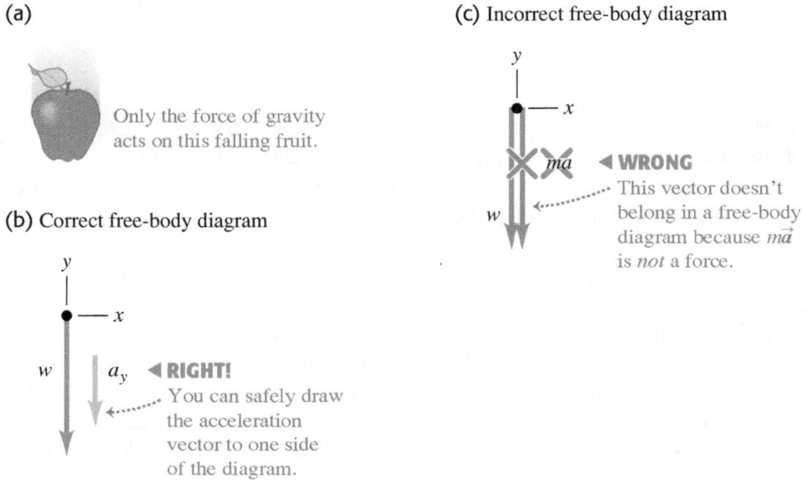
(a)
Only the force of gravity acts on this falling fruit.
(b) Correct free-body diagram
y
x
w
a_y
RIGHT!
You can safely draw the acceleration vector to one side of the diagram.
(c) Incorrect free-body diagram
y
x
$m\vec{a}$
w
WRONG
This vector doesn't belong in a free-body diagram because $m\vec{a}$ is *not* a force.

The extreme case occurs when the elevator has a downward acceleration $a_y = -g$—that is, when it is in free fall. In that case $n = 0$ and the passenger *seems* to be weightless. Similarly, an astronaut orbiting the earth with a spacecraft experiences *apparent weightlessness*. In each case, the person is not truly weightless because a gravitational force still acts. But the person's sensations in this free-fall condition are exactly the same as though the person were in outer space with no gravitational force at all. In both cases the person and the vehicle (elevator or spacecraft) fall together with the same acceleration g, so nothing pushes the person against the floor or walls of the vehicle.

5.3 Dynamics of Circular Motion

We talked about uniform circular motion. We showed that when a particle moves in a circular path with constant speed, the particle's acceleration is always directed toward the center of the circle (perpendicular to the instantaneous velocity). The magnitude a_{rad} of the acceleration is constant and is given in terms of the speed v and the radius R of the circle by

5.6 Net force, acceleration, and velocity in uniform circular motion.

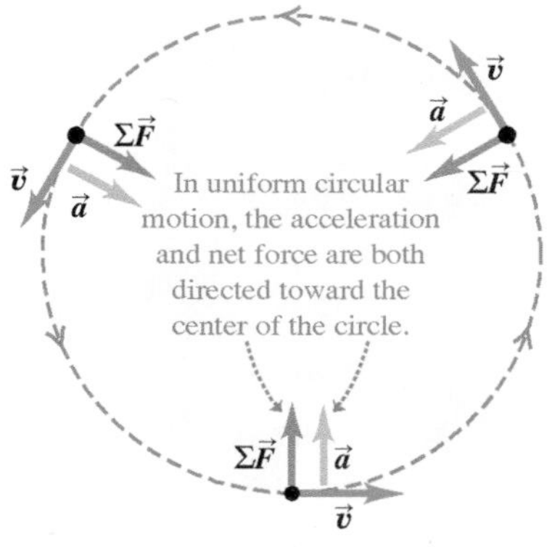
In uniform circular motion, the acceleration and net force are both directed toward the center of the circle.

$$a_{rad} = \frac{v^2}{R} \quad \text{(uniform circular motion)} \qquad (5.7)$$

The subscript "rad" is a reminder that at each point the acceleration is radially inward toward the center of the circle, perpendicular to the instantaneous velocity. We explained why this acceleration is often called *centripetal acceleration.*

We can also express the centripetal acceleration a_{rad} in terms of the *period* T, the time for one revolution:

$$T = \frac{2\pi R}{v} \qquad (5.8)$$

In terms of the period, a_{rad} is

$$a_{rad} = \frac{4\pi^2 R}{T^2} \quad \text{(uniform circular motion)} \qquad (5.9)$$

Uniform circular motion, like all other motion of a particle, is governed by Newton's second law. To make the particle accelerate toward the center of the circle, the net force $\sum\vec{F}$ on the particle must always be directed toward the center (Fig. 5.6). The magnitude of the acceleration is constant, so the magnitude F_{net} of the net force must also be constant. If the inward net force stops acting, the particle flies off in a straight line tangent to the circle (Fig. 5.7).

The magnitude of the radial acceleration is given by $a_{rad} = v^2/R$, so the magnitude F_{net} of the net force on a particle with mass m in uniform circular motion must be

$$F_{net} = ma_{rad} = m\frac{v^2}{R} \quad \text{(uniform circular motion)} \qquad (5.10)$$

5.7 What happens if the inward radial force suddenly ceases to act on a body in circular motion?

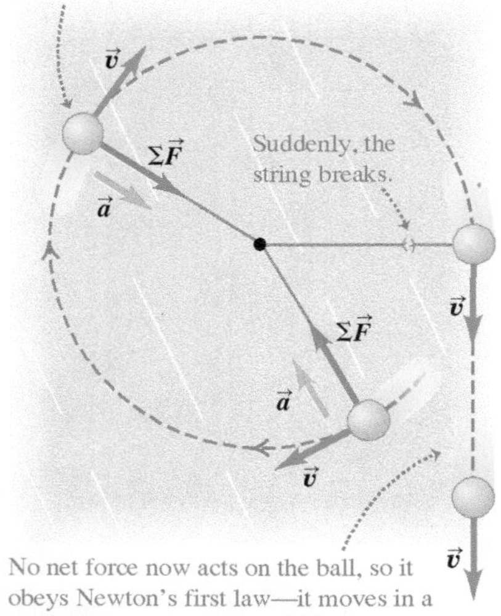
A ball attached to a string whirls in a circle on a frictionless surface.
Suddenly, the string breaks.
No net force now acts on the ball, so it obeys Newton's first law—it moves in a straight line at constant velocity.

Uniform circular motion can result from *any* combination of forces, just so the net force $\sum\vec{F}$ is always directed toward the center of the circle and has a constant magnitude. Note that the body need not move around a complete circle: Equation (5.10) is valid for *any* path that can be regarded as part of a circular arc.

CAUTION **Avoid using "centrifugal force"** Figure 5.8 shows both a correct free-body diagram for uniform circular motion (Fig. 5.8a) and a common *incorrect* diagram (Fig. 5.8b). Figure 5.8b is incorrect because it includes an extra outward force of magnitude $m(v^2/R)$ to "keep the body out there" or to "keep it in equilibrium." There are three reasons not to include such an outward force, usually called *centrifugal force* ("centrifugal" means "fleeing from the center"). First, the body does *not* "stay out there": It is in constant motion around its circular path. Because its velocity is constantly changing in direction,

5.8 (a) Correct and (b) incorrect free-body diagrams for a body in uniform circular motion.

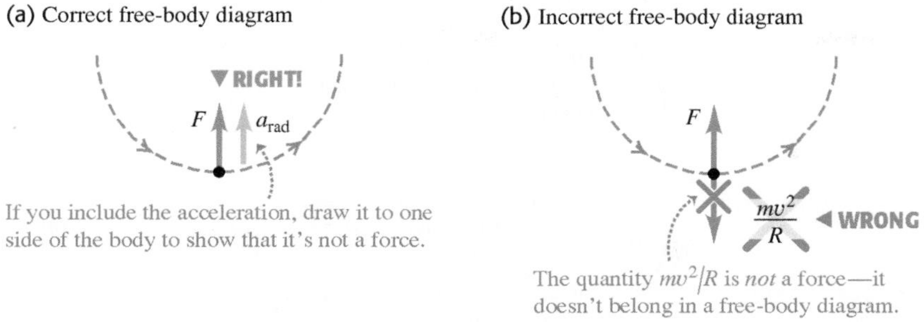

the body accelerates and is *not* in equilibrium. Second, if there *were* an additional outward force that balanced the inward force, the net force would be zero and the body would move in a straight line, not a circle (Fig. 5.7). And third, the quantity $m(v^2/R)$ is *not* a force; it corresponds to the $m\vec{a}$ side of $\sum\vec{F} = m\vec{a}$ and does not appear in $\sum\vec{F}$ (Fig. 5.8a). It's true that when you ride in a car that goes around a circular path, you tend to slide to the outside of the turn as though there was a "centrifugal force." But we saw that what really happens is that you tend to keep moving in a straight line, and the outer side of the car "runs into" you as the car turns. *In an inertial frame of reference there is no such thing as "centrifugal force."* We won't mention this term again, and we strongly advise you to avoid using it as well.

Banked Curves and the Flight of Airplanes

When an airplane is flying in a straight line at a constant speed and at a steady altitude, the airplane's weight is exactly balanced by the lift force $\vec{L}$ exerted by the air. (The upward lift force that the air exerts on the wings is a reaction to the downward push the wings exert on the air as they move through it.) To make the airplane turn, the pilot banks the airplane to one side so that the lift force has a horizontal component. (The pilot also changes the angle at which the wings "bite" into the air so that the vertical component of lift continues to balance the weight.) The bank angle is related to the airplane's speed v and the radius R of the turn: $\tan\beta = v^2/gR$. For an airplane to make a tight turn (small R) at high speed (large v), $\tan\beta$ must be large and the required bank angle β must approach 90°.

The free-body diagram for the pilot of the airplane is exactly as shown; the normal force $n = mg/\cos\beta$ is exerted on the pilot by the seat. n is equal to the apparent weight of the pilot, which is greater than the pilot's true weight mg. In a tight turn with a large bank angle β, the pilot's apparent weight can be tremendous: $n = 5.8mg$ at $\beta = 80°$ and $n = 9.6mg$ at $\beta = 84°$. Pilots black out in such tight turns because the apparent weight of their blood increases by the same factor, and the human heart isn't strong enough to pump such apparently "heavy" blood to the brain.

Motion in a Vertical Circle

Motion in a *vertical* circle is no different in principle, but the weight of the body has to be treated carefully. The following example shows what we mean.

When we tie a string to an object and whirl it in a vertical circle, the analysis isn't directly applicable. The reason is that v is *not* constant in this case; except at the instant the object is at the top and bottom of the circle, the net force (and hence the acceleration) does *not* point toward the center of the circle (Fig. 5.9). So both $\sum\vec{F}$ and $\vec{a}$ have a component tangent to the circle, which means that the speed changes. Hence this is a case of *nonuniform* circular motion. Even worse, we can't

5.9 A ball moving in a vertical circle.

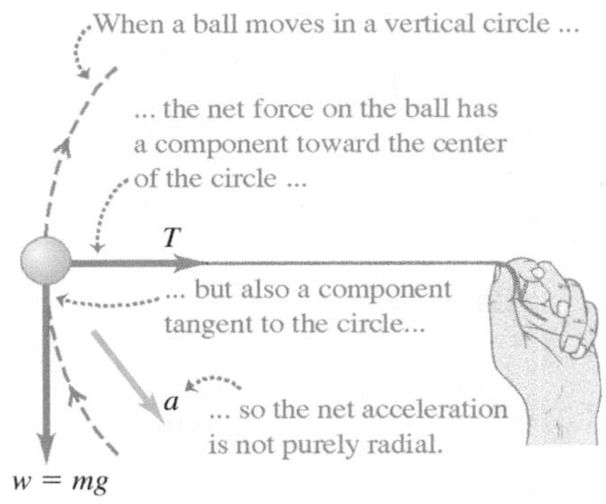
When a ball moves in a vertical circle ...
... the net force on the ball has a component toward the center of the circle ...
T
... but also a component tangent to the circle...
a
... so the net acceleration is not purely radial.
$w = mg$

use the constant-acceleration formulas to relate the speeds at various points because *neither* the magnitude nor the direction of the acceleration is constant. The speed relationships we need are best obtained by using the concept of energy.

5.4 The Fundamental Forces of Nature

We have discussed several kinds of forces—including weight, tension, friction, fluid resistance, and the normal force—and we will encounter others as we continue our study of physics. But just how many kinds of forces are there? Our current understanding is that all forces are expressions of just four distinct classes of *fundamental* forces, or interactions between particles (Fig. 5.10). Two are familiar in everyday experience. The other two involve interactions between subatomic particles that we cannot observe with the unaided senses.

Gravitational interactions include the familiar force of your *weight,* which results from the earth's gravitational attraction acting on you. The mutual gravitational attraction of various parts of the earth for each other holds our planet together (Fig. 5.10a). Newton recognized that the sun's gravitational attraction for the earth keeps the earth in its nearly circular orbit around the sun. We will study gravitational interactions in greater detail, and we will analyze their vital role in the motions of planets and satellites.

The second familiar class of forces, **electromagnetic interactions,** includes electric and magnetic forces. If you run a comb through your hair, the comb ends up with an electric charge; you can use the electric force exerted by this charge to pick up bits of paper. All atoms contain positive and negative electric charge, so atoms and molecules can exert electric forces on one another (Fig. 5.10b). Contact forces, including the normal force, friction, and fluid resistance, are the combination of all such forces exerted on the atoms of a body by atoms in its surroundings. *Magnetic* forces, such as those between magnets or between a magnet and a piece of iron, are actually the result of electric charges in motion. For example, an electromagnet causes magnetic interactions because electric charges move through its wires. We will study electromagnetic interactions in detail in the second half of this book.

On the atomic or molecular scale, gravitational forces play no role because electric forces are enormously stronger: The electrical repulsion between two protons is stronger than their gravitational attraction by a factor of about 10^{35}. But in bodies of astronomical size, positive and negative charges are usually present in nearly equal amounts, and the resulting electrical interactions nearly cancel out. Gravitational interactions are thus the dominant influence in the motion of planets and in the internal structure of stars.

The other two classes of interactions are less familiar. One, the **strong interaction,** is responsible for holding the nucleus of an atom together. Nuclei contain electrically neutral neutrons and positively charged protons. The electric force between charged protons tries to push them apart; the strong attractive force between nuclear particles counteracts this repulsion and makes the nucleus stable. In this context the strong interaction is also called the *strong nuclear force.* It has much shorter range than electrical interactions, but within its range it is much stronger. The strong interaction plays a key role in thermonuclear reactions that take place at the sun's core and generate the sun's heat and light (Fig. 5.10c).

Finally, there is the **weak interaction.** Its range is so short that it plays a role only on the scale of the nucleus or smaller. The weak interaction is responsible for a common form of radioactivity called beta decay, in which a neutron in a radioactive nucleus is transformed into a proton while ejecting an electron and a nearly massless particle called an antineutrino. The weak interaction between the antineutrino and ordinary matter is so feeble that an antineutrino could easily penetrate a wall of lead a million kilometers thick! Yet when a giant star undergoes a cataclysmic explosion called a supernova, most of the energy is released by way of the weak interaction (Fig. 5.10d).

In the 1960s physicists developed a theory that described the electromagnetic and weak interactions as aspects of a single *electroweak* interaction. This theory has passed every experimental test to which it has been put. Encouraged by this success, physicists have made similar attempts to describe the strong, electromagnetic, and weak interactions in terms of a single *grand unified theory* (GUT), and have taken steps toward a possible unification of all interactions into a *theory of everything* (TOE). Such theories are still speculative, and there are many unanswered questions in this very active field of current research.

5.10 Examples of the fundamental interactions in nature. (a) The moon and the earth are held together and held in orbit by gravitational forces. (b) This molecule of bacterial plasmid DNA is held together by electromagnetic forces between its atoms. (c) The sun shines because in its core, strong forces between nuclear particles cause the release of energy. (d) When a massive star explodes into a supernova, a flood of energy is released by weak interactions between the star's nuclear particles.

(a) Gravitational forces hold planets together.

(b) Electromagnetic forces hold molecules together.

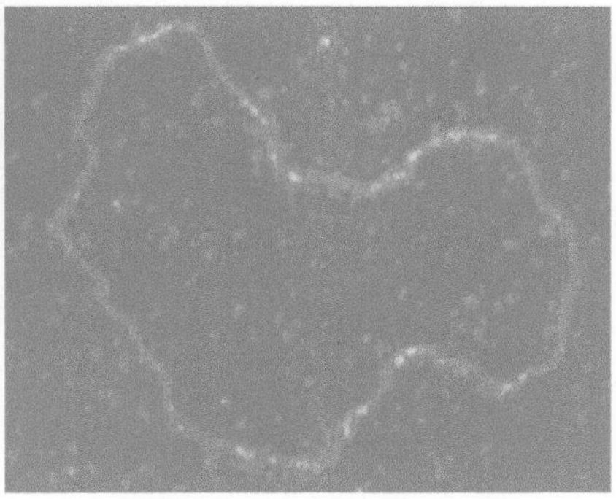

(c) Strong forces release energy to power the sun.

(d) Weak forces play a role in exploding stars.

CHAPTER 5 SUMMARY

Mass, acceleration, and Newton's second law: The inertial properties of a body are characterized by its *mass.* The acceleration of a body under the action of a given set of forces is directly proportional to the vector sum of the forces (the *net force*) and inversely proportional to the mass of the body. This relationship is Newton's second law. Like Newton's first law, this law is valid only in inertial frames of reference. The unit of force is defined in terms of the units of mass and acceleration. In SI units, the unit of force is the newton (N), equal to 1 $\text{kg} \cdot \text{m/s}^2$.

$$\sum \vec{F} = m\vec{a} \quad (5.3)$$

$$\sum F_x = ma_x$$

$$\sum F_y = ma_y \quad (5.4)$$

$$\sum F_z = ma_z$$

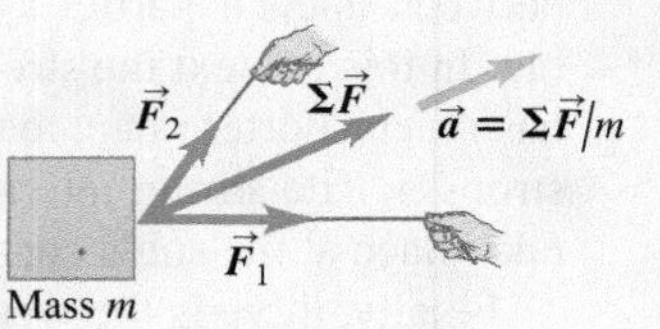

Using Newton's second law: If the vector sum of forces on a body is *not* zero, the body accelerates. The acceleration is related to the net force by Newton's second law.

Just as for equilibrium problems, free-body diagrams are essential for solving problems involving Newton's second law, and the normal force exerted on a body is not always equal to its weight.

Vector form:

$$\sum \vec{F} = m\vec{a} \quad (5.5)$$

Component form:

$$\sum F_x = ma_x \qquad \sum F_y = ma_y \quad (5.6)$$

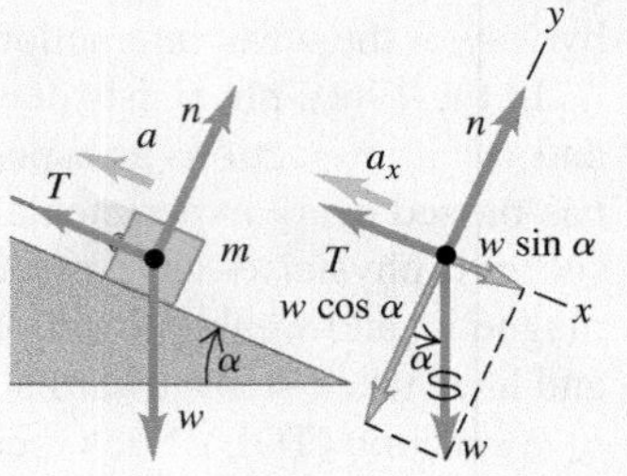

Forces in circular motion: In uniform circular motion, the acceleration vector is directed toward the center of the circle. The motion is governed by Newton's second law, $\Sigma\vec{F} = m\vec{a}$.

Acceleration in uniform circular motion:

$$a_{rad} = \frac{v^2}{R} = \frac{4\pi^2 R}{T^2} \quad (5.7), (5.9)$$

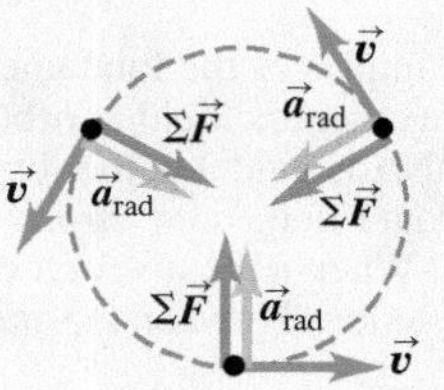

Problems

•, ••, •••: Problems of increasing difficulty. **CP**: Cumulative problems incorporating material from earlier chapters. **CALC**: Problems requiring calculus. **BIO**: Biosciences problems.

5.1 •• A 68.5-kg skater moving initially at 2.40 m/s on rough horizontal ice comes to rest uniformly in 3.52 s due to friction from the ice. What force does friction exert on the skater?

5.2 •• You walk into an elevator, step onto a scale, and push the "up" button. You also recall that your normal weight is 625 N. Start answering each of the following questions by drawing a free-body diagram. (a) If the elevator has an acceleration of magnitude $2.50\ \text{m/s}^2$, what does the scale read? (b) If you start holding a 3.85-kg package by a light vertical string, what will be the tension in this string once the elevator begins accelerating?

5.3 • A small 8.00-kg rocket burns fuel that exerts a time-varying upward force on the rocket as the rocket moves upward from the launch pad. This force obeys the equation $F = A + Bt^2$. Measurements show that at $t = 0$, the force is 100.0 N, and at the end of the first 2.00 s, it is 150.0 N. (a) Find the constants A and B, including their SI units. (b) Find the *net* force on this rocket and its acceleration (i) the instant after the fuel ignites and (ii) 3.00 s after fuel ignition. (c) Suppose you were using this rocket in outer space, far from all gravity. What would its acceleration be 3.00 s after fuel ignition?

5.4 • Two crates, one with mass 4.00 kg and the other with mass 6.00 kg, sit on the frictionless surface of a frozen pond, connected by a light rope (Fig. P5.4). A woman wearing golf shoes (so she can get traction on the ice) pulls horizontally on the 6.00-kg crate with a force F that gives the crate an acceleration of $2.50\ \text{m/s}^2$. (a) What is the acceleration of the 4.00-kg crate? (b) Draw a free-body diagram for the 4.00-kg crate. Use that diagram and Newton's second law to find the tension T in the rope that connects the two crates. (c) Draw a free-body diagram for the 6.00-kg crate. What is the direction of the net force on the 6.00-kg crate? Which is larger in magnitude, force T or force F? (d) Use part (c) and Newton's second law to calculate the magnitude of the force F.

Figure **P5.4**

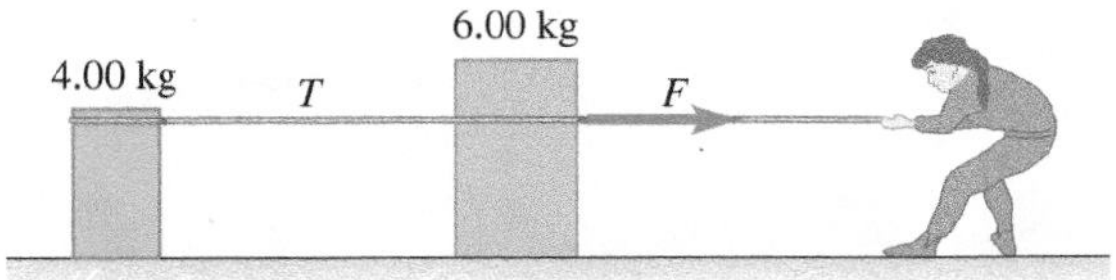

5.5 **CP** Two boxes, A and B, are connected to each end of a light vertical rope, as shown in Fig. P5.5. A constant upward force $F =$ 80.0 N is applied to box A. Starting from rest, box B descends 12.0 m in 4.00 s. The tension in the rope connecting the two boxes is 36.0 N. (a) What is the mass of box B? (b) What is the mass of box A?

Figure **P5.5**

5.6 •• **CP** A 25.0-kg box of textbooks rests on a loading ramp that makes an angle α with the horizontal. The coefficient of kinetic friction is 0.25, and the coefficient of static friction is 0.35. (a) As the angle α is increased, find the minimum angle at which the box starts to slip. (b) At this angle, find the acceleration once the box has begun to move. (c) At this angle, how fast will the box be moving after it has slid 5.0 m along the loading ramp?

5.7 •• A small car with mass 0.800 kg travels at constant speed on the inside of a track that is a vertical circle with radius 5.00 m (Fig. P5.7). If the normal force exerted by the track on the car when it is at the top of the track (point B) is 6.00 N, what is the normal force on the car when it is at the bottom of the track (point A)?

Figure **P5.7**

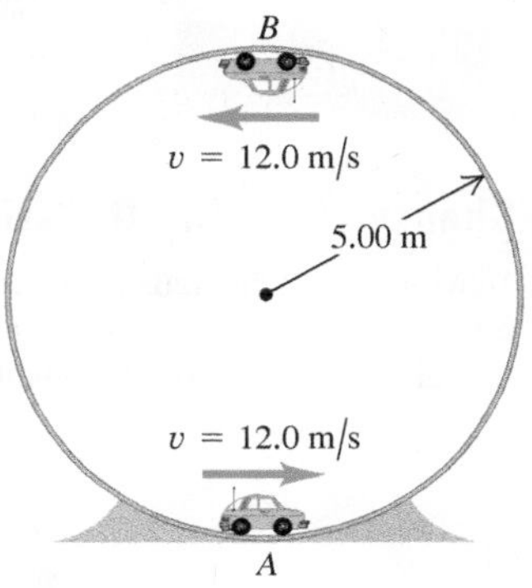

5.8 • A flat (unbanked) curve on a highway has a radius of 220.0 m. A car rounds the curve at a speed of 25.0 m/s. (a) What is the minimum coefficient of friction that will prevent sliding? (b) Suppose the highway is icy and the coefficient of friction between the tires and pavement is only one-third what you found in part (a). What should be the maximum speed of the car so it can round the curve safely?

5.9 •• In another version of the "Giant Swing" the seat is connected to two cables as shown in Fig. P5.9, one of which is horizontal. The seat swings in a horizontal circle at a rate of 32.0 rpm (rev/min). If the seat weighs 255 N and an 825-N person is sitting in it, find the tension in each cable.

Figure **P5.9**

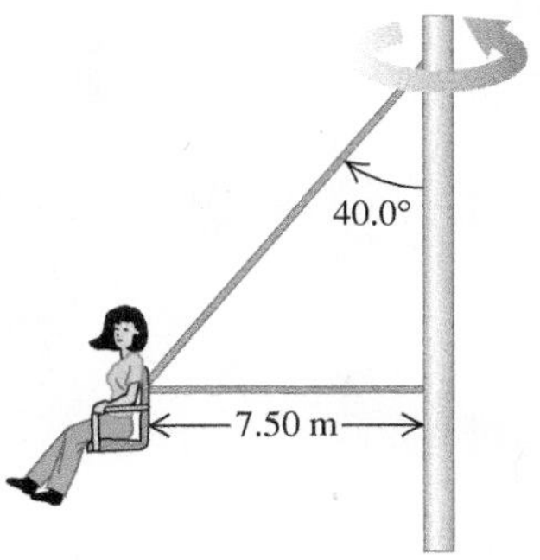

5.10 •• An airplane flies in a loop (a circular path in a vertical plane) of radius 150 m. The pilot's head always points toward the center of the loop. The speed of the airplane is not constant; the airplane goes slowest at the top of the loop and fastest at the bottom. (a) At the top of the loop, the pilot feels weightless. What is the speed of the airplane at this point? (b) At the bottom of the loop, the speed of the airplane is 280 km/h. What is the apparent weight of the pilot at this point? His true weight is 700 N.

5.11 ••• The 4.00-kg block in Fig. P5.11 is attached to a vertical rod by means of two strings. When the system rotates about the axis of the rod, the strings are extended as shown in the diagram and the tension in the upper string is 80.0 N. (a) What is the tension in the lower cord? (b) How many revolutions per minute does the system make? (c) Find the number of revolutions per minute at which the lower cord just goes slack. (d) Explain what happens if the number of revolutions per minute is less than in part (c).

Figure P5.11

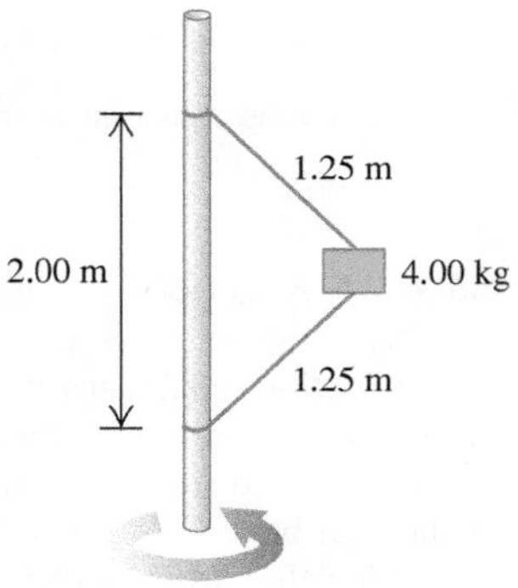
1.25 m
2.00 m
4.00 kg
1.25 m

Answers

Chapter Opening Question ?

Newton's third law tells us that the car pushes on the crew member just as hard as the crew member pushes on the car, but in the opposite direction. This is true whether the car's engine is on and the car is moving forward partly under its own power, or the engine is off and being propelled by the crew member's push alone. The force magnitudes are different in the two situations, but in either case the push of the car on the crew member is just as strong as the push of the crew member on the car.

APPLYING NEWTON'S LAWS—FORCES

6

? This skydiver is descending under a parachute at a steady rate. In this situation, which has a greater magnitude: the force of gravity or the upward force of the air on the skydiver?

LEARNING GOALS

By studying this chapter, you will learn:

- How to use Newton's first law to solve problems involving the forces that act on a body in equilibrium.
- How to use Newton's second law to solve problems involving the forces that act on an accelerating body.
- The nature of the different types of friction forces—static friction, kinetic friction, rolling friction, and fluid resistance—and how to solve problems that involve these forces.
- How to solve problems involving the forces that act on a body moving along a circular path.
- The key properties of the four fundamental forces of nature.
- How to calculate the gravitational forces that any two bodies exert on each other.
- How to relate the weight of an object to the general expression for gravitational force.
- The properties of magnets, and how magnets interact with each other.
- The nature of the force that a moving charged particle experiences in a magnetic field.

We have seen that Newton's laws of motion, the foundation of classical mechanics, can be stated very simply. But applying these laws to situations such as an iceboat skating across a froze lake, a toboggan sliding down a hill an airplane making a sharp turn, or a particle moving in an accelerator requires analytical skills and problem solving technique. In this chapter we will describe several of the forces that can cause particles to move and accelerate.

We'll learn how to describe and analyze position and velocity dependent forces that act on bodies. We will discuss how forces can vary with position, such as springs which obey Hooke's law. We will analyze the gravitational and electric forces, which despite having different origins have significant structural similarities, and we will consider fundamental forces which are exerted on moving particles.

6.1 Springs

Many objects change shape, or deform, as they are subject to a force, however they return to their original shape when the force is removed. One example of this is the cushion of a chair: as you sit down on it, it compresses and when you are sitting still the upwards force it exerts counteracts the downwards force of gravity on you. When you stand up the top of the cushion returns to approximately its original position. You may also notice that a more massive person compresses the cushion more than a smaller person - the amount that the cushion is compressed is related to the amount of force that it exerts.

To keep a spring stretched beyond its unstretched length by an amount x, we have to apply a force of equal magnitude at each end (Fig. 6.1). If the elongation x is not too great, the force we apply to the right-hand end has an x-component directly proportional to x:

$$F_x = kx \qquad \text{(force required to stretch a spring)} \qquad (6.1)$$

6.1 The force needed to stretch an ideal spring is proportional to the spring's elongation: $F_x = kx$.

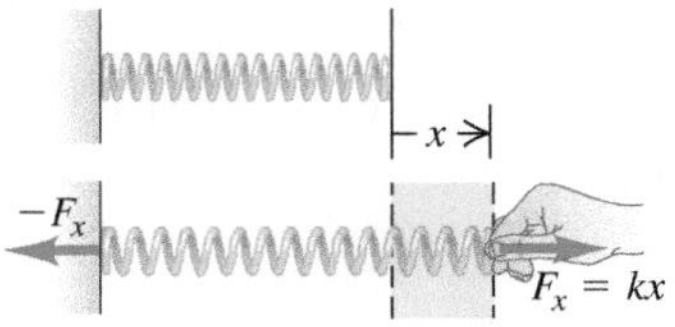

where k is a constant called the **force constant** (or spring constant) of the spring. The units of k are force divided by distance: N/m in SI units and lb/ft in British units. A floppy toy spring such as a Slinky™ has a force constant of about 1 N/m; for the much stiffer springs in an automobile's suspension, k is about 10^5 N/m. The observation that force is directly proportional to elongation for elongations that are not too great was made by Robert Hooke in 1678 and is known as **Hooke's law.** It really shouldn't be called a "law," since it's a statement about a specific device and not a fundamental law of nature. Real springs don't always obey Eq. (6.1) precisely, but it's still a useful idealized model.

6.2 Newton's Law of Gravitation

The example of gravitational attraction that's probably most familiar to you is your *weight,* the force that attracts you toward the earth. During his study of the motions of the planets and of the moon, Newton discovered the fundamental character of the gravitational attraction between *any* two bodies. Along with his three laws of motion, Newton published the **law of gravitation** in 1687. It may be stated as follows:

Every particle of matter in the universe attracts every other particle with a force that is directly proportional to the product of the masses of the particles and inversely proportional to the square of the distance between them.

Translating this into an equation, we have

$$F_g = \frac{Gm_1m_2}{r^2} \quad \text{(law of gravitation)} \tag{6.2}$$

where F_g is the magnitude of the gravitational force on either particle, m_1 and m_2 are their masses, r is the distance between them (Fig. 6.2), and G is a fundamental physical constant called the **gravitational constant.** The numerical value of G depends on the system of units used.

Equation (6.2) tells us that the gravitational force between two particles decreases with increasing distance r: If the distance is doubled, the force is only one-fourth as great, and so on. Although many of the stars in the night sky are far more massive than the sun, they are so far away that their gravitational force on the earth is negligibly small.

CAUTION **Don't confuse g and G** Because the symbols g and G are so similar, it's common to confuse the two very different gravitational quantities that these symbols represent. Lowercase g is the acceleration due to gravity, which relates the weight w of a body to its mass m: $w = mg$. The value of g is different at different locations on the earth's surface and on the surfaces of different planets. By contrast, capital G relates the gravitational force between any two bodies to their masses and the distance between them. We call G a *universal* constant because it has the same value for any two bodies, no matter where in space they are located. In the next section we'll see how the values of g and G are related.

Gravitational forces always act along the line joining the two particles, and they form an action–reaction pair. Even when the masses of the particles are different, the two interaction forces have equal magnitude (Fig. 6.2). The attractive force that your body exerts on the earth has the same magnitude as the force that the earth exerts on you. When you fall from a diving board into a swimming pool, the entire earth rises up to meet you! (You don't notice this because the earth's mass is greater than yours by a factor of about 10^{23}. Hence the earth's acceleration is only 10^{-23} as great as yours.)

6.2 The gravitational forces between two particles of masses m_1 and m_2.

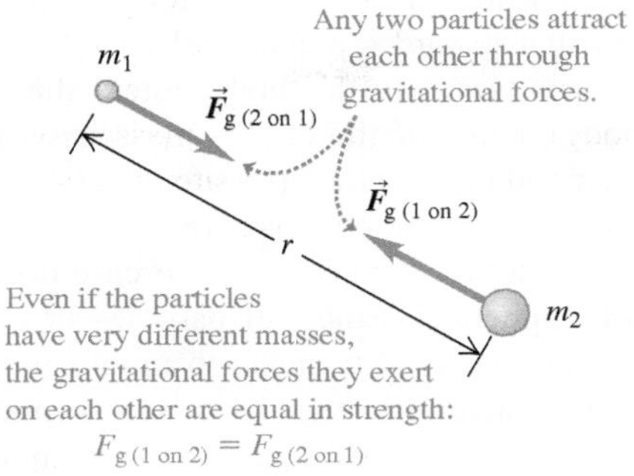

m_1
Any two particles attract each other through gravitational forces.
$\vec{F}_{g\,(2\text{ on }1)}$
$\vec{F}_{g\,(1\text{ on }2)}$
r
m_2
Even if the particles have very different masses, the gravitational forces they exert on each other are equal in strength:
$F_{g\,(1\text{ on }2)} = F_{g\,(2\text{ on }1)}$

Gravitation and Spherically Symmetric Bodies

We have stated the law of gravitation in terms of the interaction between two *particles.* It turns out that the gravitational interaction of any two bodies having *spherically symmetric* mass distributions (such as solid spheres or spherical shells) is the same as though we concentrated all the mass of each at its center, as in Fig. 6.3. Thus, if we model the earth as a spherically symmetric body with mass m_E, the force it exerts on a particle or a spherically symmetric body with mass m, at a distance r between centers, is

$$F_g = \frac{Gm_Em}{r^2} \qquad (6.3)$$

provided that the body lies outside the earth. A force of the same magnitude is exerted *on* the earth by the body.

6.3 The gravitational effect *outside* any spherically symmetric mass distribution is the same as though all of the mass were concentrated at its center.

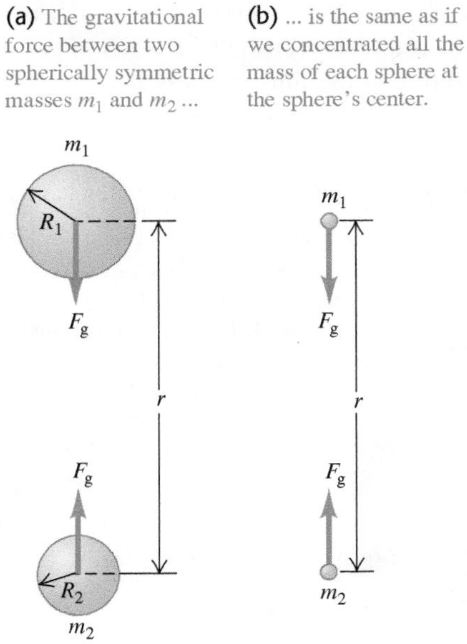

(a) The gravitational force between two spherically symmetric masses m_1 and m_2 ...
(b) ... is the same as if we concentrated all the mass of each sphere at the sphere's center.
m_1
R_1
F_g
r
F_g
R_2
m_2
m_1
F_g
r
F_g
m_2

6.4 Spherical and nonspherical bodies: the planet Jupiter and one of Jupiter's small moons, Amalthea.

Jupiter's mass is very large (1.90×10^{27} kg), so the mutual gravitational attraction of its parts has pulled it into a nearly spherical shape.

100 km
100,000 km

Amalthea, one of Jupiter's small moons, has a relatively tiny mass (7.17×10^{18} kg, only about 3.8×10^{-9} the mass of Jupiter) and weak mutual gravitation, so it has an irregular shape.

At points *inside* the earth the situation is different. If we could drill a hole to the center of the earth and measure the gravitational force on a body at various depths, we would find that toward the center of the earth the force *decreases,* rather than increasing as $1/r^2$. As the body enters the interior of the earth (or other spherical body), some of the earth's mass is on the side of the body opposite from the center and pulls in the opposite direction. Exactly at the center, the earth's gravitational force on the body is zero.

Spherically symmetric bodies are an important case because moons, planets, and stars all tend to be spherical. Since all particles in a body gravitationally attract each other, the particles tend to move to minimize the distance between them. As a result, the body naturally tends to assume a spherical shape, just as a lump of clay forms into a sphere if you squeeze it with equal forces on all sides. This effect is greatly reduced in celestial bodies of low mass, since the gravitational attraction is less, and these bodies tend *not* to be spherical (Fig. 6.4).

Determining the Value of G

To determine the value of the gravitational constant G, we have to *measure* the gravitational force between two bodies of known masses m_1 and m_2 at a known distance r. The force is extremely small for bodies that are small enough to be brought into the laboratory, but it can be measured with an instrument called a *torsion balance,* which Sir Henry Cavendish used in 1798 to determine G.

Figure 6.5 shows a modern version of the Cavendish torsion balance. A light, rigid rod shaped like an inverted T is supported by a very thin, vertical quartz fiber. Two small spheres, each of mass m_1, are mounted at the ends of the horizontal arms of the T. When we bring two large spheres, each of mass m_2, to the positions shown, the attractive gravitational forces twist the T through a small angle. To measure this angle, we shine a beam of light on a mirror fastened to the T. The reflected beam strikes a scale, and as the T twists, the reflected beam moves along the scale.

After calibrating the Cavendish balance, we can measure gravitational forces and thus determine G. The presently accepted value is

$$G = 6.67428(67) \times 10^{-11}\ \text{N} \cdot \text{m}^2/\text{kg}^2$$

To three significant figures, $G = 6.67 \times 10^{-11}\ \text{N} \cdot \text{m}^2/\text{kg}^2$. Because $1\ \text{N} = 1\ \text{kg} \cdot \text{m/s}^2$, the units of G can also be expressed as $\text{m}^3/(\text{kg} \cdot \text{s}^2)$.

Gravitational forces combine vectorially. If each of two masses exerts a force on a third, the *total* force on the third mass is the vector sum of the individual forces of the first two.

6.5 The principle of the Cavendish balance, used for determining the value of G. The angle of deflection has been exaggerated here for clarity.

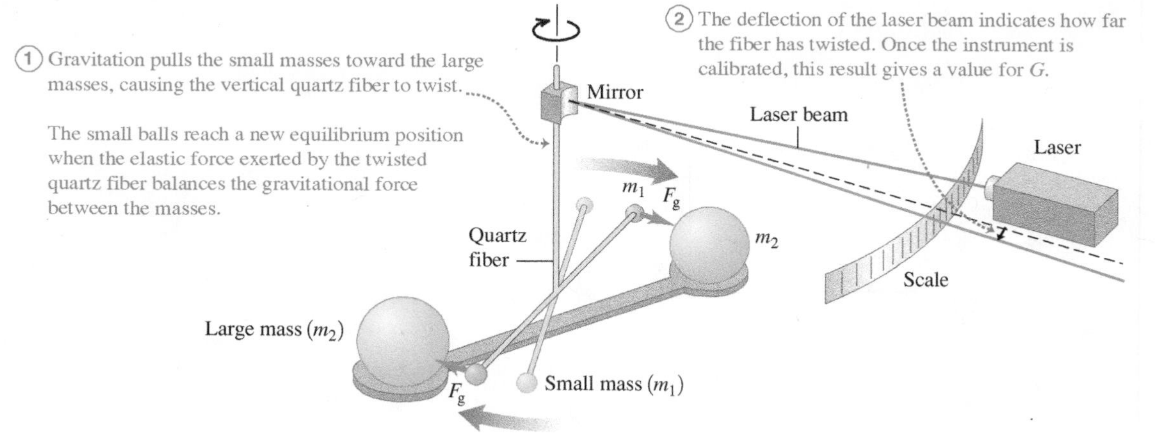
① Gravitation pulls the small masses toward the large masses, causing the vertical quartz fiber to twist.
The small balls reach a new equilibrium position when the elastic force exerted by the twisted quartz fiber balances the gravitational force between the masses.
② The deflection of the laser beam indicates how far the fiber has twisted. Once the instrument is calibrated, this result gives a value for G.
Mirror
Laser beam
Laser
m1
Fg
m2
Quartz fiber
Scale
Large mass (m2)
Fg
Small mass (m1)

Why Gravitational Forces Are Important

Gravitational forces are negligible between ordinary household-sized objects, but very substantial between objects that are the size of stars. Indeed, gravitation is *the* most important force on the scale of planets, stars, and galaxies. It is responsible for holding our earth together and for keeping the planets in orbit about the sun. The mutual gravitational attraction between different parts of the sun compresses material at the sun's core to very high densities and temperatures, making it possible for nuclear reactions to take place there. These reactions generate the sun's energy output, which makes it possible for life to exist on earth and for you to read these words.

The gravitational force is so important on the cosmic scale because it acts *at a distance,* without any direct contact between bodies. Electric and magnetic forces have this same remarkable property, but they are less important on astronomical scales because large accumulations of matter are electrically neutral; that is, they contain equal amounts of positive and negative charge. As a result, the electric and magnetic forces between stars or planets are very small or zero. The strong and weak interactions that we discussed in Section 5.4 also act at a distance, but their influence is negligible at distances much greater than the diameter of an atomic nucleus (about 10^{-14} m).

A useful way to describe forces that act at a distance is in terms of a *field.* One body sets up a disturbance or field at all points in space, and the force that acts on a second body at a particular point is its response to the first body's field at that point. There is a field associated with each force that acts at a distance, and so we refer to gravitational fields, electric fields, magnetic fields, and so on. We won't need the field concept for our study of gravitation in this chapter, so we won't discuss it further here. But we'll find that the field concept is an extraordinarily powerful tool for describing electric and magnetic interactions.

6.3 Weight

We defined the *weight* of a body as the attractive gravitational force exerted on it by the earth. We can now broaden our definition:

The weight of a body is the total gravitational force exerted on the body by all other bodies in the universe.

When the body is near the surface of the earth, we can neglect all other gravitational forces and consider the weight as just the earth's gravitational attraction. At the surface of the *moon* we consider a body's weight to be the gravitational attraction of the moon, and so on.

If we again model the earth as a spherically symmetric body with radius R_E and mass m_E, the weight w of a small body of mass m at the earth's surface (a distance R_E from its center) is

$$w = F_g = \frac{Gm_E m}{R_E^2} \quad \text{(weight of a body of mass } m \text{ at the earth's surface)} \tag{6.4}$$

But we also know that the weight w of a body is the force that causes the acceleration g of free fall, so by Newton's second law, $w = mg$. Equating this with Eq. (6.4) and dividing by m, we find

$$g = \frac{Gm_E}{R_E^2} \quad \text{(acceleration due to gravity at the earth's surface)} \tag{6.5}$$

The acceleration due to gravity g is independent of the mass m of the body because m doesn't appear in this equation. We already knew that, but we can now see how it follows from the law of gravitation.

We can *measure* all the quantities in Eq. (6.5) except for m_E, so this relationship allows us to compute the mass of the earth. Solving Eq. (6.5) for m_E and using $R_E = 6380 \text{ km} = 6.38 \times 10^6 \text{ m}$ and $g = 9.80 \text{ m/s}^2$, we find

$$m_E = \frac{gR_E^2}{G} = 5.98 \times 10^{24} \text{ kg}$$

This is very close to the currently accepted value of 5.974×10^{24} kg. Once Cavendish had measured G, he computed the mass of the earth in just this way.

At a point above the earth's surface a distance r from the center of the earth (a distance $r - R_E$ above the surface), the weight of a body is given by Eq. (6.4) with R_E replaced by r:

$$w = F_g = \frac{Gm_E m}{r^2} \tag{6.6}$$

The weight of a body decreases inversely with the square of its distance from the earth's center. Figure 6.6 shows how the weight varies with height above the earth for an astronaut who weighs 700 N at the earth's surface.

The *apparent* weight of a body on earth differs slightly from the earth's gravitational force because the earth rotates and is therefore not precisely an inertial frame of reference. We have ignored this effect in our earlier discussion and have assumed that the earth *is* an inertial system.

While the earth is an approximately spherically symmetric distribution of mass, it is *not* uniform throughout its volume. To demonstrate this, let's first calculate the average *density*, or mass per unit volume, of the earth. If we assume a spherical earth, the volume is

$$V_E = \tfrac{4}{3}\pi R_E^3 = \tfrac{4}{3}\pi(6.38 \times 10^6 \text{ m})^3 = 1.09 \times 10^{21} \text{ m}^3$$

6.6 An astronaut who weighs 700 N at the earth's surface experiences less gravitational attraction when above the surface. The relevant distance r is from the astronaut to the *center* of the earth (*not* from the astronaut to the earth's surface).

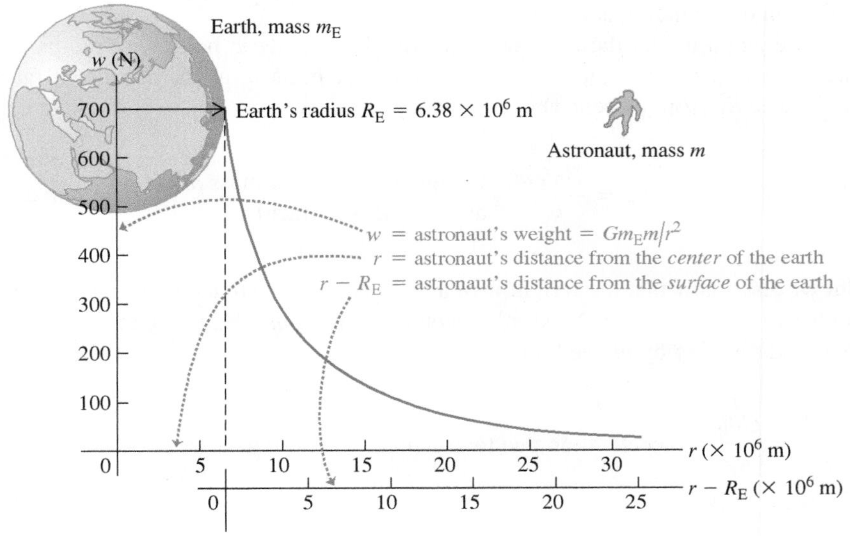

The average density ρ (the Greek letter rho) of the earth is the total mass divided by the total volume:

$$\rho = \frac{m_E}{V_E} = \frac{5.97 \times 10^{24}\ \text{kg}}{1.09 \times 10^{21}\ \text{m}^3}$$

$$= 5500\ \text{kg/m}^3 = 5.5\ \text{g/cm}^3$$

(For comparison, the density of water is $1000\ \text{kg/m}^3 = 1.00\ \text{g/cm}^3$.) If the earth were uniform, we would expect rocks near the earth's surface to have this same density. In fact, the density of surface rocks is substantially lower, ranging from about $2000\ \text{kg/m}^3$ for sedimentary rocks to about $3300\ \text{kg/m}^3$ for basalt. So the earth *cannot* be uniform, and the interior of the earth must be much more dense than the surface in order that the *average* density be $5500\ \text{kg/m}^3$. According to geophysical models of the earth's interior, the maximum density at the center is about $13{,}000\ \text{kg/m}^3$. Figure 6.7 is a graph of density as a function of distance from the center.

6.7 The density of the earth decreases with increasing distance from its center.

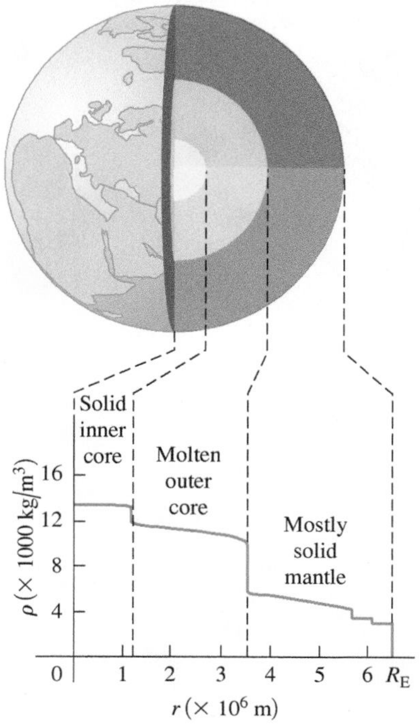

6.4 Coulomb's Law

Charles Augustin de Coulomb (1736–1806) studied the interaction forces of charged particles in detail in 1784. He used a torsion balance (Fig. 6.8a) similar to the one used 13 years later by Cavendish to study the much weaker gravitational interaction, as we discussed in Section 6.2. For **point charges,** charged bodies that are very small in comparison with the distance r between them, Coulomb found that the electric force is proportional to $1/r^2$. That is, when the distance r doubles, the force decreases to one-quarter of its initial value; when the distance is halved, the force increases to four times its initial value.

The electric force between two point charges also depends on the quantity of charge on each body, which we will denote by q or Q. To explore this dependence, Coulomb divided a charge into two equal parts by placing a small charged spherical conductor into contact with an identical but uncharged sphere; by symmetry, the charge is shared equally between the two spheres. (Note the essential role of the principle of conservation of charge in this procedure.) Thus he could obtain one-half, one-quarter, and so on, of any initial charge. He found that the forces that two point charges q_1 and q_2 exert on each other are proportional to each charge and therefore are proportional to the *product* $q_1 q_2$ of the two charges.

Thus Coulomb established what we now call **Coulomb's law:**

The magnitude of the electric force between two point charges is directly proportional to the product of the charges and inversely proportional to the square of the distance between them.

In mathematical terms, the magnitude F of the force that each of two point charges q_1 and q_2 a distance r apart exerts on the other can be expressed as

$$F = k\frac{|q_1 q_2|}{r^2} \tag{6.7}$$

where k is a proportionality constant whose numerical value depends on the system of units used. The absolute value bars are used in Eq. (6.7) because the charges q_1 and q_2 can be either positive or negative, while the force magnitude F is always positive.

The directions of the forces the two charges exert on each other are always along the line joining them. When the charges q_1 and q_2 have the same sign,

6.8 (a) Measuring the electric force between point charges. (b) The electric forces between point charges obey Newton's third law: $\vec{F}_{1\text{ on }2} = -\vec{F}_{2\text{ on }1}$.

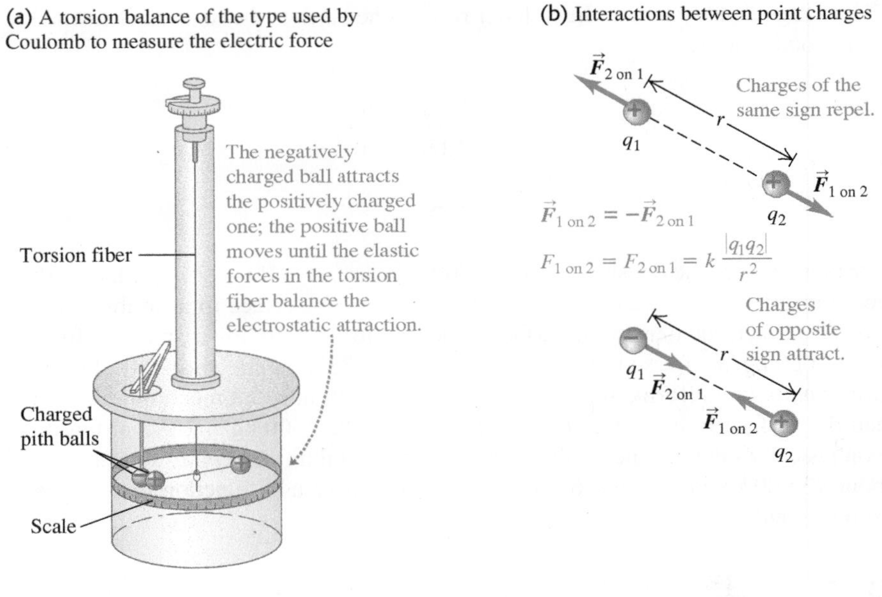
(a) A torsion balance of the type used by Coulomb to measure the electric force
The negatively charged ball attracts the positively charged one; the positive ball moves until the elastic forces in the torsion fiber balance the electrostatic attraction.
Torsion fiber
Charged pith balls
Scale
(b) Interactions between point charges
Charges of the same sign repel.
$\vec{F}_{2\text{ on }1}$
$\vec{F}_{1\text{ on }2}$
q_1
q_2
r
$\vec{F}_{1\text{ on }2} = -\vec{F}_{2\text{ on }1}$
$F_{1\text{ on }2} = F_{2\text{ on }1} = k\dfrac{|q_1q_2|}{r^2}$
Charges of opposite sign attract.

either both positive or both negative, the forces are repulsive; when the charges have opposite signs, the forces are attractive (Fig. 6.8b). The two forces obey Newton's third law; they are always equal in magnitude and opposite in direction, even when the charges are not equal in magnitude.

The proportionality of the electric force to $1/r^2$ has been verified with great precision. There is no reason to suspect that the exponent is different from precisely 2. Thus the form of Eq. (6.7) is the same as that of the law of gravitation. But electric and gravitational interactions are two distinct classes of phenomena. Electric interactions depend on electric charges and can be either attractive or repulsive, while gravitational interactions depend on mass and are always attractive (because there is no such thing as negative mass).

Fundamental Electric Constants

The value of the proportionality constant k in Coulomb's law depends on the system of units used. In our study of electricity and magnetism we will use SI units exclusively. The SI electric units include most of the familiar units such as the volt, the ampere, the ohm, and the watt. (There is *no* British system of electric units.) The SI unit of electric charge is called one **coulomb** (1 C). In SI units the constant k in Eq. (6.7) is

$$k = 8.987551787 \times 10^9\ \text{N}\cdot\text{m}^2/\text{C}^2 \cong 8.988 \times 10^9\ \text{N}\cdot\text{m}^2/\text{C}^2$$

The value of k is known to such a large number of significant figures because this value is closely related to the speed of light in vacuum. This speed is *defined* to be exactly $c = 2.99792458 \times 10^8$ m/s. The numerical value of k is defined in terms of c to be precisely

$$k = (10^{-7}\ \text{N}\cdot\text{s}^2/\text{C}^2)c^2$$

You should check this expression to confirm that k has the right units.

In principle we can measure the electric force F between two equal charges q at a measured distance r and use Coulomb's law to determine the charge. Thus we could regard the value of k as an operational definition of the coulomb. For reasons of experimental precision it is better to define the coulomb instead in terms of a unit of electric *current* (charge per unit time), the *ampere,* equal to 1 coulomb per second.

In SI units we usually write the constant k in Eq. (6.7) as $1/4\pi\epsilon_0$, where ϵ_0 ("epsilon-nought" or "epsilon-zero") is another constant. This appears to complicate matters, but it actually simplifies many formulas when we study electricity and magnetism. From now on, we will usually write Coulomb's law as

$$F = \frac{1}{4\pi\epsilon_0}\frac{|q_1 q_2|}{r^2} \quad \text{(Coulomb's law: force between two point charges)} \tag{6.8}$$

The constants in Eq. (6.8) are approximately

$$\epsilon_0 = 8.854 \times 10^{-12}\,\text{C}^2/\text{N}\cdot\text{m}^2 \quad \text{and} \quad \frac{1}{4\pi\epsilon_0} = k = 8.988 \times 10^9\,\text{N}\cdot\text{m}^2/\text{C}^2$$

In examples and problems we will often use the approximate value

$$\frac{1}{4\pi\epsilon_0} = 9.0 \times 10^9\,\text{N}\cdot\text{m}^2/\text{C}^2$$

which is within about 0.1% of the correct value.

The most fundamental unit of charge is the magnitude of the charge of an electron or a proton, which is denoted by e. The most precise value available as of the writing of this book is

$$e = 1.602176487(40) \times 10^{-19}\,\text{C}$$

One coulomb represents the negative of the total charge of about 6×10^{18} electrons. For comparison, a copper cube 1 cm on a side contains about 2.4×10^{24} electrons. About 10^{19} electrons pass through the glowing filament of a flashlight bulb every second.

In electrostatics problems (that is, problems that involve charges at rest), it's very unusual to encounter charges as large as 1 coulomb. Two 1-C charges separated by 1 m would exert forces on each other of magnitude 9×10^9 N (about 1 million tons)! The total charge of all the electrons in a copper one-cent coin is even greater, about 1.4×10^5 C, which shows that we can't disturb electric neutrality very much without using enormous forces. More typical values of charge range from about 10^{-9} to about 10^{-6} C. The microcoulomb ($1\,\mu\text{C} = 10^{-6}\,\text{C}$) and the nanocoulomb ($1\,\text{nC} = 10^{-9}\,\text{C}$) are often used as practical units of charge.

Superposition of Forces

Coulomb's law as we have stated it describes only the interaction of two *point* charges. Experiments show that when two charges exert forces simultaneously on a third charge, the total force acting on that charge is the *vector sum* of the forces that the two charges would exert individually. This important property, called the **principle of superposition of forces,** holds for any number of charges. By using this principle, we can apply Coulomb's law to *any* collection of charges. Two of the examples at the end of this section use the superposition principle.

Strictly speaking, Coulomb's law as we have stated it should be used only for point charges *in a vacuum.* If matter is present in the space between the charges, the net force acting on each charge is altered because charges are induced in the molecules of the intervening material. We will describe this effect later. As a practical matter, though, we can use Coulomb's law unaltered for point charges in air. At normal atmospheric pressure, the presence of air changes the electric force from its vacuum value by only about one part in 2000.

6.9 (a) Two bar magnets attract when opposite poles (N and S, or S and N) are next to each other. (b) The bar magnets repel when like poles (N and N, or S and S) are next to each other.

(a) Opposite poles attract.

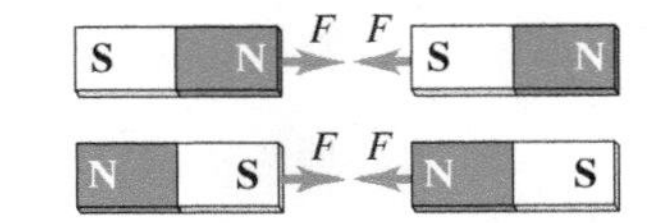

(b) Like poles repel.

6.10 (a) Either pole of a bar magnet attracts an unmagnetized object that contains iron, such as a nail.

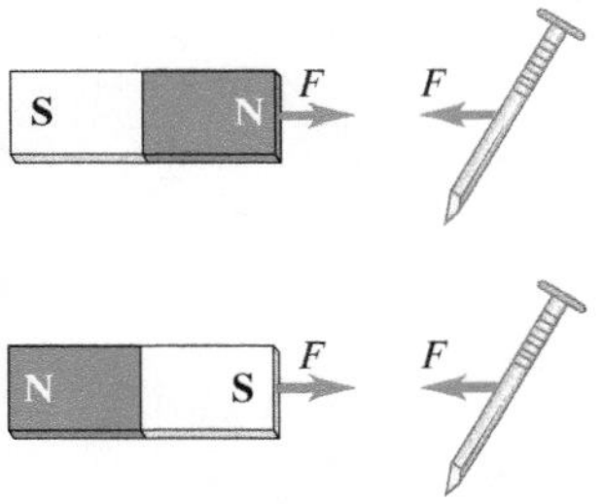

6.5 Magnetism

Everybody uses magnetic forces. They are at the heart of electric motors, microwave ovens, loudspeakers, computer printers, and disk drives. The most familiar examples of magnetism are permanent magnets, which attract unmagnetized iron objects and can also attract or repel other magnets. A compass needle aligning itself with the earth's magnetism is an example of this interaction. But the *fundamental* nature of magnetism is the interaction of moving electric charges. Unlike electric forces, which act on electric charges whether they are moving or not, magnetic forces act only on *moving* charges.

Magnetic phenomena were first observed at least 2500 years ago in fragments of magnetized iron ore found near the ancient city of Magnesia (now Manisa, in western Turkey). These fragments were examples of what are now called **permanent magnets;** you probably have several permanent magnets on your refrigerator door at home. Permanent magnets were found to exert forces on each other as well as on pieces of iron that were not magnetized. It was discovered that when an iron rod is brought in contact with a natural magnet, the rod also becomes magnetized. When such a rod is floated on water or suspended by a string from its center, it tends to line itself up in a north-south direction. The needle of an ordinary compass is just such a piece of magnetized iron.

Before the relationship of magnetic interactions to moving charges was understood, the interactions of permanent magnets and compass needles were described in terms of *magnetic poles.* If a bar-shaped permanent magnet, or *bar magnet,* is free to rotate, one end points north. This end is called a *north pole* or *N pole;* the other end is a *south pole* or *S pole.* Opposite poles attract each other, and like poles repel each other (Fig. 6.9). An object that contains iron but is not itself magnetized (that is, it shows no tendency to point north or south) is attracted by *either* pole of a permanent magnet (Fig. 6.10). This is the attraction that acts between a magnet and the unmagnetized steel door of a refrigerator. By analogy to electric interactions, we describe the interactions in Figs. 6.9 and 6.10 by saying that a bar magnet sets up a *magnetic field* in the space around it and a second body responds to that field. A compass needle tends to align with the magnetic field at the needle's position.

The earth itself is a magnet. Its north geographic pole is close to a magnetic *south* pole, which is why the north pole of a compass needle points north. The earth's magnetic axis is not quite parallel to its geographic axis (the axis of rotation), so a compass reading deviates somewhat from geographic north. This deviation, which varies with location, is called *magnetic declination* or *magnetic variation.* Also, the magnetic field is not horizontal at most points on the earth's surface; its angle up or down is called *magnetic inclination.* At the magnetic poles the magnetic field is vertical.

Figure 6.11 is a sketch of the earth's magnetic field. The lines, called *magnetic field lines,* show the direction that a compass would point at each location. The direction of the field at any point can be defined as the direction of the force that the field would exert on a magnetic north pole. In Section 6.6 we'll describe a more fundamental way to define the direction and magnitude of a magnetic field.

Magnetic Poles Versus Electric Charge

The concept of magnetic poles may appear similar to that of electric charge, and north and south poles may seem analogous to positive and negative charge. But the analogy can be misleading. While isolated positive and negative charges exist, there is *no* experimental evidence that a single isolated magnetic pole exists; poles always appear in pairs. If a bar magnet is broken in two, each broken end becomes a pole (Fig. 6.12). The existence of an isolated magnetic pole, or **magnetic monopole,** would have sweeping implications for theoretical physics. Extensive

6.11 A sketch of the earth's magnetic field. The field, which is caused by currents in the earth's molten core, changes with time; geologic evidence shows that it reverses direction entirely at irregular intervals of 10^4 to 10^6 years.

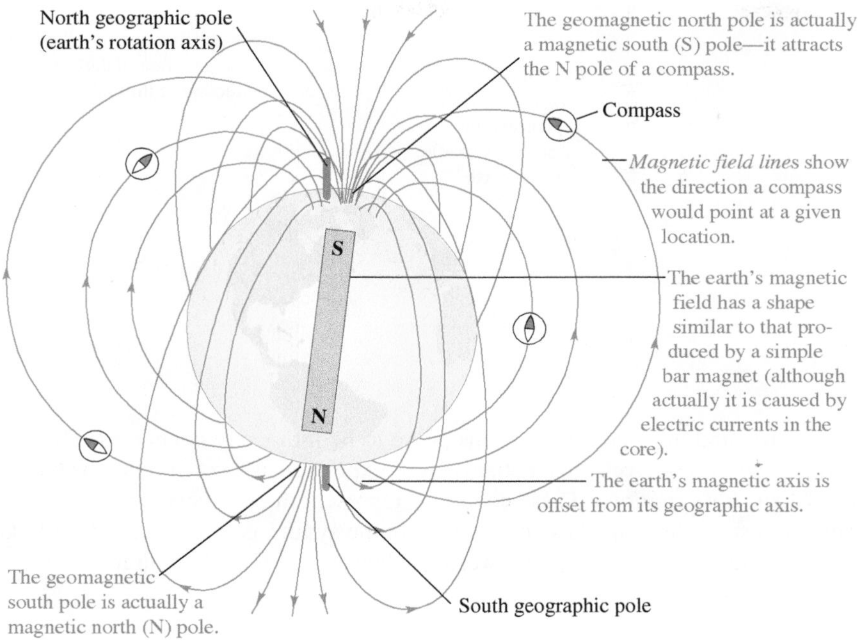
North geographic pole
(earth's rotation axis)
The geomagnetic north pole is actually a magnetic south (S) pole—it attracts the N pole of a compass.
Compass
Magnetic field lines show the direction a compass would point at a given location.
The earth's magnetic field has a shape similar to that produced by a simple bar magnet (although actually it is caused by electric currents in the core).
S
N
The earth's magnetic axis is offset from its geographic axis.
The geomagnetic south pole is actually a magnetic north (N) pole.
South geographic pole

searches for magnetic monopoles have been carried out, but so far without success.

The first evidence of the relationship of magnetism to moving charges was discovered in 1820 by the Danish scientist Hans Christian Oersted. He found that a compass needle was deflected by a current-carrying wire, as shown in Fig. 6.13 Similar investigations were carried out in France by André Ampère. A few years later, Michael Faraday in England and Joseph Henry in the United States discovered that moving a magnet near a conducting loop can cause a current in the loop. We now know that the magnetic forces between two bodies shown in Figs. 6.9 and 6.10 are fundamentally due to interactions between moving electrons in the atoms of the bodies. (There are also *electric* interactions between the two bodies, but these are far weaker than the magnetic interactions because the two bodies are electrically neutral.) Inside a magnetized body such as a permanent magnet, there is a *coordinated* motion of certain of the atomic electrons; in an unmagnetized body these motions are not coordinated.

6.12 Breaking a bar magnet. Each piece has a north and south pole, even if the pieces are different sizes. (The smaller the piece, the weaker its magnetism.)

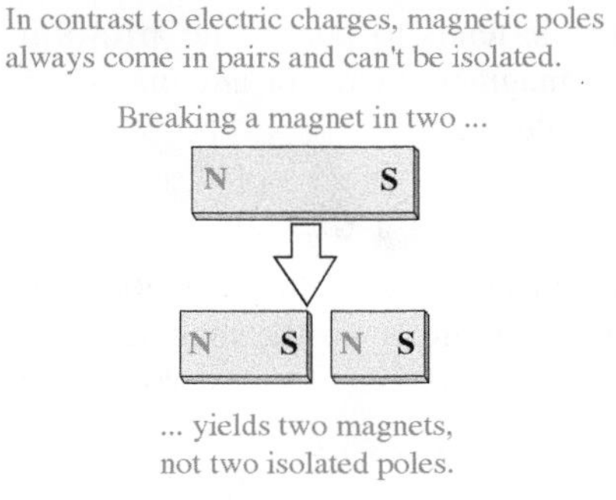
In contrast to electric charges, magnetic poles always come in pairs and can't be isolated.
Breaking a magnet in two ...
N S
N S N S
... yields two magnets, not two isolated poles.

6.13 In Oersted's experiment, a compass is placed directly over a horizontal wire (here viewed from above). When the compass is placed directly under the wire, the compass deflection is reversed.

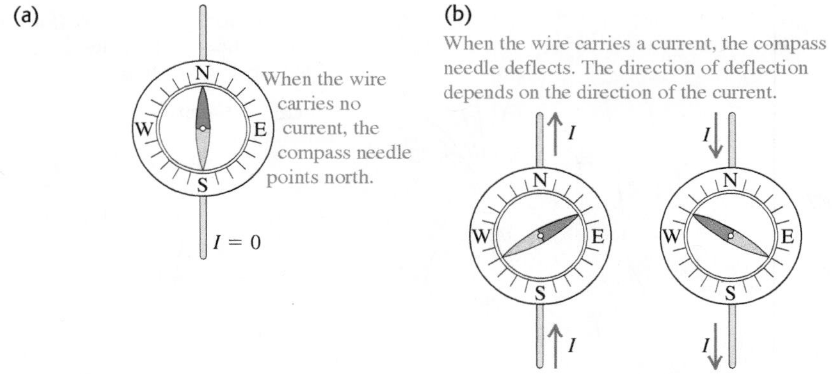
(a)
N
W
E
S
When the wire carries no current, the compass needle points north.
I = 0
(b)
When the wire carries a current, the compass needle deflects. The direction of deflection depends on the direction of the current.
I
N
W
E
S
I
I
N
W
E
S
I

Electric and magnetic interactions prove to be intimately connected. The unifying principles of electromagnetism can be expressed as a set of relations known as *Maxwell's equations.* These equations represent the synthesis of electromagnetism, just as Newton's laws of motion are the synthesis of mechanics, and like Newton's laws they represent a towering achievement of the human intellect.

6.6 Magnetic Field

To introduce the concept of magnetic field properly, let's review our formulation of *electric* interactions, where we introduced the concept of *electric* field. We represented electric interactions in two steps:

1. A distribution of electric charge at rest creates an electric field $\vec{E}$ in the surrounding space.
2. The electric field exerts a force $\vec{F} = q\vec{E}$ on any other charge q that is present in the field.

We can describe magnetic interactions in a similar way:

1. A moving charge or a current creates a **magnetic field** in the surrounding space (in addition to its *electric* field).
2. The magnetic field exerts a force $\vec{F}$ on any other moving charge or current that is present in the field.

In this chapter we'll concentrate on the *second* aspect of the interaction: Given the presence of a magnetic field, what force does it exert on a moving charge or a current?

Like electric field, magnetic field is a *vector field*—that is, a vector quantity associated with each point in space. We will use the symbol $\vec{B}$ for magnetic field. At any position the direction of $\vec{B}$ is defined as the direction in which the north pole of a compass needle tends to point. The arrows in Fig. 6.11 suggest the direction of the earth's magnetic field; for any magnet, $\vec{B}$ points out of its north pole and into its south pole.

Magnetic Forces on Moving Charges

There are four key characteristics of the magnetic force on a moving charge. First, its magnitude is proportional to the magnitude of the charge. If a 1-μC charge and a 2-μC charge move through a given magnetic field with the same velocity, experiments show that the force on the 2-μC charge is twice as great as the force on the 1-μC charge. Second, the magnitude of the force is also proportional to the magnitude, or "strength," of the field; if we double the magnitude of the field (for example, by using two identical bar magnets instead of one) without changing the charge or its velocity, the force doubles.

A third characteristic is that the magnetic force depends on the particle's velocity. This is quite different from the electric-field force, which is the same whether the charge is moving or not. A charged particle at rest experiences *no* magnetic force. And fourth, we find by experiment that the magnetic force $\vec{F}$ *does not* have the same direction as the magnetic field $\vec{B}$ but instead is always *perpendicular* to both $\vec{B}$ and the velocity $\vec{v}$. The magnitude F of the force is found to be proportional to the component of $\vec{v}$ perpendicular to the field; when that component is zero (that is, when $\vec{v}$ and $\vec{B}$ are parallel or antiparallel), the force is zero.

Figure 6.14 shows these relationships. The direction of $\vec{F}$ is always perpendicular to the plane containing $\vec{v}$ and $\vec{B}$. Its magnitude is given by

$$F = |q|v_{\perp}B = |q|vB\sin\phi \tag{6.9}$$

where $|q|$ is the magnitude of the charge and ϕ is the angle measured from the direction of $\vec{v}$ to the direction of $\vec{B}$, as shown in the figure.

This description does not specify the direction of $\vec{F}$ completely; there are always two directions, opposite to each other, that are both perpendicular to the plane of $\vec{v}$ and $\vec{B}$. To complete the description, we use the same right-hand rule that we used to define the vector product. Draw the vectors $\vec{v}$ and $\vec{B}$ with their tails together, as in Fig. 6.15a. Imagine turning $\vec{v}$ until it points in the direction of $\vec{B}$ (turning through the smaller of the two possible angles). Wrap the fingers of your right hand around the line perpendicular to the plane of $\vec{v}$ and $\vec{B}$ so that they curl around with the sense of rotation from $\vec{v}$ to $\vec{B}$. Your thumb then points in the direction of the force $\vec{F}$ on a *positive* charge. (Alternatively, the direction of the force $\vec{F}$ on a positive charge is the direction in which a right-hand-thread screw would advance if turned the same way.)

This discussion shows that the force on a charge q moving with velocity $\vec{v}$ in a magnetic field $\vec{B}$ is given, both in magnitude and in direction, by

$$\vec{F} = q\vec{v} \times \vec{B} \quad \text{(magnetic force on a moving charged particle)} \tag{6.10}$$

This is the first of several vector products we will encounter in our study of magnetic-field relationships. It's important to note that Eq. (6.10) was *not* deduced theoretically; it is an observation based on *experiment.*

Equation (6.10) is valid for both positive and negative charges. When q is negative, the direction of the force $\vec{F}$ is opposite to that of $\vec{v} \times \vec{B}$ (Fig. 6.15b). If two charges with equal magnitude and opposite sign move in the same $\vec{B}$ field with the same velocity (Fig. 6.16), the forces have equal magnitude and opposite direction. Figures 6.14, 6.15, and 6.16 show several examples of the relationships of the directions of $\vec{F}$, $\vec{v}$, and $\vec{B}$ for both positive and negative charges. Be sure you understand the relationships shown in these figures.

Equation (6.9) gives the magnitude of the magnetic force $\vec{F}$ in Eq. (6.10). We can express this magnitude in a different but equivalent way. Since ϕ is the angle

6.14 The magnetic force $\vec{F}$ acting on a positive charge q moving with velocity $\vec{v}$ is perpendicular to both $\vec{v}$ and the magnetic field $\vec{B}$. For given values of the speed v and magnetic field strength B, the force is greatest when $\vec{v}$ and $\vec{B}$ are perpendicular.

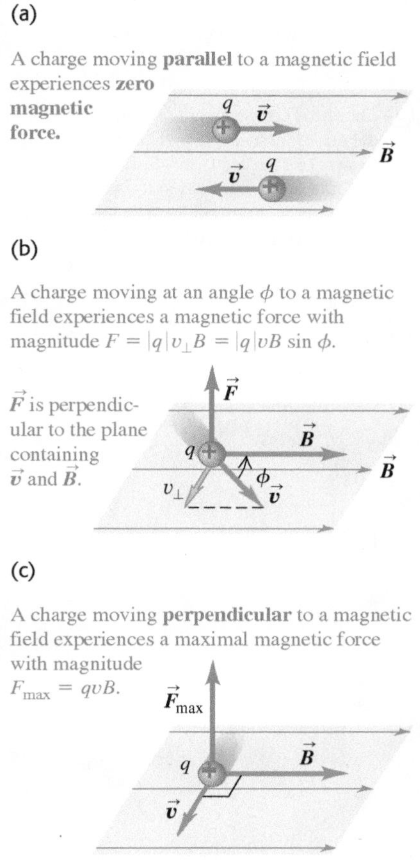
(a)
A charge moving **parallel** to a magnetic field experiences **zero magnetic force.**
(b)
A charge moving at an angle ϕ to a magnetic field experiences a magnetic force with magnitude $F = |q|v_{\perp}B = |q|vB\sin\phi$.
$\vec{F}$ is perpendicular to the plane containing $\vec{v}$ and $\vec{B}$.
(c)
A charge moving **perpendicular** to a magnetic field experiences a maximal magnetic force with magnitude $F_{max} = qvB$.

6.15 Finding the direction of the magnetic force on a moving charged particle.

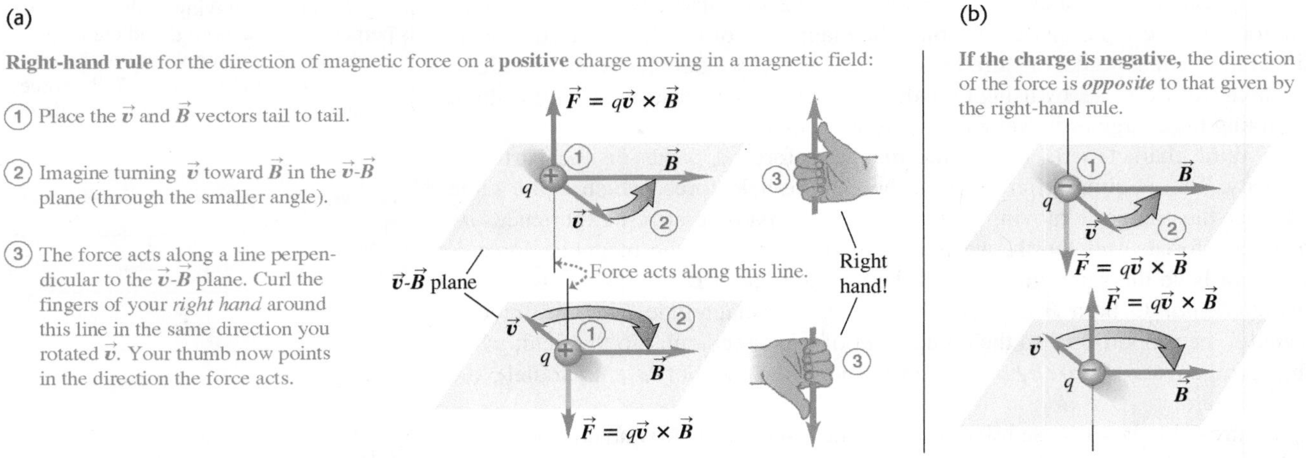
(a)
Right-hand rule for the direction of magnetic force on a **positive** charge moving in a magnetic field:
1 Place the $\vec{v}$ and $\vec{B}$ vectors tail to tail.
2 Imagine turning $\vec{v}$ toward $\vec{B}$ in the $\vec{v}$-$\vec{B}$ plane (through the smaller angle).
3 The force acts along a line perpendicular to the $\vec{v}$-$\vec{B}$ plane. Curl the fingers of your *right hand* around this line in the same direction you rotated $\vec{v}$. Your thumb now points in the direction the force acts.
$\vec{F} = q\vec{v} \times \vec{B}$
$\vec{v}$-$\vec{B}$ plane
Force acts along this line.
Right hand!
(b)
If the charge is negative, the direction of the force is ***opposite*** to that given by the right-hand rule.
$\vec{F} = q\vec{v} \times \vec{B}$

between the directions of vectors $\vec{v}$ and $\vec{B}$, we may interpret $B \sin\phi$ as the component of $\vec{B}$ perpendicular to $\vec{v}$—that is, $B_\perp$. With this notation the force magnitude is

$$F = |q|vB_\perp \tag{6.11}$$

This form is sometimes more convenient, especially in problems involving *currents* rather than individual particles.

From Eq. (6.9) the *units* of B must be the same as the units of F/qv. Therefore the SI unit of B is equivalent to $1\ \text{N}\cdot\text{s/C}\cdot\text{m}$, or, since one ampere is one coulomb per second ($1\ \text{A} = 1\ \text{C/s}$), $1\ \text{N/A}\cdot\text{m}$. This unit is called the **tesla** (abbreviated T), in honor of Nikola Tesla (1856–1943), the prominent Serbian-American scientist and inventor:

$$1\ \text{tesla} = 1\ \text{T} = 1\ \text{N/A}\cdot\text{m}$$

Another unit of B, the **gauss** ($1\ \text{G} = 10^{-4}\ \text{T}$), is also in common use.

The magnetic field of the earth is of the order of 10^{-4} T or 1 G. Magnetic fields of the order of 10 T occur in the interior of atoms and are important in the analysis of atomic spectra. The largest steady magnetic field that can be produced at present in the laboratory is about 45 T. Some pulsed-current electromagnets can produce fields of the order of 120 T for millisecond time intervals.

6.16 Two charges of the same magnitude but opposite sign moving with the same velocity in the same magnetic field. The magnetic forces on the charges are equal in magnitude but opposite in direction.

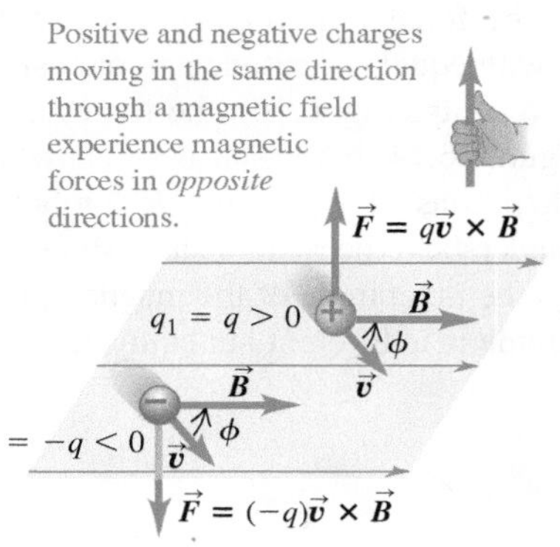
Positive and negative charges moving in the same direction through a magnetic field experience magnetic forces in *opposite* directions.
$\vec{F} = q\vec{v} \times \vec{B}$
$q_1 = q > 0$
$q_2 = -q < 0$
$\vec{F} = (-q)\vec{v} \times \vec{B}$

Measuring Magnetic Fields with Test Charges

To explore an unknown magnetic field, we can measure the magnitude and direction of the force on a *moving* test charge and then use Eq. (6.10) to determine $\vec{B}$. The electron beam in a cathode-ray tube, such as that in an older television set (not a flat screen), is a convenient device for this. The electron gun shoots out a narrow beam of electrons at a known speed. If there is no force to deflect the beam, it strikes the center of the screen.

If a magnetic field is present, in general the electron beam is deflected. But if the beam is parallel or antiparallel to the field, then $\phi = 0$ or π in Eq. (6.9) and $F = 0$; there is no force and hence no deflection. If we find that the electron beam is not deflected when its direction is parallel to a certain axis as in Fig. 6.17a, the $\vec{B}$ vector must point either up or down along that axis.

If we then turn the tube 90° (Fig. 6.17b), $\phi = \pi/2$ in Eq. (6.9) and the magnetic force is maximum; the beam is deflected in a direction perpendicular to the plane of $\vec{B}$ and $\vec{v}$. The direction and magnitude of the deflection determine the direction and magnitude of $\vec{B}$. We can perform additional experiments in which the angle between $\vec{B}$ and $\vec{v}$ is between zero and 90° to confirm Eq. (6.9). We note that the electron has a negative charge; the force in Fig. 6.17b is opposite in direction to the force on a positive charge.

When a charged particle moves through a region of space where *both* electric and magnetic fields are present, both fields exert forces on the particle. The total force $\vec{F}$ is the vector sum of the electric and magnetic forces:

$$\vec{F} = q(\vec{E} + \vec{v} \times \vec{B}) \tag{6.12}$$

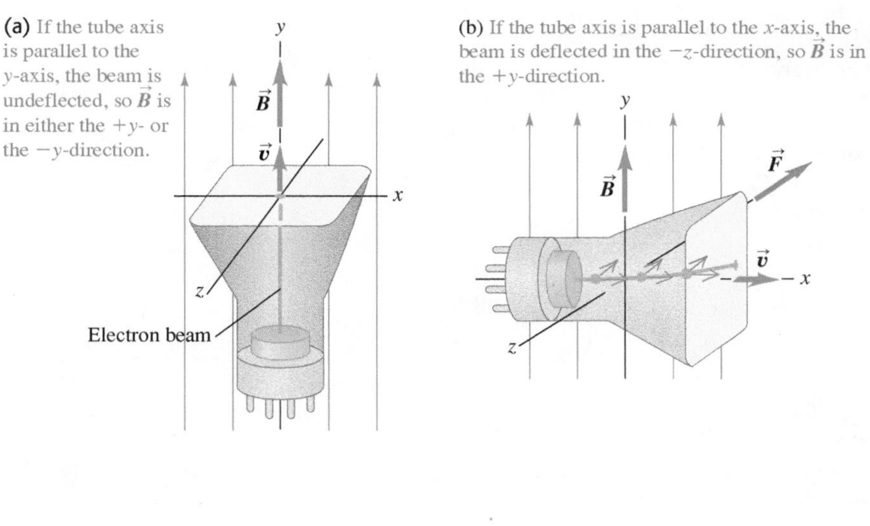
(a) If the tube axis is parallel to the y-axis, the beam is undeflected, so $\vec{B}$ is in either the +y- or the −y-direction.
y
x
z
$\vec{B}$
$\vec{v}$
Electron beam
(b) If the tube axis is parallel to the x-axis, the beam is deflected in the −z-direction, so $\vec{B}$ is in the +y-direction.
$\vec{F}$

6.17 Determining the direction of a magnetic field using a cathode-ray tube. Because electrons have a negative charge, the magnetic force $\vec{F} = q\vec{v} \times \vec{B}$ in part (b) points opposite to the direction given by the right-hand rule (see Fig. 6.14b).

CHAPTER 6 SUMMARY

Newton's law of gravitation: *Any* two bodies with masses m_1 and m_2, a distance r apart, attract each other with forces inversely proportional to r^2. These forces form an action–reaction pair and obey Newton's third law. When two or more bodies exert gravitational forces on a particular body, the total gravitational force on that individual body is the vector sum of the forces exerted by the other bodies. The gravitational interaction between spherical mass distributions, such as planets or stars, is the same as if all the mass of each distribution were concentrated at the center.

$$F_g = \frac{Gm_1m_2}{r^2} \qquad (6.2)$$

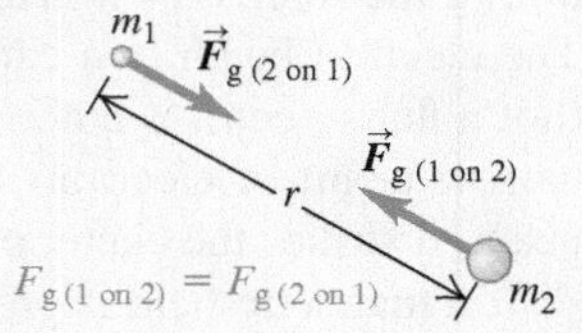

Electric charge, conductors, and insulators: The fundamental quantity in electrostatics is electric charge. There are two kinds of charge, positive and negative. Charges of the same sign repel each other; charges of opposite sign attract. Charge is conserved; the total charge in an isolated system is constant.

All ordinary matter is made of protons, neutrons, and electrons. The positive protons and electrically neutral neutrons in the nucleus of an atom are bound together by the nuclear force; the negative electrons surround the nucleus at distances much greater than the nuclear size. Electric interactions are chiefly responsible for the structure of atoms, molecules, and solids.

Conductors are materials in which charge moves easily; in insulators, charge does not move easily. Most metals are good conductors; most nonmetals are insulators.

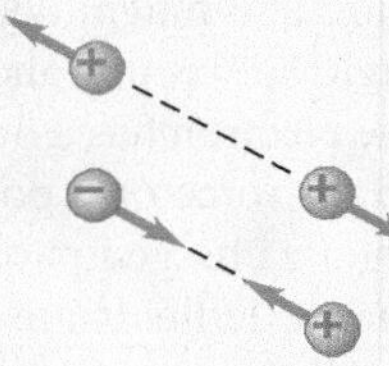

Coulomb's law: For charges q_1 and q_2 separated by a distance r, the magnitude of the electric force on either charge is proportional to the product q_1q_2 and inversely proportional to r^2. The force on each charge is along the line joining the two charges—repulsive if q_1 and q_2 have the same sign, attractive if they have opposite signs. In SI units the unit of electric charge is the coulomb, abbreviated C.

When two or more charges each exert a force on a charge, the total force on that charge is the vector sum of the forces exerted by the individual charges.

$$F = \frac{1}{4\pi\epsilon_0}\frac{|q_1q_2|}{r^2} \qquad (6.8)$$

$$\frac{1}{4\pi\epsilon_0} = 8.988 \times 10^9\ \mathrm{N\cdot m^2/C^2}$$

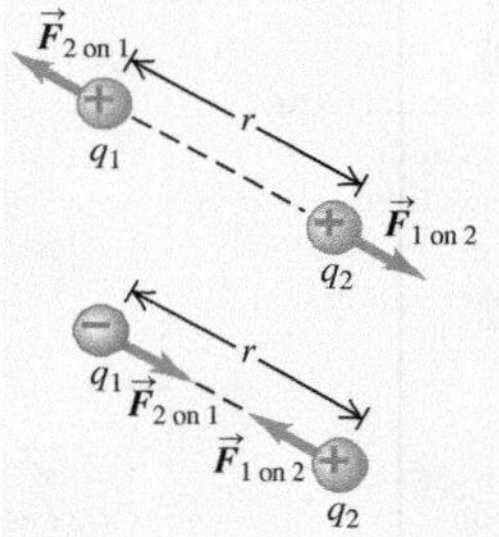

Electric field: Electric field $\vec{E}$, a vector quantity, is the force per unit charge exerted on a test charge at any point. The electric field produced by a point charge is directed radially away from or toward the charge.

$$\vec{E} = \frac{\vec{F}_0}{q_0}$$

$$\vec{E} = \frac{1}{4\pi\epsilon_0}\frac{q}{r^2}\hat{r}$$

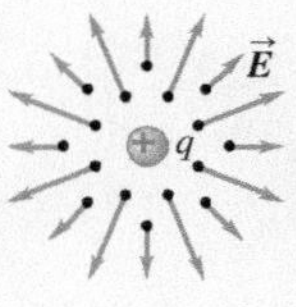

Magnetic forces: Magnetic interactions are fundamentally interactions between moving charged particles. These interactions are described by the vector magnetic field, denoted by $\vec{B}$. A particle with charge q moving with velocity $\vec{v}$ in a magnetic field $\vec{B}$ experiences a force $\vec{F}$ that is perpendicular to both $\vec{v}$ and $\vec{B}$. The SI unit of magnetic field is the tesla ($1\ \mathrm{T} = 1\ \mathrm{N/A\cdot m}$).

$$\vec{F} = q\vec{v} \times \vec{B} \qquad (6.10)$$

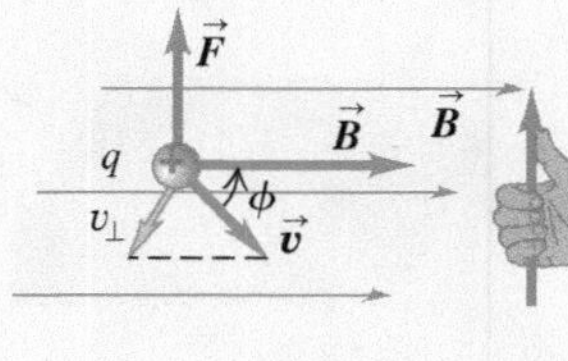

Problems

•, ••, •••: Problems of increasing difficulty. **CP**: Cumulative problems incorporating material from earlier chapters. **CALC**: Problems requiring calculus. **BIO**: Biosciences problems.

6.1 • Three identical 6.40-kg masses are hung by three identical springs, as shown in Fig. P6.1. Each spring has a force constant of 7.80 kN/m and was 12.0 cm long before any masses were attached to it. (a) Draw a free-body diagram of each mass. (b) How long is each spring when hanging as shown? (*Hint:* First isolate only the bottom mass. Then treat the bottom two masses as a system. Finally, treat all three masses as a system.)

Figure **P6.1**

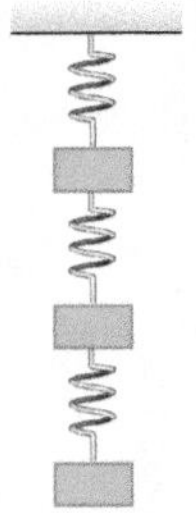

6.2 • A 2.0-kg box and a 3.0-kg box on a perfectly smooth horizontal floor have a spring of force constant 250 N/m compressed between them. If the initial compression of the spring is 6.0 cm, find the acceleration of each box the instant after they are released. Be sure to include free-body diagrams of each box as part of your solution.

6.3 • Two uniform spheres, each of mass 0.260 kg, are fixed at points A and B (Fig. P6.3). Find the magnitude and direction of the initial acceleration of a uniform sphere with mass 0.010 kg if released from rest at point P and acted on only by forces of gravitational attraction of the spheres at A and B.

Figure **P6.3**

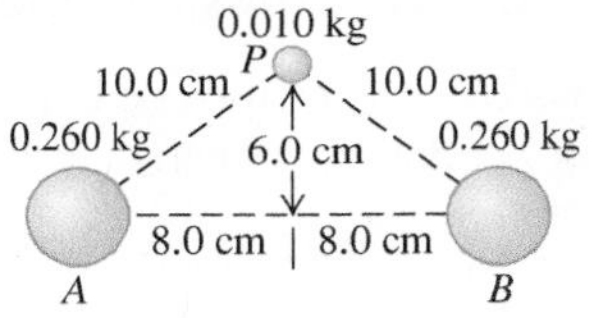

6.4 •• Find the magnitude and direction of the net gravitational force on mass A due to masses B and C in Fig. P6.4. Each mass is 2.00 kg.

Figure **P6.4**

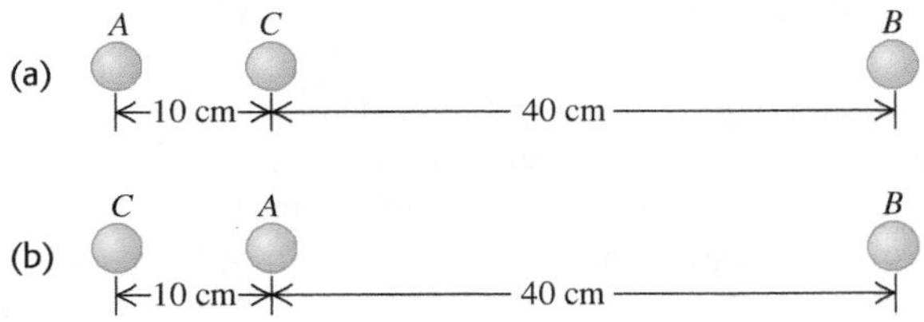

6.5 •• Two small plastic spheres are given positive electrical charges. When they are 15.0 cm apart, the repulsive force between them has magnitude 0.220 N. What is the charge on each sphere (a) if the two charges are equal and (b) if one sphere has four times the charge of the other?

6.6 •• Three point charges are arranged along the x-axis. Charge $q_1 = +3.00\ \mu C$ is at the origin, and charge $q_2 = -5.00\ \mu C$ is at $x = 0.200$ m. Charge $q_3 = -8.00\ \mu C$. Where is q_3 located if the net force on q_1 is 7.00 N in the $-x$-direction?

6.7 •• If two electrons are each 1.50×10^{-10} m from a proton, as shown in Fig. P6.7, find the magnitude and direction of the net electric force they will exert on the proton.

Figure **P6.7**

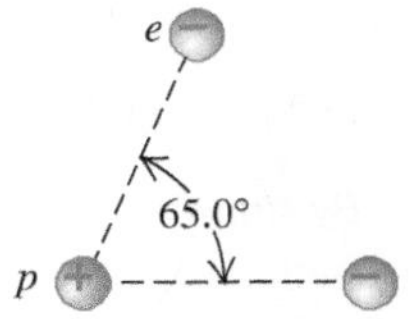

6.8 • A particle with a charge of -1.24×10^{-8} C is moving with instantaneous velocity $\vec{v} = (4.19 \times 10^4\ \text{m/s})\hat{\imath} + (-3.85 \times 10^4\ \text{m/s})\hat{\jmath}$. What is the force exerted on this particle by a magnetic field (a) $\vec{B} = (1.40\ \text{T})\hat{\imath}$ and (b) $\vec{B} = (1.40\ \text{T})\hat{k}$?

6.9 •• **CP** A particle with charge 7.80 μC is moving with velocity $\vec{v} = -(3.80 \times 10^3\ \text{m/s})\hat{\jmath}$. The magnetic force on the particle is measured to be $\vec{F} = +(7.60 \times 10^{-3}\ \text{N})\hat{\imath} - (5.20 \times 10^{-3}\ \text{N})\hat{k}$. (a) Calculate all the components of the magnetic field you can from this information. (b) Are there components of the magnetic field that are not determined by the measurement of the force? Explain. (c) Calculate the scalar product $\vec{B} \cdot \vec{F}$. What is the angle between $\vec{B}$ and $\vec{F}$?

6.10 •• Calculate the percent difference between your weight in Sacramento, near sea level, and at the top of Mount Everest, which is 8800 m above sea level.

6.11 •• **CP** Two identical spheres with mass m are hung from silk threads of length L, as shown in Fig. P6.11. Each sphere has the same charge, so $q_1 = q_2 = q$. The radius of each sphere is very small compared to the distance between the spheres, so they may be treated as point charges. Show that if the angle θ is small, the equilibrium separation d between the spheres is $d = (q^2L/2\pi\epsilon_0 mg)^{1/3}$. (*Hint:* If θ is small, then $\tan\theta \cong \sin\theta$.)

Figure **P6.11**

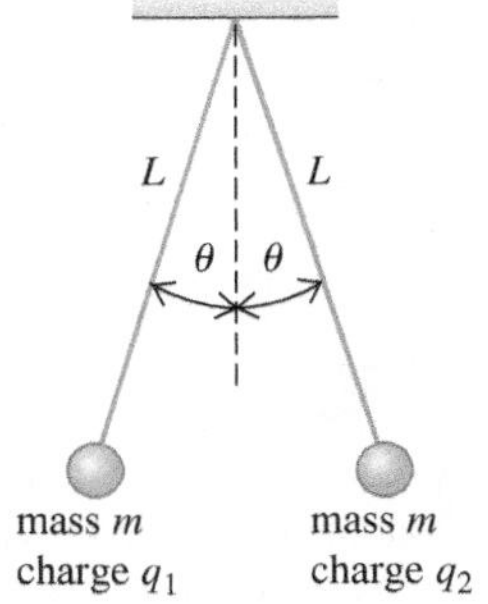

Answers

Chapter Opening Question ?

Neither; the upward force of the air has the *same* magnitude as the force of gravity. Although the skydiver and parachute are descending, their vertical velocity is constant and so their vertical acceleration is zero. Hence the net vertical force on the skydiver and parachute must also be zero, and the individual vertical forces must balance.

7 MOMENTUM, IMPULSE, AND COLLISIONS

? After billiards have been hit by the cue ball, they go in all directions. What can we say collectively about the motion of the balls immediately after they have been struck?

LEARNING GOALS

By studying this chapter, you will learn:

- The meaning of the momentum of a particle, and how the impulse of the net force acting on a particle causes its momentum to change.
- The conditions under which the total momentum of a system of particles is constant (conserved).
- How to solve problems in which two bodies collide with each other.
- The definition of the center of mass of a system, and what determines how the center of mass moves.

There are many questions involving forces that cannot be answered by directly applying Newton's second law, $\sum\vec{F} = m\vec{a}$. For example, when a moving van collides head-on with a compact car, what determines which way the wreckage moves after the collision? In playing pool, how do you decide how to aim the cue ball in order to knock the eight ball into the pocket? And when a meteorite collides with the earth, how much is the Earth's orbit changed by the impact?

A common theme of all these questions is that they involve forces about which we know very little: the forces between the car and the moving van, between the two pool balls, or between the meteorite and the earth. Remarkably, we will find in this chapter that we don't have to know *anything* about these forces to answer questions of this kind!

Our approach uses two new concepts, *momentum* and *impulse,* and a new conservation law, *conservation of momentum.* This conservation law is every bit as important as the law of conservation of energy. The law of conservation of momentum is valid even in situations in which Newton's laws are inadequate, such as bodies moving at very high speeds (near the speed of light) or objects on a very small scale (such as the constituents of atoms). Within the domain of Newtonian mechanics, conservation of momentum enables us to analyze many situations that would be very difficult if we tried to use Newton's laws directly. Among these are *collision* problems, in which two bodies collide and can exert very large forces on each other for a short time.

7.1 Momentum and Impulse

In Chapter 9 we re-expressed Newton's second law for a particle, $\sum\vec{F} = m\vec{a}$, in terms of the work–energy theorem. This theorem helped us tackle a great number of physics problems and led us to the law of conservation of energy. Let's now return to $\sum\vec{F} = m\vec{a}$ and see yet another useful way to restate this fundamental law.

Newton's Second Law in Terms of Momentum

Consider a particle of constant mass m. Because $\vec{a} = d\vec{v}/dt$, we can write Newton's second law for this particle as

$$\sum\vec{F} = m\frac{d\vec{v}}{dt} = \frac{d}{dt}(m\vec{v}) \quad (7.1)$$

We can move the mass m inside the derivative because it is constant. Thus Newton's second law says that the net force $\sum\vec{F}$ acting on a particle equals the time rate of change of the combination $m\vec{v}$, the product of the particle's mass and velocity. We'll call this combination the **momentum,** or **linear momentum,** of the particle. Using the symbol $\vec{p}$ for momentum, we have

$$\vec{p} = m\vec{v} \quad \text{(definition of momentum)} \quad (7.2)$$

The greater the mass m and speed v of a particle, the greater is its magnitude of momentum mv. Keep in mind, however, that momentum is a *vector* quantity with the same direction as the particle's velocity (Fig. 7.1). Hence a car driving north at 20 m/s and an identical car driving east at 20 m/s have the same *magnitude* of momentum (mv) but different momentum *vectors* ($m\vec{v}$) because their directions are different.

7.1 The velocity and momentum vectors of a particle.

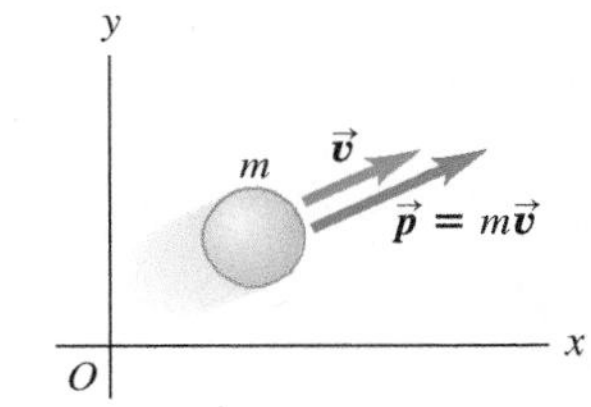

Momentum $\vec{p}$ is a vector quantity; a particle's momentum has the same direction as its velocity $\vec{v}$.

We often express the momentum of a particle in terms of its components. If the particle has velocity components v_x, v_y, and v_z, then its momentum components p_x, p_y, and p_z (which we also call the *x-momentum, y-momentum,* and *z-momentum*) are given by

$$p_x = mv_x \qquad p_y = mv_y \qquad p_z = mv_z \quad (7.3)$$

These three component equations are equivalent to Eq. (7.2).

The units of the magnitude of momentum are units of mass times speed; the SI units of momentum are kg · m/s. The plural of momentum is "momenta."

If we now substitute the definition of momentum, Eq. (7.2), into Eq. (7.1), we get

$$\sum\vec{F} = \frac{d\vec{p}}{dt} \quad \text{(Newton's second law in terms of momentum)} \quad (7.4)$$

The net force (vector sum of all forces) acting on a particle equals the time rate of change of momentum of the particle. This, not $\sum\vec{F} = m\vec{a}$, is the form in which Newton originally stated his second law (although he called momentum the "quantity of motion"). This law is valid only in inertial frames of reference.

According to Eq. (7.4), a rapid change in momentum requires a large net force, while a gradual change in momentum requires less net force. This principle is used in the design of automobile safety devices such as air bags.

The Impulse–Momentum Theorem

A particle's momentum $\vec{p} = m\vec{v}$ and its kinetic energy $K = \frac{1}{2}mv^2$ both depend on the mass and velocity of the particle. What is the fundamental difference between these two quantities? A purely mathematical answer is that momentum is a vector whose magnitude is proportional to speed, while kinetic energy is a scalar proportional to the speed squared. But to see the *physical* difference between momentum and kinetic energy, we must first define a quantity closely related to momentum called *impulse.*

Let's first consider a particle acted on by a *constant* net force $\sum\vec{F}$ during a time interval Δt from t_1 to t_2. (We'll look at the case of varying forces shortly.) The **impulse** of the net force, denoted by $\vec{J}$, is defined to be the product of the net force and the time interval:

$$\vec{J} = \sum\vec{F}(t_2 - t_1) = \sum\vec{F}\,\Delta t \qquad \text{(assuming constant net force)} \tag{7.5}$$

Impulse is a vector quantity; its direction is the same as the net force $\sum\vec{F}$. Its magnitude is the product of the magnitude of the net force and the length of time that the net force acts. The SI unit of impulse is the newton-second (N·s). Because $1\text{ N} = 1\text{ kg}\cdot\text{m/s}^2$, an alternative set of units for impulse is kg·m/s, the same as the units of momentum.

To see what impulse is good for, let's go back to Newton's second law as restated in terms of momentum, Eq. (7.4). If the net force $\sum\vec{F}$ is constant, then $d\vec{p}/dt$ is also constant. In that case, $d\vec{p}/dt$ is equal to the *total* change in momentum $\vec{p}_2 - \vec{p}_1$ during the time interval $t_2 - t_1$, divided by the interval:

$$\sum\vec{F} = \frac{\vec{p}_2 - \vec{p}_1}{t_2 - t_1}$$

Multiplying this equation by $(t_2 - t_1)$, we have

$$\sum\vec{F}(t_2 - t_1) = \vec{p}_2 - \vec{p}_1$$

Comparing with Eq. (7.5), we end up with a result called the **impulse–momentum theorem:**

$$\vec{J} = \vec{p}_2 - \vec{p}_1 \qquad \text{(impulse–momentum theorem)} \tag{7.6}$$

The change in momentum of a particle during a time interval equals the impulse of the net force that acts on the particle during that interval.

The impulse–momentum theorem also holds when forces are not constant. To see this, we integrate both sides of Newton's second law $\sum\vec{F} = d\vec{p}/dt$ over time between the limits t_1 and t_2:

$$\int_{t_1}^{t_2}\sum\vec{F}\,dt = \int_{t_1}^{t_2}\frac{d\vec{p}}{dt}\,dt = \int_{\vec{p}_1}^{\vec{p}_2} d\vec{p} = \vec{p}_2 - \vec{p}_1$$

The integral on the left is defined to be the impulse $\vec{J}$ of the net force $\sum\vec{F}$ during this interval:

$$\vec{J} = \int_{t_1}^{t_2}\sum\vec{F}\,dt \qquad \text{(general definition of impulse)} \tag{7.7}$$

With this definition, the impulse–momentum theorem $\vec{J} = \vec{p}_2 - \vec{p}_1$, Eq. (7.6), is valid even when the net force $\sum\vec{F}$ varies with time.

We can define an *average* net force $\vec{F}_{\text{av}}$ such that even when $\sum\vec{F}$ is not constant, the impulse $\vec{J}$ is given by

$$\vec{J} = \vec{F}_{\text{av}}(t_2 - t_1) \tag{7.8}$$

When $\sum\vec{F}$ is constant, $\sum\vec{F} = \vec{F}_{\text{av}}$ and Eq. (7.8) reduces to Eq. (7.5).

Figure 7.2a shows the x-component of net force $\sum F_x$ as a function of time during a collision. This might represent the force on a soccer ball that is in contact with a player's foot from time t_1 to t_2. The x-component of impulse during this interval is represented by the red area under the curve between t_1 and t_2. This

7.2 The meaning of the area under a graph of ΣF_x versus t.

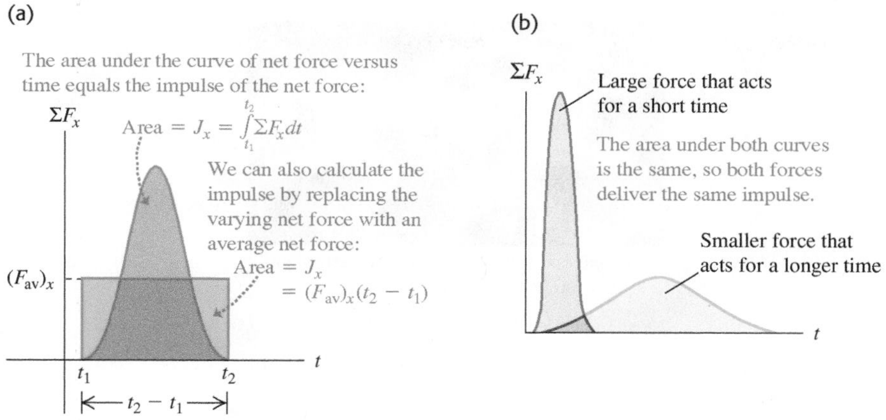
(a)
The area under the curve of net force versus time equals the impulse of the net force:
ΣF_x
Area = $J_x = \int_{t_1}^{t_2} \Sigma F_x dt$
We can also calculate the impulse by replacing the varying net force with an average net force:
Area = J_x
= $(F_{av})_x(t_2 - t_1)$
$(F_{av})_x$
t
t_1
t_2
$t_2 - t_1$
(b)
ΣF_x
Large force that acts for a short time
The area under both curves is the same, so both forces deliver the same impulse.
Smaller force that acts for a longer time
t

area is equal to the green rectangular area bounded by t_1, t_2, and $(F_{av})_x$, so $(F_{av})_x(t_2 - t_1)$ is equal to the impulse of the actual time-varying force during the same interval. Note that a large force acting for a short time can have the same impulse as a smaller force acting for a longer time if the areas under the force–time curves are the same (Fig. 7.2b). In this language, an automobile airbag provides the same impulse to the driver as would the steering wheel or the dashboard by applying a weaker and less injurious force for a longer time.

Impulse and momentum are both vector quantities, and Eqs. (7.5)–(7.8) are all vector equations. In specific problems, it is often easiest to use them in component form:

$$J_x = \int_{t_1}^{t_2} \Sigma F_x \, dt = (F_{av})_x(t_2 - t_1) = p_{2x} - p_{1x} = mv_{2x} - mv_{1x}$$
$$J_y = \int_{t_1}^{t_2} \Sigma F_y \, dt = (F_{av})_y(t_2 - t_1) = p_{2y} - p_{1y} = mv_{2y} - mv_{1y} \qquad (7.9)$$

and similarly for the z-component.

7.2 Conservation of Momentum

The concept of momentum is particularly important in situations in which we have two or more bodies that *interact*. To see why, let's consider first an idealized system of two bodies that interact with each other but not with anything else—for example, two astronauts who touch each other as they float freely in the zero-gravity environment of outer space (Fig. 7.3). Think of the astronauts as particles. Each particle exerts a force on the other; according to Newton's third law, the two forces are always equal in magnitude and opposite in direction. Hence, the *impulses* that act on the two particles are equal and opposite, and the changes in momentum of the two particles are equal and opposite.

Let's go over that again with some new terminology. For any system, the forces that the particles of the system exert on each other are called **internal forces.** Forces exerted on any part of the system by some object outside it are called **external forces.** For the system shown in Fig. 7.3, the internal forces are $\vec{F}_{B \text{ on } A}$, exerted by particle B on particle A, and $\vec{F}_{A \text{ on } B}$, exerted by particle A on particle B. There are *no* external forces; when this is the case, we have an **isolated system.**

The net force on particle A is $\vec{F}_{B \text{ on } A}$ and the net force on particle B is $\vec{F}_{A \text{ on } B}$, so from Eq. (7.4) the rates of change of the momenta of the two particles are

7.3 Two astronauts push each other as they float freely in the zero-gravity environment of space.

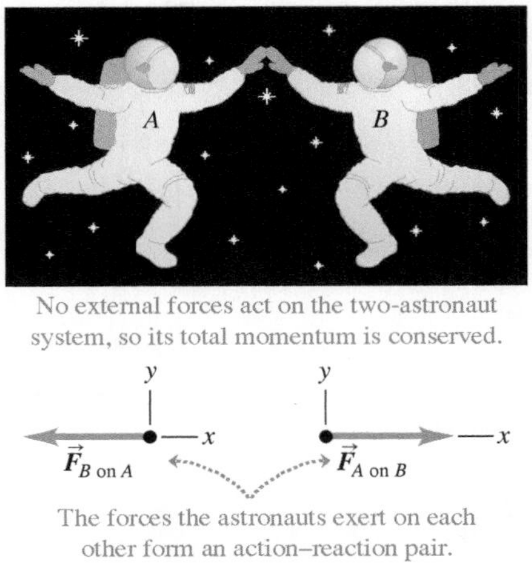
A
B
No external forces act on the two-astronaut system, so its total momentum is conserved.
y
x
y
x
$\vec{F}_{B\text{ on }A}$
$\vec{F}_{A\text{ on }B}$
The forces the astronauts exert on each other form an action–reaction pair.

$$\vec{F}_{B\text{ on }A} = \frac{d\vec{p}_A}{dt} \qquad \vec{F}_{A\text{ on }B} = \frac{d\vec{p}_B}{dt} \tag{7.10}$$

The momentum of each particle changes, but these changes are related to each other by Newton's third law: The two forces $\vec{F}_{B\text{ on }A}$ and $\vec{F}_{A\text{ on }B}$ are always equal in magnitude and opposite in direction. That is, $\vec{F}_{B\text{ on }A} = -\vec{F}_{A\text{ on }B}$, so $\vec{F}_{B\text{ on }A} + \vec{F}_{A\text{ on }B} = \mathbf{0}$. Adding together the two equations in Eq. (7.10), we have

$$\vec{F}_{B\text{ on }A} + \vec{F}_{A\text{ on }B} = \frac{d\vec{p}_A}{dt} + \frac{d\vec{p}_B}{dt} = \frac{d(\vec{p}_A + \vec{p}_B)}{dt} = \mathbf{0} \tag{7.11}$$

The rates of change of the two momenta are equal and opposite, so the rate of change of the vector sum $\vec{p}_A + \vec{p}_B$ is zero. We now define the **total momentum** $\vec{P}$ of the system of two particles as the vector sum of the momenta of the individual particles; that is,

$$\vec{P} = \vec{p}_A + \vec{p}_B \tag{7.12}$$

Then Eq. (7.11) becomes, finally,

$$\vec{F}_{B\text{ on }A} + \vec{F}_{A\text{ on }B} = \frac{d\vec{P}}{dt} = \mathbf{0} \tag{7.13}$$

The time rate of change of the *total* momentum $\vec{P}$ is zero. Hence the total momentum of the system is constant, even though the individual momenta of the particles that make up the system can change.

If external forces are also present, they must be included on the left side of Eq. (7.13) along with the internal forces. Then the total momentum is, in general, not constant. But if the vector sum of the external forces is zero, as in Fig. 7.4, these forces have no effect on the left side of Eq. (7.13), and $d\vec{P}/dt$ is again zero. Thus we have the following general result:

If the vector sum of the external forces on a system is zero, the total momentum of the system is constant.

7.4 Two ice skaters push each other as they skate on a frictionless, horizontal surface. (Compare to Fig. 7.3.)

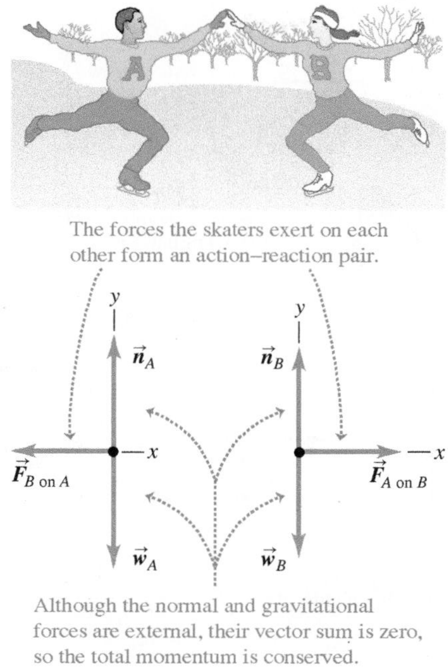
A
B
The forces the skaters exert on each other form an action–reaction pair.
y
y
$\vec{n}_A$
$\vec{n}_B$
x
x
$\vec{F}_{B \text{ on } A}$
$\vec{F}_{A \text{ on } B}$
$\vec{w}_A$
$\vec{w}_B$
Although the normal and gravitational forces are external, their vector sum is zero, so the total momentum is conserved.

This is the simplest form of the **principle of conservation of momentum.** This principle is a direct consequence of Newton's third law. What makes this principle useful is that it doesn't depend on the detailed nature of the internal forces that act between members of the system. This means that we can apply conservation of momentum even if (as is often the case) we know very little about the internal forces. We have used Newton's second law to derive this principle, so we have to be careful to use it only in inertial frames of reference.

We can generalize this principle for a system that contains any number of particles $A, B, C, \ldots$ interacting only with one another. The total momentum of such a system is

$$\vec{P} = \vec{p}_A + \vec{p}_B + \cdots = m_A\vec{v}_A + m_B\vec{v}_B + \cdots \quad \text{(total momentum of a system of particles)} \tag{7.14}$$

We make the same argument as before: The total rate of change of momentum of the system due to each action–reaction pair of internal forces is zero. Thus the total rate of change of momentum of the entire system is zero whenever the vector sum of the external forces acting on it is zero. The internal forces can change the momenta of individual particles in the system but not the *total* momentum of the system.

CAUTION **Conservation of momentum means conservation of its components** When you apply the conservation of momentum to a system, remember that momentum is a *vector* quantity. Hence you must use vector addition to compute the total momentum of a system (Fig. 7.5). Using components is usually the simplest method. If p_{Ax}, p_{Ay}, and p_{Az} are the components of momentum of particle A, and similarly for the other particles, then Eq. (7.14) is equivalent to the component equations

$$\begin{aligned} P_x &= p_{Ax} + p_{Bx} + \cdots \\ P_y &= p_{Ay} + p_{By} + \cdots \\ P_z &= p_{Az} + p_{Bz} + \cdots \end{aligned} \tag{7.15}$$

If the vector sum of the external forces on the system is zero, then P_x, P_y, and P_z are all constant.

7.5 When applying conservation of momentum, remember that momentum is a vector quantity!

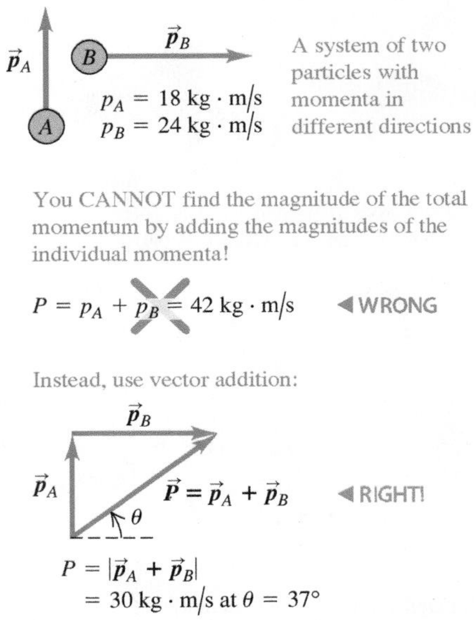
$\vec{p}_A$
$\vec{p}_B$
B
A
$p_A = 18\ \text{kg} \cdot \text{m/s}$
$p_B = 24\ \text{kg} \cdot \text{m/s}$
A system of two particles with momenta in different directions
You CANNOT find the magnitude of the total momentum by adding the magnitudes of the individual momenta!
$P = p_A + p_B = 42\ \text{kg} \cdot \text{m/s}$
WRONG
Instead, use vector addition:
$\vec{p}_B$
$\vec{p}_A$
$\vec{P} = \vec{p}_A + \vec{p}_B$
θ
RIGHT!
$P = |\vec{p}_A + \vec{p}_B|$
$= 30\ \text{kg} \cdot \text{m/s at } \theta = 37°$

To most people the term *collision* is likely to mean some sort of automotive disaster. We'll use it in that sense, but we'll also broaden the meaning to include any strong interaction between bodies that lasts a relatively short time. So we include not only car accidents but also balls colliding on a billiard table, neutrons hitting atomic nuclei in a nuclear reactor, the impact of a meteor on the Arizona desert, and a close encounter of a spacecraft with the planet Saturn.

If the forces between the bodies are much larger than any external forces, as is the case in most collisions, we can neglect the external forces entirely and treat the bodies as an *isolated* system. Then momentum is conserved and the total momentum of the system has the same value before and after the collision. Two cars colliding at an icy intersection provide a good example. Even two cars colliding on dry pavement can be treated as an isolated system during the collision if the forces between the cars are much larger than the friction forces of pavement against tires.

7.3 Center of Mass

We can restate the principle of conservation of momentum in a useful way by using the concept of **center of mass.** Suppose we have several particles with masses m_1, m_2, and so on. Let the coordinates of m_1 be (x_1, y_1), those of m_2 be (x_2, y_2), and so on. We define the center of mass of the system as the point that has coordinates given by

$$x_{cm} = \frac{m_1x_1 + m_2x_2 + m_3x_3 + \cdots}{m_1 + m_2 + m_3 + \cdots} = \frac{\sum_i m_ix_i}{\sum_i m_i}$$

$$y_{cm} = \frac{m_1y_1 + m_2y_2 + m_3y_3 + \cdots}{m_1 + m_2 + m_3 + \cdots} = \frac{\sum_i m_iy_i}{\sum_i m_i} \quad \text{(center of mass)} \quad (7.16)$$

The position vector $\vec{r}_{cm}$ of the center of mass can be expressed in terms of the position vectors $\vec{r}_1, \vec{r}_2, \ldots$ of the particles as

$$\vec{r}_{cm} = \frac{m_1\vec{r}_1 + m_2\vec{r}_2 + m_3\vec{r}_3 + \cdots}{m_1 + m_2 + m_3 + \cdots} = \frac{\sum_i m_i\vec{r}_i}{\sum_i m_i} \quad \text{(center of mass)} \qquad (7.17)$$

In statistical language, the center of mass is a *mass-weighted average* position of the particles.

For solid bodies, in which we have (at least on a macroscopic level) a continuous distribution of matter, the sums in Eqs. (7.16) have to be replaced by integrals. The calculations can get quite involved, but we can say three general things about such problems (Fig. 7.6). First, whenever a homogeneous body has a geometric center, such as a billiard ball, a sugar cube, or a can of frozen orange juice, the center of mass is at the geometric center. Second, whenever a body has an axis of symmetry, such as a wheel or a pulley, the center of mass always lies on that axis. Third, there is no law that says the center of mass has to be within the body. For example, the center of mass of a donut is right in the middle of the hole. We discussed the center of gravity in chapter 3 in the context of rigid objects; the center of mass is the same idea, just for objects which are not necessarily connected to each other.

Motion of the Center of Mass

To see the significance of the center of mass of a collection of particles, we must ask what happens to the center of mass when the particles move. The x- and y-components of velocity of the center of mass, $v_{cm\text{-}x}$ and $v_{cm\text{-}y}$, are the time derivatives of x_{cm} and y_{cm}. Also, dx_1/dt is the x-component of velocity of particle 1, and so on, so $dx_1/dt = v_{1x}$, and so on. Taking time derivatives of Eqs. (7.16), we get

$$v_{cm\text{-}x} = \frac{m_1v_{1x} + m_2v_{2x} + m_3v_{3x} + \cdots}{m_1 + m_2 + m_3 + \cdots}$$
$$v_{cm\text{-}y} = \frac{m_1v_{1y} + m_2v_{2y} + m_3v_{3y} + \cdots}{m_1 + m_2 + m_3 + \cdots} \qquad (7.18)$$

These equations are equivalent to the single vector equation obtained by taking the time derivative of Eq. (7.17):

$$\vec{v}_{cm} = \frac{m_1\vec{v}_1 + m_2\vec{v}_2 + m_3\vec{v}_3 + \cdots}{m_1 + m_2 + m_3 + \cdots} \qquad (7.19)$$

7.6 Locating the center of mass of a symmetrical object.

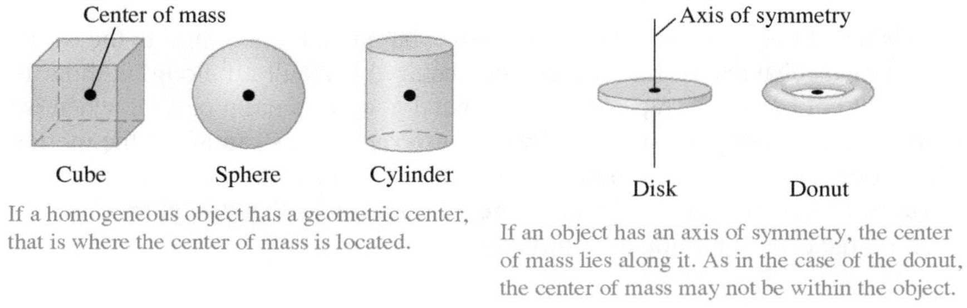
Center of mass
Axis of symmetry
Cube
Sphere
Cylinder
Disk
Donut
If a homogeneous object has a geometric center, that is where the center of mass is located.
If an object has an axis of symmetry, the center of mass lies along it. As in the case of the donut, the center of mass may not be within the object.

We denote the *total* mass $m_1 + m_2 + \cdots$ by M. We can then rewrite Eq. (7.19) as

$$M\vec{v}_{cm} = m_1\vec{v}_1 + m_2\vec{v}_2 + m_3\vec{v}_3 + \cdots = \vec{P} \tag{7.20}$$

The right side is simply the total momentum $\vec{P}$ of the system. Thus we have proved that *the total momentum is equal to the total mass times the velocity of the center of mass.* When you catch a baseball, you are really catching a collection of a very large number of molecules of masses $m_1, m_2, m_3, \ldots$. The impulse you feel is due to the total momentum of this entire collection. But this impulse is the same as if you were catching a single particle of mass $M = m_1 + m_2 + m_3 + \cdots$ moving with velocity $\vec{v}_{cm}$, the velocity of the collection's center of mass. So Eq. (7.20) helps to justify representing an extended body as a particle.

For a system of particles on which the net external force is zero, so that the total momentum $\vec{P}$ is constant, the velocity of the center of mass $\vec{v}_{cm} = \vec{P}/M$ is also constant. Suppose we mark the center of mass of a wrench and then slide the wrench with a spinning motion across a smooth, horizontal tabletop. The overall motion appears complicated, but the center of mass follows a straight line, as though all the mass were concentrated at that point.

External Forces and Center-of-Mass Motion

If the net external force on a system of particles is not zero, then total momentum is not conserved and the velocity of the center of mass changes. Let's look at the relationship between the motion of the center of mass and the forces acting on the system.

Equations (7.19) and (7.20) give the *velocity* of the center of mass in terms of the velocities of the individual particles. We take the time derivatives of these equations to show that the *accelerations* are related in the same way. Let $\vec{a}_{cm} = d\vec{v}_{cm}/dt$ be the acceleration of the center of mass; then we find

$$M\vec{a}_{cm} = m_1\vec{a}_1 + m_2\vec{a}_2 + m_3\vec{a}_3 + \cdots \tag{7.21}$$

Now $m_1\vec{a}_1$ is equal to the vector sum of forces on the first particle, and so on, so the right side of Eq. (7.21) is equal to the vector sum $\sum\vec{F}$ of *all* the forces on *all* the particles. We can classify each force as *external* or *internal.* The sum of all forces on all the particles is then

$$\sum\vec{F} = \sum\vec{F}_{ext} + \sum\vec{F}_{int} = M\vec{a}_{cm}$$

Because of Newton's third law, the internal forces all cancel in pairs, and $\sum\vec{F}_{int} = \mathbf{0}$. What survives on the left side is the sum of only the *external* forces:

$$\sum\vec{F}_{ext} = M\vec{a}_{cm} \quad \text{(body or collection of particles)} \tag{7.22}$$

When a body or a collection of particles is acted on by external forces, the center of mass moves just as though all the mass were concentrated at that point and it were acted on by a net force equal to the sum of the external forces on the system.

This result may not sound very impressive, but in fact it is central to the whole subject of mechanics. In fact, we've been using this result all along; without it, we would not be able to represent an extended body as a point particle when we apply Newton's laws. It explains why only *external* forces can affect the motion of an extended body. If you pull upward on your belt, your belt exerts an equal downward force on your hands; these are *internal* forces that cancel and have no effect on the overall motion of your body.

7.7 A shell explodes into two fragments in flight. If air resistance is ignored, the center of mass continues on the same trajectory as the shell's path before exploding.

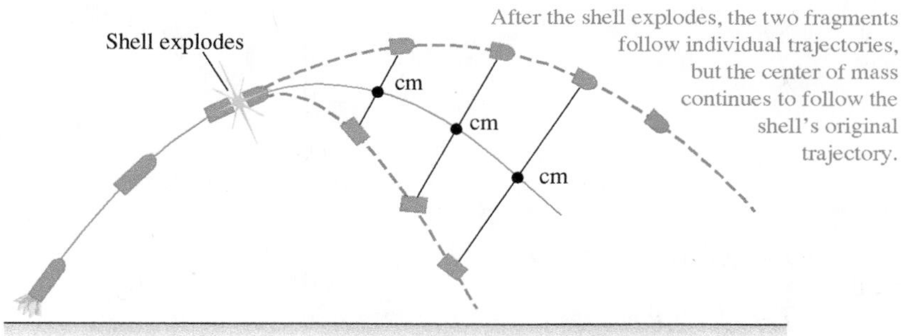
Shell explodes
cm
cm
cm
After the shell explodes, the two fragments follow individual trajectories, but the center of mass continues to follow the shell's original trajectory.

Suppose a cannon shell traveling in a parabolic trajectory (neglecting air resistance) explodes in flight, splitting into two fragments with equal mass (Fig. 7.7). The fragments follow new parabolic paths, but the center of mass continues on the original parabolic trajectory, just as though all the mass were still concentrated at that point. A skyrocket exploding in air is a spectacular example of this effect.

This property of the center of mass is important when we analyze the motion of rigid bodies. We describe the motion of an extended body as a combination of translational motion of the center of mass and rotational motion about an axis through the center of mass. This property also plays an important role in the motion of astronomical objects. It's not correct to say that the moon orbits the earth; rather, the earth and moon both move in orbits around their center of mass.

There's one more useful way to describe the motion of a system of particles. Using $\vec{a}_{cm} = d\vec{v}_{cm}/dt$, we can rewrite Eq. (8.33) as

$$M\vec{a}_{cm} = M\frac{d\vec{v}_{cm}}{dt} = \frac{d(M\vec{v}_{cm})}{dt} = \frac{d\vec{P}}{dt} \qquad (7.23)$$

The total system mass M is constant, so we're allowed to move it inside the derivative. Substituting Eq. (7.23) into Eq. (7.22), we find

$$\Sigma\vec{F}_{ext} = \frac{d\vec{P}}{dt} \quad \text{(extended body or system of particles)} \qquad (7.24)$$

This equation looks like Eq. (7.4). The difference is that Eq. (7.24) describes a *system* of particles, such as an extended body, while Eq. (7.4) describes a single particle. The interactions between the particles that make up the system can change the individual momenta of the particles, but the *total* momentum $\vec{P}$ of the system can be changed only by external forces acting from outside the system.

Finally, we note that if the net external force is zero, Eq. (7.22) shows that the acceleration $\vec{a}_{cm}$ of the center of mass is zero. So the center-of-mass velocity $\vec{v}_{cm}$ is constant. From Eq. (7.24) the total momentum $\vec{P}$ is also constant. This reaffirms our statement of the principle of conservation of momentum.

CHAPTER 7 SUMMARY

Momentum of a particle: The momentum $\vec{p}$ of a particle is a vector quantity equal to the product of the particle's mass m and velocity $\vec{v}$. Newton's second law says that the net force on a particle is equal to the rate of change of the particle's momentum.

$$\vec{p} = m\vec{v} \qquad (7.2)$$

$$\Sigma\vec{F} = \frac{d\vec{p}}{dt} \qquad (7.4)$$

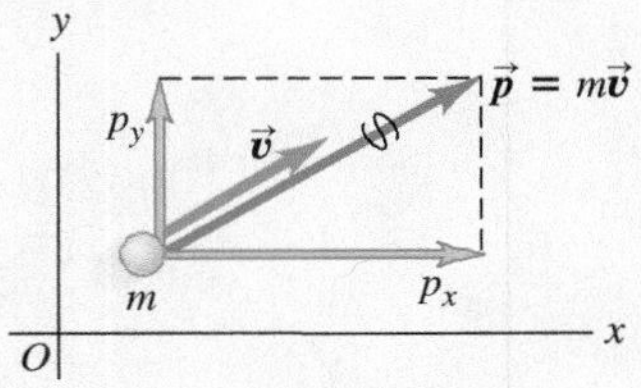

Impulse and momentum: If a constant net force $\Sigma\vec{F}$ acts on a particle for a time interval Δt from t_1 to t_2, the impulse $\vec{J}$ of the net force is the product of the net force and the time interval. If $\Sigma\vec{F}$ varies with time, $\vec{J}$ is the integral of the net force over the time interval. In any case, the change in a particle's momentum during a time interval equals the impulse of the net force that acted on the particle during that interval. The momentum of a particle equals the impulse that accelerated it from rest to its present speed.

$$\vec{J} = \Sigma\vec{F}(t_2 - t_1) = \Sigma\vec{F}\,\Delta t \qquad (7.5)$$

$$\vec{J} = \int_{t_1}^{t_2} \Sigma\vec{F}\,dt \qquad (7.7)$$

$$\vec{J} = \vec{p}_2 - \vec{p}_1 \qquad (7.6)$$

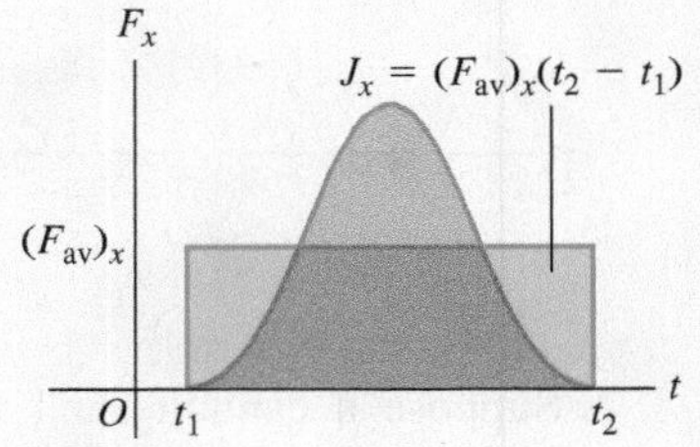

Conservation of momentum: An internal force is a force exerted by one part of a system on another. An external force is a force exerted on any part of a system by something outside the system. If the net external force on a system is zero, the total momentum of the system $\vec{P}$ (the vector sum of the momenta of the individual particles that make up the system) is constant, or conserved. Each component of total momentum is separately conserved.

$$\vec{P} = \vec{p}_A + \vec{p}_B + \cdots$$
$$= m_A\vec{v}_A + m_B\vec{v}_B + \cdots \qquad (7.14)$$

If $\Sigma\vec{F} = \mathbf{0}$, then $\vec{P}$ = constant.

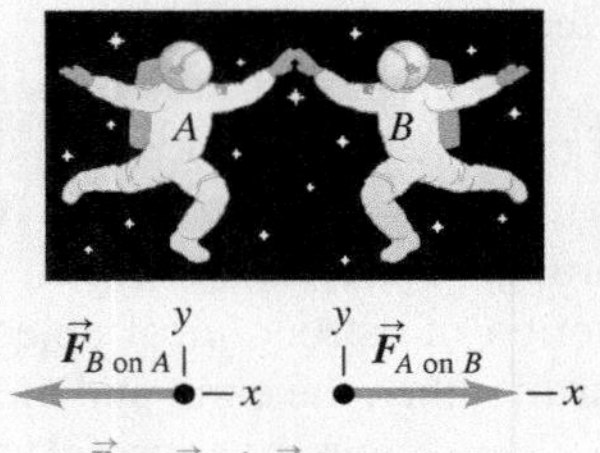

Center of mass: The position vector of the center of mass of a system of particles, $\vec{r}_{cm}$, is a weighted average of the positions $\vec{r}_1, \vec{r}_2, \ldots$ of the individual particles. The total momentum $\vec{P}$ of a system equals its total mass M multiplied by the velocity of its center of mass, $\vec{v}_{cm}$. The center of mass moves as though all the mass M were concentrated at that point. If the net external force on the system is zero, the center-of-mass velocity $\vec{v}_{cm}$ is constant. If the net external force is not zero, the center of mass accelerates as though it were a particle of mass M being acted on by the same net external force.

$$\vec{r}_{cm} = \frac{m_1\vec{r}_1 + m_2\vec{r}_2 + m_3\vec{r}_3 + \cdots}{m_1 + m_2 + m_3 + \cdots}$$
$$= \frac{\Sigma_i m_i \vec{r}_i}{\Sigma_i m_i} \qquad (7.17)$$

$$\vec{P} = m_1\vec{v}_1 + m_2\vec{v}_2 + m_3\vec{v}_3 + \cdots$$
$$= M\vec{v}_{cm} \qquad (7.20)$$

$$\Sigma\vec{F}_{ext} = M\vec{a}_{cm} \qquad (7.22)$$

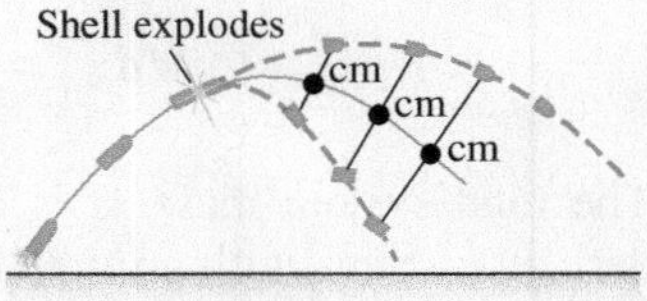

Problems

•, ••, •••: Problems of increasing difficulty. **CP**: Cumulative problems incorporating material from earlier chapters. **CALC**: Problems requiring calculus. **BIO**: Biosciences problems.

7.1 • Two vehicles are approaching an intersection. One is a 2500-kg pickup traveling at 14.0 m/s from east to west (the $-x$-direction), and the other is a 1500-kg sedan going from south to north (the $+y$-direction) at 23.0 m/s. (a) Find the x- and y-components of the net momentum of this system. (b) What are the magnitude and direction of the net momentum?

7.2 • **Force of a Baseball Swing.** A baseball has mass 0.145 kg. (a) If the velocity of a pitched ball has a magnitude of 45.0 m/s and the batted ball's velocity is 55.0 m/s in the opposite direction, find the magnitude of the change in momentum of the ball and of the impulse applied to it by the bat. (b) If the ball remains in contact with the bat for 2.00 ms, find the magnitude of the average force applied by the bat.

7.3 • A 0.160-kg hockey puck is moving on an icy, frictionless, horizontal surface. At $t = 0$, the puck is moving to the right at 3.00 m/s. (a) Calculate the velocity of the puck (magnitude and direction) after a force of 25.0 N directed to the right has been applied for 0.050 s. (b) If, instead, a force of 12.0 N directed to the left is applied from $t = 0$ to $t = 0.050$ s, what is the final velocity of the puck?

7.4 •• You are standing on a sheet of ice that covers the football stadium parking lot in Buffalo; there is negligible friction between your feet and the ice. A friend throws you a 0.400-kg ball that is traveling horizontally at 10.0 m/s. Your mass is 70.0 kg. (a) If you catch the ball, with what speed do you and the ball move afterward? (b) If the ball hits you and bounces off your chest, so afterward it is moving horizontally at 8.0 m/s in the opposite direction, what is your speed after the collision?

7.5 •• **Asteroid Collision.** Two asteroids of equal mass in the asteroid belt between Mars and Jupiter collide with a glancing blow. Asteroid A, which was initially traveling at 40.0 m/s, is deflected 30.0° from its original direction, while asteroid B, which was initially at rest, travels at 45.0° to the original direction of A (Fig. P7.5). (a) Find the speed of each asteroid after the collision. (b) What fraction of the original kinetic energy of asteroid A dissipates during this collision?

Figure P7.5

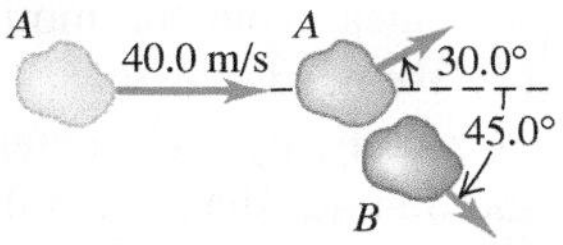

7.6 • At the intersection of Texas Avenue and University Drive, a yellow subcompact car with mass 950 kg traveling east on University collides with a red pickup truck with mass 1900 kg that is traveling north on Texas and has run a red light (Fig. P7.6). The two vehicles stick together as a result of the collision, and the wreckage slides at 16.0 m/s in the direction 24.0° east of north. Calculate the speed of each vehicle before the collision. The collision occurs during a heavy rainstorm; you can ignore friction forces between the vehicles and the wet road.

Figure P7.6

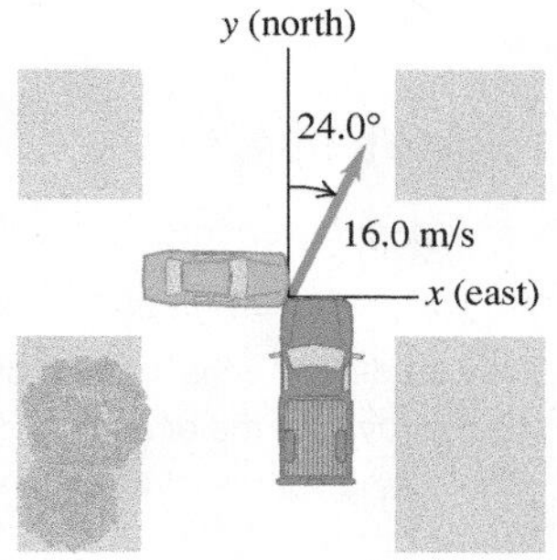

7.7 • Three odd-shaped blocks of chocolate have the following masses and center-of-mass coordinates: (1) 0.300 kg, (0.200 m, 0.300 m); (2) 0.400 kg, (0.100 m, −0.400 m); (3) 0.200 kg, (−0.300 m, 0.600 m). Find the coordinates of the center of mass of the system of three chocolate blocks.

7.8 • **CALC** A radio-controlled model airplane has a momentum given by $[(-0.75\ \text{kg}\cdot\text{m/s}^3)t^2 + (3.0\ \text{kg}\cdot\text{m/s})]\hat{\imath} + (0.25\ \text{kg}\cdot\text{m/s}^2)t\hat{\jmath}$. What are the x-, y-, and z-components of the net force on the airplane?

7.9 •• You are standing on a concrete slab that in turn is resting on a frozen lake. Assume there is no friction between the slab and the ice. The slab has a weight five times your weight. If you begin walking forward at 2.00 m/s relative to the ice, with what speed, relative to the ice, does the slab move?

7.10 •• **CP** A 20.0-kg projectile is fired at an angle of 60.0° above the horizontal with a speed of 80.0 m/s. At the highest point of its trajectory, the projectile explodes into two fragments with equal mass, one of which falls vertically with zero initial speed. You can ignore air resistance. How far from the point of firing does the other fragment strike if the terrain is level?

Answers

Chapter Opening Question ?

We know the initial velocity of the cue ball, and if we measure all of the velocities, we find that the total momentum before and after the collision is the same. In the collision, some of the balls bounce back in the direction the cue ball came from, but the center of mass moves in the same direction as the cue ball originally travelled.

8 ROTATION OF RIGID BODIES AND ANGULAR MOMENTUM

? All segments of a rotating wind turbine blade have the same angular velocity. Compared to a given blade segment, how many times greater is the linear speed of a second segment twice as far from the axis of rotation? How many times greater is the radial acceleration?

LEARNING GOALS

By studying this chapter, you will learn:

- How to describe the rotation of a rigid body in terms of angular coordinate, angular velocity, and angular acceleration.
- How to analyze rigid-body rotation when the angular acceleration is constant.
- How to relate the rotation of a rigid body to the linear velocity and linear acceleration of a point on the body.
- The meaning of a body's moment of inertia about a rotation axis.
- What is meant by the angular momentum of a particle or of a rigid body.
- How the angular momentum of a system changes with time.

What do the motions of a compact disc, a Ferris wheel, a circular saw blade, and a ceiling fan have in common? None of these can be represented adequately as a moving *point;* each involves a body that *rotates* about an axis that is stationary in some inertial frame of reference.

Rotation occurs at all scales, from the motions of electrons in atoms to the motions of entire galaxies. We need to develop some general methods for analyzing the motion of a rotating body. In this chapter and the next we consider bodies that have definite size and definite shape, and that in general can have rotational as well as translational motion.

Real-world bodies can be very complicated; the forces that act on them can deform them—stretching, twisting, and squeezing them. We'll neglect these deformations for now and assume that the body has a perfectly definite and unchanging shape and size. We call this idealized model a **rigid body.** This chapter and the next are mostly about rotational motion of a rigid body.

We begin with kinematic language for *describing* rotational motion. Next we look at the kinetic energy of rotation, the key to using energy methods for rotational motion.

8.1 Angular Velocity and Acceleration

In analyzing rotational motion, let's think first about a rigid body that rotates about a *fixed axis*—an axis that is at rest in some inertial frame of reference and does not change direction relative to that frame. The rotating rigid body might be a motor shaft, a chunk of beef on a barbecue skewer, or a merry-go-round.

Figure 8.1 shows a rigid body (in this case, the indicator needle of a speedometer) rotating about a fixed axis. The axis passes through point O and is

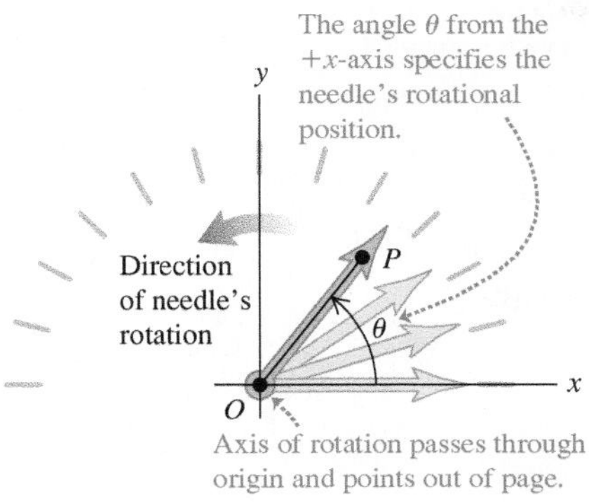
The angle θ from the $+x$-axis specifies the needle's rotational position.
y
Direction of needle's rotation
P
θ
x
O
Axis of rotation passes through origin and points out of page.

8.1 A speedometer needle (an example of a rigid body) rotating counterclockwise about a fixed axis.

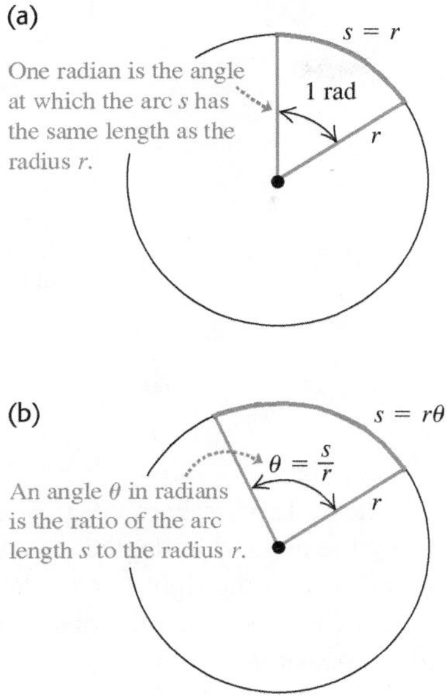
(a)
$s = r$
One radian is the angle at which the arc s has the same length as the radius r.
1 rad
r
(b)
$s = r\theta$
$\theta = \frac{s}{r}$
An angle θ in radians is the ratio of the arc length s to the radius r.
r

8.2 Measuring angles in radians.

perpendicular to the plane of the diagram, which we choose to call the xy-plane. One way to describe the rotation of this body would be to choose a particular point P on the body and to keep track of the x- and y-coordinates of this point. This isn't a terribly convenient method, since it takes two numbers (the two coordinates x and y) to specify the rotational position of the body and, since the distance from the center of rotation is fixed, x and y are related to each other. Instead, we notice that the line OP is fixed in the body and rotates with it. The angle θ that this line makes with the $+x$-axis describes the rotational position of the body; we will use this single quantity θ as a *coordinate* for rotation.

The angular coordinate θ of a rigid body rotating around a fixed axis can be positive or negative. If we choose positive angles to be measured counterclockwise from the positive x-axis, then the angle θ in Fig. 8.1 is positive. If we instead choose the positive rotation direction to be clockwise, then θ in Fig. 8.1 is negative. When we considered the motion of a particle along a straight line, it was essential to specify the direction of positive displacement along that line; when we discuss rotation around a fixed axis, it's just as essential to specify the direction of positive rotation.

To describe rotational motion, the most natural way to measure the angle θ is not in degrees, but in **radians.** As shown in Fig. 8.2a, one radian (1 rad) is the angle subtended at the center of a circle by an arc with a length equal to the radius of the circle. In Fig. 8.2b an angle θ is subtended by an arc of length s on a circle of radius r. The value of θ (in radians) is equal to s divided by r:

$$\theta = \frac{s}{r} \quad \text{or} \quad s = r\theta \tag{8.1}$$

An angle in radians is the ratio of two lengths, so it is a pure number, without dimensions. If $s = 3.0\text{ m}$ and $r = 2.0\text{ m}$, then $\theta = 1.5$, but we will often write this as 1.5 rad to distinguish it from an angle measured in degrees or revolutions.

The circumference of a circle (that is, the arc length all the way around the circle) is 2π times the radius, so there are 2π (about 6.283) radians in one complete revolution $(360°)$. Therefore

$$1\text{ rad} = \frac{360°}{2\pi} = 57.3°$$

8.3 Angular displacement $\Delta\theta$ of a rotating body.

Similarly, $180° = \pi$ rad, $90° = \pi/2$ rad, and so on. If we had insisted on measuring the angle θ in degrees, we would have needed to include an extra factor of $(2\pi/360)$ on the right-hand side of $s = r\theta$ in Eq. (8.1). By measuring angles in radians, we keep the relationship between angle and distance along an arc as simple as possible.

Angular Velocity

The coordinate θ shown in Fig. 8.1 specifies the rotational position of a rigid body at a given instant. We can describe the rotational *motion* of such a rigid body in terms of the rate of change of θ. We'll do this in an analogous way to our description of straight-line motion. In Fig. 8.3, a reference line OP in a rotating body makes an angle θ_1 with the $+x$-axis at time t_1. At a later time t_2 the angle has changed to θ_2. We define the **average angular velocity** $\omega_{\text{av-}z}$ (the Greek letter omega) of the body in the time interval $\Delta t = t_2 - t_1$ as the ratio of the **angular displacement** $\Delta\theta = \theta_2 - \theta_1$ to Δt:

$$\omega_{\text{av-}z} = \frac{\theta_2 - \theta_1}{t_2 - t_1} = \frac{\Delta\theta}{\Delta t} \qquad (8.2)$$

The subscript z indicates that the body in Fig. 8.3 is rotating about the z-axis, which is perpendicular to the plane of the diagram. The **instantaneous angular velocity** ω_z is the limit of $\omega_{\text{av-}z}$ as Δt approaches zero—that is, the derivative of θ with respect to t:

$$\omega_z = \lim_{\Delta t \to 0} \frac{\Delta\theta}{\Delta t} = \frac{d\theta}{dt} \quad \text{(definition of angular velocity)} \qquad (8.3)$$

When we refer simply to "angular velocity," we mean the instantaneous angular velocity, not the average angular velocity.

The angular velocity ω_z can be positive or negative, depending on the direction in which the rigid body is rotating (Fig. 8.4). The angular *speed* ω is the magnitude of angular velocity. Like ordinary (linear) speed v, the angular speed is never negative.

CAUTION **Angular velocity vs. linear velocity** Keep in mind the distinction between angular velocity ω_z and ordinary velocity, or *linear velocity*, v_x. If an object has a velocity v_x, the object as a whole is *moving* along the x-axis. By contrast, if an object has an angular velocity ω_z, then it is *rotating* around the z-axis. We do *not* mean that the object is moving along the z-axis.

8.4 A rigid body's average angular velocity (shown here) and instantaneous angular velocity can be positive or negative.

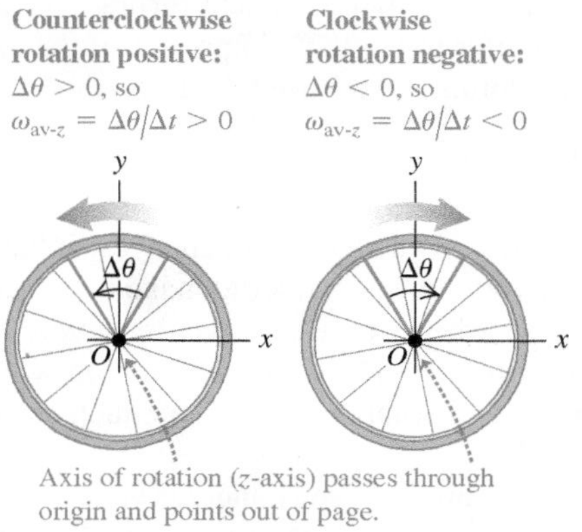
Counterclockwise rotation positive:
$\Delta\theta > 0$, so
$\omega_{av\text{-}z} = \Delta\theta/\Delta t > 0$
Clockwise rotation negative:
$\Delta\theta < 0$, so
$\omega_{av\text{-}z} = \Delta\theta/\Delta t < 0$
y
x
O
$\Delta\theta$
Axis of rotation (z-axis) passes through origin and points out of page.

Different points on a rotating rigid body move different distances in a given time interval, depending on how far each point lies from the rotation axis. But because the body is rigid, *all* points rotate through the same angle in the same time. Hence *at any instant, every part of a rotating rigid body has the same angular velocity.* The angular velocity is positive if the body is rotating in the direction of increasing θ and negative if it is rotating in the direction of decreasing θ.

If the angle θ is in radians, the unit of angular velocity is the radian per second (rad/s). Other units, such as the revolution per minute (rev/min or rpm), are often used. Since 1 rev $= 2\pi$ rad, two useful conversions are

$$1 \text{ rev/s} = 2\pi \text{ rad/s} \qquad \text{and} \qquad 1 \text{ rev/min} = 1 \text{ rpm} = \frac{2\pi}{60} \text{ rad/s}$$

That is, 1 rad/s is about 10 rpm.

Angular Velocity As a Vector

As we have seen, our notation for the angular velocity ω_z about the z-axis is reminiscent of the notation v_x for the ordinary velocity along the x-axis. Just as v_x is the x-component of the velocity vector $\vec{v}$, ω_z is the z-component of an angular velocity *vector* $\vec{\omega}$ directed along the axis of rotation. As Fig. 8.5a shows, the direction of $\vec{\omega}$ is given by the right-hand rule that we used to define the vector product. If the rotation is about the z-axis, then $\vec{\omega}$ has only a z-component; this component is positive if $\vec{\omega}$ is along the positive z-axis and negative if $\vec{\omega}$ is along the negative z-axis (Fig. 8.5b).

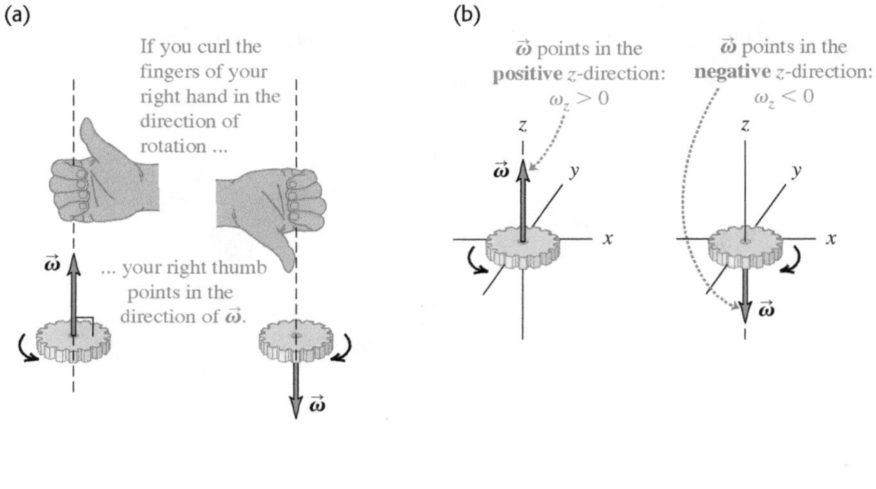
(a)
If you curl the fingers of your right hand in the direction of rotation ...
... your right thumb points in the direction of $\vec{\omega}$.
$\vec{\omega}$
(b)
$\vec{\omega}$ points in the positive z-direction:
$\omega_z > 0$
$\vec{\omega}$ points in the negative z-direction:
$\omega_z < 0$
z
y
x
$\vec{\omega}$

8.5 (a) The right-hand rule for the direction of the angular velocity vector $\vec{\omega}$. Reversing the direction of rotation reverses the direction of $\vec{\omega}$. (b) The sign of ω_z for rotation along the z-axis.

The vector formulation is especially useful in situations in which the direction of the rotation axis *changes*. In this chapter, we'll consider only situations in which the rotation axis is fixed. Hence throughout this chapter we'll use "angular velocity" to refer to ω_z, the component of the angular velocity vector $\vec{\omega}$ along the axis of rotation, which we take to be the z-axis.

Angular Acceleration

When the angular velocity of a rigid body changes, it has an *angular acceleration*. When you pedal your bicycle harder to make the wheels turn faster or apply the brakes to bring the wheels to a stop, you're giving the wheels an angular acceleration. You also impart an angular acceleration whenever you change the rotation speed of a piece of spinning machinery such as an automobile engine's crankshaft.

If ω_{1z} and ω_{2z} are the instantaneous angular velocities at times t_1 and t_2, we define the **average angular acceleration** $\alpha_{\text{av-}z}$ over the interval $\Delta t = t_2 - t_1$ as the change in angular velocity divided by Δt (Fig. 8.6):

$$\alpha_{\text{av-}z} = \frac{\omega_{2z} - \omega_{1z}}{t_2 - t_1} = \frac{\Delta\omega_z}{\Delta t} \tag{8.4}$$

The **instantaneous angular acceleration** α_z is the limit of $\alpha_{\text{av-}z}$ as $\Delta t \to 0$:

$$\alpha_z = \lim_{\Delta t \to 0} \frac{\Delta\omega_z}{\Delta t} = \frac{d\omega_z}{dt} \quad \text{(definition of angular acceleration)} \tag{8.5}$$

The usual unit of angular acceleration is the radian per second per second, or rad/s^2. From now on we will use the term "angular acceleration" to mean the instantaneous angular acceleration rather than the average angular acceleration.

Because $\omega_z = d\theta/dt$, we can also express angular acceleration as the second derivative of the angular coordinate:

$$\alpha_z = \frac{d}{dt}\frac{d\theta}{dt} = \frac{d^2\theta}{dt^2} \tag{8.6}$$

You have probably noticed that we are using Greek letters for angular kinematic quantities: θ for angular position, ω_z for angular velocity, and α_z for angular acceleration. These are analogous to x for position, v_x for velocity, and a_x for acceleration, respectively, in straight-line motion. In each case, velocity is the

8.6 Calculating the average angular acceleration of a rotating rigid body.

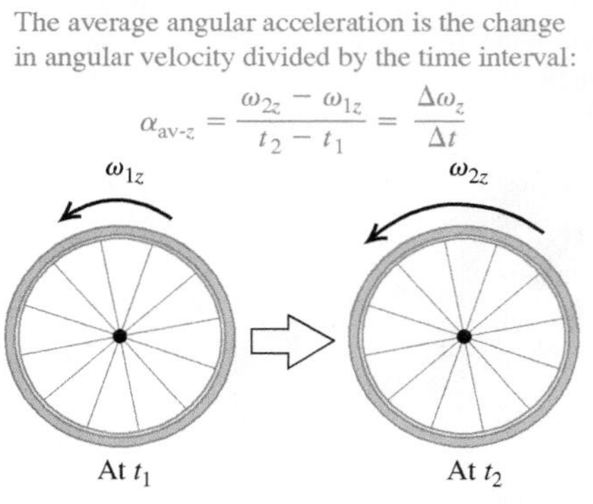

rate of change of position with respect to time and acceleration is the rate of change of velocity with respect to time. We will sometimes use the terms "*linear* velocity" and "*linear* acceleration" for the familiar quantities we defined to distinguish clearly between these and the *angular* quantities introduced in this chapter.

In rotational motion, if the angular acceleration α_z is positive, then the angular velocity ω_z is increasing; if α_z is negative, then ω_z is decreasing. The rotation is speeding up if α_z and ω_z have the same sign and slowing down if α_z and ω_z have opposite signs. (These are exactly the same relationships as those between *linear* acceleration a_x and *linear* velocity v_x for straight-line motion.

8.7 When the rotation axis is fixed, the angular acceleration and angular velocity vectors both lie along that axis.

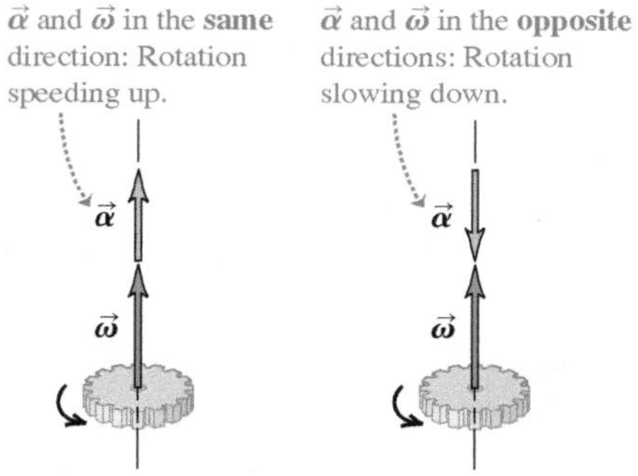
$\vec{\alpha}$ and $\vec{\omega}$ in the **same** direction: Rotation speeding up.
$\vec{\alpha}$ and $\vec{\omega}$ in the **opposite** directions: Rotation slowing down.
$\vec{\alpha}$
$\vec{\omega}$
$\vec{\alpha}$
$\vec{\omega}$

Angular Acceleration As a Vector

Just as we did for angular velocity, it's useful to define an angular acceleration *vector* $\vec{\alpha}$. Mathematically, $\vec{\alpha}$ is the time derivative of the angular velocity vector $\vec{\omega}$. If the object rotates around the fixed z-axis, then $\vec{\alpha}$ has only a z-component; the quantity α_z is just that component. In this case, $\vec{\alpha}$ is in the same direction as $\vec{\omega}$ if the rotation is speeding up and opposite to $\vec{\omega}$ if the rotation is slowing down (Fig. 8.7).

The angular acceleration vector will be particularly useful when we discuss what happens when the rotation axis can change direction. In this chapter, however, the rotation axis will always be fixed and we need use only the z-component α_z.

8.2 Rotation with Constant Angular Acceleration

We found that straight-line motion is particularly simple when the acceleration is constant. This is also true of rotational motion about a fixed axis. When the angular acceleration is constant, we can derive equations for angular velocity and angular position using exactly the same procedure that we used for straight-line motion.

Let ω_{0z} be the angular velocity of a rigid body at time $t = 0$, and let ω_z be its angular velocity at any later time t. The angular acceleration α_z is constant and equal to the average value for any interval. Using Eq. (8.4) with the interval from 0 to t, we find

$$\alpha_z = \frac{\omega_z - \omega_{0z}}{t - 0} \quad \text{or}$$

$$\omega_z = \omega_{0z} + \alpha_z t \quad \text{(constant angular acceleration only)} \tag{8.7}$$

The product $\alpha_z t$ is the total change in ω_z between $t = 0$ and the later time t; the angular velocity ω_z at time t is the sum of the initial value ω_{0z} and this total change.

With constant angular acceleration, the angular velocity changes at a uniform rate, so its average value between 0 and t is the average of the initial and final values:

$$\omega_{\text{av-}z} = \frac{\omega_{0z} + \omega_z}{2} \tag{8.8}$$

We also know that $\omega_{\text{av-}z}$ is the total angular displacement $(\theta - \theta_0)$ divided by the time interval $(t - 0)$:

$$\omega_{\text{av-}z} = \frac{\theta - \theta_0}{t - 0} \tag{8.9}$$

When we equate Eqs. (8.8) and (8.9) and multiply the result by t, we get

$$\theta - \theta_0 = \tfrac{1}{2}(\omega_{0z} + \omega_z)t \quad \text{(constant angular acceleration only)} \tag{8.10}$$

Table 8.1 Comparison of Linear and Angular Motion with Constant Acceleration

Straight-Line Motion with Constant Linear Acceleration		Fixed-Axis Rotation with Constant Angular Acceleration	
$a_x = \text{constant}$		$\alpha_z = \text{constant}$	
$v_x = v_{0x} + a_x t$	(2.8)	$\omega_z = \omega_{0z} + \alpha_z t$	(8.7)
$x = x_0 + v_{0x}t + \frac{1}{2}a_x t^2$	(2.12)	$\theta = \theta_0 + \omega_{0z}t + \frac{1}{2}\alpha_z t^2$	(8.11)
$v_x^2 = v_{0x}^2 + 2a_x(x - x_0)$	(2.13)	$\omega_z^2 = \omega_{0z}^2 + 2\alpha_z(\theta - \theta_0)$	(8.12)
$x - x_0 = \frac{1}{2}(v_{0x} + v_x)t$	(2.14)	$\theta - \theta_0 = \frac{1}{2}(\omega_{0z} + \omega_z)t$	(8.10)

To obtain a relationship between θ and t that doesn't contain ω_z, we substitute Eq. (8.7) into Eq. (8.10):

$$\theta - \theta_0 = \tfrac{1}{2}[\omega_{0z} + (\omega_{0z} + \alpha_z t)]t \qquad \text{or}$$

$$\theta = \theta_0 + \omega_{0z}t + \tfrac{1}{2}\alpha_z t^2 \qquad \text{(constant angular acceleration only)} \qquad (8.11)$$

That is, if at the initial time $t = 0$ the body is at angular position θ_0 and has angular velocity ω_{0z}, then its angular position θ at any later time t is the sum of three terms: its initial angular position θ_0, plus the rotation $\omega_{0z}t$ it would have if the angular velocity were constant, plus an additional rotation $\frac{1}{2}\alpha_z t^2$ caused by the changing angular velocity.

Following the same procedure as for straight-line motion we can combine Eqs. (8.7) and (8.11) to obtain a relationship between θ and ω_z that does not contain t. We get

$$\omega_z^2 = \omega_{0z}^2 + 2\alpha_z(\theta - \theta_0) \qquad \text{(constant angular acceleration only)} \qquad (8.12)$$

CAUTION **Constant angular acceleration** Keep in mind that all of these results are valid *only* when the angular acceleration α_z is *constant;* be careful not to try to apply them to problems in which α_z is *not* constant. Table 8.1 shows the analogy between Eqs. (8.7), (8.10), (8.11), and (8.12) for fixed-axis rotation with constant angular acceleration and the corresponding equations for straight-line motion with constant linear acceleration.

8.3 Relating Linear and Angular Kinematics

How do we find the linear speed and acceleration of a particular point in a rotating rigid body? We need to answer this question to proceed with our study of rotation.

Linear Speed in Rigid-Body Rotation

When a rigid body rotates about a fixed axis, every particle in the body moves in a circular path. The circle lies in a plane perpendicular to the axis and is centered on the axis. The speed of a particle is directly proportional to the body's angular velocity; the faster the body rotates, the greater the speed of each particle. In Fig. 8.9, point P is a constant distance r from the axis of rotation, so it moves in a circle of radius r. At any time, the angle θ (in radians) and the arc length s are related by

$$s = r\theta$$

We take the time derivative of this, noting that r is constant for any specific particle, and take the absolute value of both sides:

$$\left|\frac{ds}{dt}\right| = r\left|\frac{d\theta}{dt}\right|$$

8.8 A rigid body rotating about a fixed axis through point O.

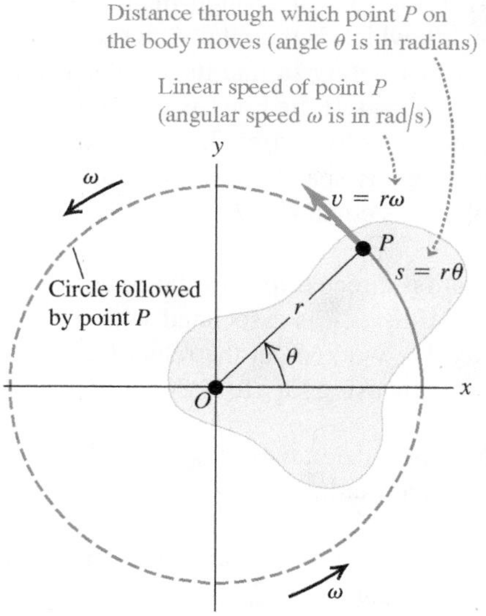
Distance through which point P on
the body moves (angle θ is in radians)
Linear speed of point P
(angular speed ω is in rad/s)
y
ω
v = rω
P
s = rθ
Circle followed
by point P
r
θ
O
x
ω

8.9 A rigid body whose rotation is speeding up. The acceleration of point P has a component a_{rad} toward the rotation axis (perpendicular to $\vec{v}$) and a component a_{tan} along the circle that point P follows (parallel to $\vec{v}$).

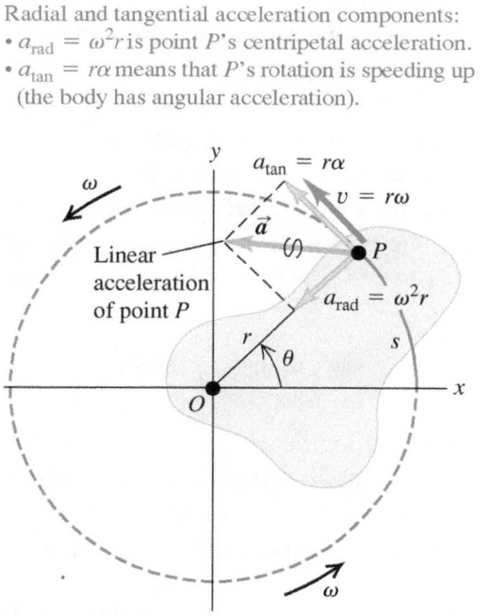
Radial and tangential acceleration components:
• $a_{rad} = \omega^2 r$ is point P's centripetal acceleration.
• $a_{tan} = r\alpha$ means that P's rotation is speeding up (the body has angular acceleration).
y
$a_{tan} = r\alpha$
ω
v = rω
$\vec{a}$
Linear
acceleration
of point P
P
$a_{rad} = \omega^2 r$
s
r
θ
O
x
ω

Now $|ds/dt|$ is the absolute value of the rate of change of arc length, which is equal to the instantaneous *linear* speed v of the particle. Analogously, $|d\theta/dt|$, the absolute value of the rate of change of the angle, is the instantaneous **angular speed** ω—that is, the magnitude of the instantaneous angular velocity in rad/s. Thus

$$v = r\omega \quad \text{(relationship between linear and angular speeds)} \tag{8.13}$$

The farther a point is from the axis, the greater its linear speed. The *direction* of the linear velocity *vector* is tangent to its circular path at each point (Fig. 8.9).

CAUTION **Speed vs. velocity** Keep in mind the distinction between the linear and angular *speeds* v and ω, which appear in Eq. (8.13), and the linear and angular *velocities* v_x and ω_z. The quantities without subscripts, v and ω, are never negative; they are the magnitudes of the vectors $\vec{v}$ and $\vec{\omega}$, respectively, and their values tell you only how fast a particle is moving (v) or how fast a body is rotating (ω). The corresponding quantities with subscripts, v_x and ω_z, can be either positive or negative; their signs tell you the direction of the motion.

Linear Acceleration in Rigid-Body Rotation

We can represent the acceleration of a particle moving in a circle in terms of its centripetal and tangential components, a_{rad} and a_{tan} (Fig. 8.10). It would be a good idea to review that section now. We found that the **tangential component of acceleration** a_{tan}, the component parallel to the instantaneous velocity, acts to change the *magnitude* of the particle's velocity (i.e., the speed) and is equal to the rate of change of speed. Taking the derivative of Eq. (8.13), we find

$$a_{tan} = \frac{dv}{dt} = r\frac{d\omega}{dt} = r\alpha \quad \text{(tangential acceleration of a point on a rotating body)} \tag{8.14}$$

This component of a particle's acceleration is always tangent to the circular path of the particle.

The quantity $\alpha = d\omega/dt$ in Eq. (8.14) is the rate of change of the angular *speed.* It is not quite the same as $\alpha_z = d\omega_z/dt$, which is the rate of change of the angular *velocity.* For example, consider a body rotating so that its angular velocity vector points in the $-z$-direction (see Fig. 8.5b). If the body is gaining angular speed at a rate of 10 rad/s per second, then $\alpha = 10\text{ rad/s}^2$. But ω_z is negative and becoming more negative as the rotation gains speed, so $\alpha_z = -10\text{ rad/s}^2$. The rule for rotation about a fixed axis is that α is equal to α_z if ω_z is positive but equal to $-\alpha_z$ if ω_z is negative.

The component of the particle's acceleration directed toward the rotation axis, the **centripetal component of acceleration** a_{rad}, is associated with the change of *direction* of the particle's velocity. We worked out the relationship $a_{rad} = v^2/r$. We can express this in terms of ω by using Eq. (8.13):

$$a_{rad} = \frac{v^2}{r} = \omega^2 r \quad \text{(centripetal acceleration of a point on a rotating body)} \tag{8.15}$$

This is true at each instant, *even when ω and v are not constant.* The centripetal component always points toward the axis of rotation.

The vector sum of the centripetal and tangential components of acceleration of a particle in a rotating body is the linear acceleration $\vec{a}$ (Fig. 8.10).

CAUTION **Use angles in radians in all equations** It's important to remember that Eq. (8.1), $s = r\theta$, is valid *only* when θ is measured in radians. The same is true of any equation derived from this, including Eqs. (8.13), (8.14), and (8.15). When you use these equations, you *must* express the angular quantities in radians, not revolutions or degrees (Fig. 8.11).

Equations (8.1), (8.13), and (8.14) also apply to any particle that has the same tangential velocity as a point in a rotating rigid body. For example, when a rope wound around a circular cylinder unwraps without stretching or slipping, its speed and acceleration at any instant are equal to the speed and tangential acceleration of the point at which it is tangent to the cylinder. The same principle holds for situations such as bicycle chains and sprockets, belts and pulleys that turn without slipping, and so on. Note that Eq. (8.15) for the centripetal component a_{rad} is applicable to the rope or chain *only* at points that are in contact with the cylinder or sprocket. Other points do not have the same acceleration toward the center of the circle that points on the cylinder or sprocket have.

8.10 Always use radians when relating linear and angular quantities.

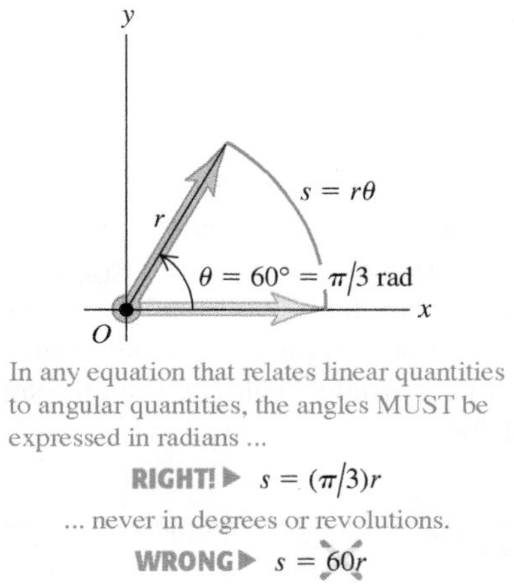
y
x
O
r
s = rθ
θ = 60° = π/3 rad
In any equation that relates linear quantities to angular quantities, the angles MUST be expressed in radians ...
RIGHT! ▶ s = (π/3)r
... never in degrees or revolutions.
WRONG ▶ s = 60r

8.4 Angular Momentum

Every rotational quantity that we have encountered is the analog of some quantity in the translational motion of a particle. The analog of *momentum* of a particle is **angular momentum,** a vector quantity denoted as $\vec{L}$. Its relationship to momentum $\vec{p}$ (which we will often call *linear momentum* for clarity) is exactly the same as the relationship of torque to force, $\vec{\tau} = \vec{r} \times \vec{F}$. For a particle with constant mass m, velocity $\vec{v}$, momentum $\vec{p} = m\vec{v}$, and position vector $\vec{r}$ relative to the origin O of an inertial frame, we define angular momentum $\vec{L}$ as

$$\vec{L} = \vec{r} \times \vec{p} = \vec{r} \times m\vec{v} \qquad \text{(angular momentum of a particle)} \qquad (8.16)$$

The value of $\vec{L}$ depends on the choice of origin O, since it involves the particle's position vector relative to O. The units of angular momentum are $\text{kg} \cdot \text{m}^2/\text{s}$.

In Fig. 8.11 a particle moves in the xy-plane; its position vector $\vec{r}$ and momentum $\vec{p} = m\vec{v}$ are shown. The angular momentum vector $\vec{L}$ is perpendicular to the xy-plane. The right-hand rule for vector products shows that its direction is along the $+z$-axis, and its magnitude is

$$L = mvr\sin\phi = mvl \qquad (8.17)$$

where l is the perpendicular distance from the line of $\vec{v}$ to O. This distance plays the role of "lever arm" for the momentum vector.

When a net force $\vec{F}$ acts on a particle, its velocity and momentum change, so its angular momentum may also change. We can show that the *rate of change* of angular momentum is equal to the torque of the net force. We take the time derivative of Eq. (8.16), using the rule for the derivative of a product:

$$\frac{d\vec{L}}{dt} = \left(\frac{d\vec{r}}{dt} \times m\vec{v}\right) + \left(\vec{r} \times m\frac{d\vec{v}}{dt}\right) = (\vec{v} \times m\vec{v}) + (\vec{r} \times m\vec{a})$$

The first term is zero because it contains the vector product of the vector $\vec{v} = d\vec{r}/dt$ with itself. In the second term we replace $m\vec{a}$ with the net force $\vec{F}$, obtaining

$$\frac{d\vec{L}}{dt} = \vec{r} \times \vec{F} = \vec{\tau} \qquad \text{(for a particle acted on by net force } \vec{F}\text{)} \qquad (8.18)$$

The rate of change of angular momentum of a particle equals the torque of the net force acting on it.

8.11 Calculating the angular momentum $\vec{L} = \vec{r} \times m\vec{v} = \vec{r} \times \vec{p}$ of a particle with mass m moving in the xy-plane.

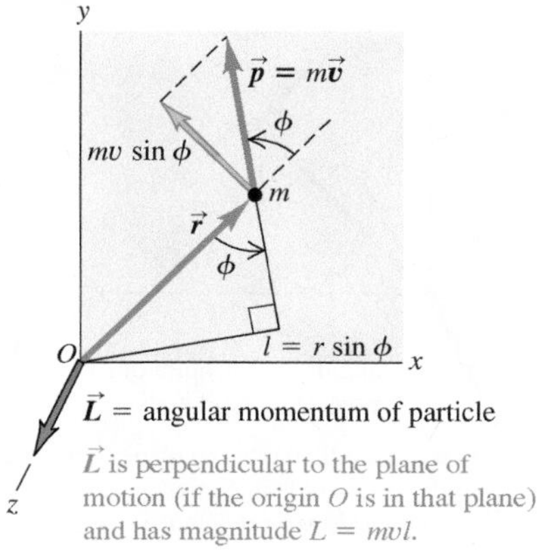

y
$\vec{p} = m\vec{v}$
ϕ
$mv \sin\phi$
m
$\vec{r}$
ϕ
O
$l = r\sin\phi$
x
$\vec{L}$ = angular momentum of particle
$\vec{L}$ is perpendicular to the plane of motion (if the origin O is in that plane) and has magnitude $L = mvl$.
z

Angular Momentum of a Rigid Body

We can use Eq. (8.17) to find the total angular momentum of a *rigid body* rotating about the z-axis with angular speed ω. First consider a thin slice of the body lying in the xy-plane (Fig. 8.12). Each particle in the slice moves in a circle centered at the origin, and at each instant its velocity $\vec{v}_i$ is perpendicular to its position vector $\vec{r}_i$, as shown. Hence in Eq. (8.17), $\phi = 90°$ for every particle. A particle with mass m_i at a distance r_i from O has a speed v_i equal to $r_i\omega$. From Eq. (8.17) the magnitude L_i of its angular momentum is

$$L_i = m_i(r_i\omega)\,r_i = m_i r_i^2\omega \qquad (8.19)$$

The direction of each particle's angular momentum, as given by the right-hand rule for the vector product, is along the $+z$-axis.

The *total* angular of the slice of the body lying in the xy-plane is the sum $\sum L_i$ of the angular momenta L_i of the particles. Summing Eq. (8.19), we have

$$L = \sum L_i = \left(\sum m_i r_i^2\right)\omega = I\omega$$

where I is the moment of inertia of the slice about the z-axis.

The quantity I, obtained by multiplying the mass of each particle by the square of its distance from the axis of rotation and adding these products, is denoted by I and is called the **moment of inertia** of the body for this rotation axis:

$$I = m_1 r_1^2 + m_2 r_2^2 + \cdots = \sum_i m_i r_i^2 \qquad \text{(definition of moment of inertia)} \qquad (8.20)$$

The word "moment" means that I depends on how the body's mass is distributed in space; it has nothing to do with a "moment" of time. For a body with a given rotation axis and a given total mass, the greater the distance from the axis to the particles that make up the body, the greater the moment of inertia. In a rigid body, the distances r_i are all constant and I is independent of how the body rotates around the given axis. The SI unit of moment of inertia is the kilogram-meter^2 ($\text{kg} \cdot \text{m}^2$).

We can do this same calculation for the other slices of the body, all parallel to the xy-plane. For points that do not lie in the xy-plane, a complication arises because the $\vec{r}$ vectors have components in the z-direction as well as the x- and y-directions; this gives the angular momentum of each particle a component perpendicular to the z-axis. But *if the z-axis is an axis of symmetry,* the perpendicular components for particles on opposite sides of this axis add up to zero (Fig. 8.13).

8.12 Calculating the angular momentum of a particle of mass m_i in a rigid body rotating at angular speed ω. (Compare Fig. 8.11.)

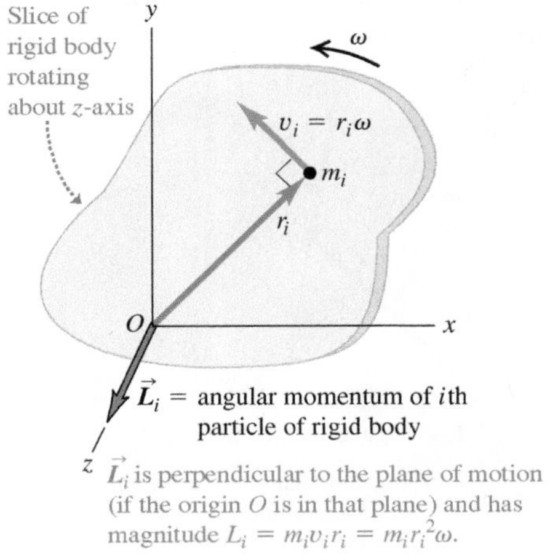

8.13 Two particles of the same mass located symmetrically on either side of the rotation axis of a rigid body. The angular momentum vectors $\vec{L}_1$ and $\vec{L}_2$ of the two particles do not lie along the rotation axis, but their vector sum $\vec{L}_1 + \vec{L}_2$ does.

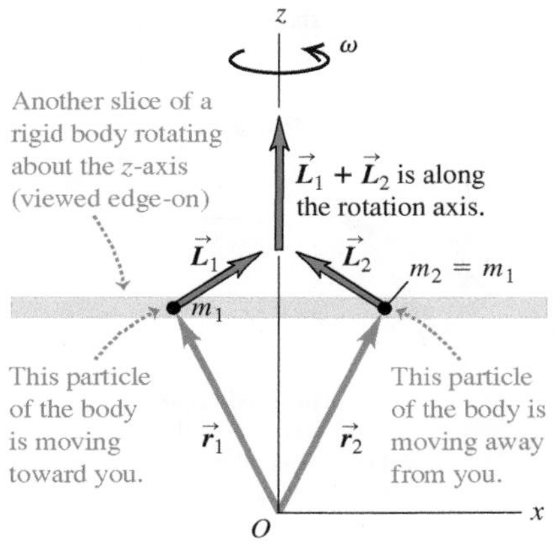

So when a body rotates about an axis of symmetry, its angular momentum vector $\vec{L}$ lies along the symmetry axis, and its magnitude is $L = I\omega$.

The angular velocity vector $\vec{\omega}$ also lies along the rotation axis. Hence for a rigid body rotating around an axis of symmetry, $\vec{L}$ and $\vec{\omega}$ are in the same direction (Fig. 8.14). So we have the *vector* relationship

$$\vec{L} = I\vec{\omega} \quad \text{(for a rigid body rotating around a symmetry axis)} \tag{8.21}$$

From Eq. (8.18) the rate of change of angular momentum of a particle equals the torque of the net force acting on the particle. For any system of particles (including both rigid and nonrigid bodies), the rate of change of the *total* angular momentum equals the sum of the torques of all forces acting on all the particles. The torques of the *internal* forces add to zero if these forces act along the line from one particle to another and so the sum of the torques includes only the torques of the *external* forces. If the total angular momentum of the system of particles is $\vec{L}$ and the sum of the external torques is $\sum\vec{\tau}$, then

$$\sum\vec{\tau} = \frac{d\vec{L}}{dt} \quad \text{(for any system of particles)} \tag{8.22}$$

Finally, if the system of particles is a rigid body rotating about a symmetry axis (the z-axis), then $L_z = I\omega_z$ and I is constant. If this axis has a fixed direction

8.14 For rotation about an axis of symmetry, $\vec{\omega}$ and $\vec{L}$ are parallel and along the axis. The directions of both vectors are given by the right-hand rule (compare Fig. 8.5).

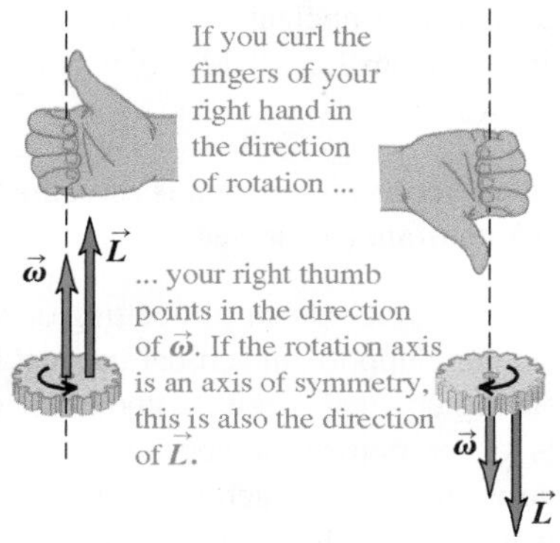

8.15 If the rotation axis of a rigid body is not a symmetry axis, $\vec{L}$ does not in general lie along the rotation axis. Even if $\vec{\omega}$ is constant, the direction of $\vec{L}$ changes and a net torque is required to maintain rotation.

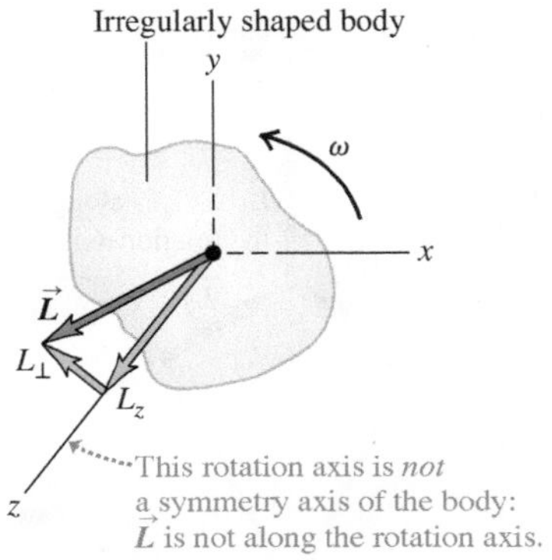
Irregularly shaped body
y
ω
x
$\vec{L}$
$L_\perp$
L_z
z
This rotation axis is *not* a symmetry axis of the body: $\vec{L}$ is not along the rotation axis.

in space, then the vectors $\vec{L}$ and $\vec{\omega}$ change only in magnitude, not in direction. In that case, $dL_z/dt = I\, d\omega_z/dt = I\alpha_z$, or

$$\sum \tau_z = I\alpha_z$$

which is again our basic relationship for the dynamics of rigid-body rotation. If the body is *not* rigid, I may change, and in that case, L changes even when ω is constant. For a nonrigid body, Eq. (8.22) is still valid, even though Eq. (10.7) is not.

When the axis of rotation is *not* a symmetry axis, the angular momentum is in general *not* parallel to the axis (Fig. 8.15). As the body turns, the angular momentum vector $\vec{L}$ traces out a cone around the rotation axis. Because $\vec{L}$ changes, there must be a net external torque acting on the body even though the angular velocity magnitude ω may be constant. If the body is an unbalanced wheel on a car, this torque is provided by friction in the bearings, which causes the bearings to wear out. "Balancing" a wheel means distributing the mass so that the rotation axis is an axis of symmetry; then $\vec{L}$ points along the rotation axis, and no net torque is required to keep the wheel turning.

In fixed-axis rotation we often use the term "angular momentum of the body" to refer to only the *component* of $\vec{L}$ along the rotation axis of the body (the z-axis in Fig. 8.15), with a positive or negative sign to indicate the sense of rotation just as with angular velocity.

8.5 Conservation of Angular Momentum

We have just seen that angular momentum can be used for an alternative statement of the basic dynamic principle for rotational motion. It also forms the basis for the **principle of conservation of angular momentum.** Like conservation of energy and of linear momentum, this principle is a universal conservation law, valid at all scales from atomic and nuclear systems to the motions of galaxies. This principle follows directly from Eq. (8.22): $\sum \vec{\tau} = d\vec{L}/dt$. If $\sum \vec{\tau} = \mathbf{0}$, then $d\vec{L}/dt = \mathbf{0}$, and $\vec{L}$ is constant.

When the net external torque acting on a system is zero, the total angular momentum of the system is constant (conserved).

A circus acrobat, a diver, and an ice skater pirouetting on the toe of one skate all take advantage of this principle. Suppose an acrobat has just left a swing with arms and legs extended and rotating counterclockwise about her center of mass. When she pulls her arms and legs in, her moment of inertia I_{cm} with respect to her center of mass changes from a large value I_1 to a much smaller value I_2. The only external force acting on her is her weight, which has no torque with respect to an axis through her center of mass. So her angular momentum $L_z = I_{cm}\omega_z$ remains constant, and her angular velocity ω_z increases as I_{cm} decreases. That is,

$$I_1\omega_{1z} = I_2\omega_{2z} \qquad \text{(zero net external torque)} \qquad (8.23)$$

When a skater or ballerina spins with arms outstretched and then pulls her arms in, her angular velocity increases as her moment of inertia decreases. In each case there is conservation of angular momentum in a system in which the net external torque is zero.

When a system has several parts, the internal forces that the parts exert on one another cause changes in the angular momenta of the parts, but the *total* angular momentum doesn't change. Here's an example. Consider two bodies A and B that interact with each other but not with anything else. Suppose body A exerts a force $\vec{F}_{A \text{ on } B}$ on body B; the corresponding torque (with respect to whatever point we choose) is $\vec{\tau}_{A \text{ on } B}$. According to Eq. (8.22), this torque is equal to the rate of change of angular momentum of B:

$$\vec{\tau}_{A \text{ on } B} = \frac{d\vec{L}_B}{dt}$$

At the same time, body B exerts a force $\vec{F}_{B \text{ on } A}$ on body A, with a corresponding torque $\vec{\tau}_{B \text{ on } A}$, and

$$\vec{\tau}_{B \text{ on } A} = \frac{d\vec{L}_A}{dt}$$

From Newton's third law, $\vec{F}_{B \text{ on } A} = -\vec{F}_{A \text{ on } B}$. Furthermore, if the forces act along the same line, their lever arms with respect to the chosen axis are equal. Thus the *torques* of these two forces are equal and opposite, and $\vec{\tau}_{B \text{ on } A} = -\vec{\tau}_{A \text{ on } B}$. So if we add the two preceding equations, we find

$$\frac{d\vec{L}_A}{dt} + \frac{d\vec{L}_B}{dt} = \mathbf{0}$$

or, because $\vec{L}_A + \vec{L}_B$ is the *total* angular momentum $\vec{L}$ of the system,

$$\frac{d\vec{L}}{dt} = \mathbf{0} \qquad \text{(zero net external torque)} \qquad (8.23)$$

That is, the total angular momentum of the system is constant. The torques of the internal forces can transfer angular momentum from one body to the other, but they can't change the *total* angular momentum of the system.

CHAPTER 8 SUMMARY

Rotational kinematics: When a rigid body rotates about a stationary axis (usually called the z-axis), its position is described by an angular coordinate θ. The angular velocity ω_z is the time derivative of θ, and the angular acceleration α_z is the time derivative of ω_z or the second derivative of θ. If the angular acceleration is constant, then θ, ω_z, and α_z are related by simple kinematic equations analogous to those for straight-line motion with constant linear acceleration.

$$\omega_z = \lim_{\Delta t \to 0} \frac{\Delta\theta}{\Delta t} = \frac{d\theta}{dt} \qquad (8.3)$$

$$\alpha_z = \lim_{\Delta t \to 0} \frac{\Delta\omega_z}{\Delta t} = \frac{d\omega_z}{dt} = \frac{d^2\theta}{dt^2} \qquad (8.5), (8.6)$$

$$\theta = \theta_0 + \omega_{0z}t + \tfrac{1}{2}\alpha_z t^2 \qquad (8.11)$$

(constant α_z only)

$$\theta - \theta_0 = \tfrac{1}{2}(\omega_{0z} + \omega_z)t \qquad (8.10)$$

(constant α_z only)

$$\omega_z = \omega_{0z} + \alpha_z t \qquad (8.7)$$

(constant α_z only)

$$\omega_z^2 = \omega_{0z}^2 + 2\alpha_z(\theta - \theta_0) \qquad (8.12)$$

(constant α_z only)

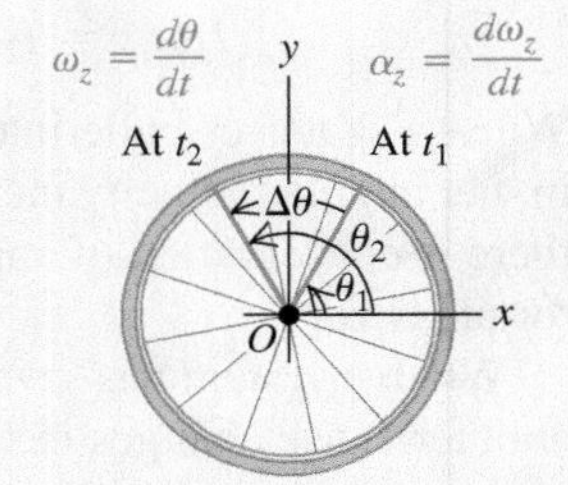

Relating linear and angular kinematics: The angular speed ω of a rigid body is the magnitude of its angular velocity. The rate of change of ω is $\alpha = d\omega/dt$. For a particle in the body a distance r from the rotation axis, the speed v and the components of the acceleration $\vec{a}$ are related to ω and α.

$$v = r\omega \qquad (8.13)$$

$$a_{\text{tan}} = \frac{dv}{dt} = r\frac{d\omega}{dt} = r\alpha \qquad (8.14)$$

$$a_{\text{rad}} = \frac{v^2}{r} = \omega^2 r \qquad (8.15)$$

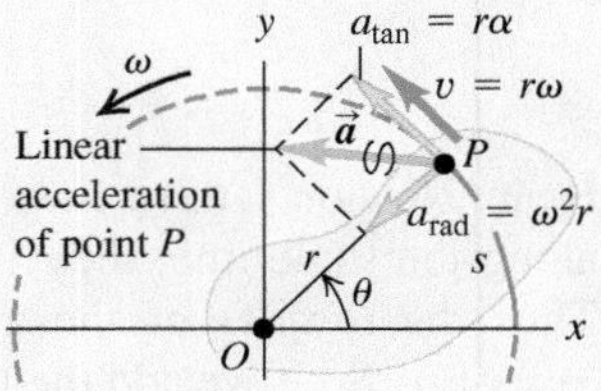

Moment of inertia and rotational kinetic energy: The moment of inertia I of a body about a given axis is a measure of its rotational inertia: The greater the value of I, the more difficult it is to change the state of the body's rotation. The moment of inertia can be expressed as a sum over the particles m_i that make up the body, each of which is at its own perpendicular distance r_i from the axis.

$$I = m_1 r_1^2 + m_2 r_2^2 + \cdots = \sum_i m_i r_i^2 \qquad (8.20)$$

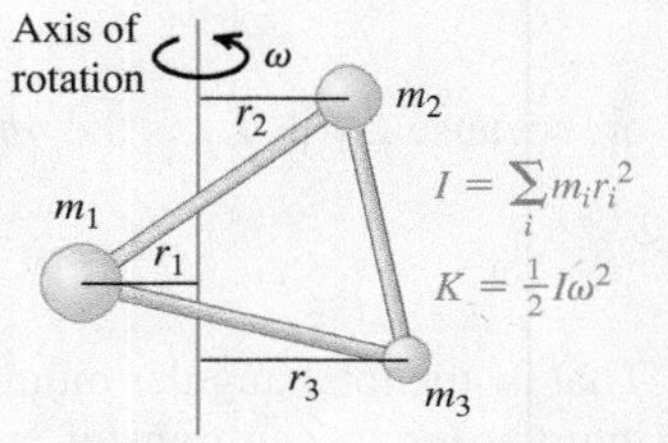

Angular momentum: The angular momentum of a particle with respect to point O is the vector product of the particle's position vector $\vec{r}$ relative to O and its momentum $\vec{p} = m\vec{v}$. When a symmetrical body rotates about a stationary axis of symmetry, its angular momentum is the product of its moment of inertia and its angular velocity vector $\vec{\omega}$. If the body is not symmetrical or the rotation (z) axis is not an axis of symmetry, the component of angular momentum along the rotation axis is $I\omega_z$.

$$\vec{L} = \vec{r} \times \vec{p} = \vec{r} \times m\vec{v} \qquad (8.16)$$

(particle)

$$\vec{L} = I\vec{\omega} \qquad (8.21)$$

(rigid body rotating about axis of symmetry)

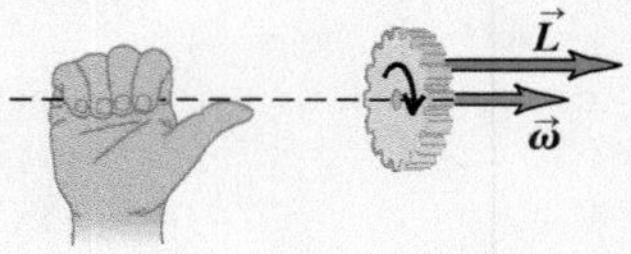

Rotational dynamics and angular momentum: The net external torque on a system is equal to the rate of change of its angular momentum. If the net external torque on a system is zero, the total angular momentum of the system is constant (conserved).

$$\sum\vec{\tau} = \frac{d\vec{L}}{dt} \qquad (8.22)$$

Problems

•, ••, •••: Problems of increasing difficulty. **CP**: Cumulative problems incorporating material from earlier chapters. **CALC**: Problems requiring calculus. **BIO**: Biosciences problems.

8.1 • (a) What angle in radians is subtended by an arc 1.50 m long on the circumference of a circle of radius 2.50 m? What is this angle in degrees? (b) An arc 14.0 cm long on the circumference of a circle subtends an angle of 128°. What is the radius of the circle? (c) The angle between two radii of a circle with radius 1.50 m is 0.700 rad. What length of arc is intercepted on the circumference of the circle by the two radii?

8.2 • A wheel is rotating about an axis that is in the z-direction. The angular velocity ω_z is -6.00 rad/s at $t = 0$, increases linearly with time, and is $+8.00$ rad/s at $t = 7.00$ s. We have taken counterclockwise rotation to be positive. (a) Is the angular acceleration during this time interval positive or negative? (b) During what time interval is the speed of the wheel increasing? Decreasing? (c) What is the angular displacement of the wheel at $t = 7.00$ s?

8.3 •• The rotating blade of a blender turns with constant angular acceleration 1.50 rad/s^2. (a) How much time does it take to reach an angular velocity of 36.0 rad/s, starting from rest? (b) Through how many revolutions does the blade turn in this time interval?

8.4 • In a charming 19th-century hotel, an old-style elevator is connected to a counterweight by a cable that passes over a rotating disk 2.50 m in diameter (Fig. P8.4). The elevator is raised and lowered by turning the disk, and the cable does not slip on the rim of the disk but turns with it. (a) At how many rpm must the disk turn to raise the elevator at 25.0 cm/s? (b) To start the elevator moving, it must be accelerated at $\frac{1}{8}g$. What must be the angular acceleration of the disk, in rad/s^2? (c) Through what angle (in radians and degrees) has the disk turned when it has raised the elevator 3.25 m between floors?

Figure **P8.4**

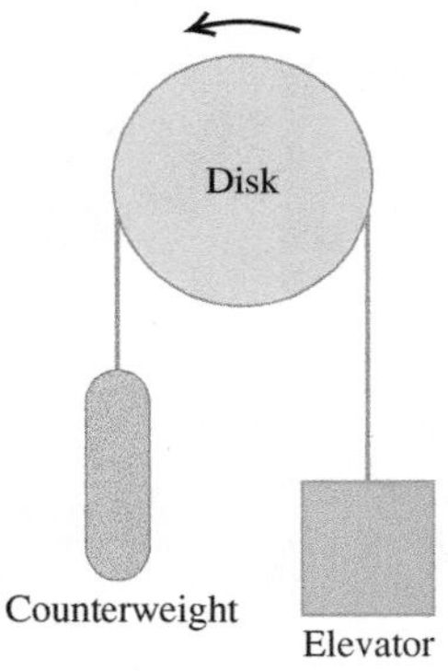
Disk
Counterweight
Elevator

8.5 • (a) Derive an equation for the radial acceleration that includes v and ω, but not r. (b) You are designing a merry-go-round for which a point on the rim will have a radial acceleration of 0.500 m/s^2 when the tangential velocity of that point has magnitude 2.00 m/s. What angular velocity is required to achieve these values?

8.6 • A 2.00-kg rock has a horizontal velocity of magnitude 12.0 m/s when it is at point P in Fig. P8.6. (a) At this instant, what are the magnitude and direction of its angular momentum relative to point O? (b) If the only force acting on the rock is its weight, what is the rate of change (magnitude and direction) of its angular momentum at this instant?

Figure **P8.6**

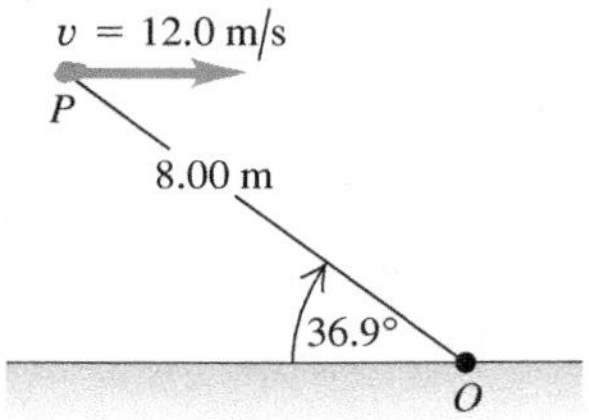
v = 12.0 m/s
P
8.00 m
36.9°
O

8.7 • **CP** A small block on a frictionless, horizontal surface has a mass of 0.0250 kg. It is attached to a massless cord passing through a hole in the surface (Fig. P8.7). The block is originally revolving at a distance of 0.300 m from the hole with an angular speed of 1.75 rad/s. The cord is then pulled from below, shortening the radius of the circle in which the block revolves to 0.150 m. Model the block as a particle. (a) Is the angular momentum of the block conserved? Why or why not? (b) What is the new angular speed?

Figure **P8.7**

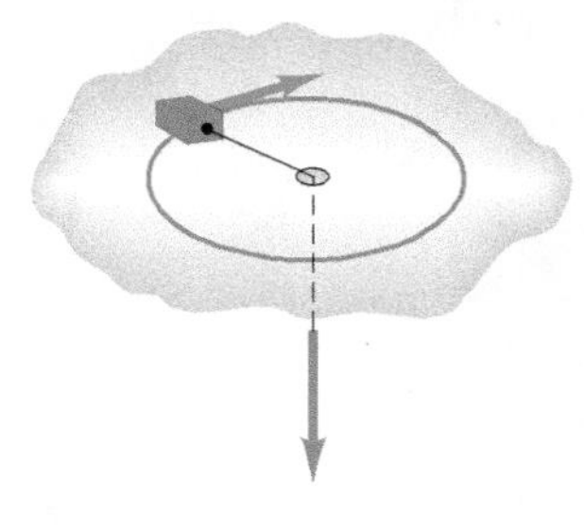

8.8 •• **The Spinning Figure Skater.** The outstretched hands and arms of a figure skater preparing for a spin can be considered a slender rod pivoting about an axis through its center (Fig. P8.8). When the skater's hands and arms are brought in and wrapped around his body to execute the spin, the hands and arms can be considered a thin-walled, hollow cylinder. His hands and arms have a combined mass of 8.0 kg. When outstretched, they span 1.8 m; when wrapped, they form a cylinder of radius 25 cm. The moment of inertia about the rotation axis of the remainder of his body is constant and equal to 0.40 kg · m^2. If his original angular speed is 0.40 rev/s, what is his final angular speed?

Figure **P8.8**

8.9 •• A diver comes off a board with arms straight up and legs straight down, giving her a moment of inertia about her rotation axis of 18 kg · m^2. She then tucks into a small ball, decreasing this moment of inertia to 3.6 kg · m^2. While tucked, she makes two complete revolutions in 1.0 s. If she hadn't tucked at all, how many revolutions would she have made in the 1.5 s from board to water?

Answers

Chapter Opening Question ?

Both segments of the rigid blade have the same angular speed ω. From Eqs. (8.13) and (8.15), doubling the distance r for the same ω doubles the linear speed $v = r\omega$ and doubles the radial acceleration $a_{rad} = \omega^2 r$.

WORK AND ENERGY

9

? After finding a piece of breakfast cereal on the floor, this ant picked it up and carried it away. As the ant was lifting the piece of cereal, did the *cereal* do work on the *ant*?

LEARNING GOALS

By studying this chapter, you will learn:

- What it means for a force to do work on a body, and how to calculate the amount of work done.
- The definition of the kinetic energy (energy of motion) of a body, and what it means physically.
- How the total work done on a body changes the body's kinetic energy, and how to use this principle to solve problems in mechanics.
- How to use the relationship between total work and change in kinetic energy when the forces are not constant, the body follows a curved path, or both.
- How to solve problems involving power (the rate of doing work).
- How to use the concept of gravitational potential energy in problems that involve vertical motion.
- How to use the concept of elastic potential energy in problems that involve a moving body attached to a stretched or compressed spring.
- The distinction between conservative and nonconservative forces, and how to solve problems in which both kinds of forces act on a moving body.
- How to calculate the properties of a conservative force if you know the corresponding potential-energy function.
- How to use energy diagrams to understand the motion of an object moving in a straight line under the influence of a conservative force.

Suppose you try to find the speed of an arrow that has been shot from a bow. You apply Newton's laws and all the problem-solving techniques that we've learned, but you run across a major stumbling block: After the archer releases the arrow, the bow string exerts a *varying* force that depends on the arrow's position. As a result, the simple methods that we've learned aren't enough to calculate the speed. Never fear; we aren't by any means finished with mechanics, and there are other methods for dealing with such problems.

The new method that we're about to introduce uses the ideas of *work* and *energy*. The importance of the energy idea stems from the *principle of conservation of energy*: Energy is a quantity that can be converted from one form to another but cannot be created or destroyed. In an automobile engine, chemical energy stored in the fuel is converted partially to the energy of the automobile's motion and partially to thermal energy. In a microwave oven, electromagnetic energy obtained from your power company is converted to thermal energy of the food being cooked. In these and all other processes, the *total* energy—the sum of all energy present in all different forms—remains the same. No exception has ever been found.

We'll use the energy idea throughout the rest of this book to study a tremendous range of physical phenomena. This idea will help you understand why a sweater keeps you warm, how a camera's flash unit can produce a short burst of light, and the meaning of Einstein's famous equation $E = mc^2$.

In this chapter, though, our concentration will be on mechanics. We'll learn about one important form of energy called *kinetic energy,* or energy of motion, and how it relates to the concept of *work*. We'll also consider *power,* which is the time rate of doing work.

9.1 Work

You'd probably agree that it's hard work to pull a heavy sofa across the room, to lift a stack of encyclopedias from the floor to a high shelf, or to push a stalled car off the road. Indeed, all of these examples agree with the everyday meaning of *work*—any activity that requires muscular or mental effort.

In physics, work has a much more precise definition. By making use of this definition we'll find that in any motion, no matter how complicated, the total work done on a particle by all forces that act on it equals the change in its *kinetic energy*—a quantity that's related to the particle's speed. This relationship holds even when the forces acting on the particle aren't constant, a situation that can be difficult or impossible to handle with the techniques you learned in Chapter 5. The ideas of work and kinetic energy enable us to solve problems in mechanics that we could not have attempted before.

In this section we'll see how work is defined and how to calculate work in a variety of situations involving *constant* forces. Even though we already know how to solve problems in which the forces are constant, the idea of work is still useful in such problems. Later in this chapter we'll relate work and kinetic energy, and then apply these ideas to problems in which the forces are *not* constant.

The three examples of work described above—pulling a sofa, lifting encyclopedias, and pushing a car—have something in common. In each case you do work by exerting a *force* on a body while that body *moves* from one place to another—that is, undergoes a *displacement*. You do more work if the force is greater (you push harder on the car) or if the displacement is greater (you push the car farther down the road).

The physicist's definition of work is based on these observations. Consider a body that undergoes a displacement of magnitude s along a straight line. (For now, we'll assume that any body we discuss can be treated as a particle so that we can ignore any rotation or changes in shape of the body.) While the body moves, a constant force $\vec{F}$ acts on it in the same direction as the displacement $\vec{s}$ (Fig. 9.1). We define the **work** W done by this constant force under these circumstances as the product of the force magnitude F and the displacement magnitude s:

$$W = Fs \qquad \text{(constant force in direction of straight-line displacement)} \tag{9.1}$$

The work done on the body is greater if either the force F or the displacement s is greater, in agreement with our observations above.

CAUTION Work = W, weight = w Don't confuse uppercase W (work) with lowercase w (weight). Though the symbols are similar, work and weight are different quantities.

9.1 The work done by a constant force acting in the same direction as the displacement.

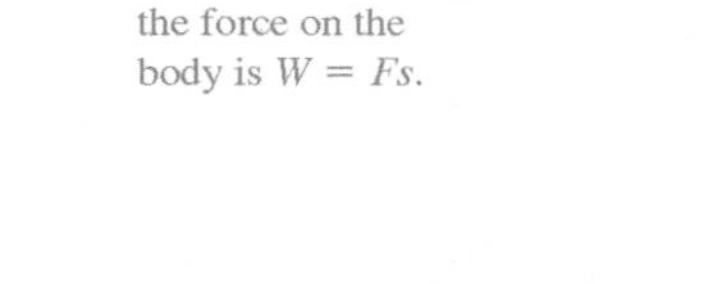
If a body moves through a displacement $\vec{s}$ while a constant force $\vec{F}$ acts on it in the same direction ...
$\vec{F}$
x
$\vec{s}$
... the work done by the force on the body is $W = Fs$.

9.2 The work done by a constant force acting at an angle to the displacement.

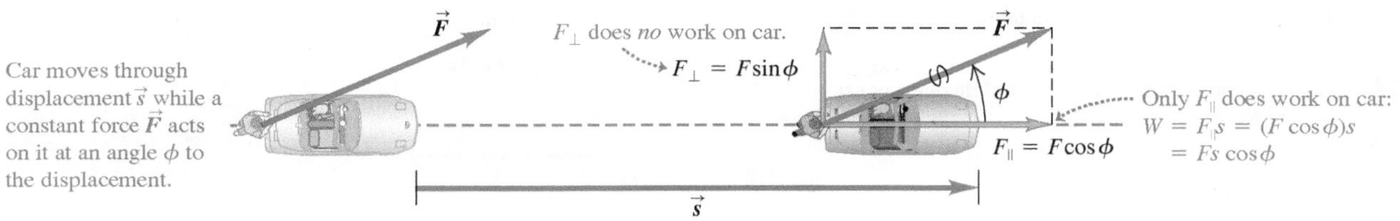
Car moves through displacement $\vec{s}$ while a constant force $\vec{F}$ acts on it at an angle ϕ to the displacement.
$\vec{F}$
$F_\perp$ does *no* work on car.
$F_\perp = F\sin\phi$
ϕ
Only $F_\parallel$ does work on car:
$W = F_\parallel s = (F\cos\phi)s$
$= Fs\cos\phi$
$F_\parallel = F\cos\phi$
$\vec{s}$

The SI unit of work is the **joule** (abbreviated J, pronounced "jool," and named in honor of the 19th-century English physicist James Prescott Joule). From Eq. (9.1) we see that in any system of units, the unit of work is the unit of force multiplied by the unit of distance. In SI units the unit of force is the newton and the unit of distance is the meter, so 1 joule is equivalent to 1 *newton-meter* $(\text{N}\cdot\text{m})$:

$$1\text{ joule} = (1\text{ newton})(1\text{ meter}) \quad \text{or} \quad 1\text{ J} = 1\text{ N}\cdot\text{m}$$

In the British system the unit of force is the pound (lb), the unit of distance is the foot (ft), and the unit of work is the *foot-pound* $(\text{ft}\cdot\text{lb})$. The following conversions are useful:

$$1\text{ J} = 0.7376\text{ ft}\cdot\text{lb} \qquad 1\text{ ft}\cdot\text{lb} = 1.356\text{ J}$$

As an illustration of Eq. (9.1), think of a person pushing a stalled car. If he pushes the car through a displacement $\vec{s}$ with a constant force $\vec{F}$ in the direction of motion, the amount of work he does on the car is given by Eq. (9.1): $W = Fs$. But what if the person pushes at an angle ϕ to the car's displacement (Fig. 9.2)? Then $\vec{F}$ has a component $F_\parallel = F\cos\phi$ in the direction of the displacement and a component $F_\perp = F\sin\phi$ that acts perpendicular to the displacement. (Other forces must act on the car so that it moves along $\vec{s}$, not in the direction of $\vec{F}$. We're interested only in the work that the person does, however, so we'll consider only the force he exerts.) In this case only the parallel component $F_\parallel$ is effective in moving the car, so we define the work as the product of this force component and the magnitude of the displacement. Hence $W = F_\parallel s = (F\cos\phi)s$, or

$$W = Fs\cos\phi \qquad \text{(constant force, straight-line displacement)} \qquad (9.2)$$

We are assuming that F and ϕ are constant during the displacement. If $\phi = 0$, so that $\vec{F}$ and $\vec{s}$ are in the same direction, then $\cos\phi = 1$ and we are back to Eq. (9.1).

Equation (9.2) has the form of the *scalar product* of two vectors, which we introduced in Section 1.9: $\vec{A}\cdot\vec{B} = AB\cos\phi$. You may want to review that definition. Hence we can write Eq. (9.2) more compactly as

$$W = \vec{F}\cdot\vec{s} \qquad \text{(constant force, straight-line displacement)} \qquad (9.3)$$

CAUTION **Work is a scalar** Here's an essential point: Work is a *scalar* quantity, even though it's calculated by using two vector quantities (force and displacement). A 5-N force toward the east acting on a body that moves 6 m to the east does exactly the same amount of work as a 5-N force toward the north acting on a body that moves 6 m to the north.

Work: Positive, Negative, or Zero

It's important to understand that work can also be negative or zero. This is the essential way in which work as defined in physics differs from the "everyday" definition of work. When the force has a component in the *same direction* as the

9.3 A constant force $\vec{F}$ can do positive, negative, or zero work depending on the angle between $\vec{F}$ and the displacement $\vec{s}$.

Direction of Force (or Force Component) | **Situation** | **Force Diagram**

(a) **Force $\vec{F}$ has a component in direction of displacement:**
$W = F_{\|}s = (F\cos\phi)s$
Work is *positive.*

(b) **Force $\vec{F}$ has a component opposite to direction of displacement:**
$W = F_{\|}s = (F\cos\phi)s$
Work is *negative* (because $F\cos\phi$ is negative for $90° < \phi < 180°$).

(c) **Force $\vec{F}$ (or force component $F_{\perp}$) is perpendicular to direction of displacement:** The force (or force component) does *no* work on the object.

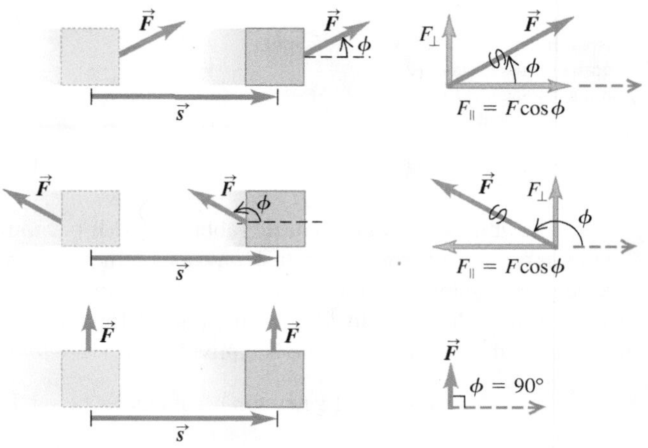

displacement (ϕ between zero and 90°), $\cos\phi$ in Eq. (9.2) is positive and the work W is *positive* (Fig. 9.3a). When the force has a component *opposite* to the displacement (ϕ between 90° and 180°), $\cos\phi$ is negative and the work is *negative* (Fig. 9.3b). When the force is *perpendicular* to the displacement, $\phi = 90°$ and the work done by the force is *zero* (Fig. 9.3c). The cases of zero work and negative work bear closer examination, so let's look at some examples.

There are many situations in which forces act but do zero work. You might think it's "hard work" to hold a barbell motionless in the air for 5 minutes. But in fact, you aren't doing any work at all on the barbell because there is no displacement. You get tired because the components of muscle fibers in your arm do work as they continually contract and relax. This is work done by one part of the arm exerting force on another part, however, *not* on the barbell. (We'll say more in Section 9.2 about work done by one part of a body on another part.) Even when you walk with constant velocity on a level floor while carrying a book, you still do no work on it. The book has a displacement, but the (vertical) supporting force that you exert on the book has no component in the direction of the (horizontal) motion. Then $\phi = 90°$ in Eq. (9.2), and $\cos\phi = 0$. When a body slides along a surface, the work done on the body by the normal force is zero; and when a ball on a string moves in uniform circular motion, the work done on the ball by the tension in the string is also zero. In both cases the work is zero because the force has no component in the direction of motion.

What does it really mean to do *negative* work? The answer comes from Newton's third law of motion. When a weightlifter lowers a barbell as in Fig. 9.4a, his hands and the barbell move together with the same displacement $\vec{s}$. The barbell exerts a force $\vec{F}_{\text{barbell on hands}}$ on his hands in the same direction as the hands' displacement, so the work done by the *barbell* on his *hands* is positive (Fig. 9.4b). But by Newton's third law the weightlifter's hands exert an equal and opposite force $\vec{F}_{\text{hands on barbell}} = -\vec{F}_{\text{barbell on hands}}$ on the barbell (Fig. 9.4c). This force, which keeps the barbell from crashing to the floor, acts opposite to the barbell's displacement. Thus the work done by his *hands* on the *barbell* is negative. Because the weightlifter's hands and the barbell have the same displacement, the work that his hands do on the barbell is just the negative of the work that the barbell does on his hands. In general, when one body does negative work on a second body, the second body does an equal amount of *positive* work on the first body.

9.4 This weightlifter's hands do negative work on a barbell as the barbell does positive work on his hands.

(a) A weightlifter lowers a barbell to the floor.

(b) The barbell does *positive* work on the weightlifter's hands.

(c) The weightlifter's hands do *negative* work on the barbell.

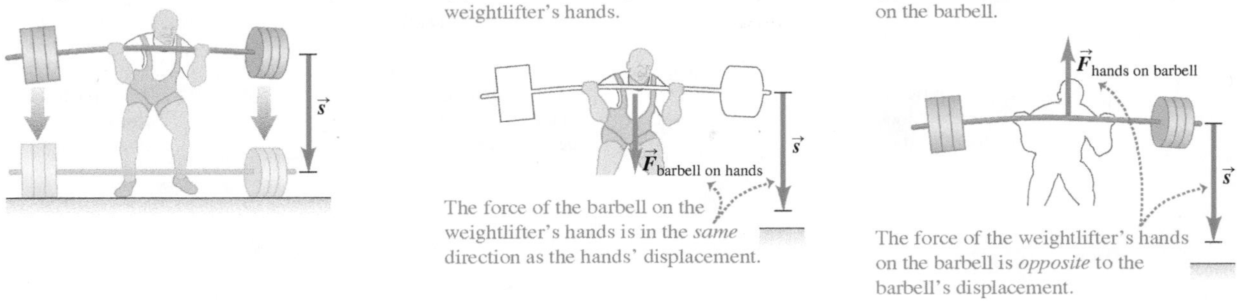

CAUTION **Keep track of who's doing the work** We always speak of work done *on* a particular body *by* a specific force. Always be sure to specify exactly what force is doing the work you are talking about. When you lift a book, you exert an upward force on the book and the book's displacement is upward, so the work done by the lifting force on the book is positive. But the work done by the *gravitational* force (weight) on a book being lifted is *negative* because the downward gravitational force is opposite to the upward displacement.

Total Work

How do we calculate work when *several* forces act on a body? One way is to use Eq. (9.3) to compute the work done by each separate force. Then, because work is a scalar quantity, the *total* work W_{tot} done on the body by all the forces is the algebraic sum of the quantities of work done by the individual forces. An alternative way to find the total work W_{tot} is to compute the vector sum of the forces (that is, the net force) and then use this vector sum as $\vec{F}$ in Eq. (9.3). The following example illustrates both of these techniques.

9.2 Kinetic Energy and the Work–Energy Theorem

The total work done on a body by external forces is related to the body's displacement—that is, to changes in its position. But the total work is also related to changes in the *speed* of the body. To see this, consider Fig. 9.5, which shows three examples of a block sliding on a frictionless table. The forces acting on the block are its weight $\vec{w}$, the normal force $\vec{n}$, and the force $\vec{F}$ exerted on it by the hand.

In Fig. 9.5a the net force on the block is in the direction of its motion. From Newton's second law, this means that the block speeds up; from Eq. (9.1), this also means that the total work W_{tot} done on the block is positive. The total work is *negative* in Fig. 9.5b because the net force opposes the displacement; in this case the block slows down. The net force is zero in Fig. 9.5c, so the speed of the block stays the same and the total work done on the block is zero. We can conclude that *when a particle undergoes a displacement, it speeds up if* $W_{\text{tot}} > 0$, *slows down if* $W_{\text{tot}} < 0$, *and maintains the same speed if* $W_{\text{tot}} = 0$.

Let's make these observations more quantitative. Consider a particle with mass m moving along the x-axis under the action of a constant net force with magnitude F directed along the positive x-axis (Fig. 9.6). The particle's acceleration is constant and given by Newton's second law, $F = ma_x$. Suppose the speed changes from v_1 to v_2 while the particle undergoes a displacement $s = x_2 - x_1$ from point x_1 to x_2. Using a constant-acceleration equation, and replacing v_{0x} by v_1, v_x by v_2, and $(x - x_0)$ by s, we have

9.5 The relationship between the total work done on a body and how the body's speed changes.

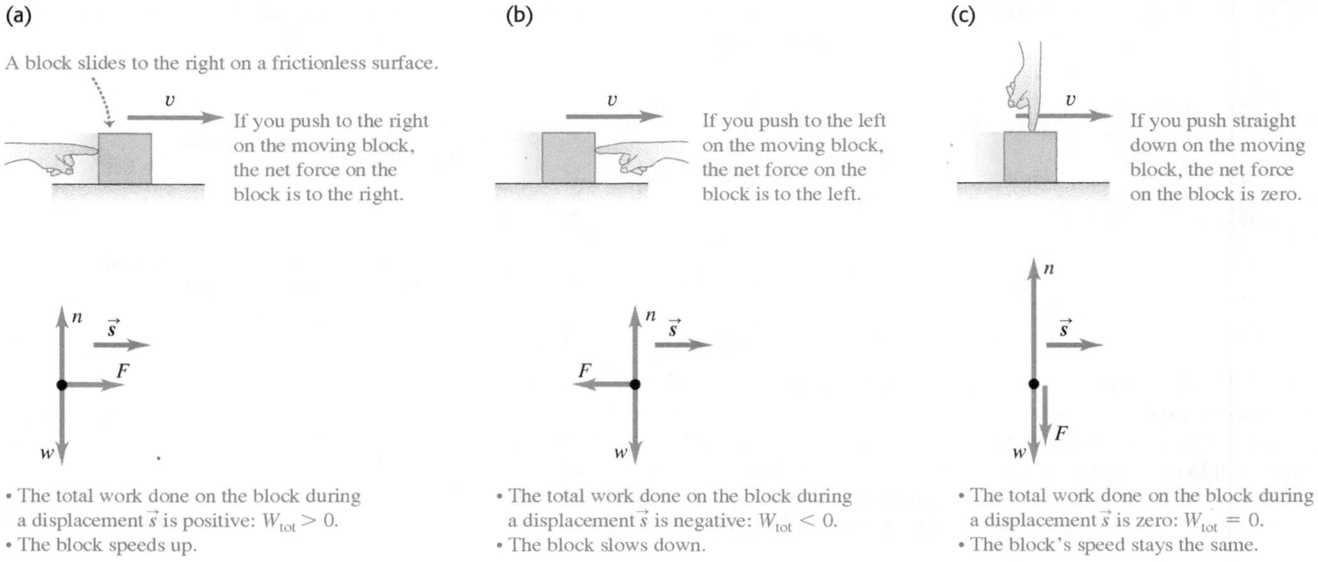
(a)
A block slides to the right on a frictionless surface.
v
If you push to the right on the moving block, the net force on the block is to the right.
n
s
F
w
• The total work done on the block during a displacement s is positive: $W_{tot} > 0$.
• The block speeds up.
(b)
v
If you push to the left on the moving block, the net force on the block is to the left.
n
s
F
w
• The total work done on the block during a displacement s is negative: $W_{tot} < 0$.
• The block slows down.
(c)
v
If you push straight down on the moving block, the net force on the block is zero.
n
s
F
w
• The total work done on the block during a displacement s is zero: $W_{tot} = 0$.
• The block's speed stays the same.

$$v_2^2 = v_1^2 + 2a_x s$$

$$a_x = \frac{v_2^2 - v_1^2}{2s}$$

When we multiply this equation by m and equate ma_x to the net force F, we find

$$F = ma_x = m\frac{v_2^2 - v_1^2}{2s} \quad \text{and}$$

$$Fs = \tfrac{1}{2}mv_2^2 - \tfrac{1}{2}mv_1^2 \tag{9.4}$$

The product Fs is the work done by the net force F and thus is equal to the total work W_{tot} done by all the forces acting on the particle. The quantity $\frac{1}{2}mv^2$ is called the **kinetic energy** K of the particle:

$$K = \tfrac{1}{2}mv^2 \quad \text{(definition of kinetic energy)} \tag{9.5}$$

Like work, the kinetic energy of a particle is a scalar quantity; it depends on only the particle's mass and speed, not its direction of motion (Fig. 9.7). A car (viewed as a particle) has the same kinetic energy when going north at 10 m/s as when going east at 10 m/s. Kinetic energy can never be negative, and it is zero only when the particle is at rest.

9.6 A constant net force $\vec{F}$ does work on a moving body.

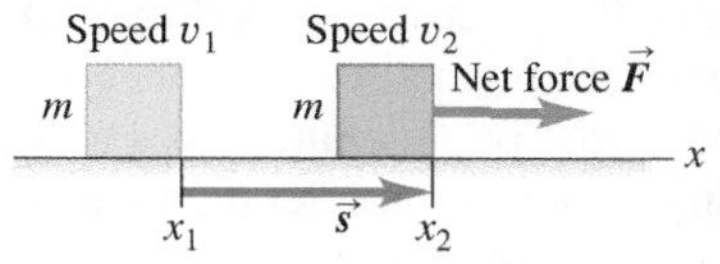
Speed v_1
Speed v_2
Net force $\vec{F}$
m
m
x
x_1
$\vec{s}$
x_2

9.7 Comparing the kinetic energy $K = \frac{1}{2}mv^2$ of different bodies.

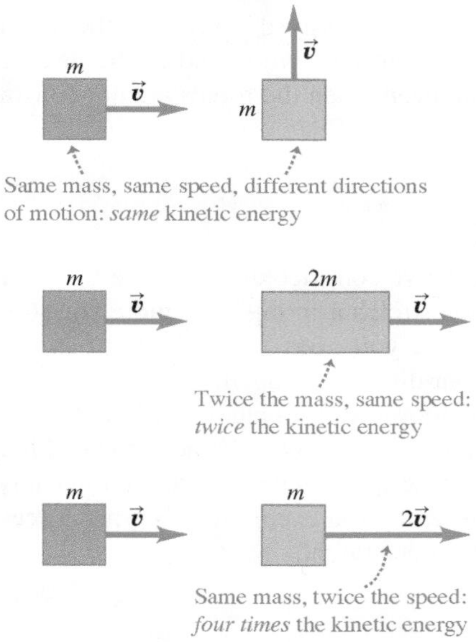
m
$\vec{v}$
m
$\vec{v}$
Same mass, same speed, different directions of motion: *same* kinetic energy
m
$\vec{v}$
2m
$\vec{v}$
Twice the mass, same speed: *twice* the kinetic energy
m
$\vec{v}$
m
$2\vec{v}$
Same mass, twice the speed: *four times* the kinetic energy

We can now interpret Eq. (9.4) in terms of work and kinetic energy. The first term on the right side of Eq. (9.4) is $K_2 = \frac{1}{2}mv_2^2$, the final kinetic energy of the particle (that is, after the displacement). The second term is the initial kinetic energy, $K_1 = \frac{1}{2}mv_1^2$, and the difference between these terms is the *change* in kinetic energy. So Eq. (9.4) says:

The work done by the net force on a particle equals the change in the particle's kinetic energy:

$$W_{tot} = K_2 - K_1 = \Delta K \qquad \text{(work–energy theorem)} \qquad (9.6)$$

This result is the **work–energy theorem.**

The work–energy theorem agrees with our observations about the block in Fig. 9.5. When W_{tot} is *positive,* the kinetic energy *increases* (the final kinetic energy K_2 is greater than the initial kinetic energy K_1) and the particle is going faster at the end of the displacement than at the beginning. When W_{tot} is *negative,* the kinetic energy *decreases* (K_2 is less than K_1) and the speed is less after the displacement. When $W_{tot} = 0$, the kinetic energy stays the same ($K_1 = K_2$) and the speed is unchanged. Note that the work–energy theorem by itself tells us only about changes in *speed,* not velocity, since the kinetic energy doesn't depend on the direction of motion.

From Eq. (9.4) or Eq. (9.6), kinetic energy and work must have the same units. Hence the joule is the SI unit of both work and kinetic energy (and, as we will see later, of all kinds of energy). To verify this, note that in SI units the quantity $K = \frac{1}{2}mv^2$ has units $\text{kg} \cdot (\text{m/s})^2$ or $\text{kg} \cdot \text{m}^2/\text{s}^2$; we recall that $1\ \text{N} = 1\ \text{kg} \cdot \text{m/s}^2$, so

$$1\ \text{J} = 1\ \text{N} \cdot \text{m} = 1\ (\text{kg} \cdot \text{m/s}^2) \cdot \text{m} = 1\ \text{kg} \cdot \text{m}^2/\text{s}^2$$

In the British system the unit of kinetic energy and of work is

$$1\ \text{ft} \cdot \text{lb} = 1\ \text{ft} \cdot \text{slug} \cdot \text{ft/s}^2 = 1\ \text{slug} \cdot \text{ft}^2/\text{s}^2$$

Because we used Newton's laws in deriving the work–energy theorem, we can use this theorem only in an inertial frame of reference. Note also that the work–energy theorem is valid in *any* inertial frame, but the values of W_{tot} and

$K_2 - K_1$ may differ from one inertial frame to another (because the displacement and speed of a body may be different in different frames).

We've derived the work–energy theorem for the special case of straight-line motion with constant forces. We'll find in the next section that the theorem is valid in general, even when the forces are not constant and the particle's trajectory is curved.

9.3 Work and Energy with Varying Forces

So far in this chapter we've considered work done by *constant forces* only. But what happens when you stretch a spring? The more you stretch it, the harder you have to pull, so the force you exert is *not* constant as the spring is stretched. We've also restricted our discussion to *straight-line* motion. There are many situations in which a body moves along a curved path and is acted on by a force that varies in magnitude, direction, or both. We need to be able to compute the work done by the force in these more general cases. Fortunately, we'll find that the work–energy theorem holds true even when varying forces are considered and when the body's path is not straight.

Work Done by a Varying Force, Straight-Line Motion

To add only one complication at a time, let's consider straight-line motion along the x-axis with a force whose x-component F_x may change as the body moves. (A real-life example is driving a car along a straight road with stop signs, so the driver has to alternately step on the gas and apply the brakes.) Suppose a particle moves along the x-axis from point x_1 to x_2 (Fig. 9.8a). Figure 9.8b is a graph of the x-component of force as a function of the particle's coordinate x. To find the work done by this force, we divide the total displacement into small segments Δx_a, Δx_b, and so on (Fig. 9.8c). We approximate the work done by the force during segment Δx_a as the average x-component of force F_{ax} in that segment multiplied by the x-displacement Δx_a. We do this for each segment and then add the results for all the segments. The work done by the force in the total displacement from x_1 to x_2 is approximately

$$W = F_{ax}\Delta x_a + F_{bx}\Delta x_b + \cdots$$

In the limit that the number of segments becomes very large and the width of each becomes very small, this sum becomes the *integral* of F_x from x_1 to x_2:

$$W = \int_{x_1}^{x_2} F_x\, dx \quad \text{(varying } x\text{-component of force, straight-line displacement)} \tag{9.7}$$

9.8 Calculating the work done by a varying force F_x in the x-direction as a particle moves from x_1 to x_2.

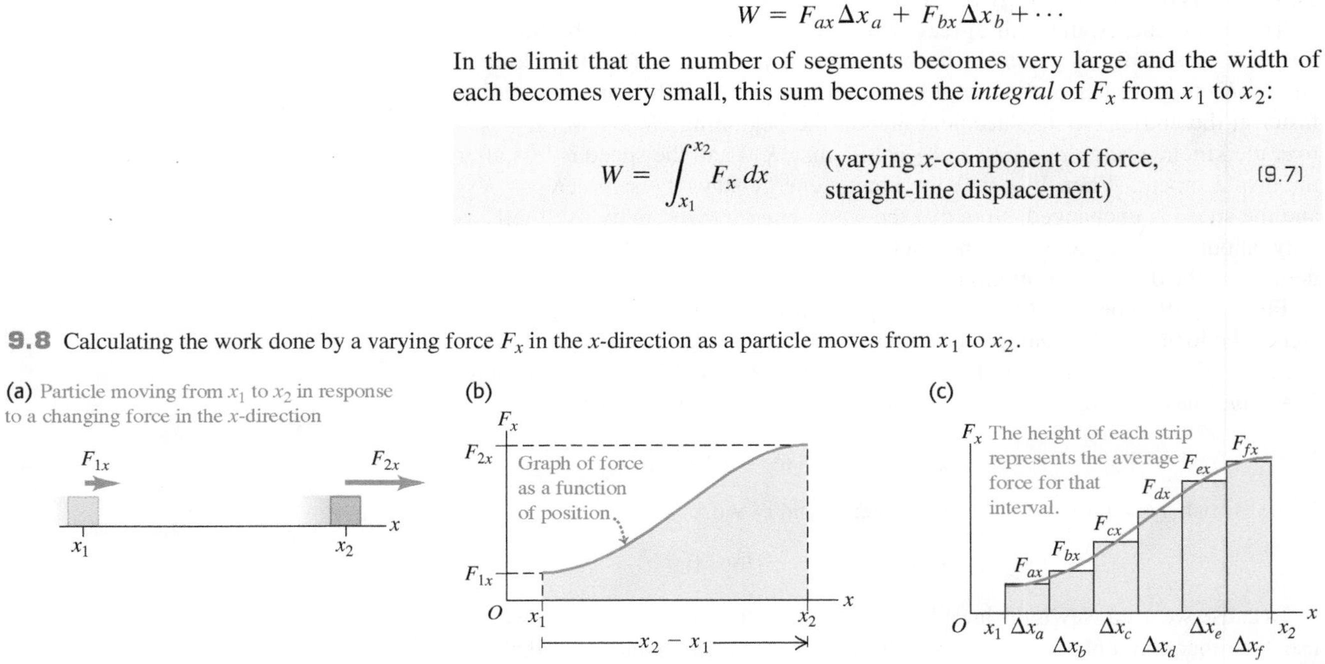

Note that $F_{ax}\Delta x_a$ represents the *area* of the first vertical strip in Fig. 9.8c and that the integral in Eq. (9.7) represents the area under the curve of Fig. 9.8b between x_1 and x_2. *On a graph of force as a function of position, the total work done by the force is represented by the area under the curve between the initial and final positions.* An alternative interpretation of Eq. (9.7) is that the work W equals the average force that acts over the entire displacement, multiplied by the displacement.

In the special case that F_x, the x-component of the force, is constant, it may be taken outside the integral in Eq. (9.7):

$$W = \int_{x_1}^{x_2} F_x\,dx = F_x\int_{x_1}^{x_2} dx = F_x(x_2 - x_1) \qquad \text{(constant force)}$$

But $x_2 - x_1 = s$, the total displacement of the particle. So in the case of a constant force F, Eq. (9.7) says that $W = Fs$, in agreement with Eq. (9.1). The interpretation of work as the area under the curve of F_x as a function of x also holds for a constant force; $W = Fs$ is the area of a rectangle of height F and width s (Fig. 9.9).

Now let's apply these ideas to the stretched spring. To keep a spring stretched beyond its unstretched length by an amount x, we have to apply a force of equal magnitude at each end (Fig. 9.10). If the elongation x is not too great, the force we apply to the right-hand end has an x-component directly proportional to x:

$$F_x = kx \qquad \text{(force required to stretch a spring)} \qquad (9.8)$$

where k is a constant called the **force constant** (or spring constant) of the spring. The units of k are force divided by distance: N/m in SI units and lb/ft in British units.

To stretch a spring, we must do work. We apply equal and opposite forces to the ends of the spring and gradually increase the forces. We hold the left end stationary, so the force we apply at this end does no work. The force at the moving end *does* do work. Figure 9.11 is a graph of F_x as a function of x, the elongation of the spring. The work done by this force when the elongation goes from zero to a maximum value X is

$$W = \int_0^X F_x\,dx = \int_0^X kx\,dx = \tfrac{1}{2}kX^2 \qquad (9.9)$$

We can also obtain this result graphically. The area of the shaded triangle in Fig. 9.11, representing the total work done by the force, is equal to half the product of the base and altitude, or

9.9 The work done by a constant force F in the x-direction as a particle moves from x_1 to x_2.

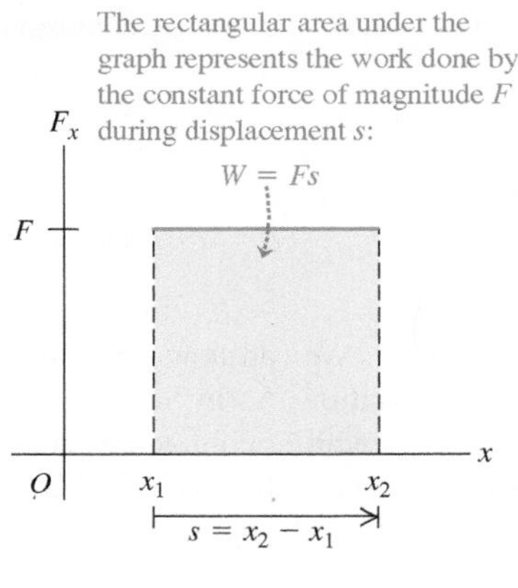
The rectangular area under the graph represents the work done by the constant force of magnitude F during displacement s:
W = Fs
F_x
F
O
x_1
x_2
x
s = x_2 − x_1

9.10 The force needed to stretch an ideal spring is proportional to the spring's elongation: $F_x = kx$.

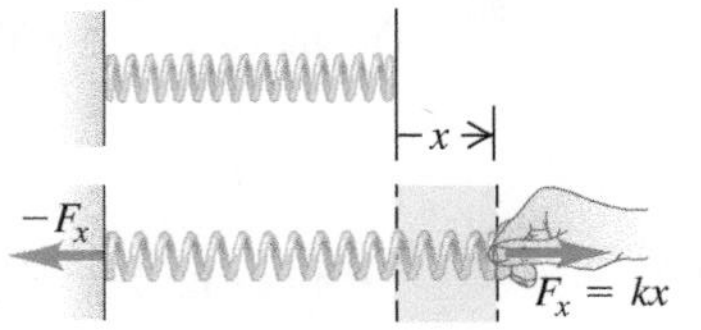
x
−F_x
F_x = kx

9.11 Calculating the work done to stretch a spring by a length X.

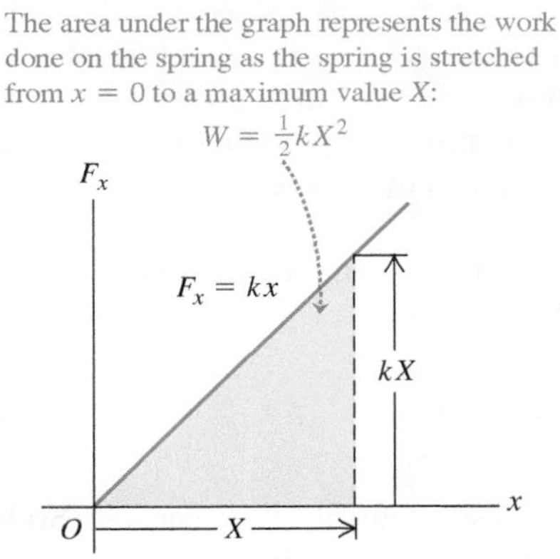

$$W = \tfrac{1}{2}(X)(kX) = \tfrac{1}{2}kX^2$$

This equation also says that the work is the *average* force $kX/2$ multiplied by the total displacement X. We see that the total work is proportional to the *square* of the final elongation X. To stretch an ideal spring by 2 cm, you must do four times as much work as is needed to stretch it by 1 cm.

Equation (9.9) assumes that the spring was originally unstretched. If initially the spring is already stretched a distance x_1, the work we must do to stretch it to a greater elongation x_2 (Fig. 9.12a) is

$$W = \int_{x_1}^{x_2} F_x\,dx = \int_{x_1}^{x_2} kx\,dx = \tfrac{1}{2}kx_2^2 - \tfrac{1}{2}kx_1^2 \tag{9.10}$$

You should use your knowledge of geometry to convince yourself that the trapezoidal area under the graph in Fig. 9.12b is given by the expression in Eq. (9.10).

If the spring has spaces between the coils when it is unstretched, then it can also be compressed, and Hooke's law holds for compression as well as stretching. In this case the force and displacement are in the opposite directions from those shown in Fig. 9.10, and so F_x and x in Eq. (9.8) are both negative. Since both F_x and x are reversed, the force again is in the same direction as the displacement, and the work done by F_x is again positive. So the total work is still given by Eq. (9.9) or (9.10), even when X is negative or either or both of x_1 and x_2 are negative.

CAUTION **Work done *on* a spring vs. work done *by* a spring** Note that Eq. (9.10) gives the work that *you* must do *on* a spring to change its length. For example, if you stretch a spring that's originally relaxed, then $x_1 = 0$, $x_2 > 0$, and $W > 0$: The force you apply to one end of the spring is in the same direction as the displacement, and the work you do is positive. By contrast, the work that the *spring* does on whatever it's attached to is given by the *negative* of Eq. (9.10). Thus, as you pull on the spring, the spring does negative work on you. Paying careful attention to the sign of work will eliminate confusion later on!

Work–Energy Theorem for Straight-Line Motion, Varying Forces

In Section 9.2 we derived the work–energy theorem, $W_{tot} = K_2 - K_1$, for the special case of straight-line motion with a constant net force. We can now prove that this theorem is true even when the force varies with position. As in Section 9.2, let's consider a particle that undergoes a displacement x while being acted on by a net force with x-component F_x, which we now allow to vary. Just as in Fig. 9.8, we divide the total displacement x into a large number of small segments Δx. We

9.12 Calculating the work done to stretch a spring from one extension to a greater one.

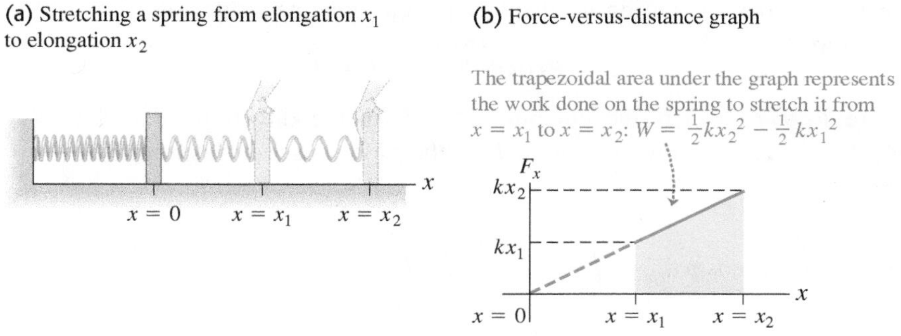
(a) Stretching a spring from elongation x_1 to elongation x_2
x
$x = 0$
$x = x_1$
$x = x_2$
(b) Force-versus-distance graph
The trapezoidal area under the graph represents the work done on the spring to stretch it from $x = x_1$ to $x = x_2$: $W = \frac{1}{2}kx_2^2 - \frac{1}{2}kx_1^2$
F_x
kx_2
kx_1
x
$x = 0$
$x = x_1$
$x = x_2$

can apply the work–energy theorem, Eq. (9.6), to each segment because the value of F_x in each small segment is approximately constant. The change in kinetic energy in segment Δx_a is equal to the work $F_{ax}\Delta x_a$, and so on. The total change of kinetic energy is the sum of the changes in the individual segments, and thus is equal to the total work done on the particle during the entire displacement. So $W_{tot} = \Delta K$ holds for varying forces as well as for constant ones.

Here's an alternative derivation of the work–energy theorem for a force that may vary with position. It involves making a change of variable from x to v_x in the work integral. As a preliminary, we note that the acceleration a of the particle can be expressed in various ways, using $a_x = dv_x/dt$, $v_x = dx/dt$, and the chain rule for derivatives:

$$a_x = \frac{dv_x}{dt} = \frac{dv_x}{dx}\frac{dx}{dt} = v_x\frac{dv_x}{dx} \tag{9.11}$$

From this result, Eq. (9.7) tells us that the total work done by the *net* force F_x is

$$W_{tot} = \int_{x_1}^{x_2} F_x\,dx = \int_{x_1}^{x_2} ma_x\,dx = \int_{x_1}^{x_2} mv_x\frac{dv_x}{dx}\,dx \tag{9.12}$$

Now $(dv_x/dx)dx$ is the change in velocity dv_x during the displacement dx, so in Eq. (9.12) we can substitute dv_x for $(dv_x/dx)\,dx$. This changes the integration variable from x to v_x, so we change the limits from x_1 and x_2 to the corresponding x-velocities v_1 and v_2 at these points. This gives us

$$W_{tot} = \int_{v_1}^{v_2} mv_x\,dv_x$$

The integral of $v_x\,dv_x$ is just $v_x^2/2$. Substituting the upper and lower limits, we finally find

$$W_{tot} = \tfrac{1}{2}mv_2^2 - \tfrac{1}{2}mv_1^2 \tag{9.13}$$

This is the same as Eq. (9.6), so the work–energy theorem is valid even without the assumption that the net force is constant.

Work–Energy Theorem for Motion Along a Curve

We can generalize our definition of work further to include a force that varies in direction as well as magnitude, and a displacement that lies along a curved path. Figure 9.13a shows a particle moving from P_1 to P_2 along a curve. We divide the curve between these points into many infinitesimal vector displacements, and we call a typical one of these $d\vec{l}$. Each $d\vec{l}$ is tangent to the path at its position. Let $\vec{F}$ be the force at a typical point along the path, and let ϕ be the angle between $\vec{F}$ and $d\vec{l}$ at this point. Then the small element of work dW done on the particle during the displacement $d\vec{l}$ may be written as

$$dW = F\cos\phi\, dl = F_{\parallel}\, dl = \vec{F}\cdot d\vec{l}$$

where $F_{\parallel} = F\cos\phi$ is the component of $\vec{F}$ in the direction parallel to $d\vec{l}$ (Fig. 9.13b). The total work done by $\vec{F}$ on the particle as it moves from P_1 to P_2 is then

$$W = \int_{P_1}^{P_2} F\cos\phi\, dl = \int_{P_1}^{P_2} F_{\parallel}\, dl = \int_{P_1}^{P_2} \vec{F}\cdot d\vec{l} \quad \text{(work done on a curved path)} \qquad (9.14)$$

We can now show that the work–energy theorem, Eq. (9.6), holds true even with varying forces and a displacement along a curved path. The force $\vec{F}$ is essentially constant over any given infinitesimal segment $d\vec{l}$ of the path, so we can apply the work–energy theorem for straight-line motion to that segment. Thus the change in the particle's kinetic energy K over that segment equals the work $dW = F_{\parallel}\, dl = \vec{F}\cdot d\vec{l}$ done on the particle. Adding up these infinitesimal quantities of work from all the segments along the whole path gives the total work done, Eq. (9.14), which equals the total change in kinetic energy over the whole path. So $W_{tot} = \Delta K = K_2 - K_1$ is true *in general,* no matter what the path and no matter what the character of the forces. This can be proved more rigorously by using steps like those in Eqs. (9.11) through (9.13).

Note that only the component of the net force parallel to the path, $F_{\parallel}$, does work on the particle, so only this component can change the speed and kinetic energy of the particle. The component perpendicular to the path, $F_{\perp} = F\sin\phi$, has no effect on the particle's speed; it acts only to change the particle's direction.

The integral in Eq. (9.14) is called a *line integral.* To evaluate this integral in a specific problem, we need some sort of detailed description of the path and of the way in which $\vec{F}$ varies along the path.

9.4 Power

The definition of work makes no reference to the passage of time. If you lift a barbell weighing 100 N through a vertical distance of 1.0 m at constant velocity, you do $(100\text{ N})(1.0\text{ m}) = 100\text{ J}$ of work whether it takes you 1 second, 1 hour, or 1 year to do it. But often we need to know how quickly work is done. We describe this in terms of *power.* In ordinary conversation the word "power" is often synonymous with "energy" or "force." In physics we use a much more precise definition: **Power** is the time *rate* at which work is done. Like work and energy, power is a scalar quantity.

9.13 A particle moves along a curved path from point P_1 to P_2, acted on by a force $\vec{F}$ that varies in magnitude and direction.

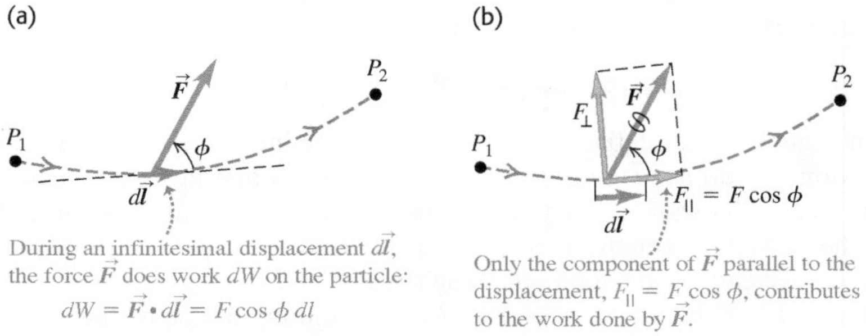

(a)
P_1
P_2
$\vec{F}$
ϕ
$d\vec{l}$
During an infinitesimal displacement $d\vec{l}$, the force $\vec{F}$ does work dW on the particle:
$dW = \vec{F}\cdot d\vec{l} = F\cos\phi\, dl$
(b)
P_1
P_2
$\vec{F}$
$F_{\perp}$
ϕ
$F_{\parallel} = F\cos\phi$
$d\vec{l}$
Only the component of $\vec{F}$ parallel to the displacement, $F_{\parallel} = F\cos\phi$, contributes to the work done by $\vec{F}$.

When a quantity of work ΔW is done during a time interval Δt, the average work done per unit time or **average power** P_{av} is defined to be

$$P_{av} = \frac{\Delta W}{\Delta t} \quad \text{(average power)} \tag{9.15}$$

The rate at which work is done might not be constant. We can define **instantaneous power** P as the quotient in Eq. (9.15) as Δt approaches zero:

$$P = \lim_{\Delta t \to 0} \frac{\Delta W}{\Delta t} = \frac{dW}{dt} \quad \text{(instantaneous power)} \tag{9.16}$$

The SI unit of power is the **watt** (W), named for the English inventor James Watt. One watt equals 1 joule per second: $1\text{ W} = 1\text{ J/s}$ (Fig. 9.14). The kilowatt $(1\text{ kW} = 10^3\text{ W})$ and the megawatt $(1\text{ MW} = 10^6\text{ W})$ are also commonly used. In the British system, work is expressed in foot-pounds, and the unit of power is the foot-pound per second. A larger unit called the *horsepower* (hp) is also used:

$$1\text{ hp} = 550\text{ ft}\cdot\text{lb/s} = 33{,}000\text{ ft}\cdot\text{lb/min}$$

That is, a 1-hp motor running at full load does 33,000 ft · lb of work every minute. A useful conversion factor is

$$1\text{ hp} = 746\text{ W} = 0.746\text{ kW}$$

The watt is a familiar unit of *electrical* power; a 100-W light bulb converts 100 J of electrical energy into light and heat each second. But there's nothing inherently electrical about a watt. A light bulb could be rated in horsepower, and an engine can be rated in kilowatts.

The *kilowatt-hour* (kW · h) is the usual commercial unit of electrical energy. One kilowatt-hour is the total work done in 1 hour (3600 s) when the power is 1 kilowatt (10^3 J/s), so

$$1\text{ kW}\cdot\text{h} = (10^3\text{ J/s})(3600\text{ s}) = 3.6 \times 10^6\text{ J} = 3.6\text{ MJ}$$

The kilowatt-hour is a unit of *work* or *energy,* not power.

In mechanics we can also express power in terms of force and velocity. Suppose that a force $\vec{F}$ acts on a body while it undergoes a vector displacement $\Delta\vec{s}$. If $F_\parallel$ is the component of $\vec{F}$ tangent to the path (parallel to $\Delta\vec{s}$), then the work done by the force is $\Delta W = F_\parallel \Delta s$. The average power is

$$P_{av} = \frac{F_\parallel \Delta s}{\Delta t} = F_\parallel \frac{\Delta s}{\Delta t} = F_\parallel v_{av} \tag{9.17}$$

Instantaneous power P is the limit of this expression as $\Delta t \to 0$:

$$P = F_\parallel v \tag{9.18}$$

9.14 The same amount of work is done in both of these situations, but the power (the rate at which work is done) is different.

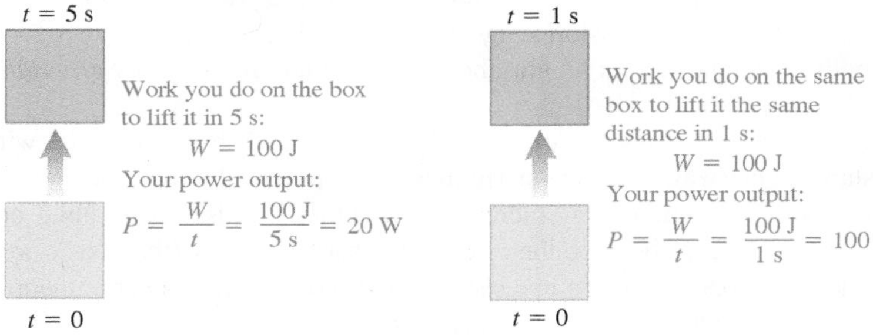

where v is the magnitude of the instantaneous velocity. We can also express Eq. (9.18) in terms of the scalar product:

$$P = \vec{F} \cdot \vec{v} \quad \text{(instantaneous rate at which force } \vec{F} \text{ does work on a particle)} \tag{9.19}$$

9.5 Gravitational Potential Energy

When a diver jumps off a high board into a swimming pool, he hits the water moving pretty fast, with a lot of kinetic energy. Where does that energy come from? The answer is that the gravitational force (his weight) does work on the diver as he falls. The diver's kinetic energy—energy associated with his *motion*—increases by an amount equal to the work done.

However, there is a very useful alternative way to think about work and kinetic energy. This new approach is based on the concept of *potential energy,* which is energy associated with the *position* of a system rather than its motion. In this approach, there is *gravitational potential energy* even while the diver is standing on the high board. Energy is not added to the earth–diver system as the diver falls, but rather a storehouse of energy is *transformed* from one form (potential energy) to another (kinetic energy) as he falls. In this chapter we'll see how the work–energy theorem explains this transformation.

If the diver bounces on the end of the board before he jumps, the bent board stores a second kind of potential energy called *elastic potential energy*. We'll discuss elastic potential energy of simple systems such as a stretched or compressed spring. (An important third kind of potential energy is associated with the positions of electrically charged particles relative to each other.

We will prove that in some cases the sum of a system's kinetic and potential energy, called the *total mechanical energy* of the system, is constant during the motion of the system. This will lead us to the general statement of the *law of conservation of energy,* one of the most fundamental and far-reaching principles in all of science.

We learned that a particle gains or loses kinetic energy because it interacts with other objects that exert forces on it. During any interaction, the change in a particle's kinetic energy is equal to the total work done on the particle by the forces that act on it.

In many situations it seems as though energy has been stored in a system, to be recovered later. For example, you must do work to lift a heavy stone over your head. It seems reasonable that in hoisting the stone into the air you are storing energy in the system, energy that is later converted into kinetic energy when you let the stone fall.

This example points to the idea of an energy associated with the *position* of bodies in a system. This kind of energy is a measure of the *potential* or *possibility* for work to be done; when a stone is raised into the air, there is a potential for work to be done on it by the gravitational force, but only if the stone is allowed to fall to the ground. For this reason, energy associated with position is called **potential energy.** Our discussion suggests that there is potential energy associated with a body's weight and its height above the ground. We call this *gravitational potential energy*.

We now have *two* ways to describe what happens when a body falls without air resistance. One way is to say that gravitational potential energy decreases and the falling body's kinetic energy increases. The other way is that a falling body's kinetic energy increases because the force of the earth's gravity (the body's weight) does work on the body. Later in this section we'll use the work–energy theorem to show that these two descriptions are equivalent.

To begin with, however, let's derive the expression for gravitational potential energy. Suppose a body with mass m moves along the (vertical) y-axis, as in Fig. 9.15. The forces acting on it are its weight, with magnitude $w = mg$, and possibly some other forces; we call the vector sum (resultant) of all the other forces $\vec{F}_{other}$. We'll assume that the body stays close enough to the earth's surface that the weight is constant. We want to find the work done by the weight when the body moves downward from a height y_1 above the origin to a lower height y_2 (Fig. 9.15a). The weight and displacement are in the same direction, so the work W_{grav} done on the body by its weight is positive;

$$W_{grav} = Fs = w(y_1 - y_2) = mgy_1 - mgy_2 \qquad (9.20)$$

This expression also gives the correct work when the body moves *upward* and y_2 is greater than y_1 (Fig. 9.15b). In that case the quantity $(y_1 - y_2)$ is negative, and W_{grav} is negative because the weight and displacement are opposite in direction.

Equation (9.20) shows that we can express W_{grav} in terms of the values of the quantity mgy at the beginning and end of the displacement. This quantity, the product of the weight mg and the height y above the origin of coordinates, is called the **gravitational potential energy,** U_{grav}:

$$U_{grav} = mgy \qquad \text{(gravitational potential energy)} \qquad (9.21)$$

Its initial value is $U_{grav,1} = mgy_1$ and its final value is $U_{grav,2} = mgy_2$. The change in U_{grav} is the final value minus the initial value, or $\Delta U_{grav} = U_{grav,2} - U_{grav,1}$. We can express the work W_{grav} done by the gravitational force during the displacement from y_1 to y_2 as

$$W_{grav} = U_{grav,1} - U_{grav,2} = -(U_{grav,2} - U_{grav,1}) = -\Delta U_{grav} \qquad (9.22)$$

The negative sign in front of ΔU_{grav} is *essential.* When the body moves up, y increases, the work done by the gravitational force is negative, and the gravitational potential energy increases $(\Delta U_{grav} > 0)$. When the body moves down, y decreases, the gravitational force does positive work, and the gravitational potential energy decreases $(\Delta U_{grav} < 0)$. It's like drawing money out of the bank (decreasing U_{grav}) and spending it (doing positive work). The unit of potential energy is the joule (J), the same unit as is used for work.

9.15 When a body moves vertically from an initial height y_1 to a final height y_2, the gravitational force $\vec{w}$ does work and the gravitational potential energy changes.

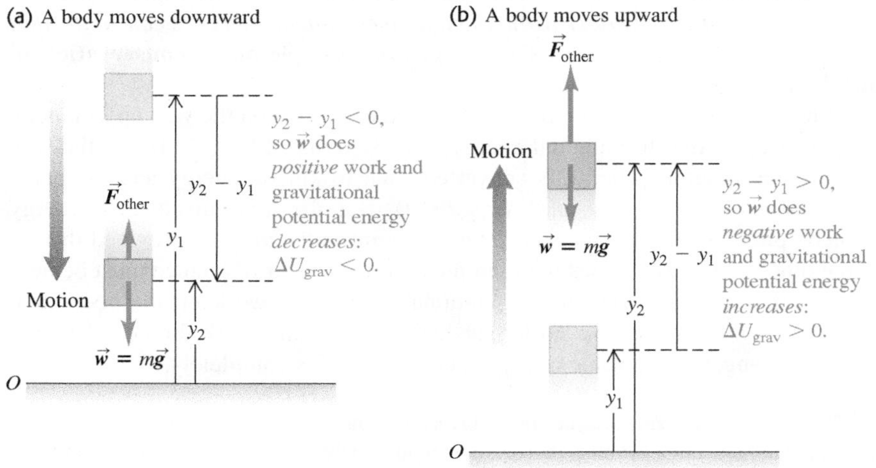

CAUTION **To what body does gravitational potential energy "belong"?** It is *not* correct to call $U_{grav} = mgy$ the "gravitational potential energy of the body." The reason is that gravitational potential energy U_{grav} is a *shared* property of the body and the earth. The value of U_{grav} increases if the earth stays fixed and the body moves upward, away from the earth; it also increases if the body stays fixed and the earth is moved away from it. Notice that the formula $U_{grav} = mgy$ involves characteristics of both the body (its mass m) and the earth (the value of g).

Conservation of Mechanical Energy (Gravitational Forces Only)

To see what gravitational potential energy is good for, suppose the body's weight is the *only* force acting on it, so $\vec{F}_{other} = \mathbf{0}$. The body is then falling freely with no air resistance and can be moving either up or down. Let its speed at point y_1 be v_1 and let its speed at y_2 be v_2. The work–energy theorem, says that the total work done on the body equals the change in the body's kinetic energy: $W_{tot} = \Delta K = K_2 - K_1$. If gravity is the only force that acts, then from Eq. (9.22), $W_{tot} = W_{grav} = -\Delta U_{grav} = U_{grav,1} - U_{grav,2}$. Putting these together, we get

$$\Delta K = -\Delta U_{grav} \qquad \text{or} \qquad K_2 - K_1 = U_{grav,1} - U_{grav,2}$$

which we can rewrite as

$$K_1 + U_{grav,1} = K_2 + U_{grav,2} \qquad \text{(if only gravity does work)} \tag{9.23}$$

or

$$\tfrac{1}{2}mv_1^2 + mgy_1 = \tfrac{1}{2}mv_2^2 + mgy_2 \qquad \text{(if only gravity does work)} \tag{9.24}$$

The sum $K + U_{grav}$ of kinetic and potential energy is called E, the **total mechanical energy of the system.** By "system" we mean the body of mass m and the earth considered together, because gravitational potential energy U is a shared property of both bodies. Then $E_1 = K_1 + U_{grav,1}$ is the total mechanical energy at y_1 and $E_2 = K_2 + U_{grav,2}$ is the total mechanical energy at y_2. Equation (9.23) says that when the body's weight is the only force doing work on it, $E_1 = E_2$. That is, E is constant; it has the same value at y_1 and y_2. But since the positions y_1 and y_2 are arbitrary points in the motion of the body, the total mechanical energy E has the same value at *all* points during the motion:

$$E = K + U_{grav} = \text{constant} \qquad \text{(if only gravity does work)}$$

A quantity that always has the same value is called a *conserved* quantity. *When only the force of gravity does work, the total mechanical energy is constant—that is, it is conserved* (Fig. 9.16). This is our first example of the **conservation of mechanical energy.**

When we throw a ball into the air, its speed decreases on the way up as kinetic energy is converted to potential energy; $\Delta K < 0$ and $\Delta U_{grav} > 0$. On the way back down, potential energy is converted back to kinetic energy and the ball's speed increases; $\Delta K > 0$ and $\Delta U_{grav} < 0$. But the *total* mechanical energy (kinetic plus potential) is the same at every point in the motion, provided that no force other than gravity does work on the ball (that is, air resistance must be negligible). It's still true that the gravitational force does work on the body as it moves up or down, but we no longer have to calculate work directly; keeping track of changes in the value of U_{grav} takes care of this completely.

CAUTION **Choose "zero height" to be wherever you like** When working with gravitational potential energy, we may choose any height to be $y = 0$. If we shift the origin for y,

9.16 While this athlete is in midair, only gravity does work on him (if we neglect the minor effects of air resistance). Mechanical energy E—the sum of kinetic and gravitational potential energy—is conserved.

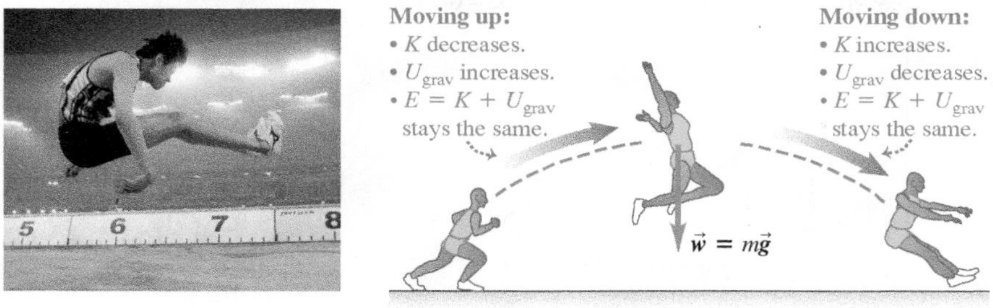
Moving up:
• K decreases.
• U_{grav} increases.
• $E = K + U_{grav}$ stays the same.
Moving down:
• K increases.
• U_{grav} decreases.
• $E = K + U_{grav}$ stays the same.
$\vec{w} = m\vec{g}$
5
6
7
8

the values of y_1 and y_2 change, as do the values of $U_{grav,1}$ and $U_{grav,2}$. But this shift has no effect on the *difference* in height $y_2 - y_1$ or on the *difference* in gravitational potential energy $U_{grav,2} - U_{grav,1} = mg(y_2 - y_1)$. As the following example shows, the physically significant quantity is not the value of U_{grav} at a particular point, but only the *difference* in U_{grav} between two points. So we can define U_{grav} to be zero at whatever point we choose without affecting the physics. ▌

When Forces Other Than Gravity Do Work

If other forces act on the body in addition to its weight, then $\vec{F}_{other}$ in Fig. 9.15 is *not* zero. For the pile driver (Section 9.2), the force applied by the hoisting cable and the friction with the vertical guide rails are examples of forces that might be included in $\vec{F}_{other}$. The gravitational work W_{grav} is still given by Eq. (9.22), but the total work W_{tot} is then the sum of W_{grav} and the work done by $\vec{F}_{other}$. We will call this additional work W_{other}, so the total work done by all forces is $W_{tot} = W_{grav} + W_{other}$. Equating this to the change in kinetic energy, we have

$$W_{other} + W_{grav} = K_2 - K_1 \qquad (9.25)$$

Also, from Eq. (9.22), $W_{grav} = U_{grav,1} - U_{grav,2}$, so

$$W_{other} + U_{grav,1} - U_{grav,2} = K_2 - K_1$$

which we can rearrange in the form

$$K_1 + U_{grav,1} + W_{other} = K_2 + U_{grav,2} \quad \text{(if forces other than gravity do work)} \qquad (9.26)$$

Finally, using the appropriate expressions for the various energy terms, we obtain

$$\tfrac{1}{2}mv_1^2 + mgy_1 + W_{other} = \tfrac{1}{2}mv_2^2 + mgy_2 \qquad (9.27)$$

The meaning of Eqs. (9.26) and (9.27) is this: *The work done by all forces other than the gravitational force equals the change in the total mechanical energy $E = K + U_{grav}$ of the system, where U_{grav} is the gravitational potential energy.* When W_{other} is positive, E increases and $K_2 + U_{grav,2}$ is greater than $K_1 + U_{grav,1}$. When W_{other} is negative, E decreases. In the special case in which no forces other than the body's weight do work, $W_{other} = 0$. The total mechanical energy is then constant, and we are back to Eq. (9.23) or (9.24).

Gravitational Potential Energy for Motion Along a Curved Path

What happens when the path is slanted or curved (Fig. 9.17a)? The body is acted on by the gravitational force $\vec{w} = m\vec{g}$ and possibly by other forces whose result-

9.17 Calculating the change in gravitational potential energy for a displacement along a curved path.

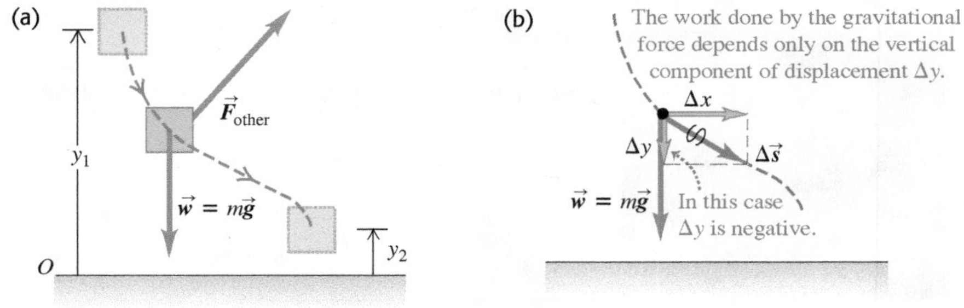

ant we call $\vec{F}_{other}$. To find the work done by the gravitational force during this displacement, we divide the path into small segments $\Delta\vec{s}$; Fig. 9.17b shows a typical segment. The work done by the gravitational force over this segment is the scalar product of the force and the displacement. In terms of unit vectors, the force is $\vec{w} = m\vec{g} = -mg\hat{j}$ and the displacement is $\Delta\vec{s} = \Delta x\hat{\imath} + \Delta y\hat{j}$, so the work done by the gravitational force is

$$\vec{w} \cdot \Delta\vec{s} = -mg\hat{j} \cdot (\Delta x\hat{\imath} + \Delta y\hat{j}) = -mg\Delta y$$

The work done by gravity is the same as though the body had been displaced vertically a distance Δy, with no horizontal displacement. This is true for every segment, so the *total* work done by the gravitational force is $-mg$ multiplied by the *total* vertical displacement $(y_2 - y_1)$:

$$W_{grav} = -mg(y_2 - y_1) = mgy_1 - mgy_2 = U_{grav,1} - U_{grav,2}$$

This is the same as Eq. (9.20) or (9.22), in which we assumed a purely vertical path. So even if the path a body follows between two points is curved, the total work done by the gravitational force depends only on the difference in height between the two points of the path. This work is unaffected by any horizontal motion that may occur. So *we can use the same expression for gravitational potential energy whether the body's path is curved or straight.*

9.6 Conservative and Nonconservative Forces

In our discussions of potential energy we have talked about "storing" kinetic energy by converting it to potential energy. We always have in mind that later we may retrieve it again as kinetic energy. For example, when you throw a ball up in the air, it slows down as kinetic energy is converted to gravitational potential energy. But on the way down, the conversion is reversed, and the ball speeds up as potential energy is converted back to kinetic energy. If there is no air resistance, the ball is moving just as fast when you catch it as when you threw it.

Another example is a glider moving on a frictionless horizontal air track that runs into a spring bumper at the end of the track. The glider stops as it compresses the spring and then bounces back. If there is no friction, the glider ends up with the same speed and kinetic energy it had before the collision. Again, there is a two-way conversion from kinetic to potential energy and back. In both cases we can define a potential-energy function so that the total mechanical energy, kinetic plus potential, is constant or *conserved* during the motion.

Conservative Forces

A force that offers this opportunity of two-way conversion between kinetic and potential energies is called a **conservative force.** We have seen two examples of conservative forces: the gravitational force and the spring force. An essential feature of conservative forces is that their work is always *reversible.* Anything that we deposit in the energy "bank" can later be withdrawn without loss. Another important aspect of conservative forces is that a body may move from point 1 to point 2 by various paths, but the work done by a conservative force is the same for all of these paths (Fig. 9.18). Thus, if a body stays close to the surface of the earth, the gravitational force $m\vec{g}$ is independent of height, and the work done by this force depends only on the change in height. If the body moves around a closed path, ending at the same point where it started, the *total* work done by the gravitational force is always zero.

The work done by a conservative force *always* has four properties:

1. It can be expressed as the difference between the initial and final values of a *potential-energy* function.
2. It is reversible.
3. It is independent of the path of the body and depends only on the starting and ending points.
4. When the starting and ending points are the same, the total work is zero.

When the *only* forces that do work are conservative forces, the total mechanical energy $E = K + U$ is constant.

Nonconservative Forces

Not all forces are conservative. Consider the friction force acting on the crate sliding on a ramp (Section 9.5). When the body slides up and then back down to the starting point, the total work done on it by the friction force is *not* zero. When the direction of motion reverses, so does the friction force, and friction does *negative* work in *both* directions. When a car with its brakes locked skids across the pavement with decreasing speed (and decreasing kinetic energy), the lost kinetic energy cannot be recovered by reversing the motion or in any other way, and mechanical energy is *not* conserved. There is *no* potential-energy function for the friction force.

In the same way, the force of fluid resistance is not conservative. If you throw a ball up in the air, air resistance does negative work on the ball while it's rising *and* while it's descending. The ball returns to your hand with less speed and less

9.18 The work done by a conservative force such as gravity depends only on the end points of a path, not on the specific path taken between those points.

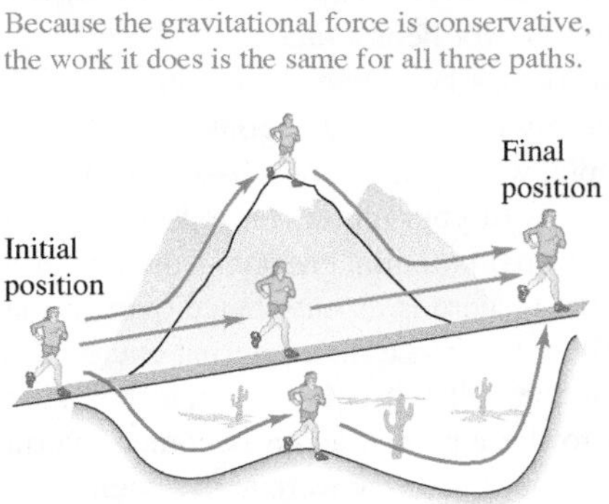
Because the gravitational force is conservative, the work it does is the same for all three paths.
Initial position
Final position

kinetic energy than when it left, and there is no way to get back the lost mechanical energy.

A force that is not conservative is called a **nonconservative force.** The work done by a nonconservative force *cannot* be represented by a potential-energy function. Some nonconservative forces, like kinetic friction or fluid resistance, cause mechanical energy to be lost or dissipated; a force of this kind is called a **dissipative force.** There are also nonconservative forces that *increase* mechanical energy. The fragments of an exploding firecracker fly off with very large kinetic energy, thanks to a chemical reaction of gunpowder with oxygen. The forces unleashed by this reaction are nonconservative because the process is not reversible. (The fragments never spontaneously reassemble themselves into a complete firecracker!)

The Law of Conservation of Energy

Nonconservative forces cannot be represented in terms of potential energy. But we can describe the effects of these forces in terms of kinds of energy other than kinetic and potential energy. When a car with locked brakes skids to a stop, the tires and the road surface both become hotter. The energy associated with this change in the state of the materials is called **internal energy.** Raising the temperature of a body increases its internal energy; lowering the body's temperature decreases its internal energy.

To see the significance of internal energy, let's consider a block sliding on a rough surface. Friction does *negative* work on the block as it slides, and the change in internal energy of the block and surface (both of which get hotter) is *positive.* Careful experiments show that the increase in the internal energy is *exactly* equal to the absolute value of the work done by friction. In other words,

$$\Delta U_{\text{int}} = -W_{\text{other}}$$

where ΔU_{int} is the change in internal energy. If we substitute this into Eq. (9.26) we find

$$K_1 + U_1 - \Delta U_{\text{int}} = K_2 + U_2$$

Writing $\Delta K = K_2 - K_1$ and $\Delta U = U_2 - U_1$, we can finally express this as

$$\Delta K + \Delta U + \Delta U_{\text{int}} = 0 \quad \text{(law of conservation of energy)} \tag{9.28}$$

This remarkable statement is the general form of the **law of conservation of energy.** In a given process, the kinetic energy, potential energy, and internal energy of a system may all change. But the *sum* of those changes is always zero. If there is a decrease in one form of energy, it is made up for by an increase in the other forms. When we expand our definition of energy to include internal energy, Eq. (9.28) says: *Energy is never created or destroyed; it only changes form.* No exception to this rule has ever been found.

The concept of work has been banished from Eq. (9.28); instead, it suggests that we think purely in terms of the conversion of energy from one form to another. For example, when you throw a baseball straight up, you convert a portion of the internal energy of your molecules to kinetic energy of the baseball. This is converted to gravitational potential energy as the ball climbs and back to kinetic energy as the ball falls. If there is air resistance, part of the energy is used to heat up the air and the ball and increase their internal energy. Energy is converted back to the kinetic form as the ball falls. If you catch the ball in your hand, whatever energy was not lost to the air once again becomes internal energy; the ball and your hand are now warmer than they were at the beginning.

9.7 Energy Diagrams

When a particle moves along a straight line under the action of a conservative force, we can get a lot of insight into its possible motions by looking at the graph of the potential-energy function $U(x)$. Figure 9.19a shows a glider with mass m that moves along the x-axis on an air track. The spring exerts on the glider a force with x-component $F_x = -kx$. Figure 9.19b is a graph of the corresponding potential-energy function $U(x) = \frac{1}{2}kx^2$. If the elastic force of the spring is the *only* horizontal force acting on the glider, the total mechanical energy $E = K + U$ is constant, independent of x. A graph of E as a function of x is thus a straight horizontal line. We use the term **energy diagram** for a graph like this, which shows both the potential-energy function $U(x)$ and the energy of the particle subjected to the force that corresponds to $U(x)$.

The vertical distance between the U and E graphs at each point represents the difference $E - U$, equal to the kinetic energy K at that point. We see that K is greatest at $x = 0$. It is zero at the values of x where the two graphs cross, labeled A and $-A$ in the diagram. Thus the speed v is greatest at $x = 0$, and it is zero at $x = \pm A$, the points of *maximum* possible displacement from $x = 0$ for a given value of the total energy E. The potential energy U can never be greater than the total energy E; if it were, K would be negative, and that's impossible. The motion is a back-and-forth oscillation between the points $x = A$ and $x = -A$.

At each point, the force F_x on the glider is equal to the negative of the slope of the $U(x)$ curve: $F_x = -dU/dx$. When the particle is at $x = 0$, the slope and the force are zero, so this is an *equilibrium* position. When x is positive, the slope of the $U(x)$ curve is positive and the force F_x is negative, directed toward the origin. When x is negative, the slope is negative and F_x is positive, again directed toward the origin. Such a force is called a *restoring force;* when the glider is displaced to either side of $x = 0$, the force tends to "restore" it back to $x = 0$. An analogous situation is a marble rolling around in a round-bottomed bowl. We say that $x = 0$ is a point of **stable equilibrium.** More generally, *any minimum in a potential-energy curve is a stable equilibrium position.*

Figure 9.20a shows a hypothetical but more general potential-energy function $U(x)$. Figure 9.20b shows the corresponding force $F_x = -dU/dx$. Points x_1 and x_3 are stable equilibrium points. At each of these points, F_x is zero because the slope of the $U(x)$ curve is zero. When the particle is displaced to either side, the force pushes back toward the equilibrium point. The slope of the $U(x)$ curve is also zero at points x_2 and x_4, and these are also equilibrium points. But when the particle is displaced a little to the right of either point, the slope of the $U(x)$ curve becomes negative, corresponding to a positive F_x that tends to push the particle still farther from the point. When the particle is displaced a little to the left, F_x is

9.19 (a) A glider on an air track. The spring exerts a force $F_x = -kx$. (b) The potential-energy function.

(a)
x
−A
O
A
The limits of the glider's motion are at x = A and x = −A.
(b)
On the graph, the limits of motion are the points where the U curve intersects the horizontal line representing total mechanical energy E.
U
U = 1/2 kx²
E = K + U
K
U
x
−A
O
A

9.20 The maxima and minima of a potential-energy function $U(x)$ correspond to points where $F_x = 0$.

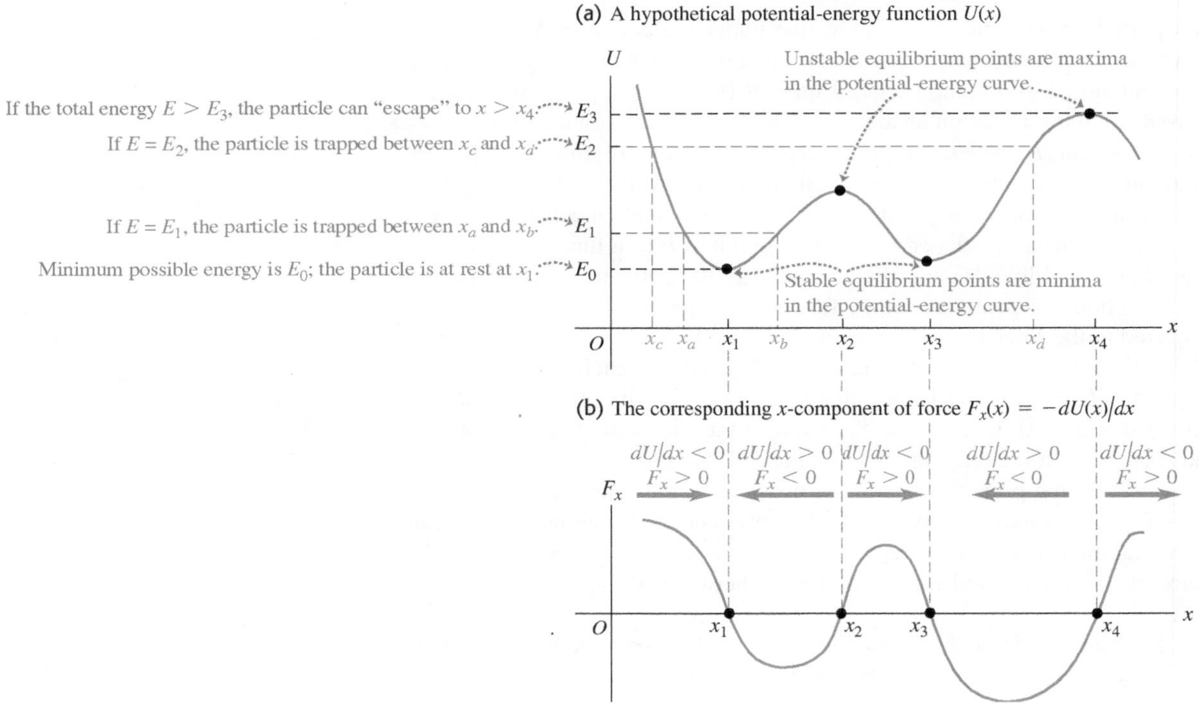
(a) A hypothetical potential-energy function U(x)
U
Unstable equilibrium points are maxima in the potential-energy curve.
If the total energy E > E3, the particle can "escape" to x > x4. E3
If E = E2, the particle is trapped between xc and xd. E2
If E = E1, the particle is trapped between xa and xb. E1
Minimum possible energy is E0; the particle is at rest at x1. E0
Stable equilibrium points are minima in the potential-energy curve.
O
xc xa x1 xb x2 x3 xd x4
x
(b) The corresponding x-component of force Fx(x) = −dU(x)/dx
dU/dx < 0 Fx > 0
dU/dx > 0 Fx < 0
dU/dx < 0 Fx > 0
dU/dx > 0 Fx < 0
dU/dx < 0 Fx > 0
Fx
O
x1 x2 x3 x4
x

negative, again pushing away from equilibrium. This is analogous to a marble rolling on the top of a bowling ball. Points x_2 and x_4 are called **unstable equilibrium** points; *any maximum in a potential-energy curve is an unstable equilibrium position.*

CAUTION Potential energy and the direction of a conservative force The direction of the force on a body is *not* determined by the sign of the potential energy U. Rather, it's the sign of $F_x = -dU/dx$ that matters. As we discussed in Section 9.5, the physically significant quantity is the *difference* in the values of U between two points, which is just what the derivative $F_x = -dU/dx$ measures. This means that you can always add a constant to the potential-energy function without changing the physics of the situation.

If the total energy is E_1 and the particle is initially near x_1, it can move only in the region between x_a and x_b determined by the intersection of the E_1 and U graphs (Fig. 9.20a). Again, U cannot be greater than E_1 because K can't be negative. We speak of the particle as moving in a *potential well,* and x_a and x_b are the *turning points* of the particle's motion (since at these points, the particle stops and reverses direction). If we increase the total energy to the level E_2, the particle can move over a wider range, from x_c to x_d. If the total energy is greater than E_3, the particle can "escape" and move to indefinitely large values of x. At the other extreme, E_0 represents the least possible total energy the system can have.

9.8 Momentum Conservation and Collisions

Momentum and Kinetic Energy Compared

There is a fundamental difference between momentum and kinetic energy. The impulse–momentum theorem $\vec{J} = \vec{p}_2 - \vec{p}_1$ says that changes in a particle's momentum are due to impulse, which depends on the *time* over which the net force acts. By contrast, the work–energy theorem $W_{tot} = K_2 - K_1$ tells us that kinetic energy changes when work is done on a particle; the total work depends on the *distance* over which the net force acts. Consider a particle that starts from rest at t_1 so that $\vec{v}_1 = \mathbf{0}$. Its initial momentum is $\vec{p}_1 = m\vec{v}_1 = \mathbf{0}$, and its initial kinetic energy is $K_1 = \frac{1}{2}mv_1^2 = 0$. Now let a constant net force equal to $\vec{F}$ act on that particle from time t_1 until time t_2. During this interval, the particle moves a distance s in the direction of the force. The particle's momentum at time t_2 is

$$\vec{p}_2 = \vec{p}_1 + \vec{J} = \vec{J}$$

where $\vec{J} = \vec{F}(t_2 - t_1)$ is the impulse that acts on the particle. So *the momentum of a particle equals the impulse that accelerated it from rest to its present speed;* impulse is the product of the net force that accelerated the particle and the *time* required for the acceleration. By comparison, the kinetic energy of the particle at t_2 is $K_2 = W_{tot} = Fs$, the total *work* done on the particle to accelerate it from rest. The total work is the product of the net force and the *distance* required to accelerate the particle.

Here's an application of the distinction between momentum and kinetic energy. Suppose you have a choice between catching a 0.50-kg ball moving at 4.0 m/s or a 0.10-kg ball moving at 20 m/s. Which will be easier to catch? Both balls have the same magnitude of momentum, $p = mv = (0.50\text{ kg})(4.0\text{ m/s}) = (0.10\text{ kg})(20\text{ m/s}) = 2.0\text{ kg}\cdot\text{m/s}$. However, the two balls have different values of kinetic energy $K = \frac{1}{2}mv^2$; the large, slow-moving ball has $K = 4.0\text{ J}$, while the small, fast-moving ball has $K = 20\text{ J}$. Since the momentum is the same for both balls, both require the same *impulse* to be brought to rest. But stopping the 0.10-kg ball with your hand requires five times more *work* than stopping the 0.50-kg ball because the smaller ball has five times more kinetic energy. For a given force that you exert with your hand, it takes the same amount of time (the duration of the catch) to stop either ball, but your hand and arm will be pushed back five times farther if you choose to catch the small, fast-moving ball. To minimize arm strain, you should choose to catch the 0.50-kg ball with its lower kinetic energy.

Both the impulse–momentum and work–energy theorems are relationships between force and motion, and both rest on the foundation of Newton's laws. They are *integral* principles, relating the motion at two different times separated by a finite interval. By contrast, Newton's second law itself (in either of the forms $\sum\vec{F} = m\vec{a}$ or $\sum\vec{F} = d\vec{p}/dt$) is a *differential* principle, relating the forces to the rate of change of velocity or momentum at each instant.

Elastic and Inelastic Collisions

If the forces between the bodies are also *conservative,* so that no mechanical energy is lost or gained in the collision, the total *kinetic* energy of the system is the same after the collision as before. Such a collision is called an **elastic collision.** A collision between two marbles or two billiard balls is almost completely elastic. Figure 9.21 shows a model for an elastic collision. When the gliders collide, their springs are momentarily compressed and some of the original kinetic energy is momentarily converted to elastic potential energy. Then the gliders bounce apart, the springs expand, and this potential energy is converted back to kinetic energy.

A collision in which the total kinetic energy after the collision is *less* than before the collision is called an **inelastic collision.** A meatball landing on a plate of spaghetti and a bullet embedding itself in a block of wood are examples of inelastic collisions. An inelastic collision in which the colliding bodies stick together and move as one body after the collision is often called a **completely inelastic collision.** Figure 9.22 shows an example; we have replaced the spring bumpers in Fig. 9.21 with Velcro®, which sticks the two bodies together.

CAUTION **An inelastic collision doesn't have to be *completely* inelastic** It's a common misconception that the *only* inelastic collisions are those in which the colliding bodies stick together. In fact, inelastic collisions include many situations in which the bodies do

9.21 Two gliders undergoing an elastic collision on a frictionless surface. Each glider has a steel spring bumper that exerts a conservative force on the other glider.

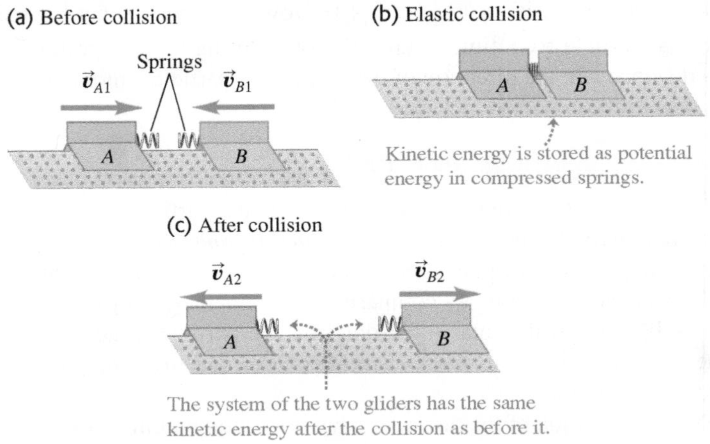
(a) Before collision
Springs
A
B
(b) Elastic collision
A
B
Kinetic energy is stored as potential energy in compressed springs.
(c) After collision
A
B
The system of the two gliders has the same kinetic energy after the collision as before it.

9.22 Two gliders undergoing a completely inelastic collision. The spring bumpers on the gliders are replaced by Velcro®, so the gliders stick together after collision.

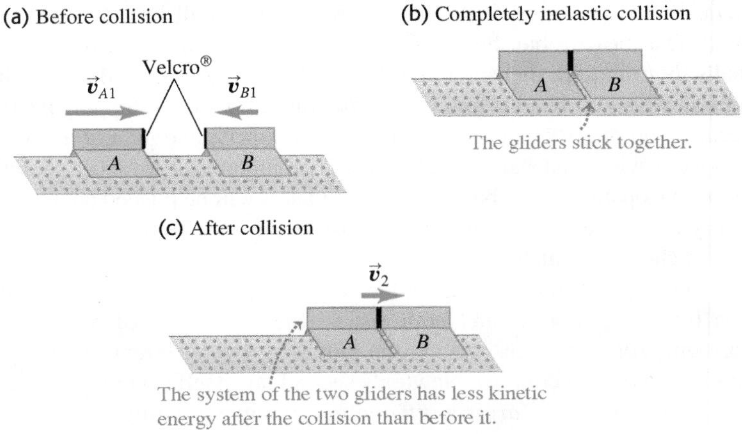
(a) Before collision
Velcro®
A
B
(b) Completely inelastic collision
A
B
The gliders stick together.
(c) After collision
A
B
The system of the two gliders has less kinetic energy after the collision than before it.

not stick. If two cars bounce off each other in a "fender bender," the work done to deform the fenders cannot be recovered as kinetic energy of the cars, so the collision is inelastic.

Remember this rule: **In any collision in which external forces can be neglected, momentum is conserved and the total momentum before equals the total momentum after; in elastic collisions *only,* the total kinetic energy before equals the total kinetic energy after.**

Completely Inelastic Collisions

Let's look at what happens to momentum and kinetic energy in a *completely* inelastic collision of two bodies (A and B), as in Fig. 9.22. Because the two bodies stick together after the collision, they have the same final velocity $\vec{v}_2$:

$$\vec{v}_{A2} = \vec{v}_{B2} = \vec{v}_2$$

Conservation of momentum gives the relationship

$$m_A\vec{v}_{A1} + m_B\vec{v}_{B1} = (m_A + m_B)\vec{v}_2 \quad \text{(completely inelastic collision)} \tag{9.29}$$

If we know the masses and initial velocities, we can compute the common final velocity $\vec{v}_2$.

Suppose, for example, that a body with mass m_A and initial x-component of velocity v_{A1x} collides inelastically with a body with mass m_B that is initially at rest ($v_{B1x} = 0$). From Eq. (9.29) the common x-component of velocity v_{2x} of both bodies after the collision is

$$v_{2x} = \frac{m_A}{m_A + m_B} v_{A1x} \qquad \text{(completely inelastic collision, } B \text{ initially at rest)} \tag{9.30}$$

Let's verify that the total kinetic energy after this completely inelastic collision is less than before the collision. The motion is purely along the x-axis, so the kinetic energies K_1 and K_2 before and after the collision, respectively, are

$$K_1 = \tfrac{1}{2} m_A v_{A1x}{}^2$$

$$K_2 = \tfrac{1}{2}(m_A + m_B) v_{2x}{}^2 = \tfrac{1}{2}(m_A + m_B)\left(\frac{m_A}{m_A + m_B}\right)^2 v_{A1x}{}^2$$

The ratio of final to initial kinetic energy is

$$\frac{K_2}{K_1} = \frac{m_A}{m_A + m_B} \qquad \text{(completely inelastic collision, } B \text{ initially at rest)} \tag{9.31}$$

The right side is always less than unity because the denominator is always greater than the numerator. Even when the initial velocity of m_B is not zero, it is not hard to verify that the kinetic energy after a completely inelastic collision is always less than before.

Please note: We don't recommend memorizing Eq. (9.30) or (9.31). We derived them only to prove that kinetic energy is always lost in a completely inelastic collision.

Classifying Collisions

It's important to remember that we can classify collisions according to energy considerations (Fig. 9.23). A collision in which kinetic energy is conserved is called *elastic.* (We'll explore these in more depth in the next section.) A collision in which the total kinetic energy decreases is called *inelastic.* When the two bodies have a common final velocity, we say that the collision is *completely inelastic.* There are also cases in which the final kinetic energy is *greater* than the initial value.

Finally, we emphasize again that we can sometimes use momentum conservation even when there are external forces acting on the system, if the net external force acting on the colliding bodies is small in comparison with the internal forces during the collision.

9.23 Collisions are classified according to energy considerations.

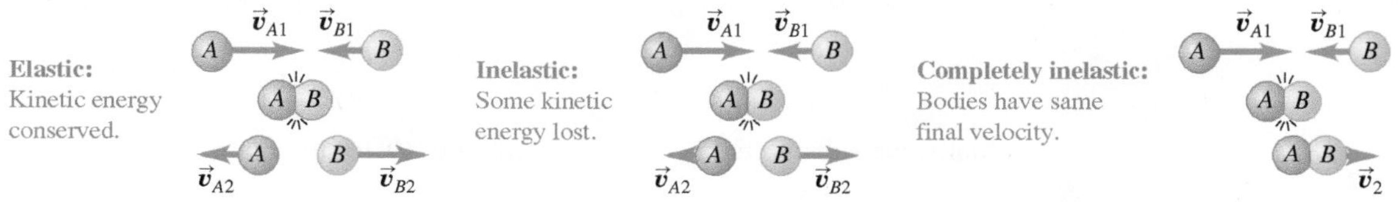

9.9 Elastic Collisions

Elastic collision in an isolated system is one in which kinetic energy (as well as momentum) is conserved. Elastic collisions occur when the forces between the colliding bodies are *conservative.* When two billiard balls collide, they squash a little near the surface of contact, but then they spring back. Some of the kinetic energy is stored temporarily as elastic potential energy, but at the end it is reconverted to kinetic energy.

Let's look at an elastic collision between two bodies A and B. We start with a one-dimensional collision, in which all the velocities lie along the same line; we choose this line to be the x-axis. Each momentum and velocity then has only an x-component. We call the x-velocities before the collision v_{A1x} and v_{B1x}, and those after the collision v_{A2x} and v_{B2x}. From conservation of kinetic energy we have

$$\frac{1}{2}m_A v_{A1x}^2 + \frac{1}{2}m_B v_{B1x}^2 = \frac{1}{2}m_A v_{A2x}^2 + \frac{1}{2}m_B v_{B2x}^2$$

and conservation of momentum gives

$$m_A v_{A1x} + m_B v_{B1x} = m_A v_{A2x} + m_B v_{B2x}$$

If the masses m_A and m_B and the initial velocities v_{A1x} and v_{B1x} are known, we can solve these two equations to find the two final velocities v_{A2x} and v_{B2x}.

Elastic Collisions, One Body Initially at Rest

The general solution to the above equations is a little complicated, so we will concentrate on the particular case in which body B is at rest before the collision (so $v_{B1x} = 0$). Think of body B as a target for body A to hit. Then the kinetic energy and momentum conservation equations are, respectively,

$$\frac{1}{2}m_A v_{A1x}^2 = \frac{1}{2}m_A v_{A2x}^2 + \frac{1}{2}m_B v_{B2x}^2 \quad (9.32)$$

$$m_A v_{A1x} = m_A v_{A2x} + m_B v_{B2x} \quad (9.33)$$

We can solve for v_{A2x} and v_{B2x} in terms of the masses and the initial velocity v_{A1x}. This involves some fairly strenuous algebra, but it's worth it. No pain, no gain! The simplest approach is somewhat indirect, but along the way it uncovers an additional interesting feature of elastic collisions.

First we rearrange Eqs. (9.32) and (9.33) as follows:

$$m_B v_{B2x}^2 = m_A(v_{A1x}^2 - v_{A2x}^2) = m_A(v_{A1x} - v_{A2x})(v_{A1x} + v_{A2x}) \quad (9.34)$$

$$m_B v_{B2x} = m_A(v_{A1x} - v_{A2x}) \quad (9.35)$$

Now we divide Eq. (9.34) by Eq. (9.35) to obtain

$$v_{B2x} = v_{A1x} + v_{A2x} \quad (9.36)$$

We substitute this expression back into Eq. (9.35) to eliminate v_{B2x} and then solve for v_{A2x}:

$$m_B(v_{A1x} + v_{A2x}) = m_A(v_{A1x} - v_{A2x})$$

$$v_{A2x} = \frac{m_A - m_B}{m_A + m_B} v_{A1x} \quad (9.37)$$

Finally, we substitute this result back into Eq. (9.36) to obtain

$$v_{B2x} = \frac{2m_A}{m_A + m_B} v_{A1x} \quad (9.38)$$

9.24 Collisions between **(a)** a moving Ping-Pong ball and an initially stationary bowling ball, and **(b)** a moving bowling ball and an initially stationary Ping-Pong ball.

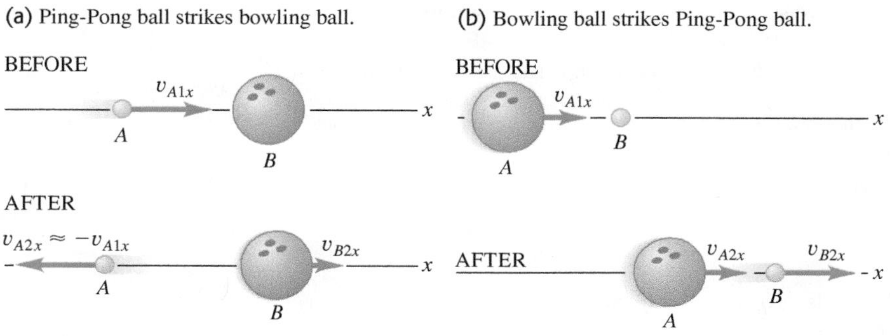
(a) Ping-Pong ball strikes bowling ball.
BEFORE
v_{A1x}
A
B
x
AFTER
$v_{A2x} \approx -v_{A1x}$
v_{B2x}
A
B
x
(b) Bowling ball strikes Ping-Pong ball.
BEFORE
v_{A1x}
A
B
x
AFTER
v_{A2x}
v_{B2x}
A
B
x

9.25 A one-dimensional elastic collision between bodies of equal mass.

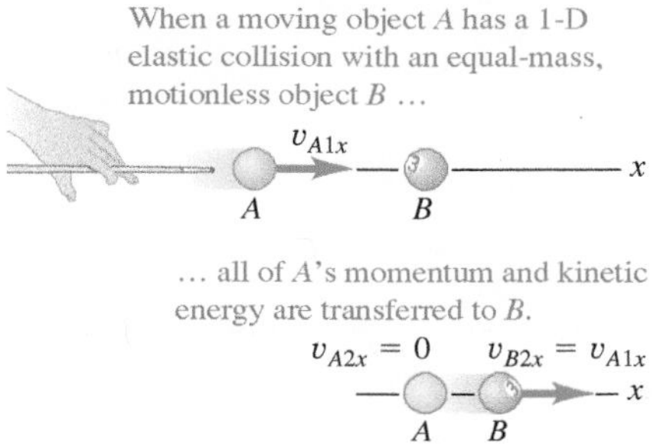
When a moving object A has a 1-D elastic collision with an equal-mass, motionless object B ...
v_{A1x}
A
B
x
... all of A's momentum and kinetic energy are transferred to B.
$v_{A2x} = 0$
$v_{B2x} = v_{A1x}$
A
B
x

Now we can interpret the results. Suppose body A is a Ping-Pong ball and body B is a bowling ball. Then we expect A to bounce off after the collision with a velocity nearly equal to its original value but in the opposite direction (Fig. 9.24a), and we expect B's velocity to be much less. That's just what the equations predict. When m_A is much smaller than m_B, the fraction in Eq. (9.37) is approximately equal to (-1), so v_{A2x} is approximately equal to $-v_{A1x}$. The fraction in Eq. (9.38) is much smaller than unity, so v_{B2x} is much less than v_{A1x}. Figure 9.24b shows the opposite case, in which A is the bowling ball and B the Ping-Pong ball and m_A is much larger than m_B. What do you expect to happen then? Check your predictions against Eqs. (9.37) and (9.38).

Another interesting case occurs when the masses are equal (Fig. 9.25). If $m_A = m_B$, then Eqs. (9.37) and (9.38) give $v_{A2x} = 0$ and $v_{B2x} = v_{A1x}$. That is, the body that was moving stops dead; it gives all its momentum and kinetic energy to the body that was at rest. This behavior is familiar to all pool players.

CHAPTER 9 SUMMARY

Work done by a force: When a constant force $\vec{F}$ acts on a particle that undergoes a straight-line displacement $\vec{s}$, the work done by the force on the particle is defined to be the scalar product of $\vec{F}$ and $\vec{s}$. The unit of work in SI units is 1 joule = 1 newton-meter (1 J = 1 N·m). Work is a scalar quantity; it can be positive or negative, but it has no direction in space.

$$W = \vec{F} \cdot \vec{s} = Fs\cos\phi \qquad (9.2), (9.3)$$

ϕ = angle between $\vec{F}$ and $\vec{s}$

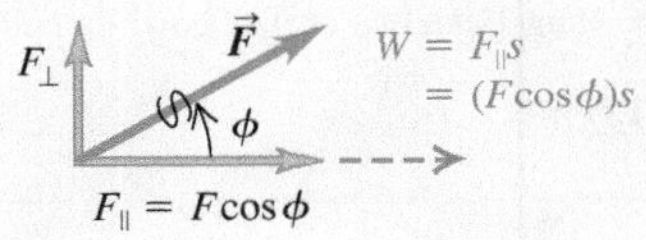

F⊥
F
s
ϕ
W = F∥s
= (F cos ϕ)s
F∥ = F cos ϕ

Kinetic energy: The kinetic energy K of a particle equals the amount of work required to accelerate the particle from rest to speed v. It is also equal to the amount of work the particle can do in the process of being brought to rest. Kinetic energy is a scalar that has no direction in space; it is always positive or zero. Its units are the same as the units of work: $1\ \text{J} = 1\ \text{N}\cdot\text{m} = 1\ \text{kg}\cdot\text{m}^2/\text{s}^2$.

$$K = \tfrac{1}{2}mv^2 \qquad (9.5)$$

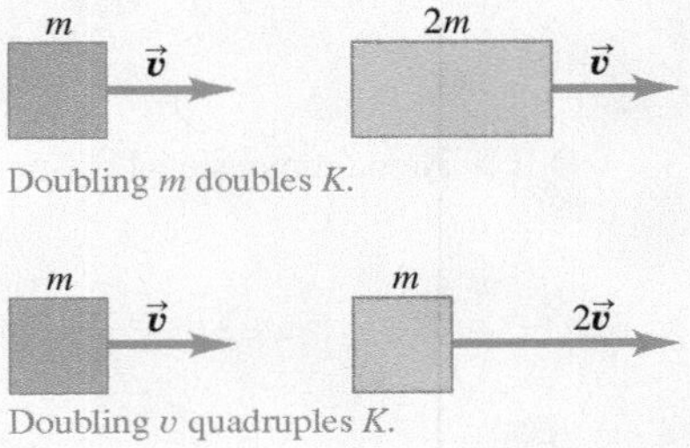

m
v
2m
v
Doubling m doubles K.
m
v
m
2v
Doubling v quadruples K.

The work–energy theorem: When forces act on a particle while it undergoes a displacement, the particle's kinetic energy changes by an amount equal to the total work done on the particle by all the forces. This relationship, called the work–energy theorem, is valid whether the forces are constant or varying and whether the particle moves along a straight or curved path. It is applicable only to bodies that can be treated as particles.

$$W_{tot} = K_2 - K_1 = \Delta K \qquad (9.6)$$

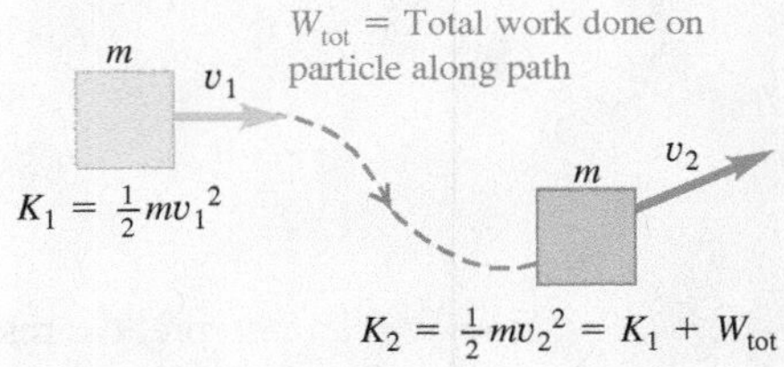

m
v1
Wtot = Total work done on particle along path
K1 = ½mv1²
m
v2
K2 = ½mv2² = K1 + Wtot

Work done by a varying force or on a curved path: When a force varies during a straight-line displacement, the work done by the force is given by an integral, Eq. (9.7). When a particle follows a curved path, the work done on it by a force $\vec{F}$ is given by an integral that involves the angle ϕ between the force and the displacement. This expression is valid even if the force magnitude and the angle ϕ vary during the displacement.

$$W = \int_{x_1}^{x_2} F_x\,dx \qquad (9.7)$$

$$W = \int_{P_1}^{P_2} F\cos\phi\,dl = \int_{P_1}^{P_2} F_{\parallel}\,dl = \int_{P_1}^{P_2} \vec{F}\cdot d\vec{l} \qquad (9.14)$$

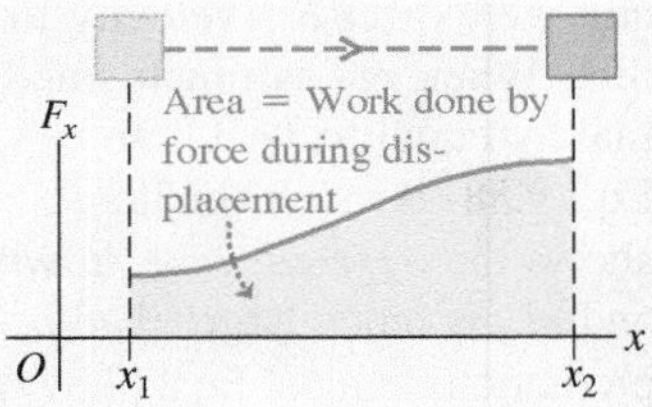

Fx
Area = Work done by force during displacement
O
x1
x2
x

Power: Power is the time rate of doing work. The average power P_{av} is the amount of work ΔW done in time Δt divided by that time. The instantaneous power is the limit of the average power as Δt goes to zero. When a force $\vec{F}$ acts on a particle moving with velocity $\vec{v}$, the instantaneous power (the rate at which the force does work) is the scalar product of $\vec{F}$ and $\vec{v}$. Like work and kinetic energy, power is a scalar quantity. The SI unit of power is 1 watt = 1 joule/second (1 W = 1 J/s).

$$P_{av} = \frac{\Delta W}{\Delta t} \qquad (9.15)$$

$$P = \lim_{\Delta t \to 0} \frac{\Delta W}{\Delta t} = \frac{dW}{dt} \qquad (9.16)$$

$$P = \vec{F} \cdot \vec{v} \qquad (9.19)$$

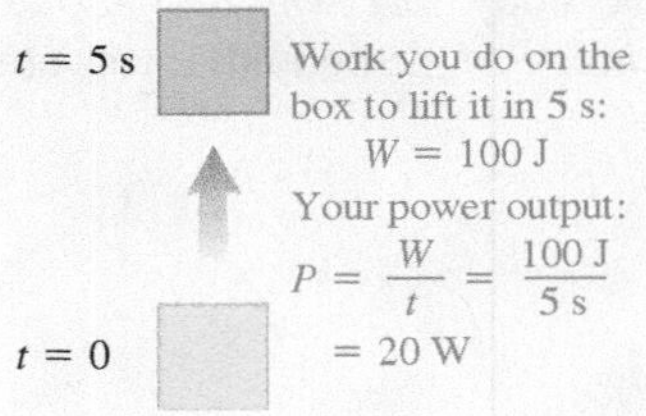

t = 5 s
t = 0
Work you do on the box to lift it in 5 s:
W = 100 J
Your power output:
P = W/t = 100 J / 5 s
= 20 W

Gravitational potential energy and elastic potential energy: The work done on a particle by a constant gravitational force can be represented as a change in the gravitational potential energy $U_{grav} = mgy$. This energy is a shared property of the particle and the earth. A potential energy is also associated with the elastic force $F_x = -kx$ exerted by an ideal spring, where x is the amount of stretch or compression. The work done by this force can be represented as a change in the elastic potential energy of the spring, $U_{el} = \frac{1}{2}kx^2$.

$$W_{grav} = mgy_1 - mgy_2 = U_{grav,1} - U_{grav,2} = -\Delta U_{grav} \quad (9.20),\ (9.22)$$

$$W_{el} = \tfrac{1}{2}kx_1^2 - \tfrac{1}{2}kx_2^2 = U_{el,1} - U_{el,2} = -\Delta U_{el}$$

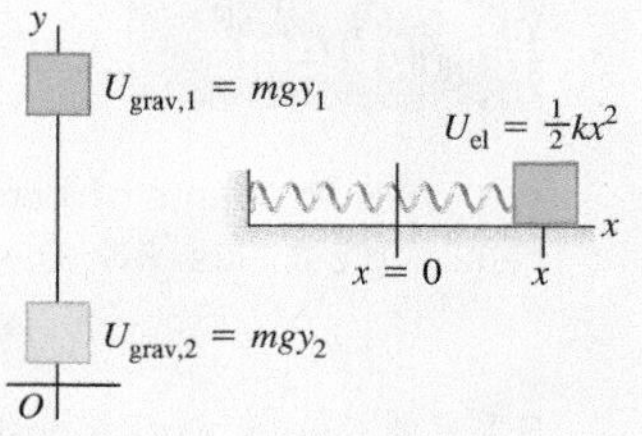

When total mechanical energy is conserved: The total potential energy U is the sum of the gravitational and elastic potential energy: $U = U_{grav} + U_{el}$. If no forces other than the gravitational and elastic forces do work on a particle, the sum of kinetic and potential energy is conserved. This sum $E = K + U$ is called the total mechanical energy.

$$K_1 + U_1 = K_2 + U_2 \quad (9.23)$$

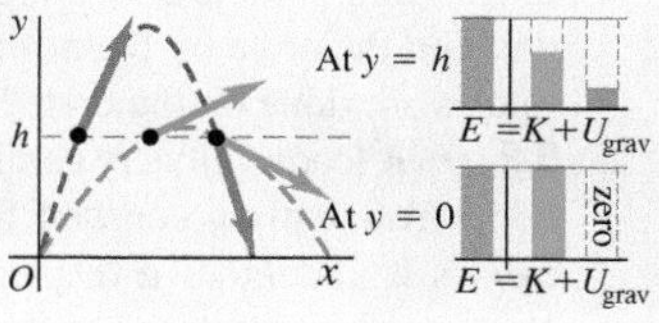

When total mechanical energy is not conserved: When forces other than the gravitational and elastic forces do work on a particle, the work W_{other} done by these other forces equals the change in total mechanical energy (kinetic energy plus total potential energy).

$$K_1 + U_1 + W_{other} = K_2 + U_2$$

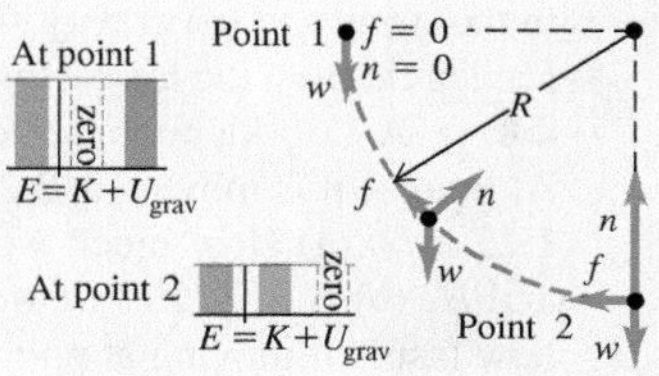

Conservative forces, nonconservative forces, and the law of conservation of energy: All forces are either conservative or nonconservative. A conservative force is one for which the work–kinetic energy relationship is completely reversible. The work of a conservative force can always be represented by a potential-energy function, but the work of a nonconservative force cannot. The work done by nonconservative forces manifests itself as changes in the internal energy of bodies. The sum of kinetic, potential, and internal energy is always conserved.

$$\Delta K + \Delta U + \Delta U_{int} = 0 \quad (9.28)$$

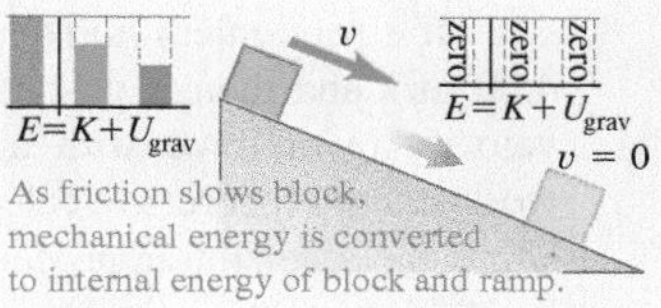

Collisions: In collisions of all kinds, the initial and final total momenta are equal. In an elastic collision between two bodies, the initial and final total kinetic energies are also equal, and the initial and final relative velocities have the same magnitude. In an inelastic two-body collision, the total kinetic energy is less after the collision than before. If the two bodies have the same final velocity, the collision is completely inelastic.

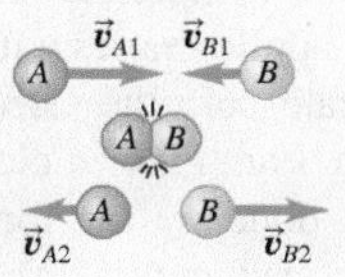

Problems

•, ••, •••: Problems of increasing difficulty. **CP**: Cumulative problems incorporating material from earlier chapters. **CALC**: Problems requiring calculus. **BIO**: Biosciences problems.

9.1 • A factory worker pushes a 30.0-kg crate a distance of 4.5 m along a level floor at constant velocity by pushing horizontally on it. The coefficient of kinetic friction between the crate and the floor is 0.25. (a) What magnitude of force must the worker apply? (b) How much work is done on the crate by this force? (c) How much work is done on the crate by friction? (d) How much work is done on the crate by the normal force? By gravity? (e) What is the total work done on the crate?

9.2 •• A loaded grocery cart is rolling across a parking lot in a strong wind. You apply a constant force $\vec{F} = (30\text{ N})\hat{\imath} - (40\text{ N})\hat{\jmath}$ to the cart as it undergoes a displacement $\vec{s} = (-9.0\text{ m})\hat{\imath} - (3.0\text{ m})\hat{\jmath}$. How much work does the force you apply do on the grocery cart?

9.3 • A 0.800-kg ball is tied to the end of a string 1.60 m long and swung in a vertical circle. (a) During one complete circle, starting anywhere, calculate the total work done on the ball by (i) the tension in the string and (ii) gravity. (b) Repeat part (a) for motion along the semicircle from the lowest to the highest point on the path.

9.4 •• A 1.50-kg book is sliding along a rough horizontal surface. At point *A* it is moving at 3.21 m/s, and at point *B* it has slowed to 1.25 m/s. (a) How much work was done on the book between *A* and *B*? (b) If −0.750 J of work is done on the book from *B* to *C*, how fast is it moving at point *C*? (c) How fast would it be moving at *C* if +0.750 J of work were done on it from *B* to *C*?

9.5 • A little red wagon with mass 7.00 kg moves in a straight line on a frictionless horizontal surface. It has an initial speed of 4.00 m/s and then is pushed 3.0 m in the direction of the initial velocity by a force with a magnitude of 10.0 N. (a) Use the work–energy theorem to calculate the wagon's final speed. (b) Calculate the acceleration produced by the force. Use this acceleration in the kinematic relationships of Chapter 4 to calculate the wagon's final speed. Compare this result to that calculated in part (a).

9.6 • A child applies a force $\vec{F}$ parallel to the x-axis to a 10.0-kg sled moving on the frozen surface of a small pond. As the child controls the speed of the sled, the x-component of the force she applies varies with the x-coordinate of the sled as shown in Fig. P9.6. Calculate the work done by the force $\vec{F}$ when the sled moves (a) from $x = 0$ to $x = 8.0$ m; (b) from $x = 8.0$ m to $x = 12.0$ m; (c) from $x = 0$ to 12.0 m.

Figure **P9.6**

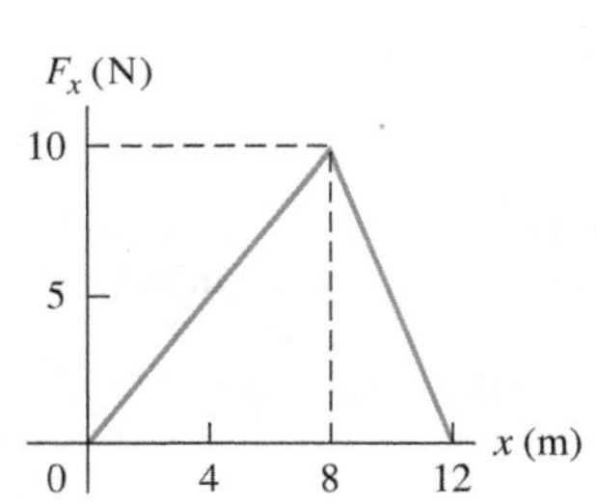

9.7 •• A ski tow operates on a 15.0° slope of length 300 m. The rope moves at 12.0 km/h and provides power for 50 riders at one time, with an average mass per rider of 70.0 kg. Estimate the power required to operate the tow.

9.8 •• **CP** A 120-kg mail bag hangs by a vertical rope 3.5 m long. A postal worker then displaces the bag to a position 2.0 m sideways from its original position, always keeping the rope taut. (a) What horizontal force is necessary to hold the bag in the new position? (b) As the bag is moved to this position, how much work is done (i) by the rope and (ii) by the worker?

9.9 •• A crate of mass *M* starts from rest at the top of a frictionless ramp inclined at an angle α above the horizontal. Find its speed at the bottom of the ramp, a distance *d* from where it started. Do this in two ways: (a) Take the level at which the potential energy is zero to be at the bottom of the ramp with *y* positive upward. (b) Take the zero level for potential energy to be at the top of the ramp with *y* positive upward. (c) Why did the normal force not enter into your solution?

9.10 •• You are testing a new amusement park roller coaster with an empty car of mass 120 kg. One part of the track is a vertical loop with radius 12.0 m. At the bottom of the loop (point *A*) the car has speed 25.0 m/s, and at the top of the loop (point *B*) it has speed 8.0 m/s. As the car rolls from point *A* to point *B*, how much work is done by friction?

9.11 • A marble moves along the x-axis. The potential-energy function is shown in Fig. P9.11. (a) At which of the labeled x-coordinates is the force on the marble zero? (b) Which of the labeled x-coordinates is a position of stable equilibrium? (c) Which of the labeled x-coordinates is a position of unstable equilibrium?

Figure **P9.11**

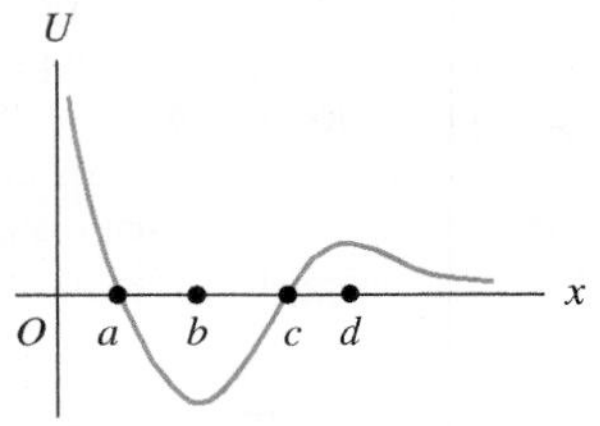

9.12 •• A 1500-kg rocket is to be launched with an initial upward speed of 50.0 m/s. In order to assist its engines, the engineers will start it from rest on a ramp that rises 53° above the horizontal (Fig. P9.12). At the bottom, the ramp turns upward and launches the rocket vertically. The engines provide a constant forward thrust of 2000 N, and friction with the ramp surface is a constant 500 N. How far from the base of the ramp should the rocket start, as measured along the surface of the ramp?

Figure **P9.12**

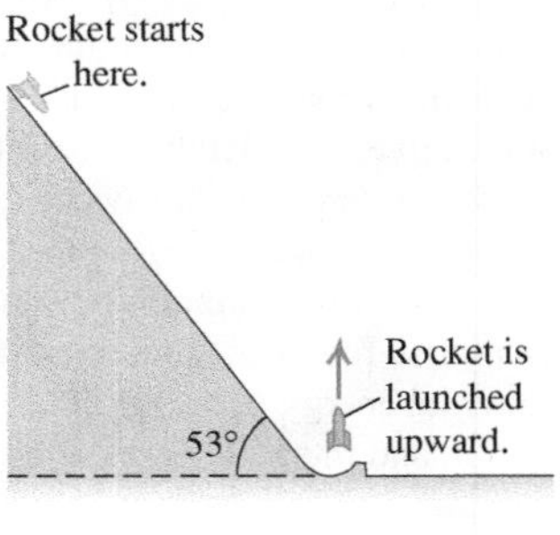

9.13 •• **A Ballistic Pendulum.** A 12.0-g rifle bullet is fired with a speed of 380 m/s into a ballistic pendulum with mass 6.00 kg, suspended from a cord 70.0 cm long. Compute (a) the vertical height through which the pendulum rises, (b) the initial kinetic energy of the bullet, and (c) the kinetic energy of the bullet and pendulum immediately after the bullet becomes embedded in the pendulum.

9.14 •• Blocks *A* (mass 2.00 kg) and *B* (mass 10.00 kg) move on a frictionless, horizontal surface. Initially, block *B* is at rest and block *A* is moving toward it at 2.00 m/s. The blocks are equipped with ideal spring bumpers, as in (Section 9.9). The collision is head-on, so all motion before and after the collision is along a straight line. (a) Find the maximum energy stored in the spring bumpers and the velocity of each block at that time. (b) Find the velocity of each block after they have moved apart.

9.15 ••• **CP** An 8.00-kg ball, hanging from the ceiling by a light wire 135 cm long, is struck in an elastic collision by a 2.00-kg ball moving horizontally at 5.00 m/s just before the collision. Find the tension in the wire just after the collision.

Answers

Chapter Opening Question ?

The answer is yes. As the ant was exerting an upward force on the piece of cereal, the cereal was exerting a downward force of the same magnitude on the ant (due to Newton's third law). However, because the ant's body had an upward displacement, the work that the cereal did on the ant was *negative* (see Section 9.1).

10 EXAMPLES OF POTENTIAL ENERGY

The rings of Saturn are made of countless individual orbiting particles. Do all the ring particles orbit at the same speed, or do the inner particles orbit faster or slower than the outer ones?

LEARNING GOALS

By studying this chapter, you will learn:

- How to use the concept of elastic potential energy in problems that involve a moving body attached to a stretched or compressed spring.
- How to use and interpret the generalized expression for gravitational potential energy.
- How to relate the speed, orbital period, and mechanical energy of a satellite in a circular orbit.
- The laws that describe the motions of planets, and how to work with these laws.
- How to calculate the electric potential energy of a collection of charges.
- The meaning and significance of electric potential.
- How to calculate the electric potential that a collection of charges produces at a point in space.

In Chapter 9 we saw how there were a class of forces (called conservative forces) for which the work done by the force only depends on where it starts and ends, not on the path it took between those locations. We saw that the work done by these forces is related to the change in potential energy of the object. In this chapter, we will learn how to analyze and apply the concept of potential energy to situations where the conservative force is non-constant.

We will consider elastic potential energy, the energy associated with the compression or stretching of a system. This sort of potential energy can be used to explain why a diver is able to jump higher if they bounce on the end of the diving board before they leap into the water; it can also be used to predict things like how much a cushion at the bottom of a slide compresses when a toddler slides into it.

We will analyze the potential energy associated with Newton's law of gravitation, and find out why planets move faster when they are closer to the Sun than when they are farther away. We will also see that the relation we derived for gravitational potential energy in chapter 6 is a special case of the more general form of gravitational potential energy derived from Newton's law.

We will also investigate the potential energy associated with the electric force. We will see that it has the same mathematical structure as gravitational potential energy, and the idea that charges move (making current) in response to differences in potential energy will be important for our studies of circuits and current in Chapter 11.

10.1 Elastic Potential Energy

There are many situations in which we encounter potential energy that is not gravitational in nature. One example is a rubber-band slingshot. Work is done on the rubber band by the force that stretches it, and that work is stored in the rubber band until you let it go. Then the rubber band gives kinetic energy to the projectile.

This is the same pattern we saw with the pile driver: Do work on the system to store energy, which can later be converted to kinetic energy. We'll describe the process of storing energy in a deformable body such as a spring or rubber band in terms of *elastic potential energy*. A body is called *elastic* if it returns to its original shape and size after being deformed.

To be specific, we'll consider storing energy in an ideal spring. To keep such an ideal spring stretched by a distance x, we must exert a force $F = kx$, where k is the force constant of the spring. The ideal spring is a useful idealization because many elastic bodies show this same direct proportionality between force $\vec{F}$ and displacement x, provided that x is sufficiently small.

Let's proceed just as we did for gravitational potential energy. We begin with the work done by the elastic (spring) force and then combine this with the work–energy theorem. The difference is that gravitational potential energy is a shared property of a body and the earth, but elastic potential energy is stored just in the spring (or other deformable body).

Figure 10.1 shows the ideal spring, with its left end held stationary and its right end attached to a block with mass m that can move along the x-axis. In Fig. 10.1a the body is at $x = 0$ when the spring is neither stretched nor compressed. We move the block to one side, thereby stretching or compressing the spring, and then let it go. As the block moves from one position x_1 to another position x_2, how much work does the elastic (spring) force do on the block?

We found in the development of equation 9.10 that the work we must do *on* the spring to move one end from an elongation x_1 to a different elongation x_2 is

$$W = \tfrac{1}{2}kx_2^2 - \tfrac{1}{2}kx_1^2 \qquad \text{(work done } on \text{ a spring)}$$

10.1 Calculating the work done by a spring attached to a block on a horizontal surface. The quantity x is the extension or compression of the spring.

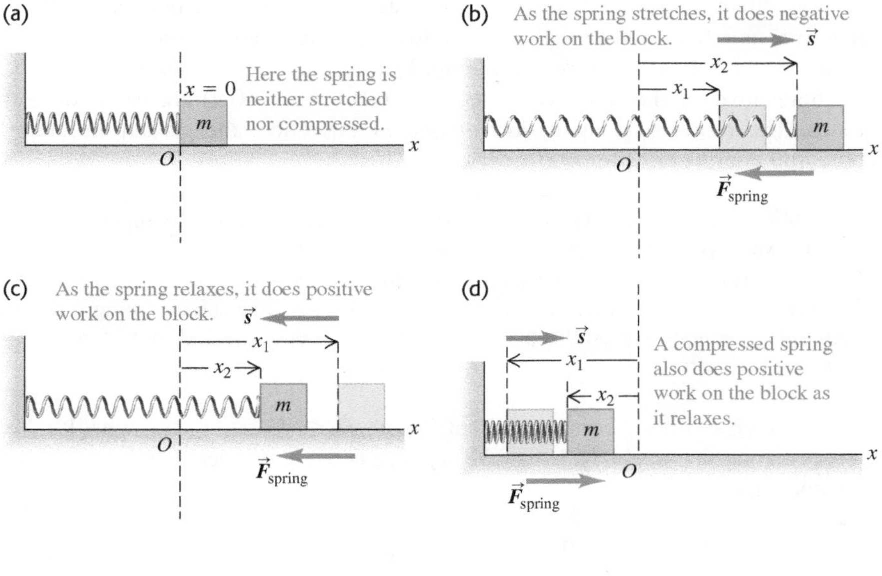

where k is the force constant of the spring. If we stretch the spring farther, we do positive work on the spring; if we let the spring relax while holding one end, we do negative work on it. We also saw that this expression for work is still correct if the spring is compressed, not stretched, so that x_1 or x_2 or both are negative. Now we need to find the work done *by* the spring. From Newton's third law the two quantities of work are just negatives of each other. Changing the signs in this equation, we find that in a displacement from x_1 to x_2 the spring does an amount of work W_{el} given by

$$W_{el} = \tfrac{1}{2}kx_1^2 - \tfrac{1}{2}kx_2^2 \qquad \text{(work done } by \text{ a spring)}$$

The subscript "el" stands for *elastic.* When x_1 and x_2 are both positive and $x_2 > x_1$ (Fig. 10.1b), the spring does negative work on the block, which moves in the $+x$-direction while the spring pulls on it in the $-x$-direction. The spring stretches farther, and the block slows down. When x_1 and x_2 are both positive and $x_2 < x_1$ (Fig. 10.1c), the spring does positive work as it relaxes and the block speeds up. If the spring can be compressed as well as stretched, x_1 or x_2 or both may be negative, but the expression for W_{el} is still valid. In Fig. 10.1d, both x_1 and x_2 are negative, but x_2 is less negative than x_1; the compressed spring does positive work as it relaxes, speeding the block up.

Just as for gravitational work, we can express the work done by the spring in terms of a given quantity at the beginning and end of the displacement. This quantity is $\frac{1}{2}kx^2$, and we define it to be the **elastic potential energy:**

$$U_{el} = \tfrac{1}{2}kx^2 \qquad \text{(elastic potential energy)} \qquad (10.1)$$

Figure 10.2 is a graph of Eq. (10.1). The unit of U_{el} is the joule (J), the unit used for *all* energy and work quantities; to see this from Eq. (10.1), recall that the units of k are N/m and that $1\ \text{N} \cdot \text{m} = 1\ \text{J}$.

We can use Eq. (10.1) to express the work W_{el} done on the block by the elastic force in terms of the change in elastic potential energy:

$$W_{el} = \tfrac{1}{2}kx_1^2 - \tfrac{1}{2}kx_2^2 = U_{el,1} - U_{el,2} = -\Delta U_{el} \qquad (10.2)$$

When a stretched spring is stretched farther, as in Fig. 10.1b, W_{el} is negative and U_{el} *increases;* a greater amount of elastic potential energy is stored in the spring. When a stretched spring relaxes, as in Fig. 10.1c, x decreases, W_{el} is positive, and U_{el} *decreases;* the spring loses elastic potential energy. Negative values of x refer to a compressed spring. But, as Fig. 10.2 shows, U_{el} is positive for both positive and negative x, and Eqs. (10.1) and (10.2) are valid for both cases. The more a spring is compressed *or* stretched, the greater its elastic potential energy.

CAUTION **Gravitational potential energy vs. elastic potential energy** An important difference between gravitational potential energy $U_{grav} = mgy$ and elastic potential energy $U_{el} = \frac{1}{2}kx^2$ is that we do *not* have the freedom to choose $x = 0$ to be wherever we wish. To be consistent with Eq. (10.1), $x = 0$ *must* be the position at which the spring is neither stretched nor compressed. At that position, its elastic potential energy and the force that it exerts are both zero.

The work–energy theorem says that $W_{tot} = K_2 - K_1$, no matter what kind of forces are acting on a body. If the elastic force is the *only* force that does work on the body, then

$$W_{tot} = W_{el} = U_{el,1} - U_{el,2}$$

10.2 The graph of elastic potential energy for an ideal spring is a parabola: $U_{el} = \frac{1}{2}kx^2$, where x is the extension or compression of the spring. Elastic potential energy U_{el} is never negative.

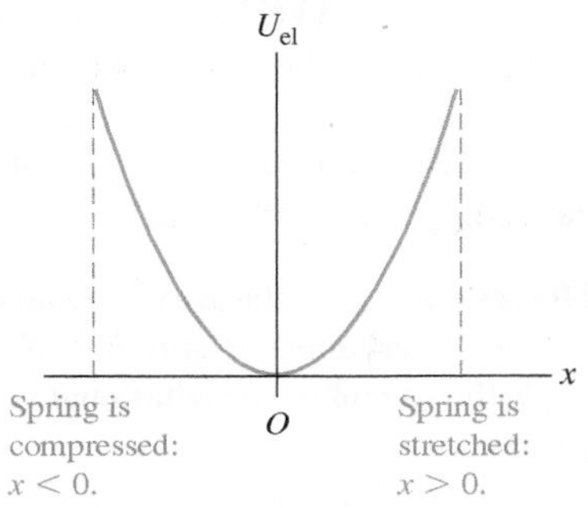

The work–energy theorem, $W_{tot} = K_2 - K_1$, then gives us

$$K_1 + U_{el,1} = K_2 + U_{el,2} \quad \text{(if only the elastic force does work)} \tag{10.3}$$

Here U_{el} is given by Eq. (10.1), so

$$\tfrac{1}{2}mv_1{}^2 + \tfrac{1}{2}kx_1{}^2 = \tfrac{1}{2}mv_2^2 + \tfrac{1}{2}kx_2^2 \quad \text{(if only the elastic force does work)} \tag{10.4}$$

In this case the total mechanical energy $E = K + U_{el}$—the sum of kinetic and *elastic* potential energy—is *conserved.* An example of this is the motion of the block in Fig. 10.1, provided the horizontal surface is frictionless so that no force does work other than that exerted by the spring.

For Eq. (10.4) to be strictly correct, the ideal spring that we've been discussing must also be *massless.* If the spring has a mass, it also has kinetic energy as the coils of the spring move back and forth. We can neglect the kinetic energy of the spring if its mass is much less than the mass m of the body attached to the spring. For instance, a typical automobile has a mass of 1200 kg or more. The springs in its suspension have masses of only a few kilograms, so their mass can be neglected if we want to study how a car bounces on its suspension.

Situations with Both Gravitational and Elastic Potential Energy

Equations (10.3) and (10.4) are valid when the only potential energy in the system is elastic potential energy. What happens when we have *both* gravitational and elastic forces, such as a block attached to the lower end of a vertically hanging spring? And what if work is also done by other forces that *cannot* be described in terms of potential energy, such as the force of air resistance on a moving block? Then the total work is the sum of the work done by the gravitational force (W_{grav}), the work done by the elastic force (W_{el}), and the work done by other forces (W_{other}): $W_{tot} = W_{grav} + W_{el} + W_{other}$. Then the work–energy theorem gives

$$W_{grav} + W_{el} + W_{other} = K_2 - K_1$$

The work done by the gravitational force is $W_{grav} = U_{grav,1} - U_{grav,2}$ and the work done by the spring is $W_{el} = U_{el,1} - U_{el,2}$. Hence we can rewrite the work–energy theorem for this most general case as

$$K_1 + U_{grav,1} + U_{el,1} + W_{other} = K_2 + U_{grav,2} + U_{el,2} \quad \text{(valid in general)} \tag{10.5}$$

or, equivalently,

$$K_1 + U_1 + W_{\text{other}} = K_2 + U_2 \quad \text{(valid in general)} \tag{10.6}$$

where $U = U_{\text{grav}} + U_{\text{el}} = mgy + \frac{1}{2}kx^2$ is the *sum* of gravitational potential energy and elastic potential energy. For short, we call U simply "the potential energy."

Equation (10.6) is *the most general statement* of the relationship among kinetic energy, potential energy, and work done by other forces. It says:

The work done by all forces other than the gravitational force or elastic force equals the change in the total mechanical energy $E = K + U$ of the system, where $U = U_{\text{grav}} + U_{\text{el}}$ is the sum of the gravitational potential energy and the elastic potential energy.

The "system" is made up of the body of mass m, the earth with which it interacts through the gravitational force, and the spring of force constant k.

If W_{other} is positive, $E = K + U$ increases; if W_{other} is negative, E decreases. If the gravitational and elastic forces are the *only* forces that do work on the body, then $W_{\text{other}} = 0$ and the total mechanical energy (including both gravitational and elastic potential energy) is conserved. (You should compare Eq. (10.6) to Eqs. (9.26) and (9.27), which describe situations in which there is gravitational potential energy but no elastic potential energy.)

Trampoline jumping involves transformations among kinetic energy, elastic potential energy, and gravitational potential energy. As the jumper descends through the air from the high point of the bounce, gravitational potential energy U_{grav} decreases and kinetic energy K increases. Once the jumper touches the trampoline, some of the mechanical energy goes into elastic potential energy U_{el} stored in the trampoline's springs. Beyond a certain point the jumper's speed and kinetic energy K decrease while U_{grav} continues to decrease and U_{el} continues to increase. At the low point the jumper comes to a momentary halt ($K = 0$) at the lowest point of the trajectory (U_{grav} is minimum) and the springs are maximally stretched (U_{el} is maximum). The springs then convert their energy back into K and U_{grav}, propelling the jumper upward.

10.2 Gravitational Potential Energy

When we first introduced gravitational potential energy, we assumed that the gravitational force on a body is constant in magnitude and direction. This led to the expression $U = mgy$. But the earth's gravitational force on a body of mass m at any point outside the earth is given more generally by $F_g = Gm_Em/r^2$, where m_E is the mass of the earth and r is the distance of the body from the earth's center. For problems in which r changes enough that the gravitational force can't be considered constant, we need a more general expression for gravitational potential energy.

We consider a body of mass m outside the earth, and first compute the work W_{grav} done by the gravitational force when the body moves directly away from or toward the center of the earth from $r = r_1$ to $r = r_2$, as in Fig. 10.3. This work is given by

$$W_{\text{grav}} = \int_{r_1}^{r_2} F_r \, dr \tag{10.7}$$

where F_r is the radial component of the gravitational force $\vec{F}$—that is, the component in the direction *outward* from the center of the earth. Because $\vec{F}$ points

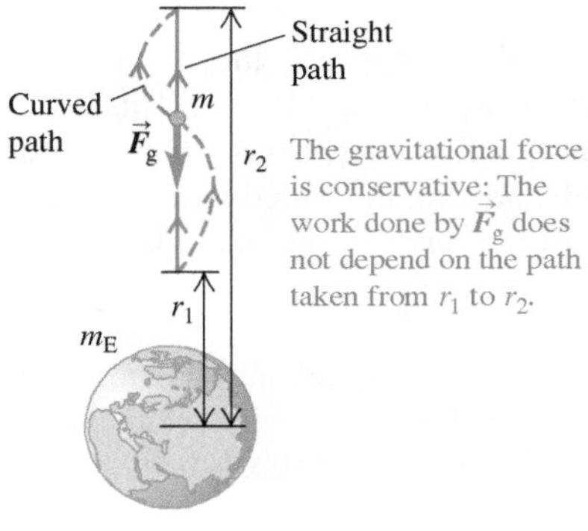

10.3 Calculating the work done on a body by the gravitational force as the body moves from radial coordinate r_1 to r_2.

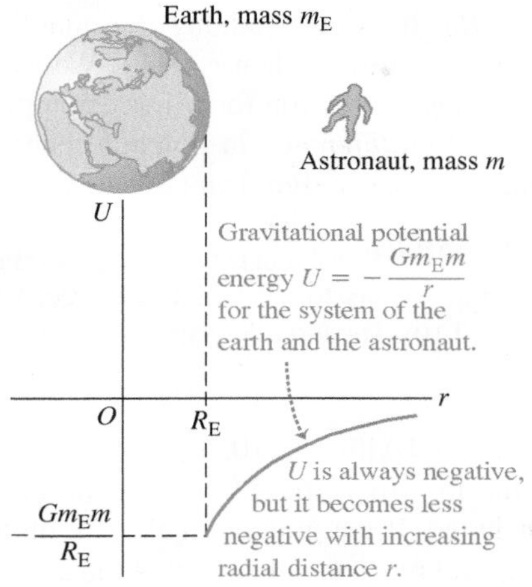

10.4 A graph of the gravitational potential energy U for the system of the earth (mass m_E) and an astronaut (mass m) versus the astronaut's distance r from the center of the earth.

directly *inward* toward the center of the earth, F_r is negative. It differs from Eq. (6.3), the magnitude of the gravitational force, by a minus sign:

$$F_r = -\frac{Gm_E m}{r^2} \tag{10.8}$$

Substituting Eq. (10.8) into Eq. (10.7), we see that W_{grav} is given by

$$W_{grav} = -Gm_E m \int_{r_1}^{r_2} \frac{dr}{r^2} = \frac{Gm_E m}{r_2} - \frac{Gm_E m}{r_1} \tag{10.9}$$

The path doesn't have to be a straight line; it could also be a curve like the one in Fig. 10.3. This work depends only on the initial and final values of r, not on the path taken. This also proves that the gravitational force is always *conservative.*

We now define the corresponding potential energy U so that $W_{grav} = U_1 - U_2$. Comparing this with Eq. (10.9), we see that the appropriate definition for **gravitational potential energy** is

$$U = -\frac{Gm_E m}{r} \quad \text{(gravitational potential energy)} \tag{10.10}$$

Figure 10.4 shows how the gravitational potential energy depends on the distance r between the body of mass m and the center of the earth. When the body moves away from the earth, r increases, the gravitational force does negative work, and U increases (i.e., becomes less negative). When the body "falls" toward earth, r decreases, the gravitational work is positive, and the potential energy decreases (i.e., becomes more negative).

You may be troubled by Eq. (10.10) because it states that gravitational potential energy is always negative. But in fact you've seen negative values of U before. In using the formula $U = mgy$, we found that U was negative whenever the body of mass m was at a value of y below the arbitrary height we chose to be $y = 0$—that is, whenever the body and the earth were closer together than some certain arbitrary distance. In defining U by Eq. (10.10), we have chosen U to be zero when the body of mass m is infinitely far from the earth ($r = \infty$). As the body moves toward the earth, gravitational potential energy decreases and so becomes negative.

If we wanted, we could make $U = 0$ at the surface of the earth, where $r = R_E$, by simply adding the quantity $Gm_E m/R_E$ to Eq. (10.10). This would make U positive when $r > R_E$. We won't do this for two reasons: One, it would make the expression for U more complicated; and two, the added term would not affect the *difference* in potential energy between any two points, which is the only physically significant quantity.

CAUTION **Gravitational force vs. gravitational potential energy** Be careful not to confuse the expressions for gravitational force, Eq. (10.8), and gravitational potential energy, Eq. (10.10). The force F_r is proportional to $1/r^2$, while potential energy U is proportional to $1/r$.

Armed with Eq. (10.10), we can now use general energy relationships for problems in which the $1/r^2$ behavior of the earth's gravitational force has to be included. If the gravitational force on the body is the only force that does work, the total mechanical energy of the system is constant, or *conserved.* In the following example we'll use this principle to calculate **escape speed,** the speed required for a body to escape completely from a planet.

More on Gravitational Potential Energy

As a final note, let's show that when we are close to the earth's surface, Eq. (10.10) reduces to the familiar $U = mgy$. We first rewrite Eq. (10.9) as

$$W_{grav} = Gm_E m \frac{r_1 - r_2}{r_1 r_2}$$

If the body stays close to the earth, then in the denominator we may replace r_1 and r_2 by R_E, the earth's radius, so

$$W_{grav} = Gm_E m \frac{r_1 - r_2}{R_E^2}$$

According to Eq. (6.5), $g = Gm_E/R_E^2$, so

$$W_{grav} = mg(r_1 - r_2)$$

If we replace the r's by y's, this is just the work done by a constant gravitational force. We used this equation to derive $U = mgy$, so we may consider gravitational potential energy to be a special case of the more general Eq. (10.10).

10.3 The Motion of Satellites

Artificial satellites orbiting the earth are a familiar part of modern technology. But how do they stay in orbit, and what determines the properties of their orbits? We can use Newton's laws and the law of gravitation to provide the answers. We'll see in the next section that the motion of planets can be analyzed in the same way.

To begin, think back to the discussion of projectile motion. A motorcycle rider rides horizontally off the edge of a cliff, launching himself into a parabolic path that ends on the flat ground at the base of the cliff. If he survives and repeats the experiment with increased launch speed, he will land farther from the starting point. We can imagine him launching himself with great enough speed that the earth's curvature becomes significant. As he falls, the earth curves away beneath

10.5 Trajectories of a projectile launched from a great height (ignoring air resistance). Orbits 1 and 2 would be completed as shown if the earth were a point mass at *C*. (This illustration is based on one in Isaac Newton's *Principia*.)

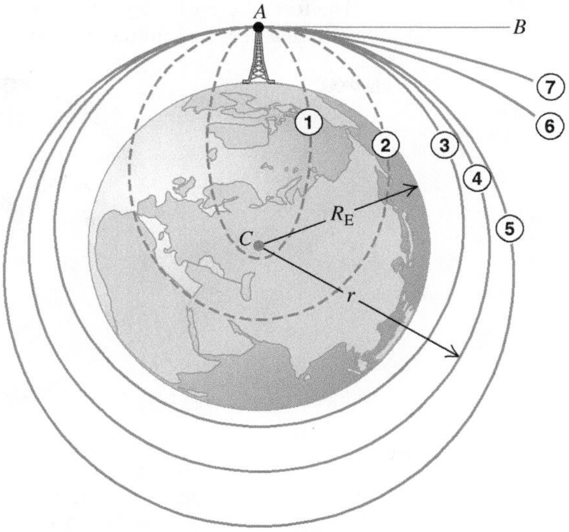

him. If he is going fast enough, and if his launch point is high enough that he clears the mountaintops, he may be able to go right on around the earth without ever landing.

Figure 10.5 shows a variation on this theme. We launch a projectile from point *A* in the direction *AB*, tangent to the earth's surface. Trajectories 1 through 7 show the effect of increasing the initial speed. In trajectories 3 through 5 the projectile misses the earth and becomes a satellite. If there is no retarding force, the projectile's speed when it returns to point *A* is the same as its initial speed and it repeats its motion indefinitely.

Trajectories 1 through 5 close on themselves and are called **closed orbits.** All closed orbits are ellipses or segments of ellipses; trajectory 4 is a circle, a special case of an ellipse. (We'll discuss the properties of an ellipse in Section 10.4.) Trajectories 6 and 7 are **open orbits.** For these paths the projectile never returns to its starting point but travels ever farther away from the earth.

Satellites: Circular Orbits

A *circular* orbit, like trajectory 4 in Fig. 10.5, is the simplest case. It is also an important case, since many artificial satellites have nearly circular orbits and the orbits of the planets around the sun are also fairly circular. The only force acting on a satellite in circular orbit around the earth is the earth's gravitational attraction, which is directed toward the center of the earth and hence toward the center of the orbit (Fig. 10.6). This means that the satellite is in *uniform* circular motion and its speed is constant. The satellite isn't falling *toward* the earth; rather, it's constantly falling *around* the earth. In a circular orbit the speed is just right to keep the distance from the satellite to the center of the earth constant.

Let's see how to find the constant speed v of a satellite in a circular orbit. The radius of the orbit is r, measured from the *center* of the earth; the acceleration of the satellite has magnitude $a_{rad} = v^2/r$ and is always directed toward the center of the circle. By the law of gravitation, the net force (gravitational force) on the satellite of mass m has magnitude $F_g = Gm_Em/r^2$ and is in the same direction as the acceleration. Newton's second law ($\Sigma\vec{F} = m\vec{a}$) then tells us that

$$\frac{Gm_Em}{r^2} = \frac{mv^2}{r}$$

10.6 The force $\vec{F}_g$ due to the earth's gravitational attraction provides the centripetal acceleration that keeps a satellite in orbit. Compare to Fig. 5.6.

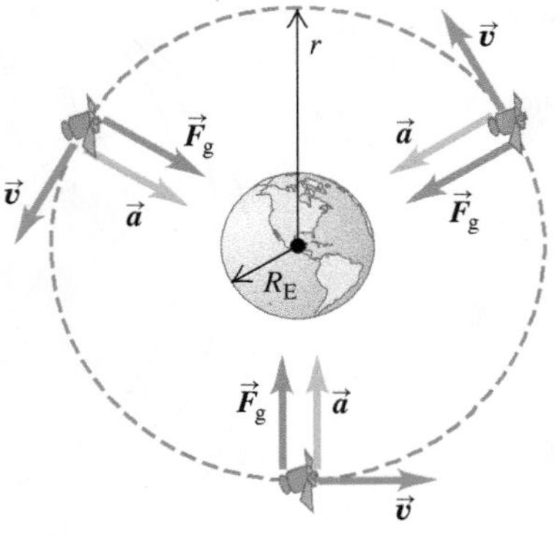

The satellite is in a circular orbit: Its acceleration $\vec{a}$ is always perpendicular to its velocity $\vec{v}$, so its speed v is constant.

Solving this for v, we find

$$v = \sqrt{\frac{Gm_E}{r}} \quad \text{(circular orbit)} \tag{10.11}$$

This relationship shows that we can't choose the orbit radius r and the speed v independently; for a given radius r, the speed v for a circular orbit is determined.

The satellite's mass m doesn't appear in Eq. (10.11), which shows that the motion of a satellite does not depend on its mass. If we could cut a satellite in half without changing its speed, each half would continue on with the original motion. An astronaut on board a space shuttle is herself a satellite of the earth, held by the earth's gravitational attraction in the same orbit as the shuttle. The astronaut has the same velocity and acceleration as the shuttle, so nothing is pushing her against the floor or walls of the shuttle. She is in a state of *apparent weightlessness,* as in a freely falling elevator; (*True* weightlessness would occur only if the astronaut were infinitely far from any other masses, so that the gravitational force on her would be zero.) Indeed, every part of her body is apparently weightless; she feels nothing pushing her stomach against her intestines or her head against her shoulders.

Apparent weightlessness is not just a feature of circular orbits; it occurs whenever gravity is the only force acting on a spacecraft. Hence it occurs for orbits of any shape, including open orbits such as trajectories 6 and 7 in Fig. 10.5.

We can derive a relationship between the radius r of a circular orbit and the period T, the time for one revolution. The speed v is the distance $2\pi r$ traveled in one revolution, divided by the period:

$$v = \frac{2\pi r}{T} \tag{10.12}$$

To get an expression for T, we solve Eq. (10.12) for T and substitute v from Eq. (10.11):

$$T = \frac{2\pi r}{v} = 2\pi r\sqrt{\frac{r}{Gm_E}} = \frac{2\pi r^{3/2}}{\sqrt{Gm_E}} \quad \text{(circular orbit)} \tag{10.13}$$

Equations (10.11) and (10.13) show that larger orbits correspond to slower speeds and longer periods. As an example, the International Space Station orbits

6800 km from the center of the earth (400 km above the earth's surface) with an orbital speed of 7.7 km/s and an orbital period of 93 minutes. The moon orbits the earth in a much larger orbit of radius 384,000 km, and so has a much slower orbital speed (1.0 km/s) and a much longer orbital period (27.3 days).

It's interesting to compare Eq. (10.11) to the calculation of escape speed. The escape speed is the minimun speed such that the total energy is 0 or greater; objects with at least this relative speed can become infinitely seperated. We see that the escape speed from a spherical body with radius R is $\sqrt{2}$ times greater than the speed of a satellite in a circular orbit at that radius. If our spacecraft is in circular orbit around *any* planet, we have to multiply our speed by a factor of $\sqrt{2}$ to escape to infinity, regardless of the planet's mass.

Since the speed v in a circular orbit is determined by Eq. (10.11) for a given orbit radius r, the total mechanical energy $E = K + U$ is determined as well. Using Eqs. (10.10) and (10.11), we have

$$E = K + U = \tfrac{1}{2}mv^2 + \left(-\frac{Gm_E m}{r}\right) = \tfrac{1}{2}m\left(\frac{Gm_E}{r}\right) - \frac{Gm_E m}{r}$$

$$= -\frac{Gm_E m}{2r} \quad \text{(circular orbit)} \tag{10.14}$$

The total mechanical energy in a circular orbit is negative and equal to one-half the potential energy. Increasing the orbit radius r means increasing the mechanical energy (that is, making E less negative). If the satellite is in a relatively low orbit that encounters the outer fringes of earth's atmosphere, mechanical energy decreases due to negative work done by the force of air resistance; as a result, the orbit radius decreases until the satellite hits the ground or burns up in the atmosphere.

We have talked mostly about earth satellites, but we can apply the same analysis to the circular motion of *any* body under its gravitational attraction to a stationary body. Other examples include the earth's moon and the moons of other worlds.

10.4 Kepler's Laws and the Motion of Planets

The name *planet* comes from a Greek word meaning "wanderer," and indeed the planets continuously change their positions in the sky relative to the background of stars. One of the great intellectual accomplishments of the 16th and 17th centuries was the threefold realization that the earth is also a planet, that all planets orbit the sun, and that the apparent motions of the planets as seen from the earth can be used to precisely determine their orbits.

The first and second of these ideas were published by Nicolaus Copernicus in Poland in 1543. The nature of planetary orbits was deduced between 1601 and 1619 by the German astronomer and mathematician Johannes Kepler, using a voluminous set of precise data on apparent planetary motions compiled by his mentor, the Danish astronomer Tycho Brahe. By trial and error, Kepler discovered three empirical laws that accurately described the motions of the planets:

1. **Each planet moves in an elliptical orbit, with the sun at one focus of the ellipse.**
2. **A line from the sun to a given planet sweeps out equal areas in equal times.**
3. **The periods of the planets are proportional to the $\frac{3}{2}$ powers of the major axis lengths of their orbits.**

Kepler did not know *why* the planets moved in this way. Three generations later, when Newton turned his attention to the motion of the planets, he discovered that each of Kepler's laws can be *derived;* they are consequences of Newton's laws of motion and the law of gravitation. Let's see how each of Kepler's laws arises.

10.7 Geometry of an ellipse. The sum of the distances SP and $S'P$ is the same for every point on the curve. The sizes of the sun (S) and planet (P) are exaggerated for clarity.

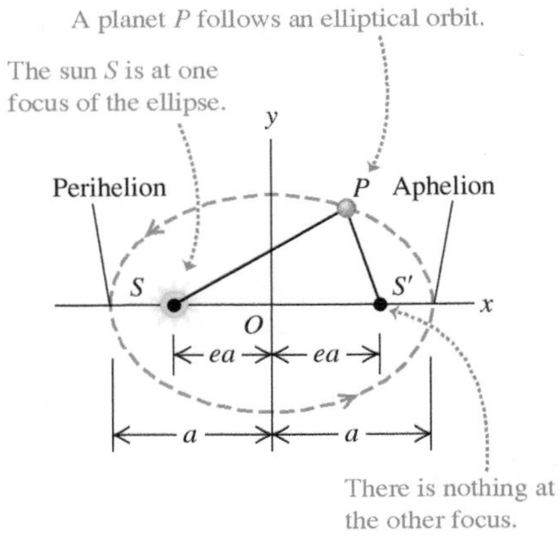

Kepler's First Law

First consider the elliptical orbits described in Kepler's first law. Figure 10.7 shows the geometry of an ellipse. The longest dimension is the *major axis,* with half-length a; this half-length is called the **semi-major axis.** The sum of the distances from S to P and from S' to P is the same for all points on the curve. S and S' are the *foci* (plural of *focus*). The sun is at S, and the planet is at P; we think of them both as points because the size of each is very small in comparison to the distance between them. There is nothing at the other focus S'.

The distance of each focus from the center of the ellipse is ea, where e is a dimensionless number between 0 and 1 called the **eccentricity.** If $e = 0$, the ellipse is a circle. The actual orbits of the planets are fairly circular; their eccentricities range from 0.007 for Venus to 0.206 for Mercury. (The earth's orbit has $e = 0.017$.) The point in the planet's orbit closest to the sun is the *perihelion,* and the point most distant from the sun is the *aphelion.*

Newton was able to show that for a body acted on by an attractive force proportional to $1/r^2$, the only possible closed orbits are a circle or an ellipse; he also showed that open orbits (trajectories 6 and 7 in Fig. 10.5) must be parabolas or hyperbolas. These results can be derived by a straightforward application of Newton's laws and the law of gravitation, together with a lot more differential equations than we're ready for.

Kepler's Second Law

Figure 10.8 shows Kepler's second law. In a small time interval dt, the line from the sun S to the planet P turns through an angle $d\theta$. The area swept out is the colored triangle with height r, base length $r\,d\theta$, and area $dA = \frac{1}{2}r^2\,d\theta$ in Fig. 10.8b. The rate at which area is swept out, dA/dt, is called the *sector velocity:*

$$\frac{dA}{dt} = \frac{1}{2}r^2\frac{d\theta}{dt} \qquad (10.15)$$

The essence of Kepler's second law is that the sector velocity has the same value at all points in the orbit. When the planet is close to the sun, r is small and $d\theta/dt$ is large; when the planet is far from the sun, r is large and $d\theta/dt$ is small.

To see how Kepler's second law follows from Newton's laws, we express dA/dt in terms of the velocity vector $\vec{v}$ of the planet P. The component of $\vec{v}$ perpendicular to the radial line is $v_\perp = v\sin\phi$. From Fig. 10.8b the displacement along the direction of $v_\perp$ during time dt is $r\,d\theta$, so we also have $v_\perp = r\,d\theta/dt$. Using this relationship in Eq. (10.15), we find

$$\frac{dA}{dt} = \frac{1}{2}rv\sin\phi \quad \text{(sector velocity)} \qquad (10.16)$$

Now $rv\sin\phi$ is the magnitude of the vector product $\vec{r} \times \vec{v}$, which in turn is $1/m$ times the angular momentum $\vec{L} = \vec{r} \times m\vec{v}$ of the planet with respect to the sun. So we have

$$\frac{dA}{dt} = \frac{1}{2m}|\vec{r} \times m\vec{v}| = \frac{L}{2m} \qquad (10.17)$$

Thus Kepler's second law—that sector velocity is constant—means that angular momentum is constant!

It is easy to see why the angular momentum of the planet *must* be constant. The rate of change of $\vec{L}$ equals the torque of the gravitational force $\vec{F}$ acting on the planet:

$$\frac{d\vec{L}}{dt} = \vec{\tau} = \vec{r} \times \vec{F}$$

10.8 (a) The planet (P) moves about the sun (S) in an elliptical orbit. (b) In a time dt the line SP sweeps out an area $dA = \frac{1}{2}(r\,d\theta)r = \frac{1}{2}r^2\,d\theta$. (c) The planet's speed varies so that the line SP sweeps out the same area A in a given time t regardless of the planet's position in its orbit.

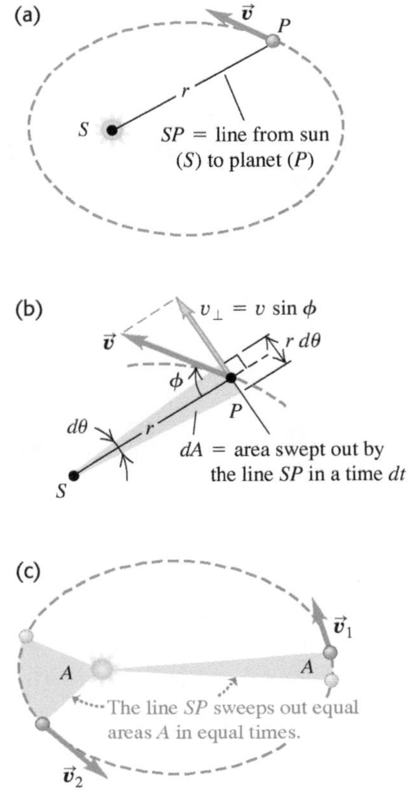

In our situation, $\vec{r}$ is the vector from the sun to the planet, and the force $\vec{F}$ is directed from the planet to the sun. So these vectors always lie along the same line, and their vector product $\vec{r} \times \vec{F}$ is zero. Hence $d\vec{L}/dt = \mathbf{0}$. This conclusion does not depend on the $1/r^2$ behavior of the force; angular momentum is conserved for *any* force that acts always along the line joining the particle to a fixed point. Such a force is called a *central force.* (Kepler's first and third laws are valid *only* for a $1/r^2$ force.)

Conservation of angular momentum also explains why the orbit lies in a plane. The vector $\vec{L} = \vec{r} \times m\vec{v}$ is always perpendicular to the plane of the vectors $\vec{r}$ and $\vec{v}$; since $\vec{L}$ is constant in magnitude *and* direction, $\vec{r}$ and $\vec{v}$ always lie in the same plane, which is just the plane of the planet's orbit.

Kepler's Third Law

We have already derived Kepler's third law for the particular case of circular orbits. Equation (10.13) shows that the period of a satellite or planet in a circular orbit is proportional to the $\frac{3}{2}$ power of the orbit radius. Newton was able to show that this same relationship holds for an *elliptical* orbit, with the orbit radius r replaced by the semi-major axis a:

$$T = \frac{2\pi a^{3/2}}{\sqrt{Gm_S}} \quad \text{(elliptical orbit around the sun)} \tag{10.18}$$

Since the planet orbits the sun, not the earth, we have replaced the earth's mass m_E in Eq. (10.13) with the sun's mass m_S. Note that the period does not depend on the eccentricity e. An asteroid in an elongated elliptical orbit with semi-major axis a will have the same orbital period as a planet in a circular orbit of radius a. The key difference is that the asteroid moves at different speeds at different points in its elliptical orbit (Fig. 10.8c), while the planet's speed is constant around its circular orbit.

Planetary Motions and the Center of Mass

We have assumed that as a planet or comet orbits the sun, the sun remains absolutely stationary. Of course, this can't be correct; because the sun exerts a gravitational force on the planet, the planet exerts a gravitational force on the sun of the same magnitude but opposite direction. In fact, *both* the sun and the planet orbit around their common center of mass (Fig. 10.9). We've made only a small error by ignoring this effect, however; the sun's mass is about 750 times the total mass of all the planets combined, so the center of mass of the solar system is not

10.9 A star and its planet both orbit about their common center of mass.

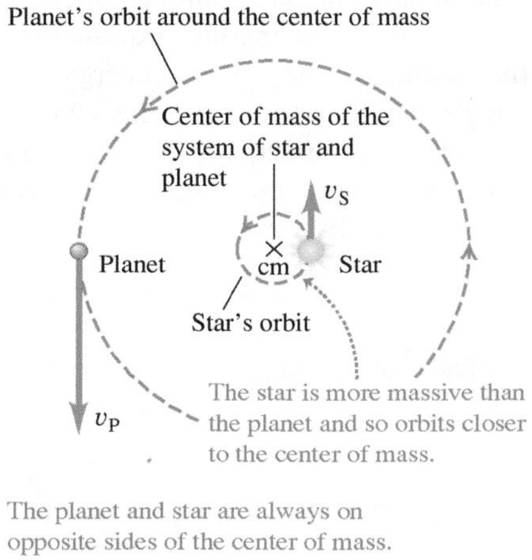

far from the center of the sun. Remarkably, astronomers have used this effect to detect the presence of planets orbiting other stars. Sensitive telescopes are able to detect the apparent "wobble" of a star as it orbits the common center of mass of the star and an unseen companion planet. (The planets are too faint to observe directly.) By analyzing these "wobbles," astronomers have discovered planets in orbit around hundreds of other stars.

Newton's analysis of planetary motions is used on a daily basis by modern-day astronomers. But the most remarkable result of Newton's work is that the motions of bodies in the heavens obey the *same* laws of motion as do bodies on the earth. This *Newtonian synthesis,* as it has come to be called, is one of the great unifying principles of science. It has had profound effects on the way that humanity looks at the universe—not as a realm of impenetrable mystery, but as a direct extension of our everyday world, subject to scientific study and calculation.

10.5 Electric Potential Energy

The concepts of work, potential energy, and conservation of energy proved to be extremely useful in our study of mechanics. In this section we'll show that these concepts are just as useful for understanding and analyzing electrical interactions.

First, when a force $\vec{F}$ acts on a particle that moves from point a to point b, the work $W_{a\to b}$ done by the force is given by a *line integral:*

$$W_{a\to b} = \int_a^b \vec{F}\cdot d\vec{l} = \int_a^b F\cos\phi\, dl \quad \text{(work done by a force)} \tag{10.19}$$

where $d\vec{l}$ is an infinitesimal displacement along the particle's path and ϕ is the angle between $\vec{F}$ and $d\vec{l}$ at each point along the path.

Second, if the force $\vec{F}$ is *conservative,* the work done by $\vec{F}$ can always be expressed in terms of a **potential energy** U. When the particle moves from a point where the potential energy is U_a to a point where it is U_b, the change in potential energy is $\Delta U = U_b - U_a$ and the work $W_{a\to b}$ done by the force is

$$W_{a\to b} = U_a - U_b = -(U_b - U_a) = -\Delta U \quad \text{(work done by a conservative force)} \tag{10.20}$$

When $W_{a\to b}$ is positive, U_a is greater than U_b, ΔU is negative, and the potential energy *decreases.* That's what happens when a baseball falls from a high point (a) to a lower point (b) under the influence of the earth's gravity; the force of gravity does positive work, and the gravitational potential energy decreases (Fig. 10.10). When a tossed ball is moving upward, the gravitational force does negative work during the ascent, and the potential energy increases.

Third, the work–energy theorem says that the change in kinetic energy $\Delta K = K_b - K_a$ during a displacement equals the *total* work done on the particle. If only conservative forces do work, then Eq. (10.20) gives the total work, and $K_b - K_a = -(U_b - U_a)$. We usually write this as

$$K_a + U_a = K_b + U_b \tag{10.21}$$

That is, the total mechanical energy (kinetic plus potential) is *conserved* under these circumstances.

10.10 The work done on a baseball moving in a uniform gravitational field.

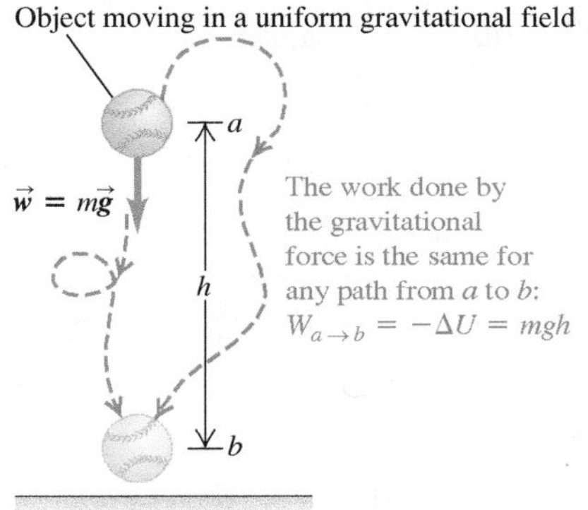

10.11 The work done on a point charge moving in a uniform electric field. Compare with Fig. 10.10.

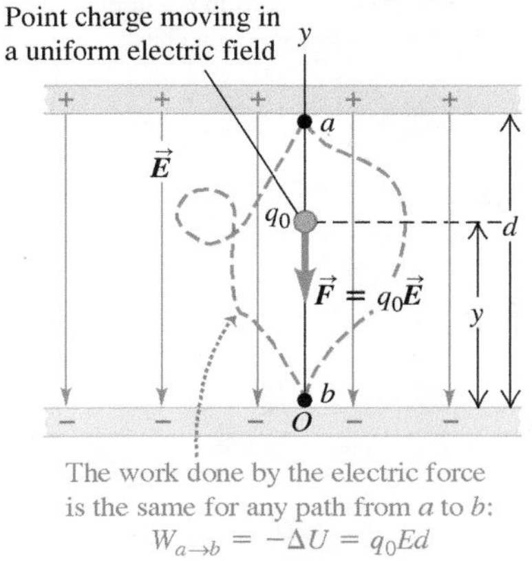

Electric Potential Energy in a Uniform Field

Let's look at an electrical example of these basic concepts. In Fig. 10.11 a pair of charged parallel metal plates sets up a uniform, downward electric field with magnitude E. The field exerts a downward force with magnitude $F = q_0E$ on a positive test charge q_0. As the charge moves downward a distance d from point a to point b, the force on the test charge is constant and independent of its location. So the work done by the electric field is the product of the force magnitude and the component of displacement in the (downward) direction of the force:

$$W_{a \to b} = Fd = q_0Ed \tag{10.22}$$

This work is positive, since the force is in the same direction as the net displacement of the test charge.

The y-component of the electric force, $F_y = -q_0E$, is constant, and there is no x- or z-component. This is exactly analogous to the gravitational force on a mass m near the earth's surface; for this force, there is a constant y-component $F_y = -mg$ and the x- and z-components are zero. Because of this analogy, we can conclude that the force exerted on q_0 by the uniform electric field in Fig. 10.11 is *conservative,* just as is the gravitational force. This means that the work $W_{a \to b}$ done by the field is independent of the path the particle takes from a to b. We can represent this work with a *potential-energy* function U, just as we did for gravitational potential energy. The potential energy for the gravitational force $F_y = -mg$ was $U = mgy$; hence the potential energy for the electric force $F_y = -q_0E$ is

$$U = q_0Ey \tag{10.23}$$

When the test charge moves from height y_a to height y_b, the work done on the charge by the field is given by

$$W_{a \to b} = -\Delta U = -(U_b - U_a) = -(q_0Ey_b - q_0Ey_a) = q_0E(y_a - y_b) \tag{10.24}$$

When y_a is greater than y_b (Fig. 10.12a), the positive test charge q_0 moves downward, in the same direction as $\vec{E}$; the displacement is in the same direction as the force $\vec{F} = q_0\vec{E}$, so the field does positive work and U decreases. [In particular, if $y_a - y_b = d$ as in Fig. 10.11, Eq. (10.24) gives $W_{a \to b} = q_0Ed$, in agreement with

10.12 A positive charge moving (a) in the direction of the electric field $\vec{E}$ and (b) in the direction opposite $\vec{E}$.

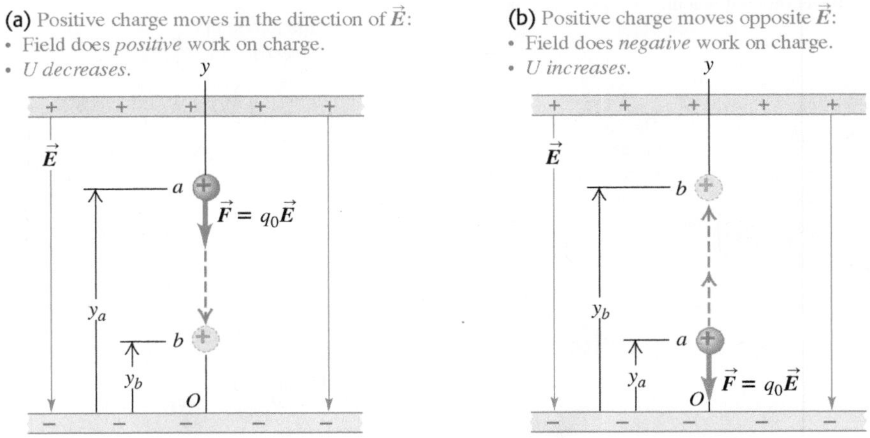

Eq. (10.22).] When y_a is less than y_b (Fig. 10.12b), the positive test charge q_0 moves upward, in the opposite direction to $\vec{E}$; the displacement is opposite the force, the field does negative work, and U increases.

If the test charge q_0 is *negative,* the potential energy increases when it moves with the field and decreases when it moves against the field (Fig. 10.13).

Whether the test charge is positive or negative, the following general rules apply: *U increases* if the test charge q_0 moves in the direction *opposite* the electric force $\vec{F} = q_0\vec{E}$ (Figs. 10.12b and 10.13a); *U decreases* if q_0 moves in the *same* direction as $\vec{F} = q_0\vec{E}$ (Figs. 10.12a and 10.13b). This is the same behavior as for gravitational potential energy, which increases if a mass m moves upward (opposite the direction of the gravitational force) and decreases if m moves downward (in the same direction as the gravitational force).

CAUTION **Electric potential energy** The relationship between electric potential energy change and motion in an electric field is an important one that we'll use often, but that takes some effort to truly understand. Take the time to carefully study the preceding paragraph as well as Figs. 10.12 and 10.13. Doing so now will help you tremendously later!

10.13 A negative charge moving (a) in the direction of the electric field $\vec{E}$ and (b) in the direction opposite $\vec{E}$. Compare with Fig. 10.12.

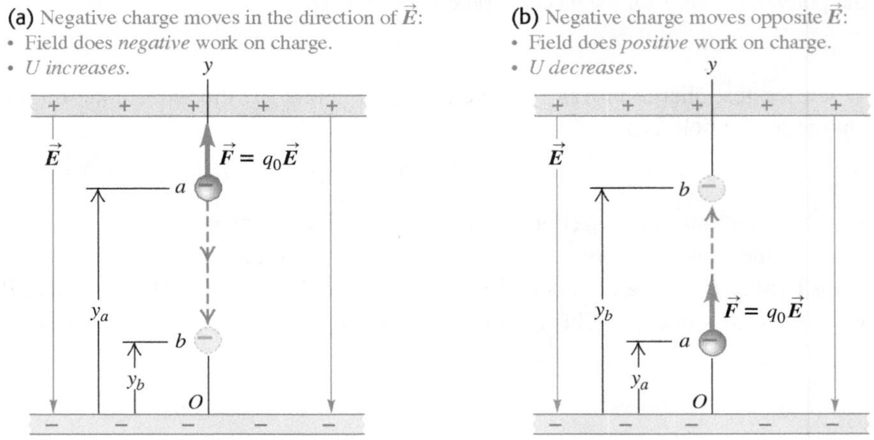

10.14 Test charge q_0 moves along a straight line extending radially from charge q. As it moves from a to b, the distance varies from r_a to r_b.

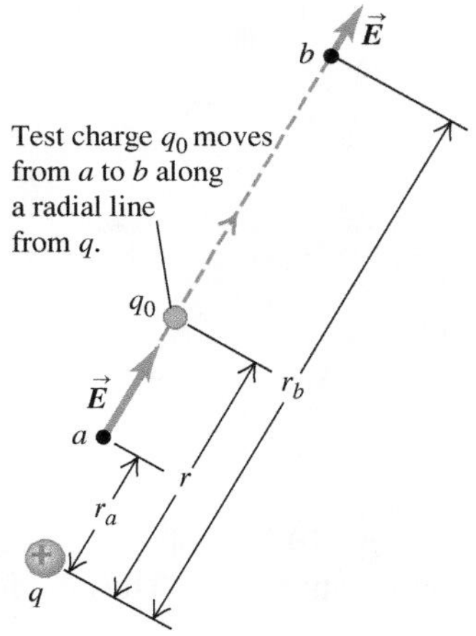

10.15 The work done on charge q_0 by the electric field of charge q does not depend on the path taken, but only on the distances r_a and r_b.

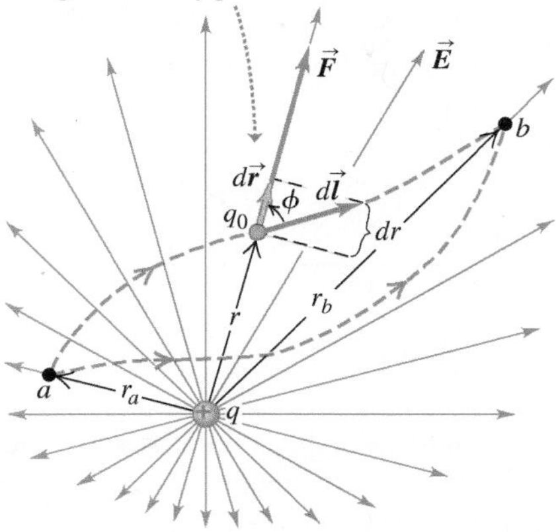

Electric Potential Energy of Two Point Charges

The idea of electric potential energy isn't restricted to the special case of a uniform electric field. Indeed, we can apply this concept to a point charge in *any* electric field caused by a static charge distribution. Recall that we can represent any charge distribution as a collection of point charges. Therefore it's useful to calculate the work done on a test charge q_0 moving in the electric field caused by a single, stationary point charge q.

We'll consider first a displacement along the *radial* line in Fig. 10.14. The force on q_0 is given by Coulomb's law, and its radial component is

$$F_r = \frac{1}{4\pi\epsilon_0}\frac{qq_0}{r^2} \tag{10.25}$$

If q and q_0 have the same sign (+ or −) the force is repulsive and F_r is positive; if the two charges have opposite signs, the force is attractive and F_r is negative. The force is *not* constant during the displacement, and we have to integrate to calculate the work $W_{a\to b}$ done on q_0 by this force as q_0 moves from a to b:

$$W_{a\to b} = \int_{r_a}^{r_b} F_r\,dr = \int_{r_a}^{r_b} \frac{1}{4\pi\epsilon_0}\frac{qq_0}{r^2}dr = \frac{qq_0}{4\pi\epsilon_0}\left(\frac{1}{r_a} - \frac{1}{r_b}\right) \tag{10.26}$$

The work done by the electric force for this particular path depends only on the endpoints.

Now let's consider a more general displacement (Fig. 10.15) in which a and b do *not* lie on the same radial line. From Eq. (10.19) the work done on q_0 during this displacement is given by

$$W_{a\to b} = \int_{r_a}^{r_b} F\cos\phi\,dl = \int_{r_a}^{r_b} \frac{1}{4\pi\epsilon_0}\frac{qq_0}{r^2}\cos\phi\,dl$$

But Fig. 10.15 shows that $\cos\phi\,dl = dr$. That is, the work done during a small displacement $d\vec{l}$ depends only on the change dr in the distance r between the charges, which is the *radial component* of the displacement. Thus Eq. (10.26) is valid even for this more general displacement; the work done on q_0 by the electric field $\vec{E}$ produced by q depends only on r_a and r_b, not on the details of the path. Also, if q_0 returns to its starting point a by a different path, the total work done in

10.16 Graphs of the potential energy U of two point charges q and q_0 versus their separation r.

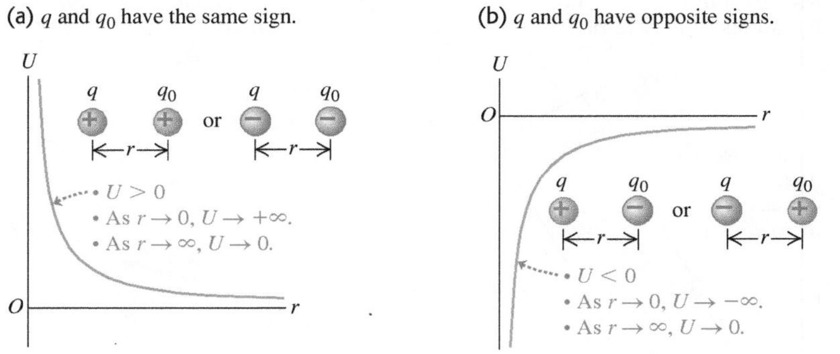
(a) q and q0 have the same sign.
U
q q0 or q q0
r r
• U > 0
• As r → 0, U → +∞.
• As r → ∞, U → 0.
O
r
(b) q and q0 have opposite signs.
U
O
r
q q0 or q q0
r r
• U < 0
• As r → 0, U → −∞.
• As r → ∞, U → 0.

the round-trip displacement is zero (the integral in Eq. (10.26) is from r_a back to r_a). These are the needed characteristics for a conservative force. Thus the force on q_0 is a *conservative* force.

We see that Eqs. (10.20) and (10.26) are consistent if we define the potential energy to be $U_a = qq_0/4\pi\epsilon_0 r_a$ when q_0 is a distance r_a from q, and to be $U_b = qq_0/4\pi\epsilon_0 r_b$ when q_0 is a distance r_b from q. Thus the potential energy U when the test charge q_0 is at *any* distance r from charge q is

$$U = \frac{1}{4\pi\epsilon_0}\frac{qq_0}{r} \quad \text{(electric potential energy of two point charges } q \text{ and } q_0) \tag{10.27}$$

Equation (10.27) is valid no matter what the signs of the charges q and q_0. The potential energy is positive if the charges q and q_0 have the same sign (Fig. 10.16a) and negative if they have opposite signs (Fig. 10.16b).

CAUTION **Electric potential energy vs. electric force** Don't confuse Eq. (10.27) for the potential energy of two point charges with the similar expression in Eq. (10.25) for the radial component of the electric force that one charge exerts on the other. Potential energy U is proportional to $1/r$, while the force component F_r is proportional to $1/r^2$.

Potential energy is always defined relative to some reference point where $U = 0$. In Eq. (10.27), U is zero when q and q_0 are infinitely far apart and $r = \infty$. Therefore U represents the work that would be done on the test charge q_0 by the field of q if q_0 moved from an initial distance r to infinity. If q and q_0 have the same sign, the interaction is repulsive, this work is positive, and U is positive at any finite separation (Fig. 10.16a). If the charges have opposite signs, the interaction is attractive, the work done is negative, and U is negative (Fig. 10.16b).

We emphasize that the potential energy U given by Eq. (10.27) is a *shared* property of the two charges. If the distance between q and q_0 is changed from r_a to r_b, the change in potential energy is the same whether q is held fixed and q_0 is moved or q_0 is held fixed and q is moved. For this reason, we never use the phrase "the electric potential energy *of* a point charge." (Likewise, if a mass m is at a height h above the earth's surface, the gravitational potential energy is a shared property of the mass m and the earth.

Equation (10.27) also holds if the charge q_0 is outside a spherically symmetric charge *distribution* with total charge q; the distance r is from q_0 to the center of the distribution. That's because Gauss's law tells us that the electric field outside such a distribution is the same as if all of its charge q were concentrated at its center.

Electric Potential Energy with Several Point Charges

Suppose the electric field $\vec{E}$ in which charge q_0 moves is caused by *several* point charges $q_1, q_2, q_3, \ldots$ at distances $r_1, r_2, r_3, \ldots$ from q_0, as in Fig. 10.17. For example, q_0 could be a positive ion moving in the presence of other ions. The total electric field at each point is the *vector sum* of the fields due to the individual charges, and the total work done on q_0 during any displacement is the sum of the contributions from the individual charges. From Eq. (10.27) we conclude that the potential energy associated with the test charge q_0 at point a in Fig. 10.17 is the *algebraic* sum (*not* a vector sum):

$$U = \frac{q_0}{4\pi\epsilon_0}\left(\frac{q_1}{r_1} + \frac{q_2}{r_2} + \frac{q_3}{r_3} + \cdots\right) = \frac{q_0}{4\pi\epsilon_0}\sum_i \frac{q_i}{r_i} \quad \text{(point charge } q_0 \text{ and collection of charges } q_i\text{)} \tag{10.28}$$

When q_0 is at a different point b, the potential energy is given by the same expression, but $r_1, r_2, \ldots$ are the distances from $q_1, q_2, \ldots$ to point b. The work done on charge q_0 when it moves from a to b along any path is equal to the difference $U_a - U_b$ between the potential energies when q_0 is at a and at b.

We can represent *any* charge distribution as a collection of point charges, so Eq. (10.28) shows that we can always find a potential-energy function for *any* static electric field. It follows that **for every electric field due to a static charge distribution, the force exerted by that field is conservative.**

Equations (10.27) and (10.28) define U to be zero when all the distances $r_1, r_2, \ldots$ are infinite—that is, when the test charge q_0 is very far away from all the charges that produce the field. As with any potential-energy function, the point where $U = 0$ is arbitrary; we can always add a constant to make U equal zero at any point we choose. In electrostatics problems it's usually simplest to choose this point to be at infinity.

Equation (10.28) gives the potential energy associated with the presence of the test charge q_0 in the $\vec{E}$ field produced by $q_1, q_2, q_3, \ldots$. But there is also potential energy involved in assembling these charges. If we start with charges $q_1, q_2, q_3, \ldots$ all separated from each other by infinite distances and then bring them together so that the distance between q_i and q_j is r_{ij}, the *total* potential energy U is the sum of the potential energies of interaction for each pair of charges. We can write this as

$$U = \frac{1}{4\pi\epsilon_0}\sum_{i<j}\frac{q_i q_j}{r_{ij}} \tag{10.29}$$

This sum extends over all *pairs* of charges; we don't let $i = j$ (because that would be an interaction of a charge with itself), and we include only terms with

10.17 The potential energy associated with a charge q_0 at point a depends on the other charges q_1, q_2, and q_3 and on their distances r_1, r_2, and r_3 from point a.

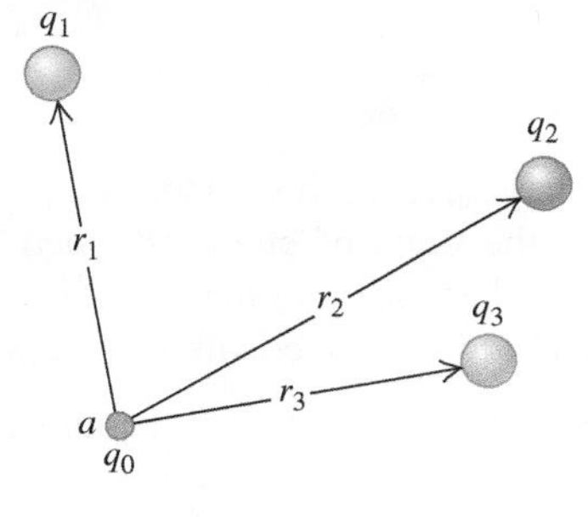

$i < j$ to make sure that we count each pair only once. Thus, to account for the interaction between q_3 and q_4, we include a term with $i = 3$ and $j = 4$ but not a term with $i = 4$ and $j = 3$.

Interpreting Electric Potential Energy

As a final comment, here are two viewpoints on electric potential energy. We have defined it in terms of the work done *by the electric field* on a charged particle moving in the field, just as we defined potential energy in terms of the work done by gravity or by a spring. When a particle moves from point a to point b, the work done on it by the electric field is $W_{a \to b} = U_a - U_b$. Thus the potential-energy difference $U_a - U_b$ equals *the work that is done by the electric force when the particle moves from a to b*. When U_a is greater than U_b, the field does positive work on the particle as it "falls" from a point of higher potential energy (a) to a point of lower potential energy (b).

An alternative but equivalent viewpoint is to consider how much work we would have to do to "raise" a particle from a point b where the potential energy is U_b to a point a where it has a greater value U_a (pushing two positive charges closer together, for example). To move the particle slowly (so as not to give it any kinetic energy), we need to exert an additional external force $\vec{F}_{ext}$ that is equal and opposite to the electric-field force and does positive work. The potential-energy difference $U_a - U_b$ is then defined as *the work that must be done by an external force to move the particle slowly from b to a against the electric force*. Because $\vec{F}_{ext}$ is the negative of the electric-field force and the displacement is in the opposite direction, this definition of the potential difference $U_a - U_b$ is equivalent to that given above. This alternative viewpoint also works if U_a is less than U_b, corresponding to "lowering" the particle; an example is moving two positive charges away from each other. In this case, $U_a - U_b$ is again equal to the work done by the external force, but now this work is negative.

We will use both of these viewpoints in the next section to interpret what is meant by electric *potential*, or potential energy per unit charge.

10.6 Electric Potential

In Section 10.5 we looked at the potential energy U associated with a test charge q_0 in an electric field. Now we want to describe this potential energy on a "per unit charge" basis, just as electric field describes the force per unit charge on a charged particle in the field. This leads us to the concept of *electric potential*, often called simply *potential*. This concept is very useful in calculations involving energies of charged particles. It also facilitates many electric-field calculations because electric potential is closely related to the electric field $\vec{E}$. When we need to determine an electric field, it is often easier to determine the potential first and then find the field from it.

Potential is *potential energy per unit charge*. We define the potential V at any point in an electric field as the potential energy U *per unit charge* associated with a test charge q_0 at that point:

$$V = \frac{U}{q_0} \quad \text{or} \quad U = q_0 V \tag{10.30}$$

Potential energy and charge are both scalars, so potential is a scalar. From Eq. (10.30) its units are the units of energy divided by those of charge. The SI unit of potential, called one **volt** (1 V) in honor of the Italian electrical experimenter Alessandro Volta (1745–1827), equals 1 joule per coulomb:

$$1 \text{ V} = 1 \text{ volt} = 1 \text{ J/C} = 1 \text{ joule/coulomb}$$

10.18 The voltage of this battery equals the difference in potential $V_{ab} = V_a - V_b$ between its positive terminal (point a) and its negative terminal (point b).

Let's put Eq. (10.20), which equates the work done by the electric force during a displacement from a to b to the quantity $-\Delta U = -(U_b - U_a)$, on a "work per unit charge" basis. We divide this equation by q_0, obtaining

$$\frac{W_{a\to b}}{q_0} = -\frac{\Delta U}{q_0} = -\left(\frac{U_b}{q_0} - \frac{U_a}{q_0}\right) = -(V_b - V_a) = V_a - V_b \quad (10.31)$$

where $V_a = U_a/q_0$ is the potential energy per unit charge at point a and similarly for V_b. We call V_a and V_b the *potential at point a* and *potential at point b*, respectively. Thus the work done per unit charge by the electric force when a charged body moves from a to b is equal to the potential at a minus the potential at b.

The difference $V_a - V_b$ is called the *potential of a with respect to b*; we sometimes abbreviate this difference as $V_{ab} = V_a - V_b$ (note the order of the subscripts). This is often called the potential difference between a and b, but that's ambiguous unless we specify which is the reference point. In electric circuits, which we will analyze in later chapters, the potential difference between two points is often called **voltage** (Fig. 10.18). Equation (10.31) then states: **V_{ab}, the potential of a with respect to b, equals the work done by the electric force when a UNIT charge moves from a to b.**

Another way to interpret the potential difference V_{ab} in Eq. (10.31) is to use the alternative viewpoint mentioned at the end of Section 10.5. In that viewpoint, $U_a - U_b$ is the amount of work that must be done by an *external* force to move a particle of charge q_0 slowly from b to a against the electric force. The work that must be done *per unit charge* by the external force is then $(U_a - U_b)/q_0 = V_a - V_b = V_{ab}$. In other words: **$V_{ab}$, the potential of a with respect to b, equals the work that must be done to move a UNIT charge slowly from b to a against the electric force.**

An instrument that measures the difference of potential between two points is called a *voltmeter.* Voltmeters that can measure a potential difference of 1 μV are common, and sensitivities down to 10^{-12} V can be attained.

Calculating Electric Potential

To find the potential V due to a single point charge q, we divide Eq. (10.27) by q_0:

$$V = \frac{U}{q_0} = \frac{1}{4\pi\epsilon_0}\frac{q}{r} \quad \text{(potential due to a point charge)} \quad (10.32)$$

where r is the distance from the point charge q to the point at which the potential is evaluated. If q is positive, the potential that it produces is positive at all points;

if q is negative, it produces a potential that is negative everywhere. In either case, V is equal to zero at $r = \infty$, an infinite distance from the point charge. Note that potential, like electric field, is independent of the test charge q_0 that we use to define it.

Similarly, we divide Eq. (10.28) by q_0 to find the potential due to a collection of point charges:

$$V = \frac{U}{q_0} = \frac{1}{4\pi\epsilon_0}\sum_i \frac{q_i}{r_i} \quad \text{(potential due to a collection of point charge)} \tag{10.33}$$

In this expression, r_i is the distance from the ith charge, q_i, to the point at which V is evaluated. Just as the electric field due to a collection of point charges is the *vector* sum of the fields produced by each charge, the electric potential due to a collection of point charges is the *scalar* sum of the potentials due to each charge. When we have a continuous distribution of charge along a line, over a surface, or through a volume, we divide the charge into elements dq, and the sum in Eq. (10.33) becomes an integral:

$$V = \frac{1}{4\pi\epsilon_0}\int \frac{dq}{r} \quad \text{(potential due to a continuous distribution of charge)} \tag{10.34}$$

where r is the distance from the charge element dq to the field point where we are finding V. We'll work out several examples of such cases. The potential defined by Eqs. (10.33) and (10.34) is zero at points that are infinitely far away from *all* the charges.

CAUTION **What is electric potential?** Before getting too involved in the details of how to calculate electric potential, you should stop and remind yourself what potential is. The electric *potential* at a certain point is the potential energy that would be associated with a *unit* charge placed at that point. That's why potential is measured in joules per coulomb, or volts. Keep in mind, too, that there doesn't have to be a charge at a given point for a potential V to exist at that point. (In the same way, an electric field can exist at a given point even if there's no charge there to respond to it.)

Finding Electric Potential from Electric Field

When we are given a collection of point charges, Eq. (10.33) is usually the easiest way to calculate the potential V. But in some problems in which the electric field is known or can be found easily, it is easier to determine V from $\vec{E}$. The force $\vec{F}$ on a test charge q_0 can be written as $\vec{F} = q_0\vec{E}$, so from Eq. (10.19) the work done by the electric force as the test charge moves from a to b is given by

$$W_{a\to b} = \int_a^b \vec{F}\cdot d\vec{l} = \int_a^b q_0\vec{E}\cdot d\vec{l}$$

If we divide this by q_0 and compare the result with Eq. (10.31), we find

$$V_a - V_b = \int_a^b \vec{E}\cdot d\vec{l} = \int_a^b E\cos\phi\, dl \quad \text{(potential difference as an integral of } \vec{E}\text{)} \tag{10.35}$$

The value of $V_a - V_b$ is independent of the path taken from a to b, just as the value of $W_{a\to b}$ is independent of the path. To interpret Eq. (10.35), remember that $\vec{E}$ is the electric force per unit charge on a test charge. If the line integral $\int_a^b \vec{E}\cdot d\vec{l}$ is positive, the electric field does positive work on a positive test charge as it moves from a to b. In this case the electric potential energy decreases as the test charge moves, so the potential energy per unit charge decreases as

10.19 If you move in the direction of $\vec{E}$, electric potential V decreases; if you move in the direction opposite $\vec{E}$, V increases.

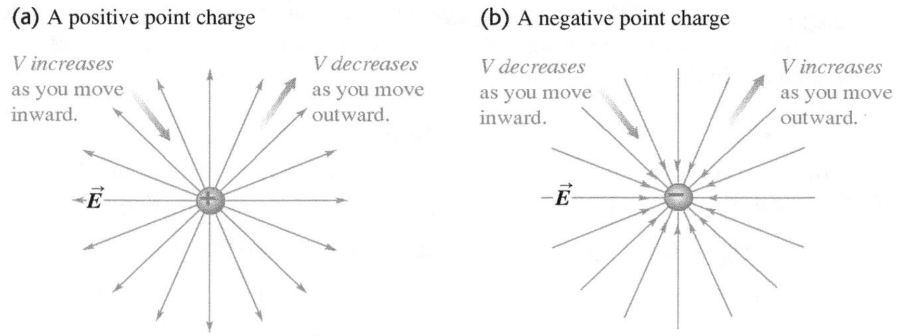
(a) A positive point charge
V increases as you move inward.
V decreases as you move outward.
E
(b) A negative point charge
V decreases as you move inward.
V increases as you move outward.
E

well; hence V_b is less than V_a and $V_a - V_b$ is positive.

As an illustration, consider a positive point charge (Fig. 10.19a). The electric field is directed away from the charge, and $V = q/4\pi\epsilon_0 r$ is positive at any finite distance from the charge. If you move away from the charge, in the direction of $\vec{E}$, you move toward lower values of V; if you move toward the charge, in the direction opposite $\vec{E}$, you move toward greater values of V. For the negative point charge in Fig. 10.19b, $\vec{E}$ is directed toward the charge and $V = q/4\pi\epsilon_0 r$ is negative at any finite distance from the charge. In this case, if you move toward the charge, you are moving in the direction of $\vec{E}$ and in the direction of decreasing (more negative) V. Moving away from the charge, in the direction opposite $\vec{E}$, moves you toward increasing (less negative) values of V. The general rule, valid for *any* electric field, is: Moving *with* the direction of $\vec{E}$ means moving in the direction of *decreasing* V, and moving *against* the direction of $\vec{E}$ means moving in the direction of *increasing* V.

Also, a positive test charge q_0 experiences an electric force in the direction of $\vec{E}$, toward lower values of V; a negative test charge experiences a force opposite $\vec{E}$, toward higher values of V. Thus a positive charge tends to "fall" from a high-potential region to a lower-potential region. The opposite is true for a negative charge.

Notice that Eq. (10.35) can be rewritten as

$$V_a - V_b = -\int_b^a \vec{E} \cdot d\vec{l} \qquad (10.36)$$

This has a negative sign compared to the integral in Eq. (10.35), and the limits are reversed; hence Eqs. (10.35) and (10.36) are equivalent. But Eq. (10.36) has a slightly different interpretation. To move a unit charge slowly against the electric force, we must apply an *external* force per unit charge equal to $-\vec{E}$, equal and opposite to the electric force per unit charge $\vec{E}$. Equation (10.36) says that $V_a - V_b = V_{ab}$, the potential of a with respect to b, equals the work done per unit charge by this external force to move a unit charge from b to a. This is the same alternative interpretation we discussed under Eq. (10.31).

Equations (10.35) and (10.36) show that the unit of potential difference (1 V) is equal to the unit of electric field (1 N/C) multiplied by the unit of distance (1 m). Hence the unit of electric field can be expressed as 1 *volt per meter* (1 V/m), as well as 1 N/C:

$$1 \text{ V/m} = 1 \text{ volt/meter} = 1 \text{ N/C} = 1 \text{ newton/coulomb}$$

In practice, the volt per meter is the usual unit of electric-field magnitude.

Electron Volts

The magnitude e of the electron charge can be used to define a unit of energy that is useful in many calculations with atomic and nuclear systems. When a particle with charge q moves from a point where the potential is V_b to a point where it is V_a, the change in the potential energy U is

$$U_a - U_b = q(V_a - V_b) = qV_{ab}$$

If the charge q equals the magnitude e of the electron charge, 1.602×10^{-19} C, and the potential difference is $V_{ab} = 1$ V, the change in energy is

$$U_a - U_b = (1.602 \times 10^{-19}\,\text{C})(1\,\text{V}) = 1.602 \times 10^{-19}\,\text{J}$$

This quantity of energy is defined to be 1 **electron volt** (1 eV):

$$1\,\text{eV} = 1.602 \times 10^{-19}\,\text{J}$$

The multiples meV, keV, MeV, GeV, and TeV are often used.

CAUTION **Electron volts vs. volts** Remember that the electron volt is a unit of energy, *not* a unit of potential or potential difference!

When a particle with charge e moves through a potential difference of 1 volt, the change in potential *energy* is 1 eV. If the charge is some multiple of e—say Ne—the change in potential energy in electron volts is N times the potential difference in volts. For example, when an alpha particle, which has charge $2e$, moves between two points with a potential difference of 1000 V, the change in potential energy is $2(1000\,\text{eV}) = 2000$ eV. To confirm this, we write

$$U_a - U_b = qV_{ab} = (2e)(1000\,\text{V}) = (2)(1.602 \times 10^{-19}\,\text{C})(1000\,\text{V})$$
$$= 3.204 \times 10^{-16}\,\text{J} = 2000\,\text{eV}$$

Although we have defined the electron volt in terms of *potential* energy, we can use it for *any* form of energy, such as the kinetic energy of a moving particle. When we speak of a "one-million-electron-volt proton," we mean a proton with a kinetic energy of one million electron volts (1 MeV), equal to $(10^6)(1.602 \times 10^{-19}\,\text{J}) = 1.602 \times 10^{-13}$ J. The Large Hadron Collider near Geneva, Switzerland, is designed to accelerate protons to a kinetic energy of 7 TeV (7×10^{12} eV).

CHAPTER 10 SUMMARY

Gravitational potential energy and elastic potential energy: The work done on a particle by a constant gravitational force can be represented as a change in the gravitational potential energy $U_{grav} = mgy$. This energy is a shared property of the particle and the earth. A potential energy is also associated with the elastic force $F_x = -kx$ exerted by an ideal spring, where x is the amount of stretch or compression. The work done by this force can be represented as a change in the elastic potential energy of the spring, $U_{el} = \frac{1}{2}kx^2$.

$$W_{grav} = mgy_1 - mgy_2 = U_{grav,1} - U_{grav,2} = -\Delta U_{grav} \quad (9.20), (9.22)$$

$$W_{el} = \tfrac{1}{2}kx_1{}^2 - \tfrac{1}{2}kx_2{}^2 = U_{el,1} - U_{el,2} = -\Delta U_{el} \quad (10.2)$$

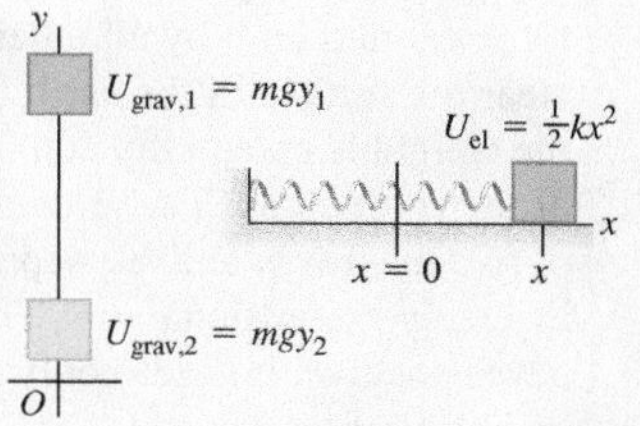

When total mechanical energy is conserved: The total potential energy U is the sum of the gravitational and elastic potential energy: $U = U_{grav} + U_{el}$. If no forces other than the gravitational and elastic forces do work on a particle, the sum of kinetic and potential energy is conserved. This sum $E = K + U$ is called the total mechanical energy.

$$K_1 + U_1 = K_2 + U_2 \quad (9.23, 10.3)$$

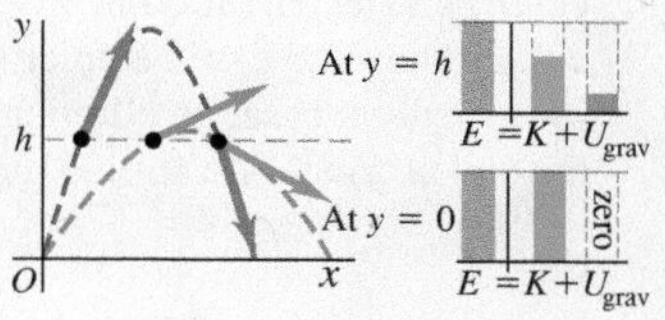

When total mechanical energy is not conserved: When forces other than the gravitational and elastic forces do work on a particle, the work W_{other} done by these other forces equals the change in total mechanical energy (kinetic energy plus total potential energy).

$$K_1 + U_1 + W_{other} = K_2 + U_2 \quad (10.6)$$

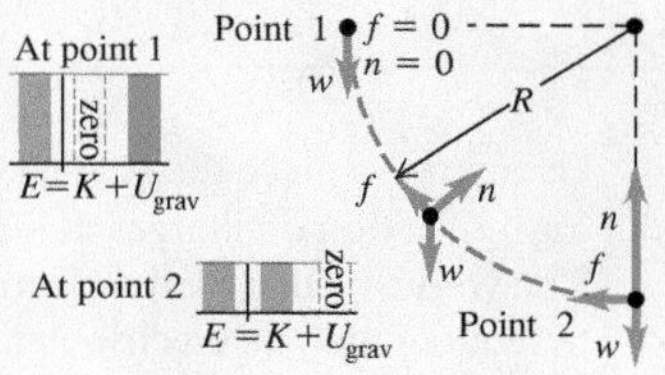

Conservative forces, nonconservative forces, and the law of conservation of energy: All forces are either conservative or nonconservative. A conservative force is one for which the work–kinetic energy relationship is completely reversible. The work of a conservative force can always be represented by a potential-energy function, but the work of a nonconservative force cannot. The work done by nonconservative forces manifests itself as changes in the internal energy of bodies. The sum of kinetic, potential, and internal energy is always conserved.

$$\Delta K + \Delta U + \Delta U_{int} = 0 \quad (9.28)$$

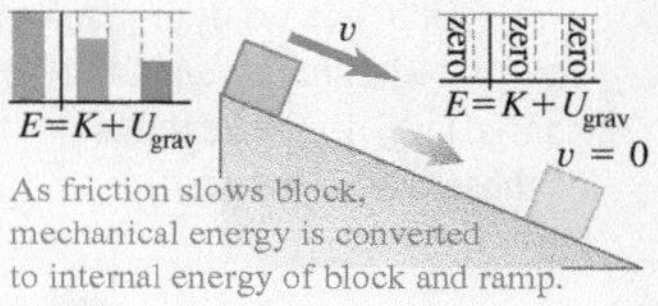

Gravitational force, weight, and gravitational potential energy: The weight w of a body is the total gravitational force exerted on it by all other bodies in the universe. Near the surface of the earth (mass m_E and radius R_E), the weight is essentially equal to the gravitational force of the earth alone. The gravitational potential energy U of two masses m and m_E separated by a distance r is inversely proportional to r. The potential energy is never positive; it is zero only when the two bodies are infinitely far apart.

$$w = F_g = \frac{Gm_E m}{R_E^2} \qquad (6.4)$$

(weight at earth's surface)

$$g = \frac{Gm_E}{R_E^2} \qquad (6.5)$$

(acceleration due to gravity at earth's surface)

$$U = -\frac{Gm_E m}{r} \qquad (10.10)$$

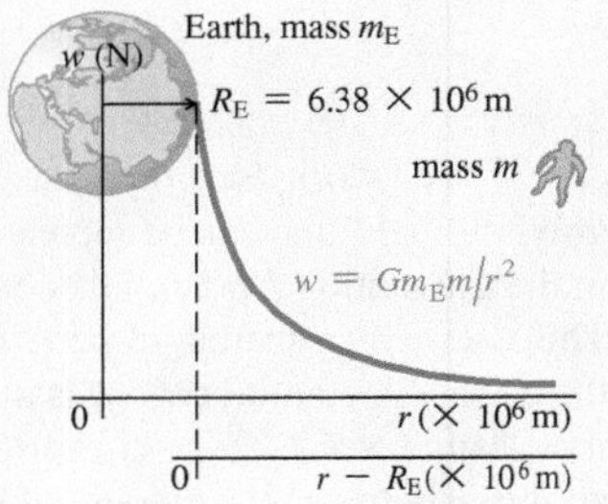

Orbits: When a satellite moves in a circular orbit, the centripetal acceleration is provided by the gravitational attraction of the earth. Kepler's three laws describe the more general case: an elliptical orbit of a planet around the sun or a satellite around a planet.

$$v = \sqrt{\frac{Gm_E}{r}}$$

(speed in circular orbit) (10.11)

$$T = \frac{2\pi r}{v} = 2\pi r\sqrt{\frac{r}{Gm_E}} = \frac{2\pi r^{3/2}}{\sqrt{Gm_E}}$$

(period in circular orbit) (10.13)

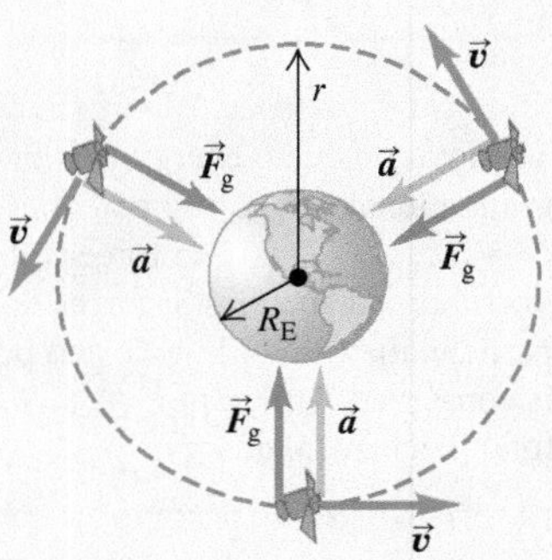

Electric potential energy: The electric force caused by any collection of charges at rest is a conservative force. The work W done by the electric force on a charged particle moving in an electric field can be represented by the change in a potential-energy function U.

The electric potential energy for two point charges q and q_0 depends on their separation r. The electric potential energy for a charge q_0 in the presence of a collection of charges q_1, q_2, q_3 depends on the distance from q_0 to each of these other charges.

$$W_{a \to b} = U_a - U_b \qquad (10.20)$$

$$U = \frac{1}{4\pi\epsilon_0}\frac{qq_0}{r} \qquad (10.27)$$

(two point charges)

$$U = \frac{q_0}{4\pi\epsilon_0}\left(\frac{q_1}{r_1} + \frac{q_2}{r_2} + \frac{q_3}{r_3} + \cdots\right) = \frac{q_0}{4\pi\epsilon_0}\sum_i \frac{q_i}{r_i} \qquad (10.28)$$

(q_0 in presence of other point charges)

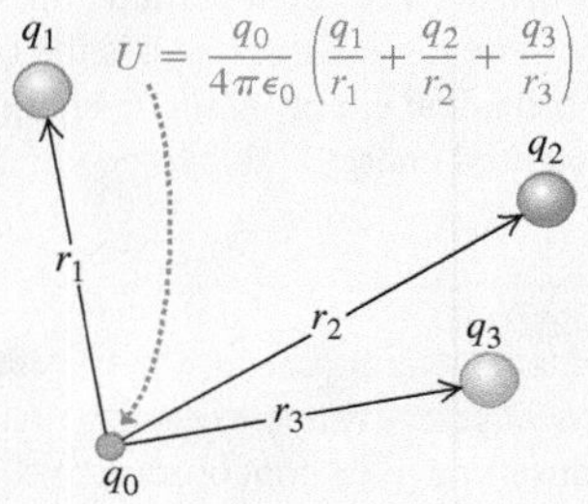

Electric potential: Potential, denoted by V, is potential energy per unit charge. The potential difference between two points equals the amount of work that would be required to move a unit positive test charge between those points. The potential V due to a quantity of charge can be calculated by summing (if the charge is a collection of point charges) or by integrating (if the charge is a distribution).

The potential difference between two points a and b, also called the potential of a with respect to b, is given by the line integral of $\vec{E}$. The potential at a given point can be found by first finding $\vec{E}$ and then carrying out this integral.

$$V = \frac{U}{q_0} = \frac{1}{4\pi\epsilon_0}\frac{q}{r} \qquad (10.32)$$

(due to a point charge)

$$V = \frac{U}{q_0} = \frac{1}{4\pi\epsilon_0}\sum_i \frac{q_i}{r_i} \qquad (10.33)$$

(due to a collection of point charges)

$$V = \frac{1}{4\pi\epsilon_0}\int \frac{dq}{r} \qquad (10.34)$$

(due to a charge distribution)

$$V_a - V_b = \int_a^b \vec{E} \cdot d\vec{l} = \int_a^b E\cos\phi\, dl \qquad (10.35)$$

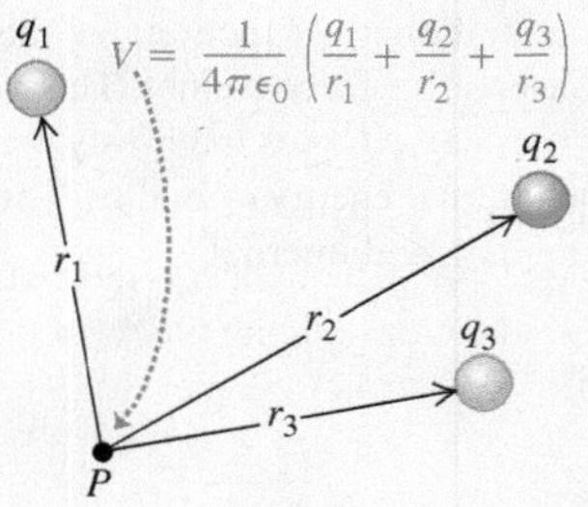

Problems

•, ••, •••: Problems of increasing difficulty. **CP**: Cumulative problems incorporating material from earlier chapters. **CALC**: Problems requiring calculus. **BIO**: Biosciences problems.

10.1 • A 5.00-kg block is moving at $v_0 = 6.00$ m/s along a frictionless, horizontal surface toward a spring with force constant $k = 500$ N/m that is attached to a wall (Fig. P10.1). The spring has negligible mass. (a) Find the maximum distance the spring will be compressed. (b) If the spring is to compress by no more than 0.150 m, what should be the maximum value of v_0?

Figure **P10.1**

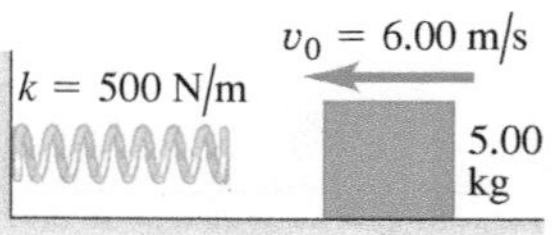

10.2 •• A force of 800 N stretches a certain spring a distance of 0.200 m. (a) What is the potential energy of the spring when it is stretched 0.200 m? (b) What is its potential energy when it is compressed 5.00 cm?

10.3 • A 2.00-kg block is pushed against a spring with negligible mass and force constant $k = 400$ N/m, compressing it 0.220 m. When the block is released, it moves along a frictionless, horizontal surface and then up a frictionless incline with slope 37.0° (Fig. P10.3). (a) What is the speed of the block as it slides along the horizontal surface after having left the spring? (b) How far does the block travel up the incline before starting to slide back down?

Figure **P10.3**

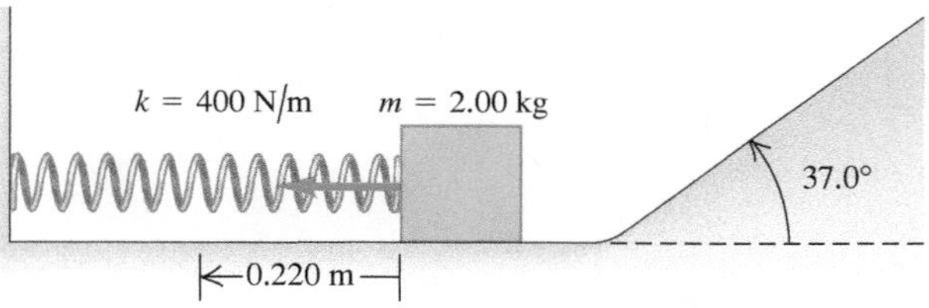

10.4 ••• **Bungee Jump.** A bungee cord is 30.0 m long and, when stretched a distance x, it exerts a restoring force of magnitude kx. Your father-in-law (mass 95.0 kg) stands on a platform 45.0 m above the ground, and one end of the cord is tied securely to his ankle and the other end to the platform. You have promised him that when he steps off the platform he will fall a maximum distance of only 41.0 m before the cord stops him. You had several bungee cords to select from, and you tested them by stretching them out, tying one end to a tree, and pulling on the other end with a force of 380.0 N. When you do this, what distance will the bungee cord that you should select have stretched?

10.5 •• **Volcanoes on Io.** Jupiter's moon Io has active volcanoes (in fact, it is the most volcanically active body in the solar system) that eject material as high as 500 km (or even higher) above the surface. Io has a mass of 8.94×10^{22} kg and a radius of 1815 km. Ignore any variation in gravity over the 500-km range of the debris. How high would this material go on earth if it were ejected with the same speed as on Io?

10.6 • Three uniform spheres are fixed at the positions shown in Fig. P10.6. (a) What are the magnitude and direction of the force on a 0.0150-kg particle placed at P? (b) If the spheres are in deep outer space and a 0.0150-kg particle is released from rest 300 m from the origin along a line 45° below the $-x$-axis, what will the particle's speed be when it reaches the origin?

Figure **P10.6**

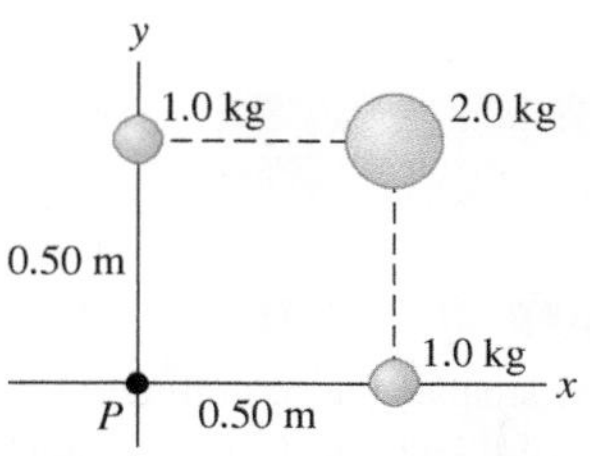

10.7 •• There are two equations from which a change in the gravitational potential energy U of the system of a mass m and the earth can be calculated. One is $U = mgy$. The other is $U = -Gm_E m/r$ (Eq. 10.10). As shown in Section 10.2, the first equation is correct only if the gravitational force is a constant over the change in height Δy. The second is always correct. Actually, the gravitational force is never exactly constant over any change in height, but if the variation is small, we can ignore it. Consider the difference in U between a mass at the earth's surface and a distance h above it using both equations, and find the value of h. Express this value of h as a fraction of the earth's radius, and also obtain a numerical value for it.

10.8 ••• Comets travel around the sun in elliptical orbits with large eccentricities. If a comet has speed 2.0×10^4 m/s when at a distance of 2.5×10^{11} m from the center of the sun, what is its speed when at a distance of 5.0×10^{10} m?

10.9 ••• **CP** Consider a spacecraft in an elliptical orbit around the earth. At the low point, or perigee, of its orbit, it is 400 km above the earth's surface; at the high point, or apogee, it is 4000 km above the earth's surface. (a) What is the period of the spacecraft's orbit? (b) Using conservation of angular momentum, find the ratio of the spacecraft's speed at perigee to its speed at apogee. (c) Using conservation of energy, find the speed at perigee and the speed at apogee. (d) It is necessary to have the spacecraft escape from the earth completely. If the spacecraft's rockets are fired at perigee, by how much would the speed have to be increased to achieve this? What if the rockets were fired at apogee? Which point in the orbit is more efficient to use?

10.10 •• A point charge $q_1 = +2.40\ \mu$C is held stationary at the origin. A second point charge $q_2 = -4.30\ \mu$C moves from the point $x = 0.150$ m, $y = 0$ to the point $x = 0.250$ m, $y = 0.250$ m. How much work is done by the electric force on q_2?

10.11 •• A small metal sphere, carrying a net charge of $q_1 = -2.80\ \mu$C, is held in a stationary position by insulating supports. A second small metal sphere, with a net charge of $q_2 = -7.80\ \mu$C and mass

Figure **P10.11**

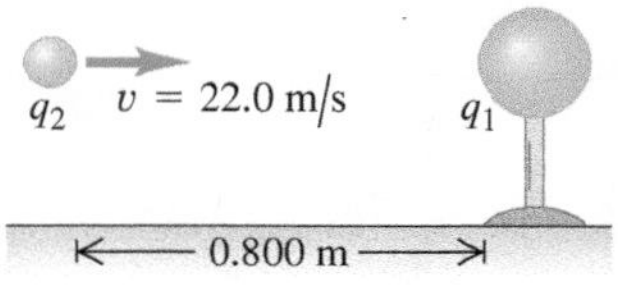

1.50 g, is projected toward q_1. When the two spheres are 0.800 m apart, q_2 is moving toward q_1 with speed 22.0 m/s (Fig. P10.11). Assume that the two spheres can be treated as point charges. You can ignore the force of gravity. (a) What is the speed of q_2 when the spheres are 0.400 m apart? (b) How close does q_2 get to q_1?

10.12 •• Three point charges, which initially are infinitely far apart, are placed at the corners of an equilateral triangle with sides d. Two of the point charges are identical and have charge q. If zero net work is required to place the three charges at the corners of the triangle, what must the value of the third charge be?

10.13 • A uniform electric field has magnitude E and is directed in the negative x-direction. The potential difference between point a (at $x = 0.60$ m) and point b (at $x = 0.90$ m) is 240 V. (a) Which point, a or b, is at the higher potential? (b) Calculate the value of E. (c) A negative point charge $q = -0.200\ \mu\text{C}$ is moved from b to a. Calculate the work done on the point charge by the electric field.

Answers

Chapter Opening Question ?

The smaller the orbital radius r of a satellite, the faster its orbital speed v [see Eq. (10.11)]. Hence a particle near the inner edge of Saturn's rings has a faster speed than a particle near the outer edge of the rings.

11 ELECTRICITY

? In a flashlight, is the amount of current that flows out of the bulb less than, greater than, or equal to the amount of current that flows into the bulb?

LEARNING GOALS

By studying this chapter, you will learn:

- The meaning of electric current, and how charges move in a conductor.
- What is meant by the resistivity and conductivity of a substance.
- How to calculate the resistance of a conductor from its dimensions and its resistivity.
- How an electromotive force (emf) makes it possible for current to flow in a circuit.
- How to do calculations involving energy and power in circuits.
- How to analyze circuits with multiple resistors in series or parallel.
- Rules that you can apply to any circuit with more than one loop.

We studied the interactions of electric charges *at rest;* now we're ready to study charges *in motion.* An *electric current* consists of charges in motion from one region to another. If the charges follow a conducting path that forms a closed loop, the path is called an *electric circuit.*

Fundamentally, electric circuits are a means for conveying *energy* from one place to another. As charged particles move within a circuit, electric potential energy is transferred from a source (such as a battery or generator) to a device in which that energy is either stored or converted to another form: into sound in a stereo system or into heat and light in a toaster or light bulb. Electric circuits are useful because they allow energy to be transported without any moving parts (other than the moving charged particles themselves). They are at the heart of flashlights, computers, radio and television transmitters and receivers, and household and industrial power distribution systems. Your nervous system is a specialized electric circuit that carries vital signals from one part of your body to another.

You must understand the basic properties of electric circuits before you can analyze electric currents and examine some practical applications of circuits. These properties are the subject of this chapter. We'll begin by describing the nature of electric conductors and considering how they are affected by temperature. We'll learn why a short, fat, cold copper wire is a better conductor than a long, skinny, hot steel wire. We'll study the properties of batteries and see how they cause current and energy transfer in a circuit. In this analysis we will use the concepts of current, potential difference (or voltage), resistance, and electromotive force. Finally, we'll look at electric current in a material from a microscopic viewpoint.

11.1 Current

A **current** is any motion of charge from one region to another. In this section we'll discuss currents in conducting materials. The vast majority of technological applications of charges in motion involve currents of this kind.

In electrostatic situations the electric field is zero everywhere within the conductor, and there is *no* current. However, this does not mean that all charges within the conductor are at rest. In an ordinary metal such as copper or alumium, some of the electrons are free to move within the conducting material. These free electrons move randomly in all directions, somewhat like the molecules of a gas but with much greater speeds, of the order of 10^6 m/s. The electrons nonetheless do not escape from the conducting material, because they are attracted to the positive ions of the material. The motion of the electrons is random, so there is no *net* flow of charge in any direction and hence no current.

11.1 If there is no electric field inside a conductor, an electron moves randomly from point P_1 to point P_2 in a time Δt. If an electric field $\vec{E}$ is present, the electric force $\vec{F} = q\vec{E}$ imposes a small drift (greatly exaggerated here) that takes the electron to point P'_2, a distance $v_d \Delta t$ from P_2 in the direction of the force.

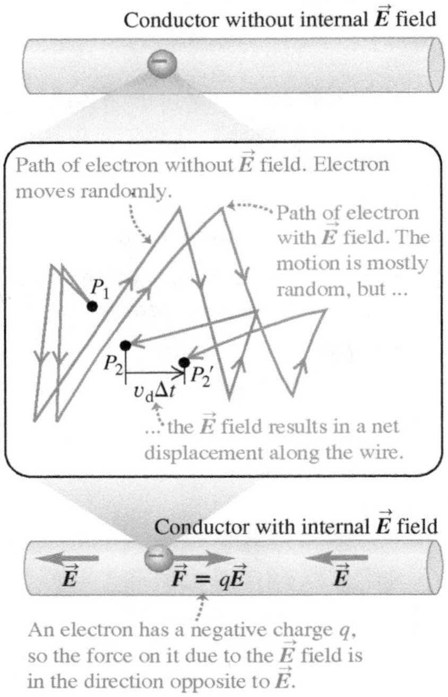

Conductor without internal $\vec{E}$ field
Path of electron without $\vec{E}$ field. Electron moves randomly.
Path of electron with $\vec{E}$ field. The motion is mostly random, but ...
P_1
P_2
P_2'
$v_d \Delta t$
...the $\vec{E}$ field results in a net displacement along the wire.
Conductor with internal $\vec{E}$ field
$\vec{E}$
$\vec{F} = q\vec{E}$
$\vec{E}$
An electron has a negative charge q, so the force on it due to the $\vec{E}$ field is in the direction opposite to $\vec{E}$.

Now consider what happens if a constant, steady electric field $\vec{E}$ is established inside a conductor. (We'll see later how this can be done.) A charged particle (such as a free electron) inside the conducting material is then subjected to a steady force $\vec{F} = q\vec{E}$. If the charged particle were moving in *vacuum,* this steady force would cause a steady acceleration in the direction of $\vec{F}$, and after a time the charged particle would be moving in that direction at high speed. But a charged particle moving in a *conductor* undergoes frequent collisions with the massive, nearly stationary ions of the material. In each such collision the particle's direction of motion undergoes a random change. The net effect of the electric field $\vec{E}$ is that in addition to the random motion of the charged particles within the conductor, there is also a very slow net motion or *drift* of the moving charged particles as a group in the direction of the electric force $\vec{F} = q\vec{E}$ (Fig. 11.1). This motion is described in terms of the **drift velocity** $\vec{v}_d$ of the particles. As a result, there is a net current in the conductor.

While the random motion of the electrons has a very fast average speed of about 10^6 m/s, the drift speed is very slow, often on the order of 10^{-4} m/s. Given that the electrons move so slowly, you may wonder why the light comes on immediately when you turn on the switch of a flashlight. The reason is that the electric field is set up in the wire with a speed approaching the speed of light, and electrons start to move all along the wire at very nearly the same time. The time that it takes any individual electron to get from the switch to the light bulb isn't really relevant. A good analogy is a group of soldiers standing at attention when the sergeant orders them to start marching; the order reaches the soldiers' ears at the speed of sound, which is much faster than their marching speed, so all the soldiers start to march essentially in unison.

The Direction of Current Flow

The drift of moving charges through a conductor can be interpreted in terms of work and energy. The electric field $\vec{E}$ does work on the moving charges. The resulting kinetic energy is transferred to the material of the conductor by means of collisions with the ions, which vibrate about their equilibrium positions in the crystalline structure of the conductor. This energy transfer increases the average vibrational energy of the ions and therefore the temperature of the material. Thus much of the work done by the electric field goes into heating the conductor, *not* into making the moving charges move ever faster and faster. This heating is sometimes useful, as in an electric toaster, but in many situations is simply an unavoidable by-product of current flow.

In different current-carrying materials, the charges of the moving particles may be positive or negative. In metals the moving charges are always (negative) electrons, while in an ionized gas (plasma) or an ionic solution the moving charges may include both electrons and positively charged ions. In a semiconductor material such as germanium or silicon, conduction is partly by electrons and

11.2 The same current can be produced by (a) positive charges moving in the direction of the electric field $\vec{E}$ or (b) the same number of negative charges moving at the same speed in the direction opposite to $\vec{E}$.

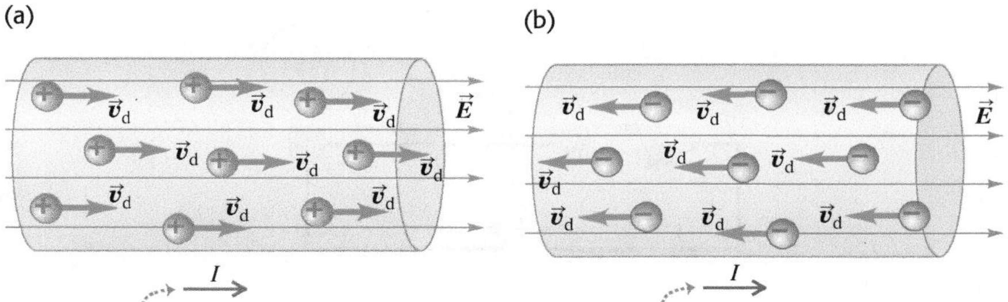

A **conventional current** is treated as a flow of positive charges, regardless of whether the free charges in the conductor are positive, negative, or both.

In a metallic conductor, the moving charges are electrons — but the *current* still points in the direction positive charges would flow.

partly by motion of *vacancies,* also known as *holes;* these are sites of missing electrons and act like positive charges.

Figure 11.2 shows segments of two different current-carrying materials. In Fig. 11.2a the moving charges are positive, the electric force is in the same direction as $\vec{E}$, and the drift velocity $\vec{v}_d$ is from left to right. In Fig. 11.2b the charges are negative, the electric force is opposite to $\vec{E}$, and the drift velocity $\vec{v}_d$ is from right to left. In both cases there is a net flow of positive charge from left to right, and positive charges end up to the right of negative ones. We *define* the current, denoted by I, to be in the direction in which there is a flow of *positive* charge. Thus we describe currents as though they consisted entirely of positive charge flow, even in cases in which we know that the actual current is due to electrons. Hence the current is to the right in both Figs. 11.2a and 11.2b. This choice or convention for the direction of current flow is called **conventional current.** While the direction of the conventional current is *not* necessarily the same as the direction in which charged particles are actually moving, we'll find that the sign of the moving charges is of little importance in analyzing electric circuits.

Figure 11.3 shows a segment of a conductor in which a current is flowing. We consider the moving charges to be *positive,* so they are moving in the same direction as the current. We define the current through the cross-sectional area A to be *the net charge flowing through the area per unit time.* Thus, if a net charge dQ flows through an area in a time dt, the current I through the area is

$$I = \frac{dQ}{dt} \quad \text{(definition of current)} \tag{11.1}$$

CAUTION **Current is not a vector** Although we refer to the *direction* of a current, current as defined by Eq. (11.1) is *not* a vector quantity. In a current-carrying wire, the current is always along the length of the wire, regardless of whether the wire is straight or curved. No single vector could describe motion along a curved path, which is why current is not a vector. We'll usually describe the direction of current either in words (as in "the current flows clockwise around the circuit") or by choosing a current to be positive if it flows in one direction along a conductor and negative if it flows in the other direction.

The SI unit of current is the **ampere;** one ampere is defined to be *one coulomb per second* (1 A = 1 C/s). This unit is named in honor of the French scientist André Marie Ampère (1775–1836). When an ordinary flashlight (D-cell size) is turned on, the current in the flashlight is about 0.5 to 1 A; the current in the wires of a car engine's starter motor is around 200 A. Currents in radio and television

11.3 The current I is the time rate of charge transfer through the cross-sectional area A. The random component of each moving charged particle's motion averages to zero, and the current is in the same direction as $\vec{E}$ whether the moving charges are positive (as shown here) or negative (see Fig. 11.2b).

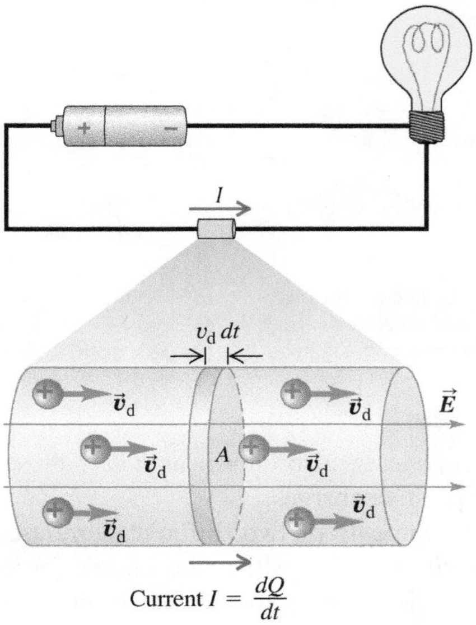

circuits are usually expressed in *milliamperes* ($1\ \text{mA} = 10^{-3}\ \text{A}$) or *microamperes* ($1\ \mu\text{A} = 10^{-6}\ \text{A}$), and currents in computer circuits are expressed in *nanoamperes* ($1\ \text{nA} = 10^{-9}\ \text{A}$) or *picoamperes* ($1\ \text{pA} = 10^{-12}\ \text{A}$).

Current, Drift Velocity, and Current Density

We can express current in terms of the drift velocity of the moving charges. Let's consider again the situation of Fig. 11.3 of a conductor with cross-sectional area A and an electric field $\vec{E}$ directed from left to right. To begin with, we'll assume that the free charges in the conductor are positive; then the drift velocity is in the same direction as the field.

Suppose there are n moving charged particles per unit volume. We call n the **concentration** of particles; its SI unit is m^{-3}. Assume that all the particles move with the same drift velocity with magnitude v_d. In a time interval dt, each particle moves a distance $v_d\, dt$. The particles that flow out of the right end of the shaded cylinder with length $v_d\, dt$ during dt are the particles that were within this cylinder at the beginning of the interval dt. The volume of the cylinder is $Av_d\, dt$, and the number of particles within it is $nAv_d\, dt$. If each particle has a charge q, the charge dQ that flows out of the end of the cylinder during time dt is

$$dQ = q(nAv_d\, dt) = nqv_d A\, dt$$

and the current is

$$I = \frac{dQ}{dt} = nqv_d A$$

The current *per unit cross-sectional area* is called the **current density** J:

$$J = \frac{I}{A} = nqv_d$$

The units of current density are amperes per square meter (A/m^2).

If the moving charges are negative rather than positive, as in Fig. 11.2b, the drift velocity is opposite to $\vec{E}$. But the *current* is still in the same direction as $\vec{E}$ at each point in the conductor. Hence the current I and current density J don't depend on the sign of the charge, and so in the above expressions for I and J we replace the charge q by its absolute value $|q|$:

$$I = \frac{dQ}{dt} = n|q|v_{\mathrm{d}}A \qquad \text{(general expression for current)} \qquad (11.2)$$

$$J = \frac{I}{A} = n|q|v_{\mathrm{d}} \qquad \text{(general expression for current density)} \qquad (11.3)$$

The current in a conductor is the product of the concentration of moving charged particles, the magnitude of charge of each such particle, the magnitude of the drift velocity, and the cross-sectional area of the conductor.

We can also define a *vector* current density $\vec{J}$ that includes the direction of the drift velocity:

$$\vec{J} = nq\vec{v}_{\mathrm{d}} \qquad \text{(vector current density)} \qquad (11.4)$$

There are *no* absolute value signs in Eq. (11.4). If q is positive, $\vec{v}_{\mathrm{d}}$ is in the same direction as $\vec{E}$; if q is negative, $\vec{v}_{\mathrm{d}}$ is opposite to $\vec{E}$. In either case, $\vec{J}$ is in the same direction as $\vec{E}$. Equation (11.3) gives the *magnitude* J of the vector current density $\vec{J}$.

CAUTION **Current density vs. current** Note that current density $\vec{J}$ is a vector, but current I is not. The difference is that the current density $\vec{J}$ describes how charges flow at a certain point, and the vector's direction tells you about the direction of the flow at that point. By contrast, the current I describes how charges flow through an extended object such as a wire. For example, I has the same value at all points in the circuit of Fig. 11.3, but $\vec{J}$ does not: The current density is directed downward in the left-hand side of the loop and upward in the right-hand side. The magnitude of $\vec{J}$ can also vary around a circuit. In Fig. 11.3 the current density magnitude $J = I/A$ is less in the battery (which has a large cross-sectional area A) than in the wires (which have a small cross-sectional area).

In general, a conductor may contain several different kinds of moving charged particles having charges $q_1, q_2, \ldots,$ concentrations $n_1, n_2, \ldots,$ and drift velocities with magnitudes $v_{\mathrm{d}1}, v_{\mathrm{d}2}, \ldots.$ An example is current flow in an ionic solution. In a sodium chloride solution, current can be carried by both positive sodium ions and negative chlorine ions; the total current I is found by adding up the currents due to each kind of charged particle, using Eq. (11.2). Likewise, the total vector current density $\vec{J}$ is found by using Eq. (11.4) for each kind of charged particle and adding the results.

We will see in Section 11.4 that it is possible to have a current that is *steady* (that is, one that is constant in time) only if the conducting material forms a closed loop, called a *complete circuit.* In such a steady situation, the total charge in every segment of the conductor is constant. Hence the rate of flow of charge *out* at one end of a segment at any instant equals the rate of flow of charge *in* at the other end of the segment, and *the current is the same at all cross sections of the circuit.* We'll make use of this observation when we analyze electric circuits later in this chapter.

In many simple circuits, such as flashlights or cordless electric drills, the direction of the current is always the same; this is called *direct current.* But home appliances such as toasters, refrigerators, and televisions use *alternating current,* in which the current continuously changes direction. In this chapter we'll consider direct current only.

11.2 Resistivity

The current density $\vec{J}$ in a conductor depends on the electric field $\vec{E}$ and on the properties of the material. In general, this dependence can be quite complex. But for some materials, especially metals, at a given temperature, $\vec{J}$ is nearly *directly proportional* to $\vec{E}$, and the ratio of the magnitudes of E and J is constant. This relationship, called Ohm's law, was discovered in 1826 by the German physicist Georg Simon Ohm (1787–1854). The word "law" should actually be in quotation marks, since **Ohm's law,** like the ideal-gas equation and Hooke's law, is an *idealized model* that describes the behavior of some materials quite well but is not a general description of *all* matter. In the following discussion we'll assume that Ohm's law is valid, even though there are many situations in which it is not. The situation is comparable to our representation of the behavior of the static and kinetic friction forces; we treated these friction forces as being directly proportional to the normal force, even though we knew that this was at best an approximate description.

We define the **resistivity** ρ of a material as the ratio of the magnitudes of electric field and current density:

$$\rho = \frac{E}{J} \qquad \text{(definition of resistivity)} \qquad (11.5)$$

The greater the resistivity, the greater the field needed to cause a given current density, or the smaller the current density caused by a given field. From Eq. (11.5) the units of ρ are $(\text{V/m})/(\text{A/m}^2) = \text{V}\cdot\text{m/A}$. As we will discuss in the next section, 1 V/A is called one *ohm* (1 Ω; we use the Greek letter Ω, or omega, which is alliterative with "ohm"). So the SI units for ρ are $\Omega \cdot \text{m}$ (ohm-meters). Table 11.1 lists some representative values of resistivity. A perfect conductor would have zero resistivity, and a perfect insulator would have an infinite resistivity. Metals and alloys have the smallest resistivities and are the best conductors. The resistivities of insulators are greater than those of the metals by an enormous factor, on the order of 10^{22}.

The reciprocal of resistivity is **conductivity.** Its units are $(\Omega \cdot \text{m})^{-1}$. Good conductors of electricity have larger conductivity than insulators. Conductivity is the direct electrical analog of thermal conductivity. We note that good electrical conductors, such as metals, are usually also good conductors of heat. Poor electrical conductors, such as ceramic and plastic materials, are also poor thermal conductors. In a metal the free electrons that carry charge in electrical conduction also provide the principal mechanism for heat conduction, so we should expect a correlation between electrical and thermal conductivity. Because of the enormous difference in conductivity between electrical conductors and insulators, it is easy to confine electric currents to well-defined paths or circuits. The variation in

Table 11.1 Resistivities at Room Temperature (20°C)

	Substance	ρ ($\Omega \cdot$m)	Substance	ρ ($\Omega \cdot$m)
Conductors			**Semiconductors**	
Metals	Silver	1.47×10^{-8}	Pure carbon (graphite)	3.5×10^{-5}
	Copper	1.72×10^{-8}	Pure germanium	0.60
	Gold	2.44×10^{-8}	Pure silicon	2300
	Aluminum	2.75×10^{-8}	**Insulators**	
	Tungsten	5.25×10^{-8}	Amber	5×10^{14}
	Steel	20×10^{-8}	Glass	10^{10}–10^{14}
	Lead	22×10^{-8}	Lucite	$>10^{13}$
	Mercury	95×10^{-8}	Mica	10^{11}–10^{15}
Alloys	Manganin (Cu 84%, Mn 12%, Ni 4%)	44×10^{-8}	Quartz (fused)	75×10^{16}
	Constantan (Cu 60%, Ni 40%)	49×10^{-8}	Sulfur	10^{15}
	Nichrome	100×10^{-8}	Teflon	$>10^{13}$
			Wood	10^{8}–10^{11}

thermal conductivity is much less, only a factor of 10^3 or so, and it is usually impossible to confine heat currents to that extent.

Semiconductors have resistivities intermediate between those of metals and those of insulators. These materials are important because of the way their resistivities are affected by temperature and by small amounts of impurities.

A material that obeys Ohm's law reasonably well is called an *ohmic* conductor or a *linear* conductor. For such materials, at a given temperature, ρ is a *constant* that does not depend on the value of E. Many materials show substantial departures from Ohm's-law behavior; they are *nonohmic,* or *nonlinear.* In these materials, J depends on E in a more complicated manner.

Analogies with fluid flow can be a big help in developing intuition about electric current and circuits. For example, in the making of wine or maple syrup, the product is sometimes filtered to remove sediments. A pump forces the fluid through the filter under pressure; if the flow rate (analogous to J) is proportional to the pressure difference between the upstream and downstream sides (analogous to E), the behavior is analogous to Ohm's law.

Resistivity and Temperature

The resistivity of a *metallic* conductor nearly always increases with increasing temperature, as shown in Fig. 11.4a. As temperature increases, the ions of the conductor vibrate with greater amplitude, making it more likely that a moving electron will collide with an ion as in Fig. 11.1; this impedes the drift of electrons through the conductor and hence reduces the current. Over a small temperature range (up to 100 C° or so), the resistivity of a metal can be represented approximately by the equation

$$\rho(T) = \rho_0[1 + \alpha(T - T_0)] \quad \text{(temperature dependence of resistivity)} \quad (11.6)$$

where ρ_0 is the resistivity at a reference temperature T_0 (often taken as 0°C or 20°C) and $\rho(T)$ is the resistivity at temperature T, which may be higher or lower than T_0. The factor α is called the **temperature coefficient of resistivity.** Some representative values are given in Table 11.2. The resistivity of the alloy manganin is practically independent of temperature.

Table 11.2 Temperature Coefficients of Resistivity (Approximate Values Near Room Temperature)

Material	α [(°C)$^{-1}$]	Material	α [(°C)$^{-1}$]
Aluminum	0.0039	Lead	0.0043
Brass	0.0020	Manganin	0.00000
Carbon (graphite)	−0.0005	Mercury	0.00088
Constantan	0.00001	Nichrome	0.0004
Copper	0.00393	Silver	0.0038
Iron	0.0050	Tungsten	0.0045

The resistivity of graphite (a nonmetal) *decreases* with increasing temperature, since at higher temperatures, more electrons are "shaken loose" from the atoms and become mobile; hence the temperature coefficient of resistivity of graphite is negative. This same behavior occurs for semiconductors (Fig. 11.4b). Measuring the resistivity of a small semiconductor crystal is therefore a sensitive measure of temperature; this is the principle of a type of thermometer called a *thermistor.*

Some materials, including several metallic alloys and oxides, show a phenomenon called *superconductivity.* As the temperature decreases, the resistivity at first decreases smoothly, like that of any metal. But then at a certain critical temperature T_c a phase transition occurs and the resistivity suddenly drops to zero, as shown in Fig. 11.4c. Once a current has been established in a superconducting ring, it continues indefinitely without the presence of any driving field.

11.4 Variation of resistivity ρ with absolute temperature T for (a) a normal metal, (b) a semiconductor, and (c) a superconductor. In (a) the linear approximation to ρ as a function of T is shown as a green line; the approximation agrees exactly at $T = T_0$, where $\rho = \rho_0$.

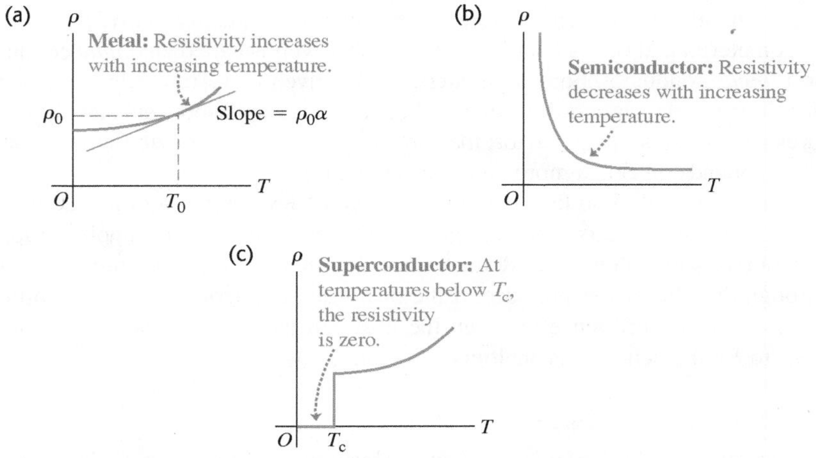

Superconductivity was discovered in 1911 by the Dutch physicist Heike Kamerlingh Onnes (1853–1926). He discovered that at very low temperatures, below 4.2 K, the resistivity of mercury suddenly dropped to zero. For the next 75 years, the highest T_c attained was about 20 K. This meant that superconductivity occurred only when the material was cooled using expensive liquid helium, with a boiling-point temperature of 4.2 K, or explosive liquid hydrogen, with a boiling point of 20.3 K. But in 1986 Karl Müller and Johannes Bednorz discovered an oxide of barium, lanthanum, and copper with a T_c of nearly 40 K, and the race was on to develop "high-temperature" superconducting materials.

By 1987 a complex oxide of yttrium, copper, and barium had been found that has a value of T_c well above the 77 K boiling temperature of liquid nitrogen, a refrigerant that is both inexpensive and safe. The current (2010) record for T_c at atmospheric pressure is 138 K, and materials that are superconductors at room temperature may become a reality. The implications of these discoveries for power-distribution systems, computer design, and transportation are enormous. Meanwhile, superconducting electromagnets cooled by liquid helium are used in particle accelerators and some experimental magnetic-levitation railroads. Superconductors have other exotic properties that require an understanding of magnetism to explore.

11.3 Resistance

For a conductor with resistivity ρ, the current density $\vec{J}$ at a point where the electric field is $\vec{E}$ is given by Eq. (11.5), which we can write as

$$\vec{E} = \rho\vec{J} \tag{11.7}$$

When Ohm's law is obeyed, ρ is constant and independent of the magnitude of the electric field, so $\vec{E}$ is directly proportional to $\vec{J}$. Often, however, we are more interested in the total current in a conductor than in $\vec{J}$ and more interested in the potential difference between the ends of the conductor than in $\vec{E}$. This is so largely because current and potential difference are much easier to measure than are $\vec{J}$ and $\vec{E}$.

Suppose our conductor is a wire with uniform cross-sectional area A and length L, as shown in Fig. 11.5. Let V be the potential difference between the higher-potential and lower-potential ends of the conductor, so that V is positive. The *direction* of the current is always from the higher-potential end to the lower-

11.5 A conductor with uniform cross section. The current density is uniform over any cross section, and the electric field is constant along the length.

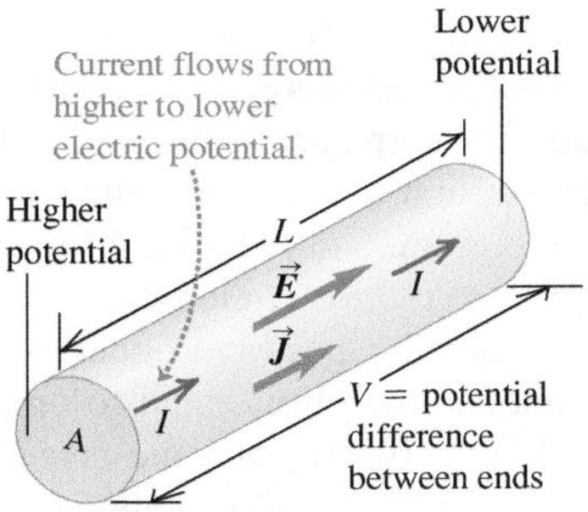
Lower
potential
Current flows from
higher to lower
electric potential.
Higher
potential
L
E
I
J
I
A
V = potential
difference
between ends

potential end. That's because current in a conductor flows in the direction of $\vec{E}$, no matter what the sign of the moving charges (Fig. 11.2), and because $\vec{E}$ points in the direction of *decreasing* electric potential (see Section 10.5). As the current flows through the potential difference, electric potential energy is lost; this energy is transferred to the ions of the conducting material during collisions.

We can also relate the *value* of the current I to the potential difference between the ends of the conductor. If the magnitudes of the current density $\vec{J}$ and the electric field $\vec{E}$ are uniform throughout the conductor, the total current I is given by $I = JA$, and the potential difference V between the ends is $V = EL$. When we solve these equations for J and E, respectively, and substitute the results in Eq. (11.7), we obtain

$$\frac{V}{L} = \frac{\rho I}{A} \quad \text{or} \quad V = \frac{\rho L}{A} I \tag{11.8}$$

This shows that when ρ is constant, the total current I is proportional to the potential difference V.

The ratio of V to I for a particular conductor is called its **resistance** R:

$$R = \frac{V}{I} \tag{11.9}$$

Comparing this definition of R to Eq. (11.8), we see that the resistance R of a particular conductor is related to the resistivity ρ of its material by

$$R = \frac{\rho L}{A} \quad \text{(relationship between resistance and resistivity)} \tag{11.10}$$

If ρ is constant, as is the case for ohmic materials, then so is R.

The equation

$$V = IR \quad \text{(relationship among voltage, current, and resistance)} \tag{11.11}$$

is often called Ohm's law, but it is important to understand that the real content of Ohm's law is the direct proportionality (for some materials) of V to I or of J to E. Equation (11.9) or (11.11) *defines* resistance R for *any* conductor, whether or not it obeys Ohm's law, but only when R is constant can we correctly call this relationship Ohm's law.

Interpreting Resistance

Equation (11.10) shows that the resistance of a wire or other conductor of uniform cross section is directly proportional to its length and inversely proportional to its cross-sectional area. It is also proportional to the resistivity of the material of which the conductor is made.

The flowing-fluid analogy is again useful. In analogy to Eq. (11.10), a narrow water hose offers more resistance to flow than a fat one, and a long hose has more resistance than a short one. We can increase the resistance to flow by stuffing the hose with cotton or sand; this corresponds to increasing the resistivity. The flow rate is approximately proportional to the pressure difference between the ends. Flow rate is analogous to current, and pressure difference is analogous to potential difference ("voltage"). Let's not stretch this analogy too far, though; the water flow rate in a pipe is usually *not* proportional to its cross-sectional area.

The SI unit of resistance is the **ohm,** equal to one volt per ampere ($1\ \Omega = 1\ \mathrm{V/A}$). The *kilohm* ($1\ \mathrm{k}\Omega = 10^3\ \Omega$) and the *megohm* ($1\ \mathrm{M}\Omega = 10^6\ \Omega$) are also in common use. A 100-m length of 12-gauge copper wire, the size usually used in household wiring, has a resistance at room temperature of about $0.5\ \Omega$. A 100-W, 120-V light bulb has a resistance (at operating temperature) of $140\ \Omega$. If the same current I flows in both the copper wire and the light bulb, the potential difference $V = IR$ is much greater across the light bulb, and much more potential energy is lost per charge in the light bulb. This lost energy is converted by the light bulb filament into light and heat. You don't want your household wiring to glow white-hot, so its resistance is kept low by using wire of low resistivity and large cross-sectional area.

Because the resistivity of a material varies with temperature, the resistance of a specific conductor also varies with temperature. For temperature ranges that are not too great, this variation is approximately a linear relationship, analogous to Eq. (11.6):

$$R(T) = R_0[1 + \alpha(T - T_0)] \tag{11.12}$$

In this equation, $R(T)$ is the resistance at temperature T and R_0 is the resistance at temperature T_0, often taken to be 0°C or 20°C. The *temperature coefficient of resistance* α is the same constant that appears in Eq. (11.6) if the dimensions L and A in Eq. (11.10) do not change appreciably with temperature; this is indeed the case for most conducting materials. Within the limits of validity of Eq. (11.12), the *change* in resistance resulting from a temperature change $T - T_0$ is given by $R_0\alpha(T - T_0)$.

A circuit device made to have a specific value of resistance between its ends is called a **resistor.** Resistors in the range 0.01 to $10^7\ \Omega$ can be bought off the shelf. Individual resistors used in electronic circuitry are often cylindrical, a few millimeters in diameter and length, with wires coming out of the ends. The resistance may be marked with a standard code using three or four color bands near one end (Fig. 11.6), according to the scheme shown in Table 11.3. The first two bands (starting with the band nearest an end) are digits, and the third is a power-of-10 multiplier, as shown in Fig. 11.6. For example, green–violet–red means $57 \times 10^2\ \Omega$, or $5.7\ \mathrm{k}\Omega$. The fourth band, if present, indicates the precision (tolerance) of the value; no band means ±20%, a silver band ±10%, and a gold band ±5%. Another important characteristic of a resistor is the maximum *power* it can dissipate without damage.

11.6 This resistor has a resistance of $5.7\ \mathrm{k}\Omega$ with a precision (tolerance) of ±10%.

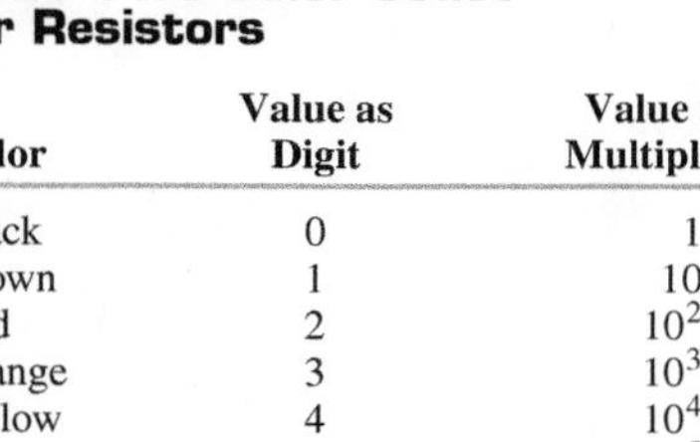
Second digit
Multiplier
Tolerance
First digit

Table 11.3 Color Codes for Resistors

Color	Value as Digit	Value as Multiplier
Black	0	1
Brown	1	10
Red	2	10^2
Orange	3	10^3
Yellow	4	10^4
Green	5	10^5
Blue	6	10^6
Violet	7	10^7
Gray	8	10^8
White	9	10^9

For a resistor that obeys Ohm's law, a graph of current as a function of potential difference (voltage) is a straight line (Fig. 11.7a). The slope of the line is $1/R$. If the sign of the potential difference changes, so does the sign of the current produced; in Fig. 11.5 this corresponds to interchanging the higher- and lower-potential ends of the conductor, so the electric field, current density, and current all reverse direction. In devices that do not obey Ohm's law, the relationship of voltage to current may not be a direct proportion, and it may be different for the two directions of current. Figure 11.7b shows the behavior of a semiconductor *diode*, a device used to convert alternating current to direct current and to perform a wide variety of logic functions in computer circuitry. For

11.7 Current–voltage relationships for two devices. Only for a resistor that obeys Ohm's law as in (a) is current I proportional to voltage V.

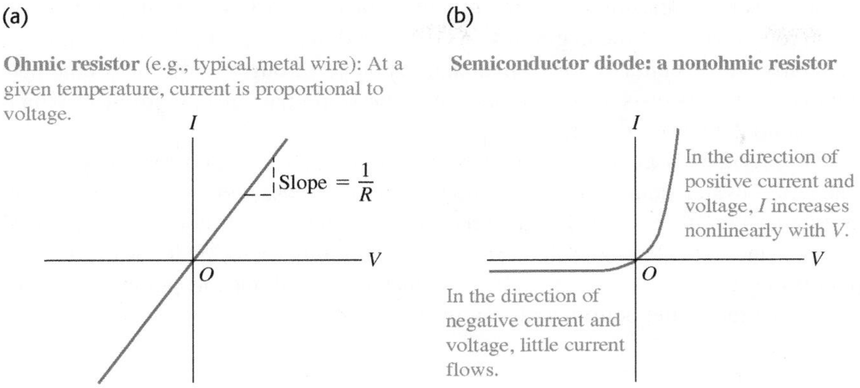
(a)
Ohmic resistor (e.g., typical metal wire): At a given temperature, current is proportional to voltage.
I
Slope = 1/R
V
O
(b)
Semiconductor diode: a nonohmic resistor
I
In the direction of positive current and voltage, I increases nonlinearly with V.
V
O
In the direction of negative current and voltage, little current flows.

positive potentials V of the anode (one of two terminals of the diode) with respect to the cathode (the other terminal), I increases exponentially with increasing V; for negative potentials the current is extremely small. Thus a positive V causes a current to flow in the positive direction, but a potential difference of the other sign causes little or no current. Hence a diode acts like a one-way valve in a circuit.

11.4 Electromotive Force and Circuits

For a conductor to have a steady current, it must be part of a path that forms a closed loop or **complete circuit.** Here's why. If you establish an electric field $\vec{E}_1$ inside an isolated conductor with resistivity ρ that is *not* part of a complete circuit, a current begins to flow with current density $\vec{J} = \vec{E}_1/\rho$ (Fig. 11.8a). As a result a net positive charge quickly accumulates at one end of the conductor and a net negative charge accumulates at the other end (Fig. 11.8b). These charges themselves produce an electric field $\vec{E}_2$ in the direction opposite to $\vec{E}_1$, causing the total electric field and hence the current to decrease. Within a very small fraction of a second, enough charge builds up on the conductor ends that the total electric field $\vec{E} = \vec{E}_1 + \vec{E}_2 = \mathbf{0}$ inside the conductor. Then $\vec{J} = \mathbf{0}$ as well, and the current stops altogether (Fig. 11.8c). So there can be no steady motion of charge in such an *incomplete* circuit.

11.8 If an electric field is produced inside a conductor that is *not* part of a complete circuit, current flows for only a very short time.

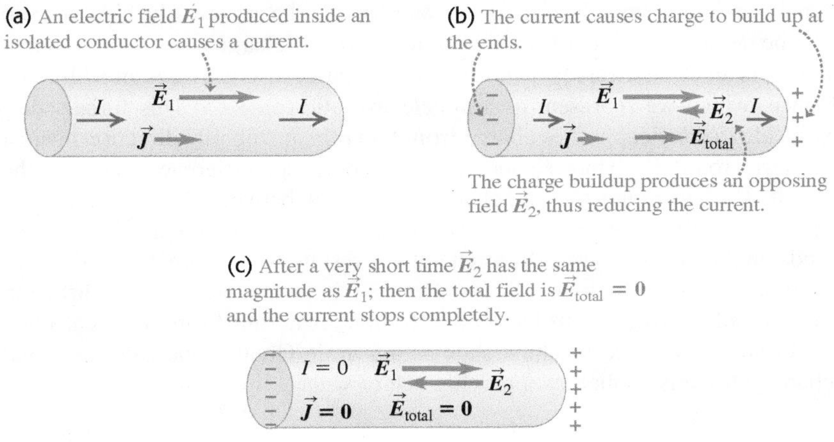
(a) An electric field E1 produced inside an isolated conductor causes a current.
E1
I
I
J
(b) The current causes charge to build up at the ends.
E1
I
E2
I
J
Etotal
The charge buildup produces an opposing field E2, thus reducing the current.
(c) After a very short time E2 has the same magnitude as E1; then the total field is Etotal = 0 and the current stops completely.
I = 0
E1
E2
J = 0
Etotal = 0

To see how to maintain a steady current in a *complete* circuit, we recall a basic fact about electric potential energy: If a charge q goes around a complete circuit and returns to its starting point, the potential energy must be the same at the end of the round trip as at the beginning. As described in Section 11.3, there is always a *decrease* in potential energy when charges move through an ordinary conducting material with resistance. So there must be some part of the circuit in which the potential energy *increases.*

The problem is analogous to an ornamental water fountain that recycles its water. The water pours out of openings at the top, cascades down over the terraces and spouts (moving in the direction of decreasing gravitational potential energy), and collects in a basin in the bottom. A pump then lifts it back to the top (increasing the potential energy) for another trip. Without the pump, the water would just fall to the bottom and stay there.

Electromotive Force

In an electric circuit there must be a device somewhere in the loop that acts like the water pump in a water fountain. In this device a charge travels "uphill," from lower to higher potential energy, even though the electrostatic force is trying to push it from higher to lower potential energy. The direction of current in such a device is from lower to higher potential, just the opposite of what happens in an ordinary conductor. The influence that makes current flow from lower to higher potential is called **electromotive force** (abbreviated **emf** and pronounced "ee-em-eff"). This is a poor term because emf is *not* a force but an energy-per-unit-charge quantity, like potential. The SI unit of emf is the same as that for potential, the volt $(1\ \text{V} = 1\ \text{J/C})$. A typical flashlight battery has an emf of 1.5 V; this means that the battery does 1.5 J of work on every coulomb of charge that passes through it. We'll use the symbol $\mathcal{E}$ (a script capital E) for emf.

Every complete circuit with a steady current must include some device that provides emf. Such a device is called a **source of emf.** Batteries, electric generators, solar cells, thermocouples, and fuel cells are all examples of sources of emf. All such devices convert energy of some form (mechanical, chemical, thermal, and so on) into electric potential energy and transfer it into the circuit to which the device is connected. An *ideal* source of emf maintains a constant potential difference between its terminals, independent of the current through it. We define electromotive force quantitatively as the magnitude of this potential difference. As we will see, such an ideal source is a mythical beast, like the frictionless plane and the massless rope. We will discuss later how real-life sources of emf differ in their behavior from this idealized model.

Figure 11.9 is a schematic diagram of an ideal source of emf that maintains a potential difference between conductors a and b, called the *terminals* of the device. Terminal a, marked +, is maintained at *higher* potential than terminal b, marked −. Associated with this potential difference is an electric field $\vec{E}$ in the region around the terminals, both inside and outside the source. The electric field inside the device is directed from a to b, as shown. A charge q within the source experiences an electric force $\vec{F}_e = q\vec{E}$. But the source also provides an additional influence, which we represent as a nonelectrostatic force $\vec{F}_n$. This force, operating inside the device, pushes charge from b to a in an "uphill" direction against the electric force $\vec{F}_e$. Thus $\vec{F}_n$ maintains the potential difference between the terminals. If $\vec{F}_n$ were not present, charge would flow between the terminals until the potential difference was zero. The origin of the additional influence $\vec{F}_n$ depends on the kind of source. In a generator it results from magnetic-field forces on moving charges. In a battery or fuel cell it is associated with diffusion processes and varying electrolyte concentrations resulting from chemical reactions. In an electrostatic machine such as a Van de Graaff generator, an actual mechanical force is applied by a moving belt or wheel.

11.9 Schematic diagram of a source of emf in an "open-circuit" situation. The electric-field force $\vec{F}_e = q\vec{E}$ and the nonelectrostatic force $\vec{F}_n$ are shown for a positive charge q.

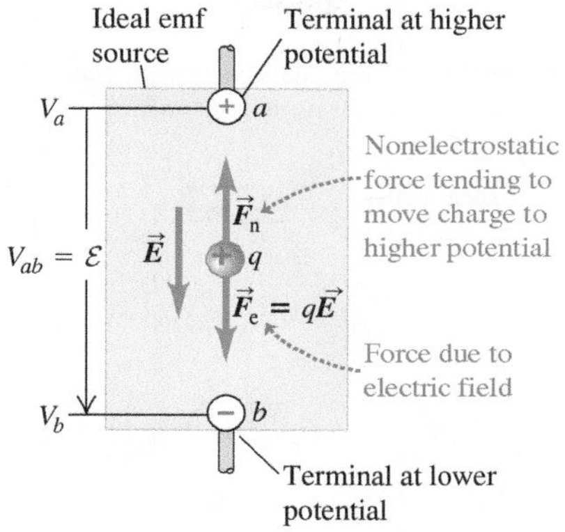
Ideal emf source
Terminal at higher potential
V_a
a
Nonelectrostatic force tending to move charge to higher potential
$\vec{F}_n$
$V_{ab} = \mathcal{E}$
$\vec{E}$
q
$\vec{F}_e = q\vec{E}$
Force due to electric field
V_b
b
Terminal at lower potential

When the emf source is not part of a closed circuit, $F_n = F_e$ and there is no net motion of charge between the terminals.

If a positive charge q is moved from b to a inside the source, the nonelectrostatic force $\vec{F}_n$ does a positive amount of work $W_n = q\mathcal{E}$ on the charge. This displacement is *opposite* to the electrostatic force $\vec{F}_e$, so the potential energy associated with the charge *increases* by an amount equal to qV_{ab}, where $V_{ab} = V_a - V_b$ is the (positive) potential of point a with respect to point b. For the ideal source of emf that we've described, $\vec{F}_e$ and $\vec{F}_n$ are equal in magnitude but opposite in direction, so the total work done on the charge q is zero; there is an increase in potential energy but *no* change in the kinetic energy of the charge. It's like lifting a book from the floor to a high shelf at constant speed. The increase in potential energy is just equal to the nonelectrostatic work W_n, so $q\mathcal{E} = qV_{ab}$, or

$$V_{ab} = \mathcal{E} \qquad \text{(ideal source of emf)} \tag{11.13}$$

Now let's make a complete circuit by connecting a wire with resistance R to the terminals of a source (Fig. 11.10). The potential difference between terminals a and b sets up an electric field within the wire; this causes current to flow around the loop from a toward b, from higher to lower potential. Where the wire bends, equal amounts of positive and negative charge persist on the "inside" and "outside" of the bend. These charges exert the forces that cause the current to follow the bends in the wire.

From Eq. (11.11) the potential difference between the ends of the wire in Fig. 11.10 is given by $V_{ab} = IR$. Combining with Eq. (11.13), we have

$$\mathcal{E} = V_{ab} = IR \qquad \text{(ideal source of emf)} \tag{11.14}$$

That is, when a positive charge q flows around the circuit, the potential *rise* $\mathcal{E}$ as it passes through the ideal source is numerically equal to the potential *drop* $V_{ab} = IR$ as it passes through the remainder of the circuit. Once $\mathcal{E}$ and R are known, this relationship determines the current in the circuit.

CAUTION **Current is not "used up" in a circuit** It's a common misconception that in a closed circuit, current is something that squirts out of the positive terminal of a battery and is consumed or "used up" by the time it reaches the negative terminal. In fact the current is the *same* at every point in a simple loop circuit like that in Fig. 11.10, even if the thickness of the wires is different at different points in the circuit. This happens because charge is conserved (that is, it can be neither created nor destroyed) and because charge cannot accumulate in the circuit devices we have described. If charge did accumu-

11.10 Schematic diagram of an ideal source of emf in a complete circuit. The electric-field force $\vec{F}_e = q\vec{E}$ and the non-electrostatic force $\vec{F}_n$ are shown for a positive charge q. The current is in the direction from a to b in the external circuit and from b to a within the source.

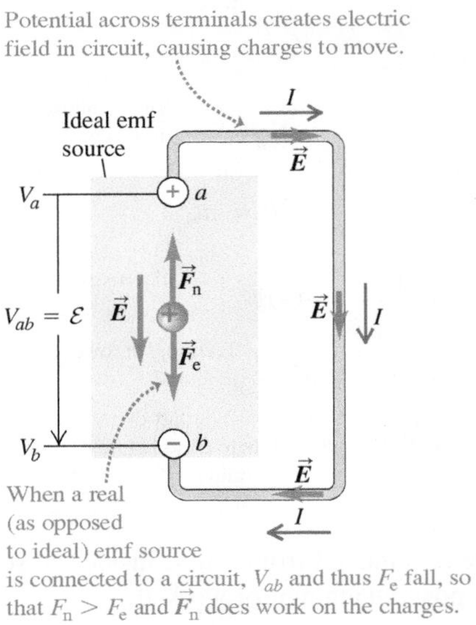
Potential across terminals creates electric field in circuit, causing charges to move.
Ideal emf source
V_a
a
I
$\vec{E}$
$\vec{F}_n$
$V_{ab} = \mathcal{E}$
$\vec{E}$
$\vec{F}_e$
I
V_b
b
When a real (as opposed to ideal) emf source is connected to a circuit, V_{ab} and thus F_e fall, so that $F_n > F_e$ and $\vec{F}_n$ does work on the charges.

late, the potential differences would change with time. It's like the flow of water in an ornamental fountain; water flows out of the top of the fountain at the same rate at which it reaches the bottom, no matter what the dimensions of the fountain. None of the water is "used up" along the way!

Internal Resistance

Real sources of emf in a circuit don't behave in exactly the way we have described; the potential difference across a real source in a circuit is *not* equal to the emf as in Eq. (11.14). The reason is that charge moving through the material of any real source encounters *resistance.* We call this the **internal resistance** of the source, denoted by r. If this resistance behaves according to Ohm's law, r is constant and independent of the current I. As the current moves through r, it experiences an associated drop in potential equal to Ir. Thus, when a current is flowing through a source from the negative terminal b to the positive terminal a, the potential difference V_{ab} between the terminals is

$$V_{ab} = \mathcal{E} - Ir \quad \text{(terminal voltage, source with internal resistance)} \tag{11.15}$$

The potential V_{ab}, called the **terminal voltage,** is less than the emf $\mathcal{E}$ because of the term Ir representing the potential drop across the internal resistance r. Expressed another way, the increase in potential energy qV_{ab} as a charge q moves from b to a within the source is now less than the work $q\mathcal{E}$ done by the nonelectrostatic force $\vec{F}_n$, since some potential energy is lost in traversing the internal resistance.

A 1.5-V battery has an emf of 1.5 V, but the terminal voltage V_{ab} of the battery is equal to 1.5 V only if no current is flowing through it so that $I = 0$ in Eq. (11.15). If the battery is part of a complete circuit through which current is flowing, the terminal voltage will be less than 1.5 V. *For a real source of emf, the terminal voltage equals the emf only if no current is flowing through the source.*

Thus we can describe the behavior of a source in terms of two properties: an emf $\mathcal{E}$, which supplies a constant potential difference independent of current, in series with an internal resistance r.

The current in the external circuit connected to the source terminals a and b is still determined by $V_{ab} = IR$. Combining this with Eq. (11.15), we find

$$\mathcal{E} - Ir = IR \quad \text{or} \quad I = \frac{\mathcal{E}}{R + r} \quad \text{(current, source with internal resistance)} \tag{11.16}$$

That is, the current equals the source emf divided by the *total* circuit resistance $(R + r)$.

CAUTION **A battery is not a "current source"** You might have thought that a battery or other source of emf always produces the same current, no matter what circuit it's used in. Equation (11.16) shows that this isn't so! The greater the resistance R of the external circuit, the less current the source will produce. It's analogous to pushing an object through a thick, viscous liquid such as oil or molasses; if you exert a certain steady push (emf), you can move a small object at high speed (small R, large I) or a large object at low speed (large R, small I).

Symbols for Circuit Diagrams

An important part of analyzing any electric circuit is drawing a schematic *circuit diagram.* Table 11.4 shows the usual symbols used in circuit diagrams. We will use these symbols extensively in this chapter and the next. We usually assume that the wires that connect the various elements of the circuit have negligible resistance; from Eq. (11.11), $V = IR$, the potential difference between the ends of such a wire is zero.

Table 11.4 includes two *meters* that are used to measure the properties of circuits. Idealized meters do not disturb the circuit in which they are connected. A **voltmeter**, introduced in Section 10.6, measures the potential difference between its terminals; an idealized voltmeter has infinitely large resistance and measures potential difference without having any current diverted through it. An ammeter measures the current passing through it; an idealized **ammeter** has zero resistance and has no potential difference between its terminals. Because meters act as part of the circuit in which they are connected, these properties are important to remember.

Table 11.4 Symbols for Circuit Diagrams

	Conductor with negligible resistance
	Resistor
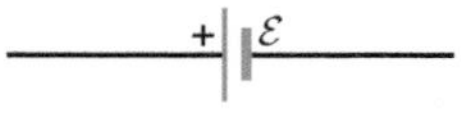	Source of emf (longer vertical line always represents the positive terminal, usually the terminal with higher potential)
 or 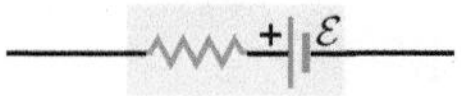	Source of emf with internal resistance r (r can be placed on either side)
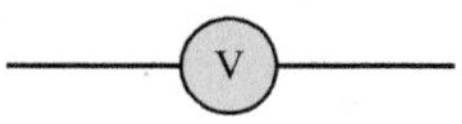	Voltmeter (measures potential difference between its terminals)
	Ammeter (measures current through it)

Potential Changes Around a Circuit

The net change in potential energy for a charge q making a round trip around a complete circuit must be zero. Hence the net change in *potential* around the circuit must also be zero; in other words, the algebraic sum of the potential differences and emfs around the loop is zero. We can see this by rewriting Eq. (11.16) in the form

$$\mathcal{E} - Ir - IR = 0$$

A potential gain of $\mathcal{E}$ is associated with the emf, and potential drops of Ir and IR are associated with the internal resistance of the source and the external circuit, respectively. Figure 11.11 is a graph showing how the potential varies. The horizontal axis doesn't necessarily represent actual distances, but rather various points in the loop. If we take the potential to be zero at the negative terminal of the battery, then we have a rise $\mathcal{E}$ and a drop Ir in the battery and an additional drop IR in the external resistor, and as we finish our trip around the loop, the potential is back where it started.

In this section we have considered only situations in which the resistances are ohmic. If the circuit includes a nonlinear device such as a diode (see Fig. 11.7b), Eq. (11.16) is still valid but cannot be solved algebraically because R is not a .constant. In such a situation, the current I can be found by using numerical techniques.

Finally, we remark that Eq. (11.15) is not always an adequate representation of the behavior of a source. The emf may not be constant, and what we have described as an internal resistance may actually be a more complex voltage–current relationship that doesn't obey Ohm's law. Nevertheless, the concept of internal resistance frequently provides an adequate description of batteries, generators, and other energy converters. The principal difference between a fresh flashlight battery and an old one is not in the emf, which decreases only slightly with use, but in the internal resistance, which may increase from less than an ohm when the battery is fresh to as much as 1000 Ω or more after long use. Similarly, a car battery can deliver less current to the starter motor on a cold morning than when the battery is warm, not because the emf is appreciably less but because the internal resistance increases with decreasing temperature.

11.11 Potential rises and drops in a circuit.

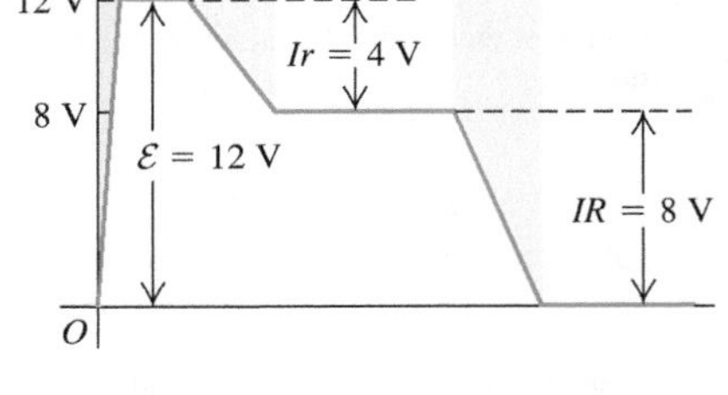

11.5 Energy and Power in Electric Circuits

Let's now look at some energy and power relationships in electric circuits. The box in Fig. 11.12 represents a circuit element with potential difference $V_a - V_b = V_{ab}$ between its terminals and current I passing through it in the direction from a toward b. This element might be a resistor, a battery, or something else; the details don't matter. As charge passes through the circuit element, the electric field does work on the charge. In a source of emf, additional work is done by the force $\vec{F}_n$ that we mentioned in Section 11.4.

As an amount of charge q passes through the circuit element, there is a change in potential energy equal to qV_{ab}. For example, if $q > 0$ and $V_{ab} = V_a - V_b$ is positive, potential energy decreases as the charge "falls" from potential V_a to lower potential V_b. The moving charges don't gain *kinetic* energy, because the current (the rate of charge flow) out of the circuit element must be the same as the current into the element. Instead, the quantity qV_{ab} represents energy transferred into the circuit element. This situation occurs in the coils of a toaster or electric oven, in which electrical energy is converted to thermal energy.

If the potential at a is lower than at b, then V_{ab} is negative and there is a net transfer of energy *out* of the circuit element. The element then acts as a source, delivering electrical energy into the circuit to which it is attached. This is the usual situation for a battery, which converts chemical energy into electrical energy and delivers it to the external circuit. Thus qV_{ab} can denote either a quantity of energy delivered to a circuit element or a quantity of energy extracted from that element.

In electric circuits we are most often interested in the *rate* at which energy is either delivered to or extracted from a circuit element. If the current through the element is I, then in a time interval dt an amount of charge $dQ = I\,dt$ passes through the element. The potential energy change for this amount of charge is $V_{ab}\,dQ = V_{ab}I\,dt$. Dividing this expression by dt, we obtain the *rate* at which energy is transferred either into or out of the circuit element. The time rate of energy transfer is *power*, denoted by P, so we write

$$P = V_{ab}I \quad \text{(rate at which energy is delivered to or extracted from a circuit element)} \tag{11.17}$$

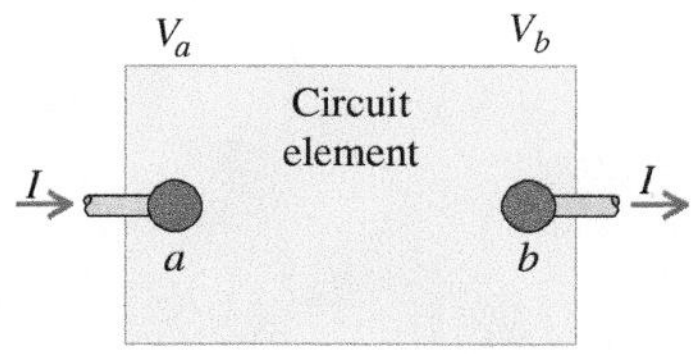

11.12 The power input to the circuit element between a and b is $P = (V_a - V_b)I = V_{ab}I$.

The unit of V_{ab} is one volt, or one joule per coulomb, and the unit of I is one ampere, or one coulomb per second. Hence the unit of $P = V_{ab}I$ is one watt, as it should be:

$$(1\ \text{J/C})(1\ \text{C/s}) = 1\ \text{J/s} = 1\ \text{W}$$

Let's consider a few special cases.

Power Input to a Pure Resistance

If the circuit element in Fig. 11.12 is a resistor, the potential difference is $V_{ab} = IR$. From Eq. (11.17) the electrical power delivered to the resistor by the circuit is

$$P = V_{ab}I = I^2R = \frac{V_{ab}{}^2}{R} \quad \text{(power delivered to a resistor)} \tag{11.18}$$

In this case the potential at a (where the current enters the resistor) is always higher than that at b (where the current exits). Current enters the higher-potential terminal of the device, and Eq. (11.18) represents the rate of transfer of electric potential energy *into* the circuit element.

What becomes of this energy? The moving charges collide with atoms in the resistor and transfer some of their energy to these atoms, increasing the internal energy of the material. Either the temperature of the resistor increases or there is a flow of heat out of it, or both. In any of these cases we say that energy is *dissipated* in the resistor at a rate I^2R. Every resistor has a *power rating,* the maximum power the device can dissipate without becoming overheated and damaged. Some devices, such as electric heaters, are designed to get hot and transfer heat to their surroundings. But if the power rating is exceeded, even such a device may melt or even explode.

Power Output of a Source

The upper rectangle in Fig. 11.13a represents a source with emf $\mathcal{E}$ and internal resistance r, connected by ideal (resistanceless) conductors to an external circuit represented by the lower box. This could describe a car battery connected to one of the car's headlights (Fig. 11.13b). Point a is at higher potential than point b, so $V_a > V_b$ and V_{ab} is positive. Note that the current I is *leaving* the source at the higher-potential terminal (rather than entering there). Energy is being delivered to the external circuit, at a rate given by Eq. (11.17):

$$P = V_{ab}I$$

For a source that can be described by an emf $\mathcal{E}$ and an internal resistance r, we may use Eq. (11.15):

$$V_{ab} = \mathcal{E} - Ir$$

Multiplying this equation by I, we find

$$P = V_{ab}I = \mathcal{E}I - I^2r \qquad (11.19)$$

What do the terms $\mathcal{E}I$ and I^2r mean? In Section 11.4 we defined the emf $\mathcal{E}$ as the work per unit charge performed on the charges by the nonelectrostatic force as the charges are pushed "uphill" from b to a in the source. In a time dt, a charge $dQ = I\,dt$ flows through the source; the work done on it by this nonelectrostatic force is $\mathcal{E}\,dQ = \mathcal{E}I\,dt$. Thus $\mathcal{E}I$ is the *rate* at which work is done on the circulating charges by whatever agency causes the nonelectrostatic force in the source. This term represents the rate of conversion of nonelectrical energy to electrical energy within the source. The term I^2r is the rate at which electrical energy is *dissipated* in the internal resistance of the source. The difference $\mathcal{E}I - I^2r$ is the *net* electrical power output of the source—that is, the rate at which the source delivers electrical energy to the remainder of the circuit.

11.13 Energy conversion in a simple circuit.

(a) Diagrammatic circuit

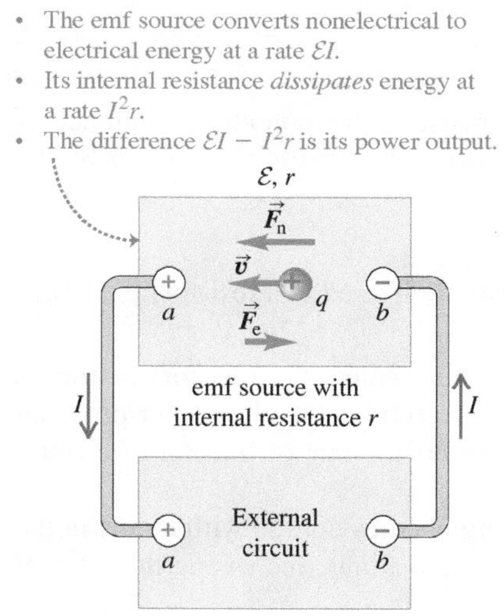
• The emf source converts nonelectrical to electrical energy at a rate $\mathcal{E}I$.
• Its internal resistance *dissipates* energy at a rate I^2r.
• The difference $\mathcal{E}I - I^2r$ is its power output.
$\mathcal{E}$, r
$\vec{F}_n$
$\vec{v}$
q
$\vec{F}_e$
+
−
a
b
emf source with internal resistance r
I
I
External circuit
+
−
a
b

(b) A real circuit of the type shown in (a)

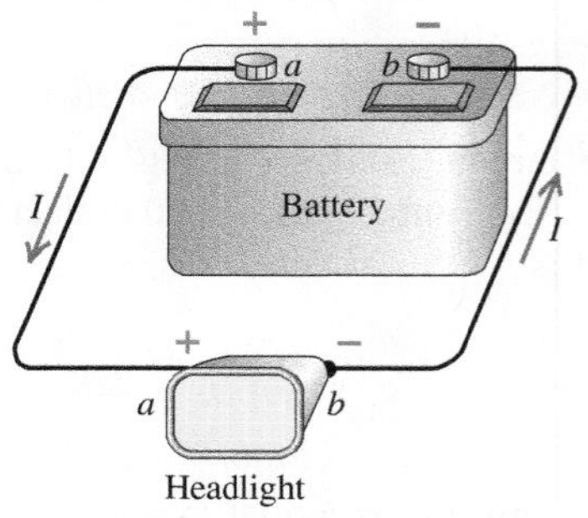
+
−
a
b
Battery
I
I
+
−
a
b
Headlight

Power Input to a Source

Suppose that the lower rectangle in Fig. 11.13a is itself a source, with an emf *larger* than that of the upper source and with its emf opposite to that of the upper source. The current I in the circuit is then *opposite* to that shown in Fig. 11.13; the lower source is pushing current backward through the upper source. Because of this reversal of current, instead of Eq. (11.15) we have for the upper source

$$V_{ab} = \mathcal{E} + Ir$$

and instead of Eq. (11.19), we have

$$P = V_{ab}I = \mathcal{E}I + I^2r \tag{11.20}$$

Work is being done *on,* rather than *by,* the agent that causes the nonelectrostatic force in the upper source. There is a conversion of electrical energy into nonelectrical energy in the upper source at a rate $\mathcal{E}I$. The term I^2r in Eq. (11.20) is again the rate of dissipation of energy in the internal resistance of the upper source, and the sum $\mathcal{E}I + I^2r$ is the total electrical power *input* to the upper source. This is what happens when a rechargeable battery (a storage battery) is connected to a charger. The charger supplies electrical energy to the battery; part of it is converted to chemical energy, to be reconverted later, and the remainder is dissipated (wasted) in the battery's internal resistance, warming the battery and causing a heat flow out of it. If you have a power tool or laptop computer with a rechargeable battery, you may have noticed that it gets warm while it is charging.

11.6 Resistors in Series and Parallel

Resistors turn up in all kinds of circuits, ranging from hair dryers and space heaters to circuits that limit or divide current or reduce or divide a voltage. Such circuits often contain several resistors, so it's appropriate to consider *combinations* of resistors. A simple example is a string of light bulbs used for holiday decorations; each bulb acts as a resistor, and from a circuit-analysis perspective the string of bulbs is simply a combination of resistors.

Suppose we have three resistors with resistances R_1, R_2, and R_3. Figure 11.14 shows four different ways in which they might be connected between points a and b. When several circuit elements such as resistors, batteries, and motors are connected in sequence as in Fig. 11.14a, with only a single current path between the points, we say that they are connected in **series.** We found that, because of conservation of charge, capacitors in series all have the same charge if they are initially uncharged. In circuits we're often more interested in the *current,* which is charge flow per unit time.

The resistors in Fig. 11.14b are said to be connected in **parallel** between points a and b. Each resistor provides an alternative path between the points. For circuit elements that are connected in parallel, the *potential difference* is the same across each element.

In Fig. 11.14c, resistors R_2 and R_3 are in parallel, and this combination is in series with R_1. In Fig. 11.14d, R_2 and R_3 are in series, and this combination is in parallel with R_1.

For any combination of resistors we can always find a *single* resistor that could replace the combination and result in the same total current and potential difference. For example, a string of holiday light bulbs could be replaced by a single, appropriately chosen light bulb that would draw the same current and have the same potential difference between its terminals as the original string of bulbs. The resistance of this single resistor is called the **equivalent resistance** of the combination. If any one of the networks in Fig. 11.14 were replaced by its equivalent resistance R_{eq}, we could write

$$V_{ab} = IR_{eq} \quad \text{or} \quad R_{eq} = \frac{V_{ab}}{I}$$

11.14 Four different ways of connecting three resistors.

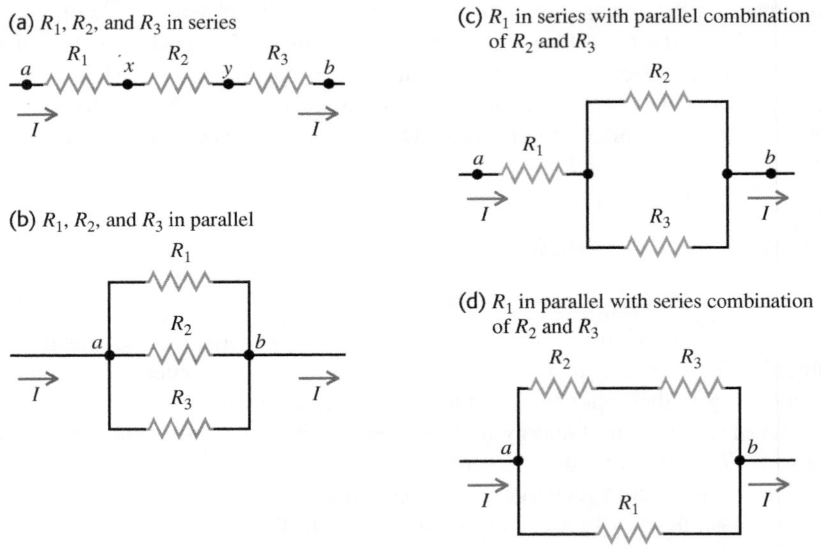
(a) R_1, R_2, and R_3 in series
R_1
R_2
R_3
a
x
y
b
I
I
(b) R_1, R_2, and R_3 in parallel
R_1
R_2
R_3
a
b
I
I
(c) R_1 in series with parallel combination of R_2 and R_3
R_2
R_1
R_3
a
b
I
I
(d) R_1 in parallel with series combination of R_2 and R_3
R_2
R_3
R_1
a
b
I
I

where V_{ab} is the potential difference between terminals a and b of the network and I is the current at point a or b. To compute an equivalent resistance, we assume a potential difference V_{ab} across the actual network, compute the corresponding current I, and take the ratio V_{ab}/I.

Resistors in Series

We can derive general equations for the equivalent resistance of a series or parallel combination of resistors. If the resistors are in *series,* as in Fig. 11.14a, the current I must be the same in all of them. (As we discussed, current is *not* "used up" as it passes through a circuit.) Applying $V = IR$ to each resistor, we have

$$V_{ax} = IR_1 \qquad V_{xy} = IR_2 \qquad V_{yb} = IR_3$$

The potential differences across each resistor need not be the same (except for the special case in which all three resistances are equal). The potential difference V_{ab} across the entire combination is the sum of these individual potential differences:

$$V_{ab} = V_{ax} + V_{xy} + V_{yb} = I(R_1 + R_2 + R_3)$$

and so

$$\frac{V_{ab}}{I} = R_1 + R_2 + R_3$$

The ratio V_{ab}/I is, by definition, the equivalent resistance R_{eq}. Therefore

$$R_{eq} = R_1 + R_2 + R_3$$

It is easy to generalize this to any number of resistors:

$$R_{eq} = R_1 + R_2 + R_3 + \cdots \qquad \text{(resistors in series)} \qquad (11.21)$$

The equivalent resistance of *any number* of resistors in series equals the sum of their individual resistances.

The equivalent resistance is *greater than* any individual resistance.

Resistors in series add directly because the voltage across each is directly proportional to its resistance and to the common current. Capacitors in series add reciprocally because the voltage across each is directly proportional to the common charge but *inversely* proportional to the individual capacitance.

Resistors in Parallel

If the resistors are in *parallel,* as in Fig. 11.14b, the current through each resistor need not be the same. But the potential difference between the terminals of each resistor must be the same and equal to V_{ab}. (Remember that the potential difference between any two points does not depend on the path taken between the points.) Let's call the currents in the three resistors I_1, I_2, and I_3. Then from $I = V/R$,

$$I_1 = \frac{V_{ab}}{R_1} \qquad I_2 = \frac{V_{ab}}{R_2} \qquad I_3 = \frac{V_{ab}}{R_3}$$

In general, the current is different through each resistor. Because charge is not accumulating or draining out of point a, the total current I must equal the sum of the three currents in the resistors:

$$I = I_1 + I_2 + I_3 = V_{ab}\left(\frac{1}{R_1} + \frac{1}{R_2} + \frac{1}{R_3}\right) \quad \text{or}$$

$$\frac{I}{V_{ab}} = \frac{1}{R_1} + \frac{1}{R_2} + \frac{1}{R_3}$$

But by the definition of the equivalent resistance R_{eq}, $I/V_{ab} = 1/R_{eq}$, so

$$\frac{1}{R_{eq}} = \frac{1}{R_1} + \frac{1}{R_2} + \frac{1}{R_3}$$

Again it is easy to generalize to *any number* of resistors in parallel:

$$\frac{1}{R_{eq}} = \frac{1}{R_1} + \frac{1}{R_2} + \frac{1}{R_3} + \cdots \quad \text{(resistors in parallel)} \tag{11.22}$$

For *any number* of resistors in parallel, the *reciprocal* of the equivalent resistance equals the *sum of the reciprocals* of their individual resistances.

The equivalent resistance is always *less than* any individual resistance.

Resistors in parallel add reciprocally because the current in each is proportional to the common voltage across them and *inversely* proportional to the resistance of each. Capacitors in parallel add directly because the charge on each is proportional to the common voltage across them and *directly* proportional to the capacitance of each.

For the special case of *two* resistors in parallel,

$$\frac{1}{R_{eq}} = \frac{1}{R_1} + \frac{1}{R_2} = \frac{R_1 + R_2}{R_1 R_2} \quad \text{and}$$

$$R_{eq} = \frac{R_1 R_2}{R_1 + R_2} \quad \text{(two resistors in parallel)} \tag{11.23}$$

Because $V_{ab} = I_1 R_1 = I_2 R_2$, it follows that

$$\frac{I_1}{I_2} = \frac{R_2}{R_1} \quad \text{(two resistors in parallel)} \tag{11.24}$$

This shows that the currents carried by two resistors in parallel are *inversely proportional* to their resistances. More current goes through the path of least resistance.

11.7 Kirchhoff's Rules

Many practical resistor networks cannot be reduced to simple series-parallel combinations. Figure 11.15a shows a dc power supply with emf $\mathcal{E}_1$ charging a battery with a smaller emf $\mathcal{E}_2$ and feeding current to a light bulb with resistance R. Figure 11.15b is a "bridge" circuit, used in many different types of measurement and control systems. To compute the currents in these networks, we'll use the techniques developed by the German physicist Gustav Robert Kirchhoff (1824–1887).

First, here are two terms that we will use often. A **junction** in a circuit is a point where three or more conductors meet. A **loop** is any closed conducting path. In Fig. 11.15a points a and b are junctions, but points c and d are not; in Fig. 11.15b the points a, b, c, and d are junctions, but points e and f are not. The blue lines in Figs. 11.15a and 11.15b show some possible loops in these circuits.

Kirchhoff's rules are the following two statements:

Kirchhoff's junction rule: *The algebraic sum of the currents into any junction is zero.* That is,

$$\sum I = 0 \quad \text{(junction rule, valid at any junction)} \tag{11.25}$$

Kirchhoff's loop rule: *The algebraic sum of the potential differences in any loop,* including those associated with emfs and those of resistive elements, *must equal zero.* That is,

$$\sum V = 0 \quad \text{(loop rule, valid for any closed loop)} \tag{11.26}$$

The junction rule is based on *conservation of electric charge.* No charge can accumulate at a junction, so the total charge entering the junction per unit time must equal the total charge leaving per unit time (Fig. 11.16a). Charge per unit time is current, so if we consider the currents entering a junction to be positive and those leaving to be negative, the algebraic sum of currents into a junction must be zero. It's like a T branch in a water pipe (Fig. 11.16b); if you have a total of 1 liter per minute coming in the two pipes, you can't have 3 liters per minute going out the third pipe. We may as well confess that we used the junction rule (without saying so) in the derivation for resistors in parallel.

The loop rule is a statement that the electrostatic force is *conservative.* Suppose we go around a loop, measuring potential differences across successive circuit elements as we go. When we return to the starting point, we must find that

11.15 Two networks that cannot be reduced to simple series-parallel combinations of resistors.

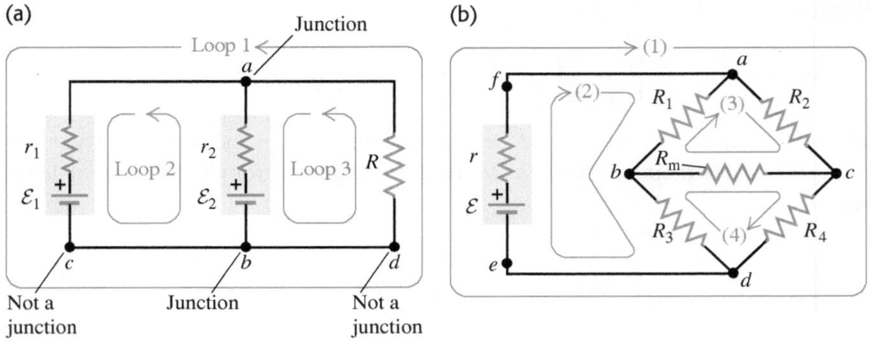

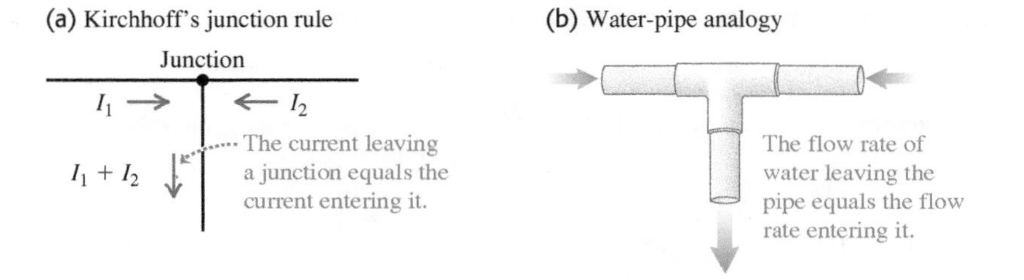
(a) Kirchhoff's junction rule
Junction
I_1
I_2
$I_1 + I_2$
The current leaving a junction equals the current entering it.
(b) Water-pipe analogy
The flow rate of water leaving the pipe equals the flow rate entering it.

11.16 Kirchhoff's junction rule states that as much current flows into a junction as flows out of it.

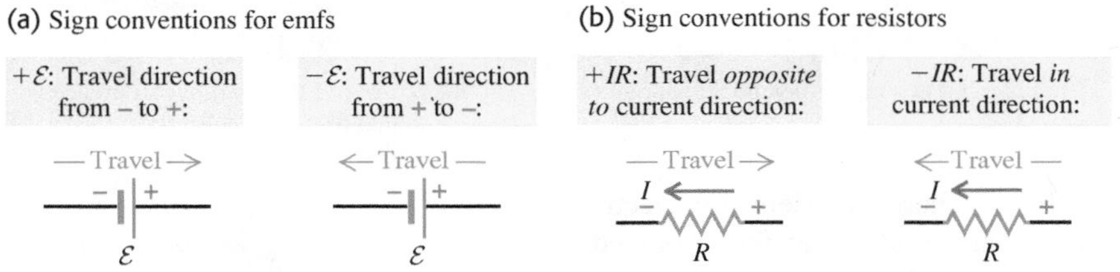
(a) Sign conventions for emfs
$+\mathcal{E}$: Travel direction from – to +:
$-\mathcal{E}$: Travel direction from + to –:
Travel
$\mathcal{E}$
(b) Sign conventions for resistors
$+IR$: Travel *opposite to* current direction:
$-IR$: Travel *in* current direction:
Travel
I
R

11.17 Use these sign conventions when you apply Kirchhoff's loop rule. In each part of the figure "Travel" is the direction that we imagine going around the loop, which is not necessarily the direction of the current.

the *algebraic sum* of these differences is zero; otherwise, we could not say that the potential at this point has a definite value.

Sign Conventions for the Loop Rule

In applying the loop rule, we need some sign conventions. We first assume a direction for the current in each branch of the circuit and mark it on a diagram of the circuit. Then, starting at any point in the circuit, we imagine traveling around a loop, adding emfs and IR terms as we come to them. When we travel through a source in the direction from $-$ to $+$, the emf is considered to be *positive;* when we travel from $+$ to $-$, the emf is considered to be *negative* (Fig. 11.17a). When we travel through a resistor in the *same* direction as the assumed current, the IR term is *negative* because the current goes in the direction of decreasing potential. When we travel through a resistor in the direction *opposite* to the assumed current, the IR term is *positive* because this represents a rise of potential (Fig. 11.17b).

Kirchhoff's two rules are all we need to solve a wide variety of network problems. Usually, some of the emfs, currents, and resistances are known, and others are unknown. We must always obtain from Kirchhoff's rules a number of independent equations equal to the number of unknowns so that we can solve the equations simultaneously. Often the hardest part of the solution is not understanding the basic principles but keeping track of algebraic signs!

11.8 The Hall Effect

The reality of the forces acting on the moving charges in a conductor in a magnetic field is strikingly demonstrated by the *Hall effect,* an effect analogous to the transverse deflection of an electron beam in a magnetic field in vacuum. (The effect was discovered by the American physicist Edwin Hall in 1879 while he was still a graduate student.) To describe this effect, let's consider a conductor in the form of a flat strip, as shown in Fig. 11.18. The current is in the direction of the $+x$-axis and there is a uniform magnetic field $\vec{B}$ perpendicular to the plane of the strip, in the $+y$-direction. The drift velocity of the moving charges (charge magnitude $|q|$) has magnitude v_d. Figure 11.18a shows the case of negative charges, such as electrons in a metal, and Fig. 11.18b shows positive charges. In both cases the magnetic force is upward, just as the magnetic force on a conductor is the same whether the moving charges are positive or negative. In either case a moving charge is driven toward the *upper* edge of the strip by the magnetic force $F_z = |q|v_dB$.

11.18 Forces on charge carriers in a conductor in a magnetic field.

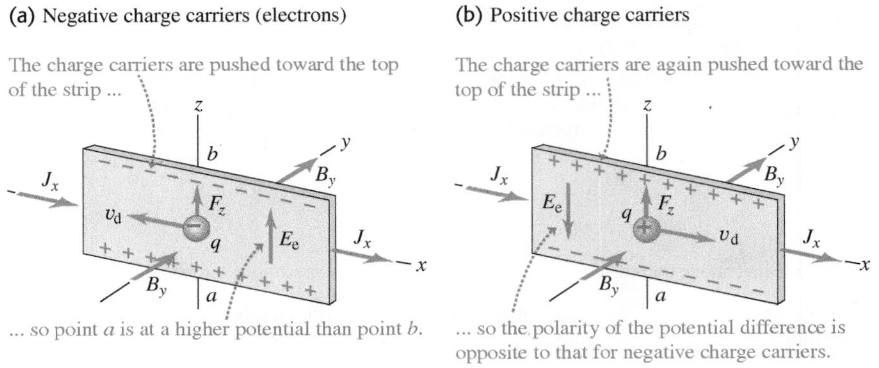
(a) Negative charge carriers (electrons)
The charge carriers are pushed toward the top of the strip ...
... so point a is at a higher potential than point b.
(b) Positive charge carriers
The charge carriers are again pushed toward the top of the strip ...
... so the polarity of the potential difference is opposite to that for negative charge carriers.

If the charge carriers are electrons, as in Fig. 11.18a, an excess negative charge accumulates at the upper edge of the strip, leaving an excess positive charge at its lower edge. This accumulation continues until the resulting transverse electrostatic field $\vec{E}_e$ becomes large enough to cause a force (magnitude $|q|E_e$) that is equal and opposite to the magnetic force (magnitude $|q|v_d B$). After that, there is no longer any net transverse force to deflect the moving charges. This electric field causes a transverse potential difference between opposite edges of the strip, called the *Hall voltage* or the *Hall emf.* The polarity depends on whether the moving charges are positive or negative. Experiments show that for metals the upper edge of the strip in Fig. 11.18a *does* become negatively charged, showing that the charge carriers in a metal are indeed negative electrons.

However, if the charge carriers are *positive,* as in Fig. 11.18b, then *positive* charge accumulates at the upper edge, and the potential difference is *opposite* to the situation with negative charges. Soon after the discovery of the Hall effect in 1879, it was observed that some materials, particularly some *semiconductors,* show a Hall emf opposite to that of the metals, as if their charge carriers were positively charged. We now know that these materials conduct by a process known as *hole conduction.* Within such a material there are locations, called *holes,* that would normally be occupied by an electron but are actually empty. A missing negative charge is equivalent to a positive charge. When an electron moves in one direction to fill a hole, it leaves another hole behind it. The hole migrates in the direction opposite to that of the electron.

In terms of the coordinate axes in Fig. 11.18b, the electrostatic field $\vec{E}_e$ for the positive-q case is in the $-z$-direction; its z-component E_z is negative. The magnetic field is in the $+y$-direction, and we write it as B_y. The magnetic force (in the $+z$-direction) is qv_dB_y. The current density J_x is in the $+x$-direction. In the steady state, when the forces qE_z and qv_dB_y are equal in magnitude and opposite in direction,

$$qE_z + qv_dB_y = 0 \qquad \text{or} \qquad E_z = -v_dB_y$$

This confirms that when q is positive, E_z is negative. The current density J_x is

$$J_x = nqv_d$$

Eliminating v_d between these equations, we find

$$nq = \frac{-J_xB_y}{E_z} \qquad \text{(Hall effect)} \qquad (11.27)$$

Note that this result (as well as the entire derivation) is valid for both positive and negative q. When q is negative, E_z is positive, and conversely.

We can measure J_x, B_y, and E_z, so we can compute the product nq. In both metals and semiconductors, q is equal in magnitude to the electron charge, so the

Hall effect permits a direct measurement of n, the concentration of current-carrying charges in the material. The *sign* of the charges is determined by the polarity of the Hall emf, as we have described.

The Hall effect can also be used for a direct measurement of electron drift speed v_d in metals. These speeds are very small, often of the order of 1 mm/s or less. If we move the entire conductor in the opposite direction to the current with a speed equal to the drift speed, then the electrons are at rest with respect to the magnetic field, and the Hall emf disappears. Thus the conductor speed needed to make the Hall emf vanish is equal to the drift speed.

CHAPTER 11 SUMMARY

Current and current density: Current is the amount of charge flowing through a specified area, per unit time. The SI unit of current is the ampere ($1\ \text{A} = 1\ \text{C/s}$). The current I through an area A depends on the concentration n and charge q of the charge carriers, as well as on the magnitude of their drift velocity $\vec{v}_d$. The current density is current per unit cross-sectional area. Current is usually described in terms of a flow of positive charge, even when the charges are actually negative or of both signs.

$$I = \frac{dQ}{dt} = n|q|v_d A \quad (11.2)$$

$$\vec{J} = nq\vec{v}_d \quad (11.4)$$

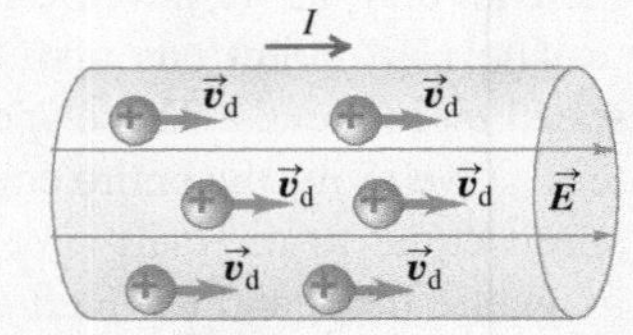

Resistivity: The resistivity ρ of a material is the ratio of the magnitudes of electric field and current density. Good conductors have small resistivity; good insulators have large resistivity. Ohm's law, obeyed approximately by many materials, states that ρ is a constant independent of the value of E. Resistivity usually increases with temperature; for small temperature changes this variation is represented approximately by Eq. (11.6), where α is the temperature coefficient of resistivity.

$$\rho = \frac{E}{J} \quad (11.5)$$

$$\rho(T) = \rho_0[1 + \alpha(T - T_0)] \quad (11.6)$$

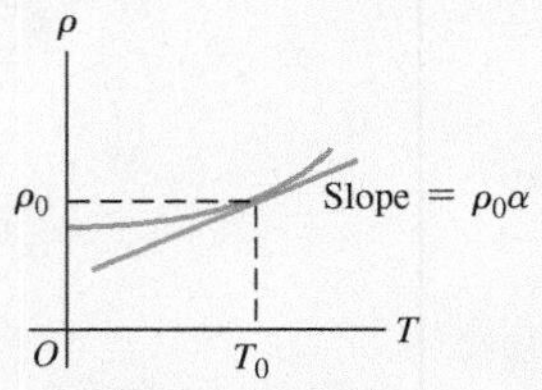

Metal: ρ increases with increasing T.

Resistors: The potential difference V across a sample of material that obeys Ohm's law is proportional to the current I through the sample. The ratio $V/I = R$ is the resistance of the sample. The SI unit of resistance is the ohm ($1\ \Omega = 1\ \text{V/A}$). The resistance of a cylindrical conductor is related to its resistivity ρ, length L, and cross-sectional area A.

$$V = IR \quad (11.11)$$

$$R = \frac{\rho L}{A} \quad (11.10)$$

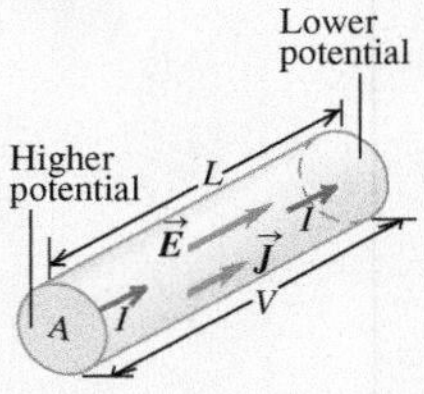

Circuits and emf: A complete circuit has a continuous current-carrying path. A complete circuit carrying a steady current must contain a source of electromotive force (emf) $\mathcal{E}$. The SI unit of electromotive force is the volt (1 V). Every real source of emf has some internal resistance r, so its terminal potential difference V_{ab} depends on current.

$$V_{ab} = \mathcal{E} - Ir \quad (11.15)$$

(source with internal resistance)

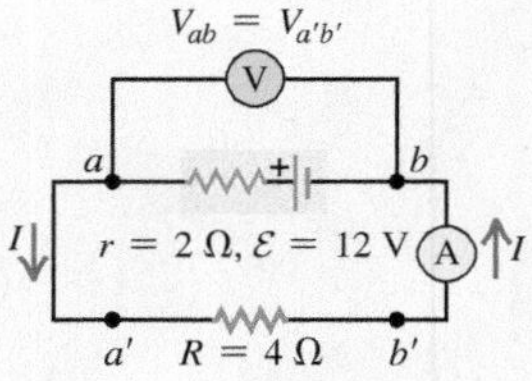

Energy and power in circuits: A circuit element with a potential difference $V_a - V_b = V_{ab}$ and a current I puts energy into a circuit if the current direction is from lower to higher potential in the device, and it takes energy out of the circuit if the current is opposite. The power P equals the product of the potential difference and the current. A resistor always takes electrical energy out of a circuit.

$$P = V_{ab}I \quad (11.17)$$

(general circuit element)

$$P = V_{ab}I = I^2R = \frac{{V_{ab}}^2}{R} \quad (11.18)$$

(power into a resistor)

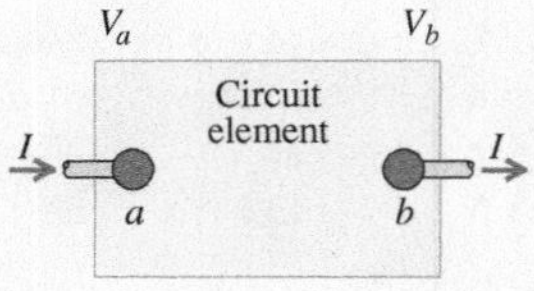

Resistors in series and parallel: When several resistors $R_1, R_2, R_3, \ldots$ are connected in series, the equivalent resistance R_{eq} is the sum of the individual resistances. The same *current* flows through all the resistors in a series connection. When several resistors are connected in parallel, the reciprocal of the equivalent resistance R_{eq} is the sum of the reciprocals of the individual resistances. All resistors in a parallel connection have the same *potential difference* between their terminals.

$$R_{eq} = R_1 + R_2 + R_3 + \cdots \quad \text{(resistors in series)} \qquad (11.21)$$

$$\frac{1}{R_{eq}} = \frac{1}{R_1} + \frac{1}{R_2} + \frac{1}{R_3} + \cdots \quad \text{(resistors in parallel)} \qquad (11.22)$$

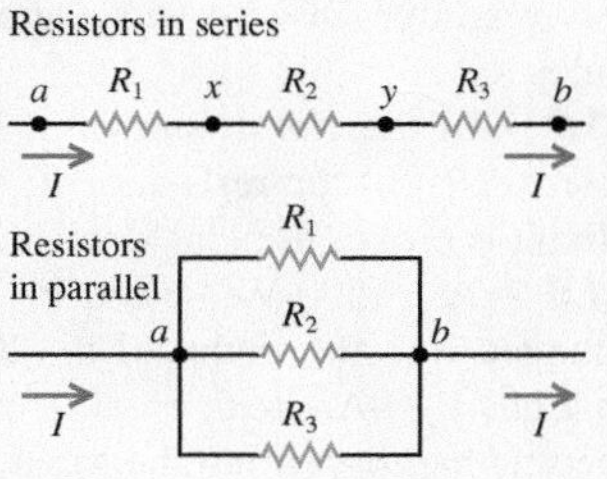

Kirchhoff's rules: Kirchhoff's junction rule is based on conservation of charge. It states that the algebraic sum of the currents into any junction must be zero. Kirchhoff's loop rule is based on conservation of energy and the conservative nature of electrostatic fields. It states that the algebraic sum of potential differences around any loop must be zero. Careful use of consistent sign rules is essential in applying Kirchhoff's rules.

$$\sum I = 0 \quad \text{(junction rule)} \qquad \sum V = 0 \quad \text{(loop rule)} \qquad (11.25)$$

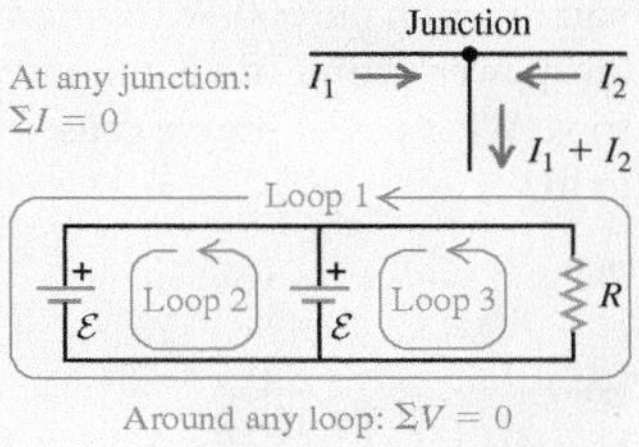

Problems

•, ••, •••: Problems of increasing difficulty. **CP**: Cumulative problems incorporating material from earlier chapters. **CALC**: Problems requiring calculus. **BIO**: Biosciences problems.

11.1 • A 5.00-A current runs through a 12-gauge copper wire (diameter 2.05 mm) and through a light bulb. Copper has 8.5×10^{28} free electrons per cubic meter. (a) How many electrons pass through the light bulb each second? (b) What is the current density in the wire? (c) At what speed does a typical electron pass by any given point in the wire? (d) If you were to use wire of twice the diameter, which of the above answers would change? Would they increase or decrease?

11.2 • A 14-gauge copper wire of diameter 1.628 mm carries a current of 12.5 mA. (a) What is the potential difference across a 2.00-m length of the wire? (b) What would the potential difference in part (a) be if the wire were silver instead of copper, but all else were the same?

11.3 • Consider the circuit shown in Fig. P11.3. The terminal voltage of the 24.0-V battery is 21.2 V. What are (a) the internal resistance r of the battery and (b) the resistance R of the circuit resistor?

Figure **P11.3**

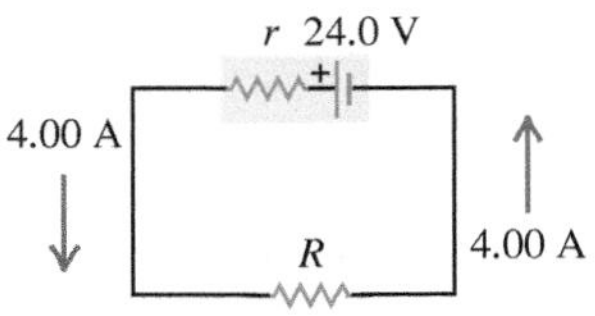

11.4 • When switch S in Fig. P11.4 is open, the voltmeter V of the battery reads 3.08 V. When the switch is closed, the voltmeter reading drops to 2.97 V, and the ammeter A reads 1.65 A. Find the emf, the internal resistance of the battery, and the circuit resistance R. Assume that the two meters are ideal, so they don't affect the circuit.

Figure **P11.4**

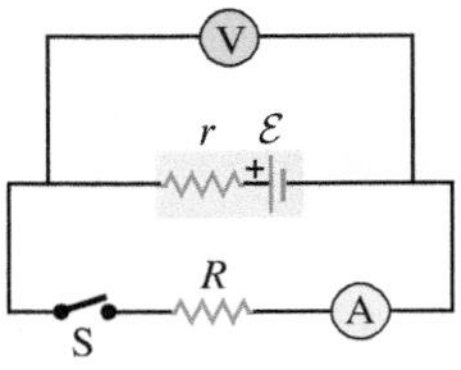

11.5 • In the circuit in Fig. P11.5, find (a) the rate of conversion of internal (chemical) energy to electrical energy within the battery; (b) the rate of dissipation of electrical energy in the battery; (c) the rate of dissipation of electrical energy in the external resistor.

Figure **P11.5**

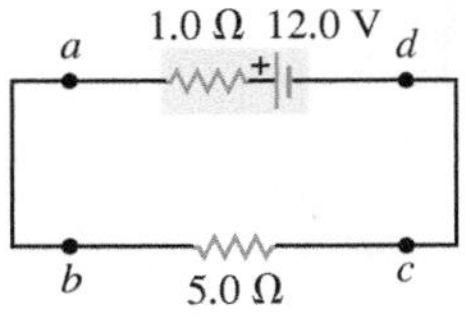

11.6 • In Fig. P11.6, $R_1 = 3.00\ \Omega$, $R_2 = 6.00\ \Omega$, and $R_3 = 5.00\ \Omega$. The battery has negligible internal resistance. The current I_2 through R_2 is 4.00 A. (a) What are the currents I_1 and I_3? (b) What is the emf of the battery?

Figure **P11.6**

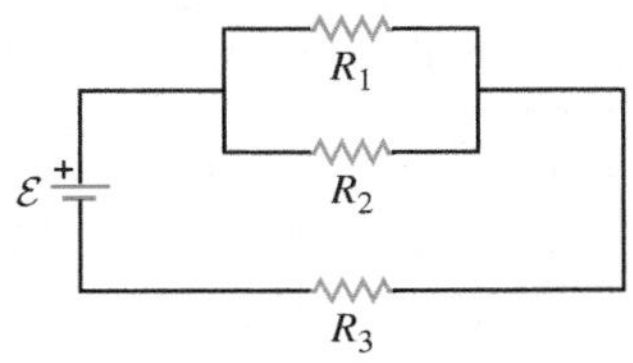

11.7 • In the circuit of Fig. P11.7, each resistor represents a light bulb. Let $R_1 = R_2 = R_3 = R_4 = 4.50\ \Omega$ and $\mathcal{E} = 9.00$ V. (a) Find the current in each bulb. (b) Find the power dissipated in each bulb. Which bulb or bulbs glow the brightest? (c) Bulb R_4 is now removed from the circuit, leaving a break in the wire at its position. Now what is the current in each of the remaining bulbs R_1, R_2, and R_3? (d) With bulb R_4 removed, what is the power dissipated in each of the remaining bulbs? (e) Which light bulb(s) glow brighter as a result of removing R_4? Which bulb(s) glow

Figure **P11.7**

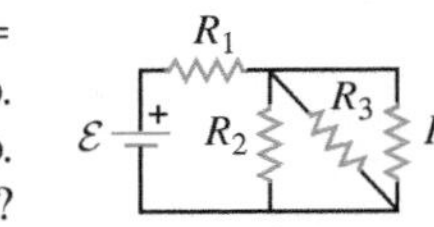

less brightly? Discuss why there are different effects on different bulbs.

11.8 • In the circuit shown in Fig. P11.9 find (a) the current in resistor R; (b) the resistance R; (c) the unknown emf $\mathcal{E}$. (d) If the circuit is broken at point x, what is the current in resistor R?

11.9 • A 1500-W electric heater is plugged into the outlet of a 120-V circuit that has a 20-A circuit breaker. You plug an electric hair dryer into the same outlet. The hair dryer has power settings of 600 W, 900 W, 1200 W, and 1500 W. You start with the hair dryer on the 600-W setting and increase the power setting until the circuit breaker trips. What power setting caused the breaker to trip?

Figure P11.9

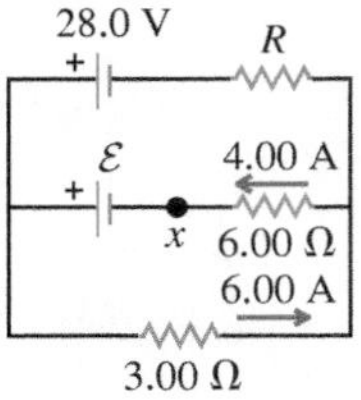
28.0 V
R
+
ℰ
+
4.00 A
x
6.00 Ω
6.00 A
3.00 Ω

11.10 •• In Fig. P11.10, the battery has negligible internal resistance and $\mathcal{E} = 48.0$ V. $R_1 = R_2 = 4.00\ \Omega$ and $R_4 = 3.00\ \Omega$. What must the resistance R_3 be for the resistor network to dissipate electrical energy at a rate of 295 W?

Figure P11.10

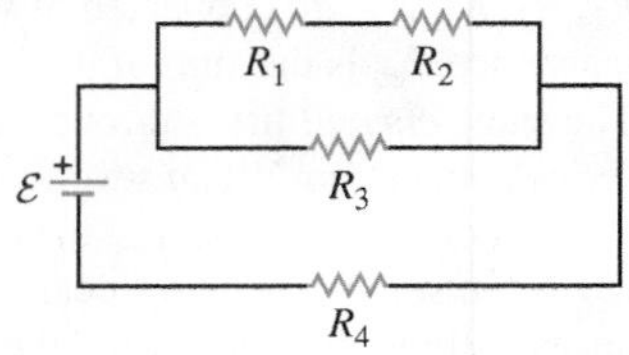
R1
R2
R3
ℰ
+
R4

Answers

Chapter Opening Question ?

The current out equals the current in. In other words, charge must enter the bulb at the same rate as it exits the bulb. It is not "used up" or consumed as it flows through the bulb.

ANSWERS TO PROBLEMS

Chapter 1

1.1 1.02 ns
1.3 31.7 y
1.4 0.45%
1.6 a) 9.01 m, 33.7° b) 9.01 m, 33.7° c) 22.3 m, 250° d) 22.3 m, 70.3°
1.7 a) 2.48 cm, 18.4° b) 4.09 cm, 83.7° c) 4.09 cm, 264°
1.9 a) $\vec{A} = (1.23\text{ m})\hat{\imath} + (3.38\text{ m})\hat{\jmath}$, $\vec{B} = (-2.08\text{ m})\hat{\imath} + (-1.20\text{ m})\hat{\jmath}$ b) $\vec{C} = (12.0\text{ m})\hat{\imath} + (14.9\text{ m})\hat{\jmath}$ c) 19.2 m, 51.2°
1.10 a) -104 m^2 b) -148 m^2 c) 40.6 m^2
1.11 a) 165° b) 28° c) 90°
1.12 a) $-63.9\text{ m}^2\hat{k}$ b) $63.9\text{ m}^2\hat{k}$
1.13 a) -6.62 m^2 b) $5.55\text{ m}^2\hat{k}$

Chapter 2

2.1 a) 0° b) 90° c) 180°
2.3 3.15 N
2.4 a) 4.49 kg b) 4.49 kg, 8.13 N
2.5 20 N
2.6 b) yes
2.9 a) 25.0 N b) 50.0 N
2.10 48°
2.14 a) 57.1 N b) 146 N up the ramp
2.15 a) w b) 0 c) $w/2$

Chapter 3

3.2 a) 8.7 N · m counterclockwise, 0, 5.0 N · m clockwise, 10.0 N · m clockwise b) 6.3 N · m clockwise
3.3 29.8 cm
3.4 5.45 kN
3.6 a) 1920 N b) 1140 N
3.7 a) $T = 2.60w$; $3.28w$, 37.6° b) $T = 4.10w$; $5.39w$, 48.8°
3.8 a) 525 N b) 222 N, 328 N c) 1.48

Chapter 4

4.1 a) 7.1 cm/s, 45° b) 5.0 cm/s, 90°; 7.1 cm/s, 45°; 11 cm/s, 27°
4.2 6.7 m/s, 6.7 m/s, 0, –40.0 m/s, –40.0 m/s, –40.0 m/s, 0
4.3 a) (i) 5.59 m/s^2 (ii) 7.74 m/s^2 b) (i) 179 m (ii) 1.28×10^4 m
4.5 b) 0.627 s, 1.59 s c) negative at 0.627 s, positive at 1.59 s d) 1.11 s e) 2.45 m f) 2.00 s, 0
4.6 a) 6.17 s b) 24.8 m c) auto: 21.0 m/s, truck: 13.0 m/s
4.7 a) 0.683 s, 2.99 s b) 24.0 m/s, 11.3 m/s; 24.0 m/s, –11.3 m/s c) 30.0 m/s, 36.9° below the horizontal
4.8 a) 3.50 m/s^2 upward b) 3.50 m/s^2 downward c) 12.6 s
4.10 a) 6.91 m c) no

Chapter 5

5.1 46.7 N, opposite to the motion of the skater
5.3 a) $A = 100$ N, $B = 12.5\text{ N/s}^2$ b) (i) 21.6 N, 2.70 m/s^2 (ii) 134 N, 16.8 m/s^2 c) 26.6 m/s^2
5.4 a) 2.50 m/s^2 b) 10.0 N c) to the right, $F > T$ d) 25.0 N
5.5 a) 4.34 kg b) 5.30 kg
5.9 1410 N, 8370 N
5.10 a) 38.3 m/s = 138 km/h b) 3580 N

Chapter 6

6.1 b) 14.4 cm, 13.6 cm, 12.8 cm
6.3 $2.1 \times 10^{-9}\text{ m/s}^2$, downward
6.5 a) 0.742 μC on each b) 0.371 μC, 1.48 μC
6.6 $x = -0.144$ m
6.7 1.73×10^{-8} N, toward a point midway between the two electrons
6.8 a) $(-6.68 \times 10^{-4}\text{ N})\hat{k}$ b) $(6.68 \times 10^{-4}\text{ N})\hat{\imath} + (7.27 \times 10^{-4}\text{ N})\hat{\jmath}$
6.9 a) $B_x = -0.175$ T, $B_z = -0.256$ T b) B_y is not determined c) 0, 90°
6.10 0.28%

Chapter 7

7.3 a) 10.8 m/s, to the right b) 0.750 m/s, to the left
7.5 a) 29.3 m/s, 20.7 m/s b) 19.6%
7.6 19.5 m/s, 21.9 m/s
7.7 (0.0444 m, 0.0556 m)
7.8 $F_x = -(1.50\text{ N/s})t$, $F_y = 0.25$ N, $F_z = 0$
7.9 0.400 m/s

Chapter 8

8.1 a) 34.4° b) 6.27 cm c) 1.05 m
8.3 a) 24.0 s b) 68.8 rev
8.6 a) $115\text{ kg} \cdot \text{m}^2/\text{s}$ into the page b) $125\text{ kg} \cdot \text{m}^2/\text{s}^2$ out of the page
8.8 1.14 rev/s

Chapter 9

9.1 a) 74 N b) 333 J c) –330 J d) 0, 0 e) 0
9.3 a) (i) 0 (ii) 0 b) (i) 0 (ii) –25.1 J
9.5 a) 4.96 m/s b) 1.43 m/s^2, 4.96 m/s
9.7 29.6 kW
9.8 a) 820 N b) (i) 0 (ii) 740 J
9.10 –5400 J
9.13 a) 2.93 cm b) 866 J c) 1.73 J
9.14 a) 3.33 J, 0.333 m/s b) –1.33 m/s, 0.667 m/s
9.15 102 N

Chapter 10

10.1 a) 0.600 m b) 1.50 m/s
10.2 a) 80.0 J b) 5.0 J
10.4 0.602 m
10.6 a) 9.67×10^{-12} N, at 45° above the $+x$-axis b) 3.02×10^{-5} m/s
10.7 $(0.01)R_E = 6.4 \times 10^4$ m
10.8 6.8×10^4 m/s
10.9 a) 7910 s b) 1.53 c) 5510 m/s (apogee), 8430 m/s (perigee) d) 2410 m/s (perigee), 3250 m/s (apogee); perigee
10.10 –0.356 J
10.11 a) 12.5 m/s b) 0.323 m
10.12 $-q/2$
10.13 a) point b b) 800 V/m c) –48.0 μJ

Chapter 11

11.1 a) 3.12×10^{19} b) $1.51 \times 10^6\text{ A/m}^2$ c) 0.111 mm/s d) both J and v_d would decrease
11.2 a) 0.206 mV b) 0.176 mV
11.4 3.08 V, 0.067 Ω, 1.80 Ω
11.5 a) 24.0 W b) 4.0 W c) 20.0 W
11.6 a) 8.00 A, 12.0 A b) 84.0 V
11.7 a) $I_1 = 1.50$ A, $I_2 = I_3 = I_4 = 0.500$ A b) $P_1 = 10.1$ W, $P_2 = P_3 = P_4 = 1.12$ W; R_1 glows brightest c) $I_1 = 1.33$ A, $I_2 = I_3 = 0.667$ A d) $P_1 = 8.00$ W, $P_2 = P_3 = 2.00$ W e) R_1 glows less brightly; R_2 and R_3 glow brighter
11.8 a) 2.00 A b) 5.00 Ω c) 42.0 V d) 3.50 A
11.9 900 W
11.10 12.1 Ω

PHOTO CREDITS

Chapter 1 Opener: Ralph Wetmore/Getty Images; 1.2a: R. Williams (STScI), the HDF-S Team, and NASA; 1.2b: SOHO (ESA & NASA); 1.2c: Courtesy of NASA/JPL/Caltech; 1.2d: Photodisc Green/Getty Images; 1.2e: PhotoDisc/Getty Images; 1.2f: Purdue University. Veeco Instruments, Inc.; 1.2g: SPL/Photo Researchers, Inc.

Chapter 2 Opener: Brian Cleary/Getty Images

Chapter 3 Opener: Ilia Shalamaev/Photolibrary

Chapter 4 Opener: Feng Li/Getty Images; 4.13: Bob Thomas/iStockphoto; 4.25: Richard Megna/Fundamental Photographs; 4.28: Richard Megna/Fundamental Photographs

Chapter 5 Opener: Brian Cleary/Getty Images; 5.10a: NASA; 5.10b: Helen Hansma, University of California; Santa Barbara; 5.10c: Nicholas Roemmelt/iStockphoto; 5.10d: David Malin, Anglo-Australian Observatory

Chapter 6 Opener: U.S. Air Force photo by Tech. Sgt. Jeremy Lock/Released; 6.4: NASA/JPL/Caltech

Chapter 7 Opener: Flickr RM/Getty Images

Chapter 8 Opener: Todd Klassy

Chapter 9 Opener: Flickr RM/Getty Images; 9.16: Robert F. Bukaty/AP

Chapter 10 Opener: NASA/JPL/Space Science Institute

Chapter 11 Opener: iStockphoto

INDEX

For users of the three-volume edition: pages 1–686 are in Volume 1; pages 687–1260 are in Volume 2; and pages 1223–1522 are in Volume 3. Pages 1261–1522 are not in the Standard Edition.

Note: Page numbers followed by f indicate figures; those followed by t indicate tables.